CLARK GABLE

THE KING OF HOLLYWOOD

VOLUME ONE (1901-1938) OF A THREE-PART BIOGRAPHY

"He had more magnetism than any man on earth."
—Joan Crawford

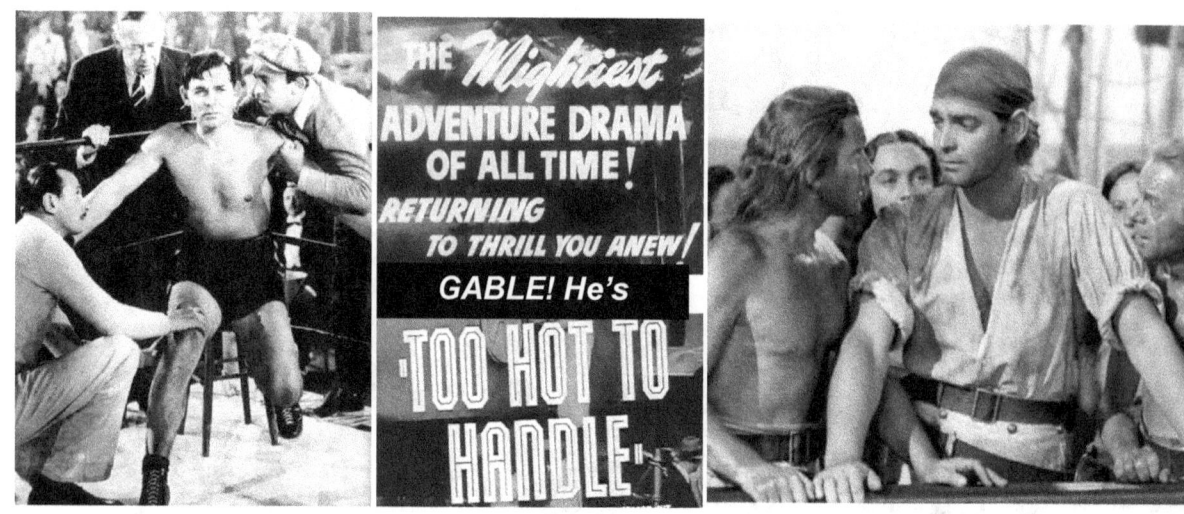

This is Volume One of a Three-Part Biography of Clark Gable.

During his heyday, he was The King of Hollywood, a role model, a patriotic symbol, and one of the most talked-about actors of the 20th Century.

The uncensored details of Clark Gable's real story might never have been known, lost to history with the passing of those who knew him personally.

Fortunately, Darwin Porter, through Blood Moon Productions, opted to change all that. Here he is, Clark Gable, the King of Hollywood.
His story has never been told...until now.

WHAT IS BLOOD MOON PRODUCTIONS?

"Blood Moon, in case you don't know, is a small publishing house on Staten Island that cranks out Hollywood gossip books, about two or three a year, usually of five-, six-, or 700-page length, chocked with stories and pictures about people who used to consume the imaginations of the American public, back when we actually had a public imagination. That is, when people were really interested in each other, rather than in Apple 'devices.' In other words, back when we had vices, not devices."

— *The Huffington Post*

CLARK GABLE
KING OF HOLLYWOOD

VOLUME ONE (1901-1938)
OF A THREE-PART BIOGRAPHY BY

DARWIN PORTER & DANFORTH PRINCE

This book describes how a roughneck from the oilfields of Ohio, with the guidance and advice of dozens of women—some of them older, some of whom he married—trained and coached him on the fine art of becoming a megastar.

CLARK GABLE
KING OF HOLLYWOOD

VOLUME ONE (1961-1938)
OF A THREE-PART BIOGRAPHY

Darwin Porter and Danforth Prince

Unless otherwise stated, all texts are copyright
© 2025 Blood Moon Productions, Ltd.
with all rights reserved.

www.BloodMoonProductions.com

ISBN 978-1-936003-95-2

Manufactured in the USA
Covers, Layouts, and Book Design by Danforth Prince

This book is distributed worldwide through
Ingram, Amazon.com, Barnes & Noble.com,
and internet vendors everywhere.

CLARK GABLE, IN THREE VOLUMES, LIKE HE'S NEVER BEEN SEEN BEFORE

At the peak of his career, flush with the success of his starring performance in history's most poignant film about the end of the Old South (*Gone With the Wind*), **Clark Gable** had become a symbol of American pride and power itself. His role as an icon was so pronounced that Adolph Hitler placed a bounty on his head and stated his intention of capturing him alive and dragging him, caged and in chains, as a trophy through the streets of Nazi Berlin.

GABLE! He's here, alive and thriving, the beneficiary of years of research from the creative team at Blood Moon. So complicated is his story that no single tome can contain all that's needed to say in this ULTIMATE OVERVIEW of CLARK, GLORIOUSLY GABLED, the focal point of a major trilogy spearheaded by film historian **Darwin Porter**.

THIS IS VOLUME ONE (1901-1938): Clark Gable, King of Hollywood

COMING SOON:

Volume Two (1938-1939): Gone With the Wind, Frankly My Dear, He DID Give a Damn

and

Volume Three (1940-1961): Clark Gable, Where Love Has Gone

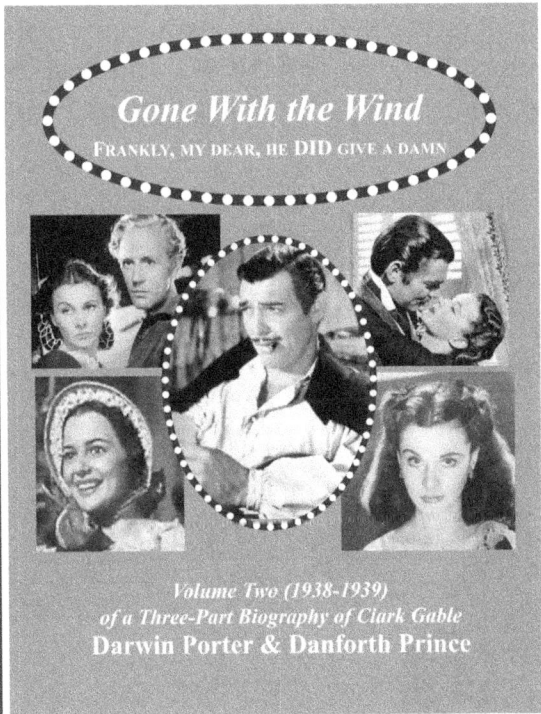

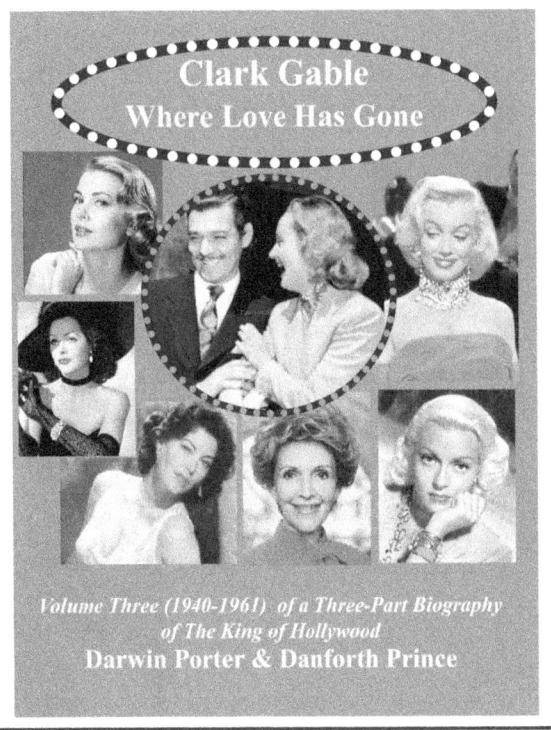

No one in Publishing Has Ever Tried this Before,

but Here It Is, New and Hot from Blood Moon Productions

He Was the King of Hollywood.

He's Clark Gable.

Although Clark Gable was probably the most-watched, and most-emulated actor of Golden Age Hollywood, no one has ever really explored his opportunistic and meteoric rise to fortune and unparalled fame. Beginning now, with the release of this, Volume One, the authors at Blood Moon Productions have changed all that. It exposes THE KING OF HOLLYWOOD, uncut, unclothed, stripped of his camouflage, and exposed.

More than any other actor of his era, he influenced America's definition of Manhood; he became a Mega-Celebrity before they invented the word; and despite intense rivalry with lesser actors, his career survived (and thrived) throughout vastly different eras of America's film-industry priorities and values.

He led a mind-bending life which Blood Moon has configured into THREE SPECTACULAR VOLUMES, each choreographed in ways never achieved, despite multiple hackneyed attempts from other publishing venues. He was THE KING, and despite many shocking revelations about the eras in which he thrived, we treat him like one.

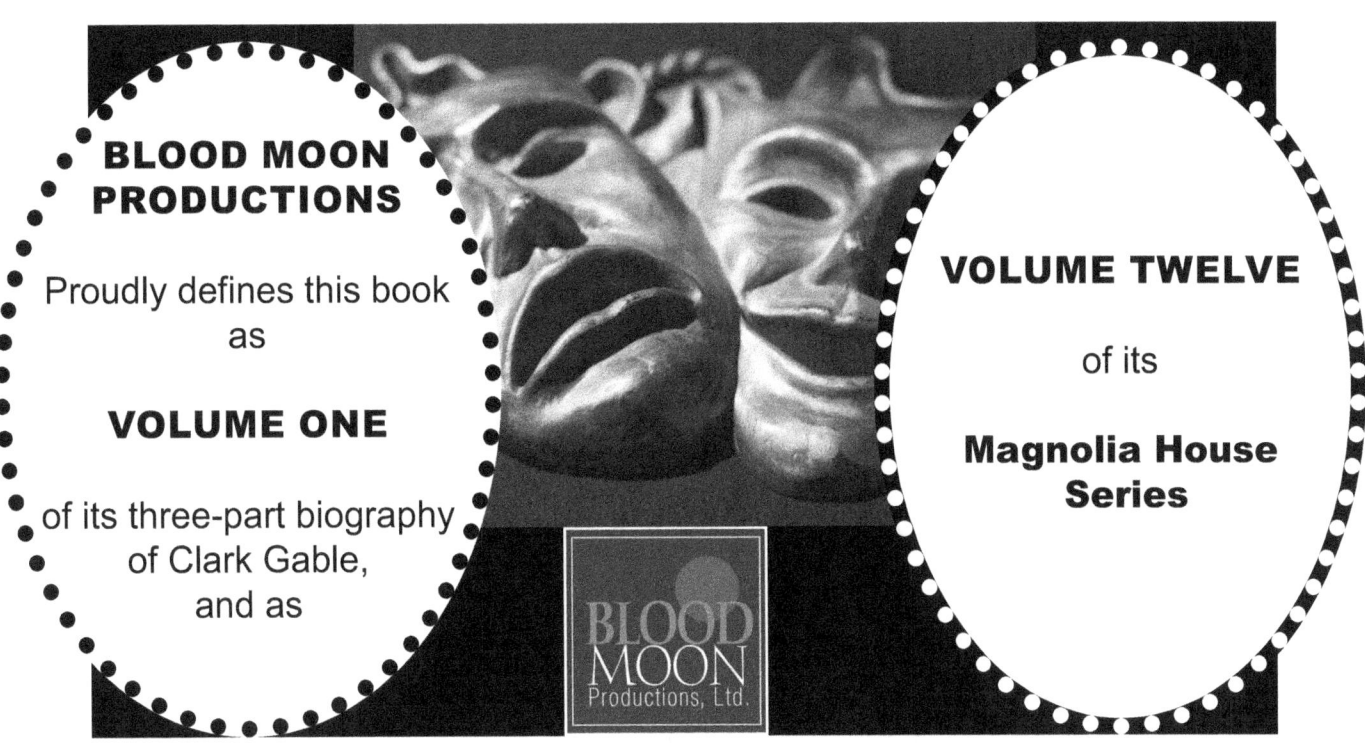

BLOOD MOON PRODUCTIONS

Proudly defines this book as

VOLUME ONE

of its three-part biography of Clark Gable, and as

VOLUME TWELVE

of its

Magnolia House Series

We've organized Clark Gable's life into episodes (or segments) defined either by the movies he made or into major transitions in his personal or professional life. Here's our

TABLE OF CONTENTS

Prelude		page 1
Episode 1	Gable: The Early Years	page 3
Episode 2	Josephine Dillon, Clark Gable's Svengali	page 13
Episode 3	Gable, Young and Struggling, Tangles with the Barrymores	page 17
Episode 4	The Roaring Twenties: Gable Climbs the Tinseltown Ladder, Rung by Rung, Seduction by Seduction	page 19

EPISODE 5	WHY GABLE NEVER REPLACED SCREEN HEARTTHROB WALLACE REID	PAGE 21
EPISODE 6	CLARK BECOMES THE KEPT BOY OF PAULINE FREDERICK, "THE GIRL WITH THE TOPAZ EYES."	PAGE 23
EPISODE 7	*WHITE MAN*: CLARK MAKES HIS FILM DEBUT	PAGE 27
EPISODE 8	JANE COWL: THE ACTRESS PROMOTED AS THE MOST BEAUTIFUL WOMAN ON BROADWAY SEDUCES CLARK GABLE	PAGE 29
EPISODE 9	*WHAT PRICE GLORY?* CLARK APPEARS AS A BIT PLAYER IN A WORLD WAR I STAGE DRAMA, AND THEN, IN A SMALL, SILLY SPOOF: *WHAT PRICE GLORIA?*	PAGE 31
EPISODE 10	*THE MERRY WIDOW.* FILMING IT WITH VON STROHEIM WAS ANYTHING BUT MERRY	PAGE 33
EPISODE 11	*THE PLASTIC AGE:* PLAYTIME WITH CLARA BOW & WILLIAM HAINES	PAGE 39
EPISODE 12	HOW THE "IT" GIRL, CLARA BOW, SEDUCED CLARK GABLE, BUT NIXED HIM AS HER LEADING MAN	PAGE 43
EPISODE 13	*NORTH STAR.* A CANINE TALE ABOUT THE FROZEN NORTH AND MAN'S BEST FRIEND	PAGE 45
EPISODE 14	DOROTHY DALTON: "I GUESS I WAS BORN TO ATTRACT MEN!"	PAGE 47
EPISODE 15	NANCY CARROLL: HOT PRE-CODE SATURDAYS WITH CLARK	PAGE 49
EPISODE 16	ARTHUR HOPKINS, "THE SPHINX OF BROADWAY," DEFINES CLARK AS A "WOOLWORTH ROMEO."	PAGE 51
EPISODE 17	GLORIA SWANSON: "CLARK GABLE WILL NOT TRESPASS ON MY TALKIE."	PAGE 53
EPISODE 18	HOLLYWOOD IN ITS GOLDEN YEARS (I.E., THE 1930S): GABLE EMERGES AS ITS KING	PAGE 55
EPISODE 19	*LOVE, HONOR, AND BETRAY:* CLARK IN THE DYING DAYS OF VAUDEVILLE	PAGE 57
EPISODE 20	OLDER AND RICH, SOCIALITE RIA LANGHAM BECOMES CLARK'S SECOND WIFE	PAGE 59
EPISODE 21	HOWARD HUGHES: HOLLYWOOD'S RICHEST PRODUCER PUTS CLARK "TO THE TEST."	PAGE 63
EPISODE 22	WHY CLARK GABLE DID NOT BECOME THE NEXT SCREEN TARZAN	PAGE 67
EPISODE 23	*LITTLE CAESAR*	PAGE 69
EPISODE 24	WUNDERKIND IRVING THALBERG LAUNCHES CLARK	

	ON THE ROAD TO STARDOM	PAGE 71
EPISODE 25	LOUIS B. MAYER TO IRVING THALBERG: *"I HATE THAT BIG-EARED SON OF A BITCH, BUT KEEP HIM AS LONG AS HE MAKES MONEY."*	PAGE 73
EPISODE 26	*THE LAST MILE.* CLARK BREAKS OUT OF JAIL	PAGE 75
EPISODE 27	*THE PAINTED DESERT:* CLARK'S DEBUT IN TALKIES	PAGE 77
EPISODE 28	PALIMONY PROBLEMS: CLARK FATHERS A CHILD BORN TO HOLLYWOOD'S THEN-LEADING GOSSIP COLUMNIST, ADELA ROGERS ST. JOHNS	PAGE 81
EPISODE 29	MGM'S "FIXERS": HOW THEY BURIED COMPROMISING SECRETS OF THEIR STARS—ESPECIALLY THOSE OF CLARK GABLE	PAGE 83
EPISODE 30	*THE EASIEST WAY:* CLARK VS. SUPERDIVA CONSTANCE BENNETT	PAGE 89
EPISODE 31	*DANCE FOOLS, DANCE:* NYMPHS, DIONYSIAN ECSTASY, AND AN "ALMOST NAKED" SWIM PARTY. ENTER JOAN CRAWFORD.	PAGE 93
EPISODE 32	GABLE AND WILLING: HOW BEN MADDOX, A PROMISCUOUS HOLLYWOOD PUBLICIST, INVITED CLARK TO LUNCH AND SERVED HIMSELF AS DESSERT.	PAGE 97
EPISODE 33	HOW CLARK, BOB HOPE, JAMES STEWART, & KING FAROUK SEDUCED PRINCESS HONEYCHILE	PAGE 101
EPISDOE 34	*THE SECRET SIX:* GABLE STARS IN IN A DETECTIVE DRAMA	PAGE 103
EPISODE 35	JOHNNY MACK BROWN: THE INTRIGUE-SOAKED STORY OF CLARK GABLE VS. THE PRIDE OF ALABAMA	PAGE 107
EPISODE 36	*THE FINGER POINTS:* GABLE VS. HOLLYWOOD'S SILENT OLD GUARD	PAGE 111
EPISODE 37 \	*LAUGHING SINNERS:* GABLE'S FIRST STAR ROLE WITH JOAN CRAWFORD	PAGE 113
EPISODE 38	*A FREE SOUL:* CLARK TEAMS WITH THE NORMA SHEARER, THE QUEEN OF MGM. IT BARELY GOT PAST THE CENSORS.	PAGE 117
EPISODE 39	*NIGHT NURSE.* GABLE, WITH STANWYCK AND BLONDELL, ANSWER THE MOST PREVALENT QUESTION OF 1931: WHAT DO NURSES REALLY WEAR BENEATH THEIR UNIFORMS?	PAGE 121
EPISODE 40	*SPORTING BLOOD:* A PRE-CODE TALE ABOUT WOMEN, HORSE FLESH, AND WINNING THE KENTUCKY DERBY. CLARK STARS WITH MADGE EVANS, A FADED QUEEN FROM THE SILENTS.	PAGE 125
EPISODE 41	*SUSAN LENOX, HER FALL AND RISE:* GARBO AND GABLE! STARRING WITH THE "THAT FRIGID SWEDE" INCLUDED, TILL THEN, THE GREATEST ACTING CHALLENGE OF GABLE'S BUDDING CAREER.	PAGE 129

EPISODE 42	THE AVANT-GARDE VS. THE MAINSTREAM: WHY GARBO & GABLE NEVER RE-APPEARED TOGETHER IN OTHER FILMS	PAGE 133
EPISODE 43	*POSSESSED:* MELODRAMA WITH JOAN CRAWFORD, WITH FIVE MORE TO FOLLOW	PAGE 137
EPISODE 44	*HELL DIVERS:* CLARK HATED IT—PARTLY BECAUSE OF HIS CO-STAR, WALLACE BEERY. OLD-TIMERS FROM THE SILENTS (DOROTHY JORDAN AND MARIE PREVOST) JOINED THE FRAY	PAGE 141
EPISODE 45	*POLLY OF THE CIRCUS.* CLARK PLAYS A CLERGYMAN IN LOVE WITH MARION DAVIES AS A BEDRIDDEN TRAPEZE ARTIST. OFFSCREEN, BUT INVOLVED, WAS HER MENTOR, MEDIA KINGPIN WILLIAM RANDOLPH HEARST.	PAGE 145
EPISODE 46	*RED DUST* CLARK, AS DEPRESSED EXPATRIATE, MEETS BLONDE VENUS (JEAN HARLOW) ON A RUBBER PLANTATION IN FRENCH INDOCHINA. MANY GABLE FANS DEFINE IT AS ONE OF HIS BEST FILMS.	PAGE 151
EPISODE 47	THE MYSTERIOUS DEATH OF PAUL BERN, THE SHADOWY HUSBAND OF JEAN HARLOW	PAGE 155
EPISODE 48	*STRANGE INTERLUDE:* AN AVANT-GARDE, EMOTIONALLY MURKY STAGE PLAY BY EUGENE O'NEILL INSPIRES A COMPLICATED AND EMOTIONALLY MURKY FILM. CLARK STARS ONCE AGAIN WITH SUPERDIVA NORMA SHEARER.	PAGE 159
EPISODE 49	*NO MAN OF HER OWN:* PRE-CODE AND SEXUALLY SUGGESTIVE, CLARK DOESN'T MAKE WHOOPEE WITH CAROLE LOMBARD. COMPETITIVE AND QUARRELSOME, BY SOME STANDARDS, THEY BARELY GET ALONG	PAGE 163
EPISODE 50	*THE WHITE SISTER.* SEPARATED BY THE HORRORS OF WORLD WAR I, CLARK AND HIS *INAMORATA* (HELEN HAYES) LOSE CONTACT, AND SHE BELIEVES HE'S DEAD. TO ASSUAGE HER GRIEF, SHE JOINS A NUNNERY, DEVOTING HER LIFE TO GOOD WORKS AND PRAYER. THEN (*TA DAH!*) THEIR PATHS CROSS ONCE AGAIN. WILL MISS HAYES RETAIN HER WIMPLE AND HER VIRTUE? PRESSURED BY CENSORS AND INSTITUTIONIST CATHOLICS, HOLLYWOOD SAID YES!	PAGE 167
EPISODE 51	*HOLD YOUR MAN.* IT WAS CLARK'S FIRST SCREEN PAIRING WITH JEAN HARLOW. THE SCRIPT CALLED FOR AN ONSCREEN PRE-MARITAL AFFAIR. CENSORS INSISTED THAT THE CHARACTERS PAY A HEAVY PRICE FOR THEIR TRANSGRESSIONS. A MORALITY TALE WITH AN UNHAPPY ENDING WAS BORN.	PAGE 171
EPISODE 52	*NIGHT FLIGHT* MGM ADAPTS AN ESOTERIC AND AVANT-GARDE FRENCH NOVELLA INTO AN AVIATION-CRAZED BLOCKBUSTER. NO ONE WAS HAPPY —INCLUDING ANTOINE DE SAINT-EXUPERY, ITS AUTHOR—WHO STARTED A LEGAL FEUD WITH MGM IN THE AFTERMATH OF ITS RELEASE.	PAGE 175
EPISODE 53	FATHER DOESN'T KNOW BEST: CLARK FACES UPHEAVALS BOTH AT MGM	

	AND IN HIS PERSONAL LIFE AFTER HIS FATHER UNEXPECTEDLY RETURNS	PAGE 179
EPISODE 54	*DANCING LADY:* ANOTHER COLLABORATION WITH THE SOARING AMBITION AND COMPLICATED ENTOURAGE OF JOAN CRAWFORD.	PAGE 183
EPISODE 55	*IT HAPPENED ONE NIGHT:* THIS IS WHAT HAPPENS WHEN AN HEIRESS (CLAUDETTE COLBERT) FLEES FROM HER OWN WEDDING. FOR CLARK, IT WAS THE BEGINNING OF THE BIGTIME	PAGE 189
EPISODE 56	*MEN IN WHITE.* IT WAS MGM'S ADAPTATION OF BROADWAY'S MELODRAMATIC SPIN ON HOSPITALS AND LIFE IN THE BALANCE. FOR THE DASHING YOUNG DOCTOR (CLARK), HIS PATIENTS CAME FIRST... UNTIL LOVE EMERGED FROM A NEARBY NURSING STATION.	PAGE 193
EPISODE 57	THE MOTION PICTURE PRODUCTION CODE: HOW THE SAUCY INNUENDOS OF CLARK GABLE, JEAN HARLOW, AND MAE WEST PROVOKED THE RAGE OF MOVIE CENSORS...AGAIN AND AGAIN AND AGAIN.	PAGE 199
EPISODE 58	*MANHATTAN MELODRAMA:* SET DEEP WITHIN A BIG, SIN-SOAKED CITY, IT WAS THE LAST OF GABLE'S PRE-CODE CRIME DRAMAS. AS "BLACKIE," HE'S A TOUGH GUY WITH A HEART OF GOLD. HIS LOVE INTEREST? MYRNA LOY. HIS COMPETITOR FOR HER AFFECTIONS? WILLIAM POWELL, WHO WINS THE GIRL IN THE END AS BLACKIE HEADS OFF TO THE ELECTRIC CHAIR. THIS IS, INDEED, A TEAR-JERKING MELODRAMA.	PAGE 203
EPISODE 59	*CHAINED.* FORBIDDEN LOVE AND GLAMOUR. MORE ABOUT CLARK AND JOAN CRAWFORD. *PHOTOPLAY* DEFINED IT AS "A NEW DIMENSION OF CLARK GABLE'S ACTING SKILLS."	PAGE 207
EPISODE 60	*FORSAKING ALL OTHERS:* IT WAS A FILM ADAPTATION, STARRING CLARK WITH CRAWFORD, OF A STAGE PLAY FAMOUSLY ASSOCIATED WITH TALLULAH BANKHEAD. AS OBSERVED BY JOSEPH MANKIEWICZ, "JOAN CRAWFORD WAKES UP MOVIE AUDIENCES. EVEN WHEN SHE GOES TO THE JOHN, SHE IS STILL A MOVIE STAR."	PAGE 209
EPISODE 61	*AFTER OFFICE HOURS*: A STYLISHLY PERMISSIVE WHODUNIT, IT ONCE AGAIN TEAMED CLEVER CLARK WITH SUPERDIVA CONSTANCE BENNETT, CAST AS ONE OF HIS EMPLOYEES. VIRTUE WINS IN THE END.	PAGE 213
EPISODE 62	*CALL OF THE WILD:* CLARK, LORETTA YOUNG, AND BUCK (AKA "SUPERDOG") UNITE TO TAME THE FROZEN NORTH. ON LOCATION, LORETTA GETS PREGNANT.	PAGE 215
EPISODE 63	MORE ABOUT CLARK'S DALLIANCE WITH LORETTA YOUNG, AND ITS CONVOLUTED AFTERMATH, DURING THE FILMING OF *CALL OF THE WILD*,	PAGE 221
EPISODE 64	JOAN CRAWFORD GETS MARRIED. (NO, NOT TO CLARK, BUT TO FRANCHOT TONE)	PAGE 225
EPISODE 65	*CHINA SEAS:* HOT AND HANDSOME, A SPIRITUALLY TORMENTED	

Sea Caption (Clark) meets a Trampy Adventuress (Jean Harlow) far from home. It's love at "second sight," and movie audiences fall in love with both of them. PAGE 227

EPISODE 66 *MUTINY ON THE BOUNTY.* Empire-Building and Men Togehter at Sea. It was the first of several film adaptations of a 1932 novel about a mutiny in the British Navy in the early 1800s. Clark did it best—much better than Marlon Brando's remake in 1962. PAGE 233

EPISODE 67 How Merle Oberon seduced Clark Gable: Everything you ever wanted to know about what her detractors called "That Trampy Half-Caste with Perfect Taste" PAGE 239

EPISODE 68 Hal LeSueur, Joan Crawford's "Incestuous Brother from Hell" tries to seduce Clark Gable PAGE 247

EPISODE 69 Lupe Velez, The Mexican Spitfire PAGE 249

EPISODE 70 The Death of Irving Thalberg and its complicated aftermath PAGE 257

EPISODE 71 *WIFE Vs. SECRETARY:* Clark's wife (Myrna Loy) plays her marital vows badly until she's jolted awake by Clark's attraction to his secretary, as portrayed by Jean Harlow. Virtue wins in the end as Clark returns to Myrna PAGE 259

EPISODE 72 *SAN FRANCISCO:* The Mother of every disaster film that followed, it combined Armageddon with Clark Gable and the blockbusting show tunes of operatic megadiva Jeanette MacDonald. Although cynics view it today as Campy but rousing good fun, audiences of the '30s found it inspirational. Decades later, its theme song is indelibly associated with the City on the Bay. PAGE 263

EPISODE 73 *CAIN AND MABEL:* It was conceived and funded as an acting vehicle for his protegee, Marion Davies, by William Randolph Hearst. Into this hotbed of ambition stepped their mutual friend, Clark Gable, who rescued it, critically. Here's the story of the frothy comedy that turned out surprisingly well for everyone involved. PAGE 269

EPISODE 74 Marlene Dietrich & Clark Gable. Getting Bilingual with *Der Blaue Engel.* PAGE 273

EPISODE 75 *LOVE ON THE RUN:* Its casting represented some of the most sophisticated (or indulgent) sexual couplings of an onscreen trio in the history of Hollywood. In reference to who was sleeping with whom (Gable and Crawford and Franchot Tone), no one outside the triangular pairing of the co-stars was entirely sure. PAGE 277

EPISODE 76 *PARNELL:* Perhaps it was its frumpish prudery that doomed it to

FAILURE, OR PERHAPS BY NOW, MYRNA LOY AND CLARK GABLE WERE TOO HIP AND LIBERATED TO CONVINCINGLY PLAY LOVERS TRAPPED IN THE BELIEF PATTERNS OF THE *HAUTE* VICTORIAN AGE. SO DESPITE ITS BRILLIANT COSTUMES AND A ROSTER OF SAVVY CHARACTER ACTORS, THIS TRIBUTE TO THE UNCROWNED "KING OF IRELAND" (CHARLES STEWART PARNELL) NEVER MORPHED INTO A BLOCKBUSTING HIT. .... PAGE 279

EPISODE 77 — THE ORIGIN OF CLARK GABLE'S PASSIONATE ROMANCE WITH CAROLE LOMBARD .... PAGE 283

EPISODE 78 — *SARATOGA*. IT WAS A RACETRACK DRAMA WHOSE CO-STARS WERE INFINITELY MORE INTERESTING THAN THE FILLIES RUNNING AROUND THE TRACK. JEAN HARLOW DIED BEFORE FILMING WAS FINISHED. THIS IS ABOUT THE LENGTHS EVERYONE INVOLVED TOOK TO FILL IN THE FINAL CRUCIAL SCENES WITHOUT HER. .... PAGE 287

EPISODE 79 — THE DEATH (1937) AND BURIAL OF JEAN HARLOW THE PLATINUM BLONDE GOES DARK .... PAGE 291

EPISODE 80 — *TEST PILOT:* AS SABERS RATTLED ACROSS EUROPE AND ASIA, *TEST PILOT* MORPHED INTO A HIGH-TECH TRIBUTE TO AMERICA'S ENGINEERING SAVVY. CLARK, ONCE AGAIN PAIRED WITH MYRNA LOY, CELEBRATE EVERYTING ABOUT AVIATION AND AMERICA'S POTENTIAL FOR CONTROLLING THE SKY. .... PAGE 295

EPISODE 81 — *TOO HOT TO HANDLE:* CLARK, STILL IN CAHOOTS WITH MYRNA LOY AS AN AVIATRIX, PROVES HIS METTLE AS NEWSREEL JOURNALIST. THE FILM'S ACTION-PACKED SPECIAL EFFECTS PROBABLY SAVED THE GABLE-LOY PAIRING FROM THE PERCEPTION THAT AS A SCREEN TEAM, THEY WERE OVER-EXPOSED. .... PAGE 299

EPISODE 82 — *IDIOT'S DELIGHT*: IT ORIGINATED ON BROADWAY AS A STYLISH AND AVANT-GARDE STAGE DRAMA SOAKED WITH EXISTENTIAL AND PACIFIST MESSAGES. THIS, THE FILM ADAPTATION, TEAMED CLARK FOR THE LAST TIME WITH NORMA SHEARER. WHIPLASHED DURING PRODUCTION BY THE POLITIC PRESSURES OF ITS ERA, IT WAS ARCH, ARTSY, AND NOT ALTOGETHER SUCCESSFUL, DESPITE THE VALIANT EFFORTS OF EVERYONE INVOLVED. .... PAGE 303

EPISODE 83 — CLARK DIVORCES RIA LANGHAM AND MARRIES CAROLE LOMBARD. THEIR FANS WENT WILD, AMERICA STOPPED IN ITS TRACKS, AND THAT'S THE END OF OUR CLARK GABLE, VOLUME ONE. .... PAGE 309

AUTHORS BIOS .... PAGE 313

Previous Works by Darwin Porter
Produced In Collaboration with Blood Moon

Biographies

Blood Moon Productions: Its Origins, Its Oeuvre, Its Sources, and Its Legacy
Entertainment About How America Interprets its Legends, Icons, & Celebrities

Henry Fonda, He Did It His Way,
(Volume One — 1905-1960 — of a Two-Part Biography)

The Fondas, Henry, Jane, and Peter
(Volume Two — 1961-1982 — of a Two-Part Biography)

Lucille Ball & Desi Arnaz: They Weren't Lucy & Ricky Ricardo
(Volume One — 1911-1960 — of a Two-Part Biography)

The Sad & Tragic Ending of Lucille Ball
(Volume Two-1961-1989) of a Two-Part Biography

Marilyn: Don't Even Dream About Tomorrow
(a 2021 revised version of the best-selling
Marilyn at Rainbow's End: Sex, Lies, Murder, & the Great Cover-Up (2012)

The Seductive Sapphic Exploits of Mercedes de Acosta
Hollywood's Greatest Lover

Jacqueline Kennedy Onassis, Her Tumultuous Life & Her Love Affairs

Judy Garland & Liza Minnelli, Too Many Damn Rainbows

Historic Magnolia House: Celebrity & The Ironies of Fame

Glamour, Glitz, & Gossip at Historic Magnolia House

Burt Reynolds, Put the Pedal to the Metal

Kirk Douglas, More Is Never Enough

Playboy's Hugh Hefner, Empire of Skin

Carrie Fisher & Debbie Reynolds,
Princess Leia & Unsinkable Tammy in Hell

Rock Hudson Erotic Fire

Lana Turner, *Hearts & Diamonds Take All*

Donald Trump, *The Man Who Would Be King*

James Dean, Tomorrow Never Comes

Bill and Hillary, *So This Is That Thing Called Love*

Peter O'Toole, *Hellraiser, Sexual Outlaw, Irish Rebel*

Love Triangle, *Ronald Reagan, Jane Wyman, & Nancy Davis*

Pink Triangle, *The Feuds and Private Lives of Tennessee Williams, Gore Vidal, Truman Capote, and Famous Members of their Entourages.*

Those Glamorous Gabors, *Bombshells from Budapest*

Inside Linda Lovelace's Deep Throat,
Degradation, Porno Chic, and the Rise of Feminism

Elizabeth Taylor, *There is Nothing Like a Dame*

J. Edgar Hoover and Clyde Tolson
Investigating the Sexual Secrets of America's Most Famous Men and Women

Frank Sinatra, *The Boudoir Singer. All the Gossip Unfit to Print*

The Kennedys*, All the Gossip Unfit to Print*

The Secret Life of Humphrey Bogart *(2003), and*
Humphrey Bogart, The Making of a Legend *(2010)*

Howard Hughes, *Hell's Angel*

Steve McQueen, *King of Cool, Tales of a Lurid Life*

Paul Newman, *The Man Behind the Baby Blues*

Merv Griffin, *A Life in the Closet*

Brando Unzipped

Katharine the Great, Hepburn, Secrets of a Lifetime Revealed

Jacko, His Rise and Fall, The Social and Sexual History of Michael Jackson

Damn You, Scarlett O'Hara,
The Private Lives of Vivien Leigh and Laurence Olivier

FILM CRITICISM
Blood Moon's 2005 Guide to the Glitter Awards
Blood Moon's 2006 Guide to Film
Blood Moon's 2007 Guide to Film, and
50 Years of Queer Cinema, 500 of the Best GLBTQ Films Ever Made

NON-FICTION
Hollywood Babylon, It's Back!

Hollywood Babylon Strikes Again!

Hollywood Babylon with Detours to Gomorrah
An enlarged, more shocking new edition of the scandal-soaked anthologies
that made Blood Moon famous.

Hollywood Remembered: Glamour, Glitz, Triumph, & Tragedy
A Tribute to the Glory Days of Entertainment & the Way We Were

NOVELS

Blood Moon,
Hollywood's Silent Closet,
Rhinestone Country,
Razzle Dazzle
Midnight in Savannah

OTHER PUBLICATIONS BY DARWIN PORTER
NOT DIRECTLY ASSOCIATED WITH BLOOD MOON

NOVELS

The Delinquent Heart
The Taste of Steak Tartare
Butterflies in Heat
Marika (a roman à clef based on the life of Marlene Dietrich)
Venus (a roman à clef based on the life of Anaïs Nin)
Sister Rose

TRAVEL GUIDES

Many Editions and Many Variations of The Frommer Guides, The American Express Guides, and/or TWA Guides, *et alia* to:

Andalusia, Andorra, Anguilla, Aruba, Atlanta, Austria, the Azores, The Bahamas, Barbados, the Bavarian Alps, Berlin, Bermuda, Bonaire and Curaçao, Boston, the British Virgin Islands, Budapest, Bulgaria, California, the Canary Islands, the Caribbean and its "Ports of Call," the Cayman Islands, Ceuta, the Channel Islands (UK), Charleston (SC), Corsica, Costa del Sol (Spain), Denmark, Dominica, the Dominican Republic, Edinburgh, England, Estonia, Europe, "Europe by Rail," the Faroe Islands, Finland, Florence, France, Frankfurt, the French Riviera, Geneva, Georgia (USA), Germany, Gibraltar, Glasgow, Granada (Spain), Great Britain, Greenland, Grenada (West Indies), Haiti, Hungary, Iceland, Ireland, Isle of Man, Italy, Jamaica, Key West & the Florida Keys, Las Vegas, Liechtenstein, Lisbon, London, Los Angeles, Madrid, Maine, Malta, Martinique & Guadeloupe, Massachusetts, Melilla, Morocco, Munich, New England, New Orleans, North Carolina, Norway, Paris, Poland, Portugal, Provence, Puerto Rico, Romania, Rome, Salzburg, San Diego, San Francisco, San Marino, Sardinia, Savannah, Scandinavia, Scotland, Seville, the Shetland Islands, Sicily, St. Martin & Sint Maarten, St. Vincent & the Grenadines, South Carolina, Spain, St. Kitts & Nevis, Sweden, Switzerland, the Turks & Caicos, the U.S.A., the U.S. Virgin Islands, Venice, Vienna and the Danube, Wales, and Zurich.

BIOGRAPHIES

From Diaghilev to Balanchine, The Saga of Ballerina Tamara Geva

Greta Keller, Germany's Other Lili Marleen

Sophie Tucker, The Last of the Red Hot Mamas

Anne Bancroft, Where Have You Gone, Mrs. Robinson?
(co-authored with Stanley Mills Haggart)

Veronica Lake, The Peek-a-Boo Girl

Running Wild in Babylon, Confessions of a Hollywood Press Agent

HISTORIES

Thurlow Weed, Whig Kingpin

Chester A. Arthur, Gilded Age Coxcomb in the White House

Discover Old America, What's Left of It

Challenging the Status Quo's Beliefs about Classic Hollywood

Biographies
from Blood Moon Productions

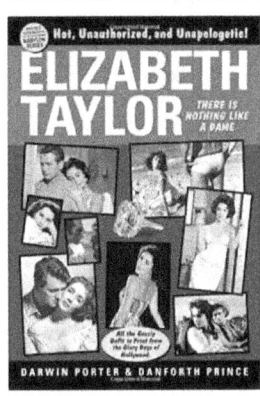

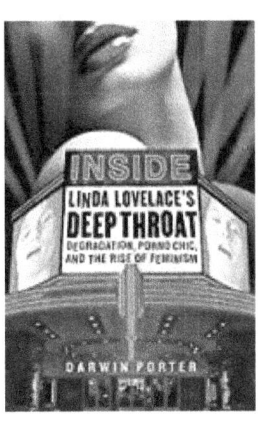

More Biographies
from Blood Moon Productions

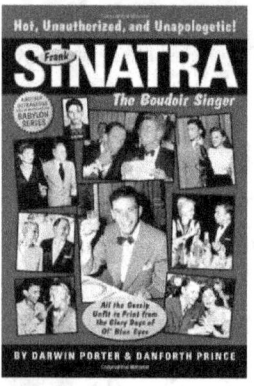

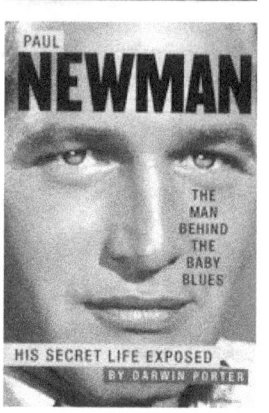

PRELUDE

Clark Gable used the casting couch to break into films, and he married two older women to further his career. Then he became the most enduring actor in the history of motion pictures.

His rugged good looks, except for his big ears, and that devilish Rhett Butler smile, made Clark Gable the King of Hollywood during its Golden Age.

Early in his MGM career, he co-starred with the legendary Greta Garbo. In his last picture, *The Misfits,* he appeared opposite the sex siren of the 1950s, Marilyn Monroe, the last picture for both of them.

Especially in his heyday, the 1930s, he seduced a bevy of leading ladies who ranged from Jean Harlow to Joan Crawford, from Marion Davies to Hedy Lamarr.

His real life commando raids into the boudoirs of celebrated actresses competed with his celluloid *clichés*.

Sometimes it's fashionable to say that the legendary actor's death marked the end of an era. Actually, in Gable's case, the Golden Age of Hollywood was tolling its death knells after he returned to the screen following military service in World War II.

He held on through the Eisenhower 1950s, often appearing in Westerns such as *Lone Star* (1952) and *Mogambo* (1953), a white hunter on a safari with Ava Gardner and Grace Kelly.

He lived to see television threaten the movie industry in the 1950s. And he survived the vanilla sequels of *Ozzie and Harriet.*

In November of 1960, when he died just after his completion of *The Misfits,* the Hollywood he knew had come and gone.

Today, many movie fans have seen him in only one picture, *Gone With the Wind* (1939), in which he played Rhett Butler opposite Vivien Leigh as Scarlett O'Hara.

He is being discovered anew by people all over the world, as all his movies are now in international distribution.

Episode 1

Clark Gable

THE EARLY YEARS

"No son of mine is going to become a fairy boy actor."
—William Gable

Clark, aged 17, on the verge of one of the most spectacular careers in the history of America's entertainment industry.

William Clark Gable, later nicknamed "Billy," came late into the world on the cold morning of February 1, 1901, in Cadiz, Ohio, weighing 11 pounds. It was a difficult pregnancy for his ailing mother, Adeline Hershelman. The doctor charged ten dollars for the delivery.

His father was William Henry Gable, a heavy-drinking wildcatter, a self-styled "he-man," who was always pursuing "liquid gold" in the oil fields of Ohio, Pennsylvania, Oklahoma, and Texas, but never bringing in a gusher.

When he was six months old, Adeline had her son baptized as a Catholic. She died when Billy was only ten months old. Perhaps she was suffering from a brain tumor. Upon her death, Will refused to have his son raised as a Catholic.

Billy's ancestors included Dutch Rhinelanders and Bavarian Germans.

In April of 1903, his father married Jennie Dunlap, whom he'd met when living with her parents in their boarding house in Hopedale, Ohio.

Jennie, 33, was not the most attractive woman in town, but she was the best-dressed, always stylishly coiffed and attired. She ran a millinary shop in the middle of town, selling hats she had designed herself.

No one who visits Clark Gable's birthplace of **Cadiz, Ohio**, is allowed to ignore its association with its famous native son. *Left to right*, above: an oversized portrait of Clark (as Rhett Butler) in the downtown shopping district; his birthplace (now a museum; and a granite monolith with his image in bas-relief as a monument to his memory.

After the marriage, Jennie's brothers helped Will build a wood-framed house for his new family.

In her late teens, Jennie had wanted to be a performer on the stage, or at least a musician.

Unlike many children with their stepmothers, Billy adored Jennie, and they became very close. She taught him how to play the piano, and brought in a musician to teach him how to play a brass instrument. Billy became so good, he was invited to join the local band. At night, she read to him from the works of Shakespeare.

She and Will often got into arguments, as he claimed "you're raising a sissy. You dress him up for school in such finery the bullies on the playground sometimes beat him up. Just remember one thing, bitch. I brought a boy to this house—not a gal. If I had the time, I'd take him fishing and hunting, doing what a man should do."

Clark's birth mother, **Adeline Hershelman Gable**, was warned by her doctors that having a child might kill her, but tragically, she defied them. Above *right*, **Baby Clark**.

Will wasn't home most of the time, often on one of his wild "black gold" hunts. When he was home, he taught his son how to repair cars. When he was old enough, he purchased a Ford Roadster for him for $175. When school let out in the summer, Clark took odd jobs such as delivering sacks of flour to local households from a nearby mill. Later, for $5 a day, he supplied coal miners with food and water.

At the age of fifteen, Billy stood six feet tall and weighed 157 pounds. For six weeks, he worked as a delivery boy for a grocery store. On a delivery to the home of Florence Wilson, a 59-year-old widow, he was invited into her home, since it was his last delivery of the day. She was overweight, with sagging breasts, and heavily made up. She gave him a slice of pecan pie.

She was struck by the rawness of this young boy with his bad teeth and slightly shy charm. She didn't go in for pretty boys, and her two previous husbands had been rugged he-men.

Before the afternoon ended, she had lured him into her bed, where he lost his virginity. She complained that he climaxed too soon, but she gave him two dollars nonetheless.

It is said that Wilson, "the town Jezebel," was the woman who began Clark Gable's involvement with older women, two of whom he would later marry.

As he moved into his teen years, he soon learned how to make extra money. "I no longer settled for $2. My price had gone up to $5. If one of the older queers in town wanted me, the bastard had to shell out $10. With women, you had to work harder. With men, you just lay back, dreaming of a beautiful gal while they took care of business down below. Easy money, wouldn't you say?"

Baby Clark in 1902: Camera-ready for his close-up, even at the age of one.

When Billy was 16, his father sold the small wood-framed house he'd built and moved to Ravenna, Ohio, where he bought a homestead. In summer, Billy plowed the fields, rising at 4AM to feed the chickens and livestock.

He hated farm work and soon dropped out of school and fled to nearby Akron, Ohio, 21 miles away. There was a great shortage there of male labor, since so many of Akron's young men were away, fighting World War I.

His first day in town, he was hired by the Firestone Tire and Rubber Company, molding treads on the tires of heavy-duty tractors and trucks.

This was the era of Prohibition, and it was rumored that at night, Billy delivered bootleg gin to speakeasies. Akron—the world's rubber capital—was dubbed "a mecca for bootleggers."

One night, he attended the Akron Music Hall, where he sat through a showing of *The Bird of Paradise*. It had opened on Broadway in 1912. An adventure story set in the South Seas, it contained brief nudity— shocking for the Akron audience—and an elaborate dance sequence.

He was enthralled.

Only 17 years old, Billy recalled, "that very night I decided I wanted to become a stage actor. I knew if I confessed that to Will, he would give me a severe beating."

He began to hang out at the theater until the manager decided to use him as an errand boy, working for no salary. He was first assigned toilet duty. He swept the stage floor and moved props around. Sometimes, he "put out" for some of the homosexual actors, hoping they might recommend him to the director for at least a walk-on.

"As an errand boy, I served hot coffee to the cast and crew, which I made myself backstage.," he said. "I sewed on buttons, and I ran errands in town, even picking up laundry for some of the actors. At night, I slept backstage on a cot. The next morning, I visited the YMCA for a shower."

[Flash forward to Hollywood of 1931, when then 30-year-old Clark Gable is making A Free Soul *with Norma Shearer and Lionel Barrymore.*

It was Barrymore who alerted him that Bird of Paradise *was being adapted into a movie. King Vidor had been signed as its director for a 1932 release. Clark had already confided in him how much the play had meant to him as a teenager.*

The aging actor suggested that Clark "would be perfect for the role of Johnny Baker," who arrives on a Pacific island and becomes involved with a young maiden.

When he got to the studio for his try-out, Lionel ordered him to strip naked, claiming that he would apply his body makeup. "Although you don't play a native, you're far too pale. You need a dark suntan."

"He even applied makeup to my genitals, which had a predicted effect. I was always horny back then. Good old Lionel. He knew how to take care of a young man."

"Finally, I was ready to go onto the set. Before leaving, Lionel stuck a rose behind my ear."

As Clark walked out, attired only in a skimpy leotard, the grips whistled at him. One yelled, "Pansy, have I got a big surprise for you!"

Young **Clark** with his stepmother, **Jennie**, whom he liked, loved, and respected. She read to him, listened to him, and cultivated a love of music.

The traveling road show (*The Bird of Paradise*, circa 1912) that got young Clark hooked on show biz. The play was marketed with tag lines that touted Hawaii as an exotic island where native girls play ukuleles, live in grass huts, dance the hula, and worship volcano gods. At the age of 17, at a theater in Akron, young Clark was mesmerized.

After Lionel introduced him to Vidor, the director appraised him up and down. "Just who are you trying to be? Tarzan's boyfriend?" He turned to Lionel. "Get this thing out of here."

The next day he gave the male lead in this Pre-Code drama to Joel McCrea, the female lead going to the sultry Dolores del Rio as "Luana."

Even though this film was Pre-Code, one scene was particularly shocking to audiences. On a boat, McCrea was depicted stripping down before donning his swimming trunks. As he does, the camera caught him stark naked, showing off his genitals.]

***

With the war coming to an end, soldiers returned to Akron to reclaim their jobs. Billy was fired, and he went back to the farm in Ravenna.

On January 11, 1920, when he was nineteen, his beloved stepmother died. With Jennie gone, Will sold the farm and demanded that Billy go with him to the oil fields outside Tulsa, Oklahoma. Billy's job involved removing sludge from the field.

In the summer of 1920, Jennie's father died, and Billy received a $300 bequest from the Hershelman estate.

Without telling Will where he was going, Billy ran away. He got into his Ford Roadster one night and headed northwest to Portland, Oregon, where he hoped to join a stock company he'd heard about.

After checking into a cheap hotel in Portland, Billy, the next morning, put on his finest suit to answer a HELP WANTED ad in the local newspaper.

He was interviewed by the manager of Maier and Frank's Department Store and hired right away. He was assigned to sell neckties behind a counter.

Later that morning, he met Earle Larrimore, a good-looking 23-year-old actor, who was holding down a temporary job waiting for the arrival of the Red Lantern Players. He told Billy he had the lead in their upcoming play, which they planned to take on tour.

The two wannabe actors had dinner together that night. Larrimore invited Billy to check out of his cheap hotel and move in with him. He lived at a boarding house run by Sarah August, a former burlesque queen from Seattle.

She greeted Billy warmly with a knowing smile. "My house is always open to boys like you," she said. "I'll serve you a hearty breakfast of ham and eggs in the morning at 8AM. In the meantime, I expect to hear those springs rattling upstairs, but not after midnight."

Billy woke up nude in the bed with Larrimore at seven the next morning. As he turned over, he saw that Larrimore was awake. "I've fallen in love with you," Larrimore proclaimed.

Robert Jordan, a fellow actor working in a part time job, recalled, "Earle and Billy were practically bonded at the hip. They could be Siamese twins."

That domestic bliss would become more complicated after a week had passed. Larrimore told him that he had a girlfriend, an actress named Peggy Martin.

Clark as a late teenager, a hip newcomer to the ins and outs of a brave new world getting ready for talkies and Pre-Code licentiousness, both on film and behind the scenes.

Clark with his gay, jaded, and world-weary mentor, **Lionel Barrymore**, as they appeared in Clark's breakthrough role, *A Free Soul*.

At this "on the way to the top" stage of Clark's career, some sexual indiscretions had transpired between the two actors, long ago and far away. But long after Clark's ascendancy to the "big-time," no one really wanted to talk about or mention them.

"She'll stay with me, and I'll get Sarah to put you in the room next to mine. I'll visit you every night before returning to bed with Peggy. She's very understanding about such things, and she sees other guys on the side."

Before Martin arrived, Larrimore held out the promise of going to New York with Billy. They could stay in the apartment of the actress, Laura Hope Crews. "I'm her cousin."

Born in San Francisco, Crews was an established actress, having appeared on a stage at the age of four. "She'll help us break into Broadway. I know she will."

Martin arrived with the Red Lantern Players, and she was immediately accepting of her beau's relationship with Billy, since it freed her to continue other involvements on the side. On some nights, she didn't return to the boarding house at all, and Larrimore slept with Billy.

It was late one hot morning in June of 1922 when Larrimore brought Billy to the little theater where the Red Lantern Players were going to rehearse before departing on a summer tour. Billy was introduced to Rex Jewell, the manager of the troupe, and his actress wife, Rita Cordero.

At Larrimore's request, Jewell let Billy audition for a small part in the upcoming play. Later, Jewell told Larrimore, "The guy is a damn clumsy brute. He flubbed his lines and even bumped into a prop."

Larrimore could be persistent, and he prevailed upon Jewell to give Billy a second chance. He promised that he'd rehearse him every night, and that he'd be ready to go on the road with the other members of the troupe. Since Larrimore was his leading man, Jewell reluctantly hired Billy.

That night, Peg Martin didn't return to the bedroom she shared with Larrimore. He began to rehearse Billy in his new role. He also made a suggestion that would become known around the world. "How are you going to bill yourself in the program?"

"William Gable."

"Fuck that! I've got a better idea. Why not use your middle name? It's more dramatic. You should call yourself Clark Gable."

AMERICAN GOTHIC
from the fields and forests of Ohio

The Gables: A punitive father poised side-by-side with his rebellious son.

Two views of Clark's early "lunch money," the successful stage actor and matinee idol, **Earle Larrimore**.

Right photo, Earle Larrimore onstage with his then-wife, the stage diva **Selena Royle**, in *Days Without End*, a four-act play that ran on Broadway for a successful eleven-month run in 1934. Royle's stage and film career ended abruptly during the "Red Scare" after members of Congress questioned her "loyalty" during one of HUAC's anti-Communist witch hunts.

***

"At the first rehearsal, Jewell was still uncertain which plays that he wanted to produce and direct. He kept changing his mind, telling the cast he would have selected the debut play by the time all of them returned from lunch.

As the newly named Clark was leaving the theater, he met a doe-eyed actress who stood five feet, two inches. She was a brunette and wore her hair in a bob, a style which Clara Bow would make fashionable in silent picture later in the 1920s.

Using his new name, Clark introduced himself to Franz Dorfler, an actress with the Red Lantern Players.

Impulsively, he invited her for lunch, where both of them got to know each other, each creating a somewhat exaggerated biography.

Larrimore had said he was in love with Clark after their first time together. He really wasn't. However, it seemed that Clark did fall in love with Franz after their first date. He even confessed that to Larrimore the day after his dinner with her.

The actor had no objection to Clark having a girlfriend, since he had one, too. "You may feel free to screw around with Franz, but I'm not leaving your life. How can I object? I have my Peggy."

Five days later, "Clark and Franz," along with "Earle and Peggy" stood together on the deck of the sternwheeler, the *Bailey Gatzert*, as it left Portland, heading 97 miles northwest to the town of As-

Two views of Clark Gable's early sweetheart, actress **Franz Dorfler**. *Left*, as an *ingénue* actress around the time she was dating the then-unknown **Clark**, and *right*, in 1937, when she made herself available to testify on his behalf, in court, against allegations of having impregnated Violet Wells Norton.

Thanks in part to Dorfler's favorable testimony, Norton's allegations were, for the most part, dismissed by the movie-going public as those of a fortune-hunting "adventuress."

MILESTONES: CLARK'S FIRST PATRIMONY LAWSUIT

In their edition of April 21, 1937, the *Cushing (Oklahoma) Daily Citizen* ran the news shown on the right, and "accessorized' it with the following caption: *Left to right:* **W.H. Gable**, *father of* **Clark Gable** *(center), and* **Jack Powell,** *assistant Federal Attorney, in court in Los Angeles, CA, to assist government in mail fraud trial of* **Mrs. Violet Wells Norton** *(on right), who allegedly claimed that the movie actor was the father of her child*

toria, Oregon. Positioned at the junction of the Columbia River with the Pacific Ocean, it had a reputation as a bustling, booming, hell-raising town.

[Founded in 1811, Astoria was the oldest city in Oregon, the first permanent settlement west of the Rocky Mountains. It had been named for John Jacob Astor, an investor from New York who had founded the American Fur Company of Fort Astoria, providing fur coats for women in the East. Today, Astoria is known to Clark Gable fans as the town in which he made his stage debut at the old Astoria Theatre.]

"I was falling more in love night after night," he said. "So was she." He made this confession years later.

Jewell kept Franz and even Clark in the show as they traveled aboard milk boats, migrating between settlements along the river for one-night stands. "Clark and I had to take bit parts that weren't suited for us because we were such a small group. Believe it or not, Jewell once had Clark play a baby hidden in a big crib. Once, when his so-called baby voice was heard, the audience burst into laughter."

At the end of the run, Franz invited Clark to come home to live at the farm of her mom and dad. At first, they rejected him, but he won them over with his hard work in the fields, wearing a worn-out pair of her brother's jeans.

When the cold weather came, he was hired by the Silver Falls Lumber Company for $3 a day. At this time, Franz was touring in a musical in Washington State.

When she came home, she found him selling ads for the local paper, *The Oregonian*. It was January of 1923, and soon, she was off again. They wrote love letters to each other. But then one week she didn't hear from him again. When they did have a reunion, months later, he bluntly told her, "I don't love you anymore."

She learned later that he was living with an aging grey-haired acting coach, Josephine Dillon. She was "making him over" for the stage and would marry him in 1924.

Franz entered into a long depression after losing him. She would never marry. "How does a girl replace THE Clark Gable in her life?" she asked a reporter years later.

In 1962, she contributed a testimonial of her love affair to the book *The Films of Clark Gable*.

She never saw Clark again until she reappeared in his life on April 22, 1937 when he was a big star at MGM and hailed as the King of Hollywood. She showed up in court to testify on his behalf when he was on trial in a paternity suit.

A Londoner, Violet Norton, was suing him for child support, claiming that he was the father of her 13-year-old daughter, Gwendolyn, who coincidentally did bear a close resemblance to him.

Norton gave the details of his alleged affair with her in London when he was known as "Frank Billings."

Tracing back to that long-ago summer when Violet gave birth, Franz testified that he was in Oregon with her. Cancelled paychecks from employers there also beefed up her case.

Based partly on the testimony of Franz, Clark won the case.

He met with Franz later in the day, where he learned that she was doing poorly financially. He used his power at MGM to get her a minor job at the studio. She had hoped that he would resume dating her

TOURISM, Circa 1900

Here's a poster advertising **River Cruises along the Columbia River.** The outfitter's "Fast Steamers" included the *Bailey Gatzert*, a panoramic riverboat named after the then-mayor of Seattle. Clark Gable, with his then-*inamorata*, Franz Dorfler, were aboard it during some of the transits to and from their stage gigs in Portland and Astoria, Oregon.

Astoria, Oregon: A salty river town with a "grand dowager' architectural past. Here's one of its meticulously restored historic homes, circa 1892.

again, but that didn't happen. She heard that he was being sought after by thousands of female fans and by most of the leading ladies at the studio.

Weeks later, after getting her that job, he walked past her on the MGM lot, either failing to recognize her or just pretending that he didn't. She knew then that her love affair with Clark had gone with the summer winds over Oregon. The winter chill had set in. But he would always live in her memory.

Norton was indicted by the U.S. Post Office for using the mail to try to defraud. She was sentenced to one year in prison. Upon her release, she fled to Canada and was never heard of again.

Franz Dorfler even faded from most biographies of Clark Gable. The last word on her was that in her early 80s, she died in a dreary nursing home in Portland.

***

Earle Larrimore did not disappear completely from the life of Clark Gable. They came together in 1925 when Larrimore was starring on Broadway in *Made in America* (1925). Meeting in Manhattan, Larrimore renewed his invitation for Clark to stay with him in the guest room of his cousin, the Broadway actress, Laura Hope Crews.

At the time, she was starring as Judith Bliss in the original Broadway production of Noël Coward's *Hay Fever*, which she co-directed with him.

She welcomed Clark into her home as the roommate of her cousin, and gave them orchestra seats the following night to see her Broadway play.

Clark and Crews bonded, and she found him most appealing. She had never married, but often seduced actors in the plays in which she appeared. One afternoon, when Larrimore was at an audition, she invited Clark into her boudoir. Before he left for Hollywood, she lured him back again for a repeat performance.

[Clark would not see her again until 1938 when she had been cast as Aunt Pittypat in Gone With the Wind. *She immortalized herself in the role, especially in that iconic scene where she flees Atlanta as it's being torched by Union soldiers.*

"Laura was old and fat when we met again, but I found her adorable," Clark said. Apparently, they never spoke of any romantic liaison that had occurred between them so long ago.

Time had been cruel to her fading body, but Clark looked much handsomer and manly than he had back in 1925. In fact, his screen image by then was idolized around the world.

Crews made her final stage appearance on Broadway in 1942 in the original run of Arsenic and Old Lace.

Four views of the distinguished stage actress, **Laura Hope Crews**, left to right: 1) As an Edwardian-era beauty, circa 1910; 2) From around the time of her "brief encounter" with Clark Gable; 3) as the focal point of a poster that promoted her then-famous silent film, *Blackbirds* (1915); and *4)* fluttery, flustered, and confused as Aunt Pittypat in *Gone With the Wind (1939).*

She had to drop out of the cast because of illness. Death followed on November 12, 1942 when she was 62 years old.]

Larrimore and Clark came together again in 1928 when he was starring on Broadway in *Strange Interlude,* that Eugene O'Neill drama staged at the John Golden Theatre. Ironically, in 1932, Clark would star in its film adaptation. That was the year Larrimore entered into a decade-long marriage to the actress, Selena Royle.

Larrimore's last appearance in Clark's life came in 1934 when Clark had completed *Forsaking All Others,* co-starring Robert Montgomery and Joan Crawford.

Larrimore was the leading man on Broadway in the stage version of *Dark Victory* starring Tallulah Bankhead. Backstage, after the show, she invited both actors to her suite at the Gotham Hotel, where the night before, she had hosted a party for Dame Sybil Thorndike.

Here's **Laura Hope Crews** (*left figure in left-hand photo*) with then-superstar **Constance Bennett** in the Pre-Code show-biz drama, *Rockabye* (1932). *The New York Times* reviewed it as: "There are tears enough in *Rockabye* to drown a plot, a circumstance which is a form of mercy in the case of this particular plot."

Insiders cited Clark's affair with Crews as his lesson in coping with the emotional and physical demands of *grand* theatrical *dames*—-and for the gossip he learned about Constance Bennett, Crew's co-star.

Bennett and Clark, in 1935, would co-star in *After Office Hours*.

Details of what happened that night became the subject of rumors along Broadway.

A.J. Liebling, a reporter for the *New York Telegraph* speculated, off the record, that Tallulah, Larrimore, and Clark conjoined in a *ménage à trois*. That item never appeared in his paper.

Shortly after Clark returned to Hollywood, he heard from Larrimore that he was out of a job. Tallulah had to drop out of her *Dark Victory* because of a sudden illness, and the production was subsequently canceled.

As she later confessed, "My face was swollen to twice its size. My mouth and lips were distorted. The skin across my cheeks and forehead was stretched taut. If I had been able to totter out on that stage, I could only have played pantomime. My voice had vanished. A doctor told me that he might have had to cut away my upper lip out of fear that the infection would spread to my brain."

When Clark, back in Hollywood, heard this disaster report, he told Larrimore, "Thank God it wasn't catching."

Alone and alcoholic, his career long faded, Larrimore died in Manhattan on October 22, 1947 at the age of 48. That ended a little-known chapter in the early life of Clark Gable.

Tallulah was furious when Warner Brothers cast **Bette Davis** in the 1939 film adaptation of *Dark Victory*. Whereas Tallulah failed in its Broadway version, Davis scored a triumph on celluloid.

Long recovered from her illness, Tallulah had tested for the screen role but was rejected by producer Hal Wallis. Barbara Stanwyck was also rejected.

Davis was cast with George Brent, **Humphrey Bogart** (shown with Davis above), and Ronald Reagan, who was paid $1,258.

The plot concerns a dying young heiress suffering from a mysterious brain ailment.

Tallulah Bankhead as Judith Traherne in the original Broadway production of *Dark Victory* (1934).

It opened to disastrous reviews. More trouble followed as Tallulah became desperately ill with a rare head infection that began when she squeezed a big pimple on her lip.

Before her illness, she had invited Clark Gable and his friend, Earle Larrimore, to share her bed in a short-term *ménage à trois*. This overnight conquest was not revealed until years later.

Clark Gable usually does not appear on most lists citing Tallulah's male conquests. Other members included Johnny Weissmuller (Tarzan), Gary Cooper, John Barrymore, and Sir Winston Churchill.

Episode 2

Josephine Dillon
Clark Gable's Svengali

Clark's First Wife was a Gray-Haired Acting Coach 17 Years His Senior

When his girlfriend, Franz Dorfler, got a job with another stock company in Seattle, Clark remained behind in Portland. He had already proposed marriage to her, with the understanding that they'd tie the knot upon her return.

In the meantime, he worked in odd jobs. Then he heard of Josephine Dillon, who had opened an acting school.

Born in Denver, Colorado, in 1884, she was one of six children. Her father was Judge Henry Clay Dillon, and his wife was a socialite in the area.

As a little girl, she'd grown up in an artistic family, where her fellow siblings studied art, listened to opera and other musical compositions, and read from the works of Shakespeare at night.

As a teenager, she went abroad, studying acting in Rome before returning to the United States to enroll in Stanford Universithy.

After her graduation in 1908, she joined the stock company of Edward Everett Horton. This Brooklyn-born actor in the 1930s would become a familiar face in Hollywood talkies. He had a beaked nose and always wore a pained look on his face. In his prissy, jittery voice, he was always uttering "oh, dear," on the screen.

His major competitor was Franklin Panghorn, whose droopy puss was also frequently seen on the 1930s screen, competing with Horton in putdowns of W.C. Fields.

Years later, after Horton was introduced to Clark, he told Dillon, "Your *protégé* is the kind of man I'd like to lock up in my boudoir for three months until I released him for an hour to get some sun before summoning him back to perform unspeakable acts, crimes against nature, with me."

"I have no intention of doing that," she said. "I have enough trouble keeping sex-crazed women from him."

Dillon was a short woman with very white skin, a low forehead, a broad nose, oversized nostrils, and thin lips. She was noted for her erect posture and a melodious speaking voice which was ideal for the stage.

After their first meeting, she appraised Clark as a "gorgeous skeleton," who needed work done on his front teeth and with a voice that was too high-pitched. One of her first recommendations was for him to wander into the forest somewhere and scream for an hour or two until he damaged his vocal

Josephine Dillon (*seen in the upper photo with a "stage prop" dog and in the lower photo with a well-tailored Clark in his early 20s*) invested time and effort in her younger *protégé*. She paid to get his teeth fixed, his hair styled, and his "drawing room" manners improved. Thanks to her training, he lowered his vocal registers, gained confidence as an actor, and improved his grammar and social skills.

After long and rigorous training in acting, **stage** presentation, and diction, she considered him prepped and ready for a film career.

chords and emerged with a much lower voice, not the high-pitched tone in which he had first greeted her.

Dillon also encouraged her young suitor to build up his body, for which he did daily exercises. He enjoyed her nourishing food at night.

It's only a guess, but in Dillon, Clark may have relived or found some of the love he'd had for his beloved stepmother Jennie, who had died far too young. There is little doubt that Dillon was a motherly figure to him.

In spite of his faults, she took this untrained youth "under her wing," as it was called back then. Her attraction to him had been immediate. Right to her face, he had appraised her in flattering terms. "You're a hell of a woman, a fine-looking lady. You've got beautiful eyes and a seductive voice."

No man had ever appreciated her like that before. "I wanted to adopt him that very day. I did, too."

Right from their first meeting, she sensed he was undernourished and living on almost no money.

She urged him to move out of his cheap hotel room and share her apartment. It had only three rooms—a combined kitchen and dining room, a small living room with a radio, and a bedroom with a double bed.

He packed all his belongings into one battered suitcase and moved in. She invited him to share her bed. He told her he didn't own a pair of pajamas and slept naked. She informed him, "I have no problem with that."

On his first night with her, she asked him what his favorite meal was. He told her "a big juicy steak." She immediately went out and bought one from a nearby butcher. At a market, she bought him potatoes for French fries and his stated favorite, a pecan pie.

Little did he know at the time, but she was training the future actor who would compete to play Tarzan on the screen He didn't get that role, but time and time again, he would have to strip off his shirt and reveal that physique that Dillon had encouraged him to work on beginning in the early 1920s.

Years later, a rumor spread that Clark's marriage to Dillon was never consummated.

It is highly unlikely that they never had sex, as he slept in the nude with her night after night. "I was one horny bastard in those days and for years to come," he admitted.

In the July 1932 issue of *Motion Picture*, years after he'd left her, **Josephine Dillon** *(photo above)* wrote an open letter to Clark Gable about his acting.

In print, she asked him, "Are you on the screen to make a show of yourself, merely letting the girls look you over, or are you there to make an entertaining show of the story?"

Despite Dillon's deep-seated respect for the stage and for stage acting, young Clark, under her tutelage, became fixated on morphing himself into a replacement for macho/flashy stars of silent films. News of the sudden death of western icon **Tom Mix** *(both illustrations above)* sparked a belief that one day, "with enough lucky breaks," he might replace him as a celluloid cowboy.

The super star died in a car accident in the Arizona desert in 1940.

She later admitted to her close friends, "Clark was the only man I've ever loved."

Her months-long training of Clark as an actor went on day by day. She envisioned a stage career for him. But after two weeks, he informed her that he would rather go to Hollywood and break into films.

His pronouncement was spurred by his visit to a movie house the night before, where he had watched a western with the reigning star of that genre, Tom Mix.

"I could replace him one day," he told her. "Of course, I'll have to learn how to ride a horse."

He didn't want to hear she was stage oriented. To her, Hollywood was a "boulevard of broken dreams," where hundreds of wannabee actors arrived every month and only a small handful ever became stars like Theda Bara or Mary Pickford or Douglas Fairbanks Sr.

"Most of the hopefuls who go to Hollywood end up pumping gas or waiting on tables, even carrying out the garbage," she warned him.

Still, he persisted night after night that they should leave Portland and head for Hollywood.

"With that in mind, I began to teach him to be more evocative with his facial expressions, something he had to conquer if he became a film star. I also worked with him, teaching him to be more natural and convincing in whatever role he might be offered."

Leaving him temporarily in Portland, she went ahead to Hollywood to prepare for his arrival. To support them, she got a day job typing manuscripts for Paramount, although she planned to open an acting school in time.

Knowing he would have to get around Hollywood, visiting the various studios, waiting at the gates to get a job as a $3-a-day extra, she bought a used car for him. It cost her $60 from her savings. She also rented a two-room bungalow for $20 a month.

Clark followed her to Hollywood and began making the rounds. Week after week went by, and he didn't get one job. He was living off Dillon.

Author Jane Ellen Wayne described his life at that time: "Clark felt like a caged gigolo, a frustrated philanderer, a lost child clinging to his mother for survival."

Sometimes, he didn't arrive at their bungalow for "Dinner at Eight," the name of a future MGM movie. She knew he was out seeing other women, but she was so afraid of losing him that she never confronted him with accusations.

Dillon, a firm believer in the artistic merits of the stage, but not necessarily of the film industry, was acutely aware of the treacheries that awaited actors as they aged.

Everyone in the film community was aware of the ruin that had already descended on silent screen actors such as **Theda Bara** *(photo above)*, and several hundred others.

One night, as she later recalled, she received "the shock of my life. After dinner, he asked me, 'Will you marry me?'"

"I broke down in tears," she claimed. "Tears of joy. I used to feel I would be a spinster for the rest of my life."

On December 18, 1925, Clark Gable married Josephine Dillon. There was no honeymoon. He listed his age as 24, and she claimed she was 36.

In the weeks ahead, he decided that waiting at a studio gate for a $3-a-day job was not for him. He wanted to be a movie star.

Along the way, he met a very handsome and well-built blonde-haired actor from Kansas. His name was Rex Wheeler. Over beer at a tavern at around five o'clock one afternoon, he told Clark he was getting steady work "no starring roles, but I'm living the good life." The well-dressed young man pointed to a new Ford parked outside.

"The game is you've got to let an established male star, director, or producer suck your cock. You don't have to return the favor, either. That's the easy road to success. Trust me."

A few months later, Clark encountered Wheeler again. "This time, the would-be actor confessed that he was leaving Hollywood and giving up trying to break into the movies.

"Your gig of surrendering your meat didn't work out?" Clark asked.

"It worked out better than I thought. At a party, I met this multi-millionaire who has a large estate in Sussex over in England. I'm going to be his kept boy and live in luxury. All I have to do is strip down every night and let him have his fill."

"Sounds like you've struck gold," Clark said. "That sounds like a gig I should find."

"Good luck and come and visit me in England some day," Wheeler said. "I'll give you my new address. I'll leave word with the butler to admit you."

Dillon was well aware of such offers made to handsome young men. "I think there were more homosexuals in Hollywood in the 1920s and beyond than straights," she later claimed. "Young men like Clark were their prey."

She forged ahead and opened her acting school. One of her early pupils was Gary Cooper, a handsome young man from Montana who had gone to school in England. "Gary wanted to learn to act," she said, "and I coached him. In time, he became the reigning king at Paramount while Clark ruled over MGM. Gary, I soon learned, was climbing the lavender ladder, a term for men selling their favors to other men such as producers and directors."

"As the years went by, word spread about Gary. He was letting men have their way with him. Everyone from Howard Hughes to Rod La Rocque. For his own amusement, he was seducing Clara Bow or Lupe Velez...later on, Marlene Dietrich."

Cooper was the first of the name actors Dillon coached. As the years went by, her pupils included Bruce Cabot, Donna Reed, Rita Hayworth, and Linda Darnell.

At long last, roles both on the stage and screen came to Clark, and he was *en route* to super stardom beyond his wildest dreams.

Yet it seemed inevitable that he came to Dillon one night and asked for a divorce.

He didn't tell her at the time, but he had met a rich socialite and planned to become her "kept man."

For a long time, Dillon resisted the divorce. In desperation, Clark learned that for $100, he could get a Mexican divorce. He went to Mexico to obtain the papers, but he needed her signature.

Two years after the divorce, she admitted, "Long before our divorce, he had come to me on several occasions and asked for one. I knew he was sleeping with other women, some quite well known actresses. Finally, I could no longer hold out on him, and I signed the document."

She also took it upon herself to file for a separation on the grounds of desertion on March 28, 1929. The final divorce decree came in on April 1, 1930.

The "impossibly handsome" **Gary Cooper**, known for a long and sometimes illustrious roster of financial benefactors, was another of Josephine Dillon's pupil/proteges. Here's how he appeared, vulnerable, horny, and available, in 1926.

***

Under query from a reporter in 1932, Clark denied that he had married Dillon for career advancement. He didn't really want to talk about that episode in his past. He had little to say. "I owe her a debt of gratitude for helping me become an actor."

A female cousin who was close to Dillon claimed, "Josephine never married again. She carried a torch for Gable until the end of her life. He was her one and only."

In the 1950s, a reporter discovered the first Mrs. Clark Gable living in a very modest home in San Fernando Valley.

In July of 1956, she was the subject of an *exposé* in *Confidential* magazine The story claimed that she was down and out and about to be evicted.

It also charged that Clark Gable was made aware of this but had refused to help her.

In August of 1957, Dillan testified against the magazine, charging them with libel.

With all this bad publicity, Clark ordered his business manager to send her money to avoid foreclosure.

When Gable died in 1960, his will stipulated that the remainder of Dillon's latest mortgage should be paid in full.

Throughout most of the rest of the 1960s, Dillon continued working as an acting coach until illness forced her to give it up. After Clark's death, many biographies came out, telling various tales about their marriage.

Many of them were misinformed. She was accused of being a lesbian.

She never publicly disparaged Clark in interviews. When biographies were published, she received many threatening and insulting letters from his loyal fans, many calling her "an old bag."

After prolonged illness, death came to Dillon on November 11, 1971 at a sanatorium in Glendale, California. She was 87 years old.

Episode 3

Gable
— Young and Struggling —

Tangles with the Barrymores,

John and Lionel

Three ferociously talented siblings (*left to right*, **John, Ethel,** and **Lionel Barrymore**) as they appeared in 1904. Eccentric and with massive egos and (in the case of the two men) problems with alcohol, they collectively morphed into the most revered and gossiped-about stage dynasty in Broadway's history.

Lionel (focus of the illustration from 1933 inserted below), segued between coaching young Clark and molesting him, always in a way the younger star indulged and accepted, often with bemused nonchalance and a wry sense of inevitablitiy.

As a young, wannabee actor, Clark Gable dreamed of becoming a stage star. He got a job as a $15-a-month "callboy," joining the backstage crew of *The Jest*, set for an opening at the New Plymouth Theater on Broadway, where it ran for 77 performances beginning in April of 1919.

His job involved knocking on a performer's door, warning him or her about their being due on stage in five minutes.

"The two stars of the play were John and his older brother Lionel," Clark recalled. "In the case of John, I had to knock much earlier because he was always a bit drunk, sometimes more than a bit. Once I found him stark naked, and I had to get him fully attired. I remembered he got semi-erect as I struggled to fit him into his boxer shorts."

One night, after the final curtain went down, Lionel invited Clark into his dressing room. "I was in need of a new job and nearly broke. I gladly accepted that shiny $20 he laid on me in return for letting him unbutton my pants and give me a blow-job."

"It was the beginning of a beautiful friendship that would last until his death in 1954." Clark remembered. "We made a few films together. When he starred on Broadway in *The Copperhead*, he got me cast in it, too."

The older actor asked young Clark to share his dressing room. One day, after a sweaty afternoon

Left: Pipe-smoking and flamboyantly alcoholic, **John Barrymore** was brilliant portraying oratorical heroes and Shakespearean kings. His fame as a stage actor during the 1920s cannot be overstated. Audiences forgave him virtually anything—including falling down drunk in public.

Right: His ferociously competitive, less attractive older brother, **Lionel Barrymore.** Gay, outspoken, and more involved in filmmaking than his brother, he's seen here with his second wife, **Irene Fenwick**, dressed to the nines in the finery of 1923.

on the set, Clark showered. As he stepped out from beneath the running water, Lionel was waiting with a bath towel. He rubbed or patted it over every inch of Clark's body, giving him an erection. Lionel took advantage and fellated him, continuing a sexual act that would be repeated over the course of the many years they appeared in films together.

"In addition to sucking me off, Lionel was like an acting coach to me," Clark confessed. "He didn't mind telling me if I stunk or if I blew a scene. Later, he'd blow me. He really helped me as an actor, and I was only too happy to reward him."

Playing opposite Lionel in *The Copperhead* was the stage actress and silent movie star Mabel Julienne Scott, a native of Minnesota.

She admitted, however, that she preferred film work to the stage. "Youth lasts for such a short time. You're younger than me, and you still have a little more time to break into pictures. I want to get ahead in Hollywood before I'm assigned to character parts."

Left photo: **Lionel Barrymore** as the focal point of a promotional poster, circa 1919, for *The Copperhead*. a stage drama about espionage during the early years of the Civil War. Clark Gable worked backstage as his gopher, acolyte, and "lust object." The arrangement included invaluable acting lessons, stage tips, and a decades-long friendship with the alcoholic but very savvy older actor.

Right photo: Stage diva **Mabel Julienne Scott**, a keen observer of the *zeitgeists* unfolding around her, shown during her jazz-age heyday.

[Many months later, Clark would reunite with her once again when she succeeded in getting him cast in another play, The Lullaby.]

Augustus Thomas wrote the historical drama, *The Copperhead*. At the beginning of the Civil War, Abraham Lincoln asks Milt Shanks (Barrymore) to join The Copperheads, a clandestine quasi-political crew in the North whose loyalties lie with the South. Shanks is to serve as a spy.

Clark and Lionel would make several films together, beginning in 1931 with *A Free Soul*, starring Norma Shearer, the Queen of MGM.

In *Night Flight* (1933), Clark would appear with both John and Lionel. In *Test Pilot* (1938), Lionel starred with Spencer Tracy and Clark.

Lionel's last appearance in a Gable film was in 1952 when they shot *Lone Star* with Ava Gardner.

Today, Lionel, born in Philadelphia in 1878, is still seen on television every Christmas as the villainous Mr. Potter in the Frank Capra movie, *It's a Wonderful Life* (1946) starring James Stewart.

***

At the Pasadena Playhouse in California, Clark had a reunion with the aging actress Mabel Julienne Scott, who had been instrumental in getting him cast in the play, *Lullaby*, by Edward Knoblock.

"I warned you how important it was to become a movie star while you're still young," she said. "I'm only a decade or so older than you, and here I am, cast in the role of a mother."

The author of *Lullaby*, Knoblock, who was also a novelist, arrived to greet the cast. He was known for turning out two or three plays a year, his most successful being *Kismet* (1911).

He also became involved with the creative ambitions of both Mary Pickford and her husband, Douglas Fairbanks Sr. For the swashbuckler, he adapted from their original format as novels *The Three Musketeers* (1921), *Robin Hood* (1922), and *The Thief of Baghdad* (1924). For Pickford, he wrote a script for *Rosita*, a film she brought to the screen in 1923.

"Edward sat through a dress rehearsal and gave me several pointers about how to sharpen my performance," Clark said. "He predicted a bright future for me as an actor, although admitting I had a lot to learn."

Episode 4

The Roaring Twenties:
Climbing the Tinseltown Ladder

Clark Gable Climbs It Rung by Rung, Seduction by Seduction

Ready, willing, able, and hot to trot. **Clark Gable** in the 1920s.

The Roaring Twenties descended on Hollywood as it became the film capital of the world, with dozens of young men and women—each dreaming of stardom—arriving daily from across America.

It was an era of great affluence, as mansions were erected and stars drove around in made-to-order automobiles, some of them painted purple.

It was also a time of cultural ferment and innovation in Pre-Code Hollywood.

The film industry's financial hub was still on Manhattan's Wall Street, but its creative production center was in California. Directors could "get away with almost anything"—providing that their silent flickers made money.

This era of excess and debauchery saw flappers dancing Charlestons and drinking bootleg gin with their handsome beaux. Hundreds of good-looking men came from the plains of Utah or the ports of New Jersey, thinking they would get cast in movies based on their looks alone. The women did the same, especially if they'd won a beauty contest such as Miss Indiana.

Clara Bow and John Gilbert were typical of those hopefuls. Legends such as Valentino and Wallace Reid had arrived, as had Gloria Swanson, Greta Garbo, and Pola Negri. Mary Pickford and Douglas Fairbanks Sr., already wore their crowns.

Studios such as Metro-Goldwyn-Mayer rose out of the heap, as did Paramount, 20th Century Fox, Warner Brothers, and Columbia.

At the beginning, studios ruled by men such as Louis B. Mayer or Jack Warner had near monopolistic control, from pre-production to release where they often controlled distribution. They could make or break stars. Weekly, they churned out flickers which were enjoyed around the world, including in Europe.

There was a nightmarish underside to the dream factory. Drugs, heavy drinking, and sexual debauchery were on display at many a party. Dreaming of stardom, a beautiful young woman often ended up on the casting couch of a producer or director. Handsome young men were also told to take off their pants, and many did so, even future "he men" of the screen.

At parties, especially in the mid-1920s, both young men and women were having sex without gender preference. The rule of the night was "anything goes

Josephine Baker, a black *chanteuse* born in St. Louis, MO, emigrated to Paris during the Roaring Twenties. There, consistent with the era's fast-emerging libertine tastes, she thrived as an "exotic," strutting her stuff as a role model to other entertainers with dreams of show-biz applause,

Here, she appears at the *Folies Bergère* against a then-newfangled Art Deco representation of an urbanopolis. What did she wear? Her trademark costume consisted only of a short skirt of artificial bananas and a beaded necklace, With nicknames that included the "Black Pearl," the "Bronze Venus," and the "Creole Goddess," she became an iconic image and a symbol of the Roaring Twenties.

Ambitious newcomers like Clark Gable either thrived or were demolished in the *tsunamis* of change, maneuvering their ways with the help of whatever assets or talents they could muster.

as long as it feels good." Actor Ramon Novarro later privately revealed, "As long as one hot mouth was working me over, I didn't bother to look down."

Rudolph Valentino became America's heartthrob until his untimely death in 1926 in Manhattan. He was the midnight dream of many a woman. At the time, his actual sexual preference was known only within the most limited chambers of homosexual Tinseltown.

The star system came into vogue, and millions of fans had their favorites.

Even back in the Pre-Code days, there were outcrys from the heartland "to clean up La La Land."

As one writer put it: "Will Hays, the former chairman of the Republican National Committee, was hired to clean up the movies, although it would take him some time. He wanted to prevent profanity, nudity, sex, and "ridicule of the clergy" from creeping into the flickers of the era. In time, he would succeed, but as the mid-1920s moved on, there were a lot of "shockers" yet to be screened.

As another author put it, "By the 1920s, consumer and popular culture were thriving. Women had the right to vote. European immigration and African American migration were descending on the land. Much of white Christian America feared the changes, seeking to re-establish cultural homogeneity and control over the motion picture industry."

By 1925, 50 million Americans were going to movie houses every week. That was half of the nation's population. In poorer areas, a movie ticket cost ten cents. Audiences in rural areas were often rowdy, as mothers brought their crying babies and drunks arrived cursing. There were cheers, jeers, shouts, and whistles aimed at the screen, along with stamping feet.

As time went on, theaters in major cities became luxurious, with carpets, plush seats, and pipe organs priced at $15,000 to $20,000 each.

Into this world marched a young and daring Clark Gable, who was destined to become the leading male star of his era. He was a gruff but dashing figure, attractive to both leading actresses of the day as well as some homosexual directors or producers.

"I had shoveled horseshit in the barn on a farm in Ohio. I hauled sludge from the oil fields of Oklahoma. I had cleaned crap from toilets in theaters. Taking off my pants and pulling down my underwear to lie on some producer's elegant couch was among the easiest tasks I performed. It could even be enjoyable, especially if I got a movie role. I dreamed of the day when I would be the seducer in total command. I'd be the star!"

Left: A gauzy illustration of Victrolas, wind-up devices that brought dance music to a generation desperate for high jinx, good times, and escapes from the morally repressive strictures of their Victorian parents.

Right photo: Flappers in Harlem, circa 1925.

When Clark arrived in silent-era Hollywood, the film industry was new, fun, sexually *piquant*, horny, and virtually immoral.

This circa 1923 magazine cover promises fast money and easy-going sex—a winning formula in any era.

Episode 5

Why Clark Gable Never Replaced Screen Heartthrob

Wallace Reid

Two Views of **Wallace Reid**

Upper photo, as a conquistador (*center figure*) with **Geraldine Farrar** as an Aztec princess (*right figure*) in *The Woman God Forgot* (1917).

Lower photo,, with his wife, **Dorothy Davenport**. After Reid's death, she aimed her professional and romantic crosshairs at Clark.

Born into a show business family in 1891 in St. Louis, Missouri, actor Wallace Reid became for a while the leading silent screen heartthrob before the ascendancy of Rudolph Valentino.

Reid's father, James Halleck Reid, was a successful playwright and actor, and his mother, Bertha Westbrook, was a stage actress. By the age of eight, young Reid himself was on the stage.

But he abandoned it and went on to enroll in the Freehold Military School in New Jersey, where he became an all-around athlete. When he wasn't on the football field, he studied music, learning to play the violin and the piano.

"To make him more of a man" (*his father's words*), he was sent to a ranch in Wyoming, where he became an expert horseman.

Wherever he went, he was praised for his good looks and his sculpted physique. There was later a rumor that when he first arrived in Hollywood, he posed as a nude model.

Producers at Vitagraph Studios spotted him and began to cast him in films. He was on his way to becoming the leading heartthrob of the Silent Screen.

Film mogul Allan Dawn was a major factor in building up Reid's film career.

In 1913, while working at Universal, Reid met actress Dorothy Davenport and was captivated by her beauty and charm. They were married a few months later.

Davenport was also born into a show business family in 1895 in Boston. Her father, Harry Davenport, had been a Broadway star, and her mother, Alice, an actress too.

Reid and Davenport began to appear in dozens of movies together, including *His Only Son* (1912), on the set of which they had first fallen in love.

They produced a son, naming him Wallace Reid, Jr.

D.W. Griffith spotted Reid and cast him in his two most famous movies: *Birth of a Nation* (1915) and *Intolerance* (1916).

Soon, Reid was playing the leading man to such reigning stars of the silent era as Gloria Swanson, Lillian Gish, Geraldine Farrar, and Florence Turner.

Jessie Lasky signed Reid to become the leading man at Lasky's Famous Players, which later morphed into Paramount Pictures.

His auto-racing films attracted male viewers, and his romantic scenes made him the idol of millions of American women.

The beginning of Reid's fall from grace came on a train ride to Oregon where he was set to film *Valley of the Giants* in 1919. The train had a wreck, and his scalp was seriously injured. At the local hospital, his

Wallace Reid (*right figure*) in a still shot from *Birth of a Nation* (1915).

doctors injected him with morphine in heavy doses.

This marked the beginning of a lifetime addiction. His wife, Dorothy, didn't try to seek a cure for his addiction, but actually supplied his morphine herself.

At the age of 31, on January 16, 1923, newspapers across America announced the untimely death of the former screen idol.

In the wake of Reid's death, Davenport went on a search for a leading man who could star opposite her. One day she spotted Clark on a studio lot and asked who he was.

The next day, she got the phone number of Josephine Dillon after being told that she managed the young actor's career.

Davenport was a name well known to Dillon, who viewed her unfavorably. She believed some newspaper accounts that Davenport had contributed to (some said, "caused") the death of her drug-addicted husband by giving him increasingly potent doses of morphine.

When Davenport called Dillon, she slammed down the phone on her. At the time, Clark was unaware of the call from the actress.

Dillon told Clark that before he broke into the movies, he needed more experience on stage. She secured him a position with a stock company in Houston, Texas. He left Los Angeles for Houston aboard the next train.

At the Palace Theater in Houston, Clark became a leading man. In fact, he made such a masculine, sexy appearance that young women began assembling at the stage door seeking his autograph. This marked the beginning of his being hailed as a matinee idol. He admitted, "I love the attention."

He also began a series of seductions. Word of them eventually got back to Dillon in Hollywood.

The plays changed every week. Clark scored his biggest success when he came onstage as the leading man in Eugene O'Neill's *Anna Christie*. In 1930, it would become Greta Garbo's first talkie. In it, she played a prostitute. It would have been impossible to imagine at that time that Clark himself would be her leading man in *Susan Lennox— Her Fall and Rise* (1931).

Weeks later, when Clark learned of Davenport's offer, he was furious that Dillon had not presented it to him. He asked for a divorce, the first of eight times he would seek to separate himself from Dillon before she finally acquiesced.

Davenport's star status in Hollywood faded, but she continued to work in show business as a screenwriter and in some cases, as a film director.

As the years went by and Reid's former young female fans faded away, Davenport lived to see the emergence of the new screen idol, Clark Gable.

She often bragged that she was the first to discover his potential as a screen heartthrob.

"Had it not been for that Dillon bitch, Clark and I might have challenged John Gilbert and Garbo as screen lovers. I think Dillon didn't want him to become a star, because she knew that if he did, he'd dump her, which he did, of course."

Dorothy Davenport in 1916. Decades later, in reference to how she supplied her then-husband with the morphine he craved, she said, "What happened to Wally had happened to many a soldier released from hospitals after World War I, and had happened to patients--released from hospitalization, cured perhaps of their injuries, but made into hopeless addicts through the then abysmal ignorance of the medical profession. It was worse, in a way, with Wally, because he was confident that he knew enough about medicine to believe that addiction wouldn't happen to him." *(Films in Review, April 1966)*

Episode 6

Clark Becomes the Kept Boy of
PAULINE FREDERICK,
"The Girl with the Topaz Eyes"

As a Gigolo, Clark Moves Onward and Upward

For two years in the early 1920s, Clark was financially supported, more or less full-time, by the stage and film actress Pauline Frederick, nicknamed "The Girl with the Topaz Eyes."

A Bostonian, she was born in 1883 and was around 43 years old when she met this struggling young actor fresh from the sludge of the oil fields of Oklahoma.

In their backgrounds, both Clark and Frederick had at least one thing in common: Each of their fathers had objected violently to their going into show business. Miss Frederick's father, in fact, had disowned her, bequeathing his sizable fortune instead to the family of his second wife.

When she was 17, Frederick had been hired as a chorus girl in *The Rogers Brothers at Harvard*. She was fired from that role four days later. Horribly disappointed, she cried for two days before seeking other roles and getting cast in some small parts.

The break that every aspirant showgirl dreams of came to her when she was discovered by the illustrator, Harrison Fisher, who defined and packaged her as "The Purest American Beauty."

By 1906, she was touring in such stage shows as *The Girl in White*. She met Frank Mills Andrews in 1909 and married him, temporarily leaving the stage. She returned to it in 1913 in the wake of their divorce.

Frederick was already in her 30s when she made her film debut in *The Eternal City* (1915). A decade and a half later, she gracefully made the transition to talkies when she played Joan Crawford's mother in *This Modern Age*, released by MGM in 1931. It was during its filming that Crawford (who co-starred in it with Neil Hamilton) learned a lot about Clark Gable's affair with her.

What was it about? Socialite Valentine Waters (portrayed by Crawford), reared by her father, goes to Paris to visit her mother, Diane (played by Frederick). There, she learns for the first time that her mother is the mistress of a wealthy Frenchman.

According to their director, Nicholas Grinde, "When they weren't needed on the set, Joan and Pauline spent a lot of their time dishing Clark Gable. They both knew him—how shall I put this?—as David knew Bathsheba."

Crawford later wrote, "Acting with Pauline Frederick was a stirring experience for me. The celebrated actress I'd met backstage with Paul Bern when I was a novice in Hollywood was the first legitimate theater actress I had ever seen. Now we were working together every day, and I had the

---

The distinguished but scandal-soaked **Pauline Frederick** (1883-1938), as she appeared onstage emulating Elizabeth I.

Her beauty was legendary. When the German-American sculptor, Ulric Ellerhusen, was a teenager, he saw a picture of her in a magazine and throughout the rest of his life, "defined" that memory of her as "the typical American girl."

The effigy he created from her photo won him a prize, and he continued to use that same "remembered image" of her as the pattern for many of his later sculptures. As stated by biographer Muriel Elwood, "Thus, unbeknownst to Pauline Frederick until later, her face and figure were molded in stone and bronze for several decades and appeared on many famous buildings, gracing memorial parks, state capitols and sculptured facades. She was the figure of the twenty-one life-size statues on the Chapel of the University of Chicago and the model of Wonderment on the San Francisco Palace of Fine Arts, as well as the four fifty-foot figures on the State Capitol in Louisiana" among others.

opportunity of knowing her, savoring her quality. Her voice had the tone and range of a rare instrument, but that was just one adjunct of her charm, as were her physical beauty and dramatic ability. At the core of this woman was an exquisite maturity. She had utilized her intelligence, expanded it, and was living proof of what a woman and an actress could become. Imagine my reaction when she told everyone, 'If they give this child a chance, she'll do big things. Joan is an actress.'"

In *This Modern Age*, Frederick vied with Mary Pickford as one of the top earners in Hollywood. However, after an unprofitable, unfulfilling filmmaking association with Samuel Goldwyn, she suffered through a number of flops. Seeking respite from talkies, and reaffirming that she preferred stage work, Frederick opted for a starring role in the road show reprise of *Madame X*, with the intention of touring it as a stage play through California and the West.

[Frederick had previously starred in a successful silent film version of that drama in 1920, and she had, shortly before her filming of This Modern Age, *starred in a stage production of* Madame X *in London. It had morphed into a smashing success. Reviewers in London, after its opening there in March of 1927, cited how the English accorded her "the greatest ovation given to a foreign (i.e., non-British) actress since Sarah Bernhardt."*

In time, Madame X *evolved into one of the most durable entertainment themes in history. Based on a French novel first published in 1918, it inspired adaptations in countries around the world 65 times, the first in 1910. After Frederick's silent version of 1920, Ruth Chatterton starred in a 1929 reprise. Gladys George updated the film in 1937. Even an aging Lana Turner, in one of her most memorable dramatic performances, made a tear-jerking version of it in 1966.]*

Madame X is the story of a fallen woman who is kicked out of her household and forced to leave her son behind. As the young boy grows up, he is told that "your mom has died."

The son becomes an attorney who, ironically, is assigned the legal defense, in court, of his mother on a murder charge. Neither the son nor the mother

Two testimonials to the fame and adulation accorded to Pauline Frederick:

Poster, left: **Frederick**, in her first major film role, evokes an ancient Roman Muse in *The Eternal City (1915)*. Its filming was interrupted by the breakout of World War I.

Poster, right: Promotional material for **Frederick**'s starring performance in *The Woman on the Index* (1919), a gangster drama about parental abuse, police misconduct, Bolshevism, betrayal, and suicide. It is believed that no copies of either of these silent films remain.

In 1931, **Pauline Frederick,** with second billing, co-starred with the top-billed (and younger) female lead, **Joan Crawford** in *This Modern Age,* a Pre-Code "morality tale" about social mores and sex. Between takes, Frederick (a previous sexual patron of Clark Gable) and Crawford (a future sleepover pal of his) gossiped shamelessly about his charm (or lack thereof), performance traits, and stamina. Both appear in the photo above, **Frederick** on the left, **Crawford** on the right.

Each was a discreet but unapologetic (and very promiscuous) bisexual, rumors spread about possible sexual dalliances between them.

knows of their primal relationship.

Frederick met Clark when he showed up to audition as her attorney/son for yet another road show reprise. "His reading lacked fire, but he looked like one hunk of a man. I hired him to tour with me, providing he joined me in bed every night."

[Frederick already had a reputation in Hollywood as a "female Casanova." Despite the difference in their ages, Clark found her alluring. Over the course of a long, eventful, and sometimes tragic life that included five husbands, punitive lawsuits, bankruptcy, and a swain whose suicide had been based, it was said, on unrequited love, it was bruited throughout show biz that "It's unlucky to marry Pauline Frederick."]

Over the course of the next two years, Frederick provided young Clark with a lavish lifestyle he never thought possible.

After moving into her mansion on Sunset Boulevard, he was seen riding around Hollywood in a Duesenberg Roamer painted purple. She dressed him in tailored suits and the best shoes, shirts, and hats, turning him into an elegant (young) gentleman.

In the privacy of her bedroom, she always insisted that he walk around naked. She had an insatiable appetite for sex, and often invited other young and aspirant actors to join them for three-ways.

She also secured the best dentist in Beverly Hills to work on his rotting teeth.

Clark left her at the end of his contract. After that, she married her third husband, Charles A Rutherford, a physician, in 1922. The union lasted two years.

She would be married five times, each of her husbands a bisexual or homosexual. Her favorite form of sex still remained a threesome.

She also had a stretch of lesbianism, seducing Joan Crawford, Jeanne Eagels, and Lilyan Tashman.

In an obituary in the *Montreal Gazette* published in September of 1938, a writer defined her as "Once America's favorite actress, stately in carriage, black-haired, and talented, she regally portrayed society dowagers and mothers. But whereas young theatregoers saw Miss Frederick as a tall, grey-haired woman, to the gay blades of a previous generation, she had been the epitome of seductive and sophisticated womanhood."

Older, wiser, and still fabulous: **Pauline Frederick** as she looked around the time of her extended dalliance, onstage and in bed, with Clark Gable.

Fast Forward to 1966: *MADAME X*

In 1920, **Pauline Frederick** starred in a silent film adaptation of a French-language stage play (*Madame X, see illustration, left*) about a tormented mother forced into a life of dereliction by her vengeful husband. Her 1920 version was only one of several other adaptations. Regardless of which version you might have seen, it managed to elicit tears from virtually everyone who saw it.

In 1966, **Lana Turner**—a scandal-soaked film icon noted for some occasionally frivolous roles—famously hoisted it into one of her most memorable performances.

In 2017, the authors of this biography of Clark Gable—as diehard and lifelong fans of LUSCIOUS LANA—celebrated her tumultuous life, her film career, and her niche in American history in a biography of her own.

Driving Pauline Frederick's custom-made Duesenberg inspired **Clark Gable** *(above)* to order one of his own when he became a highly paid movie star.

He already knew that his chief rival, Gary Cooper, on the screen and in the bedroom of female stars, already owned a Duesenberg, which he'd dubbed "The Yellow Peril."

Clark sent a spy to measure the length of Cooper's vehicle, and then ordered the manufacturer to make his one foot longer.

As the 1930s deepened, Clark was seen driving Carole Lombard around in his Duesenbarg. When Gary heard that, he bragged, "I got a Duesenberg before Gable did...and I got into the panties of Lombard before Big Ears did, too."

Instead of with Lombard, Gary was spotted driving along Hollywood Boulevard with his new co-star, Claudette Colbert.

Both Clark and Gary were in good company as owners of a Duesenberg. Fellow owners included Greta Garbo, Tyrone Power, Mayer Jimmy Walker of New York, press baron William Randolph Hearst, King Alfonso of Spain, and Prince Nicolas of Romania.

Episode 7

WHITE MAN

Clark Gable Makes His Film Debut

Copies of *White Man* **(1924)** have all been lost to history, but the images displayed above show some of the sexual hysteria associated with its release in 1924.

It's best known today as the first credited movie role Clark Gable nabbed. Even so, his role was minor. He played the affable brother of **Alice Joyce** (*the woman being abused in the lower photo*), a silent movie diva famous as a damsel in distress.

A lot of people in the film industry, both male and female, have claimed that they discovered the young Clark Gable. B.P. Schulberg, a pioneer film producer and studio executive, might have made the claim himself, but he never did. However, he did cast Clark in a minor role in the silent film, *White Man* in 1924.

Schulberg was born in Connecticut in 1892. As soon as he finished his schooling, he headed west to Hollywood, where he broke into the film industry. After some success followed by failure, he founded Preferred Pictures, which he built around the silent screen star, Katherine MacDonald. He also hired Clara Bow, 18, giving her a three-month option. He may not have claimed Clark as a discovery, but he had found "The It Girl," the bob-haired flapper who rose to super stardom as the late 1920s rolled on.

Schulberg, as a marketing genius, dubbed Mary Pickford "America's Sweetheart." A fixture linked with Paramount, he did much to promote the film careers of such legends as Cary Grant, Marlene Dietrich, and the French star, Maurice Chevalier. In the early 1930s, he discovered child star Shirley Temple, who—for a brief reign—became a box office champ.

However, by 1950, the film industry shoved him aside. He suffered a stroke and retired to Florida, where he died at the age of 65 in 1957.

Silent Film Esoteria: Did You Know?

That B.P. Schulberg, the marketing genius (and gambling addict) who produced *White Man*, Clark Gable's first film, was the film entrepreneur who "discovered" (some say "created") **Clara Bow** (*photo above*).

***

Schulberg hired Louis J. Gasnier to direct *White Man*. Another film pioneer himself, he became famous for the hit series, *Perils of Pauline,* starring Pearl White.

Gasnier returned to France in the early 1930s but was back in Hollywood in time to direct *Reefer Madness,* an anti-marijuana movie, in 1937.

Today, *Reefer Madness* is usually evaluated as ridiculous, ludicrous, and campy. It was re-released in theaters in 1972 for rowdy midnight audiences of pot-smokers, who screamed and yelled at the screen. Actress Thelma White, cast as Mae, later complained, "It bombed, and it ruined my film career."

In Hollywood, Gasnier ended up on "Poverty Row," turning out low-budget films for Monogram Pictures. He died, destitute, at the age of 87 in Hollywood in 1963.

In the plot of *White Man*, Lady Andrea Pellor consents to enter into a loveless marriage to Mark Hammer to preserve the ancestral estate of her impoverished family. She sails to South Africa, where the groom owns a diamond mine. On the night before her wedding, she wanders along a deserted beach and meets an aviator, the "White Man" of the title. She begs him to fly her away. Gallantly, he agrees.

They arrive in a jungle, where she begins to fall in love with him. She is shocked to find that in the jungle, he is worshipped by the natives, who know him only as "White Man."

Later, she is kidnapped by a river pirate who attempts to return her, with hopes of collecting a ransom, to Hammer and his diamonds. The pirate doesn't succeed

By now deeply in love, Lady Andrea and White Man fly together to London, where she consents to marry him. In London, Andrea re-connects with her brother, who, as it happily turns out, was a loyal buddy and soldier-comrade of White Man, the object of her affection

The role of Lady Andrea's brother was cast with Clark Gable in his inaugural movie role. He was paid $150. His scenes took ten days to shoot.

Cast as White Man, Kenneth Harland, a Bostonian, was often assigned romantic leading roles as heroes in action/adventure films.

In Hollywood, he was also known for marrying five wives, The best-known of the lot, in a marriage that lasted from 1924-1929, was the silent film star Marie Prevost.

Harland's leading ladies included Mary Pickford, Constance Talmadge, Lois Weber, and Anna Mae Wong.

Alice Joyce was cast as Lady Andrea. Although D.W. Griffith told her, "You remind me of a cow," she was a great beauty who became known as "The Madonna of the Screen," appearing in some 200 films.

Clark looked exceedingly well groomed and very handsome in his brief appearance and received 18 fan letters, 17 from young women and one from an older man.

He was launched on the rocky road to stardom.

**Silent Era Esoteria:
DID YOU KNOW?**

That the director (**Louis Gasnier**, *upper photo*) of Clark Gable's first film was

1) a Frenchman famous for directing such celluloid oddities as the first *Perils of Pauline* and *Reefer Madness* (1936), and

2) That he died in obscurity and poverty, and that

3) one of *Reefer Madness*'s stars, **Thelma White** *(bottom photo)* insisted, years later, that her involvement in it ruined her career.

Episode 8

JANE COWL

The Actress Promoted as the Most Beautiful Woman on Broadway Seduces Clark Gable

Clark Gable launched an affair with the actress voted "the most beautiful on Broadway." She was Jane Cowl, notorious for playing lachrymose parts—many of them by Shakespeare— and for her marvelous bovine eyes. The future movie star Jane Russell was named after her.

It all began when Josephine Dillon sent Clark to audition for a minor role in *Romeo and Juliet* (1925). Even though she was 41 at the time, she'd been cast as a very young Juliet.

She first spotted Clark when he was a shy young man lumbering down the aisle of a theater in Los Angeles to audition for a small part. Cowl said, "That kid has something. I don't know what it is, but I'm going to find out. Hire him!" she told producer David Belasco.

That day, without an audition, Clark was hired as a spear-carrier at $30 a week. Cowl was married at the time to Adolph Klauder, the drama critic for *The New York Times*, but that didn't stop her. "She was a real nymph," Belasco said. "She got off on teenage boys, claiming their semen kept her skin young and gorgeous. Having a husband didn't matter. During the run of *Romeo,* she virtually devoured Gable. He became not only her lover, but her servant, fetching her a drink of water, putting on her slippers, massaging her back."

Romeo & Juliet opened on Broadway and was praised by critics, including the leading lady's husband, who called her "the best Juliet in the history of Broadway." Perhaps he was prejudiced.

When the production went on the road, Clark went with it, his salary raised to $40 a week. They played Vancouver, Seattle, and Portland before landing in Los Angeles, where the play ended.

So did his torrid romance with Cowl. She would find other young men to do her bidding, and he, too, would move on to a string of other conquests.

***

Jane Cowl as Juliet in ad for one of the performances in which newcomer Clark Gable appeared onstage as an uncredited bit player silently carrying a spear.

Three images of the stage diva **Jane Cowls**: *Top and middle photos,* as editors displayed her on covers of their magazines in 1914 and 1927, respectively; and *bottom photo,* as she appeared during her sexual dalliance with her (younger) personal assistant and gopher, Clark Gable.

In one of his early gigs, Clark was seen on the screen in the 1924 silent drama, *Forbidden Paradise*. He had an uncredited role as one of the soldiers guarding the Czarina, Catherine the Great.

In 1922, the play, by then renamed *The Czarina*, migrated to Broadway in a production that starred Doris Keane as Catherine and Basil Rathbone as her leading man, Captain Alexei Czerny.

[Famous Players-Lasky, later acquired the screen rights, casting Pola Negri and Rod LaRocque in the leads, and Adolphe Menjou as the Chancellor.]

Initially, Clark planned "to put the make" on Negri, who had been widely publicized for her notoriously extravagant (some said, "fake") grieving at the Manhattan funeral of Rudolph Valentino, insisting that he had been the love of her life, which was not really true.

Two views of the silent era's debonair matinee idol **Rod LaRocque**, who "courted" (some said "pursued") Clark despite his flirtations with media outlets (*right photo*) about conflicting details of his engagement to his fellow Hungarian, silent screen diva **Vilma Banky.**

On the set, Clark soon learned that Negri was having an affair with the film's director, Ernst Lubitsch, so he stayed clear of her.

As a reigning screen vamp at the time, Negri, born in Poland, was the major competitor of Gloria Swanson.

Ironically, instead of Negri, it was LaRocque, the tall, handsome, and macho leading man, who pursued Clark. It began when they had ten days off. LaRocque invited Clark on a yachting trip to Catalina Island.

Having appeared in silent films since 1914, he was three years older than Clark.

There, LaRocque's lust for Gable became more obvious. They were seen visiting nightclubs together in the permissive Roaring Twenties before homophobia set in during the Depression-drenched 1930s and the activation of its strict Production Code.

When a newspaper item appeared about LaRoque's associations with Gable, they were each warned that their respective careers could be destroyed.

Since LaRocque was the star, he was the only one really vulnerable, so he rushed into what was called a "lavender marriage" with the Hungarian actress, Vilma Banky.

There were predictions that their union would be brief, but it survived until LaRocque's death in 1969. *[Throughout the course of their marriage, they slept in different rooms and maintained discreet affairs with same-sex partners.]*

Because of her thick Hungarian accent, Banky's film career ended at the dawn of the talkies. LaRocque, however, continued to work throughout the 1930s. His onscreen allure (and his career) effectively ended in 1941 when he appeared in *Meet John Doe*, starring Gary Cooper, another of his all-time "crushes."

Although only a lowly extra, Clark hoped the Prussian director, Lubitsch, might notice him. Whenever he could, without being too annoying, he tried to talk to him.

"He always had a cigar in his mouth. In spite of that, he was building a reputation as the most elegant and sophisticated director in Tinseltown," claimed Clark.

An actor himself, Lubitsch had made his last screen appearance opposite Pola Negri. Now he was her director.

"Kid," he addressed Clark, after looking him up and down with a frown. "I specialize in romantic comedies of manners, with my leading man often in a tuxedo, the leading lady beautifully gowned. You don't belong in an elegant drawing room, but in the barnyard, smelling of horse shit. You've got cowboy written all over you. Now run along and stop annoying me. I've got to return to thinking how much I detest Mary Pickford."

***

Episode 9

Clark appears as a bit player in a World War I Stage Drama,

What Price Glory?

And then in a small, silly role in a small silly spoof:

What Price Gloria?

The cruelly outspoken **Lillian Albertson** as a silent-era stage diva. She called acting newbie Clark Gable "a pansy."

Lillian Albertson, Indiana-born in 1881, was a stage and screen actress who became better known as a theatrical producer. She spent much of her life (dying in 1962) proclaiming that she "discovered the future film star, Clark Gable."

Lillian's husband, Louis Macloon, was also a theatrical producer, and for years, he also took partial credit for discovering the young Clark.

Their "discovery" got off with them to a rough start. He was seeking a role in a Los Angeles stage production of Maxwell Anderson's 1924 stage play, *What Price Glory?*

After Clark read for Lillian, she confronted him: "You sound just like a pansy. This roughneck role calls for a he-man, not a fairy."

Her brutal words echoed what his father used to label him.

He stood up to her and pleaded with her to give him another reading. Somehow, he managed to lower his voice based on the extensive coaching he'd received from his wife, Josephine Dillon.

The play depicted the rivalry between the U.S. Marine Corps officers fighting in France during World War I. It morphed into such an onstage success that it allowed Anderson to give up his teaching job and become a full-time playwright.

"Against my better judgment," according to Lillian, she cast him in the minor role of Private Kiper. Later, when actor Hale Hamilton left the play, Lillian promoted Gable to the second lead of Sergeant Quirt.

During rehearsals, Dillon showed up every day to coach her husband in the role. After three days, Lillian ordered her "to get your fat ass out of here. This play has only one director."

In 1926, in a film adaptation of Maxwell's stage play, director Raoul Walsh cast Victor MacLaglen and the gay actor, Edmund Lowe, as the soldiers, with Dolores Del Rio as the leading lady.

A raffishly charming **Clark Gable** as a young, untested actor in a minor stage production of *What Price Glory?* This was his first real part on the stage—a hardy, virile roughneck known as Kiper.

***

What Price Gloria?

A short time later,, Clark was cast in a bit part in a short, somewhat silly spoof of *What Price Glory* in which no one was particularly blatant about trying to seduce him. Entitled *What Price Gloria?* (a spoof of the title, *What Price Glory?*), it was the tenth in the (easily forgettable, not very well known, even at the time) *Pacemaker* film series. *[Each title within the series was a word play on one of the popular feature films of the silent era.]*

Its director was Wesley Ruggles, who was soon to helm Clark in another small role in silent romantic comedy, *The Plastic Age* (1925), starring Clara Bow.

Moving Picture World described the storyline of *What Price, Gloria* as: "George and Stanley are competitors in a swimming race and, as usual, Stanley tries to pull some crooked work to prevent George from winning, but fails. Stanley hires a woman named Gloria to aid him by claiming she is George's wife."

The lead role of George went to George O'Hara, a New Yorker who was born in the last year of the 19th Century. Reared in Hollywood, he had been "discovered" a few years before by director Mack Sennett, who defined the handsome, cleft-chinned young actor as a potential leading man after demanding that he strip naked in his office during an audition. After inspecting his body, he pronounced, "I think you can photograph sexier than Valentino."

Whereas *What Price Glory?* was produced in several film versions, including this version released in 1926, Gable's short-term gig in a frothy spinoff with a similar name (*What Price Gloria?*) never reached a platform of national importance.

This poster promotes the mainstream war drama from 1926 (co-starring **Victor McLaghlin** and **Dolores del Rio**) that movieland was talking about at the time.

[In the 1920s, O'Hara managed to leverage himself into a matinee idol. In 1926, he co-starred with John Barrymore and Dolores Costello in The Sea Beast, *a silent film adaptation of* Moby Dick. *In it, he played Barrymore's evil half-brother. Critics pointed out that the two actors resembled each other so closely that they could have been brothers.]*

O'Hara's glory days didn't survive the 1920s. He ended up in uncredited roles in just a handful of other films, the most important of which was *The Grapes of Wrath* (1940) starring Henry Fonda.

Stanley Taylor, a son of Minnesota, took the second lead in *What Price Gloria?* He was later cast in a few films such as *The Guilty One* (1924) and *The Romantic Age* (also 1924).

The female lead went to a coquettish Kentucky-born belle, Alberta Vaughn. In 1924, she (along with Clara Bow) had been designated as WAMPAS Baby Star. Success probably came too early for Vaughn. Although she co-starred with John Wayne in *Randy Rides Again* (1934), she was more or less washed up in show-biz by the time she was 31. Her life deteriorated after that. In the 1940s, she was in and out of jail on drunk-driving charges.

In *What Price Gloria?*, Clark appeared with a mustache and with his hair plastered down in a style inspired by Valentino. He sits at a soda fountain, watching Alberta squirt soda on another extra.

When Clark met H.C. Witwer, who had created the Pacemaker film series, and who was known for his successful adaptation of baseball and boxing stories for films, he cajoled him with "I wish you could make my role a little bigger. I have sixth billing, and I'm better looking than George O'Hara."

Witwer, responding after glancing at Clark's physique, recommended that he appear in boxing trunks. "That will appeal to the gals and fags."

Clark probably listened to his advice. In his successful 1936 film, *Cain and Mabel* (in which he portrayed a prizefighter) he displayed his body in black trunks. His co-star was Marion Davies, the mistress of press baron William Randolph Hearst.

***

Episode 10

The Merry Widow (1925)

Most of Erich Von Stroheim's silent films were visually glorious. Here's **Mae Murray** emotiong with **John Gilbert in** *The Merry Widow.*

This silent romantic drama was both written and directed by "that arrogant bastard," Erich Von Stroheim. He based it on the 1905 opera with the same name by Franz Lehár.

Von Stroheim lives today not for his past achievements in film, but because he played "that damn butler role" in *Sunset Blvd.* (1950). It starred Gloria Swanson as the fading silent screen goddess, Norma Desmond.

Born in Vienna in 1885, the future trend-setter had fled from military service in Austria and escaped to Ellis Island at the Port of New York in 1909. By 1914, in Hollywood, he was a stuntman in silent pictures. His break came in 1919 when he wrote, directed, and starred in *Blind Husbands.*

He became known for his dictatorial, demanding, and eccentric personality and his cynical view of human nature.

His most notorious film was *Greed (1924),* whose first cut ran for ten hours, and which required "drastic butchering."

The Merry Widow had been filmed before in Budapest. Entitled *A Víg özvegy,* and released in 1918, it was a silent directed by Michael Curtiz.

As a talkie, director Ernst Lubitsch cast Maurice Chevalier and Jeanette MacDonald in a 1934 version.

Finally Lana Turner and Fernando Lamas would bring it to the Technicolor screen in 1952. By then, it seemed pretentious, dated, and trite.

But when MGM announced *The Merry Widow* for a release in 1925, rumors surged through Hollywood that the studio was bringing a trio of its most unstable stars and director together. Many insiders predicted disaster. Von Stroheim was to direct Mae Murray ("fragile as glass") opposite John Gilbert, the rising screen heartthrob known as "Big, Bad Jack."

Von Stroheim had wanted Norman Kerry, the

Erich von Stroheim, a combative actor and sometimes brilliant film director, falsely claimed to be a decorated war hero and a member of the Austrian nobility. He had, in fact, been rejected by the Austrian army as unfit, the son of a Jewish haberdasher whose chances of advancement in Vienna were almost nonexistent. (Even the "von" in his name was fiction.) But in early Hollywood, his talent as a "fibber incarnate" (as stated by his biographer, Arthur Lenning) found an ideal home.

He's depicted above with **Miss DuPon**t in *Foolish Wives* (1922), during the frenzy of Hollywood's early film industry. Nicknamed by both his colleagues and movie audiences as "The Man You Love to Hate," he excelled at playing "dirty Huns" arrogantly leering at virtuous women.

lover of Valentino, for the role, but Irving Thalberg, the "Boy Wonder" of MGM, demanded John Gilbert. Thalberg warned the director that the film could not exceed a running time of two hours, and the budget had to be under $600,000.

Eventually, the film would earn $2 million, which was impressive, since many small town theatres charged ten cents a seat.

On the first day of filming, Von Stroheim warned Murray that "there will be no cutey-cute close-ups of your famous bee-stung lips." He would later be praised for "making Murray an actress," an almost unbelievable feat.

Little known except by fanatic film junkies, *The Merry Widow's* 1925 version brought together two screen legends, each rising from the Talkies of the 1930s as co-stars: Joan Crawford and Clark Gable. She was a lowly extra, and he was cast as a ballroom dancer in the background.

In the plot, Prince Danilo Petrovich (John Gilbert) meets Sally O'Hara (Mae Murray), a dancer. He falls in love with her and proposes marriage. Queen Milena (Josephine Crowell) objects because the proposed bride is a commoner.

Some of the crew compared Crowell, a native of Nova Scotia, born one year before America's Civil War, to Josephine Dillon, Clark's older wife.

A New Yorker, Murray was born in 1885. She had begun her Broadway career in 1906 when she danced with Vernon Castle. Two years later, she was in the chorus line of the Ziegfeld Follies, morphing into a headliner by 1915.

She danced with Clifton Webb and Rudolph Valentino. She also starred with Valentino in *The Delicious Little Devil* and *Big Little Person*, both released in 1919. She made sexual overtures to him, but was disappointed when she learned that he preferred men as bed partners.

Before he fell irretrievably under the spell of the Swedish actress Greta Garbo, Gilbert developed a crush on Murray, "the blonde goddess," as she was known back then. When she starred with him, she was in the process

John Gilbert with **Mae Murray** in Erich Von Stroheim's ode to Viennese schmaltz: *The Merry Widow* (1925). Darwin Porter's friend and partner, Stanley Mills Haggart, was an extra in it, dancing the waltz to endless repetitions of Johann Strauss's *Blue Danube*, and gossiping about the politics associated with its filming.

Decades later, co-author Darwin Porter drank and dined with her, listened to her travails, and recorded the anecdotes she relayed, sometimes with fury, about the tormented "glory days" of silent films.

  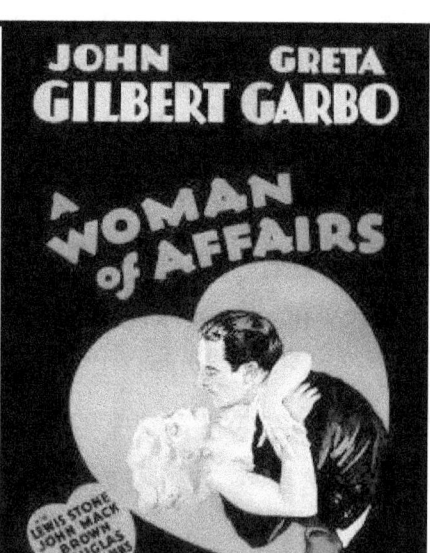

Two views of **John Gilbert**: *Left*, in the early 1920s, and *right*, as a mature and confident silent film superstar, accepting the onscreen adoration of **Greta Garbo** in *A Woman of Affairs* (1928).

It was inspired by a best-selling novel, *The Green Hat* published in the UK by Michael Arlen and adapted into a controversial (i.e.,racy) Broadway play a year later. Hollywood censors were so horrified by its decadence that they demanded that the producers rename it (*A Woman of Affairs*) as a means of disassociating it from its original "prurience." Additionally, its screenwriters were forced to eliminate all references to syphilis, heroin use, and homosexuality—all of them at the core of the original novel's (and the play's) plot. Only Garbo's mysterious allure managed to save it from ruin.

of divorcing Robert Z. Leonard, who would evolve into a future director of Clark Gable.

He sent her roses every day. Their budding (and very visible) courtship was bruited around Hollywood.

For Murray, the highlight of the movie involved her dancing "The Merry Widow Waltz" in the arms of Gilbert. When Stroheim told her, "There will be no waltz," she began arguing with him. Later, she appealed his decision to Irving Thalberg, who demanded that Von Stroheim film the waltz or else he would be fired.

Many of his creative ideas for scenes within the movie were opposed by Thalberg and discarded. Von Stroheim wanted to depict orgies, and as a means of establishing the "depravity" he wanted to replicate. He planned to hire at least three deformed people, two men and a woman.

Thalberg found one of Von Stroheim's proposals "deplorable." He planned to depict Prince Danilo as a foot fetishist invading the clothes closet of Sally O'Hara. As envisioned by Von Stroheim, Danilo would be seen kissing and licking her shoes. Thanks to Thalberg's intervention, that scene never appeared in the final version of the film.

Clark, as a mere extra, wasn't frequently needed except for the filming of two very small and short scenes. Nonetheless, he wanted to be close to the stars—not only Murray and Gilbert, but those visiting the set—that he agreed to work as a member of the crew, doing odd jobs. That way, he could eavesdrop while discreetly distant."

At one point, he heard Gilbert talking to Von Stroheim: "Everywhere I go, I hear nothing but whispers and giggles from love-starved women."

Gibert's biggest films lay in his immediate future. They included a role as Garbo's leading man in *Flesh and the Devil* (1926) and *The Big Parade* (1929), each of them important—some say "immortal"—touchstones of their respective eras.

Until she was "discovered" by Erich Von Stroheim, **Mae Murray** self-defined as a dancer more than as an actress. Unaware that she was on the cusp of movie stardom, she was one of the most popular (and gossipped-about) stars of the early Silent Era, the first ever acknowledged as "The Queen of MGM."

Years after her decline and fall from movie grace, she defined *The Merry Widow* as her best movie, despite the screaming arguments she sustained (some said "provoked") with Von Stroheim, her "impossibly difficult" director,

Accessorized with high-button shoes, a parasol, and the lacy fashion accessories of the Edwardian Age, here's **Mae Murray**, in a publicity photo for Florenz Ziegfeld's *Follies of 1915*,

NYC newspaper columnists described her as one of the "Favorites of the Footlights"—in this case at the rooftop "Jardin de Danse" at the New York Theatre, on Broadway at 44th Street. As described by historian John Douglas Eames, "You could call her affected, artificial, absurd; but who could deny that she was the very personification of Hollywood in its dizziest days of extravagance and glamour?"

At the time, Clark could not have imagined that in only a few years, he would replace Gilbert as the leading man at Metro and become Garbo's leading man himself.

***

Emerging from the wild plains of Utah in 1897, John Cecil Pringle (later known as John Gilbert) became the rival of Rudolf Valentino, who was to die in 1926.

Screenwriter Ben Hecht claimed, "Jack drank with carpenters and made love to whores but also to movie queens. Not just Garbo, but Lila Lee, Miriam Hopkins, Jeanne Eagels, and even Mary Pickford. He seduced starlet Carole Lombard years before Clark married her."

As far as male actors go, Robert Taylor is the only actor known to have seduced both Clark and Gilbert.

Gilbert was also a frequent patron at Lee Frances' exclusive bordello in Beverly Hills, which employed twenty of the most beautiful young women in Hollywood. Each of them had come to Tinseltown with hopes of becoming a star.

Frances also hired five studly young men for her bordello for clients, who liked variety in their sexual diet or wanted to engage in a *ménage à trois*. When Clark earned a higher paycheck, he also became one of her patrons.

Clark had seen *Heart of the Hills* (1919) in which Gilbert had co-starred with Mary Pickford. He had also seen two of the movies he'd made with Norma Shearer: *He Who Gets Slapped* (1924); and *The Snob* (also 1924). Even in his dreams, he probably could not imagine that in the not-so-distant future, he would become Shearer's leading man.

With the release of *The Big Parade* in 1925—the same year *The Merry Widow* was filmed— Gilbert was on the dawn of becoming known as "The Great Lover," thanks in part to those silents he made with Garbo. Ironically, with the debut of talkies, Gilbert's reign would be short. In contrast, with the advent of sound, Gable's career was just beginning.

Lionel Barrymore helmed Gilbert in the Ruritanian romance, *His Glorious Night* (1929), a talkie. Into a microphine, to his leading lady, Catherine Dale Owen, he uttered "*I love you, I love you, I love you.*" At the sound of his high-pitched voice, movie audiences burst into mocking laughter.

During his filming of *The Merry Widow*, Gilbert was in the process of divorcing actress Leatrice Joy. She had learned of his affairs with Barbara La Marr, Laurette Taylor, and Bebe Daniels.

Clark got her first, but Gilbert later seduced the newly renamed Joan Crawford when they co-starred in *Twelve Miles Out* (1927). His seduction of Crawford continued when they co-starred again in *Four Walls* (1928). She told Clark, "Jack does not make love to a woman. A woman makes love to him."

When Clark had first met Crawford, her name was Lucille LeSueur. Born in Texas one year after Clark entered the world, she was the daughter of a broken, spectacularly dysfunctional home.

Her girlhood read like a book of horrors. Her brother, Hal, frequently forced her to have sex with him, and he made extra money by bringing home tough buddies to seduce (or rape) her for fifty cents.

As she grew older and faced starvation, she appeared in some porn flicks. Years later, after she'd morphed into a big star on the MGM lot, these "blue movies" (as they were called back then) came back to haunt her.

With dreams of fame and glory, she headed to Hollywood, where she would do virtually anything to become a movie star. She also had a voice that would survive silent films and be perfectly recorded through microphones.

She later gave Clark some advice about "getting ahead," although he had already figured it out on his own.

"The casting couch is better than the cold hard floor," she told him. "Time is running out for both of us. We're not going to look this young and pretty forever. We've got to become stars before we turn 30."

Crawford later reflected on the number of handsome young men who came to Hollywood during the Roaring Twenties and who formed liaisons with established homosexuals in the industry.

"Sex with men may not have been their heart's desire, but it was an easy way to pay the rent because jobs were hard to come by unless you knew someone in the industry."

As time went by, the long-enduring love affair of Clark and Crawford would become embedded in the lore of Golden Age Hollywood. They would have sex to-

Who's that emoting (frenziedly) with then-superstar **John Gilbert**, cast as a reformed gangster in his hit 1928 romantic drama, *Four Walls?*

It's one of America's then-most-famous flappers, **Joan Crawford**, about a year before her unhappy marriage into Hollywood Royalty (i.e. with Douglas Fairbanks Jr.), long before she became an über-star herself.

F. Scott Fitzgerald described Crawford like this: "Joan Crawford is doubtless the best example of the flapper, the girl you see in smart night clubs, gowned to the apex of sophistication, toying iced glasses with a remote, faintly bitter expression, dancing deliciously, laughing a great deal, with wide, hurt eyes. Young things with a talent for living."

gether for years, and would also star together in pictures of the 1930s. But they would never marry.

Later, Bette Davis, who "despised" Joan and attacked Clark's "manhood," told a reporter, "Beginning with John Gilbert and Clark Gable, Crawford slept with every male star at MGM except Lassie, and I'm not so sure about that. Clark bragged about going through the roster of MGM's leading ladies, although he had a tougher time with those more lez-oriented like Garbo and Claudette Colbert."

"Lucille—I mean, Joan—behaved like a star before she became one," Clark said. "I adored her. As a flapper, she competed with Clara Bow for a while. She raided MGM's wardrobe department and appeared in night clubs beautifully gowned with a string of beaux. I was never jealous. We didn't have that kind of relationship."

"She would go on to marry three bisexual husbands. She was a great dancer, and the two of us often whirled around the floor before retiring to some secluded rendezvous for a night of sex. I was married but what the hell! God gave men—and women, too—sexual desires, and I'm sure he wanted us to put them to good use. However, beyond Joan's façade of glamour and a fun-loving gal on the make, if you looked closely, rather deeply, into her big, beautiful eyes, you saw a deep hurt that she could not conceal."

A publicity photo of **Clark** from shortly after his involvement as an uncredited stage hand and extra in Von Stroheim's strife-soaked 1925 version of *The Merry Widow*.

It was snapped with the intention of stressing his talents as a dapper urbanite familiar with the ways and morals (or lack thereof) of "high society".

Since Clark was a lowly extra and a sometimes "coffee boy," he had almost no encounters with Von Stroheim. When the director did take notice of him one hot afternoon, he looked him up and down. "You look exactly like a Hun," Von Stroheim said to Clark, as he slapped his whip against his black-booted leg.

Clark continued to be mesmerized by the stars who wandered onto the set of *The Merry Widow* when they weren't otherwise needed elsewhere on the lot.

He was already a friend of Lionel Barrymore. One afternoon, he had a reunion with Lionel's handsome brother, John Barrymore, who visited the set. "You're that Gable kid," The Great Profile said to him. "Lionel told me about you. I remember you. He gave you a rave and predicted stardom for you. Some advice, if you don't mind. Just keep giving Lionel what he wants, and he'll open doors for you."

After that pronouncement, he walked across the set to where Von Stroheim was speaking to Gilbert.

It would seem like "the impossible dream," but in a few years, Clark would be starring in a talkie with both of the Barrymore brothers.

***

New to Hollywood, Greta Garbo also arrived on the set one afternoon. Clark heard her speaking in a heavy Swedish accent to Gilbert He didn't get to meet her, but in a few years he would be her leading man, replacing Gilbert, whose career by then would be in decline.

In the years to come, when the Garbo/Gilbert love affair flickered out, he began an affair with Marlene Dietrich. In fact, it was at her residence, in January of 1936, where he died.

Rod LaRocque had already seduced Clark when they appeared in *Forbidden Paradise* (1924) His best friend was actor Roy D'Arcy, who was cast in *The Merry Widow* as Crown Prince Mirko.

Born in San Francisco in 1894, D'Arcy was just beginning his film career with the release of *Pretty Ladies* (1925). [*Also in the film,*

Bette Davis, a sworn enemy of Joan Crawford, was known both for her acting talent and her brilliantly vindictive put-downs.

Here's how she looked as a streetwalking harridan in *Of Human Bondage* (1934).

uncredited, appeared Carole Lombard and Myrna Loy as showgirls, and Joan Crawford, credited as Lucille Le-Sueur.) D'Arcy was on his way, appearing in film after film, including *The Gay Deceiver* in 1926 and *The Temptress*, also in 1926, this one starring Greta Garbo.

LaRocque must have told D'Arcy about his seduction of Clark because on their first meeting, the actor came on strongly. In Clark's later words to Crawford, "He approached me like a hungry panther seeking fresh meat."

Over lunch, Clark and D'Arcy bonded, and Clark accepted his invitation for a three-day sail to Catalina Island. Neither of them was needed on the set for a few days.

As Clark later confessed to Crawford, "He kept praising my macho charm. He claimed that I made Gilbert look like a pansy flower. I didn't see much of Catalina. The guy was insatiable. He just could not get enough."

"The thing with D'Arcy was a one-time thing," Clark allegedly told Crawford, "because I have other conquests in mind, including repeat performances with you. Oh, and another thing…I'm going to be in Clara Bow's (your fellow flapper's) next picture."

**Seductive Brouhahas
from the Film Sets of Yesteryear**

Here are two views of **Roy D'Arcy,** a talented, gay, and sometimes predatory staple in films of Classic Hollywood.

Left photo: **D'Arcy** as Crown Prince Mirko in *The Merry Widow* (1925); and

Right photo: **D'Arcy** as an Afghan lieutenant entertaining **Myrna Loy** in *The Black Watch* (1929), a costume drama about British intelligence (and imperialism) in India on the dawn of World War I.

Episode 11

Clara Bow, William Haines, and Clark Gable in

The Plastic Age (1925)

Before Clark met Clara Bow on the set of her latest picture, *The Plastic Age* (1925), the reputation of this flapper had preceded her. She thrilled audiences with her fashionably bobbed hair, Cupid's bow lips, and her devil-may-care *joie de vivre*.

She'd had a tough girlhood, growing up in a poverty-stricken family in Brooklyn.

Her father, Robert Bow, who was, it was said, plagued with mental problems, raped her on her sixteenth birthday.

One night, her mother woke Clara up at 3AM with a butcher knife at her throat. That afternoon, the young girl had told her, "I'm going to be an actress."

With the knife poised and ready to plunge in, her mother said, "You're going to hell. I'll see you dead before you become an actress."

A break came when she competed in "Fame and Fortune," an annual nationwide acting contest, in September of 1921. Among other benefits, the winner received a screen audition. One judge claimed that she had "a genuine spark of divine fire."

After that audition, Bow was on her way to super stardom in the silents of the late 1920s. By 1928 and 1929, she had morphed into the leading box office attraction in America.

Thanks to her private life, she developed a notorious reputation, seducing a string of movie stars, producers, and directors. She had a knack for bedding future screen legends. They included Gary Cooper, Clark himself, and John Wayne. *[Bow was rumored to have seduced every member of the USC football team, which included Wayne.]*

Believe it or not, Bela Lugosi can be added to Bow's list of lovers. He kept a frontal nude of her positioned near his bed for the rest of his life.

During her career, she became the subject of wild rumors about her sex life. The tabloids of the day accused her of exhibitionism, lesbianism, bestiality, drug addiction, and alcoholism.

Three views of **Clara Bow** in *The Plastic Age*. *Center photo*, with insights into the vulnerabilities of her wounded soul, and *left and right photos*, "making whoopee' with **Donald Keith**. Her heady promise of good times, bathtub gin, and easy intimacies proved almost irresistable to the movie-going public.

The Los Angeles-born director Wesley Ruggles had assigned Clark a small role in an episode of the two-reel comedy series *The Pacemakers* in 1925, and hired him again for *The Plastic Age*, produced by Bud Schulberg. Before too long, Ruggles would be helming Clark as the male lead of *No Man of Her Own* (1932) alongside his future wife, Carole Lombard.

The plot of *The Plastic Age* was based on a best-selling 1924 novel by Percy Marks.

It chronicles the lives of the "fast set" at an American University. An athlete, Hugh Carver (Donald Keith), meets party girl Cynthia Day (Bow), a hard-drinking, Charleston-dancing roadhouse hottie. He falls for her, although he has to face competition from Carl Peters (Gilbert Roland)

Amazingly, the film captured the performances of four future movie stars, each in uncredited roles: Janet Gaynor, Clark Gable, William Haines, and Carole Lombard. Those future married lovers, Lombard and Gable, first met on the set of *The Plastic Age*. Lombard later remembered the introduction. He did not particularly impress her, probably because he was in pursuit of Bow at the time. However, he was losing out to Roland, who was spending a lot of time in her dressing room.

A native of Mexico, Roland was viewed as competition for Clark. He had intended to become a bullfighter, but hopped a freight train to Hollywood, where, dreaming of stardom, he became an extra in films.

His birth name (Luis Antonio Dámasco de Alonso) was too big for the marquee, so he changed it to Gilbert Roland. He took his first name from the actor John Gilbert, and his last from his favorite actress, Ruth Roland.

In *The Plastic Age*, Donald Keith was Bow's leading man. A Bostonian, he was the same age as Clark, and was tall and rather good looking, as revealed in a number of movies in the early 1920s. He had worked with Bow before and had had a brief fling with her. When asked if he'd ever seduced her, he said he had not. "She seduced me."

Clara Bow's "unhappiness quotient" morphed from flamboyantly miserable to "hellishly psychotic," depending on what stage of her life she was at.

Her path to movietime glory began by submitting an application to a *Fame and Fortune* contest, similar to the one inserted above, in 1921.

Bela Lugosi, famous as "the ultimate vampire," as publicized for the 1931 film that launched his career, fell madly in love with, guess who? Clara Bow.

One afternoon on the set of *The Plastic Age,* Clark was surprised to encounter John Gilbert, fresh from starring in *The Merry Widow*. He'd arrived to pick up Bow for a hot date. The following evening, he was seen out with another "latest conquest," Greta Garbo.

Clark began to think he didn't have a chance with Bow, but one afternoon she didn't seem to have a date and turned to him She asked if he'd escort her out that night for some "hot time Jazz Club hopping and drinking bootleg gin from a silver flask."

As they headed out in his Ford, she told him, "I fuck on the first date. Why wait around?"

She kept her promise. As he whispered to William Haines the next day, "Clara is one hot tamale. She'll do every known sexual act, even one I had never tried before." He didn't describe what act that was.

Her other beau, B. P. Schulberg, later said, "Clara Bow lays everything but linoleum."

Her affair with Gary Cooper heated up when he was cast as one of the actors in *Wings* (1927), one of the most famous of all silents. During its filming, she continued her affair with Cooper, but also seduced Buddy Rogers, the future husband of Mary Pickford.

Clark had tried to persuade Bow to use her influence to get him cast in *Wings* in the role that eventually went to Cooper. *[By now, Cooper's nickname, "the Montana Mule," based on the size of his endowment, had been widely bruited throughout the movie colony.]*

Clark soon learned that Cooper, like himself, "swung both ways," generously offering himself to such figures as Howard Hughes, William Haines, Rod LaRocque, Randolph Scott, and Cary Grant. Eventually, Cooper formed a long-term relationship—in his case with Anderson Lawler, the tobacco heir, who lavished expensive gifts on the rising star.

Bow later claimed that "Coop was hung like a horse and could go all night."

If its director (Ruggles) had had his way, *The Plastic Age's* movie audiences might have seen distant but full frontal nude views of both William Haines and Clark Gable, each emerging from showers in a Pre-Code locker room scene.

Fearing censorship, Schulberg ordered that the scene be reconfigured and reshot. It still remains homoerotic. Clark was moved to a position closer to the camera, this time half-clad alongside the film's (also partially -clad) leading men, Gilbert Roland and Donald Keith.

Had someone saved that clip of Haines with Gable, each frontally nude, it would be worth a lot of money as a collector's item.

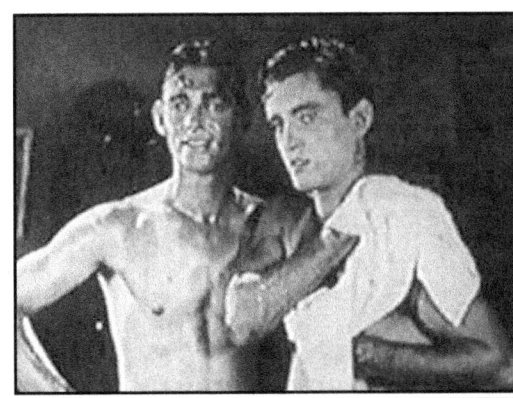

Clark's "studliness quotient" had never been more intense than when he appeared as a horny, uncredited extra in *The Plastic Age*. Here, he appears as the figure on the left, arms akimbo, with an unidentified colleague.

Full frontal nudes of the actors, including Clark emerging from a shower in a locker room, had to be cut.

***

The sexual mating of Haines with Clark became part of Hollywood's lore. A rumor involved Haines sodomizing Clark in a toilet booth in the men's room of the Beverly Wilshire Hotel.

William Mann, in his biography of Haines *[Wisecracker]*, quoted "a friend" who claimed that "Billy (Haines) fucked Clark in the men's room of the hotel. Billy was a fucker, not a fuckee."

That alleged incident is highly unlikely, indeed. They were seen by another person at the same event at the Beverly Wilshire, emerging from a booth in the men's toilet. Haines, however, was also known in Hollywood for "giving the best head" in town. It is more likely that he fellated Clark that night instead of sodomizing him.

Joan Crawford was the best friend of Haines, whom he nicknamed "Cranberry."

Here's **Clara Bow** as the poster girl for Howard Hughe's "psychotically disorganized" 1927 aviation drama, *Wings*. On the right is **Gary Cooper**, cast in a small role as a World War I flying ace. As part of the plot, he accepts a chocolate bar from his fellow pilot (Richard Arlen), and heads out to his plane, saying, "When your time comes, you're going to get it." Moments later, moviegoers learn that his plane has crashed.

Paramount was inundated with letters asking, "Who is that handsome pilot?" Clark had wanted Clara to use her influence to get him that role ."She preferred Coop over me. My day will come."

She did admit that Clark and Haines had a sexual relationship on and off for a period of more than a year and a half. "Billy and I passed Clark back and forth," she claimed.

Haines would go on to reach super stardom before Clark.

***

Haines was born on the second day of the 20th Century in Virginia. At the age of 14, he and his young male lover ran away from home, never to return.

The wild life of Haines and his exploits in New York's Greenwich Village would fill book and film scripts. Handsome, smart, and charismatic, the young actor was discovered by a homosexual talent scout who seduced him before sending him off to sign with Goldwyn Pictures in 1922.

In Hollywood, like so many other actors, he got off to a slow start, appearing in bit parts, uncredited. Slowly, he worked his way up the ladder. His first success arrived with his appearance in *Brown of Harvard* (1926) opposite Jack Pickford, brother of the reigning queen of Hollywood, Mary Pickford.

Shown here *(left photo)* during his movie-making peak in silent films, **William Haines** reigned briefly as Hollywood's number one box office draw. He was talented, handsome, and a wisecracker. He was also a homosexual.

Clark *(right)* was also handsome and virile. At age 24, he had his first sexual encounter with Haines, then age 25.

He was hoping that Haines would use his star power to help him get roles—in essence "prostituting" himself," in the words of Joan Crawford, Haines' best woman friend.

During a trip to Manhattan in 1926, Haines met Jimmie Shields and seduced him that very night. He had found the love of his life. The couple would be together until Haines' death, the day after Christmas in 1973 when he was 73 years old.

That same year, Shields committed suicide, claiming that he could not live without his lover at his side. Joan Crawford had referred to them as "the happiest couple in Hollywood."

To go back in time to 1930, the Quigley Poll had listed Haines as the number one box office attraction in America, but when he was arrested and involved in a sex scandal at the Los Angeles YMCA, Louis B. Mayer summoned him to his office.

There, Haines was ordered to drop Shields and enter into a lavender marriage with any of the willing starlets at MGM.

But Haines refused to give up Shields and was subsequently ousted from MGM. In the aftermath of "his fall," he morphed into one of the best-connected and most successful interior decorators in Hollywood. His clients included not just Joan Crawford, but Jack Warner, Gloria Swanson, Carole Lombard, Marion Davies, George Cukor, and in time, Ronald and Nancy Reagan.

Episode 12

The "It" Girl,
CLARA BOW

How She Seduced Clark Gable But Nixed Him as Her Leading Man

Silly, silent, and reeking of barely suppressed sexual hysteria, two of **Clara Bow's** greatest hits are illustrated in the photos above. Clark, as a newbie tooling his way across Hollywood, was emphatically aware of their content and the actress who became typecast (and trapped) by their implications.

Clara Bow continued to date Clark on occasion, but he grew disappointed with her when she vetoed him as her leading man in her next pictures. The first was *Mantrap* in 1926; the second was "It" in 1927.

Producer B. P. Schulberg felt that Bow had great potential to become a major star as the Roaring Twenties moved on. He had tried to promote her as "The Brooklyn Bonfire," but that label didn't stick.

After he read *Mantrap* by Sinclair Lewis, he became convinced that its film adaptation would shoot Bow into the upper ranks.

He met with Victor Fleming who signed to helm the project. Ironically, this was the same director who would direct Clark Gable in *Gone With the Wind* in 1939.

During the first week of rehearsals, Fleming began an affair with his leading lady.

The setting was a camp in Mantrap, Canada, where bachelor Joe Easter (Ernest Torrence) runs a dry goods store. He soon meets and calls for a flirtatious manicurist, Alverna (Bow).

The drama has just begun.

The movie became popular and helped make Bow a star. Its main detractor, ironically, was Sinclair Lewis himself. "I did not recognize my book from this film."

After Clark went to a movie house to see *Mantrap*, he discussed it with William Haines. "She let Ernest Torrence be her leading man. That's insane. I would have been terrific in the role. Torrence might be better cast as her drunken uncle."

Producer Schulberg came up with another idea for Clara Bow that he thought would go over even bigger. "It" *(stylized in quotation marks)* originated as a novel by Elinor Glyn.

He hired Clarence G. Badger and Josef von Sternberg (who later "created" Marlene Dietrich) to turn the plot into a vehicle for Bow.

Schulberg was right about "It." This star vehicle for Bow turned her into "The It Girl" of the flapper era. When asked to define "It," she told the press, "The term is defined as the quality possessed by some which draws all others with its magnetic force."

When meeting Bow, Glyn, who also appeared briefly in the film, explained to Bow that "It" was a reference to "a seductive siren of incredible animal magnetism, a virtual mantra for the ages." The writer was paid $50,000 for allowing Bow to be promoted as "The 'It' Girl."

In the film, Bow played a spunky shopgirl who has a crush on her handsome employer, Cyrus Waltham Jr. (Antonio Moreno).

Born in Madrid in 1887, Moreno had emigrated to New York in 1901. He became a stage actor before moving to Hollywood to work in films. By 1914, he was co-starring in a series of highly successful serials for Vitagraph opposite Norma Talmadge, a reigning diva of the silent screen.

He predated Valentino as the screen's "Latin Lover," co-starring with Gloria Swanson, Blanche Sweet, Dorothy Gish, and Pola Negri. Before working with Bow, he co-starred with Greta Garbo in *The Temptress* (1926).

Moreno was rumored to have had a number of sexual liaisons with homosexuals in the movie colony. However, he married heiress Daisy Emma Canfield in 1923, filing for divorce ten years later. Shortly before going to court, she was killed in an automobile accident.

Once again, Clark was disappointed with the love scenes between Moreno and Bow, claiming, "I could have done them better. Besides, I hear that even though he's married, he prefers men."

Clark decided never again would he have to try to convince Bow to be her leading man. "We stopped dating. My interest had drifted."

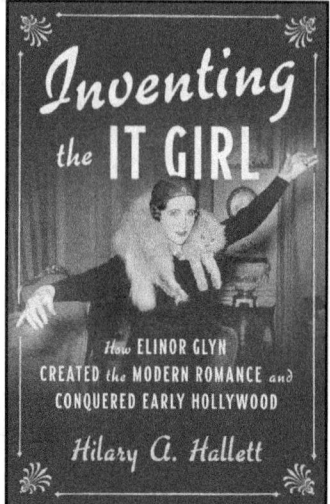

Elinor Glyn's (1864–1943) story began in 1892 after she married her way up the social ladder and into the English gentry. When her *belle époque* husband, Clayton, gambled their fortune away, she began writing "modern romance novels." Their notorious success changed publishing, the concept of love, and movie-making forever, infusing celluloid with sex in ways that set audiences aflame.

It was Glyn who endorsed Clara as **the "It" Girl**, thereby morphing her into a symbol of America's first sexual revolution.

In the photo above, **Clara Bow** and **Elinor Glyn** pose as the pair who regularly made "it" happen.

Three views of **Antonio Moreno**, then the pre-eminent cinematic stud of the entertainment industry. *Center photo*, with **Clara Bow** in *It* (1927), and *right photo* with **Greta Garbo** in *The Temptress* (also 1927).

Episode 13

North Star (1925)

Of all the co-stars proposed for Clark Gable, none was more outrageous than teaming him with "Strongheart" a male German Shepherd, one of the early canine stars of silent films in the 1920s.

He had been trained as a police dog in Berlin during World War I. After the war, its owner ended up in poverty. He shipped his beloved dog to a friend who ran a kennel in White Plains, New York.

At the sixth annual Shepherd Dog Show, in October of 1920, the future Strongheart won the event's third prize. He was described as "immense in body and hind leg formation."

The dog was spotted by film director Laurence Trimble, who bought him with the intention of morphing him into a star at Vitagraph in Hollywood. Trimble directed him in four films beginning with *The Silent Call* in 1921.

Clark Gable didn't work with the dog until 1925 when director Paul Powell cast him in a role in an adventure film, *North Star*.

The then-most-famous dog in the world, **Strongheart,** as he was publicized in this poster for *North Star (1925)*. Although the humans who starred in it (**Stuart Holmes** and **Virginia Lee Corbin**) have been for the most part forgotten, two of its uncredited, "eye candy" bit players included both **Clark Gable** and **Gary Cooper**.

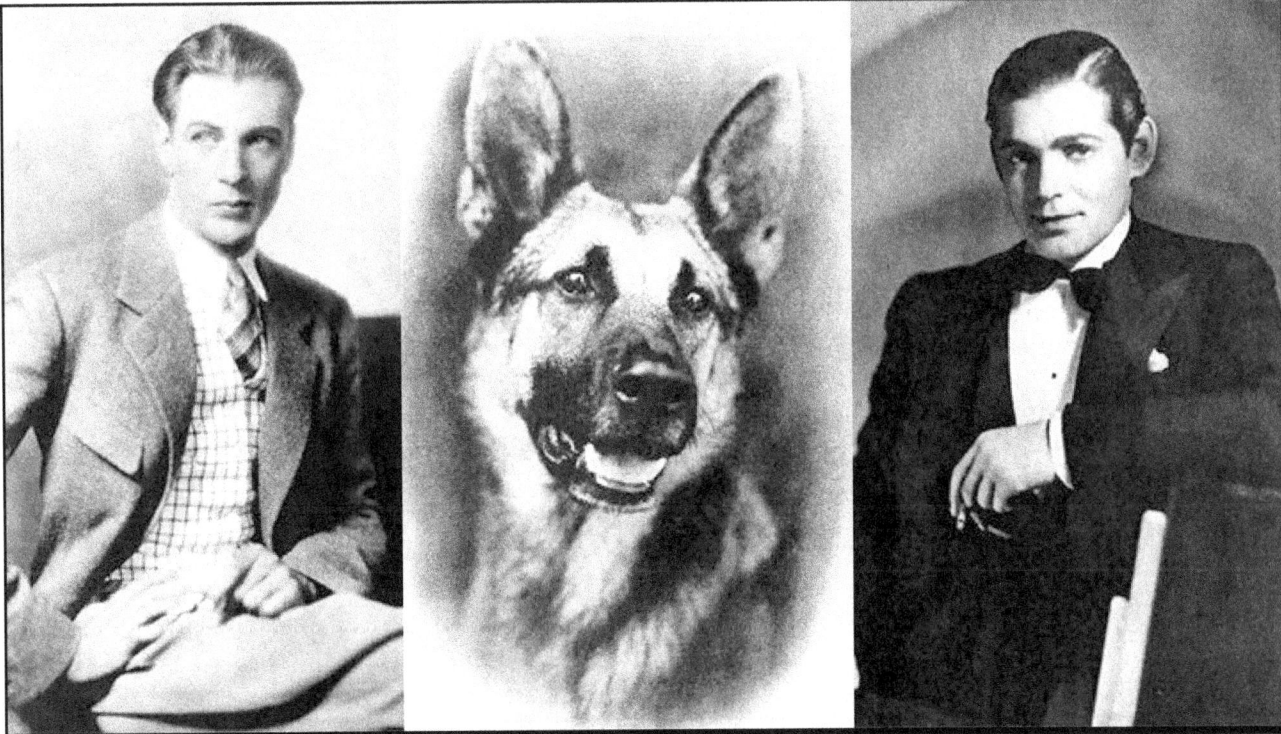

Ironically, when this portrait *(center photo)* of **Strongheart** was snapped in 1922, he was a MUCH bigger film star than either **Gary Cooper** *(left photo,* from 1927) and **Clark Gable** *(right photo,* from 1931).

From the beginning, Strongheart seemed to worship Clark, and spent time licking him whenever he could. If someone approached Clark, the dog growled as if protecting his private property.

In Clark's scene, he sits, playing the piano, at a party. With his front legs on the piano bench, Strongheat barks a solo. "It's fortunate that the film was silent," the director quipped.

Intrigued by how dog and man emoted together on film, Powell came up with the idea of casting them together in a series of adventure films.

"Clark and Strongheart might have been a hit duo in forthcoming movies, but he balked at the idea," said Powell.

Strongheart was viewed as the major competition for Rin Tin Tin, who was rescued by an American soldier from the battlefields of France during World War I and brought to Hollywood. Named "The Wonder Dog," Rin Tin Tin appeared in 27 movies, gaining international fame. He and Strongheart set off a craze among dog lovers for German Shepherds.

Rin Tin Tin's first starring role was in *Where the North Begins* (1923). It became such a huge success, eventually saving Warners from bankruptcy.

Rin Tin Tin died in 1932. Other dogs were groomed to replace him.

As for Strongheart, he died in 1929. During filming, he was accidentally burned by a scalding hot studio light. He developed a tumor which led to his untimely death.

It wasn't until 1960 that he was inducted into the Hollywood Walk of Fame.

Two views of **Laurence Trimble**, the intensely intuitive pioneer of Hollywood dog trainers. *Left photo*, in 1916 as a fast-emerging "man to call" about finding the right dog, and training him or her to "act" in any of the then-popular "Adventures in the Frozen North" films.

Middle photo: **Trimble** in 1921 during a shared expression of affection with **Etzel von Oeringen,** a German Shepherd originally trained as an attack dog by the Kaiser's military police during World War I. Trimble rescued him from the ruins of Imperial Germany, renamed him **Strongheart**, and morphed him into the then-most-famous dog in Hollywood.

En route to Strongheart's success, Trimble found and trained *(right photo above)*, **Jean** a Scottish Collie who became known as **The Vitagraph Dog.** Beautifully attentive and "as emotive as any actress in Hollywood at the time," she became a celebrity in her own right during the tear-jerking peak years of Silent Film.

MOVIE ICONS WE LOVE: More about Jean, The Vitagraph Dog.

In this movie still from *The Church Across the Way* (1912), child star **Helene Costello** and **Jean the Vitagraph Dog**—as a unified team—put themselves up for sale. Jean, a female collie, was the first canine to have a leading role in motion pictures

Episode 14

Dorothy Dalton

Clark Gable was available in 1927 for either screen or stage work. He became furious when he learned that an offer to tour with screen vamp Dorothy Dalton had come in for him, and that Josephine Dillon, as his agent, had rejected it, no doubt out of jealousy. In the 1920s, the sultry Dalton had a reputation of "devouring" handsome young men.

Arriving in Hollywood in 1914, Dalton became a screen goddess almost overnight. She appeared opposite William S. Hart in *The Disciple*. With his cigar-store Indian look, he'd become a Western star at the age of 50, having won acclaim on the stage in plays by Shakespeare.

During the course of her career, Dalton made 56 silent films, each before 1924. Thirty-five of them are lost to history. Kay Anthony wrote, "She was a shatterer of hearts. She made the pulses of men beat hard and fast."

Asked about her sex appeal, Dalton demurely told a reporter, "I guess I was just born to attract men."

Dalton's reputation as a screen vamp rose quickly. Off the screen, at one point, she set her eye on the then-unknown Clark Gable, whom she had met at a party.

Two views of screen vamp/siren **Dorothy Dalton**: *Lower photo* as a two-timing frontierswoman with too many children in *The Disciple* (1915).

The next day, she phoned Clark's agent, Josephine Dillon (Clark's lover at the time, and later, his wife) with the clear implication that she was calling about professional, not personal, reasons. Dalton wanted Clark to accompany her on a vaudeville tour of several states, including Texas, for a salary of $200 a week, the highest amount he'd ever been offered. The tour, it was said, would end with performances at the fabled Palace Theatre on Broadway in New York City, where his paycheck would rise to $500 a week, a "dream salary" back then.

The proposal was tempting, but Dillon—afraid of Dalton's sexual and marital aspirations, rejected the offer, asserting (falsely) that Clark was already committed to other bookings.

Weeks later, Clark "discovered" the full extent of what Dillon had rejected. "Clark never forgave me," Dillon reminisced, years later. "He considered it a betrayal, and accused me of trying to block his rise to stardom."

***

Dalton's big moment came in 1922 when she was cast opposite Rudolph Valentino in *Moran of the Lady Letty* (1922). She had planned to seduce the reigning heartthrob of the silent screen,

Dalton *(right)* with **Rudolph Valentino** in her breakout film, *Moran of the Lady Letty.*

but after a few days of filming with him, she learned a secret: He preferred male lovers, especially one named Paul Ivano.

Learning that, Dalton focused her radar instead on muscle-bound George O'Brien, only to learn that he was involved in a *ménage à trois*—ironically, with Ivano and Valentino.

Dalton had married actor Lew Cody in 1913, but the union lasted for only a few turbulent months.

[In 1931, on the set of Sporting Blood *(1931), Clark and Cody had a long talk about Dalton and why Cody's marriage with her had failed.]*

In 1924, Dalton wed Arthur Hammerstein, uncle of the lyricist Oscar Hammerstein II.

In the 1930s, Clark encountered Dalton at another party in Beverly Hills. In a chat, both of them reflected on "what might have been."

He later bragged to reporter Ben Maddox, "If I had been allowed to go on tour with that 'She Devil,' Dorothy Dalton, I could have taken away her pitchfork and taught her what a 'He-Devil' is like."

In 1972, when Dalton died at the age of 78 in her home in Scarsdale, New York, she was a forgotten star from an era in film history long gone.

***

Years after his "failure to connect" with Dorothy Dalton's offer of a nationwide touring gig, **Clark** (*left figure above*) co-starred with Dalton's ex-husband, **Lew Cody** (*right*) during the filming of a movie about racetrack politics, *Sporting Blood* (1931). In the center is **Madge Evans**.

It wasn't until then, during conversations and "replays" with Cody, that some of the mysteries about Dalton (and the involvement of Josephine Dillon, Clark's first wife) became more obvious.

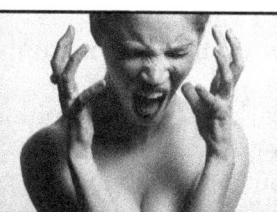

Clark probably paid a price for his sometimes cavalier treatment of his first wife, **Josephine Dillon** (*right photo*).

Prompted by jealousy and perhaps hatred of rivals for Clark's affection, it was she who sabotaged Clark's road-trip "elopement" with the sexually compelling *über*-vamp **Dorothy Dalton**, depicted *above on the left*.

Episode 15

Nancy Carroll

Nancy Carroll might be a forgotten name today had she not become the widely publicized mistress of mogul Joseph P. Kennedy, competing with Gloria Swanson for his affections and attention. Kennedy's wife, Rose (*née* Rose Fitzgerald, of the deeply entrenched political clan in Boston), was back on the East Coast, either giving birth to his children or tending to their brood.

Carroll also became known in Cary Grant biographies for having the lead in *Hot Saturday* (1932). That was the movie on the set of which the "real-life" Grant fell in love with their co-star, Randolph Scott.

The play, *Chicago,* brought Carroll together with Clark. Originally, it had premiered on Broadway with Florence Larrimore in the lead role.

Carroll and Clark took the play on tour. Its plot was based on two unrelated court cases in Chicago in which two women were each accused of murdering their lovers. Both were later acquitted.

Party girl and flapper, **Nancy Carroll.** A fan of hot jazz, chilled champagne, and cold gin, she was as famous in silent films as Gable later became in Talkies.

Carroll played Roxie Hart, "the prettiest woman ever charged with murder in Chicago." Cast as Jake, Clark portrayed a reporter on *The Morning Gazette,* covering Roxie's trial.

In years to come, he would portray a reporter nine times in films. But it was in the play, *Chicago,* that he first pioneered his simulated skills as a newsman. His hat was tilted back, he wore his coat collar up, and he maintained what was called "a cocky grin and a lumberman's stride."

Even when Carroll was emoting, Clark was still a scene stealer, "with a smirk on his face and the devil in his eyes," in the words of one critic.

During the run of the play, Carroll took Clark on as her lover. Unlike many of the women he'd seduced, she was two years younger than him.

He was glad to be working again. In the previous

Despite her flourishing film career, **Nancy Carroll** *(above, left)* is most frequently cited as one of the players in the Hollywood love triangle she became the victim of with **Joseph Kennedy Sr.** *(center photo),* and Silent-Era über-diva **Gloria Swanson** *(right photo).* Each of them appears as they were around 1918.

Ironically, the ultimate winner in the race for Kennedy's affection was **Rose** *(inset photo, right),* his long-suffering wife and mother of his nine children—three of whom (JFK, RFK, and Teddy Kennedy) morphed into some of the most influential politicians of the 20th Century.

two years, he had earned only two thousand dollars, his expenses being paid by his wife, Josephine Dillon.

During the run of the play, talent scouts from Hollywood offered Clark a screen test, but he rejected their offer. "I like to watch films. I don't like to be in them."

In contrast, Carroll was delighted when she was offered a contract with Paramount. In Hollywood, she became an immediate success. By the early 1930s, at least for a brief period, she was receiving more fan mail than any other actress in Tinseltown.

In many ways, the play, *Chicago*, would mark a turning point in Clark's career.

During a performance in San Francisco, an agent for a stock company in Houston, Texas, came backstage and pitched an offer to him. "For $150 a week, he was invited to join their company from the autumn of 1927 until March of 1928.

He would perform in various capacities and roles. Dillon was delighted, thinking it would give him the actor's training that he needed.

His first role would be Mat Burke in Eugene O'Neill's *Anna Christie*.

As 1928 rolled around and his time in Houston was running out, an offer came in for him to head to Broadway for a role in *Machinal*, starring Zita Johann.

Clark *(left figure)*, as a minor character, standing with an unidentified colleague onstage during a performance of *Chicago* in 1927.

Three views of **Nancy Carroll** on the set of the saucy/naughty PreCode "assault on public morality," *Hot Saturday*. Even its title offended the Victorian parents of many of its most avid fans.

Left photo: Carroll emotes with **Cary Grant**, the suave courtier who rescues her character from the small-town blahs, and

Center photo: At this point in her career, no one needed to add Carroll's name to her image and the title of the film that had been built around her. Everyone already knew it.

Right photo: **Letting 'em eat cake. Cary Grant** appears here with the fast-emerging object of his affections, handsome **Randolph Scott**, who played one of Carroll's onscreen love interests as *Hot Saturday's* third lead.

Episode 16

ARTHUR HOPKINS

The Sphinx of Broadway

Defines Clark Gable as a "WOOLWORTH ROMEO"

Within New York theatrical circles, producer Arthur Hopkins was known as "The Sphinx of Broadway" because he said little, his facial expressions indicating his approval or dislike.

He earned a reputation for casting unknown actors in key roles, notably Humphrey Bogart, Barbara Stanwyck, Spencer Tracy, and Edward G. Robinson. Clark Gable could be added to that list.

At the time, he worked with him, Hopkins had also cast a spunky New England redhead, Katharine Hepburn, in the play, *These Days*.

Hopkins gave Clark Gable his first big break when he cast him in a minor role with 22 other actors in the Broadway play *Machinal*, a drama which opened on Broadway at the Plymouth Theatre on September 7, 1926, where it ran for 91 performances.

The undemonstrative and enigmatic **Arthur Hopkins** one of the princes of the Broadway theater.

Over a period of 36 years, he produced and staged two plays a year, many written by (or starring) then-obscure writers and actors revered today as giants in their fields.

Question: What did detractors say about **THE MUMMY**, the silent film starring Zita Johann, an "import" from Franz-Josef's Austrian Empire? *Answer*: "*She's Three-Thousand Years Old, and STILL Without a Man of Her Own?*"

Zita Johann's scantily clad interpretation of a rescuscitated Egyptian princess prompted screams of horror, sighs of desire, and a sense of fascination from moviegoers across America.

In the *center photo, above*, she appears as a pre-destined mate for the evil High Priest (**Boris Karloff**) of an ancient Egyptian fertility cult.

Gable was assigned the role of "A Man." Most of the characters in the play did not have a name, even the lead actress, Zita Johann, whose character was simply named "A Young Woman." When Hopkins told her that Clark Gable would be her leading man, she asked, "Who in hell is Clark Gable?"

When he was also told that Zita Johann was the female star, he asked somewhat the same question: "Who in the fuck is that?"

Born in 1904 in what is now Romania, Johann and her family had come to America in 1911. By 1924, she made her Broadway debut in a minor play. Her first film was D.W. Griffith's 1931 *The Struggle.* Today, she is known for starring in Karl Freund's film, *The Mummy* (1932) with Boris Karloff.

Before working with Clark, Johann had been a *protégée* of Alfred Lunt and Lynn Fontanne.

At the time she worked with Clark, she was dating John Houseman. She married him in 1929. [*The marriage lasted till 1933.*]

Machinal was by playwright Sophie Treadwell, an early feminist of her day. It was based on a real-life case of convicted and executed murderer Ruth Snyder. She was strapped to an electric chair at Sing Sing in January of 1928. A reporter with a concealed camera snapped her photo at the moment electric waves shot through her body. The picture, which appeared within hours of her death, was replicated on front pages of newspapers throughout the country.

"Gable is a Woolworth Romeo," Hopkins told Johann, "But, trust me, he'll rise to the occasion."

The producer's prediction came true. Clark received good critical appraisals, one reviewer calling him "brutally masculine," a label he would carry throughout all of his future movies.

During rehearsals, he had become estranged from his wife, Josephine Dillon. In defiance of his wishes, and uninvited, she tried to crash rehearsal sessions of the play in Manhattan, sometimes interfering wth the production's orchestrators. As a reward for her interest, she was evicted from the theater.

Her last words to Gable were, "I hope you make it as an actor. You certainly never made it as a man."

During the early rise of Zita Johann, one of her claims to fame involved her association with (and her endorsement by) **Alfred Lunt** and his wife, **Lynn Fontanne**.

They were revered for their willingness to bring theatrical classics of Shakespeare (among others) to medium-sized cities of the American heartland during their reign as the most admired theatrical actor/entrepreneurial teams of their era.

Above (*left*) they appeared onstage, on tour, perhaps inspiring thousands of show-biz wannabees like young Clark Gable. Above (*right*), as they were honored by the U.S. Postal Service in 1999.

The theme of the Broadway play (***Machinal***) in which Clark Gable would appear with Zita Johann was based on one of the most grisly and sensationalist executions in the legal history of New York State. Shortly after it was "fried' in the then-newfangled electric chair, the body of a convicted murderer (**Ruth Snyder**) was displayed on the front page of the January 14, 1928 edition of New York's ***Daily News.***

Episode 17

"Clark Gable Will Not Trespass on My Talkie."
—Gloria Swanson

The future vamp of silent pictures, Gloria Swanson, entered the world in the spring of the final year of the 19th Century. Born in Chicago to a military family, she lived from Army base to base throughout her girlhood.

When she was fifteen, she had a brief walk-on in a film shot in Chicago. That sparked her migration to Hollywood, where she worked at Mack Sennett's Keystone Studios.

At Famous Players/Lasky/Paramount Pictures, she became a global superstar. She starred in films directed by Cecil B. De Mille, including *Male and Female* (1919) and *Beyond the Rocks* (1922) with Rudolph Valentino.

Her greatest acclaim came when she both produced and starred in *Sadie Thompson* (1928), earning her a Best Actress nomination, in 1929, at the first annual Academy Awards. Based on a short story by W. Somerset Maugham, it focused on the travails of a prostitute selling her services to soldiers and sailors in American Samoa.

By the end of 1927, the costs associated with her lavish lifestyle left her with only $69 in the bank. She turned to Joseph P. Kennedy to manage her financial affairs.

Sound films were on the way, but Kennedy advised her to make another silent, *Queen Kelly*, directed by Erich von Stroheim. He also took her as his mistress.

Under the banner of Gloria Productions, *Queen Kelly*, disastrously, went into production. After endess delays and constant retakes, it went way over budget even when it was nowhere near completion. Kennedy shut it down.

Before ***Sunset Blvd.***, ***Sadie Thompson*** was the most successful talkie **Gloria Swanson** ever made. In the film adaptation of a story by W. Somerset Maugham, she played a South Seas prostitute in defiance of the censors at the Hays Office.

She interpreted the character with such gusto that she was nominated for a Best Actress Academy Award for the 1927-1928 season. She lost to Janet Gaynor for three films, *Seventh Heaven, Street Angel*, and *Sunrise*. It was the only time an actress was nominated for acting excellence as spread across three separate pictures.

Swanson being courted by **Byron Kelly** in *Queen Kelly* (1929). Producer Joseph P. Kennedy and "the big spender," director Erich von Stroheim, collaborated in the creation of one of the alltime disasters of the silent era. The film was so over budget that it was never completed, leaving behind $600,000 of wasted footage. In *Sunset Blvd*, Norma Desmolnd showed a scene from Queen Kelly to Joe Gillis (William Holden).

To salvage her career, director Edmund Goulding and Laura Hope Crews (the future Aunt Pittypat in *Gone With the Wind*) worked on the script of *The Trespasser*.

Its plot focused on Marion Donnell (Swanson), a stenographer in Chicago, who elopes with Jack Merrick. The marriage is opposed by his rich father, who demands that his son have the union dissolved.

A Britisher, Goulding set about casting the movie. Previously, he had written screenplays for Mae Murray, and he had directed Garbo in *Love* (1927), a film adaptation of Leon Tolstoy's *Anna Karenina.* Joan Crawford, Bette Davis, and Tyrone Power each lay in his future as a director.

Goulding's writing partner, Crews, recommended Clark Gable for the role of Jack Merrick. She'd had a brief fling with him during her younger days.

Goulding phoned Clark, and he agreed to a screen test. Swanson agreed to test with him, something she rarely did. Years later, she told De Mille, "He was so rugged and masculine, I feared he'd steal the film from me, and I was desperate to succeed in talkies."

"I needed a more delicate man who looked at home in a dinner jacket," Goulding said "Gable looked like he was a former lumberjack. Perhaps he could play a hard-boiled gangster mauling a dame."

He had to find a meeker actor and one not so good looking. He settled on Robert Ames. Born in Connecticut in 1889, he'd had a long career in stock companies. Previously, he'd appeared onstage with such stars as Ruth Chatterton in *Come Out of the Kitchen.*

The Trespasser (1929), a Talkie, was a hit, garnering **Gloria Swanson** an Academy Award nomination. She lost to Norma Shearer for *The Divorcee.* Its plot focused on a "kept woman" who maintains a lavish lifestyle.

Swanson later said, "I turned down Clark Gable becuse of his huge ears, and I thought he would be mistaken for a truck driver. Robert Ames was a better choice for my leading man."

At its opening in New York, she thought she woul be crushed by hundreds of her fans. On October 29, 1929, the stock market crashed, as thousands lost all their savings. Joseph P. Kennedy was delighted. He had sold all his stock and was on the verge of picking up massive tracts of real estate "for pennies."

In Hollywood, Ames became Swanson's leading man. Years later, reflecting on her as a scene-stealer, he said, "When she came before the camera, she hogged the screen. No actor had a chance opposite her."

Tragically, after a run of other films he made in 1929 and 1930, Ames was found dead in a room at the Hotel Delmonico in Manhattan. Although he was only 42 at the time of his death, it was not ruled a suicide. He had been taking a non-narcotic medication for alcohol withdrawal delirium. He had divorced his fourth wife shortly before his death.

As for Swanson, *The Trespasser* (1930) morphed into one of only two hit talkies that she appeared in, and one of three for which she was Oscar-nominated. *[Actually* The Trespasser *was initially released as a silent film and then re-released as a talkie.]*

Swanson's other Oscar nominations had been for her performance in Sadie Thompson *(1929) and 21 years later for her interpretation of the demented silent screen star, Norma Desmond, in* Sunset Blvd. *(1950). Many of the other films she made were flops.*

As for her performance in *Sunset Blvd.,* director Billy Wilder had offered the female lead to Pola Negri, Mae West, and Mary Pickford before turning to Swanson. Swanson was nominated for a Best Actress Oscar, along with Bette Davis and Anne Baxter for *All About Eve.* All of them lost to Judy Holliday for her work in *Born Yesterday.*

Director Billy Wilder dared to "paint Hollywood naked" by shooting the film classic **Sunset Blvd**. (1950). **Gloria Swanson** was cast as the fading vamp of the silent screen, living in a deranged version of yesterday "when I was the greatest star in Hollywood, appealing to all those wonderful people out there in the dark." To everlasting regret, she lost the Best Actress Oscar that year to Judy Holliday for *Born Yesterday.*

William Holden, in the male lead as Joe Gillis, lost the Best Actor Oscar to Jose Ferrer for his interpretation of *Cyrano de Bergerac.*

Episode 18

Hollywood in its Golden Years
(i.e., the 1930s)

Clark Gable Emerges as Its King

In spite of the Wall Street Stock Market Crash of 1929, Hollywood in the upcoming 1930s entered its Golden Age. Silent pictures were out and talkies were in. Dozens of established stars faded into film history since many of them had voices, accents, or speech defects not suited to sound. By the dozens, many of their movies were either lost or crumbled into dust. Others would be preserved for future film historians. Such was the case with *Beyond the Rocks* (1922), starring Gloria Swanson with Rudolph Valentino. Its only surviving copy was "rediscovered" in 2003 in the attic of a decaying movie house in Amsterdam.

After a long and difficult climb up the Tinseltown ladder, rung by rung, Clark suddenly found himself cast opposite such leading ladies as Greta Garbo, Joan Crawford, Jean Harlow, and Norma Shearer.

HOLLYWOOD IN THE '30s:
*Escapist,
Sexually Rebellious,
and "Modern"*

Desperate for players who conjured a sense of swaggering, All-American chivalry, Clark had it made.

This photo was associated with a press campaign for *Broadway Serenade* (1939). By the time it was released, two years before America's entry into World War II, the era it celebrated was almost over.

In 1931, MGM released eleven films in which Clark starred. Movie magazines hailed him as "the most sensationalist personality of the year." He became so well known that a sarcastic new reprimand *"Who do you think you are? Clark Gable?"* swept across the country.

He already knew the Barrymores (Lionel and John), and he'd already seduced Joan Crawford. Now, he began to meet other stars at MGM, a studio that boasted, "We have more stars than there are in heaven."

Clark found himself taking over roles originally slated for John Gilbert, the unlucky heartthrob of the 1920s in those silent romances with Garbo.

Clark would soon be sustaining affairs with such leading ladies as Mary Astor and Marion Davies, the mistress of the immensely wealthy William Randolph Hearst. And as his own career fizzled, Ramon Novarro, the fast-fading hero of the silent film, *Ben-Hur* (1925), developed a crush on Clark, too.

His frequent co-star of the future, Jean Harlow, would also come running at his command.

Another of his leading ladies, Helen Hayes, claimed, "There are only two actors in Hollywood that I would leave my husband for—Gary Cooper and Clark Gable."

Soon Clark was seen dining with Marie Dressler and Wallace Beery (his future co-star).

In the Pre-Code era, the talkies became increasingly risqué, especially in their depiction of the battle

THE KING OF HOLLYWOOD: It's difficult to estimate how often Clark appeared as an editorial focal point during the 1930s. Here are cover photos of six of them. Casting directors responded by virtually bombarding him with movie roles throughout the course of a decade defined today as the entertainment industry's Golden Age.

of the sexes. For those who could afford the meager price of a ticket, movies, especially on crowded Saturday nights, were an escape from landscapes with massive unemployment, near-starvation, and large-scale crime as the "have-nots" robbed the "haves."

The flickering silent films of the 1920s were by now a distant memory. Stage actors were flooding into southern California from New York and sometimes London to replace stars like Pola Negri or Vilma Banky who spoke with heavy accents. The screen's reigning heartthrob, Rudolph Valentino, had died in 1926.

Actors who had previously been allocated only small, sometimes uncredited roles, were becoming stars. Notable among them were Myrna Loy, Jean Arthur, Bette Davis, Carole Lombard, William Powell, and Constance Bennett.

Legends were being born: James Cagney, Edward G. Robinson, Humphrey Bogart, and Mae West. From vaudeville emerged such stars as Bing Crosby, Rudy Vallee, Alice Faye, and Bob Hope.

Paramount was not the only studio challenging MGM. Competition was intense from Warner Brothers, 20th Century Fox, RKO, and Columbia, too.

As war clouds thundered over Europe, America remained isolated, most of its citizens not wanting to get involved in foreign wars. They'd rather go to the movie to watch "Fred and Ginger" dance. Escapism ruled the night.

Dracula and Frankenstein elevated Bela Lugosi and Boris Karloff into cultish stars. That swashbuckler of the 1920s, Douglas Fairbanks Sr., was replaced with the dashing and even handsomer Errol Flynn, a native of Tasmania.

Katharine Hepburn had burst onto the scene and had become a major star almost overnight. Cary Grant, assisted by Mae West, became the epitome of sophisticated masculine glamour.

Pint-sized Mickey Rooney morphed into a box office champ in all those Andy Hardy movies. By the end of the decade, Judy Garland was " over the rainbow."

If Mary Pickford had a replacement, it was the sugar-coated "Little Miss Lollipop," Shirley Temple, who reigned briefly as box office gold.

Censorship was forced onto Hollywood filmmakers with the introduction of the Hays Code, the first large-scale attempt at an organized "cleanup" of motion pictures.

In 1935, Clark starred in *Mutiny on the Bounty* the highest-grossing film of that year. His other movie released that year, *China Seas,* came in second.

In 1936, his movie, *San Francisco,* became the nation's second-highest grossing film.

In 1938, *Test Pilot* came in third in box office receipts.

Before the decade ended, Clark, against his better judgment, starred in Margaret Mitchell's *Gone With the Wind* opposite Vivien Leigh. For her efforts, she would win the Best Actress Oscar that year. Clark would be nominated, but lost to Robert Donat for his performance in the syrupy *Goodbye, Mr. Chips.*

Film historians rate 1939 as the greatest year in the history of filmmaking. In that benchmark year, *Gone With the Wind* would win the gold as its Best Picture.

Runners-up included *Dark Victory* with Bette Davis; *Goodbye, Mr. Chips; Love Affair* with Irene Dunne and Charles Boyer; *Mr. Smith Goes to Washington* with James Stewart; *Ninotchka* with Greta Garbo; *Of Mice and Men* with Lon Chaney Jr. and Burgess Meredith; *Stagecoach* with Claire Trevor and John Wayne; *The Wizard of Oz* with Judy Garland; and *Wuthering Heights* with Merle Oberon and Laurence Olivier.

1939 also loomed large in Clark's book of memories. He married Carole Lombard, his third wife, defining for the world at large as "the love of my life."

Then America (and Hollywood along with it) abruptly changed. Hitler's Nazi troops invaded Poland on September 1, 1939. A few days later, Britain and France declared war on Germany. World War II had begun. But hostilities would not directly involve the United States until Japanese forces on sea and in the air attacked Pearl Harbor early on the Sunday morning of December 7, 1941.

Clark would make a few movies that year, and Lombard would die in a 1942 plane crash before he joined America's fighting forces.

Hollywood's Golden Age: Clark was its King.

Episode 19

Clark in the Dying Days of Vaudeville
Love, Honor, and Betray (1930)

Clark Gable with Alice Brady in *Love, Honor, Betray*

A theater producer, A.H. Woods, born in Budapest in 1870, arrived at the Port of New York while still an infant. Growing up in the slums of the lower East Side of Manhattan, he dreamed of becoming a theater producer. As a young man, he joined two other struggling producers, and they formed touring companies, bringing popular melodramas of the day to the "provinces."

In time, he became so successful that he built his own theater on Broadway, naming it the Eltinge Theatre. He took the name from his rumored lover, Julian Eltinge, who at the time was the most famous female impersonator in America.

Over the course of his career, Woods fought many censorship battles waged against his bedroom farces. Some of his plays were raided by the police, who shut them down. A prominent rabbi, Sam S. Wise, denounced him. "No Jewish producer should sponsor such filth. It hurts the reputation of Jews generally."

In the spring of 1930, during the most dire months of the Great Depression, he staged a drama at his own theater, *Love, Honor, and Betray*. He had seen Clark Gable perform, and he offered him a key role in it as "The Lover."

> Thrust into a theatrical setting that was starved for blatantly macho men who knew how to kiss onstage, then relatively-unknown **Clark Gable** *(left)* rose to the occasion. Here, he appears with the then-celebrated **Alice Brady** onstage at Al Wood's controversial (and always *risqué*) Broadway theater.

He also hired Lester Lonergan to direct it. A native of Ireland, he had been in America for a half-century, staging plays from San Francisco to Boston. He had also helmed silent pictures for Fox and Paramount.

Unknown to Woods at the time, Clark and Lonergan had tangled before when they worked together on a play, *House Unguarded*, in 1928. Clark had been cast as a Navy lieutenant. After two days of rehearsal, Lonergan fired Clark, telling him, "You're the worst actor who has ever walked on stage. You're fired! Get out of this theater."

During an early rehearsal of *Love, Honor, and Betray*, Clark and the director once again conflicted, this time almost to the point of violence. Woods happened to arrive at the moment that Clark was being fired.

"Gable stays in the play," he told Lonergan.

"Then I'm out of here!" the director shouted, heading for the exit.

Woods took over the play's direction and assembled the final cast for a Broadway opening on March 12, 1930.

Settings for the three-act drama included a cemetery, a living room, and a "Love Nest."

Cast as "The Woman," Alice Brady was assigned the lead in this play adapted from a French drama by André Antoine. She was the daughter of William A. Brady, a major Broadway producer who used his influence to get his aspiring actress and daughter work. An example of that included her casting in the silent film *A Thief for the Night* (1913), in which she appeared opposite John Barrymore.

In time, Brady went to Hollywood to star in silent pictures and was around to survive the advent of the talkies. She played Carole Lombard's flighty mother in *My Man Godfrey* (1936). She also won a Best Supporting Actress Oscar for *In Old Chicago* (1937).

In all, she made 80 films, her last appearance in *Young Mr. Lincoln* (1939), the year *Gone With the Wind* was released. She died of cancer later that year.

Lombard learned that Clark, her future husband, had had a brief fling with Brady during the 45-night Broadway run of *Love, Honor, and Betray*.

"I had divorced my husband, James L. Crane, in 1922, and I was hoping to get hitched again. Clark and I were an item during the run of the play, but on closing night, he faded. I heard he married some old dame."

In addition to Clark, Woods also cast two other future movie stars into his play: George Brent and Glenda Farrell. Each of them would become stars in the 1930s. A handsome Irishman, Brent, three years younger than Clark, is best remembered today for the eleven films he made with Bette Davis. They included *Jezebel* (1938) and *Dark Victory* (1939). Their offscreen romance continued on and off for years.

Brent was married five times, most notably to actress Ruth Chatterton (1932-1934) and to Ann Sheridan (1942-1943).

Emerging from the plains of Oklahoma, Glenda Farrell began stage acting as a child. Her goal was stardom. As a young woman, she arrived in Hollywood and worked for the next half century. She came to personify the smart, fast-talking, sassy, wise-cracking blonde. Her most notable role was Torchy Blane in *Smart Blonde* (1937). It was so successful that her role was reprised in several sequels. Joan Blondell was her most frequent co-star.

Comic book writer Jerry Siegel later admitted that Farrell had been his inspiration for the character of reporter Lois Lane in all those *Superman* comics and films.

A.H. ("Al") Woods was the ultimate impresario, famous during his heyday for introducing the Bedroom Farce to Broadway.

Examples of his showmanship included **The Girl With the Whooping Cough** (*see poster, below*).

He also sponsored the career of the female impersonator, **Julian Eltinge** (above *right*) who—more famously than anyone before—brought drag to the saloons, stages, and mining camps of the early 20th century.

Other stars "discovered" by A.H. Woods include **George Brent** *(left)* and **Glenda Farrell**.

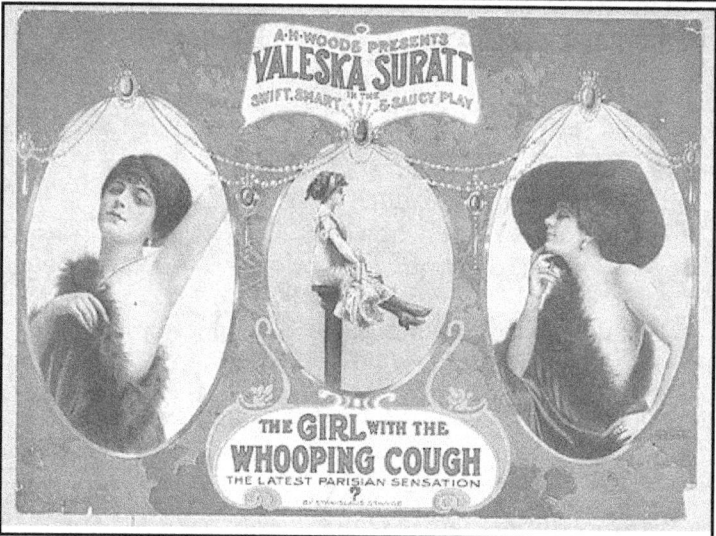

In April of 1910, almost a decade before Clark Gable's audition at his theater, **A.H. Woods** (*see photo at top*) mounted the production of a *risqué* romance/comedy, **The Girl with the Whooping Cough** that enraged Broadway censors. Highly suggestive, it was based on a Belle Epoque beauty who spreads whooping cough through frequent kissing of good-looking men. The mayor of New York eventually forced Woods to shut it down.

Clark's arrival on Broadway a few years later as the romantic co-star (and kisser) of **Alice Brady** (see photo, previous page) helped Woods keep his theater open and the lights on. Woods eventually became one of New York's most prolific theatrical producers, staging more than 140 plays in various neighborhoods of Manhattan, including some blockbusters.

Episode 20

Older and Rich, Socialite
RIA LANGHAM
Becomes Clark's Second Wife

Clark, then 30 years old, appears with his 47-year-old bride, **Ria Langham,** around the time of their wedding ceremony in Santa Ana, California. Each was outfitted in the best and most formal attire money could buy.

Some members of the press speculated that their wedding in Santa Ana was a repeat ceremony because the one that had been performed months earlier in New York was suddenly discovered to be invalid in California. Or was that just his studio's way of sweeping adultery under the rug?

Although still married to Josephine Dillon, young Clark Gable became the "kept boy" of a rich socialite. Her name was Maria ("Ria") Franklin Langham, born in 1884 in Kentucky.

She had been reared in Illinois. When she was 17, she married William Prentiss, a union that lasted for four years.

When her mother died, she moved to Texas to look after her ailing father, who was suffering from tuberculosis.

There, she met and married Alfred Thomas Lucas, a rich widower 22 years her senior. With him, she gave birth to two children, George Jana and Alfred Jr.

When her husband died six years after he married her, he left her a fortune. She became one of the richest socialites in Houston.

In 1925, she married for the third time to Denzil Langham, but divorced him after two horrible years.

She and her children, with all of her money, relocated in Manhattan. Previously, she had seen Clark perform in a play in Houston and "re-discovered" him when he was appearing with Zita Johann onstage in *Machinal*.

Her half brother, Booth Franklin, knew Clark, and escorted Ria backstage to meet him.

She virtually "adopted" him that night, and he went home with her.

During the weeks ahead, she began to re-groom him, getting his hair restyled, his teeth fixed, his wardrobe upgraded, and even teaching him more social graces.

She paid for his divorce from Dillon in 1930 and moved with him to Hollywood, where he wanted to launch a movie career.

He had changed his mind about the movies since the flickers had begun to talk. To him, at least, the stage appeared less and less compelling.

She was introduced throughout the movie colony as Mrs. Clark Gable. It was announced, but never really proven, that the couple had married in Manhattan before

A double-barreled view of **Clark Gable** with his second wife, **Ria Langham**. A rich socialite from Houston, Texas, Ria was one of the backers of a theatrical stock company that hired him in 1927. His raw sexuality attracted her, and she demanded that his weekly salary be raised from $75 to $200 a week. He paid her back the only way he knew how.

heading to California.

In May of 1930, she paid $5,000 for a Roamer sports car and gave it to him so that he could get around Los Angeles. Ria also financed the stage production of *The Last Mile*, demanding that Clark be cast as Killer Mears, the male lead. Because of its visibility to the movie colony, that more or less launched him, almost overnight, into an immediate screen career, thanks in part to the advent of talkies.

Several Hollywood agents and two film directors watched his onstage performance and were impressed. Some of them judged him ideal for "pictures which had learned to talk." With hordes of actors getting fired because of their "unsuitable" voices, many roles were opening up for stage actors.

Clark, Ria, and her brood moved into the Ravenswood Apartments underneath Mae West, who remained, for decades, famously associated with that address.

[Designated as a Los Angeles Historic-Cultural Monument in 2003, the Ravenswood (570 North Rossmore in the Hancock Park neighborhood of L.A.,) was built by Paramount Pictures in 1930 about five blocks from their studios on Melrose Avenue. Mae West lived in its penthouse from its opening until her death in 1980.]

Mae encountered Clark in the elevator one afternoon and invited him "to come up and see me sometime." As legend has it, that "sometime" transpired the following night.

While living with Ria, Clark was also secretly dating other women, avoiding his regular Hollywood haunts, but instead driving to some remote tavern or motel in the San Fernando Valley. Also, he and Joan Crawford continued to meet privately whenever they could. Her marriage to Douglas Fairbanks Jr. had unraveled and was entering its final months.

Since Clark repeatedly rejected Ria's offer to get married, she decided to force him into a legal (and binding) union.

She made an appointment to visit Howard Strickling at his offices at MGM. She was aware that he was managing publicity for Clark, and she'd found two magazine articles offensive. One was headlined CLARK GABLE—HOLLYWOOD'S DON JUAN. Another ran under the banner: CLARK GABLE—WHAT A MAN!.

Ironically, and unknown to her, Strickling himself still harbored a crush on Clark. One of his duties at MGM involved keeping Clark out of trouble and covering up his indiscretions.

Inside his office, Ria confessed that they

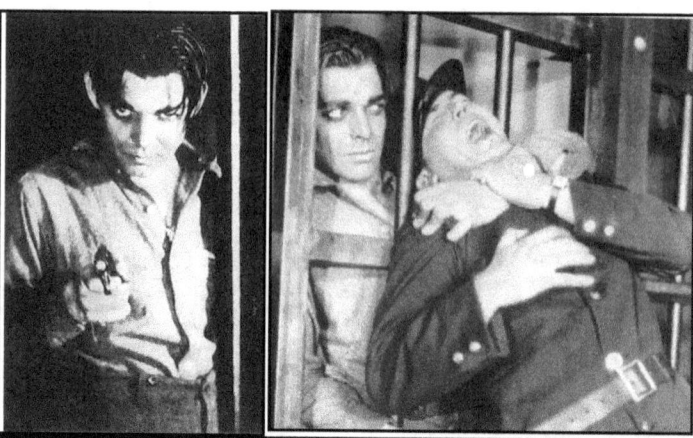

Clark Gable's *Jailhouse Rock*, circa 1930

Long before Elvis Presley broadcast entertainment from a (simulated) jail cell, Clark Gable morphed himself into a scary-looking desperado locked behind bars. Presented at a theater in Los Angeles, and attended by casting directors from the major-league studios, *The Last Mile* showed **Clark**, as Killer Mears, at his most menacing.

His friends and associates noticed a remarkable improvement in **Clark Gable**'s tailoring, thanks to new-built links to Ria Langham, the social-climbing socialite who morphed herself into his second wife

weren't officially married, and that she feared that reporters writing about Clark would make that discovery and publicize it widely. She pointedly reminded Strickling that since they were openly living together, news like that might wreck his career.

Then she delivered a threat. If he and Irving Thalberg could not convince Clark to marry her, she would deliver incriminating news directly to the press. Then she reminded him that there was a morality clause within the contract he had signed. As Strickling fully understood, Clark's career could (and probably would) be wrecked just as it was beginning to boom.

Before leaving, Ria turned to Strickling and said, "The stink I could cause would be smelled all the way to San Diego."

The next day, Clark was summoned to Thalberg's office. He held up the actor's signed contract, waving it in his face, and reminding him of its "moral turpitude" clause. "Living openly with a woman and not married to her could wreck what is looking like a promising career. I pray that Will Hays, our so-called 'defender of Hollywood morals,' doesn't get hold of this."

After an hour's heated discussion, Clark agreed to get married, but that he'd conduct the marriage ceremony in secret.

Discreetly, he applied for a license under the name of William C. Gable. The wedding would take place at the courthouse in Santa Ana, in Orange County, about 80 miles southeast of Los Angeles. Clark hoped to avoid any press coverage.

Clark's second wedding was on June 19, 1931. As the newlyweds emerged from the courthouse, about twenty reporters converged around them. Someone had leaked the news of their marriage. Ria fled in horror, and Clark refused any interviews.

Once inside their car, he grabbed her arm and said, "You have just married Clark Gable. I'm public property now. Get used to it!"

There was no honeymoon.

Previously, she had moved them out of the Ravenswood and into a large and lovely house on San Ysidro Drive in Beverly Hills, not too far from Pickfair, the home of Mary Pickford and Douglas Fairbanks Sr. Bedrooms for the newly married couple were at different ends of the building.

However, he continued to escort her to public events and night clubs, with every intention of slipping off into the night for sexual encounters with other women. Many of these were neophyte starlets from MGM, each

Here's where it happened, long ago and far away: The **Santa Clara Courthouse**, site of Clark and Ria Langham's wedding. First opened in 1901, it now operates as a museum.

Irving Thalberg, seen here with his actress wife, Norma Shearer, in 1929.

Mae West *(left)* and *(right photo)* the **Ravenswood Apartment Complex**, her stamping ground, home and investment

desperate to become the next Constance Bennett or Joan Crawford.

As time went by, Langham learned to tolerate this. Being a major-league socialite who attended chic parties and who mingled with the elite meant more to her than having Clark to herself every night. For intimacies, she hired young and attractive aspirant actors as her house manager, chauffeur, or whatever.

Clark even paid occasional visits to the home of the widely read columnist Adela Rogers St. Johns. "It seems that the rising MGM star, Clark Gable, need only snap his fingers and the gals come running," she claimed. "When he appears on the screen, many women in the audience get an immediate orgasm." Of course, she only told that to friends. She couldn't print anything that graphic in her column.

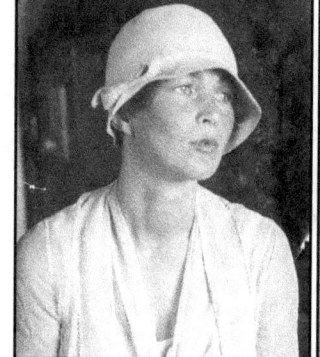

Two views of **Adela Rogers St. Johns,** *left* from 1928 and *right*, from 1967. A columnist, she was rumored to have given birth to Clark's child, which was secretly put up for adoption.

***

Clark hoped that his first wife, Josephine Dillon, had disappeared from his life forever. She had not. Blackmail was on her mind.

Reporters digging into Clark's early life "discovered" his youthful marriage to this much older woman. The press sought her out, and she received offers of money for revelations about her life with the then-struggling aspirant actor.

At the time, she had almost no money. She was desperate enough to write a letter to Louis B. Mayer, dated August 2, 1931.

In it, she claimed that Clark had never made any effort to pay her back for what she had invested in his career. She claimed she was getting lucrative offers to sell her story, but that she was holding them off, hoping that MGM might make a financial offer for her silence, hereby protecting their rising new star from career-destroying scandals.

"I am in desperate need of financial help," she pleaded.

A deal was struck, providing her with $200 a month, funds which Mayer deducted from Clark's salary. That deal remained in place about a year (until July 25, 1932), when Dillon placed an urgent call to Mayer's secretary, claiming, "The monthly checks have stopped."

She never got any more checks. And indeed, she went on to sell stories to the yellow press. Her first *exposé* was headlined *I CREATED CLARK GABLE.*

Here's **Ria Langham** years after her separation and divorce from Clark, still "dining out" on their former association.

Her contemporaries might have evaluated her fashion sense as "the height of *haute*."

Hipster women of today, however, would probably refer to it as restrictive, frumpy, and "suffocating."

Clark had many defenders, notably Adela Rogers St. Johns, who wrote, "If anyone made Clark Gable a good actor, it was not Josephine Dillon.... You remember your elocution teacher in high school? That's what Dillon looks like and acts like."

Back at MGM, Strickling had learned not to trust Clark around reporters. In interviews, he seemed too candid, too skeptical, unrepentant, and "morally neutral."

In his latest encounter with a reporter from *Variety,* Clark had said, "They say I'm a success as an actor on the rise. But just what is success? Did I seduce her or did she seduce me? Would you call it rape?"

Episode 21

HOWARD HUGHES

—Hollywood's Richest Producer— Puts Clark Gable "To the Test"

Howard Hughes, a dysfunctional and later insane billionaire, as he appeared in the mid-1940s with superstar and sex symbol **Ava Gardner**.

After three flops in a row *(Sky Devils* really hadn't prospered), the film industry had begun to view Hughes as a has-been. To prove them wrong, he launched what would eventually be interpreted as two of the most prestigious pictures of the early talkies—*The Front Page* (1931) and *Scarface* (1932).

The best writing team in the business, Ben Hecht and Charles MacArthur, had scored a hit on Broadway with a zany play about the newspaper business, *The Front Page*. Hughes bought the screen rights to the play for $125,000, an astonishing figure back then. *[A few years later, the rights to Gone With the Wind would sell for only $50,000.]* Hecht and MacArthur then demanded an additional $80,000 to write the scenario. Hughes balked at this final demand, hiring two lesser-known writers, Bartlett Cormack and Charles Lederer, instead.

For *The Front Page*, he brought back his favorite director, Lewis (Milly) Milestone, who had won an Oscar for his direction of *All Quiet on the Western Front* (1930). The overriding fear was that *The Front Page*, a one-set film, would look like a Broadway play. Milestone overcame that hurdle by using a tracking camera to keep pace with the "machine-gun" dialogue on screen.

The grotesquely ugly Louis Wolheim, who had played the lead in *Two Arabian Knights,* was cast as the lovably conniving newspaper editor, Walter Burns, but only three weeks after filming began, he collapsed on the set. He was taken to a Los Angeles hospital where a doctor informed Milestone that Wolheim was "eaten up with cancer." He died a few days later.

Adolphe Menjou, the dashing but sarcastic actor with a mustache evocative of a stage villain from a Victorian play, was cast subsequently as the lead.

Menjou and Hughes detested each other on sight, in spite of their shared right-wing views. Behind Hughes's back, Menjou called him a "cocksucking pervert." Hughes was kinder to the actor, suggesting that "he looks like a repainted Rolls Royce."

Hughes, in the 1920s, had followed the example of his famous father, often appearing in bespoke tailoring. But by the time *The Front Page* was released, he had adopted his sloppy dress code for life. His suits looked like he'd slept in them, which he probably had. Menjou, on the other hand, was

Adolphe Menjou, Mary Brian, and **Pat O'Brien** in the movie Clark Gable didn't get a role in: *The Front Page* (1931). To find out why, keep reading.

famous for his sartorial style. Thinking that Hughes knew nothing of tailoring, the actor foolishly suggested that he could help him improve his wardrobe. Taking one cynical look at Menjou, Hughes spoke not a word but walked away from the set, never to speak to the actor again.

Cast in the second lead, that of a newspaper reporter named Hildy Johnson, was the New York stage actor, Pat O'Brien. Milwaukee-born, Irish, and a drunk much like his best friend, Spencer Tracy, O'Brien also didn't impress Hughes, although he'd agreed to the casting.

When he met Hughes for the first time, O'Brien tried to impress him to

Waterloo Bridge was the tear-jerking story of an impoverished English lass who—wild with grief—turns to prostitution when her *fiancé* goes missing in action during wartime.

Mae Clarke (*poster, left*) starred in the 1931 version with **Kent Douglass**. **Vivien Leigh** (*poster right*) was the even more poignant star (with **Robert Taylor**) of its reconfiguration in 1940.

no avail. First, he told him that he'd seen a stage version of *The Front Page* performed by an all-black cast in Hoboken, New Jersey, for a tails-and-white tie crowd. Hughes didn't reveal his distain for blacks, and said nothing.

Trying to connect, O'Brien quipped, "California's a great place to live if you're an orange," a line he stole from comedian Fred Allen. Again, Hughes wasn't impressed. Like his friend Spencer Tracy, O'Brien didn't click with him.

Milestone introduced him to his two leading ladies. Famous today for the way James Cagney smashed a grapefruit into her face, Mae Clarke was cast as a prostitute, and Mary Brian played Pat O'Brien's sympathetic girlfriend. Hughes was less than enthralled with Mary Brian. "She's a nice girl," he told Milestone. "A nice, open, honest face. Nice smile. Nice teeth. Nice blue eyes. She has the same emotion in every scene. *Nice*."

"But she's from Texas like yourself," Milestone said.

"She's not like any Texas broad I've ever met," Hughes said before turning away.

Mary Brian would re-enter Hughes's life unattractively once again several years later, when his lover, Cary Grant, announced that he was going to marry her, angering Hughes. In later life, her career over, Brian took up painting portraits as a hobby. One of her first paintings was of Hughes, depicting him as a giant prick. She ultimately got her revenge on both Cary and Hughes simply by outliving them, dying in the final hours of 2002.

Hughes found the film's other leading lady, Mae Clarke, a bit more to his liking. "Clarke should always play whores," he said to Milestone. "Unhappy ones." In a way, he was right, as the role of the hooker in the 1931 version of *Waterloo Bridge* became one of her more memorable pictures until, nine years later, Vivien Leigh took over the role, making it her own.

In Vivian Leigh's version of the film, she was cast opposite Hughes's future boyfriend, Robert Taylor. Hughes was mildly titillated to learn from Milly Milestone that Clarke was a bisexual like himself. She'd had an affair with Barbara Stanwyck in New York in 1926 when

Here's the college athlete and cowboy star **Johnny Mack Brown**, shown "against character" in a tailored suit that would have fitted into any society cocktail party of its era.

Broad-shouldered, affable, and macho, he morphed, briefly and early, into a *bona fide* screen competitor of Clark Gable.

they'd appeared together in the stage drama, *The Noose*.

Hughes accurately predicted that both Clarke and O'Brien would be awarded with star parts for only a few more short years before fading. "This film belongs to the boys," Hughes said to Milestone. "The ladies are just for window dressing. Any actress in Hollywood could play these parts."

Uncharacteristically, Hughes didn't interfere in the production of *The Front Page*, letting the very talented Milestone direct as he saw fit.

Taking him at his word, the director arranged for the establishment of a bar, a few steps from the sound stage, where both crew and actors could take a drink whenever they wanted. That ran up a big bill for Hughes. Milestone didn't like to get up before noon, so he scheduled his daily filmings to begin every afternoon at one o'clock. Often, after a dinner break, they would resume shooting until one o'clock the next morning. A genuine craps table was set up off set, and there was a continuous game going on throughout the entire shoot.

Almost from the moment the film was released, Hughes knew he had a hit. *The Front Page* became the quintessential newspaper movie and inspired a host of other films, even remakes. Starring Rosalind Russell and Cary Grant, *His Girl Friday* did even better box office in 1940 than Hughes's 1931 hit. The director of *His Girl Friday* was none other than Howard Hawks, Hughes's on-again, off-again friend and sometimes rival.

The Front Page was nominated for Best Picture, Menjou for Best Actor, and Milestone for Best Director. The only sour note was the film's banning in Chicago. Local politicians didn't like the premise that they were crooks.

Milestone later recalled, "What's more interesting even than the casting of Pat O'Brien and Menjou in the lead roles was my original cast. Howard Hughes nixed both of the actors I wanted as replacements for O'Brien—James Cagney and Clark Gable."

Why did Clark Gable and James Cagney miss out as the stars of *The Front Page?* Read on.

***

On their first meeting, Clark Gable and Howard Hughes hit it off. In many ways, the ruggedly handsome and masculine star was Hughes's type. William Haines had already told Hughes that he'd "had" Gable back in 1925 when he was a struggling bit player. The almost aggressively heterosexual Gable had allegedly told Haines, "I'll do anything to become a star—and I mean *anything!*" Now that Gable's star was on the rise, Haines wondered out loud if that offer were still available. Hughes had already admitted to Haines that he was attracted to the actor's good looks and devilish grin, two characteristics that would eventually turn him into the most widely recognized male sex symbol of the Thirties.

Milestone arranged the meeting after learning that Gable was available and that he wanted the role of the newspaper reporter, Hildy Johnson, in *The Front Page*.

The director later recalled the first encounter between Gable and Hughes: "Howard was not a talkative man but he was chattering away with Gable. They seemed to speak the same language. Whether the stories were true or not, Gable was spinning yarns about his days as an oil wildcatter that must have evoked memories of Big Howard for Howard Jr. Gable also claimed that he'd been a garage mechanic, and Hughes had a long history of being attracted to men in that field. Then Gable claimed to have been both a lumberjack and a telephone lineman."

After they had been talking for about fifteen minutes, and again according to Milestone, Gable said, "Howard, you and I have the same goal in Hollywood."

"And what might that be?" Hughes asked.

"To become the two biggest shits in Tinseltown and to fuck every big movie star out here."

From across the desk from him, Hughes set down his glass of milk and smiled at Gable. "You're my kind of man, Clark."

Gable could not have been unaware of the intense scrutiny he was getting from Hughes. For the occasion of their meeting, he had worn casual riding breeches and a battleship gray turtleneck sweater.

Finally, Hughes called attention to Gable's looks. "I've seen you on screen before. You somehow look different. Like you've changed."

"I'm a new man," Gable said. He flashed a smile showing his teeth. "New dentures. Some faggot over at

MGM insisted I part my hair on my left. That kept that natural cowlick I have. In photographs they let it break loose and dangle over my right eye. That's supposed to make women cream in their bloomers. They also plucked my eyebrows. I ain't Joan Crawford yet, but I'm getting there— if they come at me with those tweezers again. I work out every day in the studio gym. The goal is broader shoulders and trim waistline. Women go for that."

"And others," Hughes quipped..

"What was that again?" Gable asked.

"Never mind."

"I've got a rival over at MGM," Gable said. "It's Johnny Mack Brown. He's about twenty-six or so. Irving Thalberg is pitting Johnny boy against me. They're giving him the big push with rugged he-man promotion like they're doing with me. He's a good-looking fucker like me and has a lot going for him. One of us is going to win out."

Totally left out of the conversation, Milestone hastily added, "It's going to be you, Clark. I know Johnny. He's got that languid southern drawl. You don't. Your voice will record better. I hear MGM is lining up all its big stars to appear with you. If you aren't bedding them now, you'll soon be starring opposite—both on and off the screen— the usual suspects: Jean Harlow. Norma Shearer. Joan Crawford. Greta Garbo."

"I hear Garbo's pussy is so big that any man who fucks her falls in," Gable said. "Bring 'em on. I'll sleep with all of them, although any gal in bed with me isn't going to get much sleep. The gals don't have to be big name stars. Hash slingers or call gals…all pussies are dark at night. One woman is just like another to me. Love 'em and leave them. In some ways, call gals are better. Unlike call gals, the good girls stick around and want a big romance. I want to keep moving. A different one every night will suit me fine. And despite my past or future marriages, I'll never be faithful to just one pussy."

"You do have a graphic way of speaking," Hughes said. "You'd be perfect cast as a newspaper reporter."

Milestone claimed that Hughes invited Gable to fly with him that weekend to San Francisco, and the actor accepted. Milestone never learned any details of that trip. Hughes never spoke to him about what happened.

But when Hughes returned to his office the following Monday, he angrily announced to Milestone that Gable was not going to get the role. The director had really wanted Gable for the part, but Hughes would not hear of it. Finally Milestone asked why.

"His ears are so big they make him look like a taxi with both doors wide open," Hughes said.

Milestone recalled Hughes making a final enigmatic comment before dropping the subject. "And besides, his tits are too small."

Although he tried, Haines never learned the details of that weekend. However, he told such pals as Joan Crawford and Ramon Novarro, plus countless others, what he suspected the problem was.

"Clark is the worst lay in Hollywood, and amazingly he'll admit that himself," Haines later said. "His foreskin is so tight it's difficult for him to draw it back over his glans. He also doesn't keep that little charger clean. Not only that, he's a premature ejaculator. Not Howard's cuppa!"

With Gable not cast in *The Front Page*, Milestone called Darryl Zanuck and asked if James Cagney would be available. Zanuck said Cagney was available.

The next day, Cagney was ushered into Hughes's office. Before the two men were introduced, Hughes gave a fast appraisal of Cagney: "Throw this fucking little runt out of my office!" he shouted.

Here's the former vaudevillian, dancer, and drag performer, **James Cagney.**

Irrepressible and egomaniacal, he offended many— including Howard Hughes, who almost immediately ejected him from his office when he arrived to audition for a role in *The Front Page* in 1931.

Episode 22

Why Clark Gable Did Not Become the Screen

Tarzan

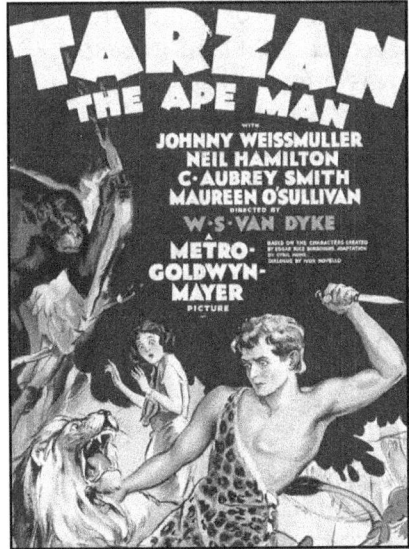

One little-known aspect of Clark Gable's climb to stardom was that he tried to become the screen Tarzan of the 1930s.

MGM had decided to bring Tarzan back to the screen in a Pre-Code adventure movie (*Tarzan the Ape Man*; 1932) featuring the jungle hero created by Edgar Rice Burroughs in 1912.

The film would mark the debut of Tarzan's famous jungle yell, perfected later by Carol Burnett.

Cyril Hume was adapting the tale for the screen. As its director, MGM hired W.S. Van Dyke, who set out to find a suitably muscled athlete who would look "sexy and thrilling," with his genitals concealed with a leopard skin loincloth, but showing off his body.

Buster Crabbe seemed perfect for the role. He was a two-time Olympic swimmer, and he had a muscled physique that seemed suitable for the role. For some reason, he didn't like the terms offered.

[Ironically, he later became a rival Tarzan when cast in Tarzan the Fearless *(1932), launching a career in which he starred in more than 100 movies.]*

Stonefaced Tom Tyler also donned a loin cloth. As a young man, he'd been an amateur weightlifter during the late 1920s and had "the perfect body." But he was viewed as "too wooden." Later, he became known for his portrayal of superhero Captain Marvel in the 1941 serial.

A New Englander, Neil Hamilton tried out,

HE DOES MORE THAN SWING FROM VINES

HERE'S JANE (Ireland-born **Maureen O'Sullivan**), maintaining her dignity while falling for the seductive charms of "the Ape Man," **Johnny Weissmuller.**

In this publicity still for the 1932 version of the Tazan series, **Maureen O'Sullivan, Johnny Weissmuller**, and **Cheeta**, then the world's most famous chimp, present their version of *See, Hear, and Speak No Evil*.

67

but Van Dyke found him more suitable for the second male lead in *Tarzan*. Consequently, he was offered the role (and accepted) of Harry Holt, who travels to Africa on a quest for elephant burial grounds and ivory.

Van Dyke also tested John Mack Brown but didn't think he was tall enough for the role. A former football star from Alabama, he certainly had the athletic build, and his powerful physique had appeared on Wheaties cereal boxes. In 1929, he'd played the love interest of Mary Pickford in her first talkie, *Coquette*, for which she won an Oscar.

Clark always remembered what happened after he was advised to try out for the role: "Two fairy queens were told to make me up to look like Tarzan. They ordered me to strip jaybird naked and spent far too much time sizing up my junk. Finally, they took a long time fitting this very little strip of a loincloth onto me."

"I asked them for a jock strap in case I had to jump around, and they assured me that if I got the role, wardrobe would design such a strap for me."

"Van Dyke did a screen test for me in which I swung from a vine. I think he captured on film everything that loincloth didn't conceal. Then he rejected me, saying my body was not athletic enough."

Somewhere, screen shots of Gable's genitals are either lost to history or in some buried archive that will turn up for future generations to see on the internet.

Hume, the project's screenwriter, was a member of the Hollywood Athletic Club, where the men swam nude. One day, he spotted John Wayne and his new buddy, Johnny Weissmuller, emerge naked from the pool. He rejected Wayne, but instantly intuited that Weissmuller would make the perfect Tarzan. He was one of the champion Olympic swimmers of the world.

Hume recommended him to Van Dyke, who immediately cast him as Tarzan. The star athlete would go on to make a dozen other Tarzan films, thanks, in part, to his male model good looks and physique.

Applause for the Beefcake of Yesteryear

Two views of **Tom Tyler:** *Left* in 1928, the year he won first prize in a weightlifting contest, and *right*, as a silent-screen cowboy who's ready to rodeo.

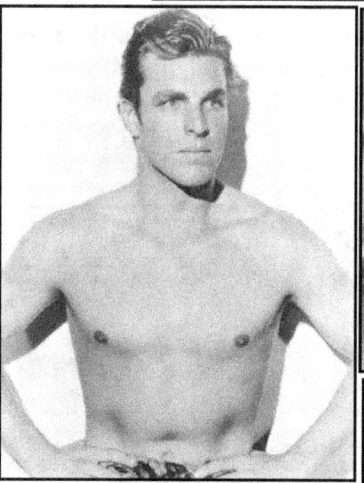

Two views of **Buster Crabbe**. *Left*, as Tarzan, *right* as Flash Gordon.

Famous as a foil for flappers drinking bathtub gin, **Neil Hamilton** (*photo, left*) was a screen hero of the Jazz Age.

He wasn't designated as Tarzan, but as the "city slicker" whose firearms don't deter the brave heart of the Ape Man.

Episode 23

Little Caesar (1931)

Had casting gone differently, Clark Gable might have ruled over the kingdom of Warner Brothers instead of being crowned at MGM. Director Mervyn LeRoy had been intrigued with Clark as an actor ever since he sat through his performance in *The Last Mile.*

LeRoy contacted him the following day and Clark agreed to shoot a screen test for the upcoming film *Little Caesar. Variety* had already announced that Edward G. Robinson had agreed to play the title role of the Chicago mob boss Rico Bandello, nicknamed "Little Caesar."

Glenda Farrell would star as the female lead of Olga Stassoff. She was instructed to appear in the test in tandem with Clark.

The director had wanted Clark as the film's second male lead, the character of Joe Massoff, a friend of Rico. Massoff arrives in Chicago with the goal of succeeding as a dancer. His girlfriend, Olga (Farrell), is his dance partner. Joe tries to break free of the gang, but Rico lures him to participate in a robbery which quickly explodes into disaster.

After Clark completed his screen test, LeRoy set up an appointment with Darryl F. Zanuck and Jack Warner to watch it. At the end, Zanuck gloomily predicted, "The lug will never make it…crude as hell."

Warner then attacked LeRoy for wasting $500 of studio funds. "Forget this shit. Jug ears. He's monster ugly and lumbers around like a big ape looking for a banana. I'll deduct the money from your next paycheck."

Years later, Warner claimed, "I spent the rest of my life regretting that I did not sign Big Ears."

Instead, the role went to Douglas Fairbanks Jr., who so far had been coasting on the reputation of his father, Douglas Fairbanks Sr., the "ultimate swashbuckler" of silent pictures.

Losing the role to Fairbanks Jr. marked the beginning of Clark's long rivalry with that actor. Their jealousy became even more intense after Fairbanks learned that "the bastard had been banging my wife (Joan Crawford) for years before I got her."

Warner initially approved of Fairbanks, but months later, regretted it. "Every time I saw him, he's hanging out with the studio fags. I'm sure he's their Fairy Princess."

When Fairbanks Jr. was named as an accessory in a Hollywood divorce case, Warner was delighted by its "reaffirmation" of his heterosexual credentials.

The actor would marry three times but was rarely faithful within the context of any of them. One could ask Tallulah Bankhead, Marlene Dietrich, Lupe Velez, Gertrude Lawrence, or Loretta Young, among many others.

Fairbanks Jr. turned down Clifton Webb, but Noël Coward may have gotten lucky. In Fairbanks Jr.'s honor, Coward later composed that memorable lament, "Mad About the Boy."

The Ultimate Noir

Moviegoers were frantic, drowning in the darkest (early) years of the Great Depression. To distract them from their woes, consumers flocked to gangster films, none more natable than *Little Caesar* (1930).

As Caesar Enrico Bandello, **Edward G. Robinson** morphs into a bigshot mobster.

Two views of :"the ugliest villain in Hollywood," **Edward G. Robinson**. *Lower photo*: Robinson, *left*, aims a gun at **Douglas Fairbanks Jr.** as **Glenda Farrell** pleads for mercy.

Clark attended a showing of *Little Caesar,* carefully observing the performance of Edward G. Robinson and becoming highly critical of Fairbanks Jr., too. "Warners thought I was ugly. What about Robinson? He's the ugliest actor in Hollywood!"

During his 50-year run as a highly visible Hollywood actor, Robinson would star in more than 100 movies. He's best remembered for his tough guy performance in *Key Largo* (1948) with Humphrey Bogart.

Both Jack Warner and LeRoy, who had cast Robinson in *Little Caesar,* were pallbearers at his funeral in January of 1973.

Some critics referred to **Edward G. Robinson** *(left)* and **Douglas Fairbanks Jr.** as "The Beauty and the Beast." They appear together in this scene from *Little Caesar.* "Some people have youth, others beauty," Robinson said. "I have menace." Despite his looks, he managed to seduce (as did Doug Jr.) both Marlene Dietrich and Lupe Velez.

Doug Sr. was appalled (and threatened) when his son told him he wanted to become an actor. "There is only one Douglas Fairbanks!" he bellowed.

Seen here at the Santa Monica beach with his faithful dog, **Douglas Fairbanks Jr.** reigned as the unofficial Prince of Hollywood.

Despite his dashing good looks, he struggled all his life to carve out a distinctive career of his own,

He was forever eclipsed by the shadow of his celebrated and egotistical father, the swashbuckler of silent films.

Joan Blondell *(left)* with **Glenda Farrell** *(right)*. The sassiest, fast-and-loose gun molls in Pre-Code Hollywood often worked in tandem as "Sass Mouthed Dames."

Blondell became the bigger star and entered into two famous marriages, first to Dick Powell and then to Michael Todd. After seeing her on the screen, Jack Warner ordained, "For God's sake, put a brassière on Big Tits."

At the time this photo was taken, **Mary Pickford** and **Douglas Fairbanks Sr.** were the most famous couple on earth. During his marriage to heiress Anna Beth Sully, he sired Doug Jr.

Fairbanks Sr. later married "America's Sweetheart," Mary Pickford, making her the stepmother of young Doug Jr. When Junior married Joan Crawford, she warned him "not to bring that trash to Pickfair."

With a happy glow on her face, flapper **Joan Crawford** married **Douglas Fairbanks Jr.** in 1929. Whereas she was a neophyte actress and a former porn star and prostitute, he was the son of one of the ten most famous men on the planet—better known than Thomas Edison and King George V.

Episode 24

Irving Thalberg

Launches Clark Gable on the Road to Stardom

Irving Thalberg, basking in the romance and glamour of marriage to his movie-star wife, **Norma Shearer**. Her detractors attributed at least some of her success to him.

Irving Thalberg was born on the last day of May in the closing year of the 19th Century. Emerging from Brooklyn, he made it to Hollywood in the early years of motion pictures.

He had been born with a congenital heart disease, and doctors warned him that he'd be lucky to live until the end of his thirties. Nonetheless, he became a workhorse, nicknamed "The Boy Wonder" of MGM.

In partnership with Louis B. Mayer, he turned out some of the most successful of the studio's box office bonanzas in the 1930s, including *Grand Hotel* (1932) and *Mutiny on the Bounty* (1935).

For twelve years at MGM, in spite of his young age and declining health, he produced forty movies.

Thalberg had not been impressed with Clark's screen test for MGM, but his wife, Norma Shearer, thought otherwise. She con-

Thalberg and **Shearer** in a moment of camaradarie with the unfunny "autocrat of MGM," **Louis B. Mayer**

vinced her husband that Clark had a seductive, masculine look that would enthrall female movie-goers across the country.

Over the course of his short but illustrious career, Thalberg groomed some of the biggest stars of all time. Clark Gable joined a list that included Joan Crawford, Jean Harlow, Greta Garbo, John Gilbert, Lon Chaney, Ramon Novarro, Spencer Tracy, two-time Oscar winner Luise Rainer, and Norma

Thalberg and (almost) everyone else at MGM worked hard to sustain and nurture MGM's network of distributors in Nazi Germany. Modern-day historians attribute that to that fact that atrocities later inflicted on the Jews (and homosexuals and gypsies and dissidents) by the Nazis were, at the time, almost unthinkable. Ironically, clues were emerging in places like **Petaluma, California**, site of a Pro-Nazi rally (*see photo, above*), in the mid-1930s.

Shearer herself, whom he married in 1927.

On December 4, 1930, Clark signed a one-year contract with MGM for $650 a week. By now, he had gleaming (false) white teeth, compliments of Ria Langham's fat bank account.

In Thalberg's office, Clark was instructed to remove his shirt. Thalberg said he'd probably have to appear without it in some closeups, and because of that, he was ordered to work out at the MGM gym every day. At the time, he was in recovery from a bout of hepatitis, and he'd lost a lot of weight.

During his first week with MGM, he landed in the studio's makeup department, where two experts labored to create what later became "the Clark Gable look," thanks in part to what was known back then as the "kiss curl" dangling over his right eye. Thalberg warned his chief cameraman never to photograph Clark face-on, because "his ears stuck out one and a half miles."

Roland Flamini, the biographer of Thalberg, wrote, "His films carved out an international market, projecting a seductive image of American life brimming with vitality and rooted in democracy and personal freedom."

During his short reign, Thalberg was the most savvy of Hollywood producers, despite having been dismissed as "just a kid" at first. Yet despite his ethnicity as a Jew, he was not savvy about Nazism, and wanted to protect the then-thriving demand for MGM films being screened at theaters throughout Germany.

"Hitler and Hitlerism will pass. Dictators come and go. Jewry is embedded in every walk of German life. Jews will be strong enough to stand up to Hitler."

The Führer himself *(center figure in left photo)* morphed into a huge fan of (some) Hollywood films, praising Mickey Mouse and sappy melodramas in particular.

The consequences of World War II ended tragically for everyone depicted in the photo *(right)*:

An American Film the Nazis Loved
(...and used...and polluted...
and plagiarized)

The press photo above shows **Loretta Young** romancing **Robert Young** in *The House of Rothschild* (1934), a historical drama based on the banking family's tenuous grasp on wealth and power across five countries during Europe's "Age of Revolution."

Despite mocking long streches of it, the Nazis plagiarized extended scenes for insertion into propaganda films of their own. They were then promoted as "proof" of a worldwide Jewish conspiracy to rob "good Germans" of their hard earned savings.

An American Film the Nazis Hated

All Quiet on the Western Front (1930), the film adaptation of Erich Maria Remarque's novel about the horrors and romantic delusions of war, enraged the Nazi hierarchy, who viewed it as an critique of their war effort and banned it from screenings throughout Germany.

Episode 25

"I hate that big-eared son of a bitch, but keep him as long as he makes money."

—Louis B. Mayer to Irving Thalberg

MGM's studio slogan was, indeed, correct..... But "more stars than there are in Heaven" meant that any individual actor within its constellation was, therefore, "replaceable."

Louis B. Mayer emerged from the Russian Empire in 1884, and he eventually made it to New York, where he paraded through the streets as a junk dealer.

By 1918, he'd moved to Hollywood, where he made a prediction: "I grew up a poor boy, but I'll die a rich Jew."

His big breakthrough came in 1924 when Metro-Goldwyn-Mayer (MGM) was created. He later teamed with Irving Thalberg, "The Boy Wonder." Together, they created the most successful studio in Hollywood, boasting, "We have more stars than there are in heaven."

"The idea of a star being born is *bush-wah*," Mayer said. "A star is made, created, carefully and cold-bloodedly built up from nothing. A perfect example of that is Clark Gable. He was nothing until he met Irving and me. Although I made him a star, the bastard hated my guts."

"I discovered Greta Garbo, Hedy Lamarr, Norma Shearer, even that whoring bitch, Joan Crawford."

In public, he boasted about the glories of these stars. In private, he shared different opinions: "Garbo is a lez. Clark Gable and Joan Crawford are bisexuals."

Early in hs career, Clark came to him, demanding an increase in his salary and better roles. Mayer told him, "an actor like you is a dime a dozen in Hollywood. Garbo is unique. I can't replace her. But as for you, all I'd have to do is to look out my window until I saw the first good-looking stud pass by. I'd call him into my office and have the studio go to work on him. We could turn him into a star…your replacement. Oh, I would be kind to you. Give you one-way train fare back to Ohio."

[After his departure from MGM, Mayer was frank in his appraisal of Clark. "I couldn't stand the son of a bitch. But he made money for the studio. Any actor who did that, I could tolerate. Actually, MGM made $25 million when I loaned Gable to David O. Selznick for Gone With the Wind. *Gable didn't see one damn penny of that money. I saw to that. Even so, the big-eared lug was drawing $4,500 a week."]*

In 1951, Mayer was kicked out of MGM and replaced by Dore Schary.

Joan Crawford *(right)* at the 1953 premiere of *Torch Song*, clinging to the arm of MGM Studio Head **Louis B. Mayer**.

How did she describe him, officially and in public? "To me,"L.B. Mayer was my father, my father confessor, the best friend I ever had."

To insiders and friends, and in private, her point of view was radically different.

73

SMILING FOR THE CAMERA: For the actors who survived Louis B Mayer's rigorous (some said "cruel") process of elimination, life at MGM could be wonderful and sweet, indeed. Here's a view of the celebrants, each a mega-star during MGM's pinnacle, at Lionel Barrymore's 61st birthday party in 1939.

Standing, left to right: **Mickey Rooney, Robert Montgomery, Clark Gable, Louis B. Mayer, William Powell,** and **Robert Taylor**.

Seated, left to right: **Norma Shearer, Lionel Barrymore,** and **Rosalind Russell**.

Some of the films produced by MGM, including many with **Clark Gable** (shown *left* with **Vivien Leigh**) and **Judy Garland** *(photo right)* are interpreted today as quintessential expressions of *The American Experience.*

Despite the often bizarre aspects of the studio system it crafted and enforced, somebody (Louis B. Mayer?) must have been doing something right.

Episode 26

The Last Mile (1930)

The Last Mile, a play written by John Wexley, made Spencer Tracy a star in a Broadway production where he was cast as "Killer Mears," the leader of a prison mutiny. Later, it gave the career of Clark Gable a major boost, too.

Set on "Death Row," it is a grim drama that ran for 289 performances on Broadway. Hollywood agents attended its premiere in February of 1930, and would later lure Tracy to Hollywood.

Ironically, Tracy would, in time, become a lifelong friend of Gable, although there was always a certain rivalry between them. Sometimes, they had affairs with the same women. Such was the cast with Loretta Young.

At the time, Clark was being considered for the role of the male lead in *Secrets* (1933), starring Mary Pickford. *[That film was a remake of a circa 1924 silent film that had starred Norma Talmadge, based on a 1922 play with the same name.]* At the time, Pickford was frantically but unsuccessfully trying to evolve from America's Silent Sweetheart to equivalent recognition in the Talkies.

Clark was also being evaluated by producer Albert H. Woods for a role on Broadway in a stage adaptation of Ernest Hemingway's *A Farewell to Arms*.

Lillian Albertson, who had directed Clark in *What Price Glory?*, hired him again to take over the Spencer Tracy role in San Francisco and Los Angeles.

In Los Angeles, during the peak of the Great Depression, the play opened on June 7, 1930.

Lillian was entering the final weeks of her marriage to the play's producer, Louis Macloon.

Clark was favorably reviewed, one critic claiming, "Gable has all the fearsome likeness of a caged panther."

As reviewed by Elza Schallert in the *Los Angeles Times*, "In the role of convict Killer Meers, who waits to walk the last mile to the chair, Gable literally knocked everyone in the audience between the eyes with the fierce, bloodthirsty, vindictive, and blasphemous way he tore the part open."

The final performance of *The Last Mile* was a financial disaster. Producer Macloon disappeared with the box office receipts. His wife, Lillian, later divorced him on grounds of desertion.

The Last Mile was adapted into a 1932 feature film directed by Samuel Bischoff and starring Preston Foster. In 1959, it was vastly rewritten and formatted as the script for a film directed by Howard W. Koch and cast with pint-sized Mickey Rooney as "Killer Mears."

***

Neophyte stage actor **Clark Gable**, aiming a gun from this circa 1930 publicity picture promoting him as a half-crazed desperado on the verge of a prison breakout. Some critics cite his stage performance as "Killer Mears" as his *entrée* into the celluloid bigtime.

The Last Mile: Before Clark replaced him, **Spencer Tracy** *(photo above)* appeared in the same production, as the same character ("Killer Mears").

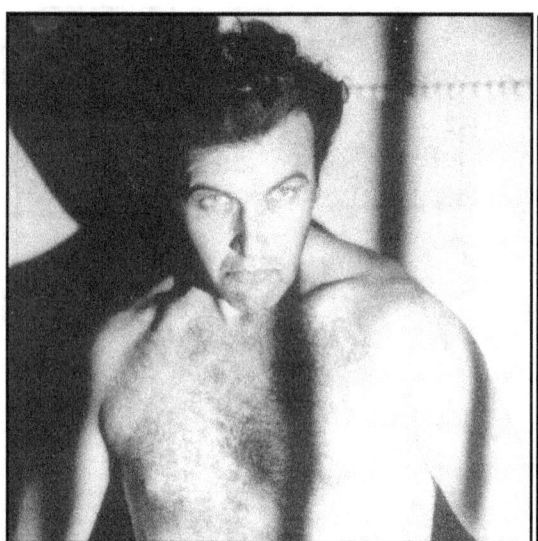

Beefcake Under Pressure (aka, The Prison Drama that Wouldn't Die

Left photo: Here's brooding **Preston Foster** as Killer Mears in the 1932 film adaptation of 1929-1930 stage play, *The Last Mile*.

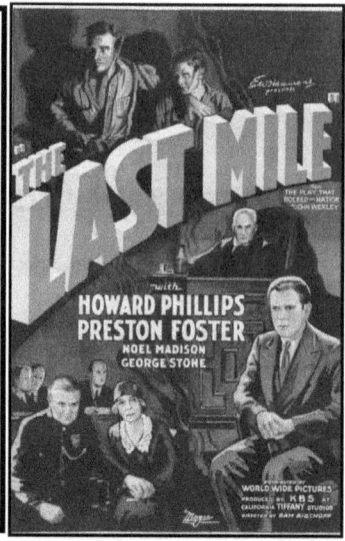

Trouble on Death Row

Two views of **Mickey Rooney** in the 1959 remake of *The Last Mile*.

Left photo: as the focal point of a poster promising gun violence and mayhem; and *right photo*: the former teenage prodigy, now an unattractive inmate (*Killer Mears*), strangling a prison guard.

Right photo: Here's that smooth-talking "imported Englishman," **Leslie Howard**, sweet-talking America's Sweetheart, **Mary Pickford**, in a 1933 cattle-rustling romantic drama for which Clark might have been better suited. It was Pickford's second attempt with the same script. Unhappy with the first version, even after spending $300,000 of her own money to film it, she'd ordered all the celluloid destroyed before starting anew.

Episode 27

The Painted Desert (1931)

Clark Gable made his debut in talking films for the soon-to-be-bankrupt Pathé Exchange, the trailblazing American filmmaking and distribution company that had thrived during the silent era since 1904. The film was evocatively titled *The Painted Desert*. Configured as a Pre-Code Western, it placed him in fifth billing among actors who included William Boyd (later Hopalong Cassidy), Helen Twelvetrees., William Farnum, and J. Farrell MacDonald.

Farnum (as Cash Holbrook) and MacDonald (as Jeff Cameron) come across an abandoned covered wagon on a remote and arid plain. No one can be found. Suddenly, they hear the cry of a baby bundled in the back. They argue over which of them is better suited to raise the boy. Cash (Farnum) prevails, taking the child, thereby creating a lifelong feud.

The baby grows up to be Bill Holbrook (Boyd) who works with his adoptive father on their family's cattle ranch. Meanwhile, Cameron, the "loser" in the argument over who would adopt the lost boy as his own, has become the father of the beautiful Mary Ellen, with whom Bill falls in love.

Cash wants access to the water hole on Jeff's property, but Jeff resists. Their ongoing feud continues to simmer.

To complicate matters, an itinerant cowboy, Rance Brett (Clark Gable), goes to work for Jeff. He, too, becomes smitten with Mary Ellen. Appearing rough and often unshaven in some scenes, this dangerous interloper looms as a threat.

Clark Gable *(right)* wasn't the only actor making his debut in then-newfangled talkies: Virtually everyone else in the entertainment industry was, too. Only the brave (and actors with voices that projected well) survived.

When Bill discovers tungsten on Jeff's property, he attempts to excavate a mine, hoping to end the feud between his two "fathers." But Rance, in an act of savagery and misdirected revenge, blows up the mine.

The age of talkies had arrived. Filming of *The Painted Desert* began late in 1930 for a January release.

Howard Higgin was designated as the film's director. He had started his career designing stage sets, and in time, he became the production designer of Cecil B. De Mille's *Forbidden Fruit* (1921).

His first duty as a director, involved helming Wallace Reid and Lila Lee in the silent comedy, *Rent Free* (1922). Over the course of his career, Higgin would direct such stars as Bette Davis, Mae Clark, Robert Armstrong, Basil Rathbone, Alan Hale, Pat O'Brien, and Carole Lombard.

Clark's agent at the time, Minna Wallis, the sister of producer Hal B. Wallis, had secured the role for Clark. It would be his highest-paid role to date. For a seventeen-week shoot in the Arizona desert, he'd be paid $750 a week.

Wallis had assured Higgin that Clark was a skilled horseman, which he was not. Before filming began, she enrolled him the Griffin Park Riding Academy. There, he was vigorously trained by Art Wilson, and old time cowpoke who, as a youth, was riding horses across the then wide-and-open

Two views of **Clark Gable** in *Painted Desert*. *Upper photo*: Face to face with veteran silent film star **William Boyd**.

Lower photo: **Clark,** rugged, unshaven, and macho enough for anything a Western action/adventure could throw at him.

plains of Montana. He later said, "Gable has the guts of an Army mule. When I finish with him, he could hire out as a rodeo rider."

Higgin later claimed that Clark and Boyd hated each other on sight. Actually, they had more in common than they wanted to admit. Both of them, as young men, had lain on the casting couch of directors or producers to break into silent pictures.

Born in Ohio (like Clark), Boyd was six years older than his competitor. After his arrival in Hollywood, he'd been an orange picker, a tool dresser, a surveyor, and an auto salesman.

He later found work as an extra, where his good looks, physique, and masculine charm attracted homosexuals in positions of power. Like Clark, he became "gay for pay" before the term was coined. He was rumored to have spent time, briefly, in the bed of Rudolph Valentino.

His rise in the film industry came much faster than it did for Clark. Cecil B. De Mille cast Boyd in *The Road to Yesterday* (1925). He won critical approval for his performance, leading De Mille to make him a leading man in *The Volga Boatman* (1926).

De Mille also cast him in *The King of Kings* (1927), and D.W. Griffith hired him for *Lady of the Pavements* (1929).

At his peak, Boyd was earning $100,000 a year, an amount whose spending power was roughly equivalent to $1.8 million, adjusted for inflation, in 2024,.

Perhaps with the intention of concealing his past, he became very homophobic. He seemed aware of Clark's background and made disparaging remarks about him.

Actually, Boyd's reputation had been severely damaged when a newspaper ran his picture on its front page, claiming he'd been arrested on gambling and liquor charges. It was later revealed that he'd been defamed. The crook that the police had arrested was an unrelated man with a roughly equivalent name, William "Stages" Boyd. The actor, William Boyd, was hoping that his performance in *The Painted Desert* would restore his tarnished reputation.

Brooklyn-born Helen Twelvetrees, whom both Boyd and Clark lusted for on screen, arrived in Hollywood with the advent of sound in 1929. She would continue to be cast in pictures for a decade, often playing suffering women in lachrymose dramas. Maurice Chevalier and Spencer Tracy were among her leading men. "The best roles I sought went to Katharine Hepburn," she asserted, years later.

Her birth name was Jurgens, but she billed herself as Twelvetrees after marrying Clark Twelvetrees, and actor, in 1927. At a dinner party in Manhattan, he attempted suicide by jumping out of an eighth-floor window. Breaking the impact of his attempt at death, he hit two awnings before landing on top of a parked car. He was hospitalized for four months. She divorced him in 1931.

[*In 1938, Clark Twelvetrees died of a skull fracture after striking his head on a sidewalk when a man— who saw him hit a woman to the ground with whom he was arguing—physically intervened. Murder charges against the man, 29-year-old painter James Paskovics, were dismissed.*]

Helen Twelvetrees, too, would die an early death at the age of 49 in Middletown, Pennsylvania.

The Painted Desert: What was it all about? A tungsten miner (**Bill Boyd**, *right*) loves his father's rival's daughter (**Helen Twelvetrees**, *left*) and fights off her other suitor (Clark Gable).

Helen Twelvetrees is a forgotten name today, but she had a brief reign as a screen queen in the 1930s.

"The young Clark Gable came on to me but got rebuffed. He was unshaven and looked like a cowpoke in need of a bath. How was I to know he would become the matinee idol of the 1930s?"

Born in Boston in 1876, William Farnum was a dashing leading man before he descended into character roles. Reared in a family of actors, he had portrayed the title character of *Ben-Hur* on Broadway in 1900.

Farnum's most famous scene came in the 1914 silent film, *The Spoilers,* in which he and actor Tom Santschi staged a fight that lasted for a full reel. *[Ironically, he was hired as a staff member for a remake of The Spoilers in 1930. His duties included teaching Gary Cooper and William Boyd how to fight their way through that same scene.]*

Tragically, most of Farnum's films were destroyed in a fire. *[In July of 1937, an out-of-control fire broke out in a 20th-Century-Fox film-storage facility in Little Ferry, New Jersey. It resulted in one death, two injuries, and the obliteration of almost every film in the vaults, i.e., most of the silent films produced by Fox before 1932.]*

A Yankee from Connecticut, J. Farrell MacDonald was both a director and an actor, playing supporting roles or occasional leads in an astounding 325 movies between 1911 and 1952, the year of his death at the age of 77.

Over the course of his career, MacDonald would work with Hal Roach, Harold Lloyd, John Ford, Raoul Walsh, and Preston Sturges.

He also played a detective in the first version of *The Maltese Falcon* (1931), starring Ricardo Cortez and Bebe Daniels. He even played the hobo, "Mr. Tramp," in *Our Little Girl* (1935) with Shirley Temple.

Clark Gable's career almost ended in the Arizona desert during his portrayal of the vengeful cowboy

(Above left) In ads like this, **Pathé Exchange** *(aka Pathé Studios)*, the Hollywood branch of the France-based filmmakers, promoted the careers of its most-recognized stars. *Counterclockwise from the left poster's upper left*, are **Constance Bennett, Ann Harding, Bill Boyd,** and **Helen Twelvetrees,** as they appeared in 1930.

(Above right) shows the brilliant illustrative skills of Pathés press and PR department. It's devoted to the second of a three-film (1927-28) serial that followed the passion and resurrection of Jesus. Each film within the series was conceived and orchestrated by Cecil B. De Mille.

who blows up a tungsten mine. "Something went horribly wrong. The debris was supposed to go in one direction, but it went where I was on horseback. Flying rocks killed one crew member and injured 28 others."

"I was trying to guide my horse away from the blast. Had the horse obeyed me, I would have been killed. The animal must have sensed impending doom and began galloping with me away from the huge blast. All I got was a lot of dirt blowing my way. That brave animal rode me to safety. At the end of the ride, I gave it a big, juicy kiss, the only time in my life I kissed a horse."

Around the time that *The Painted Desert* was released, his agent, Minna Wallis, delivered bad news: Pathé had gone bankrupt. She told Clark that she was trying to negotiate a deal for Clark at MGM. What she didn't tell him was that she had already contacted Warner Brothers, where Jack Warner had mocked his "big ears."

The columnist Adela Rogers St. Johns "gushed" over Clark's film debut in *The Painted Desert*. Perhaps that had something to do with his visiting her home late at night once a week.

Film Daily wrote, "Clark Gable wasn't very good, but lady fans liked him. His brutish mannerisms were appropriate for the role.

The *Hollywood Reporter* praised the Arizona scenery but found that "much of the dialogue is unconvincing and serves chiefly to slow up the action."

Motion Picture Magazine found the film "worth seeing" and complimented Clark's acting. "You could call the plot hokum if you will, but it's the hokum of which life is made."

Picture Play lauded the acting, but found the film "dull and pointless, more so than any we have ever seen."

Years later, on Johnny Carson's *The Tonight Show,* the host (Carson) sustained a running, oft-repeated gag: "Who was Rin Tin Tin's favorite actress?" The answer?: "Helen Twelvetrees."

In 1958, the holders of the copyright of *The Painted Desert* did not renew their rights. It is now in the public domain.

***

WHATEVER HAPPENED TO WILLIAM BOYD?

As often detailed within pulp magazines by the author Clarence E. Mulford, the original character of Hopalong Cassidy was a hard-drinking, rough-living, redheaded wrangler. For a film series, he was "reconfigured" into a cowboy hero with no vices. Instead of alcohol, he drank sarsaparilla.

In 1935, William Boyd signed to bring Hopalong to the screen. Rivaled mostly by Gene Autry and Roy Rogers, he became a hero to young boys attending Saturday matinees across the land,

The Hopalong Cassidy series, which ended in 1948, generated millions.

Boyd then made one of the smartest financial moves of any actor in the history of Hollywood. Emptying his bank account and mortgaging every property he owned, he bought the rights to all the Hopalong Westerns. He sold them to television, where they became the building blocks for a freshly reconfigured series. It generated millions for him. He made yet another fortune licensing merchandise that included a comic strip, watches, cups, trading cards, and cowboy outfits. In all, he sold 106 television shows and 104 Hopalong radio broadcasts.

As an actor, Cecil B. De Mille brought Boyd back for a cameo role in the 1952 circus movie, The Greatest Show on Earth, *starring Betty Hutton. Later, however, Boyd rejected De Mille's offer to play Moses in* The Ten Commandments *(1956) fearing that his cowboy fame would impair the credibility of his portrayal of an Old Testament patriarch (i.e., Moses). That role was ultimately assigned to Charlton Heston.*

Throughout most of his retirement, Boyd refused to be photographed, as he did not want his young fans to see him as an old man.

In 1972, at the age of 77, he died in Laguna Beach, California.

If appearing on the cover of *Life* magazine implies a degree of immortality, **William Boyd** won every benchmark of fame prevalent at the time. Here, he appears as **Hopalong Cassidy** on the cover of the June 12, 1950 edition of the then-most-widely read magazine in the world.

Episode 28

Palimony Problems

Clark Gable Fathers a Boy Born to Hollywood's Then-Leading Gossip Columnist, Adela Rogers St. Johns

Hardworking, well-connected, and eccentric, **Adela Rogers St. Johns**, during her heyday, was one of the leading entertainment/gossip columnists in the world. Here she is, as she appeared with a corsage and stylishly turbaned, in the late 1920s.

Before there was a Louella Parsons, before there was a Hedda Hopper, there was Adela Rogers St. Johns. A daughter of Los Angeles born in 1894, she was a journalist, screenwriter, and novelist. She is best known for her reporting about Hollywood movie stars in the 1920s and 1930s, when she was the major writer for *Photoplay* magazine.

It is said that she fell in love with the screen image of Clark Gable when she saw his performance in *The Painted Desert*, a 1931 Pre-Code Western starring William Boyd.

In her glowing review, she referred to him as "almost too beautiful."

Ever the opportunist, he phoned her two days later and asked to meet privately with her. She was married at the time to Ivan St. Johns, the chief copy editor at the *Los Angeles Herald*. He didn't get home until 11pm on work nights, so she invited Clark for a private dinner. Before her husband's return that night, Clark was in her bed, beginning a series of seductions that stretched over several years.

She always wrote glowingly of him. "Clark Gable is the same man on or off the screen, which is true of only a few stars. He has a charm that no psychologist can explain. It probably is the same feeling that Eve had when she first spotted Adam in the Garden of Eden."

In a subsequent article for *Liberty* magazine, she referred to him as "The Great God Gable. A year ago, not a soul in Hollywood had heard of him. Today, he ranks ahead of any established favorites."

Clark and St. Johns were soon seen riding around Los Angeles in a $10,000 automobile presented to him by press baron William Randolph Hearst, the boss of St. Johns.

The most persistent rumor that arose was that Clark made her pregnant, and she had to conduct her interviews for several months over the phone. She was said to have given birth to a boy.

Eddie Mannix from MGM's publicity department covered up the birth. He told a few friends, "Somewhere in America today there is a school kid being mocked by the other boys on the playground for his big ears. The poor boy doesn't know that Clark Gable is his father."

Once, on *The Merv Griffin Show,* the TV host asked her about

In her 1969 memoir, *The Honeycomb*, **Adela Rogers St. Johns** ran a photograph of herself with **Clark Gable** as they emerged from the MGM commissary. Whereas she was madly in love with him, as the photo reveals, he was accused of seducing her for career advancement.

the rumors that she once produced a child with Clark Gable.

"What woman would deny that Clark Gable was the father of her child?"

Once, in one of her columns, St. Johns ran a widely publicized quote from Clark: "I'm no Adonis. I'm as American as the telephone poles I used to climb to make a living. Other men see me on the screen making love to Jean Harlow, Norma Shearer, or Joan Crawford. They say that if I can do it, so can they. They go home and make passionate love to their wives."

In her column, St. Johns would later write about the divorce of Clark from his second wife Ria Langham. "Their parting makes my heart ache. The two of them seemed to have an ideal marriage."

As she wrote that, she knew it wasn't true. In the early years, Ria kept Clark as her "kept boy," and he constantly cheated on her.

After Gable's death in 1960, St. Johns wrote, "The King is dead. Long live the King. There is no successor to his crown. Nor will there be. The title died with the death of Gable."

St. Johns would go on to live until 1988, always treasuring her memory of Clark, someties referring to him as "My only true love."

KISS & TELL!

HEEEERE'S MERV! as he appeared on his syndicated talk show coaxing indiscretions from his guest, **Adela Rogers St. Johns.** By this stage in his career, he'd developed a reputation for interviewing "everyone who mattered" in contemporary American life.

The date was January 28, 1963, when as many as 20 million viewers heard and saw her more or less confess to an affair with Clark.

The "New Romance" referred to in the March 7, 1936 edition of *Liberty* was **Clark Gable's** romance with Carole Lombard, "The Queen of Screwball Comedy."

The two leading gossip columnists, **Adela Rogers St. Johns** and **Louella Parsons** wrote extensively about it. It is believed that Clark is the only actor in Hollywood who seduced both of these gossip mavens.

HEEEEERE'S MERV!

DID YOU KNOW? That in 2009, Porter and Prince, the authors of this overview of Clark Gable, wrote and released a tell-all about one of the then-richest men in Hollywood (**Merv Griffin**) that generated headlines and "*oooh-la-las*" in some of the world's biggest tabloids

Episode 29

How MGM's "Fixers"
Buried the Most Compromising Secrets of Their Stars—

Especially Those of Clark Gable

As author E.J. Fleming said, "Eddie Mannix and Howard Strickling are virtually unknown outside of Hollywood and little remembered even there, but as general managers and as heads of publicity at MGM, they were lords of the star-studded universe of Hollywood's Golden Age from the 1920s through the 1940s. When MGM stars found themselves in trouble, it was 'Eddie and Howard' who solved their problems, hid their crimes, and kept their secrets. They were known as 'The Fixers.'"

Some secrets were relatively minor, such as Joan Crawford's adulterous affair with Clark Gable, who was also married. Sometimes, they were much more serious, such as when Wallace Beery murdered Ted Healy, the creator of *The Three Stooges*. When MGM executive Paul Bern was found dead in the home he shared with his newlywed wife, Jean Harlow, Strickling was the first man called.

When Clark made his co-star, Loretta Young, pregnant on the set of *Call of the Wild* (1935), the urgent message went out: "Get Strickling on the phone and get Young out of town until she has Gable's kid."

As other scandals continued to surface, Strickling hated hearing the ring of his phone at 2AM. Maybe it was a security guard informing him that he'd rescued a drunk and belligerent Spencer Tracy, who had been stopped by the police in his car with a 15-year-old boy he'd "rented" for the night. Maybe it was Marlene Dietrich calling to tell him that John Gilbert had died in her bedroom.

One of their biggest tasks involved concealing abortions, especially those of Jean Harlow, Judy Garland, and Lana Turner.

Indeed, one of the most outrageous stories was spread about Turner. And of course, it could have been true. According to the rumor, when

It embarrassed and humiliated everyone, a lurid tale about Clark's long-suffering first wife, **Josephine Dillon**. Had **MGM's Fixers** prevailed, stories like this would never have been published.

This embarrassing exposé in *Confidential* was one of the rare instances where the "smooth-over skills" of Eddie Mannix and Howard Strickland didn't work.

 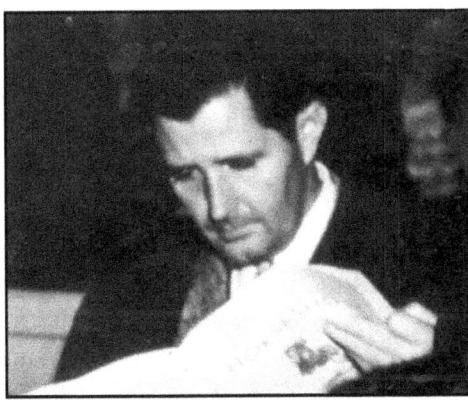

To achieve a "cleansing" of any whiff of scandal from their corps of contract players, **Eddie Mannix** *(left photo)*, along with MGM's head of publicity, **Howard Strickling** *(right photo)*, nurtured contacts with hospitals, the police, the district attorney's office, and members of the press.. A tour through MGM, or a face-to-face with some movie stars, was usually enough to charm (and divert) many writers and law enforcement officials. In more obstinant cases, some were added to MGM's payroll.

Turner's gangster boyfriend, Johnny Stompanato, was stabbed to death inside her home, Strickling intervened.

If the legend is to be believed, he immediately summoned Fred Otash, the master private investigator, to get at once to the Turner home. There, he was said to have removed the knife from the gangster's body, wiping off Turner's fingerprints and replacing them with those of her daughter, Cheryl Crane.

Turner could have ended up in prison, but Strickling knew that the law would let Crane (then a teenager) off with no more than a brief juvenile internment.

Strickling later admitted, "I knew scandals, or aided in cover-ups that would have brought shame and disgrace on such heavyweights as Gary Cooper, Tallulah Bankhead, Charles Laughton, Cary Grant, Barbara Stanwyck, Robert Taylor, Jeanette MacDonald, Jean Harlow, Nelson Eddy, and that horny little runt, Mickey Rooney."

The fixers also covered up the seemingly endless (and convoluted) sexual affairs of "The Mexican Spitfire," Lupe Velez, the former wife of Johnny Weissmuller, the screen Tarzan.

During the 1930s, she was the most notorious nymphomaniac in Hollywood. Clark Gable was one of her many conquests.

Actor Charles Bickford said, "Lupe was a sex-driven, drug-crazed wreck."

To conceal Van Johnson's homosexuality in the 1940s, Mannix arranged for him to marry the wife of his best friend and lover, Keenan Wynn.

[Interestingly, Strickling sometimes diverged from his role as an enforcer and fixer: When MGM agreed to release David O. Selznick's Gone With the Wind (1939), they hired tough-talking Strickling to provide voiceovers for several of the trailers that promoted it.]

Just who were these two men, Mannix and Strickling, who kept the secrets?

***

Strickling was born far, far away from Hollywood in the wilds of West Texas in 1896. He had been discovered while working in construction at an amusement park in Fort Lee, New Jersey. *[Josh Brolin portrayed him in* Hail Caesar!, *a fictional 2016 comedy loosely based on Strickling's exploits.]*

Brothers Nick and Joseph Schenck brought Strickling to Hollywood, where he ended up in the MGM publicity department. The studio had been on the lookout for a "gangster type," not to generate publicity or to advance the plots of any of their movies,, but to squelch scandals.

Strickling's partner was Eddie Mannix. Born in Fort Lee, New Jersey, in 1891, he was a tough-talking and macho, formerly a bouncer in an unruly bar.

Like Strickling, he, too ended up at MGM after "bouncing around from job to job."

He climbed the MGM ladder rung by rung, eventually being promoted to the rank of general manager and VP.

Mannix was married twice and had no children. Because of a weak heart, he suffered poor health on occasion. In 1959, after several heart attacks, he was more or less permanently confined to a wheelchair.

[Actor Bob Hoskins portrayed Mannix in the 2006 biographical film, Hollywoodland, *starring Ben Affleck as actor George Reeves, who had portrayed Superman in the television series* The Adventures of Superman

Poor **Loretta Young**...So prone to Catholic guilt...and SUCH a movie star... soooo unmarried...and soooo pregnant. The father was Clark. Thanks in part to the media spins of Strickling and Mannix, the public never knew..until decades later.

One of the most flaunted "open secrets' of the Silent Screen involved the bisexual dramas of **Rudolph Valentino** with his wife, that formidable lesbian and egomaniac, **Natacha Rambova**.

(1952-1958).]

Mannix has long been suspected of having Reeves murdered. Mannix's second wife, Toni Larrier, a former Ziegfeld Follies dancer., and been engaged in a torrid affair with Reeves.

When he got angry one day at Strickling, Mannix told Irving Thalberg, "My buddy, Strickling, has had only two great loves of his line: Rudolph Valentino and Clark Gable."

Strickling got a job as a press agent for director Rex Ingram. He was next assigned to generate publicity for Rudolph Valentino.

Strickling had been introduced to Valentino by columnist Adela Rogers St. Johns. According to her, "Howard fell hard. They slipped around and banged each other every chance they got. Rudi went on to other adventures before his untimely death, but I think Howard carried a torch for him for the rest of his life—that is, until he met Clark Gable, who, coincidentally, was also my lover. Hollywood was a small town back then. Lovers often overlapped."

Lots of insiders knew that **Wallace Beery** *(right photo)* was a mean, sometimes violent drunk. Ask his first wife, Gloria Swanson (married from 1916-1918), who bruited it around Hollywood. He probably played a direct role in the murder of comedian **Ted Healy** *(left figure in left photo)*. Strickling and Mannix covered it up.

It was widely known among Hollywood insiders, but unknown to the public at large, that the three most famous lovers of the silent screen were each homosexuals—Rudolph Valentino, Ramon Novarro, and Antonio Moreno.

During the course of his short life, "The Sheik," as he was known—a reference to Valentino— married twice—first to Jean Acker in 1919 and later, to Natacha Rambova in 1923. Both women were lesbians. Rambova had formerly been a lover of Nazimova, who, for a brief time in the early 1920s, had been the Queen of MGM.

Both Acker and Rambova later admitted that their marriages to Valentino had never been consummated.

After his image-crafting for Valentino, Strickling became a publicist for John Barrymore and Greta Garbo.

He always remembered his first meeting with Clark Gable. It was in November of 1930 at the apartment of Minna Wallis, his agent.

Years later, Strickling in an interview said, "Clark was the biggest man I ever saw. His hands were tremendous. His feet were tremendous. He had a tremendous, big head. His ears were tremendous. I would say he was one of the most powerful men. One of his great fears, I learned as I got to know him, was that he could hurt someone. Physically. He never did. He always knew he had tremendous strength, but he never used it. I thought Gee whiz. What a tremendous guy. What a hell of a man."

Although that statement explicitly described Gable's physicality for anyone who didn't pick up on it, Strickling might as well have written, "I fell in love with 'Tremendous' the first time I spotted him across a crowded room on that enchanted evening."

Author Chrystopher J. Spicer characterized what Strickling became in Clark's life: "A security squad, a nursemaid, a go-between with Louis B. Mayer, a counselor, and a cover-up expert."

He didn't include the word "lover."

"Keep it cheerful and keep it hetero," was a byline adopted by any starlet paired with the closeted **Van Johnson**, typecast by MGM as "the boy next door" even until he reached late middle age.

Here, he appears with perky **Janet Leigh** in the relentlessly heterosexual rom-com, *Wives and Lovers* (1963).

85

"If it were not for Howard Strickling, I probably would have ended up a truck driver," Clark later said, "or else a stunt man risking my life in some dumb movie."

St. Johns claimed, "Until Howard met Gable, I never thought he would get over the death of Valentino."

***

When stardom finally came to Clark, it arrived fast and furious in 1931, thanks in part to his involvement in eleven separate movies, each in circulation at the same time. By December of that year, his name was familiar to movie-goers across the nation. His on-screen (and sometimes off-screen) lovers included Constance Bennett, Joan Crawford, Fay Wray, Norma Shearer, Barbara Stanwyck, Greta Garbo, and Joan Blondell, among others. It didn't seem to matter to him that he was still married to Ria Langham—at least officially.

At this point in his career, since Clark had been elevated to the status of leading man, the management at MGM was ferociously committed to protecting his reputation.

Mayer himself, horrified at the possibility of one of his star's public involvement in a sex scandal, began defining both Clark and Spencer Tracy as "walking time bombs."

A bordello pro, Lee Francis, had opened the "House of Francis," a whorehouse that staffed eighteen beautiful young women, all of whom had come to Hollywood with hopes of becoming movie stars.

Mayer ordered Mannix to open an corporate expense account with Francis, so that none of the stars sent there would have to exchange dollars.

Mannix warned Clark to stop parking his "instantly recognizable" custom-made automobile in front of the bordello.

John Gilbert became a regular patron, as did John Barrymore, Milton Berle, Bob Hope, Douglas Fairbanks Jr., John Huston, William Powell, George Raft, and in time, Mickey Rooney and Errol Flynn.

Francis soon found out that many of the male stars then thriving at MGM were either bisexual or closeted homosexuals. Thus, she began recruiting extraordinarily handsome young men, all of whom had arrived in Hollywood hoping to break into the movies. They quickly became popular, and some nominally straight men "decided to try a boy for a change."

When the House of Francis became too well known, Mayer ordered Strickling to open "Mae's," a much more private bordello, within a sprawling mansion in Beverly Hils. Billie Bennett, its madam, looked like and talked exactly like Mae West.

Her gimmick involved dressing and making up

In April of 1958, did **Lana Turner** stab her gangster lover, Johnny Stompanato? Or was it her daughter, Cheryl Crane, who killed him when she caught him threatening her mother with death? At this point, the actual truth may never be known.

If Lana were convicted, it could mean the end of her career and a sentence of life in prison. In contrast, a guilty verdict for Cheryl might mean only a few months in reform school.

Long before the police were called, attorney Jerry Giesler was summoned to the Turner residence. He was the man you called when you murdered someone.

Dresed as a sailor, **Lupe Velez**, "The Mexican Spitfire," rode the high seas of romance during her short reign in Hollywood before her untimely death. Clark Gable was only "a passing diversion" as she later proclaimed that Gary Cooper was the true love of her life. She married only once, to Johnny (Tarzan) Weissmuller, but was never faithful, not with Charlie Chaplin and Errol Flynn lurking nearby.

her prostitutes to look like famous stars of their era. Clients who included Clark could arrive and request Carole Lombard (long before he married the real one), Marlene Dietrich, Ginger Rogers, Alice Faye, Constance Bennett, or Barbara Stanwyck. Ironically, Clark didn't have to ask for the Joan Crawford impersonator, since he was getting the real thing.

Billie (aka "Mae") soon learned that no man wanted Katharine Hepburn or Greta Garbo. "I think those two dykes frightened men," she claimed.

***

As press baron William Randolph Hearst told his (very cooperative) columnist, Louella Parsons, "If you don't know the truth, print the legend."

According to a rumor that still persists today, a drunken Clark Gable, in the summer of 1933, ran through a red light and killed a woman in her sixties who was walking across Sunset Blvd. After killing her, he drove away, fleeing into the night.

Eddie Mannix, if reports are to be believed, was immediately alerted by an employee at MGM whose job included the monitoring of police calls. Mannix is said to have arrived on the scene soon thereafter and bribed two policemen before the dead woman was hauled away in an ambulance.

Within a few hours, Howard Strickling, who had also been alerted, was *en route* to his rented cottage in Palm Springs with a still-drunk Clark snoring in his back seat.

In the meantime, Louis B. Mayer was informed of Clark's involvement. Fearing that he would be outed as the hit-and-run driver, he made a deal that morning that preserved the career of his now-valuable property, even though, personally, he intensely disliked his rising star.

As the unproven story rambles on, Mayer got a low-level manager at MGM to take the blame for the accident. At the most, he would serve a jail term of less than a year. For that inconvenience, Mayer would guarantee him a weekly salary of $500 a month, increased as time went by to keep abreast of inflation.

The manager was said to have accepted the deal. Eventually, MGM lawyers arranged to have him committed to, and later released from, an "honor farm" (a minimum security correctional facility that allows inmates to work and perform community service) after only eight months.

Mayer also had his attorneys contact the relatives of the dead pedestrian and offer them $125,000 for not bringing charges. During the depth of the Depression, the poverty-stricken family eagerly accepted this life-changing windfall.

These stories, as related above, have each been widely reported over the course of many years. Other sources, however, have asserted that the accident never happened.

An alternate story circulated that Clark's car accident was invented as a racy, attention-grabbing explanation for Clark's medium-term absence from public life at around the same time.

Those rumors claim that he had spent several unexplained weeks in a hospital having some of his rotted teeth pulled and replaced with gleaming dentures.

Other rumors conclude that he had endured cosmetic surgery to reduce the size of his ears, and that MGM's brass feared

Back when costume parties were in vogue, **William Randolph Hearst** choreographed a birthday party, in his honor, and got his picture taken, sandwiching **Bette Davis** (*center*) between himself and **Louella Parsons** (*right*), who's unflatteringly outfitted as a drum majorette.

An enduring Hollywood fable in 1924 claims that Parsons, a guest aboard Heart's yacht off the coast of Southern California, witnessed a fatal shooting.

It was dark, and Hearst was alleged to have shot producer Thomas Ince, mistaking him for Charlie Chaplin. The Little Tramp was having an affair with Hearst's mistress, Marion Davies.

Parsons, according to reports, blackmailed Hearst into beefing up her career as a columnist.

The legend has gained popularity over the years, although it has been discredited by those who investigated Ince's untimely death at the time.

that news of that would undermine Clark's romantic image.

There is no dispute that during the course of his early career, Clark had false teeth inserted However, it isn't likely that he had cosmetic surgery ever performed to "correct" the size of his ears.

On the other hand, some sources allege that there was never any car accident at the alleged time and place involving Clark, since he was on a trip to Alaska.

Nonetheless, E. J. Fleming, author of *The Fixers*, convincingly asserted, "I believe the accident did occur involving Gable. Over the years, dozens of industry executives at MGM have confirmed that the Gable accident did occur."

Fleming, however, after extensive research of newspaper archives never uncovered that a low-level MGM executive was sentenced to an honor farm to serve time for the accident. That part of Mayer's pay-off may be the stuff of legend.

Confusing the issue at its core, Gable had several other accidents that were known about and carefully documented at the time, even though their worst aspects were never officially reported

At this date, and probably forever more, the actual details associated with the death of that pedestrian on Sunset Blvd. will never be known.

***

The mother of actor **George Reeves**, outfitted as Superman above, did not believe that he killed himself with a gunshot. Neither did his friends, Alan Ladd and Gig Young. Actor Rory Calhoun told a reporter, "No one in Hollywood believes that suicide crap. George was murdered."

In their book, *Hollywood Kryptonite*, Nancy Schoenberger and Sam Kashner, make a case that Eddie Mannix was behind his murder, perhaps because of his affair with his wife. Since Mannix had ties to the Mafia, it would have been easy for him to have arranged a hit man to do the dirty deed.

Actor George Reeves (1914-1959) became best known for portraying Clark Kent/Superman in the hit television series, *Adventures of Superman,* on television from 1952 to 1958. He could never escape the association of his personal identity with that superhero, try as he did.

His film career began in 1939 when he was cast as one of the suitors of Scarlett O'Hara in *Gone With the Wind.* He appears in that film's opening scene (the Barbecue at Tara) before the Civil War has begun.

That was followed by a series of mainly B pictures, two with Ronald Reagan and three with James Cagney. Reeves even made five Hopalong Cassidy pictures.

After service in World War II, he returned to Hollywood and found that roles had more or less dried up. At one point, he dug cesspools. Along came the *Adventures of Superman* series that marked the peak of his career.

In the meantime, he was having an affair with Toni Mannix, the wife of Eddie Mannix, "the Fixer" over at MGM. Her husband was having affairs of his own.

Right before his death, Reeves had broken off his affair with Toni and had begun a sexual relationship with the society playgirl, Leonore Lemmon. They were making plans for their honeymoon.

That would not happen. On January 16, 1959, Reeves, aged 45, was found dead at his home. The official ruling was suicide.

Episode 30

The Easiest Way (1931)

As a director, Jack Conway was given a tough assignment by Irving Thalberg. "For *The Easiest Way*, you've got a big star in Constance Bennett, who is hauling in $30,000 a week. She'll boss you. I'm sending over a young, tough former lumberjack, Clark Gable. Mayer and I are going to sign him. He's a mass of raw meat that I want you to turn into a sexy hunk of juicy steak."

"You don't want much, do you, Irving?" Conway said.

The Easiest Way had originated on Broadway in 1909 as a starring vehicle for the then-famous stage actress Frances Starr, as produced by David Belasco. In 1917, Select/Selznick Studio adapted it into a silent film starring Clara Kimball Young.

Robert Montgomery (the film's male lead, a bitter rival of Clark Gable) with its superstar blonde, **Constance Bennett.**

Hollywood wits quickly (but privately) renamed the film "*The Easiest Lay.*"

On at least three other occasions, producers or directors set out to turn it into a film but met with obstacles "because the plot is immoral, dealing with a prostitute."

Cecil B. De Mille embarked on filming it in 1928, but that "nasty little censor," Will H. Hays, talked him out of it.

Hays also lobbied to persuade Thalberg to abandon plans to adapt it into a movie, but the MGM mogul defied him, forging ahead with plans to produce it in a format that included Clark Gable.

Bennett, as Lolly Murdock, received top billing within an all-star cast. Her leading men were Adolphe Menjou as William Brockton and Robert Montgomery as Jack Madison. Anita Page played Peg Murdock, her sister, married to a laundryman named Nick Feliki (Clark Gable).

The father of the women is Ben Murdock, cast with J. Farrell MacDonald, who had just finished filming *The Painted Desert* (1931) with Clark.

In an uncredited, very minor role, the future gossip columnist, Hedda Hopper, played Mrs. Cara Williams.

Clark also met and befriended a future screen legend, James Stewart, also cast in an uncredited role as a cigar store clerk.

Reared in the slums, Lolly (Constance Bennett)

Two views of Clark Gable as Nick Feliki (the second male lead) in *The Easiest Way*

Left photo: Dressed in his workaday "everyman" garb as a laundryman; and

Right photo: Dolled up and glam, seducing "uptown girl" **Constance Bennett,** with hints of the dapper and debonaire king he'd eventually become.

lands a job at a department store. There, she meets William Brockton (Menjou), head of the Brockton Advertising Agency. She becomes his mistress, and he lavishes gifts and money on her.

In a chauffeur-driven limousine, she arrives at the modest home of her sister, Peg (Anita Page). Peg's husband Nick (Gable) rejects her, objecting to her prostituting herself.

Before the end of the final reel, facing rejection from all corners, Lolly ends up walking the streets, peddling her wares to any paying customer.

By now, Clark had proved his versatility as an actor, going from playing a villainous cowpoke in his previous movie to a hardworking, morally upright and proper husband.

Jack Conway, a son of Minnesota, would become one of Clark's favorite directors. In the late 1920s, he had helmed both William Haines and Joan Crawford, and he was made aware of the time Clark had spent on various casting couches. He did not hold that against him. "To get ahead, an actor has to do what an actor has to do."

Over the course of his distinguished career, Conway would direct such stars as Lon Chaney, Marie Dressler, Wallace Beery, Jean Harlow, Myrna Loy, William Powell, and Spencer Tracy. Gloria Swanson asserted, "Making a film with Jack is like attending an elegant party."

As "the best-dressed man in Hollywood," the Pittsburgh-born son of an Irish mother and a French-born father, Adolph Menjou's film career would stretch from 1916 to 1960. He'd co-starred with Valentino in *The Sheik* (1921), and appeared opposite Gary Cooper, Marlene Dietrich, Janet Gaynor, and Fredric March, among others. Menjou appraised Clark as "a diamond in the rough."

The daughter of Richard Bennett, the stage and silent screen star, Constance was also the older sister of actress Joan Bennett.

"Based on my press," she quipped, "I am the female Casanova of Hollywood."

Irene Mayer Selznick

Dapper? Prissy? Or one of the best-dressed men in America?

Here's **Adolphe Menjou**, the Franco-Irish-American political conservative who represented the best of well-dressed (male) Americana over the course of a career that spanned both silent films and talkies.

Left photo: **Constance Bennett,** a "Park Avenue Dame" ill-suited to plebeian comedy

Constance elicited envy from many of the society-conscious women she frequented, in part because of the aristocratically "spectacular" title of the third of her five husbands.

He was *(right photo)* **Henry de La Falaise, Marquis de La Coudraye**, who's seen here with Constance around the time of their wedding. A French translator, war hero, film director & producer, and scion of the Hennessy cognac family, he was best known for his high-profile marriages to two leading Hollywood actresses: Gloria Swanson (married 1925-1931) and Constance Bennett. Their glam but not-particularly happy marriage began in 1931 and ended in 1940.

claimed, "Constance is crazy about money and sex."

Clark denied spending a weekend at her residence, a smart thing for a married actor to have said. "There was nothing between us. She didn't seem to take notice that I was even alive."

Joan Bennett, however, later revealed that her sister told her she did, indeed, have a fling with Clark. The handsome Mexican-American heartthrob, Gilbert Robert, during their filming of *Our Betters* (1933), said, "Gable got to her before I did." He waited until 1941 to marry her, a marriage that lasted until 1946.

***

As Clark admitted, "Anita Page, who played my wife in *The Easiest Way*, got a rise out of me the first day I met her."

Page had first met Clark when she was appearing opposite William Haines in the 1928 comedy-drama *Telling the World*. "Gable dropped by the set late one afternoon and walked off with Haines. I assumed he was Haines' boyfriend."

"I also encountered Clark when I was filming *Our Dancing Daughters* with Joan Crawford, also in 1928," Page said. "When he came by at the end of a day's shoot and made off with Crawford, I then guessed Gable to be at least bisexual."

MGM promoted Page as "a blonde-haired, blue-eyed Latina," and also as "the girl with the most beautiful face in 1920s Hollywood."

Clark inaugurated an affair with her that continued on and off for at least two years, seeing her only on occasion His competition was (believe it or not) Benito Mussolini, dictator of Fascist Italy.

During the course of his infatuation with her, Mussolini sent Page an airline ticket to Rome and three separate proposals of marriage.

At the peak of her fame, Page was receiving more fan mail at MGM than any female star except Garbo.

When she died in September of 2008 at the age of 98, newspapers hailed her as "the last star of the silents."

Two views of **Anita Page:** *Upper photo*, as a hard drinking flapper in *Our Dancing Daughters*, and *lower photo*: as the working-class wife of **Clark Gable**, cast as a laundry worker, in *The Easiest Way*.

***

Although they were very different types, Robert Montgomery, three years younger than Clark, would be his rival for certain roles. On Broadway, he had appeared on stage with George Cukor, who must have informed him of Clark's "gay-for-pay" past. On the set of *The Easiest Way*, Montgomery made a number of disparaging remarks about Clark, and word reached him that the actor was calling him a pansy. Clark threatened to beat him up, and Montgomery shut up.

Author Scott Eyman wrote, "Robert Montgomery off-screen has a reputation as one of the chilliest, most pompous actors ever to find his way to Hollywood."

Before working with Clark, Montgomery had just appeared opposite Garbo in *Inspiration* (1930). That same year, Norma Shearer chose him as her leading man in *The Divorcée*. For about three weeks, he had been Thalberg's choice to appear with both Garbo and Shearer again. But after seeing Clark in *The Easiest Way*, Thalberg cast him in *A Free Soul* (1931) with Shearer and again in 1931 with Garbo in *Susan Lennox—Her Fall and Rise*.

***

During Tallulah Bankhead's brief stint in Hollywood in the early 1930s, fresh from a spectacular series of stage triumphs in London, she was cast in *Faithless* (1932), playing a prostitute alongside Robert Montgomery.

"I went to Hollywood to fuck that divine Gary Cooper in *The Devil and the Deep* (1932). Then, I wanted to fuck that hot rod, Clark Gable, but I ended up with Robert Montgomery. I seduced him off screen instead. He delivers what is known as a gentleman's fuck."

Coincidentally, Montgomery ended up appearing opposite Carole Lombard, Clark's then-wife, in Alfred Hitchcock's *Mr. and Mrs. Smith* (1941). Months later, Lombard died in an airplane crash over Nevada.

In 1954, Montgomery, an avid Republican, ended up with an unpaid job at the White House as a consultant to President Eisenhower, coaching him in how to look, dress, and talk during his addresses to the nation.

[Elizabeth Mongomery, the actor's daughter, became a household name in the 1960s, thanks to her distinctive performances in the hit TV series, Bewitched *(1964-1972).*]

Tallulah Bankhead, known for her wanton ways both on and off the screen, as she appeared as a prostitute in *Faithless* (1932).

***

The Easiest Way would mark the first of several films in which Marjorie Rambeau appeared with Clark, the last being *Any Number Can Play* (1949).

Born in San Francisco back in 1889, she'd moved to Alaska at the age of eight when her parents divorced. Her mother cut her hair and dressed her as a boy when she sang and danced in taverns, rowdy dives and music halls. She didn't want drunken men to molest "my little girl."

Rambeau made a name for herself on Broadway before hitting Hollywood, where she worked for decades until bowing out in 1957. Along the way, she co-starred with such legends as James Cagney, Ginger Rogers, Jean Harlow, Marie Dressler, Ronald Reagan, Jane Wyman, and John Wayne. In 1953, she was nominated for a Best Supporting Actress Oscar for her performance in *Torch Song,* starring Joan Crawford.

***

The Easiest Way opened to mixed reviews and was banned in Alberta, Nova Scotia, and Dublin.

Photoplay found that "newcomer Clark Gable shines brightly in this mildly entertaining adaptation of a slightly dated Broadway play."

Variety wrote that "Adolphe Menjou looks prissy in his elegant men's wear, especially when compared to Clark Gable in his dirty workman's clothes."

Another reviewer found "Gable, with his boyish charm, (is) enchanting, irresistible, and even adorable."

Critic Tobey Garnet found the movie "an outdated and unsatisfactory adaptation of an old Broadway play that wowed them at the turn of the century. Constance Bennett is not convincing as a child of the slums. She is strictly a penthouse on Fifth Avenue dame."

DID YOU KNOW? That even the dreaded **Hedda Hopper** *(shown above in an MGM press and PR photo before she morphed into a gossip columnist)* had a minor, unmemorable role in ***The Easiest Way***?

Episode 31

Dance, Fools, Dance (1931)

The badly named Pre-Code Drama, *Dance, Fools, Dance,* became the first of eight films in which Clark would co-star with Joan Crawford. She took the star role of Bonnie Jordan, and he got sixth billing as mob boss Jake Luva. Its plot was inspired by the St. Valentine's Day Massacre in Chicago.

Many biographers have made the claim that these two stars met for the first time on the set of this film. However, her best friend, actor William Haines, revealed that their affair had begun in 1925 when both of them were cast as extras on the set of *The Merry Widow.*

Since then, however, Crawford had married into Hollywood royalty, tying the knot with Douglas Fairbanks Jr., the son of the silent screen swashbuckler, Douglas Fairbanks Sr. and his first wife, heiress Anna Beth Sully. He'd later married America's Sweetheart, Mary Pickford, his co-star in *The Taming of the Shrew* (1929). During their reign as Hollywood's superstars, they were the most famous couple in the world.

Being married did not prevent Crawford from sleeping around. By the time she co-starred with Clark, her marriage was winding down. As she confessed to him, "Doug is only good for the missionary position—and he's not too good at that."

"An extramarital affair now and then is good for a marriage," Crawford claimed. "It adds spice and keeps married life from getting boring. I ought to

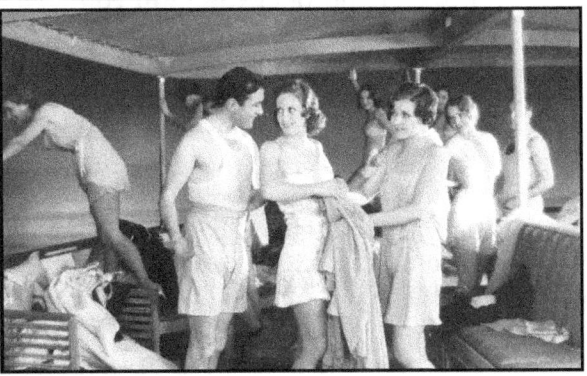

Nymphs, Dionysian dancing, and an "almost naked" swim party: In its way, this Pre-Code *oooh-la-laa* was its era's equivalent of BEACH BLANKET BINGO with prohibition-era bathtub gin.

In it, Pre-Code audiences felt included in the exhibitionistic frenzy of Hollywood's then fastest-rising hot-to-trotter, **Joan Crawford**, fore-playing in the center with **Lester Vail.**

Elders from the Victoran Age were horrified.

know. Actually, having a lot of sex gives me a clear complexion, although I'd rather do it for love."

Originally, it was Crawford who had given Clark advice for career advancement, recommending that he make himself available on the casting couch, "whenever it mattered."

She also recommended her own special diet for keeping one's figure "lean and mean for the camera. Survive for ten days on a strict diet of black coffee, soda crackers, and mustard."

She confessed to Clark that Pickford and Fairbanks Sr. looked down on her. He referred to his daughter-in-law as a "flapper whore screwing every producer or director she could."

Pickford, in contrast, merely viewed her as "common." It would be eight months into her marriage before Crawford was allowed to attend a dinner party at Pickfair, one of the most elegant and exclusive mansions in Hollywood.

"The dumb broad didn't know which fork to use," Fairbanks Sr. said. "She was white trash."

As for Junior, his father issued a warning when he, too, announced his intention of pursuing a screen career. "There can be only one Douglas Fairbanks."

Star status was judged by salary, with Crawford taking in $150,000 a year, her husband earning $75,000. In contrast, Clark got a weekly check for $850.

Gable had yet to be crowned King of Hollywood, but in the early 1930s, Crawford was voted Hollywood's top female star along with Greta Garbo and Norma Shearer, each a member of MGM's "stable."

Unlike the glamourous roles her rivals played, Crawford was often cast as a working-class girl striving for a better life.

James Merrick, an MGM publicist who in time worked to promote more than a dozen Crawford movies, was interviewed by author Roy Newquist. He spoke candidly about "Joan & Clark."

"I don't think sex was the main attraction, but they probably did all right in that department. Joan was an outlet for him. He could talk with her about all his problems, including his disastrous marriage to socialite Ria Langham."

"She'd listen and offer the right comments and usually the right advice A lot of us thought she'd marry Clark after her divorce from Fairbanks. I think he came close on several occasions of proposing marriage. It wouldn't have worked out. She was stronger than he was, and he had an image to protect. He once told me, 'Joan swings more balls than I do.'"

During the filming of *Dance, Fools, Dance*, Fairbanks Jr. visited the set several times, chatting with its director, Harry Beaumont.

He later said, "It was obvious to me that Doug knew that his wife was carrying on with our brash new star, Clark Gable. He didn't seem upset, as he was also getting plenty of pussy on the side. Both he and Clark had had torrid affairs with Lupe Velez, that Mexican siren. Around the corner for Doug waited Tallulah Bankhead, Gertrude Lawrence, Loretta Young, and especially, a firecracker involvement with Marlene Dietrich."

"Doug and I became friends, and I knew him over a period of years," Beaumont, the film's director, said. "When he and his third wife bought a townhouse in London, he became friends with Prince Philip and was entertained frequently at Buckingham Palace. He confessed to me that Queen Elizabeth had developed a powerful crush on him, but he was reluctant to put the make on her. He did know that Philip had a number of affairs on the side."

Beaumont had been ordered to star Crawford in the *Dance, Fools, Dance* by Irving Thalberg and to assign a key role to Clark. His job after that involved rounding up the rest of the cast. He had been born in 1888 in the then-frontier town of Abilene, Kansas. He had arrived in then small-town Hollywood as a young man, later evolving into an actor, screenwriter, and director.

Among his achievements, he directed John Barrymore in *Beau Brummel* (1924) and Crawford in *Our Dancing Daughters* (1928). He then directed MGM's first talkie musical, *The Broadway Melody of 1929*. It won an Academy Award that year for Best Picture, and he was nominated for Best Director.

"Clark and I were too wild in nature to settle into marriage," Crawford said. "We would never have been faithful. You see, both of us have delinquent hearts."

Here's Pickfair, the ultimate destination for anyone who was anyone in Hollywood. In the foreground of this postcard are America's Sweetheart (**Mary Pickford**) with "the Egomaniacal Swashbuckler," her husband, **Douglas Fairbanks Sr**. Each seemed to delight in the fact that they're in a canoe floating on the waters of their then-novel accessory, a swimming pool.

Visitors admired the place but complained about its uptight social codes and rigorous teetotaling—no liquor was ever served.

The owners' emotionally abused son, Douglas Fairbanks, Jr., was at first strictly forbidden to bring his then-wife (Joan Crawford) by for a visit—simply because she was deemed by his mega-celebrity parents as "too parvenue" and "too trashy."

Nearly Forgotten Arbiters of a Nearly Forgotten Aristocracy

At Pickfair, *left to right*, **Douglas Fairbanks Sr.** with his wife, **Mary Pickford, Charlie Chaplin,** and the biggest director/producer of the silent screen, **D.W. Griffith.**

"We did talk about marriage one day, but we feared settling down would eventually destroy our relationship. He was my dream lover, and I figured it would be better to live with a dream alive than a dream broken."

"In spite of his very macho aura, he was a very sensitive and loving man," Crawford continued. "He feared that showing his tender side would destroy his screen image. He was both a woman's man and a man's man. He represented man at his most primeval—valiant, rough, and ready, with passion. He had absolutely no fancy airs or parlor games. He had more balls than any man."

Although Fairbanks Jr. thought they were silly, Clark was amused at the nicknames Crawford "assigned" to her body parts. She referred to her breasts as "ninny pies," and to screwing as "going to heaven." She nicknamed Clark's penis as "Willie" and referred to her vagina as "the gateway to paradise."

Dance, Fools, Dance opens with one of the most controversial scenes in Pre-Code Hollywood. As socialite Bonnie Jordan, Crawford is hosting a chic party aboard a yacht. To enliven the gala, she breaks into a frenzied (some said "highly suggestive") four-minute dance to the tune of "Oh, He Is a Gay Caballero."

She then orders her guests to strip down to their underwear and dive from the yacht into the water, illuminated only by the dim rays of the moon.

When it was shown across the nation, *Dance, Fools, Dance* created *tsunamis* of both titillation and disapproval.

According to the plot, a few days later, Bonnie and her brother, Rodney (William Bakewell), receive terrible news: Their father, Stanley (William Holden—*no not the star of* Stalag 17…*we mean the character actor born in 1862*) tells them he has lost everything in the Wall Street Crash of 1929. He dies soon after that, and both Bonnie and Rodney have to go to work for the first time in their lives.

Bonnie has been having an affair with Bob Townsend (Lester Vail), and he gallantly offers to marry her, but she doesn't want to accept charity. Instead, she gets a job as a cub reporter for a newspaper. In contrast, Rodney innocently stumbles into a bootlegging gang. His troubles escalate.

The gang's leader, Jake Luva (Clark), is the leading bootlegger in Chicago. Despite having been rejected for an equivalent role in *Little Caesar* (1931), Clark as a mob boss plays the part (without a mustache) with a certain bravura. *Variety* would later define his performance as "a vivid and authentic bit of acting."

He stages a gangland slaying of seven rivals, but the police can't prove it.

Meanwhile, working undercover as a cub reporter, Bonnie becomes a night club dancer, attracting the sexual interest of Luva, who owns the club.

She is not really interested in an affair with him, as she's secretly investigating his involvement in the massacre. And although she may be maneuvering her way to betraying him, her hip-to-hip, groin-against-groin scene with him is convincingly steamy.

In a bar scene, Rodney innocently reveals too much to Bert Scranton (Cliff Edwards), an undercover reporter and a newspaper colleague of Bonnie's.

Luva (Clark) orders Rodney to assassinate Scranton, under penalty of death. When he finds out who Bonnie really is, he announces his intention of killing her, too.

In the subsequent shootout, Luva and Rodney are both killed

Bonnie, conflicted and horrified, cradles Luva's head in her arms as he dies. She's got her scoop on the gangland slaying, but at a heavy price. She resigns as a reporter.

As she exits from the newspaper's office, she encounters Bakewell, her original beau. This time, she's ready for marriage.

Incidentally, during the filming of *Dance, Fools, Dance*, William Haines, Crawford's best friend, came onto the set

The on-screen affection between **Gable** and **Crawford**, seen here in a press and PR photo for *Dance, Fools, Dance*, wasn't just a celluloid flash: It endured for years after its completion.

several times to "retrieve" Bakewell. Despite his deep (and "known throughout Hollywood") emotional commitment to Jimmie Shields, he was still having affairs on the side. Clark, at this point, avoided any encounter with his former fellator.

A native of Los Angeles, Bakewell began his career as an extra, and in time would appear in 170 film and television roles. He played a German soldier in *All Quiet on the Western Front* (1930).

By the end of the 1930s, his career had sagged. He is seen briefly as a mounted soldier in *Gone With the Wind* (1939). Scarlett O'Hara asks him when Yankee soldiers are going to invade Atlanta.

Bonnie's (i.e., Crawford's) romantic interest in *Dance, Fools, Dance*, Bob Townsend, was essayed by Lester Vail. The Denver-born actor thrived as a stage, screen, and radio star from the 1920s until the end of the 1940s. He spent a decade on the Great White Way in Manhattan. During the course of his career, he would co-star with Lily Damita (married to Errol Flynn), Irene Dunne, Gary Cooper, and Carole Lombard.

Cliff Edwards was cast as the reporter (Burt Scranton) slated for death. On the screen, he enjoyed wide popularity in the 1920s and 1930s. As a teenager, he dropped out of school and went to work as a performer, singing and playing the ukulele. His nickname became "Ukulele Ike."

Edwards' all-time greatest movie role occurred within the musical context of *The Hollywood Revue of 1929,* when his ukulele rendition of *Singin' in the Rain* was accompanied by members of the MGM chorus dancing their way across a water-soaked Art Deco set. *[Edwards' rendition preceded by more than two decades Gene Kelly's rain-soaked reprise that was featured within the 1952 film with the same name.]* Edwards would also appear again onscreen with Crawford and Gable in *Laughing Sinners* (1931).

According to MGM, the film earned $848,000 in Canada and the U.S., and $420,000 elsewhere, resulting in a profit of $524,000. Critics denounced it as "hokum, but good hokum."

Although marketers aimed the film at "mature audiences," the publishers of mags for horny teenagers got into the act, too.

On the cover of this 1931 edition of ***Boy's Cinema***, *Dance, Fools, Dance* was marketed as "A GRIPPING CROOK DRAMA" (with lots of sauce and skin) instead.

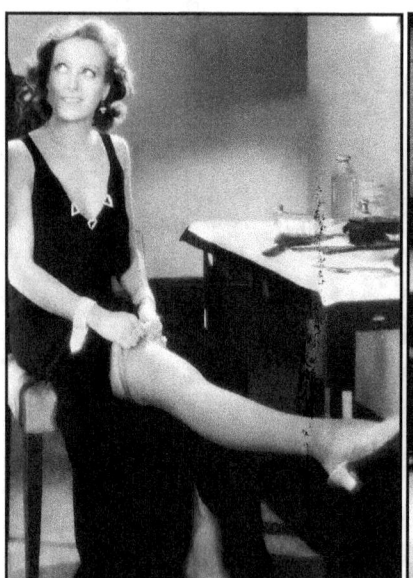

A Mommie Dearest Quadriplex: Four views of **CRAWFORD** in the Pre-Code "gangster vs. public morals" drama, ***Dance, Fools, Dance***. Her fans accept them today as proof that a gal's gotta do what a gal's gotta do.

Episode 32

Gable & Willing

How BEN MADDOX,

A Promiscuous Hollywood Publicist, Invited Clark Gable to Lunch and Served Himself as Dessert

Right photo shows the first page of the "slatheringly smitten" puff piece that Ben Maddox wrote about **Clark Gable** for the October, 1932 edition of *Screenland*. Hipsters snickered at the adulation the author expressed for virtually everything associated with Clark.

Left photo shows the magazine's girly-glam cover. Perhaps as compensation for too strong a dose of Clark, it focused on an illustration of **Constance Bennett** looking *über*-glam. Other features included a denial by **George Raft** that he was a gigolo, and an overview of then-First Lady **Eleanor Roosevelt's** movie tastes.

Reporter Jim Prevenzano wrote, "For decades of his career, the syndicated columnist, (yellow) journalist Ben Maddox remained a close confidant and sexual pal of Clark Gable, including being his companion on several vacations. Maddox's interfering confidant status, however, led to some stupid decisions on his part, including urging Gable to turn down *Mutiny on the Bounty* (1935). Maddox's pernicious role as a double-talking gossip trader resulted in other people's heterosexuality being traded as fodder for the tabloids, in exchange for his, Gable's, and other gay men's affairs being kept secret."

Of all the Gable biographies, it was David Bret's *Tormented Star* that exposed Maddox in the most detail. A promiscuous bisexual, Maddox was the lead reporter for the movie magazine, *Screenland*. Clark was said "to have lent his manly charms for high-profile, flattering interviews that not only advanced his film career, but led to salary increases going from $650 a week to $2,000 a week.

Although Maddox knew that Clark's marriage to the rich socialite Ria Langham was a bit of a sham, he nonetheless published, in *Screenland*, the following appraisal:

> *Clark Gable is a he-man with dimples, the movie gangster who went heroic by the demand of his fans, who turned hin into one of the most desired of screen lovers today. Where does he go from here? Can it be true that fame is splitting up his second marriage? Nine out of ten great stars in Hollywood spoil their home life. Clark Gable won't. So here's the marriage to Ria Langham that we can depend on. He married a cultured, charming woman who has the knack of completely satisfying him in every way. Will it last? I think so. He isn't temperamental and high-*

William Haines, Hollywood's most Out and outspoken gay movie star, with **Marion Davies** in *Show People* (1928). The mistress of press baron William Randolph Hearst was known on occasion for seducing her leading men, notably Clark Gable. She knew not to pursue Haines. "We were gossipy sisters but found we had the same taste in men, notably this blonde-haired, 22-year-old hunk of male flesh who worked as an assistant cameraman."

strung like John Gilbert, nor is he Sheikish like late Valentino. Gable has depth and virility that those stars lacked.

In David Bret's biography, William Haines is reported to have said that "Clark Gable is one hot suck."

According to Bret, "Gable was the archetypal bisexual, the hallmarks of which were clear in his early years. Throughout his life, like Cary Grant and Rock Hudson, he would overplay the machismo and conceal the feminine side that would have made him a great actor instead of an inordinately good one—the result of being raised by a bigoted father who had persistently drummed into him that all actors are sissies. And, of course, he became involved with three of the 20th Century's acknowledged 'fag hags'—Joan Crawford, Carole Lombard, and later, Marilyn Monroe."

Bisexual Maddox must have had great sex appeal, as he seduced both male and female movie stars he interviewed. As time went by, he was said to be the only man, except for Howard Hughes, who seduced not only Clark, but Errol Flynn, Tyrone Power, and Robert Taylor.

Maddox was very handsome, rather brawny, and stood six feet, two inches tall. He had piercing blue eyes and was said to be capable of "charming the pants off any man and the bloomers off any woman," in the words of director George Cukor.

His seduction of movie stars began in 1923 when he visited Rudolph Valentino at his home (Falcon Lair) in Hollywood.

In his private diary, which was later discovered, "The Sheik" wrote, "I let Ben ride my favorite Arabian steed on my grounds and later, he rode me."

Just three years after that eventful afternoon, Maddox would be one of eight pallbearers at Valentino's heavily attended funeral in Manhattan.

"I seduced Jean Harlow before Gable got around to doing it offscreen in *Red Dust*," Maddox claimed.

Screenland assigned Maddox to write a feature entitled "Hollywood's Bachelor Maidens" about Marian Marsh, Sylvia Sidney, Sidney Fox, and Anita Page.

In just one week, he was said to have interviewed and seduced all four of them.

"Before I set out to interview this glamourous quar-

No stranger to bisexual intrigue, **Clark Gable** portrays an exhausted captain about to be tortured in *China Seas* (1935). In the background is a muscled desperado, evocatively shirtless but wearing a bandolier. Was it homoerotic?

Considering the omnisexual promiscuity that was rampant in Pre-Code Hollywood Ben Maddox's penchant for collecting male trophies was neither surprising nor uncommon. In the trio of photos *arranged clockwise, beginning on the left*, are three of his most prized (bisexual) conquests: **Rudolph Valentino, Robert Taylor** (show here with **Lana Turner**), and "the ultimate *débauché*," **Errol Flynn.**

tet, my editor told me he'd heard they were a bit lez oriented," Maddox told Gable. "All of them were raging tigresses in bed, and couldn't seem to get enough. I recommend that you try out each of them."

Marian Marsh was the first to grant Maddox an interview. Born in Trinidad to a German chocolate manufacturer, she eventually left the Caribbean and made her way to Hollywood, where Howard Hughes not only noticed her, but seduced her. He gave her a bit role in his classic *Hell's Angels* (1930). Her big break came in 1931 when she was cast opposite John Brrymore in *Svengali.*

Sylvia Sidney, born in the Bronx in New York City, also made it to Hollywood, dreaming of stardom. She became one of the leading stars of the Depression era, often cast as a working-class heroine.

During the course of her career, she appeared opposite Joel McCrea, Cary Grant, Henry Fonda, Spencer Tracy, Gary Cooper, and Fredric March. Two years after Maddox seduced her, she married author, editor, and publisher Bennett Cerf (co-founder of Random House, Inc.) in 1935. The marriage lasted only two months.

Sidney Fox, born in Ukraine, made her Hollywood debut in 1931 in *Bad Sister* starring Bette Davis and Humphrey Bogart. She also became the mistress of movie executive Carl Laemmle Jr. At the age of 31, in 1942, she overdosed on sleeping pills.

Another of Maddox's conquests was Anita Page, born in Queens, New York City. The blue-eyed, blonde-haired Latina had been cast as Clark Gable's wife in *The Easiest Way*, at which time they had an affair.

Before that, she had enjoyed a lesbian fling with Joan Crawford when they co-starred in

They were "Hollywood's Bachelor Maidens"

or so said **Ben Maddox**, who described, promoted, and probably slept with some of them as part of his "journalistic process."

Everyone in this montage was spectacularly famous during their Pre-Code peaks.

Photo #1: Sylvia Sidney. Her most improbable (and short-lived) marriage was to Bennett Cerf, then-president and publisher of Random House.

Photo #2 Sidney Fox had advice for starlets: "If you can't seduce the producer, become the mistress of his son."

Photo #3 Anita Page. Even **Benito Mussolino, (Photo #4)** fascist dictator of Italy, adored her from afar, proposing marriage from faraway Rome. Each had a talent for gesticulating expressively with his or her right arm.

Photo #5 Marian Marsh shown here with the billionaire aviator and oddball, **Howard Hughes**, in 1934.

Our Dancing Daughters (1928). Their affair continued as the two stars followed that with performances in *Our Modern Maidens* (1929) and *Our Blushing Brides* (1930).

The Crawford movies were followed by Fox's biggest hit when she starred in *The Broadway Melody*, which won an Academy Award in 1929 as Best Picture.

As has been noted before, Anita Page received but rejected marriage proposals from Benito Mussolini, the Fascist dictator of Italy.

Maddox "struck out" with Barbara Stanwyck, but years later seduced her attractive (some said, "pretty boy") husband, Robert Taylor.

Tallulah Bankhead arrived in Hollywood in the early 1930s, hoping for a film career. After Maddox seduced her, she nicknamed him, "Big Ben."

While making *The Devil Is a Woman* (1935), Marlene Dietrich was interviewed by Maddox in her dressing room. He told her, "Just looking at you gives me an erection."

She invited him to use her bathroom to take a cold shower.

Maddox had seduced Rod La Rocque and William Haines before he was powerfully attracted to Phillips Holmes, an handsome actor born in Grand Rapids, Michigan, in 1907. Early in the 1930s, he became a popular leading man in such films as *American Tragedy* (1931), directed by Josef von Sternberg and in *Broken Lullaby* (1932), helmed by Ernst Lubitsch.

Maddox also seduced Ramon Novarro, who had shot to international fame after the release of *Ben-Hur* (1925). Maddox took up with him after he'd made *Mata Hari* (1931) with Greta Garbo.

Actor George O'Brien, hailed as "The Body Beautiful," became Maddox's all-time crush. The San Francisco-born actor (1899) became a star in silents. His career survived the advent of the talkies.

John Ford, a closeted homosexual, put O'Brien on the casting couch before shooting began on *The Iron Horse* (1924). O'Brien would go on to be cast in nine more films for Ford. Privately, Ford made a short underground reel of O'Brien masturbating.

Maddox linked up with O'Brien when he met him on the set of *Noah's Ark* (1928), in which he starred alongside Doris Costello.

For years to come, Maddox took credit, among others, for discovering Clark Gable and promoting him early in his career. "My involvement with Clark lasted over the years. He knew that I could destroy his career at any minute by writing his true story. For that reason, he always obeyed my command when I wanted to see him privately. Call it blackmail if you will. Such a filthy word. But what is the benefit of having power if you don't use it?"

With his career in decline, Maddox joined the Royal Canadian Air Force at the debut of World War II. On August 12, 1942, he was killed in a mid-air collision in northwest Ontario.

The bisexual, predatory, and on-the-make journalist, **Ben Maddox** (died 1942) had a knack for morphing his research for Hollywood fan magazines into post-interview romps. In addition to Clark Gable—who wasn't averse (during his climb up the Hollywood ladder) to "gay for pay"— others of Maddox's conquests included **Ramon Novarro** (shown in *left photo* as *Ben-Hur* in 1925); **Rod La Rocque** (as he appeared in in *Captain Swagger* in 1928); and *(right photo)* **George O'Brien**, who always seemed willing to strip naked for a photographer.

Episode 33

A Story about Rich Eccentrics from the Jazz Age

Clark Gable, Bob Hope, James Stewart, & King Farouk Seduce

"Princess Honeychile"

Patricia Wilder was born in the land of cotton (Macon, Georgia) in 1913. Her father was Oscar Wilder, which evoked a far more famous (but unrelated) name, and she grew up with a dozen brothers and sisters.

In the mid-1930s, referring to herself as "Honeychile," she made her way to Broadway, appearing as a showgirl with Bob Hope at the Palace Theater. She got her first mink coat by sleeping with "Ski Nose."

"I always had a girl back then, and the money was good," Hope said.

Honeychile now appears on Hope's long list of seductions, joining other attractive women who included Rhonda Fleming, Marilyn Maxwell, Barbara Payton, Dorothy Lamour, Paulette Goddard, Betty Hutton, Frances Langford, and Janis Paige. From there, the list goes on and on until it stretches around the block.

In Hollywood, Honeychile was assigned her first film role, a minor part, in *Speed* (1936) alongside James Stewart.

In his bachelor days, Stewart seduced more beautiful women than Hope himself. As he claimed, "My bachelor years were wonderful. Boy, did I have some good times." The difference between Hope and Stewart seductions was that whereas Stewart seduced legends, Hope slept with showgirls.

Stewart's seductions read like a *Who's Who* from the film industry's golden age: June Allyson, Wendy Barrie, Diana Barrymore, Olivia de Havilland, Marlene Dietrich, Mitzi Gaynor, Jean Harlow, Rita Hayworth, Grace Kelly, Katharine Hepburn, Ginger Rogers, Jeanette MacDonald, Rosalind Russell, Norma Shearer, Margaret Sullavan,

The most famous, charming, and socially adroit girl to ever emerge from Macon, Georgia, **Patricia Honeychile Wilder.**

Two views of **Patricia Honeychile Wilder,** both from her days in showbiz: *Left photo,* with **Bob Hope** in their act, "Hope and Honeychile," and *right photo,* flexing her comic timing and looking fabulous with **Milton Berle** in *New Faces of 1937*.

Lana Turner, and Loretta Young.

Clark had met Stewart when they had co-starred in *Wife vs. Secretary* (1936) with Jean Harlow. One late afternoon, he phoned Clark to ask if he'd help him out of a dilemma he had become trapped in: Confusing his calendar dates, he had invited both Harlow and Honeychile on the same round of nightclub hops through Hollywood. At that point in his bachelor life, Stewart's main interest involved seducing Harlow, so he asked Clark to escort Honeychile. "If you can understand her thick southern accent, you'll be rewarded later that night with one of the better lays in Tinseltown."

Clark accepted, and he and Honeychile got along fabulously. He ended up in her bed that night, and "we hit if off," he later confided to Stewart.

Thus began Clark's series of occasional sexual trysts with this Georgia peach.

Clark was later spotted with Honeychile in both New York and Hollywood. In Manhattan, she became a "regular" during lunch at "21" with her beau of the moment. In a typical late-night spree, she could be seen at the Stork Club, Café Pierre, and El Morocco.

Conde Nast would send his limousine to take her to black tie dinners where she met the elite of New York society. George Gershwin asked her to sit next to him at the piano while he was composing *Porgy and Bess*. She went bar hopping with columnist Walter Winchell and his pal, J. Edgar Hoover.

Gable was so taken with her that he even promised to marry her, pending his divorce from Ria Langham. *[That, of course, never happened.]*

Honeychile Wilder with her third husband, the charming, handsome, and spectacularly prestigious Austrian **Prince Alexander zu Hohenlohe-Valdenburg Schillingfürst.**

Farouk, then-deposed former King of Egypt, in Cannes, in 1957, with the oldest of his three daughters, **Ferial.**

Honeychile had an affair with Milton Berle when he cast her in *New Faces of 1937*. She also had many celebrated liaisons in Paris and Rome, including with the deposed (and debauched) former King of Egypt, King Farouk.

After divorcing her first two husbands Honeychile married Prince Alexander zu Hohenlohe-Valdenburg Schillingfürst in 1951. After that, she became known as "Princess Honeychile."

She told Winchell, "For the life of me, I can't understand why so many women get cotton-pickin' mad at me when their husbands spend the night devouring Honeychile's honeypot."

She survived a widely publicized encounter on the night of February 22, 1941 at the Café Pierre in Manhattan. Beverly Paterno—whose husband was the heir to a real estate fortune, calculated at 63 million in 1941 dollars—confronted her, slapped her face, and then peppered her with a flurry of rights and lefts. Honeychile fought back, pulling her hair and ripping her gown. Then, Paterno picked up a pitcher of water and doused Honeychile. The fight made headlines the next day.

Honeychile later said, "Everyone was my friend, even Clark Gable himself, but I never fell in love. That was, not until I met my Prince Alexander. He was my dreamboat, what I had been looking for all my life and never found."

She married him in 1951. Their union lasted until his death in 1984. After that, Honeychile spent the rest of her life visiting rich friends at their estates around the world.

Death came in August of 1995 when she was 81 years old.

It was said about heiress **Beverly Paterno** *(photo above)* that the only thing she did that ever made her famous was a fistfight at the Café Pierre with the girl who later became Princess Honeychile.

Episode 34

The Secret Six (1931)

The Secret Six, a crime film that eventually starred Clark Gable, began when director George Hill and his wife, Frances Marion, a screenwriter he'd recently married, crafted a screenplay they entitled "Slaughterhouse Scorpio," loosely based on the Chicago gangster, Al Capone.

Irving Thalberg at MGM went for the idea, and Hill and his wife (a close friend and collaborator of Mary Pickford) were commissioned to adapt the project into a star vehicle for Wallace Beery.

Hill, a son of Kansas born in 1895, already boasted an impressive record of helming stars who included Lon Chaney, Marion Davies, Jackie Coogan, and Wallace Beery. Hill had, in fact, already directed Beery in two of his biggest hits, *The Big House* (1930), a stark prison drama, and *Min and Bill* (1931).

The latter of those two films had paired Beery and Marie Dressler as alcoholic tugboat owners with a virginal daughter to protect. As a screen team, they were ridiculed as the ugliest film stars in America, but because of the way they conveyed a rough kind of loyalty and affection for one another, they enjoyed a brief but eccentric reign as box office champions.

In fact, for a brief period, Beery became the highest-paid actor in Hollywood. Louis B. Mayer, his boss, said, "The guy is a son of a bitch. But he's our son of a bitch."

His co-star, Marie Dressler, detested her co-star, calling him a baboon. "I wanted to serve his head to Mayer on a platter. When fans asked for an autograph, he often spat at them."

During filming of *The Secret Six*, Marion's marriage to Hill crumbled as he devolved into an abusive alcoholic.

Along with June Mathis and Anita Loos, Marion was one of the most renowned female screenwriters of the 20th Century, turning out more than 325 scripts. She was the first to win two Academy Awards.

[Ironically, a few months after the release of *The Secret Six*, Hill and Marion were in the divorce courts. Three years later, in 1934, Hill was seriously injured in an accident whose aftereffects spiraled into weeks of agonizing pain. He committed suicide at the age of 39.]

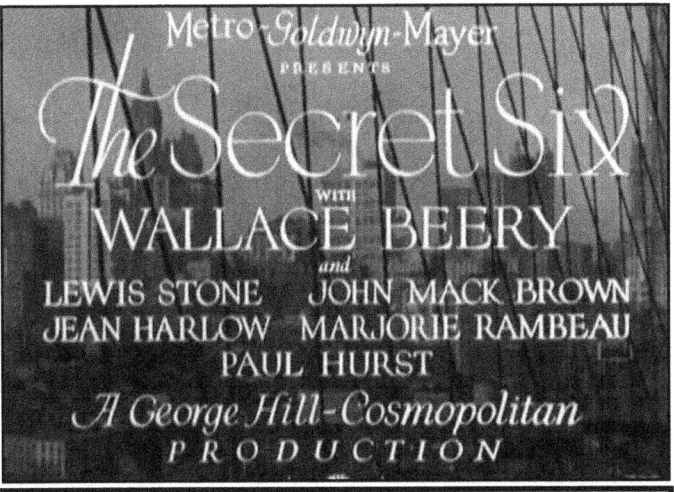

As a relatively unknown newcomer, Clark Gable celebrated his casting in *The Secret Six* alongside its much better-known stars—especially Wallace Beery. As noted in the title shot above, Clark's name is glaringly absent from the "short list" of its players.

Well versed in the flamboyant characterizations of the Silent Screen, **Marjorie Rambeau**, *left*, portrayed her aggrieved character ("Peaches') with emotions that bordered on hysteria. She's shown here with Slaughterhouse, her meatheaded gangland manfriend, as played by **Wallace Beery.**

***

Born in America's heartland (Missouri) in 1885, Wallace Beery was the youngest of three boys. He was an ugly baby, and in time, became a rough and ugly movie star—and a box office champ. At the age of 16, he dropped out of school and joined the Ringling Brothers as an elephant trainer. He fled two years later after being clawed by a leopard.

Heading for Manhattan in 1904, he got his first showbiz gig, adapting his baritone voice to comic opera, and later, working for many months in summer stock.

By 1933, he was in Chicago as an employee of Essanay Studios, making his debut in a short film, *His Athletic Wife* (1913).

Between 1914 and 1916, he was a drag queen in a series of comedic shorts. *[Surprisingly, future movie gangster and tough guy James Cagney also got his start in show biz as a drag queen.]*

In *Sweetie Goes to College* (1915), Beery co-starred with Gloria Swanson and married her the following year. Predictably, their union was a disaster. A virgin at the time, she later wrote about her wedding night where he whispered filth in her ear as he sexually mauled her. She ended the evening by retreating to the bathroom, where she locked herself in for the remainder of the night, trying to control her bleeding. By 1918, their divorce officially ended their marriage, even though it had ended very soon after it began.

Five husbands lay in Swanson's self-enchanted future. Her most notorious affair was with Joseph P. Kennedy, a Hollywood investor and later, Franklin Roosevelt's Ambassador to London.

In *The Secret Six*, Beery, as "Slaughterhouse Scorpio," becomes the leading bootlegger in Chicago during Prohibition. The crooked lawyer for his gang, "Newt" Newton, was played by Lewis Stone. A young Jean Harlow was cast as Anne Courtland, Beery's mistress.

Harlow's character, however, is actually in love with a newspaper reporter, Hank Rogers, portrayed by John Mack Brown. Clark Gable was cast as Carl Luckner, a rival "scoop artist."

Harlow, born as Harlean Carpenter in 1911, burst onto the screen near the end of the flapper era as defined by Clara Bow and Joan Crawford.

As a voluptuous "bottle blonde bombshell," Harlow became an instant sensation after Howard Hughes cast her in *Hell's Angel* (1930). She became a star overnight. During the making of that film, she temporarily morphed into "The Aviator's" mistress.

Lewis Stone, born in Worcester, Massachusetts, in 1879, was a contract player at MGM for 29 years. In the late 1930s, he became known across America as the onscreen father of Mickey Rooney in all those Andy Hardy movies. Before that, he had starred as a leading man, appearing in seven movies with the great Greta Garbo. One of them was *Grand Hotel (1932)*.

Instead of letting Hill cast the rest of the film, Thalbeg intervened, because he wanted to promote some young actors he'd signed. Jean Harlow got the role of Annie Courtland, a gangster moll. Clark Gable (portraying Carl Luckner) and John Mack Brown

Depicted above are two of the most successful women in the entertainment industry during the transition from silents to talkies.

On the left is **Mary Pickford**, "America's Sweetheart" who had, since her silent heyday, morphed into an independent producer/director of enormous influence, and *right*, **Frances Marion**, a scriptwriter whose plots and scenarios were among the best of the early 1930s.

Marion's script for *The Secret Six*, especially the character of "Slaughterhouse" (Wallace Beery), was based on the life and exploits of Al Capone.

Newlyweds on the Verge of a Disastrous marriage

The year was 1916 and **Wallace Beery** had just joined hands in a brief (very short) marriage with **Gloria Swanson**.

In this photo, taken years before she became the celluloid dragon whose legend persists today, Swanson appears shell-shocked, waiting in dread for honeymoon horrors to come.

(as Hank Rogers) played rival reporters.

John Mack Brown's character is later assassinated by Scorpio's boys in a subway slaying, dying in the arms of Anne (Harlow), who loves him, even though she's the paid girlfriend of Scorpio.

Thalberg also wanted to promote Ralph Bellamy in the role of Johnny Franks, one of the leaders of the bootleg gang.

The Secret Six would mark the first of several films in which Clark portrayed a hard-boiled newspaper reporter.

The title, *The Secret Six,* does not refer to Scorpio's gangsters, but to a small group of concerned Chicago businessmen committed to the downfall of Scorpio and his gang, despite the meddling of a crooked police department "on the take." When the morally upright members of the Secret Six appear on screen, their faces are concealed behind black masks.

[Some history-minded movie-goers went to screenings of The Secret Six *with the belief that they'd witness a historical drama set in 1859, a year before the Civil War. The Secret Six was a nickname assigned to the half-dozen men who secretly funded the historic raid on Harper's Ferry, West Virginia, by the abolitionist, John Brown.]*

On the set, Clark had a reunion with character actress Marjorie Rambeau, cast as a whorish saloon keeper named "Peaches." She has a crush on Johnny Franks (Bellamy), and Scorpio (Beery) has a crush on her. In reaction, she mockingly calls him "The Missing Link."

Years later, Rambeau admitted, "In the script, I was ready to rock with Bellamy, but in real life I found Gable hot. I'd heard that he dug older women, and even married a grandma type, so I went after him. All I got was a pat on my fat ass and a kiss on the cheek."

As for Bellamy, he was just getting started. Born in Chicago in 1904, he would enjoy one of the longest careers of any actor in Hollywood, a range of 65 years. In the months after working with Clark on *The Secret Six*, he appeared in twenty-two films before the end of 1933.

"I was often typecast as the second male lead, the Joe who lost the gal at the end of the movie to the leading man—including Cary Grant, for example. One of my leading ladies was Little Miss Lollipop, Shirley Temple. We made a film called *Rebecca of Sunnybrook Farm.*"

[Bellamy showed what a fine actor he really was when he was cast in his widely praised emulation of Franklin D. Roosevelt in Sunrise at Campobello *(1960).]*

Cast in a minor role as "Smiling Joe" Colimo, John Miljan would soon be working in a picture alongside Greta Garbo and Clark Gable. For nearly four decades, he would play tall, smooth-talking villains, later essaying top-ranking military officers. One of his last screen appearances would be in Cecil B. De Mille's *The Ten Commandments* (1956) in which he was cast as a blind Israelite grandfather.

On a minor note, Clark had a few beers with the actor Paul Hurst, who was billed as the gangster "Nick the Cougar."

A son of California, born in 1888, Hurst was half-Che-

For reasons that seem murky by modern-day standards, the plot called for the character played by **Jean Harlow** (the blonde) to marry the character played by **Clark Gable** (the reporter) before he's hauled off to jail.

Here's Clark, handcuffed and about to be thrown into the slammer—kissing his bride goodbye before a happy ending rescues them from too long a separation. Audiences loved it—and cheered.

Actually, although newcomer Clark got seventh billing, his part kept getting expanded by his champion, Irving Thalberg. And when filming ended, MGM offered (and he accepted) a long-term contract.

Gable *(left)* and **Johnny Mack Brown**: Onscreen, as shown in this publicity pic for *The Secret Six*, their bromance was "enlarged" to include a Platinum Blonde: in this case, **Jean Harlow**.

rokee, half-Seneca. Raised on a ranch, Hurst drifted to Hollywood as a young man. He appeared in small roles in 250 movies during the 1920s, '30s, and '40s. He had a stocky build and a squinty demeanor and spoke with a raspy voice which made him ideal for roles as villains, cops, and comedy sidekicks.

He is remembered today as the Yankee Union deserter who trespasses at Tara in *Gone With the Wind* and is shot in the face by Scarlett O'Hara.

Late in 1952, Hurst was diagnosed with terminal cancer. Unable to stand the subsequent agony, he committed suicide on February 27, 1953. He was 64 years old.

Hill, *The Secret Six's* director, later said, "No one knows for sure what was really going on between Clark and Johnny, but it was the best case of male bonding I've ever seen. As two hunks of male flesh, they seemed to find something in each other that no woman could provide."

Audiences might, before the end of *The Secret Six*, have grown tired of mean-spirited, ugly-mugged Wallace Beery in favor of the newer, more "modern" aesthetics of **Harlow with Gable.**

"My wife, Frances Marion, seemed much more knowing about male/male relationships than I did. She told me that it was entirely possible that two men could make love to each other yet be satisfactory straight lovers too. Some men she knew had an occasional homosexual fling, although seducing a host of women as their main preference."

"Men such as Johnny and Clark may want some variety in their sex lives," Marion said.

"Then Frances got dirty," Hill continued. She told me that wives or girlfriends rarely bring erotic thrills to one of man's most erotic zones, his rosebud."

According to John Mack Brown, "With women, you've got to do a lot of sucking up, a lot of pretending, telling them the gown they put on looks gorgeous when no self-respecting drag queen would be seen wearing it. With a buddy like Clark, I don't need to pretend. I can share my hopes and dreams of being an actor with him, and also tell him of my fears that I won't make it. He gives me something my wife does not. Too bad my close friendship with him had to come to such a bad end."

***

Years later, a drunken Wallace Beery indiscreetly talked to a reporter who could not reveal what he said in print. "I tried to fuck that dyed blonde little whore, Harlow, but the bitch slapped my face. But I'll tell you something you didn't know about those two so-called he-men, Clark Gable and John Mack Brown. They were a couple of pansies getting their rocks off every night with each other until they turned into bitter enemies."

***

The censors at the Hays office felt that a more apt title for *The Secret Six* should be *Slaughterhouse*, since there was so much violence depicted on the screen. Pressure was applied to Thalberg, and he had the original blood-soaked and tragic ending reshot.

Scorpio (Beery) was originally depicted getting killed as a herd of runaway cattle stampeded over him. In the reshoot, he is seen handcuffed and being led into a gas chamber

The New York Times wrote, "Clark Gable, who has been seen mostly as a gangster, undertakes the role of a newspaper reporter. He does valiant work and his acting is forceful."

Variety reported, "*The Secret Six* features two actors, John Mack Brown and Clark Gable, who are destined for super stardom. It's a race between these two handsome hunks to see who will become the biggest box office attraction at MGM. Our money is on Gable. His ears are bigger."

***

John Mack Brown (later billed as "Johnny" Mack Brown) rose from the cottonfields of Alabama, where he was born in 1904. His parents were shopkeepers, and he was one of eight siblings. The details of the short but intense relationship between John Mack Brown and Clark Gable immediately follows.

Episode 35

Clark Gable & Johnny Mack Brown

Was It Just a Bromance?

The Secret Six marked the beginning of Jean Harlow and Clark Gable being marketed as co-stars, but its timing didn't coincide with the launch of their affair. After her affair with Howard Hughes, she moved into a soon-to-be tragic involvement with Paul Bern, an executive at MGM.

"I liked Harlow a lot," Clark told its director, George Hill, "but I'm holding back, not making the moves on her. She's a hot little number. Don't ask me how I know, but I learned she never wears panties. On two occasions, I saw the bush. It's blonde. She dyes it, too."

Unknown to John Mack Brown at the time, casting politics were brewing, and they didn't bode well for him. Hill and his screenwriter/wife Frances Marion had ordered experimental rewrites of the scenes between Harlow and Brown, adapting them instead with "test encounters" between Harlow and Clark.

Before *Hell's Angels*, Harlow had portrayed minor characters in fourteen silent films, including *The Saturday Night Kid* (1929) and *The Unkissed Man* (also 1929). The characters she'd portrayed had included everything from a "winged ballerina" to a streetwalker.

After *Hell's Angel*, Hughes sold her contract to MGM for $60,000. Subsequently, Harlow's career shot skyward. Among other accomplishments, she became Clark Gable's favorite leading lady.

Regrettably, in the months ahead, she would get sucked into the controversies associated with one of the most scandalous deaths in Hollywood, that of her then-newlywed husband, Paul Bern.

New to Hollywood, the football hero Johnny Mack Brown, had became an overnight sensation. In contrast, Clark Gable, his future "best buddy," had come up the hard way.

In no time at all, Brown was cast as a leading man to such stars as Greta Garbo, Joan Crawford, Norma Shearer, and Mary Pickford.

He had helped the 1925 Alabama Crimson Tide football team win a national championship in that year's Rose Bowl. He'd been designated as the team's Most Valuable Player after scoring two of the

Best of (equivalently dressed and on-the-make) Buddies—at least on the surface.

Here's **Clark Gable** *(left)*, emoting amicably with **Johnny Mack Brown** in *The Secret Six*

"The Dothan Antelope," Johnny Mack Brown, Most Valuable Player at the 1926 Rose Bowl

Johnny Mack Brown's heroism on the football field carried the University of Alabama's Crimson Tide to its first national title. Young, handsome, and charismatic, he appears as a focal point amid a sea of admirers, circa 1926, with flowers strewn at his feet.

The event this photo commemorates was Alabama's nail-biting victory over the Washington Huskies. It was recorded in sports history as "The Football Game that Changed the South."

team's three touchdowns in an upset over the heavily favored Washington Huskies.

Nicknamed "the Dothan Antelope" after his hometown in Alabama, he stood five feet, 11 inches. His "biggest asset" was covered up by his football uniform. In the shower stalls of the locker room, he inspired penis envy in some of his fellow players.

Although these assets might have been ignored (or unknown) on the football field, when Brown's handsome face appeared on boxes of Wheaties breakfast cereal (then the best-selling brand in America) across the nation, it morphed him into a national icon.

MGM reached Brown first, giving him a screen test and rewarding him with a five-year movie contract.

Soon after his arrival in Hollywood, Brown stirred up the libidos of horny female stars, homosexual matinee idols, and those who were "merely bisexual." After wardrobe changes for his screen test, news of his "best asset" spread quickly through the Hollywood grapevine.

Movie star William Haines was perhaps the first to seduce him, spreading the word to his best friend, Joan Crawford. "Cranberry, you've got to take on this hunk of meat." He set up a meeting.

Crawford later told Haines, "You'd have to look long and hard to find a lover like that." Soon, Brown would become her co-star.

No one seemed to take notice that Brown, in 1926, had married Cornelia ("Connie") Foster. Their union would last until his death in 1974. She must have been a very loving and tolerant wife, since her husband wasn't home on many a night. She seemed to have settled in for the good life he offered her, even if she couldn't expect sexual loyalty from him

***

The race to de-pants Brown was on.

A young actor, Humphry Bogart, then new to Hollywood, for a time did some "pimping" for the aviator/producer Howard Hughes. He was richly rewarded, making far more money from Hughes than he did from his salary as an actor. In time, he would also set up a rendezvous between Brown and his closeted friend, Spencer Tracy.

Brown was assigned a minor role in Greta Garbo's *The Divine Woman* (1926). Her leading man was Lars Hanson, a fellow Swede like herself. Shooting began the day her boss, Irving Thalberg, married Norma Shearer, Brown's future co-star.

Two Early Press Photos of Johnny Mack Brown

Movie studios didn't quite know what to do with him: Was he a romantic hero of the drawing room? Or a quick-on-the draw roughneck from the Western Frontier?

His advantages included a physique better than Clark Gable's, a personality that audiences tended to relate to, and a boyish, All-American charm that required some acting lessons to develop and polish. But whereas Clark had spent years navigating lavender ladders and the political minefields of stage acting, Johnny Mack Brown was a relative neophyte to show-biz.

So whereas Clark eventually emerged as the film industry's Megastar, Brown became a durable but repetitive hero of a flood of low-budget pictures, many of them from "Poverty Row."

Handsome, blond, gay, and Swedish, **Nils Asther** *(left)*, a frequent screen counterpart to Greta Garbo, negotiates with his onscreen rival, **Johnny Mack Brown** *(right)* in the intrigue-soaked romantic drama, *The Single Standard* (1929).

Onscreen, Asther lost Greta to Brown. Nonetheless, offscreen, he managed some "between the sheets" intrigue with Alabama's Finest.

That Garbo film was thought to have been lost to history until an excerpt (a single reel with only nine minutes of usable film) was discovered in a vault in Moscow.

That was followed by Brown's being cast in another Garbo film, *A Woman of Affairs* (1928). Brown was billed before Douglas Fairbanks Jr. but beneath the names of both John Gilbert and Lewis Stone.

In yet another Garbo vehicle, *A Single Standard* (1929), Brown becomes the man who marries Garbo. She bears him a son that both of them adore.

However, her character's true love is Nils Asther, a wealthy ex-boxer who, before their marriage, takes her on a yachting trip through the South Seas.

During its filming, it wasn't Garbo who seduced Brown, but Asther himself. He was a notorious homosexual. In advance of their kissing scenes, Garbo, in fact, stridently complained to her director, "I don't know where his mouth was the night before."

In 1930, Joan Crawford used her prestige to get Brown cast opposite her in *Montana Moon*. On the second day of the shoot, she invited him to her dressing room where, to his surprise, she was sitting nude before the mirror at her makeup tale. That afternoon marked the beginning of their affair.

Montana Moon (1930) was one of Hollywood's experimental tryouts of an established star (**Crawford**) co-starring with a hot and handsome newcomer, the celebrity football hero, **Johnny Mack Brown**.

From it came an incongruous scene of **Joan** (*center photo*) wearing English (not Western) riding garb and (*right photo*) one of the campiest photos of Miss Crawford ever taken. In it, she shoots "directly from the titties," ignoring all preconceived notions of shooting from the hip.

He was new, hot, and popular—enough so that even the Empress of the Silent Screen (**Mary Pickford**) made **Johnny Mack Brown** her (nominal) co-star in the jazz age romcam, *Coquette* (1929).

Interestingly, it was Mary Pickford's name (but not Johnny Mack Brown's) that appeared alone on much of that film's press and PR, including the lobby card depicted on the *right*.

Brown also got lucky with another leading lady, Norma Shearer, who had recently married Irving Thalberg. Over the course of many months, she had discovered that because of his ailing health, he had a very low sexual appetite.

As then 16-year-old Mickey Rooney, years later, asserted, Shearer was "hotter than a half-fucked fox in a forest fire."

During the shooting of *A Lady of Chance* (1928), Shearer summoned Brown to her dressing rooms on several occasions. [Lady of Chance *entered the public domain on January 1, 2024.*]

Brown was also cast as the love interest of Mary Pickford in *Coquette* (1929), her first talkie. Movie-goers got to hear "America's Sweetheart" talk for the first time. It brought Pickford a Best Actress Academy Award.

Brown was cast in a Western, *Billy the Kid* (1930), where he got star billing over Wallace Beery.

Before filming began, Brown had tried to get cast in *Tarzan, The Ape Man* (1932). His body was perfect for a portrayal of the jungle hero, but the director found him too short, awarding the role instead to Johnny Weissmuller. Unknown to Brown, Clark Gable had also tried out for the role, but was rejected "because his chest wasn't developed enough."

Almost from the first day they met, Clark and the ex-footballer, John Mack Brown, became instant buddies. When they weren't needed on the set, they were seen together in the commissary or else spending long hours in their shared dressing room.

Sometimes, they went on "escapist weekends" to such destinations as Catalina Island or Palm Springs. On three separate occasions, they drove south to watch the bullfights in Tijuana. Both of them had wives, but that didn't seem to matter.

Hill had a front row seat for views of the growing intimacy between the two handsome actors. "Within a week, these two had formed a close bond. I often hung out with them, waiting for whatever set was being prepared for our next shot. Often, the talk was about what kind of character they wanted to be on screen, Two very different types."

Early in his career, producers opted to cast him in roles set in boudoirs with the *über-*glam. Here are two views of **Johnny Mack Brown:** *Left* with **Greta Garbo** in *A Woman of Affairs* (1928), *and right,* when he was 22, as a swain to **Marion Davies** in *The Fair Co-Ed* (1927)

Left: Young **Johnny Mack Brown** as the star of a shoot-em-up 1930 tale of an American icon and near-mythical hero, *Billy the Kid*

Right *Oklahoma Justice* (1951). No longer a newcomer, and no longer a candidate for roles in stylish urban comedies, here's **Johnny Mack**, as the "typecast in concrete" staple of this B-list action-adventure from "Poverty Row's" Monogram Pictures.

"Clark saw himself as a 'he-guy' instead of as a 'he-man.' His desire was to project an overly masculine presence on the screen. He didn't want to look like some prissy grad from an East Coast Ivy League College. He wanted his face and mannerisms to reflect his rough-and-tumble background—telephone lineman, lumberjack, and a wildcatter in the oil fields of Oklahoma."

In contrast, according to Hill, "Brown wanted to be more of a strong, silent type, the camera focusing on his polite manners and good looks."

As the actor himself put it, "I want to be the type of leading man the heroine settles down with after her adventures with wild men who want to use women and then dump them."

Episode 36

The Finger Points (1931)

When Clark Gable complained that he didn't want to portray any more gangsters, Irving Thalberg, his boss, not knowing what else to do with him, lent him to First National.

As a newcomer at the new studio, he was introduced to director John Francis Dillon, who informed him that in *The Finger Points*, he'd be cast as a gangland leader, Louis Blanco.

A former New Yorker, Dillon was "multi-functional," having appeared in the 20-year period between 1914 and 1934 as an actor in 74 films and as a director of 130 movies.

That morning, Clark also learned that the film's leading man would be Richard Barthelmess and its leading lady Fay Wray.

In 1928, Dillon had helmed Barthelmess, a fellow New Yorker, in *The Noose* (1928), which brought the star a nomination for an Academy Award.

Many contemporary viewers drew a sharp contrast between Clark and the better-established star. In 1922, *Photoplay* had labeled Barthelmess "the idol of every girl in America." Exactly one decade after that (i.e., in 1932), that magazine would be describing Clark Gable the same way.

Tastes had changed over the previous decade. With his slicked-back black hair, his piercing eyes, sharp nose, and thin lips, Barthelmess looked like "Central Casting's" definition of a respectable businessman or a preacher.

The Russian actress, Alla Nazimova, discovered him and cast him in *War Brides* (1916). His performance attracted the attention of D.W. Griffith, who cast him opposite Lillian Gish in *Broken Blossoms* (1919) and in *Way Down East* (1920).

Clark, as a rugged he-man with a somewhat devil-may-care look, stood in sharp contrast. Privately, they had something in common. Each of them had seduced journalist Adela Rogers St. Johns, the difference being that Clark had impregnated her.

Hailing from Alberta, Canada, where she was born in 1907, Fay Wray was on the dawn of starring in *King Kong* (1933), an adventure/horror film that would make her internationally famous and lead to her being known as one of Hollywood's early "scream queens." Her role in *King Kong* had originally been envisioned for Jean Harlow.

Later in his life, Clark bragged that he'd seduced practically every one of his leading ladies at MGM. That didn't apply, however, to the actresses at First National. In her memoir, entitled *On the Other Hand* (an obvious reference to *King Kong*), Wray wrote that Clark Gable had a small part in *The Finger Points*— and that's all she had to say.

However, her name would be tenuously linked to his years later when Darryl F. Zanuck of Fox summoned her to his office. He told her that he was securing Clark Gable as her leading man in her next picture. It can be assumed that she was thrilled by the news, since Clark, at the time, was the hottest male star in the film industry.

In retrospect, *The Finger Points* appears mired in the aesthetics and priorities of the late Silents. Visibly younger (and better looking) than its deeply entrenched holdovers from the Silents, (including its male lead, **Richard Barthelmess)** Clark appears as a virile, fast-talking archetype of moviegoing tastes for new kinds of heroes.

On the left in this newsroom confrontation is **Richard Barthelmess**, no longer a matinee idol, and *(right figure)* newcomer **Clark Gable.**

Note that whereas the younger actor looks fabulous in a bowler, like Barthelmess, it, too, was hurtling toward fashion obsolescence.

Then something went wrong: Zanuck rose from his desk and began chasing after her, trying to run his hands up her dress. She escaped from his office and phoned his wife, Virginia Fox, that afternoon to inform her of the incident. To Mrs. Zanuck, news of her husband's philandering was tired, old, and familiar. She listened for a minute or two before dismissively hanging up the phone.

Then Zanuck's feverishly anticipated film deal with the King of Hollywood collapsed, and Wray (temporarily) left the screen in 1942 in anticipation of her marriage to Robert Riskin.

A son of Pittsburgh, Regis Toomey had third billing over Clark. He began his career as a singer on Broadway at the right time—just before the advent of talkies. Hollywood needed actors who could talk. He was summoned to audition, emerging as a leading man in a handful of minor films before resigning himself to a long tenure (without his *toupée*) as a character actor.

[As a historical footnote, he co-starred with Jane Wyman (aka Mrs. Ronald Reagan) in the 1941 comedy, You're in the Army Now. *It featured the longest kiss (between Wyman and himself) till then in film history. It lasted for a total of three minutes and five seconds, and infuriated Wyman's then-husband, future U.S. President Ronald Reagan, when he first saw it screened.]*

According to the plot of *The Finger Points*, Breck Lee (Barthelmess) is a naïve kid from the South. He lands in New York and is hired as a reporter. His first assignment involves exposing the illegal gambling parlor run by a gangster, Louis J. Blanco (Clark). When he "outs" Blanco, he is beaten up by the mob.

After his recovery, he falls for a fellow reporter, Marcia Collins (Fay Wray), but he can't afford to marry her. Soon, however, he makes "a deal with the devil."

The critic for *Film Daily* wrote: "As a gangster-newspaper talker, *The Finger Points* doesn't hold much. Barthelmess stands well and where the gangster fever is in high, plus the phase of the reporter who runs the underground of the town, this picture should do well. Clark Gable again scores with his fine voice and magnetic personality."

Variety wrote, "The leading characterization must have been a tough one for the writers. Even when the reporter goes bad, the script attempts to keep him clean. If not of hand, at least of heart. This permits a sob sister angle. Fay Wray interprets this assignment constantly, remonstrating with the lad to get out of the blood money class. A breezy and booze-loving reporter, also enamored of Barthelmess' girl, is excellently interpreted by Regis Toomey. Story takes the conventional twist by having him get the gangster yarn which cleans up the local situation, but not before he is paid in full with machine gun bullets by the gangland cast, portrayed characteristically by Clark Gable."

TEMPTATION

The Power of Love vs. Gangland Corruption

The lower photo, above, part of a newspaper ad for *The Finger Points*, illustrates **Barthelmess'** emotional torments from that siren of the silent screen, **Fay Wray**.

In 1931, both **Clark**, *left*, and **Fay Wray** were on the verge of bigger roles in bigger movies.

On the *right*, **Wray** appears as a vestal virgin, an object of sacrifice to **King Kong** (1933), the ape-hero of the movie that made her a camp and cult icon.

Episode 37

Laughing Sinners (1931)

Director Harry Beaumont had helmed Joan Crawford and Clark Gable in *Dance, Fools, Dance* (1931), and he wanted to re-team them in another film. The project he proposed had originally been titled *Complete Surrender*, but later retitled *Laughing Sinners*.

Irving Thalberg ordained a variation of that idea: "I was impressed with John Mack Brown when he co-starred with Joan in *Our Dancing Daughters*. Reteam them!"

However, after only 20 minutes of film had been recorded, Thalberg sat through the rushes. "Reshoot all those scenes with Brown," he ordered, " and replace him with Clark Gable."

When news of that reached Brown, it ended, forever, his "best buddy bromance" with Clark.

Brown's dream had involved becoming one of the leading matinee idols of the 1930s, but that position went to Clark instead.

With a downturn in his career, Brown re-invented himself and changed his name to "Johnny" Mack Brown. He began to make low-budget Westerns for independent producers. He became one of the screen's top B picture cowboys.

He was a popular star at Universal before moving to Monogram Pictures on "Poverty Row." In 1943, he was tapped to replace cowboy star Buck Jones, who had died. At Monogram, he would make 60 pictures over the next decade.

All in all, Brown appeared in more than 160 movies between 1927 and 1966 in a career spanning almost 40 years.

He died in California at the age of 70 in 1974, having been inducted into the Hollywood Walk of Fame and the Alabama Sports Hall of Fame.

***

When Clark received a copy of the script for *Laughing Sinners*, he was at first thrilled, but later, not so much. "I told Thalberg that I didn't want to play any more gangsters. But now they want

Laughing Sinners was the second instance of a screen pairing that went on and on and on for years. **Crawford** was already an established star in need of an onscreen male staple. **Clark Gable** stepped into the breach as a Salvation Army Evangelist (a role he found embarrassing), and *voila!* film history was made.

MGM promoted it with *(upper photo)* lobby cards whose banners defined it as ***"Crawford's Most Dramatic Talkie!*** *The amazing drama of a song-and-dance girl who is first cheated by love, then finds real romance. The star's finest from the stage hit "Torch Song."*

With promotions like that, who WOULDN'T want to see it?

me to play a member of the Salvation Army? That's WAY too goodie-two-shoes."

In this Pre-Code drama, a café entertainer, Ivy Stevens (Joan Crawford) experiences an spiritual redemption.

Neil Hamilton was her leading man, with Clark billed in third place.

Hamilton, born in Massachusetts in 1899, was four years older than Clark and was believed to have more box office appeal. Of course, that would change within a few months.

Nonetheless, Hamilton would have a career spanning half a century, starring in more than 260 films, both silent and sound.

As a leading man in the 1920s, he often was cast opposite Bebe Daniels. He played Ronald Colman's brother in the silent version of *Beau Geste* (1926), and he was cast as Nick Carraway in the first film adaptation of *The Great Gatsby* (1926).

Although every copy of that particular film adaptation is believed to have been lost, future film adaptations of the F. Scott Fitzgerald novel would later star Alan Ladd and later still, Robert Redford.

In *Laughing Sinners,* Hamilton plays the cad, Howard Palmer, who deserts Ivy, leaving her broken-hearted. After working with Crawford and Clark, he would appear in two upcoming Tarzan movies. Hamilton is best remembered today for playing Police Commissioner Jim Gordon in 120 episodes of the *Batman* television series (1966-1968).

Cast as Ruby, Marjorie Rambeau had worked with Clark before. When they met again, he gave her a bear hug and a sloppy kiss. "I'm still trying to seduce you," she said, half jokingly.

"One night when I'm drunk enough, I'll let you rape me," he promised.

Laughing Sinners was based on a play, *Torch Song,* which had opened on Broadway, the work of Kenyon Nicholson. Ironically, in 1953, Rambeau would be cast as Crawford's mother in its film adaptation, also called *Torch Song.*

As Cass Wheeler, Guy Kibbee had the fifth lead. A son of Mississippi, he'd begun his career on riverboats and later became an actor in stock companies. He'd made his stage debut in *Torch Song,* a performance that earned him a Hollywood contract.

After finishing *Laughing Sinners,* he joined the cast of *Rain* (1932), starring Crawford as a South Seas prostitute.

By the end of 1932, after appearances in fifteen talkies, Kibbee had become a familiar face to audiences across America.

IN CASE YOU DIDN'T KNOW, The transition from Silents to Talkies was packed with movie themes focussing on **Bad Girls Gone Good,** or **Good Girls Gone Bad,** with **Love as Their Road to Redemption.** Audiences wept, applauded, and cheered.

Here's **Clark**, fresh from portrayals of violent, sometimes depraved gangsters, outfitted as a Salvation Army Sergeant rescuing an exotic *danseuse* (**Joan Crawford**) from jumping off a bridge—a solution to her romantic anguish and atonement for her evil ways.

Left to right: **Neil Hamilton, Clark Gable,** and **Joan Crawford**, three players in a Romantic Triangle. As the headline at the top of this lobby card indicates, Joan was "far and away" the film's highlighted star.

During the filming of *Laughing Sinners,* Clark had a few beers with Cliff Edwards, cast as Mike. He had worked with both Crawford and Clark in *Dance, Fools, Dance.* Clark's role in their latest movie involves luring Ivy away from her shady past and into a union with him that is righteous, good, and even romantic—but only after they're legally married.

When Louis B. Mayer heard that Thalberg had cast Clark in the latest Crawford picture, he warned, "Tell the cameraman to do all he can to conceal his elephant ears. Frankly, I detest both Crawford and Gable, but I think I can make some money out of them. Film fans have such low taste."

Variety said, "The original star of *Laughing Sinners,* John Mack Brown, would hav been more convincing with his Sunday-go-to-meeting honest face. In contrast, Clark Gable is unconvincing as a worker for the Salvation Army. He'd have been more convincing putting up money to open a bordello."

The New York Times wrote, "Clark Gable, a leading man, is rather unconvincing as the savior of fallen Joan Crawford, who is better than usual in a film that is less than average in its overall scheme. It doesn't live up to its publicity."

Film Daily claimed, "Clark Gable doesn't have the high moments that Hamilton does, but is more consistent, however average. He has done better. So has Miss Crawford."

Crawford and Gable: THEY CLICKED!

Here's **Neil Hamilton** *(left)* confronting an always photogenic **Joan Crawford** as a repentant "new believer" in the message—as promulgated by **Clark Gable**—of the Salvation Army.

Is it True? that Joan Crawford's face, physicality, and acting intensity made it hard for her NOT to look good in photos?

As the star of *Laughing Sinners,* Brown was visiting Crawford's dressing room at least once a day. After he was fired, Crawford entertained Clark, instead, and often spent her nights with him, since her marriage to Fairbanks Jr. had entered the "not-speaking-to-each-other" phase.

When Clark did return to his home with his wife, Ria Langham, she often happened to be hosting one of her many dinners or parties. Often, after briefly greeting (or not) her guests, he retreated to his separate bedroom for the night. At least she appeared to be enjoying her status as "Gable's wife," if in name only.

Crawford later told the press, "I want Clark to be my leading man in future films with a far better and more scalding plot than *Laughing Sinners.* We just were not convincing as Salvation Army workers."

At the end of its filming, a gossip columnist wrote, "What married star over at MGM is romantically involved with her co-star? She's a top actress and a grand gal, but her hunk is also married. She's running a risk being wide-eyed and in love on and off the screen."

WHY? one wonders, did the art directors opt to depict an angry-looking **Joan Crawford**, clad in funereal Salvation Army drag, as the focal point of this poster?

It (incorrectly) implies, contrary to the plot, that her character's REAL miseries didn't begin until AFTER her religious conversion.

More About Johnny Mack Brown *(continued from Episode 35)*

As described in the text of this episode (Number 37), during the initial setups for *Laughing Sinners*, **Johnny Mack Brown** *(photo above, left)* had originally been cast into the role later filled by Clark Gable.

After seeing early rushes that focused on the Alabama athlete, MGM bigwig Irving Thalberg opted to "de-cast' him. It was a decision that instantly chilled the bromance of Brown with Gable, MGM's rising, studly, and very competitive, stars.

It wasn't as if Brown hadn't already been filmed as a romantic swain to **Joan Crawford**. They appear together in the *photo right* acting through some serious foreplay in this scene from *Our Dancing Daughters* (1928).

So They Made Her Do It AGAIN?

Here's **Joan Crawford** shocking the bourgeoisie and dancing up a storm, this time in *Laughing Sinners*. She's acting her way through a plot about the inner **"bad girl, good girl"** conflicts that only get resolved AFTER her rescue by **Clark Gable** as a sexy emissary of the Salvation Army.

Episode 38

A Free Soul (1931)

Director Clarence Brown, born in Massachusetts in 1890, was assigned the awesome task of directing Norma Shearer, the Queen of MGM, in a film that brought together the future Rhett Butler and Ashley Wilkes (Clark Gable and Leslie Howard) in a Pre-Code drama, *A Free Soul*. Its script had been adapted from a racy, *avant-garde* novel, published in 1927, by Adela Rogers St. Johns.

A former car salesman and fighter pilot in World War I, Brown was the right man for the job. He'd directed his first film in 1920 and eventually moved to MGM where he set a record, helming Greta Garbo seven times and Joan Crawford six times.

Over the years, he was nominated for an Oscar six times as a director. His films also received Best Picture nominations 38 times.

In terms of billing, Norma Shearer, as the wife of MGM's Irving Thalberg, received billing above the title, followed (in smaller fonts) by the names of Leslie Howard, Lionel Barrymore, James Gleason, and Clark Gable.

Lionel Barrymore, Clark's longtime mentor and ardent admirer, became known for his famous courtroom scene—delivered with oratorical panache—near the climactic end of *A Free Soul*. It was cited as the main reason he won the Best Actor Oscar that year.

Leslie Howard, a Londoner born in 1893, was an actor, director, producer, and writer. He was one of the biggest box office draws of the 1930s, often cast as the quintessential English gentleman. One of his greatest successes was opposite Bette Davis in *Of Human Bondage* (1934).

In *A Free Soul*, Howard played Dwight Winthrop, the boyfriend of Jan Ashe (Shearer).

Author Adela Rogers St. Johns was delighted that Thalberg had given her novel his endorsement, despite his fears about objections from the Hays Office.

"I've seen too many gooey virgins on the screen, giving fans diabetes from all that sugar," St. Johns said. "It's time for some rough-and-tumble sex. Gable is the man for that. I should know."

Cast as "Eddie," James Gleason, a New Yorker born in 1882, usually played tough-talking, world-weary guys with secret hearts of gold. As an actor, he'd made his film debut in *Polly of the Follies* (1922), starring Constance Talmadge. Soon, his balding head and craggy voice became familiar to movie-goers across America.

Gable's performance as the gangster (Ace Wilfong) who "roughs up" (and fascinates) Shearer propelled him up the Hollywood ladder, morphing him into an actor widely acknowledged

Feverishly promoted, and with lurid intensity, *A Free Soul* promised (and delivered) sexual heat between the players. Both **Clark Gable** and **Norma Shearer** (the wife of one of MGM's top executives) performed with a believability that barely got past the censors.

Norma Goes Slumming (*aka* **"Ready to Be Ravished"**). Having orchestrated a midnight supper for two, alone with a notorious mob boss (**Clark**), she appears supremely confident, creamy smooth, and in total control of the sexual dynamic. As noted by film critic Mick LaSalle, "Shearer never rids herself of a taint of the *grande dame* manner, but her plunge into a rogue sexuality is fascinating."

"Norma the Shearer" her jealous enemies called her, perhaps for her ability to (stylishly) control most of the men around her—including, they said, her frail husband, Irving Thalberg, studio supervisor of most of her films.

Daddy's Favorite: Always able to bypass the strictures of her wealthy and indulgent father (**Lionel Barrymore**), Jan (**Norma Shearer**) comforts him during one of his alcoholic binges. Tormented by the thought of his daughter sharing intimacies with the gangland boss he defended in court, he drinks himself into the gutter...Until he's resurrected during his defense of "her beau" in court.

Is it true that spoiled uptown girls like to get slapped around? Scriptwriter Adela Rogers St. Johns thought so...and added it to her filmscript.

In this then-startling encounter with **Clark**, who's on the verge of seriously roughing her up, Jan (**Norma**) seems emotionally unrehearsed. What happens next? She falls madly, deliriously in love with him. Audiences lapped it up.

after that as a leading man.

Shearer, cast as Jan Ashe, daughter of the drunken attorney Stephen Ashe (Lionel Barrymore), is engaged to Winthrop (Leslie Howard). Their relationship is threatened by the roguish charms of Ace (Clark).

Enraged and psychotically jealous, Winthrop arrives at Ace's gambling club and shoots him before turning himself in to the police.

Jan rescues her drunken lawyer/father, Stephen Ash (Barrymore) from a flophouse, where he'd retreated after a drinking binge. After she sobers him up, as a defense lawyer he goes into court to defend Winthrop. As part of his defense of Winthrop, he accepts blame for everything that happened, explaining "with Barrymore flourish" that his alcoholism prevented him from being a proper father to his daughter. At the end of his defense arguments before the jury, he collapses to the floor and dies.

Two views of "that English import," Leslie Howard

Adept at playing dull but respectable counterparts to his flashier, testosterone-soaked two-time rival (Clark Gable), he appears *(left photo)* with **Norma Shearer** in *A Free Soul*, and

Right photo as Ashley Wilkes with Melanie (**Olivia De Havilland**) in *Gone With the Wind* (1939).

The wardrobe that Adrian designed for Shearer shocked (and titillated) audiences because viewers could see through the semi-transparent fabric for views of her legs and thighs. As Clark later revealed to his director, " I learned, during our love scenes together, that she doesn't wear underwear, either."

As he shoves her roughly onto a couch, he tells her: "You're an idiot—a spoiled, silly brat that needs a hairbrush now and then!"

Barrymore later appraised the forceful, "game-changing" assault by gangster Clark upon Shearer, his on-screen mistress (*aka* Barrymore's on-screen daughter). "He delivered a *bona-fide* sockeroo that rocked Norma off her feet. In the role, she was sexual dynamite, though speaking in the voice of Minnie Mouse."

After seeing the film, James Quirk at *Photoplay* wrote an article he entitled, "Why Women Go Crazy About Clark Gable": "Clark meets every woman with a challenge in his eyes, a mocking grin culminating in a laughing dimple. He is an adroit opponent in a duel of the sexes. He is like a magnet that both attracts and repels."

He also defined Shearer as "a hottie who burns up the celluloid. She can simmer, seethe, and scintillate."

St. Johns later, in private, outed the affair between Gable and Shearer: "He made her hormones jump, something her husband, Thalberg, could not do."

As St. Johns later whispered to friends, "Poor Clark not only had to appear before the camera but had to run between the dressing rooms of both Lionel and Norma, too."

A Free Soul was Gable's first really big screen role, but he held his own against the seductive and alluring Shearer. He played a gangster, rough and tough, a role conceived by the scriptwriters as "an unpolished rhinestone."

In spite of her marriage to Thalberg, Shearer had a penchant for seducing her leading men. Gable, Shearer, and everyone else quickly realized that their sexual involvement was merely a fling, and rather brief.

Shearer's pattern of seduction had begun with John Gilbert during their filming of *The Wolf Man* (1924), continuing with Lew Cody in *A State of Fashion* (1925) and John Pickford (the brother of Mary Pickford) in *Waking Up the Town* (also 1925).

By 1928, she moved in on Johnny Mack Brown in *A Lady of Chance,* followed by Ralph Forbes in *The*

Actress (1929). She seduced Robert Montgomery when they made *The Divorcée* in 1930.

Shearer was reunited with Gable when they co-starred once again in *Strange Interlude* (1932). However, by then her romantic radar was focused on the film's third male lead, Alexander Kirkwood.

Burgess Meredith seduced her when they co-starred in *Idiot's Delight* (1939). She also sustained affairs with Howard Hughes, James Stewart, David Niven, and director Victor Fleming. Author Gavin Lambert summed up Shearer: "She was the personification of elegance. Throughout the 1920s and 30s, she was the most versatile actress at the most opulent studio in Hollywood. Without ever appearing on stage, she inherited the great Broadway roles of Katharine Cornell, Lynn Fontanne, and Gertrude Lawrence."

Lambert continued: "No star ever worked harder to create an image of glamour. Shearer was unfailingly attentive to her costumes, her make-up, and, above all, that her scenes be perfect. She embodied sophisticated charm, and audiences adored her subtle balance of refinement and playful eroticism."

***

The Motion Picture Herald wrote: "Clark Gable and Leslie Howard are both grand. At the time they made *A Free Soul*, they were unimportant players. After the film's release, both of them were on the road to super stardom"

The critic for *The New York Herald Tribune* wrote, "Clark Gable is a fascinating villain who will convince female viewers that he is naughty but nice. He stands out as a major character, although in fifth billing."

The film cost $550,000 to make, earning $1.5 million at the box office.

Although Shearer and Clark would spark the screen together again, she almost became his co-star in *Gone With the Wind* (1939), when she was offered the role of Scarlett O'Hara against his Rhett Butler. She rejected the proposal after she received a ton of mail from fans who protested her playing Scarlett. Most of the letters maintained that Shearer was far too sophisticated and refined to cheapen herself by playing a Southern vixen like Scarlett. As Buddy Segal, president of her fan club in New York wrote, "our beloved Norma could never play a woman born in Georgia."

Shearer also rejected the title role in *Mrs. Miniver* (1942), an assignment that was eventually awarded to Greer Garson.

Perhaps even more ironic, before its filming began in 1949, director Billy Wilder offered Shearer the role of Norma Desmond in *Sunset Blvd.* Although she rejected the role, he adopted her first name (Norma) as the moniker for the faded (and homicidally demented) grand diva of silent films.

Shearer later issued her own appraisal of Clark: "He was beautiful from head to feet. He was rhythmic, unconsciously alive with a powerful grace, like a jungle animal. He is a new kind of man in a new kind of world."

Gossipy Cal York in his column wrote: "One of the main objects of conversation over Hollywood tea tables is the change that has taken place in Norma Shearer. Once the discreet little lady of films, she is now appearing in gowns so sensational that they make even hard-boiled Hollywood gulp a few gulps. When she is having her clothes designed for picture purposes, she insists that they show as much of her anatomy as the law and Will Hays will allow."

> **Norma Shearer's** husband, Irving Thalberg, asked her why she wanted **Clark Gable** as her co-star. "He's nothing but a big-eared mug with bad teeth."
>
> The novel on which both the play and film had been based had been written by Adela Rogers St. Johns, who had had an early affair with Gable, and who "sold" the commercial appeal of his masculine charms to Shearer. "His virility will excite you."

Episode 39

Night Nurse (1931)

Lent to Warner Brothers for his next film, Clark had to postpone his dream of becoming a romantic hero.

"As a black-uniformed chauffeur, 'Nick,' I not only give Barbara Stanwyck the alltime beating of her cinematic life, but I scheme to starve two kids to death so that I and her horrible mother, with whom I'm having an affair, can take over their trust fund left to them by their wealthy father."

Clark was widely written about in the press for the way he'd mauled Shearer. That was nothing compared to his violent scenes with Stanwyck. In two different instances, he hauls off and smashes her face, knocking her down onto the floor.

She suggests to Nick that the world has a place for men like him—the electric chair. She stands up to the men in the cast with fiery denunciations—a harbinger of the tough girls she'd later play.

Directed by William A. Wellman, this Pre-Code "crime drama mystery" starred Stanwyck, Ben Lyon, Joan Blondell, and Clark.

Stanwyck portrays the film's title role: the night nurse, Lora Hart, who struggles to save the dying children. Ben Lyon, a bootlegger, is her love interest. Blondell is Nurse Maloney, Lora's sidekick.

During pre-production, it was a "**BARBARA STANWYCK**" film. Then it was a vehicle for "**STANWYCK AND BEN LYONS.**"

But after its release, as fans discovered the roughshod charm of Clark Gable, it morphed into "**A CLARK GABLE SHOWCASE.**"

Charlotte Merriam was the devious alcoholic mother who's in love with her loutish chauffeur, Nick (aka Clark Gable), and Charles Winninger plays the self-absorbed but decent and morally upright Dr. Arthur Bell.

Jack Warner had originally objected to Clark after seeing his screen test. But he changed his mind when he learned how extensive the actor's fan base had become. For $750 a week, he borrowed Clark from MGM, warning his cameramen to avoid focusing on his big ears,

Born in Massachusetts in 1896, William W. Wellman was one of Clark's alltime best drectors, In Hollywood, he turned out numerous films, often with crime, adventure, or aviation themes. His first big success had been the memorable *Wings* (1927). During the course of a career that stretched from 1918 to 1954, he helmed eighty movies. Many were major hits, such as *A Star is Born* (1937) for which he was nominated for a Best Director Academy Award.

In 1939, he would direct *Beau Geste,* starring Gary Cooper, a role that Clark had coveted. *[Instead of that, he had to take the role of Rhett Butler in* Gone With the Wind *(1939).]*

Not since Valentino, as **The Shiek** in 1921, had a damsel been roughnecked like **Clark Gable** did to **Babs.**

Here, fresh-faced but forceful, and without a mustache, **Gable** portrays an abusive beast.

***

Born Ruby Stevens in Brooklyn in 1907, Barbara Stanwyck made 85 films in 38 years before turning to television. Director Frank Capra called her "the greatest emotional actress the screen has yet known." She combined beauty and brains.

When Clark met her, she was in an unhappy marriage to Frank Fay, a well-known show biz personality of his day.

She'd made her debut at the age of sixteen in the chorus as a Ziegfeld Girl in 1923. In 1929, she shot her first talking picture after Frank Capra cast her in his romantic drama, *Ladies of Leisure*—a picture credited with making her a star.

After *Night Nurse*, she'd make one more picture with Clark, a film about auto racing called *To Please a Lady* (1950).

Wellman and Clark had several talks on the set, some of them reminiscences of their boyhood days. The director said he got kicked out of high school after he threw a stink bomb which landed on the bald head of the school's principal.

He was arrested for car theft before running off to join the French Foreign Legion during World War I. His fellow pilots called him "Wild Bill."

He told Clark he had hated working as an actor in his early days. "Acting is not a manly profession. I'm a real he-man, and I think you are, too. Nearly all actors are pansies."

Right before filming Clark, Wellman had had a big success with *The Public Enemy* (1931).

His friendship with Clark led to him casting the actor in *Mutiny on the Bounty* (1935), one of his most memorable films.

***

Cast as a bootlegger, Ben Lyon as "Mortie" encounters Nurse Stanwyck in a hospital emergency room, where she treats him for a bullet wound in the arm. He is immediately attracted to her and pursues her. He begs her not to report his injury, which is against hospital rules.

Lyon emerged in Atlanta, Georgia, the same year (1901) Clark was born. He became a star long before Clark. In 1918, he co-stared opposite the legendary Jeanne Eagels.

His box office hit was the silent film, *Flaming Youth* (1923). It shot him to stardom. He then starred opposite such silent-era vamps as Gloria Swanson, Barbara La Marr, Viola Dana,

Saucy and silly: What do nurses REALLY wear beneath their uniforms?

In naughty, Pre-Code formats, **Night Nurse** did its best to answer that question. Here are two cheesecakey views of **Stanwick** and **Blondell** "getting girlie" in ways their nursing supervisor would not have approved.

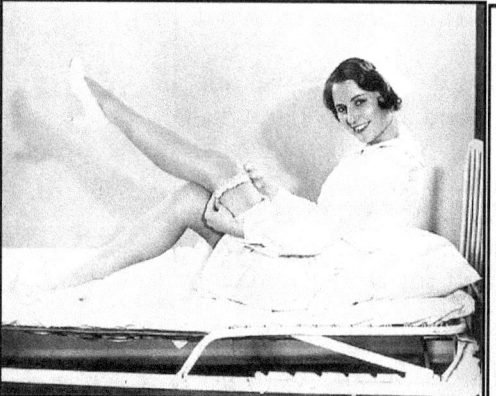

Press and PR photos of **Night Nurse**'s female stars: *Photo above:* **Bloody Babs** wearing starchy whites with a garter belt; and *photo right:* **Blondell**, looking likable and sexy, playing with a tripod.

Colleen Moore, Mary Astor, and Blanche Sweet. In 1930, he married actress Bebe Daniels.

Lyon is best remembered today for starring in the memorable *Wings* (1930) in a role that Clark tried out for but lost.

Film historians lament that nearly all of Lyon's films are now lost. Examples include *So Big* (1924) and *Bluebeard's Seven Wives* (1926). One reel of *Flaming Youth* (1923) survives.

As his career as a screen idol faded, Lyon morphed into a studio executive at Fox. On July 12, 1946, he met a young hopeful, Norma Jean Dougherty. "She is Jean Harlow come back to life," he told his bosses after organizing a screen test for her.

It was with a certain irony that this actress, as Marilyn Monroe, would co-star with Clark in the last movie both of them ever made, *The Misfits* (1961).

***

In *Night Nurse,* Clark, as Nick the sadistic chauffeur, appears in a smartly tailored black uniform with knee-high shiny black boots. He is having an affair with Mrs. Ritchey (Charlotte Merriam), the larcenous drunken mother of the two children. She is gradually starving them to death. She and Nick plan to then take over the inheritance left to the children by their wealthy (deceased) father.

After the advent of sound, most of Merriam's roles had her cast as a tarnished society woman. In *Night Nurse,* she had dyed Jean Harlow hair, and in every scene plays a sloppy, scheming, alcoholic mother with tarnished morals.

After *Night Nurse,* she was awarded the role of the syphilis-infected Elsie in *Damaged Lives* (1934).

Character actor Charles Winniger is Dr. Bell, whom Nurse Stanwyck appeals to for help in saving the starving children.

He'd begun his career in vaudeville and later portrayed Cap'n Andy Hawks in the original Broadway production of *Show Boat.* He essayed the role a second time in the 1936 film adaptation.

"When Babs (Stanwyck) and I first saw Clark Gable walk onto the set, we both had to sit down to control our fluttering hearts," claimed Joan Blondell, a friend of co-author Darwin Porter. She'd been cast as the film's third lead, Nurse Maloney, Stanwyck's blonde, gum-chewing, wise-cracking roommate.

The previous year, **Ben Lyon**, had been awarded a better part in a bigger film (*Hell's Angels*, 1930).

This photo shows how he appeared in it as the love interest of the voluptuously blonde and spectacularly scandalous **Jean Harlow**.

Gable, as a degenerate lowlife between con jobs, hangs out with (and "sizes up') good girl **Stanwyck** at a malt shop

As Blondell remembered it years later, "Clark was around to watch Babs and me strip down to our underwear in scenes that barely made it past the censors. Babs salivated over him, but I was the one who got him. Maybe he preferred blondes. I don't know."

Born in 1906 to a vaudeville family in Manhattan, Blondell had become famous in Pre-Code Hollywood working for Warner Brothers. She often portrayed wisecracking, sexy characters, a total of 100 over the course of fifty years. . She and the also blonde, also wise-cracking Glenda Farrell starred in nine films together.

Blondell became one of the highest-paid actresses in Hollywood during the Depression.

James Cagney was one of her early co-stars in such movies as *The Public Enemy* (1931).

"For the rest of my life, wherever I went, I was always asked the same question: "What was Cagney really like?"

In the 1930s, she had an affair with Bing Crosby and much later, with George C. Scott. He said, "For me, at least, the sexiest woman on the screen was Joan Blondell. What tits!"

"I had a brief fling with Clark," Blondell admitted to author Darwin Porter during the course of a weekend she spent at his home. "Any dame would be a fool, or perhaps a lesbian, if she turned down Gable. I welcomed his advances and managed to get him in the sack three times before he moved on to other conquests. In contrast, I resisted the lesbian advances of Stanwyck. I don't go that route."

Before the end of the final reel of *Night Nurse*, Stanwyck and Lyon are united at last. An ambulance passes nearby with the corpse of a man killed within the previous few minutes by a bullet. It's clad in a smartly tailored chauffeur's uniform with shiny, knee-high black boots. Nick is on his way to the morgue.

In a review in *Variety*, a critic wrote, "Clark Gable goes through socking everybody, including mauling Miss Stanwyck, and the menace is finally done away with. This is his macho of all macho roles. Miss Stanwyck plays her dancehall type of girl on one note and is shy of shading to lend her performance some color."

The *Hollywood Reporter* wrote, "The best scenes in *Night Nurse* are watching Misses Stanwyck and Blondell strip down to their underwear two or three times."

"My billing in *Night Nurse* changed after the opening of *A Free Soul*," Stanwyck said. "Our little thriller had its premier on Broadway, where the billing was listed as starring **Ben Lyon and Barbara Stanwyck**. On the second day, the billing was changed to a trio—**Lyon, Stanwyck, and Gable**." By the end of the first week, huge black letters appeared, hyping the name of **Clark Gable as the star of Night Nurse**. Ben and I got demoted to second and third billing."

***

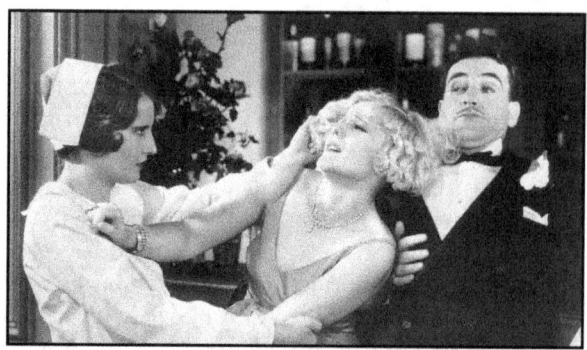

Nice girls can get tough, too—especially if they're a nurse on the night shift.

Here, Stanwyck deals with a violent drunken mother trying to starve her children to death. As a nurse, she confronts her: "*You're a cruel, inhuman mother. You're a rotten parasite. Don't blame it on the booze. It's you!*"

Director Wellman's only direction to Gable for the character he was playing was "He's a loathsome brute."

From there, **Gable** forged a memorably sexy sleazeball who convincingly delivered lines that included "*Never mind that. Get busy with her! Give her a stomach wash!*"; "*I'll break your neck!*"; "*Aw, shut up!*"; "*Hey, just what's the idea behind that crack?*"; "*You're speaking right out, ain't you?*"; "*I'd run along if I was you.*"

In the wake of its release, girls surged to enroll in nursing schools, and men tried to mimic Gable's hard-to-define interpersonal style.

Episode 40

Sporting Blood (1931)

At long last, Clark Gable got top star billing in his latest film. a Pre-Code drama released by MGM entitled *Sporting Blood,* its theme centered on horse racing. Its plot originated in 1930 as a short story, *Horse Flesh*, by Frederick Brennan, as it appeared in *The Saturday Evening Post*.

MGM bought the rights and asked Charles Brabin, the husband of screen vamp Theda Bara, to draft a screenplay and direct the picture. In it, Clark would play a gambler, "Rid" Riddell.

Born in Liverpool, England, in 1882, Brabin emigrated to the Port of New York around the turn of the 20th Century, taking whatever odd jobs he could.

Eventually, he became a stage actor. By 1908, he joined the Edison Manufacturing Company, where he acted in silent films, later writing and directing them.

He made a number of silent films. They included *The Raven* (1915), and *Red, White, and Blue Blood* (1917).

In the gossipy Hollywood press, Brabin was mostly known for his marriage, in 1921, to Theda Bara. It lasted until her death in 1955.

Three years afer directing Clark in *Sporting Blood*, he would retire from the screen after completing *A Wicked Woman* (1934) for MGM.

Although he got top billing, Clark later agreed with a reviewer at *Time* magazine that the film was about "horses and nonsense."

Clark's co-star, Ernest Torrence, had the second lead as Jim Rellence, who breeds racehorses. His favorite horse, "Tommy Boy," is sold to Jerry Hardwick (J. Farrell MacDonald). On the set, Clark had a reunion with his old character actor friend, with whom he had co-starred in his first movie, *The Painted Desert* (1931).

Then Hardwick sells Tommy Boy to a rich married couple, Bill and Angie Ludeking (Hallam Cooley and Marie Prevost). The dilettantish new owners overwork and abuse the animal.

After Ludeking loses a lot of money betting on Tommy Boy, he stumbles into the gambling joint of Tip Scanton (Lew Cody), hoping to win back his losses. *[Rid Riddell (Clark) works for Scanton.]* But after he loses even more money, Ludeking is forced to transfer his ownership of Tommy Boy over to Scanton.

To his fellow gangsters, Scanton virtually guarantees that Tommy Boy will win a major race. As such, the crooks bet heavily on the horse. When he loses, gang members go after Scanton and murder him.

Before Scanton's death, he transfers the ownership of Tommy Boy to Missy Ruby (Madge Evans). She and "Rid" (Clark) restore the horse's health, and he wins the Kentucky Derby. Rid ends up with Missy, and they live happily ever after.

One of the ironies of *Sporting Blood* (the film) is that **Clark** didn't appear until 45 minutes after its opening credits, and only belatedly did he emerge as the film's most important star.

Here, he appears with an equine lookalike named (in the film, at least) as **"Tommy Boy,"** a reference to "Sporting Blood," one of the most famous racehorses in America in the early 1920s

The real-life owners of Sporting Blood were major-league mobsters forever linked to corruption in the racing world.

***

Although almost completely unknown today, the cast was familiar to audiences of yesterday.

A New Yorker born in 1909, Madge Evans, the film's leading lady was a child performer and model before becoming a stage and screen star. When she was two years old, she was the model featured as the "Fairy Soap Girl."

She was eight when she appeared on Broadway in 1917 in a play starring John Barrymore and Laura Hope Crews, who later portrayed Aunt Pittypat in *Gone With the Wind* (1939).

Beginning in 1914, in the silent film, *The Sign of the Cross*, Crews worked steadily, appearing in dozens of films during the Silent Era, including a co-starring role, with Richard Barthelmess, in *Classmates* (1924).

MGM signed her in 1927, casting her in various roles that included the love interest of Al Jolson in *Hallelujah, I'm a Bum* (1933), which she made after working with Clark. She was married to playwright Sidney Kingsley, known for his plays *Dead End* and *Detective Story*.

Ernest Torrence was a Scottish character actor born in 1875. He made a name for himself playing cold-eyed and imposing villians. He appeared in *Mantrap* (1926) with Clara Bow and in *Fighting Caravans* (1931) with Gary Cooper.

After working with Clark, Torrence was assigned to star with Clark's upcoming leading lady, Claudette Colbert in *I Cover the Waterfront* (1933). After completing that film, he suffered an attack of gallstones en route to Europe. Death came at the age of 54 on May 15, 1933.

Lew Cody, born in Maine in 1884, was a stage and film actor. In the late 1910s, he became known for playing "male vamps," a term heretofore used for female stars, most notably, Theda Bara.

After he moved to Hollywood, he made a hundred films between 1914 and 1934, when he died at the age of 50.

He famously married screen legend Mabel Normand in 1926. She died in 1930, four years later, of tuberculosis.

During the filming of *Sporting Blood*, Clark, off screen, became sexually attracted to the Canadian-born actress, Marie Prevost. Stunningly beautiful, she was born in 1896 and became one of Mack Sennett's Bathing Beauties by the late 1910s. After signing with Warners' in 1922, her career flourished, especially when Ernst Lubitsch helmed her.

By the time Prevost worked with Clark, her career was in decline. Their off-screen relationship began when she invited him to go on a night crawl with her. She was on her way to becoming a full-fledged alcoholic. On the night of their first date she invited him to spend the night in her apartment.

The distinguished stage and screen actress **Madge Evans,** as she appeared as the love interest of Clark Gable in *Sporting Blood.*

Mabel Normand *(photo above)*, famously married to *one of Sporting Blood's* stars, **Lew Cody.** as she appeared in *Barney Oldfield's Race for a Life*, an early slapstick silent released in 1913.

Very famous but almost forgotten today, Normand derived from Staten Island and lived a few houses from what today is Blood Moon's editorial headquarters in historic Saint George, Staten Island.

Despite many other films, here's **Laura Hope Crews** as she appeared in the (relatively) minor role that made her famous with modern film fans: dotty Aunt Pittypat in *Gone With the Wind.*

Lew Cody, known early in his career as "the male vamp" and famously married to **Mabel Normand**, is shown above as he appeared in his obituary in 1933.

Another view of the saucy, Pre-Code household name, **Mabel Normand.**

During the shoot, he spent several more nights with her, finding her highly seductive. "That talented tongue of hers begins at a man's feet and works its way north," he told Charles Brabin, their director.

After seeing Prevost in F. Scott Fitzgerald's *The Beautiful and the Damned*, Howard Hughes cast her as the lead in *The Racket* (1928). The couple had a brief affair.

In 1930, Prevost starred with Joan Crawford in *Paid* (1930). Crawford became attracted to her and seduced her.

Films in Review claimed that "Clark Gable heads the cast, but Ernest Torrence steals the show."

Time wrote, "Only the race sequences offer any promise for the fan. This one is indubitably not Mr. Gable's best work, though far from his worst. If his stardom is to last, Gable better find more thrilling roles than as a gambler on horse races, or else he might go the way of John Gilbert."

***

Here's **Marie Prevost**, two years before her appearance with Clark Gable in *Sporting Blood*.

The wife of the director, Theda Bara, visited the set on three different occasions for lunch with her spouse, Charles Brabin, and Clark.

She had been one of the most popular actresses of the silent era and one of Hollywood's first sex symbols. Nicknamed "The Vamp" (short for "vampire") she starred in *femme fatale* roles based on exoticism and sexual domination.

Her biggest hit was in the epic *Cleopatra* (1917). No complete print of that film exists today, although dozens of still photographs do.

In promoting the film, Fox executives falsely claimed that Theda Bara's name was an anagram of "Arab Death," and that she was "the daughter of an Arab sheik and a Frenchwoman born in the Sahara."

Actually, she was born Theodosia Burr Goodman on July 29, 1885 in Cincinnati, Ohio. The Burr in her name came from the daughter of Vice President Aaron Burr. Theda was of Jewish and Swiss origin.

Between 1914 and 1926, she made forty films, only six of which still exist. The rest were destroyed in the fire that, in 1937, swept through Fox's storage vaults in Little Ferry, New Jersey.

On four different occasions, Clark was invited for dinner at the home of the Brabins. He listened endlessly to her desire to remake a talkie version of *Cleopatra*, with him cast as Mark Antony.

Sporting Blood's screenwriter and director, Charles Brabant, was famously married for more than 30 years to the Silent Screen's "ultimate vamp," **Theda Bara.** She appears above as *Cleopatra* in 1917.

Although her star power no longer existed, Clark fully supported the plan, partly because of Brabin's cachet as a director, thanks to which financing might be arranged. But Brabin was soon to make his last film.

What really killed the deal was Claudette Colbert, who starred in a talkie version of *Cleopatra* in 1934, right after she and Clark had won Oscars for *It Happened One Night* that same year.

***

Thalberg and Louis B. Mayer disliked Gable, but he remained their best hope at the box office. They each knew that they would have to get rid of John Gilbert when his contract expired, and their vision involved replacing him with Gable, despite their mutual distaste for him.

The Hollywood Reporter claimed, "A star in the making has been made, one that will outdraw every other male actor in Tinseltown. His name is Clark Gable."

Studio executive Howard Strickling had been busy keeping Clark's former and present life out of the scandal sheets, especially his whoring past from the 1920s.

"Clark earned his reputation as the least selective lover in the hemisphere," said Eddie Mannix,

MGM's "Fixer."

"Our boy will screw anything. She didn't even have to be pretty...or clean; age wasn't all that important, either."

After their initial encounter, Greta Garbo and Clark had intrigued each other during the final weeks of shooting of *Susan Lenox* (1931). That was, until she overheard him calling her "a stuck-up Swedish lez."

Early in her career, starlet Joan Crawford was seduced by Mayer. Years later, she had only insults about his performance in bed. "Mayer is also a pedophile. He seduced that dancer, Ann Miller, when she had not shed her diapers."

[In 1944, the studio boss would propose marriage to Miller, even though he was already wed at the time.]

As the years went by, Crawford also alleged that "Louis B. not only seduces the starlets, he fucked their mothers, too. I know he screwed Mabel Cooper, the mother of child star Jackie Cooper."

Later in the 1940s, he would be accused of seducing Gladys O'Brien, the mother of child star Margaret O'Brien.

Mayer once told MGM lawyer Mabel Willebrandt, "There is one thing I will not do—and that is fuck a woman in the ass. As far as I'm concerned, her rosebud is reserved for her husband's pleasure."

If Clark hadn't been generating a healthy box office for MGM, he would surely have been fired after Mayer heard a comment he was spreading across the studio lot: "Mayer is the type of guy who can't get laid in a whorehouse."

He equally infuriated Thalberg when he spoke to yellow journalist Ben Maddox: "When I co-starred with Norma Shearer in *A Free Soul,* I found she kisses like a whore in heat. She doesn't wear any bloomers. After our big love scene, I found her as wet as November rain."

After hearing that, Thalberg said, "I don't always agree with Mayer, but on one subject, we are in complete accord: Both of us detest Clark Gable."

As the Depression deepened across the land, many couples could not put food on the table, much less spend 50¢ for two tickets to the local movie house. Studios such as RKO and Warners went in the red in 1931, the year Clark Gable made more movies than he ever did before or would do again.

MGM declared a profit of $12 million that dreadful year when a lot of Americans were going hungry.

Every day, Mayer's faithful secretary delivered to her boss the latest press assessments of Clark.

The editor and publisher of *The Hollywood Reporter,* William R. Wilkerson, wrote: "A star in the making has been one that, to our reckoning, will outdraw every other star pictures have developed. Never have we seen audiences work themselves into such enthusiasm as when Clark Gable appears on the screen."

Screenland dubbed him "a lumberjack in evening clothes, the answer to ten million maidens' prayers."

In 1931, the first Joan Crawford fan clubs would appear and then thrive for three decades. A founding member was a young Van Johnson, who also dreamed of stardom one day for himself.

Charter members hailed from virtually everywhere, from Ireland to South Africa.

Stridently, Mayer once told Crawford, "Families go to movies, and I'm not going to put any actor or actress on the screen who isn't a fit subject for father, mother, and their kids to watch. The only exception to my mandate is casting pictures with you and Clark Gable as the stars. For you two, perhaps we should put up a sign in front saying 'Adult Entertainment.'"

Mayer also told his secretary, Ida Koverman, "My greatest desire is that one day in the future, I will be able to summon Crawford and Gable to my office. There, I'll order both of them to get their asses off the MGM lot within the hour. Once they go through those gates, they are never to return. That will be the day when I will see the last of those two has-been whores."

Mavericks and iconoclasts: **Clark Gable** with **Joan Crawford.** Louis B. Mayer, MGM's autocratic studio chief, voraciously hated both of them, lamenting why he couldn't easily fire them and referring to them as "has-been whores."

Episode 41

Susan Lenox: Her Fall and Rise
(1931)

Clark Gable faced the acting challenge of his life when he read in *Variety* that his next picture would star Greta Garbo, the Queen of MGM. As for Clark, he was years away from being acknowledged as "King of Hollywood."

He was "seriously pissed off" that Irving Thalberg had not even consulted him about appearing as Garbo's leading man. His fear was that he was not up to the challenge. "That Swedish block of ice, this so-called Love Goddess, will eat up the screen. Who is going to notice me while she goes through all her melodramatic emoting?"

Garbo wanted Clarence Brown to direct her, but after their last picture together, he told the press, "I will not work with Garbo again." He had recently directed Clark and Norma Shearer in *A Free Soul*.

Instead, Thalberg hired Robert E. Leonard, the film director, actor, producer, and screenwriter. A son of Chicago born in 1889, he had been married to "The Merry Widow" (Mae Murray) from 1918 to 1925.

He had been nominated for an Academy Award as Best Director for *The Divorcée* (1930) starring Thalberg's wife, Norma Shearer.

Whereas Thalberg and Louis B. Mayer had dictated the pairing of Garbo with Gable, Leonard was allowed to cast the other roles.

Early in the film, Garbo's character would be introduced as Helga Ohlin, later (based on nuances of the plot) changing it to Susan Lenox. As her leading man, Clark was assigned the character name, Rodney Spencer.

The cast was rounded out with Jean Hersholt as Karl Ohlin; John Miljan as Wayne Burlington; Alan Hale Sr. as Jeb Mondstrum; Hale Hamilton as Mike Kelly; and Ian Keith as Robert Lane.

Born in Copenhagen in 1886, Jean Hersholt became famous when he starred in the CBS radio series (1937-1954).

During a career that spanned 1906 to 1955, he starred in 75 silent films and 85 talkies. His film appearances ranged from Erich von Stroheim's *Greed* (1924) to his playing the beloved

Almost everyone, including Clark, interpreted *Susan Lenox* as an MGM showcase for "That Frigid Swede," **Greta Garbo**.

Above, she's drenched in a display of her legendary enigma, half-hiding behind a diaphanous but glittery gauze— a standard, much-used "trick" that her enemies sometimes ridiculed.

Clark found her evasive devices infuriating.

grandfather of Shirley Temple in the 1937 film version of the 1880 children's classic, *Heidi*.

Clark had worked with Miljan before on the set of *The Secret Six* (1931). The actor had made his first sound film appearance in a trailer for Al Jolson's *The Jazz Singer* (1927), Hollywood's first talkie.

During the filming of *Susan Lenox*, this very conservative actor had begun to campaign for the 1932 re-election of Herbert Hoover.

Born in Chicago in 1892, Alan Hale Sr. is best remembered today for his many character roles, most notably as a sidekick for Errol Flynn. He'd begun as a leading man in 1913 for Biograph Company. In supporting roles, he co-starred with Wallace Beery, James Cagney, Douglas Fairbanks Sr., Cary Grant, Humphrey Bogart, and even Ronald Reagan.

Clark also renewed his acquaintance with Hale Hamilton, with whom he had co-starred in *Dance,*

Fools, Dance (1931) with Joan Crawford.

Ian Keith first entered the world in 1899 in Boston before growing up in Chicago. He played many a colorful role in silent films before D.W. Griffith cast him as John Wilkes Booth in his first talkie, *Abraham Lincoln,* in 1930. He had a major role as a gambler in Raoul Walsh's 1930 Western, *The Big Trail,* starring a young John Wayne, who was no longer using his birth name of "Marion."

Right after working with Clark, Cecil B. De Mille cast Keith in *The Sign of the Cross* (1932).

The plot of *Susan Lenox* was based on a 1917 novel by David Graham Phillips (1867-1911), a son of Madison, Indiana. He launched his career as a muckraker journalist for a newspaper in Cincinnati. At the turn of the 20th Century, he was a controversial columnist for *New York World.*

Jean Hersholt   John Miljan

The writer cut a striking figure, as he always dressed in a tailored white suit with a large chrysanthemum in his lapel. That was what he was wearing on January 24, 1911 when at age 43 he was assassinated outside the Princeton Club on Gramercy Park in Manhattan.

His killer was the Harvard-educated musician, Fitzburgh Coyle Goldsborough, a violinist with the Pittsburgh Symphony Orchestra. He was convinced that Phillips' novel, *The Fashionable Adventures of Joshua Craig,* had cast literary aspersions on his family.

In the wake of his death, Phillips' sister, Carolyn, organized his manuscript and arranged for its publication as *Susan Lenox: Her Fall and Rise.* Shopped around the studios, it finally found a buyer at MGM. The studio acquired the novel as a vehicle for Garbo.

As the film opens, Garbo, as Helga Ohlin, lives in a hovel with her brutal farmer uncle, Karl Ohlin (Jean Hersholt).

The plot reveals that she was an illegitimate child born and reared in an abusive home. Her uncle wants to get rid of her and marry her off to Jeb Mondstrum (Alan Hale Sr.), an odious dirt farmer who tries to rape her.

In a rainstorm, she flees into the night, seeking refuge in a cabin owned by Rodney Spencer (Clark). At first, she is leery of him after he suggests that she remove her wet clothing. But she quickly begins to trust him. He gets her a pair of pajamas, and in the morning, he cooks breakfast for her. Their affair has just begun.

When Rodney leaves for work, Ohlin and Mondstrum arrive to kidnap her and bring her back, but she flees again, this time to a railway station in the nearby small town of Lenoxville.

She boards the first train. It's filled with circus performers. She changes her name to Susan Lenox.

GABLE & GARBO: Two views of a short-lived and experimental screen team.

The boss of the circus troupe, Wayne Burlingham (John Miljan) takes her under his wing and hires her as a dancer. It's clear, however that in return, she'll have to become his mistress.

A reunion with Rodney (Clark) fails after they argue, and she lands in Manhattan as the mistress of a crooked politician, Mike Kelly (Hale Hamilton).

In time, Susan heads for South America working as a dancer, this time in a sleazy dance hall.

There, she begins an affair with a rich sea captain, Robert Lane (Ian Keith), who wants to marry her.

By chance, she comes together again with Rodney, who has fallen on bad days. She convinces him that he is the only man she ever really loved.

John Gilbert, Garbo's frequent co-star and real-life lover at the time, had been slated to appear opposite her once again in *Susan Lenox*, but at the last minute, his avowed enemy, MGM mogul Louis B. Mayer, ordered that Gilbert be fired.

Garbo and Gilbert had become the most famous lovers of the silent screen. But with the dawn of the talkies and his feud with Louis B. Mayer, Gilbert's career was heading toward oblivion. He hoped that *Susan Lenox* would lead to his comeback. But when he was kicked off the picture, he never really recovered.

A new type of film hero was needed for the Depression-ravaged 1930s, and Gable fit the need. As biographer Karen Senson stated, "Gable was a new hero for a new era, a rough, straight-shooting average Joe with an urge for life and for women. He had no time for phonies. His success would irretrievably seal Gilbert's fate at MGM."

Gable had just turned 30, like the decade itself, and he dreaded facing the reigning screen queen. He feared he was too inexperienced to face such an intimidating presence. In their first scene together, she arrives drenched with rain, seeking refuge from the clutches of an uncouth farmer, Alan Hale—nobody's idea of a leading man.

He invites her in and suggests she should remove her water-soaked clothes. At first, she's afraid, perhaps fearing rape. But they seem to warm to each other. After several days together on the set, Garbo took an interest in MGM's newest male star.

Director Robert T. Leonard later claimed that he believed that Gable and Garbo had a sexual tryst. He'd seen Gable, on three different occasions, enter her dressing room and remain there each time for about two hours. "Of course, the Swede and the former lumberjack might have been playing poker, but I don't think so."

Garbo later said she felt that Gable might develop a screen *persona* of magnetic appeal, but that he was "not there yet."

As she told her lover, the arts-industry socialite Mercedes de Acosta, "Gable has not developed a magnetic presence as a lover. He leaves much to be desired. I think he really doesn't know how to satisfy a woman."

"Of one thing I am certain," Garbo continued. "I will not be making any more movies with him. Instead of me, Gable should be cast with a very different type of woman, a real-life whore like Joan Crawford."

According to Gable, "Garbo made me feel inadequate as a man, and I didn't like that one god damn bit. I also didn't like our movie."

Upper photo: Clark, suave as a male courtesan in a drawing room in Mayfair, emotes with Garbo in well-dressed style

Lower photo: Rough but ready, Clark, here, plays it like a highly sexual "Everyman," with all the Tomcat charm necessary to thaw "The Frigid Swede."

His fans couldn't seem to agree on which version of him they preferred.

Many of the reviews were negative, but not *Photoplay's*: "If you like your romance spread thick, your passion strong, and your Garbo hot, don't miss *Susan Lenox*. And take notice, you Garboites! If you were mad about her before, just wait until you see her teamed up with this manifestation of masculine sex appeal called Clark Gable."

"As the 1930s rolled on," Gable said, "I became the King of Hollywood as Garbo's luster faded—and that was even before I joined the military in the war-torn 40s. GIs wanted a different type of screen goddess, gals like Betty Grable and Rita Hayworth."

"After her last picture bombed," he continued, "Garbo faded from the screen and tried to hide from the world for the remainder of her life."

***

Censors in London banned *Susan Lenox* and refused to change its censored status until 125 feet of its footage was removed. As an edited "shadow" of its original, it was finally released with the title *The Rise of Helga*.

A London critic wrote "Once again, Greta Garbo convinces us she can play a whore." He was referring to her performance in her first talkie, *Anna Christie* (1930).

Although praised in general by the American press, Clark didn't fare so well in the view of many a Londoner. Hannen Swaffer wrote: "Whatever started all this fuss about Clark Gable? He is moderately good looking. But there is nothing to distinguish him from hundreds of similar young actors. If he died, or lived, or went on not living, you would still refrain from noticing what he could not do."

When Clark read that review, he said, "The idiot who wrote that confusing last line must have had his 18th mug of beer in some lowly tavern in the East End."

Susan Lenox cost $600,000 to make, generating $1.5 million at the box office. That is a more impressive figure than it sounds, since a movie ticket to see it cost 25¢.

After its release, columnist Adela Rogers St. Johns claimed that the sheer animal magnetism of Clark Gable had not been equaled since a nude Adam walked into the Garden of Eden, 'turning on' Eve, who sat under an apple tree."

In many newspapers, Clark was hailed for his masculinity. He replaced those "powder puffs of the silent screen, both Valentino and John Gilbert," wrote Foster Browne.

Variety wrote, "Teaming with Greta Garbo marks the peak of the Clark Gable vogue."

The noted film critic James Agee found Clark's performance "excellent."

London Film Weekly cited Clark "for giving a straightforward performance as Garbo's lover."

Mayer and Thalberg viewed the final cut of *Susan Lenox* together. "Gable has the power to heat up the screen with this Swede iceberg," Mayer said. "Let's recast Garbo and Gable in their next movie."

"I've got the perfect script for them," Thalberg said. "It's called *Red Dust*."

At the end of filming, despite the short-term heat they'd generated, **Greta Garbo** *(photo above)* remained resolutely alone, and Clark sealed their collaborative doom by defining her—and word spread through Hollywood's gossipy grapevine—as "a frigid lesbian."

***

As **John Gilbert's** foothold within MGM grew increasingly fragile, thanks to his feud with its director, Louis B. Mayer, his frenzied jealousy of Clark Gable—who he interpreted (correctly) as his replacement—increased.

In the photos above, each of them shot during "the success years" of his collaboration with **Garbo**, he declares his undying love. With the advent of Talkies *(his voice, his detractors claimed, sounded high-pitched and girlish)*, and the arrival of Clark Gable, his career collapsed.

Episode 42

The Avant-Garde at War with
THE MAINSTREAM

WHY GARBO & GABLE Never Re-Appeared Together in Other Films

Garbo in one of her early European hits, The Swedish *Saga of Gosta Berlings*, directed by her mentor, Mauritz Stiller in 1924.

At the time of the production of *Susan Lenox—Her Fall and Rise* a bizarre legend whirled around Garbo and her links to two (flamboyant) foreign directors.

Irving Thalberg is credited with teaming Garbo with Clark as a replacement for John Gilbert despite his many hits in silent pictures. Like Clark, Garbo had become one of MGM's biggest stars, getting more fan mail than anybody else at the studio. Their movies, those filmed separately and *Susan Lenox* (the one they'd made together), had morphed into huge box office draws.

How did Garbo's exposure to American audiences originate? During a trip to Europe in 1924, Louis B. Mayer stopped over in Berlin. There, he sat through a screening of Maurice Stiller's *The Saga of Gosta Berlings,* starring a plump 19-year-old Greta Gustafsson. He invited both the director and his actress to dinner and held out the possibility that they might, if they migrated to America and followed his instructions, join the elite circle of MGM's star-studded studio. As part of the process, he issued a warning to the shy teenager: "We don't like fat girls in America."

In the months that followed, she lost at least 21 pounds. The MGM mogul lured them to Hollywood, and they arrived at the Port of New York on July 6, 1925. They lingered at the moderately priced Hotel Commodore for two months before they got MGM's summons to continue their journey by train to Los Angeles.

It was Irving Thalberg, not Mayer, who cast Garbo in *The Temptress* (1926). Stiller, who had been waiting impatiently for weeks in his hotel room, was finally summoned to direct Garbo in that film. But after two weeks, and in the aftermath of an argument (and ongoing feud) with Thalberg, he was fired and replaced with director Fred Niblo. Stiller then migrated to Paramount Pictures, where he worked briefly and unhappily before they dismissed him. Shattered, he told Garbo and others that he regretted ever leaving Sweden.

He had been born in the Duchy of Finland in 1883 when it was part of the Russian Empire. When he was drafted into the Imperial

Greta Garbo with **Mauritz Stiller** en route, for the first time, to America, young and hopeful players in the early film industry, aboard the *Drottningholm* in 1925.

Ultra *avant-garde*, and homosexual, here's **Mauritz Stiller** in 1926, shortly after his (unhappy) emigration to Hollywood.

Army of Czar Nicholas II, he fled to Sweden. There, he became a director, later credited with "discovering" Greta Garbo.

On his final night in Hollywood, Stiller arranged a farewell dinner with Garbo. Suffering from pleurisy, he would die the following year at the age of 45.

Garbo entered a period of depression. Hollywood insiders thought she was mourning a lost lover. *[Actually, Stiller was a homosexual.]*

Thalberg was also responsible for the mandate to cast Garbo alongside John Gilbert in their immensely popular silent film, *Flesh and the Devil* (1926).

Garbo soon moved into Gilbert's mansion. He later proposed marriage to her, and she reluctantly accepted. The wedding was set, and even Mayer showed up as one of the guests. Ironically, Garbo was the only one missing at the ceremony.

Garbo's popularity grew, as did Clark's. More and more reporters were snooping into their respective backgrounds. Rumors were rampant that Garbo was a closeted lesbian, and that Clark had morphed into a male prostitute for easier access up the Hollywood ladder, renting himself out ("gay for pay") to leading stars and directors.

After Clark's brief sexual encounter with Garbo, he decided that she genuinely preferred bedding women instead.

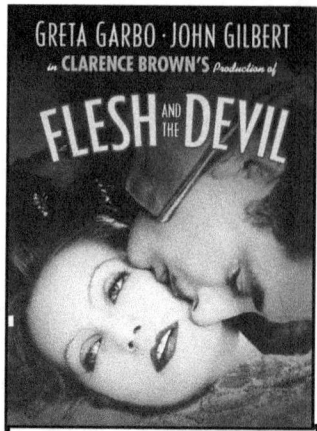

Thanks in part to Irving Thalberg, whereas Garbo's career thrived, that of her mentor, Mauritz Stiller, didn't.

Here's **John Gilbert** with **Greta Garbo** in one of her early U.S.-based hits.

***

Almost four years later, another death of one of Garbo's close friends occurred, this time during the production of *Susan Lenox—Her Fall and Rise*.

Director F.W. Murnau had also moved to Hollywood. A producer, director, and screenwriter had been born in Germany in 1888, and had grown up to become one of the key players in the cinematic world of silent films.

As an erudite child Friedrich was said to have already read books by Nietzche, Schopenhauer, Shakespeare, and Ibsen before he was 12. He showed an early, almost obsessive interest in films. He served in the Imperial German Army during World War I, and had survived several airplane crashes.

His 1922 silent film, *Nosferatu*, an adaptation of Bram Stoker's 1897 novel, *Dracula*, earned international acclaim. Today, it's viewed as a masterpiece of German Expressionist cinema.

Hollywood beckoned. There, he joined Fox as a director and helmed George O'Brien and Janet Gaynor in *Sunrise: A Song of Two Humans* (1927). Some film historians interpret it as the greatest silent film ever made, and one of the ten greatest

A short-lived cinematic genius **F.W. (Friedrich Wilhelm) Murnau**. Soaked in post-mortem scandal, he was revered by Greta Garbo

Scenes from F.W. Murnau's South Seas Idyll, **Tabu**. Filmed in 1931, it's revered as a cinematic legacy of Tahiti before it was commercialized and "westernized."

films of any genre ever made.

At the first Academy Awards ceremony, in 1929, Janet Gaynor won the Best Actress award not only for *Sunrise*, but for two other movies she made that year. *[That was the first and only time an actress would receive the coveted prize for three films in just one year.] Sunrise* itself won an Oscar for Best Unique and Artistic Production, the only time such an Oscar was ever awarded.

In Hollywood, the brilliant (and somewhat alienated) Murnau joined Garbo's closely knit entourage of Europeans. His next two films, including the (now lost) *4 Devils* (1928) and *City Girl* (1930), did not fare well at the box office.

During the filming of *Susan Lenox*, he visited the set several times and was introduced to Clark Gable. As a homosexual, he was very intrigued by the actor. To boost his career, he met with them several times for dinner to discuss possible film projects that would include him, with Garbo, as a co-starring team. Coincidentally, Irving Thalberg and Louis B. Mayer had the same idea.

On a personal level, Murnau became very attracted to Clark. Through William Haines and other gay actors, Murnau made several overtures to Clark. He was rejected. Thanks in part to his high weekly paycheck, and with a wife (Ria Langham) who was meeting all his household expenses, he no longer sold his body.

Murnau then journeyed to Bora Bora in French Polynesia for the filming of the 1931 film, *Tabu, A Story of the South Seas*, using Polynesians in the picture. A local boy, Matahi, starred in the lead role as a pearl diver. According to rumor, he spent his nights in the director's bed.

Back in Hollywood, Murnau hired the young actor David Rollins to pose nude for him beside his swimming pool.

On March 10, 1931, only one week before the world premiere of *Tabu*, Murnau was heading up the Pacific Coast Highway in his Packard touring car, driven by Eliazar Garcia Stevenson.

He swerved to avoid a large truck that unexpectedly veered into the northbound lane. To avoid collision, Murnau's driver plunged off an embankment and rolled over twice as it crashed down 35 feet, landing with its undercarriage facing the sky.

The driver suffered minor injuries. However, Murnau was rushed to the Santa Monica Hospital, where it was discovered that he had several bones broken and serious internal injuries He died the following morning.

Soon, a Hollywood rumor spread quickly through the gossip vine. That rumor still exists and has even appeared in some biographies.

Murnau had hired a young Filipino houseboy who double-dutied as his lover. As the story goes, it was the 14-year-old who was driving the car when it crashed. Rescuers found the driver's pants pulled down below his knees, within the remains of the ruined car. An autopsy, according to the rumor, revealed cuts on the boy's penis that were consistent with lacerations from human teeth. It was suggested that Murnau had been fellating the fourteen-year-old at the moment of impact, and that he had bit down

A view of **Nosferatu**, the protagonist of F.W. Murnau's seminal horror film.

Whereas Garbo, Murnau, and their entourages represented the underground and the *avant-garde*, MGM with its rigorously supervised studio system, stood for the mainstream film industry.

To his enormous credit, it was Irving Thalberg, second-in-command at MGM, who recoganized the genius of F.W. Murnau.

But after Thalberg's early death in 1936, Murnau, too, died, thereby "condemning" the dilletantish and the edgy to the periphery of American tastes, in favor, instead, of bigger, mainstream films embraced by MGM.

In the photo above, **Irving Thalberg**, with his wife, **Norma Shearer**, appear with **Louis B. Mayer**, the autocratic kingpin of MGM.

on the boy in horror.

The rumor spread fast, and soon reached the offices of Thalberg and Mayer. Based on the fear that its implications might adversely affect Garbo's career, they instructed Howard Strickling to do everything he could to keep the information away from, and out of, the tabloids.

Thalberg phoned Garbo and ordered her not to attend the funeral. She defied him and announced that she was going.

Her lover, the socialite Mercedes de Acosta, wanted to accompany her, but Garbo didn't want their picture taken together. Consequently, she asked Clark to escort her instead, but he declined. At the funeral, fewer than a dozen mourners showed up.

Future films starring Garbo and Clark never materialized. She had a death mask crafted from the face of Murnau's corpse, and she displayed it atop her piano, along with a photograph of Stiller, for many years to come.

In the aftermath, In lieu of any of the much-discussed ideas for another film that paired him with Garbo, Clark was cast in *Possessed* (1931), another picture with Crawford as his female lead.

As Garbo's personal tastes increasingly defined themselves as avant-garde, Europeanized, and bisexual, she increasingly moved away from mainstream studio tastes.

Here are two views of the Cuban-American poet, playwright, socialite and heiress **Mercedes de Acosta** *(photo left)* **in** an unguarded moment with **Greta Garbo.** Her "unclosetedness" was rare and daring during her heyday, and devastatingly dangerous to the careers of the lesbian superstars she favored.

In 2020, the authors of this book released a biography of the fabled "superlesbian," **Mercedes de Acosta,** who had managed to seduce greater numbers of female celebrities than anyone else in the history of show-biz. Alla Nazimova, Katharine Cornell, Marlene Dietrich, Pola Negri, and Isadora Duncan were only a few of those she later publicized.

(Photo left) The very durable, spectacularly talented, and always reliable Joan Crawford eventually emerged as an easier, less fraught, screen partner than Garbo.

Here's **Clark Gable** with **Joan Crawford** in *Possessed* (1931)

Episode 43

Possessed (1931)

It was Louis B. Mayer who thought Gable and Crawford would be "dynamite together" onscreen. He ordered that they be cast together in movies that included *Dance, Fools, Dance*; *Laughing Sinners* and *Possessed* (each released in 1931); *Chained* and *Foresaking All Others* (both released in 1934); *Love on the Run* (1936); and *Strange Cargo* (1940).

"We often talked about marriage, but in some way feared it would be the end of our love affair," Crawford later claimed. "He was my dream lover, and I figured it would be better to live with a dream unfulfilled than to live with a dream broken."

"In spite of his very macho aura, Clark was a very sensitive and loving man," she said. "He was afraid to show his tender side, fearing it would destroy his image. He was both a woman's man and a man's man. A lot of men can't perform both roles."

"Clark represented man at his most primeval—valiant, rough and ready with the passion of a wild beast. He had absolutely no fancy airs or parlor graces. Gable had more balls than any man I ever knew, although the prick needed a little work."

Crawford's first husband, Douglas Fairbanks Jr., resented her nicknames for body parts—a kiss was "a goober;" her breasts were "ninny pies;" and screwing was "going to heaven." In contrast, Gable found these pet names amusing. She nicknamed his penis "Willie," and referred to her vagina as "the gateway to paradise."

When confronted with assessments that he was a lousy lay, Gable told Spencer Tracy, "Well, that means I need to practice a lot more."

Joan Blondell once claimed, "Any woman who doesn't fall for Clark is dead meat."

Once, when he and Tracy were standing before an array of glamourous enlarged photographs of leading female stars of MGM, Gable bragged, "I've had every one of them."

Later, after standing beside Franchot Tone at a urinal, he said, "Now I know why Joan's second husband is known as 'Jawbreaker.'"

"When I first met Clark," Crawford confessed to director Clarence Brown, "he sent an electric bolt through me. I couldn't wait for him to deflower me."

"Our ambitions were grandiose. I would lay on any casting couch, and Clark even let my best buddy, (actor) William Haines, fuck him in the ass in exchange for getting him small roles in three of his next movies."

Indeed, **Joan Crawford**—inspired, no doubt, by her growing disenchantement with her real-life husband (Fairbanks, Jr.) and her increasing infatuation with Clark Gable, gave every indication of being POSSESSED throughout the course of filming it.

"Clark and I had too wild a nature to settle into a marriage with each other," Crawford recalled. "We would never be faithful. You see, both of us had delinquent hearts."

Clark Gable and Joan Crawford had not seen each other for several weeks when they came together for lunch at MGM with Clarence Brown. He had last helmed Clark in *A Free Soul* (1931), in which he co-starred with Norma Shearer.

The day before, scriptwriter Lenore J. Coffee had personally delivered to them the script for their new movie, entitled *Possessed*. She had begun her screenwriting career by working, for $50 a week, on a script that would feature Clara Kimball Young. *[Famous during the Silent Era for her portrayal of virtuous heroines, by 1915, Young's popularity was equivalent to that of Mary Pickford, the Gish sisters, and Mabel Normand.]*

In time, Coffee would be twice Oscar nominated for Best Adapted Screenplay—the first for *Street of Chance* (1929) and the second for *Four Daughters* (1938), based on a short story Fannie Hurst.

When she handed Clark a copy of her most recent screenplay, she seemed disillusioned and disenchanted. "I'm tired of the studio system. They pick your brain, break your heart, and ruin your digestion. What do you get out of it? Nothing but a lousy fortune!"

Brown had already cast the major roles: Crawford would take top billing as Marian Martin, with Clark, her leading man, as Mark Whitney.

In supporting roles, the lackluster Wallace Ford would be cast as Al Manning; "Skeets" Gallagher as Wally Stuart; Frank Conroy as Horace Travers; Marjorie White as Vernice LaVerne; and John Miljan as John Driscoll.

Possessed would be the picture that established "Crawford & Gable" as a screen duo, with her receiving top billing, much to his displeasure.

The script included a heady mix of sex and politics. Crawford's use of sex to advance herself in the world ran afoul of censors.

The film opens with Crawford as a bored worker in a small town paper factory. She dreams of greater things, especially replacing her dull factory worker boyfriend, Al Manning (Ford).

At the rail station, she encounters Wally Stuart (Gallagher), who suggests she might find a better life in New York. She gets "incorrect signals," and imagines, wrongly, that he might "sponsor" her if and when she lands in Manhattan.

In his elegant apartment, he rejects her. In the elevator on the way back to the lobby, she encounters Mark Whitney (Clark), who is immediately smitten with her, and then follows him back into Stuart's apartment. In a short time, she becomes his mistress, living in luxury and dressed in finery.

Because he's running for political office, a cover-up is conceived. She will claim to be Mrs. Moreland, a reputed rich divorcée.

Near the end of the film, when he is at a campaign rally running for governor, sheets of paper litter the auditorium after being dropped from balcony seats. Issued by his adversaries, they link him with his mistress.

Marian rises to the challenge and delivers an impassioned speech to the audience defending her lover and

Joan Crawford, seen here as a factory girl in Erie, PA who's miserably frustrated with her circumstances and with her hayseed onscreen husband, **Wallace Ford.**

She flees to the Big City. There, she becomes emotionally "possessed" by the character played by Clark.

Moviegoers (many of them frustrated with their lives, too) agreed that no one could portray abject despair and raw ambition better than Joan.

Crawford's entree into Hollywood Royalty began with her marriage, in 1929, to **Douglas Fairbanks Jr.** Even at the time—confronted as she was by the savage hostility of Fairbank's family—she didn't seem that happy. From its beginning to its dismal end, neither of them was faithful to each other.

candidate.

Before THE END is splashed across the screen, we see him chasing after her, grabbing her, and holding her in a tight embrace. The viewer never knows if he will become the new governor or not.

***

Wallace Ford, as the actor who instigated the Crawford character's migration to the big city, was born Samuel Grundy Jones in England in 1898. His working-class parents were too poor to raise him, and he was placed in an orphanage at the age of three. When he was seven, he was shipped to Canada as part of Britian's program to populate Commonwealth countries.

Moved from one family to another, he finally could take it no more and fled. At the age of eleven, he joined a traveling vaudeville troupe, performing with the Winnipeg Kiddies.

In 1914, when he was sixteen, Samuel and another youth named Wallace Ford headed south from Canada to the U.S. to seek their fortune. The train in which they were stowaways crashed, and Ford was killed. That very night, Samuel adopted his name of Wallace Ford.

The newly named Ford served n the U.S. Cavalry during World War I, later becoming an actor with a stage company that led to roles on Broadway.

He made his first credited film debut in *Possessed* and was given third billing, after Crawford and Clark. After that, he was assigned the lead in MGM's *Freaks*, one of the most controversial movies of the 1930s.

His career was launched, leading to 150 films over a span of three decades. Most of his work was in B movies, where he was often cast as a "regular Joe."

Richard ("Skeets") Gallagher, born in Indiana in 1891, had blue eyes and naturally blonde hair that was tinged with gray from the age of 16. As a young man, he studied to become a lawyer, later switching to vaudeville. He signed with Paramount, appearing in his first feature film, Frank Capra's *For the Love of Mike* (927), a silent film lost to history.

Frank Conway, born in England in 1890, launched his career by appearing in plays by Shakespeare in his home country. He emigrated to the United States in 1915. He later appeared in 40 Broadway plays from 1913 to 1962. In 1939, he co-starred with Tallulah Bankhead in Lillian Hellman's *The Little Foxes*.

On the set of *Possessed*, Clark had a reunion with actor John Miljan, with whom he had last appeared in *The Secret Six*.

***

Possessed was shot for a budget of $380,000, taking in $1.6 million at the box office.

James B. Quirk in *Photoplay* wrote, "If Joan Crawford weren't so good, Clark Gable could have had the picture to himself."

The New York Times found his performance "nicely restrained."

Variety dug into Clark the actor: "He is again the stiff, cold-blooded, manly leading man. Since graduating from gangster parts, he failed to register any strong emotions. Happy or sad, it's always the same Gable. Only when the script calls for him to slap Miss Crawford in the face, calling her a 'little tramp' and telling her to

SUAVE SWAIN: **Gable** getting histrionic with **Crawford** in *Possessed*. Audiences loved it.

The backdrop of *Possessed* was the grinding depths of the Great Depression. But fear not....**Joan** (economically, at least) has hit the jackpot.

Here's an Art Deco view of an *uber* glam cocktail hour in which **Joan** is loved...by a fomally dressed and terribly attractive State Governor, as portrayed by **Clark**. The audience sees, up close and personal, that dreams can, indeed, come true.

scram, does anything register on the Gable horizon. One sobbie said that in Gable's face, there is cruelty, so maybe that's what his fans like."

Film Daily wrote, "This man, Clark Gable, that we've been waiting for a little over a year, has come a long way from his villain roles. His performance suggests he may become a solid actor. A personality he already is, but so much talent will take him a good deal farther than just good looks."

Still harboring a crush on Clark, Adela Rogers St. Johns wrote, "In *Possessed*, Clark Gable is so hot he almost burns down Hollywood."

A gross exaggeration, of course, but she was making a point.

Ben Maddox, who had sampled Clark's charms, exclaimed, "The day of fairy pansies as leading men died with silent pictures. John Gilbert, Valentino, and Ramon Novarro are dead meat. Using his fists and filled with sarcastic wisecracks, this masculine hero of 1931, Gable himself, brings a new screen image. He has no competitor at MGM. His major rival over at Paramount is Gary Cooper. Each of them has horny women wetting their underwear and homos drooling at the mouth."

[Of course, Maddox's editor had to cut several lines of that appraisal.]

During the pre-production of *Possessed*, Crawford discovered that she was pregnant. She knew it was Clark's child, since she was no longer sharing intimacies with her husband, Douglas Fairbanks Jr.

She appealed to Howard Strickling, MGM's fixer. As ordered by Louis B. Mayer, he arranged to have her sent to the doctor who performed abortions for MGM stars,.

"I actually wanted the child," she said. "I just knew it would be a boy. Could you imagine what a son of Clark Gable and Joan Crawford would look like? He would probably grow up to become the most fabulous-looking screen actor of all time."

Clark, as Crawford later admitted in a memoir, offered her great comfort during the making of *Possessed*. She was in the final chapter of her marriage to Fairbanks.

"I felt saturated with defeat in my personal life. That was actually good for the role I was playing, where I had to suggest pathos. Doug was leaving me, but Clark was there for me. This magnetic man had more sheer male magic than anyone in Hollywood. Every woman looked at him with desire. He knew it, too. It was as much of him as breathing."

"When our on-screen love scenes ended, our love for each other didn't stop there," she said. "We were playing characters very much like ourselves. All day long, we would look in each other's eyes. The reflections were both glorious and hopeless. We both were in marriages where love had gone. In his case, love was never there to begin with."

Rumors spread of the Crawford/Gable affair. Tantalizingly, Louella Parsons wrote, "What star is interested in her leading man?"

When Irving Thalberg learned that rumors about Crawford's abortion of Clark's child were sweeping through Hollywood, he summoned both of them into his office. Then he delivered a stern ultimatum: If they didn't end their affair, Mayer would probably have them fired.

Crawford was sent on a month-long press and PR tour of Europe with her alienated husband, with a special emphasis on London. There, they booked into different suites at the same hotel, where he was rumored to have engaged in seductions of three other women.

Shortly after they returned to Hollywood, she filed for divorce.

Small-town virtue, in Joan's case, eventually triumphs. In *upper photo*, **Joan** nobly testifies in favor of her paramour before (*lower photo*) fleeing from the scene in tears.

In the aftermath, Clark is exonerated, they marry, and live happily ever after.

Episode 44

HELL DIVERS (1932)

"Right from the beginning, I didn't want to star in *Hell Divers*," Clark said, years after it was wrapped. "Especially with Wallace Beery again in the male lead. When I sat through the final cut, I liked it even less. I regretted I was forced to make the picture."

Both Clark and Beery were cast as petty officers in the U.S. Naval Air Force. As in private life, they were also intensely competitive rivals on screen.

Hell Divers was both produced and directed by George W. Hill, who had previously helmed both Beery and Clark in *The Secret Six*. "Shall I take credit for discovering THE Clark Gable?" Hill asked the actor.

"Better not," Clark said. "Too many people already claim that dishonor."

The very complicated military plot was based very loosely on the silent screen classic *What Price Glory?* in which Clark made a small, uncredited appearance.

The current film was shot before Clark grew his famous mustache.

He not only regretted Beery's star billing, but he resented the fact that his salary far exceeded his own—in fact, Beery, during that brief period, was still the highest paid actor in Hollywood.

Encountering Clark again, Beery told him, "I'm tired of reading that you and Gary Cooper are the leading He-Men of Hollywood. Hell, I'm the leading He-Man. With my ugly mug, I just ooze masculinity. I make you two homos look like sissies."

Instead of slugging Beery, Clark turned and walked away.

Beery had been cast as "Windy" Riker; Clark as Steve Nelson; Conrad Nagel as "Duke" Johnson; Dorothy Jordan as Ann Mitchell; Marjorie Rambeau as Mame Kelsey; Marie Prevost as Lulu Farnsworth; Cliff Richards as "Baldy"; John Miljan as Lt. Commander Jack Griffin; and Frank Conroy as the ship's chaplain. In an uncredited role, the future movie star, Robert Young appears very briefly, near the end, as a pilot named Graham.

Clark survived a provocative introduction to Conrad

Hell Divers was released during the peak years of Hollywood's aviation craze. It had peaked with the release, a year before, of Howard Hughes' *Hell's Angels* (1930; *see photo, left*) an ode to the aerial gymnastics of experimental warplanes and the sexual dynamics of the men who flew them. In the photo above, from *Hell Divers*, **Clark** —before strapping himself into a cockpit, delivers a raffish, daredevil salute.

Nagel: "Guys like you are making me a memory of yesterday."

He wasn't joking. He had been one of those handsome leading men of the 1920s like John Gilbert and Ramon Novarro, all of whom made women swoon.

Nagel stood six feet tall, with blue eyes, wavy blonde hair. and an All-American charm.

A son of Iowa, born in 1892, he became both a stage and film actor. He achieved stardom in his first film, based on the classic novel *Little Women*, written by Louisa May Alcott in 1868. When sound came, his baritone voice was ideal for talkies.

Nagel recalled a night in the 1920s at the peak of his film popularity: He and his first wife, Ruth Helms (they were married from 1924 to 1934), wanted to go to the movies. "We couldn't find a theater nearby in which I was not starring. We'd already seen my films, so we went home, instead."

In May of 1927, Nagel and three dozen other industry insiders founded the Academy of Motion Pictures Arts and Sciences. Fellow founders included both Mary Pickford and Douglas Fairbanks Sr. Nagel was also a founding member of the Screen Actors Guild (SAG).

A daughter of Tennessee, Southern belle Dorothy Jordan, born in 1906, had a short career in early talkies. She made her debut in the 1929 film, *The Taming of the Shrew*. Over the next four years, she would star in 22 movies before leaving the screen in 1933.

She had co-starred in *Min and Bill* (1930) with Beery and Marie Dressler, and in *Cabin in the Cotton* (1932) with a very young Bette Davis.

Jordan married Merian C. Cooper, who co-wrote, produced, and directed *King Kong* (1933).

In 1938, she attempted a comeback, showing up for a screen test for *Gone With the Wind*, auditioning for the role of Melanie Wilkes. The results of her test were rejected by

Based on the feigned camaraderie of **Wallace Beery** and **Clark Gable** in the photos above, it's hard to recognize that the two actors genuinely hated each other.

But whereas Beery's career was on the verge of a crash-landing, Clark's was about to soar into the wild blue yonder.

 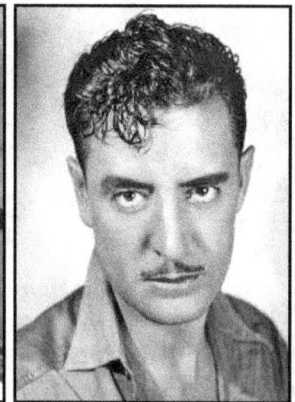  

HOMOPHOBIC TERROR: The once-illustrious matinee idol and household name, **Conrad Nagel** *(far right)* noted that with the arrival of Clark Gable on the cinema circuit, he had devolved into being perceived as "one of those fairy pansies your journalist friend (Ben Maddox) writes about."

Other leading men slurred as "fairy pansies" by Maddox and by other cruel and mean-spirited publicists of their day included *(left to right, above)*, **Rudolph Valentino, John Gilbert,** and **Ramon Novarro.**

David O. Selznick, who awarded the role, instead, to Olivia de Havilland.

In *Hell Divers*, Clark renewed his friendship with Marie Provost, with whom he'd had a brief fling during the filming of *Sporting Blood*. In *Hell Divers*, the hottest scene in the movie is when she, as the seductive Lulu, comes on to him.

Tragically, Provost came to a horrible ending on January 21, 1937. She died alone, except for her dog, at the age of 40, suffering from acute alcoholism and malnutrition. Her imprisoned pet, locked up in the room with her, survived by eating part of her left leg.

It was his barking that led to her body being discovered. In her bedroom were several empty liquor bottles and a promissory note *(aka, an I.O.U.)* to Joan Crawford for $110.

Like Clark himself, Crawford, too, had a brief fling with Prevost.

Crawford also paid for Prevost's funeral, which was attended by, among others, Barbara Stanwyck, Douglas Fairbanks Jr., and Clark.

On the set of *Hell Divers*, Clark also had reunions with several actors with whom he had starred. Those included what he called "that good ol' gal," Marjorie Rambeau. She cautioned him, "Don't worry. I won't be begging you to bang me this time. After two husbands, I married Francis Gudger in 1931. It took a couple of years, but I finally taught him how to satisfy me."

"I'm sorry I missed my chance," he said gallantly, but with a smirk.

Clark told actor John Miljan, "I think you follow me around." Miljan had last been cast with Garbo and Clark in *Susan Lenox: Her Fall and Rise*.

Clark had appeared with Frank Conroy in *Possessed*, also with Crawford.

He also was cast once again with Cliff Edwards ("Ukulele Ike") with whom he had recently co-starred alongside Joan Crawford in *Laughing Sinners*.

***

As **Gable**'s cinematic fame increased, so did his supposed "responsibility" for demonstrating how a man will inevitably have to deal with "tipsy, out of control broads."

In the photo above, a press and PR shot for *Hell Divers*, "good girl" **Dorothy Jordan** watches with dismay as "that tramp" played by **Marie Prevost** gets amorous.

Hell Divers emerges as a movie about men and machines. Although Jordan provides a token of "genuine love" interest, she is eliminated from the script before the end of the third reel.

Marjorie Rambeau—a by-then over-the-hill argument for the allure of bawdy older women—emoting over cocktails with **Clark Gable** in *Hell Divers*.

Even **Robert Young** appeared briefly, almost as an afterthought, as a bit player in *Hell Divers*.

Decades later, as part of an irony-soaked confession, he said, "All those years at MGM I hid a black terror behind a cheerful face."

Variety wrote, "No other actor than Beery and Gable is important on performance. It boils down to those two. The women have bit parts, while Gable is not placed to advantage in this assignment. So it boils down to him and Beery. There has been much written about Beery and also about Gable. But, as a combination, they don't promise much."

Film Daily interpreted *Hell Divers* as "an intense study of and a celluloid display of naval aviation. It is unusually long on aerial display and short on ground entertainment. Women will like the inclusion of Gable."

The Hollywood Reporter claimed, "Clark Gable and Dorothy Jordan provide the love interest. Miss Jordan is eliminated from the screen by the end of the third reel."

Hell Divers earned $1,250,000 at the box office in the U.S. and Canada, and another $920,000 abroad.

***

Hot on the heels of Howard Hughes' pioneering (and way overbudget **Hell's Angels**, **Hell Divers** was assessed as a showcase of America's aviation superiority, with special focus on the then-novel Curtiss F8C-4 Helldiver as the undercover star of the show. **Clark Gable** appears above as the photogenic symbol of American grit and technological ingenuity, firing from a precarious perch as a Top Gun.

Episode 45

Polly of the Circus (1932)

After his disappointing role in *Hell Divers*, Clark was hoping for a more exciting part in his next picture. To his disappointment, he learned that he had been assigned as the leading man to Marion Davies, the mistress of press baron William Randolph Hearst.

Ironically, as a struggling actor in 1922 in Portland, Oregon, he had appeared in "that old chestnut," a revival of the 1907 Broadway staple, *Polly of the Circus*, by Margaret Mayo. It involved a romance between a clergyman and a circus tart. He didn't like it then, and he liked it even less during the waning weeks of 1931.

In reference to his leading lady, he also lodged a complaint with the director, Albert Santell: "I'll probably have to screw the bitch, since I hear Hearst is past his prime in the boudoir."

He had detested the original script, where he would be cast as a Catholic priest, and Davies as a trapeze artist in a circus. In a rewrite, his role was changed to a Protestant pastor. He also told Santell, "The role would be better suited for Robert Montgomery."

At the time *Polly* went into production, Marion Davies was an unofficial Empress, reigning over Hollywood's most glittering era.

Born Marion Cecille Douras in Brooklyn in 1897, she was educated in a convent. When she ws old enough, she fled from school and found work on Broadway as a dancer in *The Ziegfeld Follies*. It was on stage in 1916 that the 19-year-old dancer was spotted by the fabulously wealthy 52-year-old tycoon. He began showing up every night, sitting in the front row to watch Davies.

Within two weeks, she became his mistress. Hearst also took over the management of her career, promising her a quick road to stardom.

To promote her as a film star, he founded Cosmopolitan Pictures, with links to MGM. By 1924, Davies was the number one box office attraction in America, at least temporarily.

At the time, she'd already starred in two "big hit" silent movies: *When Knighthood Was in Flower* (1922), and *Little Old New York* (1923). He invested $7 million to promote her career, the equivalent of $145 million in today's currency.

Over a 20-year period, Davies appeared in 45 feature films.

During Hearst's long affair with Davies, he remained married to Millicent Veronica Willson, born in New York in 1882. She had been a vaudeville performer whom Hearst had been at-

Thrown into circumstances that in other instances would have guaranteed undying jealously and hatred, **Marion Davies** had a gift for morphing potential enemies into allies and friends. Such was the case with **Clark Gable**. In the *lower photo*, wearing a clerical collar, he gazes in admiration—with other spectators—at *Polly of the Circus* during one of her high-trapeze stunts.

tracted to, marrying her in 1903.

When his affair with Davies began, she refused to give him a divorce. She died in 1974 at the age of 92. She had remained close to their five sons for all her life. Their names were William Jr., George, John, Randolph, and David.

In California, Hearst erected the legendary castle, San Simeon, north of Los Angeles, overlooking the Pacific Ocean. The sprawling estate was filled with Greek statues and celestial suites at which Hearst and Davies entertained not only the elite of Hollywood, but major figures in politics, science, and the arts.

With what was called "a passion for acquisition," Hearst bought (at Depression-era prices) art, antiques, statuary, textiles, and silverware on a scale described as "epic." Of special interest were historically important architectural elements (including entire rooms, doors, porticos, stonework, and paneling, all of them priceless art objects of historic merit, from Europe, especially Spain. When the playwright, George Bernard Shaw visited, he quipped, "This is the kind of castle God would have erected if he had the money."

Davies became known for her sense of humor. When Albert Einstein came to visit, she asked him, "Why don't you get a haircut? I'll lend you the money."

President Calvin Coolidge, a teetotaler, was also an honored guest. She served him a vintage Tokay wine from their cellar, telling him it was a luscious non-alcoholic fruit drink. He liked it so much he asked for another glass and another glass, pronouncing it "the most refreshing drink I've ever had."

***

Assigned the difficult task of director, Albert Santell was born in San Francisco in 1895 and became both a director and film producer. Over the course of his career (1915-1946), he helmed more than sixty motion pictures.

With his rising new power at MGM, Clark wanted more money. Mayer tried to bribe him with the offer of a $10,000 custom-made car, but, wisely, Clark wanted that salary hike more than the vehicle.

After the first day on the set, he disappeared, opting to hide out in Palm Springs. Only his agent, Minna Wallis, knew where he was. Louis B. Mayer threatened to fire him, telling Wallis, "If he doesn't report to work, I'll not only can him, but see that he doesn't work again in this town."

As justification for his demand for a salary increase, Clark claimed that he had been the screen replacement for John Gilbert, who had once drawn $520,000 a year. Clark had demanded a salary hike to $2,000 a week.

Finally, in part to appease his mistress, Marion Davies, Hearst himself intervened. Clark ended up with a two-year contract that specified a salary of $2,000 a week. Mayer's lack of *largesse* stemmed in part from

Whereas the splendours of Hearst's hilltop estate at San Simeon are described in the text of this episode, his beach house in Santa Monica (aka "**Ocean House**') elicited jealousy, wonder, and amazement from virtually everyone in L.A.

Actress Colleen Moore described it as "the biggest house on the beach – the beach between San Diego and Vancouver." Built on what had been 15 separate oceanfront lots, it had 100-plus rooms, 36 fireplaces and 55 bathrooms.

Views of **William Randolph Hearst** with his mainstream, "official" family; Upper photo, at home with **Millicent Willson Hearst** and some of their children in 1902, and *(lower photos)* portraits of Millicent and William from the time of his service as U.S. Congressman (1903-1907) from Brooklyn and Staten Island

MGM's million dollar deficit from the previous season. Although Gable's movies had made a profit, many others produced by MGM had not.

With a revised script, shooting began. The circus arrives in a small town where the Rev. John Hartley (Gable) administers a small congregation.

The star, Polly Fisher (Davies), is a trapeze artist. In one daring stunt, she falls fifty feet, hitting the ground. There was no net.

Unconscious, and on the verge of death, she's carried to the nearest house, which is where Hartley lives. A doctor advises that she is not to be moved. During his prolonged term as her caregiver, Hartley falls in love.

They eventually get married, over the objections of Bishop James Northcott (C. Aubrey Smith). After his wedding to this "wicked show trollop," Hartley is dismissed as a pastor. *[Fear not: It will all work out for a happy ending.]*

A Londoner, Smith was born in 1863. As a young man, he'd become a noted cricketer and film and stage actor. He took time off to head to South Africa in 1888 to prospect for gold but caught pneumonia and was pronounced dead. Obviously, the doctor was wrong.

In Hollywood in 1932, he founded a cricket club, inviting Clark to join. He rejected the offer, but English actors who included Laurence Olivier, David Niven, and Leslie Howard joined up. Before that, in 1895, Smith had appeared on Broadway as Henry Higgins in George Bernard Shaw's *Pygmalion*.

In Hollywood, Smith found a niche playing officer-and-gentleman roles, co-starring with such actors as Greta Garbo, Vivien Leigh, Elizabeth Taylor, Ronald Colman, Maurice Chevalier, and Gary Cooper.

Cast as Eric Alvarez in *Polly*, Guinn ("Big Boy") Williams was the Hollywood star that Clark detested more than all others. Crude, opinionated, toxically macho, and standing six feet, two inches, he had emerged from Texas in 1899. His nickname derived from his muscular build, which he had developed while riding a vast ranch as a cowboy.

Will Rogers discovered him and cast him in a movie. Williams would go on to work with such stars as Charles Farrell, Janet Gaynor, and Fannie Brice.

He usually starred in Westerns, co-starring with Errol Flynn, Gary Cooper, John Wayne, and Robert Mitchum, often wearing his trademark ten-gallon hat.

When he worked with Johnny Mack Brown in *The Great Meadow*, Williams heard gossip that Brown and Clark had once been "an item."

At one point, Big Boy was engaged to marry Lupe Velez, that "Mexican Spitfire." At a wild party at the home of Flynn, she broke off their engagement, before breaking a framed portrait of her betrothed, pulling down her panties, and urinating on it.

Confronting Clark on the set of *Polly of the Circus*, he told Clark, "I hear you're a cocksucking fairy. If you come on to me, I'll see that you end up in the hospital."

Enraged, Clark headed toward him, but was restrained by two stagehands.

In contrast, Clark met and befriended a young, then-unknown actor named Ray Milland. He appeared near the end of *Polly* in an uncredited role as a church usher. A dazzling film career awaited him reaching its peak when he won a Best Actor Oscar for *The Lost Weekend* in 1945.

Bette Davis once pronounced Milland "a shit," but he managed very well at Paramount, starring with Gene Tierney, Veronica Lake,

An unconventional but high-functioning love affair: **Marion Davies** with **William Randolph Hearst.**

Belligerent, obnoxious, mean-spirited, and provocative, C-list cowboy star **Guinn Williams** offended collegues from every aspect of the film industry, including Clark Gable. His status as a box office draw diminished as his reputation as an a**hole grew. He was eventually relegated to low-end sh**-kicking roles in D-list westerns.

Jean Arthur, Marlene Dietrich, Lana Turner, Maureen O'Hara, Loretta Young, and Jane Wyman.

Years later, when asked about working with Clark Gable, Milland said, "The only thing we had in common is that both of us fucked Grace Kelly."

***

Polly of the Circus did little to further the careers of either Clark Gable or Marion Davies.

Motion Picture Herald wrote: "Don't try to foist off Clark Gable as a preacher. He simply does not register as a member of the clergy. Casting of this picture showed gross carelessness."

Film Daily found that the casting of Clark as a clergyman "will disappoint many of his female fans."

John Gammie in *London Film Variety* wrote: "American critics favor the view that the screen's fashionable heavy lover is wasted in a role that gives him absolutely no scope for his caveman tactics. I disagree. I think Gable makes a much better minister than a 'typed' actor of the milksop variety would have done. He rubs off the edges of his film personality in a characterization that is virile without being tough."

A failure at the box office, *Polly* earned $350,000 in the U.S and $170,000 elsewhere, resulting in a profit of only $20,000.

Years later, a book was published called *The Golden Turkey Awards* by Harry and Michael Medved. Within it, they quipped: "What a man of the cloth Clark Gable makes. He plays a minister like an overgrown altar boy. The beatific smile he affects for the party looks greasy and obsequious—as if Uriah Heap has taken Holy Orders."

[Uriah Heap was a rock band formed in London in 1969. They were pioneers of the hard rock, heavy metal, and progressive rock genres, selling 40 million records worldwide.]

***

Marion Davies was famous for her stutter, and many of her film scenes had to be reshot. She often said words such as "*v-v—very*" and "*s-s-short*."

Although she was widely known (and sometimes condemned) for her long-running affair with Hearst, she was never faithful. She could be quite frank about him at times: "When he starts jawing, he bores me stiff. And certainly, he's not so wonderful behind the barn. I can find a million better lays any Wednesday. You know what he gives me, sugar? He gives me the feeling I'm worth something. He has sons as old as I am. He's kind and good to me, and I will never walk out on him."

Even before Clark co-starred with her, he knew of her reputation for seducing her leading men. Exception to that

Ray Milland in his most famous role, that of an alcoholic struggling to quit drinking in ***The Lost Weekend*** (1945). Directed by Billy Wilder and winner of multiple film awards, it (brutally) addressed one of the era's most vexing and widespread addictions: Alcoholism.

There had been an earlier version of ***Polly of the Circus***, a silent version starring **Mae Marsh** released in 1917. Re-releasing it in 1932 with a different set of stars (i.e., Marion Davies and Clark Gable) "seemed like a good (and wholesome) idea at the time." As the means to getting it made as a starring vehicle for his *inamorata*, Hearst established and funded an all-new studio, **Cosmopolitan Pictures.**

included gay actors William Haines and Nils Asther.

Her list of lovers is long—not just with movie stars, but with such luminaries as Joseph Kennedy, father of a future president. She was reported to have had an early fling with Valentino, and she had a long-running affair with Charlie Chaplin that lasted for many years in the 1920s.

She also seduced Lawrence Gray, her co-star in *The Floradora Girl* (1930); Leslie Howard in *Five and Dime* (1931), and Dick Powell in *Hearts Divided* (1936).

Cast in the romantic comedy, *Five and Ten* (1931), Marion played a rich girl of the Fannie Hurst variety. Because of her star power, she could also select her leading man. Its plot had been inspired by the Woolworth heiress, Barbara Hutton.

In a private screening room at MGM, Davies had ordered film clips of some of the leading men being considered as her co-star. Clark appeared on the screen in an episode from his recent *A Free Soul* (1931) in which he roughs up Norma Shearer.

After watching it, Marion announced to Irving Thalberg, "That bruiser Gable is not right for my movie. He'd be better cast as a boxer, a gangster or a villain I don't want him to appear in a picture with me. The part calls for a society man. Gable would not look right in a tuxedo with tails. He looks like Jack Dempsey, a little dumb but muscled."

To her astonishment, when the lights went on, Thalberg made her aware that Clark was sitting nearby, as he had requested the lead in *Five and Ten.*

She looked back at him as he was making his way to the exit, having heard her review of him.

Two days later, after Leslie Howard had been cast as her leading man, Clark walked by her on the studio lot and said: "Hello, Miss Davies. Remember me? I'm the pug who looks like Jack Dempsey."

During the shoot, Thalberg convinced her that Clark Gable was on the verge of becoming the biggest star at MGM.

She changed her mind and demanded him as her co-star in *Polly of the Circus,* her next film.

When Clark learned of this, he told Thalberg, "The dame is out of her mind. She typecast me before. Now she wants me to play a fucking clergyman. Women! Sometimes, I'd like to boil them in oil. They can drive a man crazy with their demands."

During the filming of *Polly,* Davies certainly didn't opt to commute the long distance to and from San Simeon every day, opting to sleepover instead at her 118-room beach house at Santa Monica.

She invited Clark to invent some excuse for Ria Langham and spend his nights there, too. They often dined *à deux,* and were seen walking along the moonlit beach holding hands.

Davies was a very generous person. At the end of the shoot, she promised she would make him her leading man again in a future picture.

On two occasions, when they took off early from the studio, he drove her to Venice, where they enjoyed amusements that included riding the roller coaster.

With *Polly of the Circus* wrapped, Davies invited Clark to go with her to Palm Springs. After a night of love-making, she asked him to drive her two miles from Palm Springs. There, they stopped at a small villa on two acres of land.

He thought they were calling on her friends, but she used a key to unlock the door and casually entered the fully and comfortably furnished six-room villa, which had a beautiful new kitchen.

"Is this your retreat?" he asked.

"No, it's yours. I'm giving it to you as a present."

He grabbed her and hugged and kissed her, suggesting, "You'd better come with me to the bedroom. I'm overheated."

After *Polly of the Circus* wrapped, Clark became part of Davies' inner circle of star-studded friends. He often drove to San Simeon, which lay midway between Los Angeles and San Francisco, on weekends. And he was invited to all the parties she hosted (without Hearst) at the 118-room beach house at Santa Monica.

***

Over the ears, Davies' reputation has been trivialized, maligned, and destroyed, even though Orson Welles claimed she was not the inspiration for Susan Alexander, the mogul's mistress in *Citizen Kane* (1941). That film character—a larcenous, untalented, gold-digging, dim-witted floozie, is familiar to film devotees of *Citizen Kane,* which is still popular. Film historians regard *Citizen Kane* as one of the greatest films ever made, rivaling Humprey Bogart's *Casablanca.*

Of course, newer generations, for the most part, never heard of Marion Davies and have never seen even one of her films.

Many reporters and journalists have described Davies as a dumb blonde, even though she wasn't. She was a woman of wit and charm, who captivated the likes of Sir Winston Churchill, Albert Einstein, George Bernard Shaw, Charles Chaplin, Joseph P. Kennedy, and the King of Siam.

When Louis B. Mayer exited from a private screening of *Citizen Kane*, he was in tears. He tried to buy the negative so he could destroy it.

Davies was devastated by what she felt was her caricature. Hearst advised her, "Ignore the clamor. Go on with your life and hold your head up proudly. Continue to entertain your coterie of friends and admirers. Living well and thriving is the best revenge over the "screeching hyenas."

Originally, Davies had obtained a copy of the film and had it previewed at a screening room in her massive beach house in Santa Monica. Clark Gable was among those invited that night to see it. At several points during the screening, her guests heard Davies cry out. At the end, she ran to her bedroom and locked herself away for several days.

A portrait of Davies reached a new generation in 1999 when the movie *RKO 281* was released. It focused on how Hearst suppressed accounts of it in his newspapers. Melanie Griffith portrayed the Davies character, displaying irritation with Hearst's lifestyle and political views.

In this publicity still from *Citizen Kane* (1941), **Dorothy Comingore** appears with **Orson Welles** in a "knock 'em dead" commentary on the vanity and financial excesses of William Randolph Hearst.

Comingore's acceptance of the role that unattractively trivialized the brains and talent of Hearst's mistress (i.e., Marion Davies) earned Hearst's undying enmity until the end of her unhappy life and her blacklisted career.

There have been several other depictions of Davies in the movies, including the 2010 Netflix release of *Mank,* centering on Herbert J. Mankiewicz, the screenwriter of *Citizen Kane*. Amanda Seyfried portrayed Davies, and for her effort, she won a Best Supporting Actress Oscar.

In recent years, there has been increased speculation as to who Dorothy Comingore (aka Linda Winters) was. She had portrayed Susan Alexander (Kane's mistress) in *Citizen Kane*.

A native daughter of Los Angeles, she was born in 1913. Much of her life is something of a mystery. She was "discovered" by Charlie Chaplin, who did little more for her than seducing her.

Comingore had played small parts in films until Orson Welles selected her for the controversial role of Susan Alexander, a thinly veiled reference to Marion Davies. Thanks to her portrayal, she acquired a powerful enemy — the 78-year-old Hearst himself.

After the release of *Citizen Kane*, the Hearst papers, especially entertainment columnists Walter Winchell and the ferociously conservative Hedda Hopper, did much to damage Comingore's reputation.

When all acting jobs vanished, she morphed into a political activist, championing the civil rights of African Americans and often working with the musician, Lead Belly, and singer Paul Robeson. She wanted to desegregate USO clubs, which were "whites only."

She was later accused of distributing Communist literature and ended up before the House Un-American Activities Committee, where she refused to testify. That was the end of her film career.

On March 10, 1953, she was arrested for prostitution in West Hollywood. She spent the rest of her life struggling with alcoholism, dying in December of 1971 at the age of 58.

***

On a trivia note, the word "Rosebud" featured as a theme in *Citizen Kane* became known to millions. There is much dispute over its origins: In *The New York Review of Books,* author Gore Vidal wrote that Rosebud was Hearst's nickname for the clitoris of Marion Davies, his mistress.

Episode 46

Red Dust (1932)

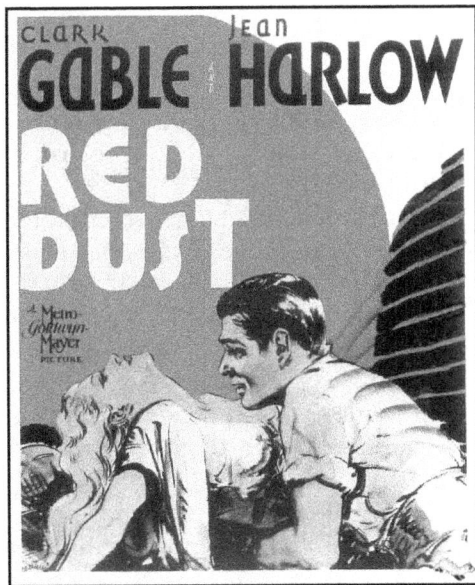

Red Dust originated as a play by Wilson Collison in 1928. MGM ordered John Mahin to tailor it into vehicle for John Gilbert, a leading heartthrob of the silent screen. Unfortunately for Gilbert, during screenings of his first talkie, *His Glorious Night* (1929), his squeaky voice prompted audiences to roar with laughter, especially during his love scenes.

Director Victor Fleming, who would later helm Clark Gable in *Gone With the Wind* (1939), cast "the rugged He-Man" (Gable) in it instead.

His two leading ladies would include Jean Harlow and Mary Astor, with Gene Raymond in fourth billing as the engineer husband of Barbara Willis (Astor).

The setting is a rubber plantation in French Indochina (now Vietnam). The plantation owner, Dennis Carson (Gable) becomes involved in a love triangle with the whorish Vantine (Harlow) and the dour but more ladylike Astor character.

In one of its most memorable scenes, Harlow stripped nude for a bath in a rainbarrel full of drinking water. At the end of her scene, she stood up, exposing her breasts to the camera, and calling out, "Here's one for the boys in the lab!" Of course, although that moment was removed from the final cut, photos of Harlow with her breasts exposed gained wide (private) circulation.

Nigel Cawthorne wrote: "Harlow and Gable made love as if the camera were not there. Even when the camera wasn't rolling, they couldn't keep from touching each other."

Fleming recalled, "I wish I could have filmed their love scenes in her dressing room. I bet they were hot. From the sounds that emerged from her dressing room, Harlow seemed to enjoy 'the Gable rape.' I found later that our horndog also slipped around and plugged Astor on three different occasions."

John Mahlin, after he turned in his screenplay, remained on the set to see the scenes shot. He admitted to Fleming, "I've got a crush on Clark. He's got the eyes of a seductive woman, but the physique of a raging bull. One night in my bed, I can make him give up gals for life."

Producer Hunt Stromberg also developed a crush on Gable and had some X-rated scenes filmed. They never made it into the final cut, but became part of the producer's large (personal) inventory of porn.

Gene Raymond also developed a years-long crush on Gable. They shared the same dressing room.

In *Red Dust*, **Gable** and his wisecracking co-star, the much-younger platinum blonde vixen **Jean Harlow**, got along beautifully both on the set and during their "impossible to conceal" sexual affair.

This photo captures the spontaneous humor that elevated *Red Dust* into a genuinely charming (thanks, in large part, to Harlow) love story..

At the end of the shoot, Fleming told Louis B. Mayer, "I made a great picture, even though I was working with a coven of pansies who seemed to feel that the male penis was God's gift to the world."

Fleming and Gable bonded, and years later, Gable would demand that Fleming commandeer the direction of *Gone With the Wind* (1939) after the gay director George Cukor was booted.

"Clark and I shared at least one thing in common," Fleming told his friends. "When I directed *Red Dust*, I was coming off affairs from both Clara Bow and Norma Shearer. Of course, Gable had had them both before I got into their snatches."

***

Gene Raymond, born in Manhattan in 1908, was an actor, singer, composer, screenwriter, director, producer, and decorated pilot in World War II.

He'd made his stage debut at the age of 17, appearing with Humphrey Bogart in *The Cradle Snatchers* (1925).

His blonde good looks, classic profile, and youthful exuberance got him a summons to Hollywood, where he began appearing with such stars as W.C. Fields, Loretta Young, and Charles Laughton, who chased after him.

Raymond wrote songs and appeared in musicals with Ann Sheridan. He met the MGM songbird Jeanette MacDonald who sang many of the songs he'd written.

Victor Fleming noted that Raymond was love struck by Clark when they co-starred with Mary Astor and Jean Harlow in *Red Dust*.

In a deliberately provocative move, Fleming assigned Raymond to Gable's dressing room.

Clark could have kicked him out, but he was won over by Raymond's charm and personality.

"I knew the kid was hot for me, but I wasn't putting out. I'd never had anyone who worshipped even my dirty underwear before. I never let him go for the goodie, but he was always there waiting with a bath towel when I emerged from the shower."

"Gene spent a lot of time fussing with my hair," Clark claimed. "I credit him for giving me that seductive look whenever a strand of my hair fell down over my forehead. Gene even shined my shoes and took care of my clothing, helping me get dressed. I should have given in to him, but I merely teased him. On looking back, I feel ashamed for my tantalizing tease of the guy."

Raymond had excelled in gymnastics and tennis, and he urged Clark to work out more and build up a more muscular frame.

George Sidney later called Raymond "the most gorgeous thing that the world has ever seen."

Although he didn't get Clark, Raymond was known for seducing some of the major box office stars of Hollywood, including John Barrymore, Errol Flynn, Gary Cooper, Ramon Novarro, and Tyrone Power. Hollywood insiders predicted that Raymond's marriage to Jeanette MacDonald would last less than two weeks. Amazingly, their marriage staggered on for 28 years, ending with MacDonald's death in 1965.

She certainly knew he was gay. Biographer Sharon Rich wrote that on their honeymoon, MacDonald caught her husband in bed with Buddy Rogers, the third husband of Mary Pickford.

Throughout their long marriage, Raymond and MacDonald maintained separate bedrooms, and they never had any kids. It was revealed that Raymond "was physically unable to produce a child."

MacDonald, however, did have pregnancies from other men— including her singing co-star, Nelson

In *Red Dust*, **Gene Raymond** *(left)* played the naïve, self-involved young husband to the "utterly without humor" emotionally isolated character played by **Mary Astor**. Midway through the film, she falls briefly (but madly) in love with Gable.

Portrait of a Marriage: *Upper left*: The temperamental songbird **Jeanette MacDonald** poses operatically next to a headshot of her sometimes notorious husband, blonde and beautiful **Gene Raymond**.

In the lower photo, **MacDonald** and **Raymond** are seen together at the races in the 1930s. No one expected their marriage to survive. Surprisingly, for decades, it did.

Eddy—but each ended in miscarriage.

MacDonald's diary was sold at auction in 2015. She wrote of living in separate bedrooms during her marriage to Raymond, and of his physical neglect and abuse of her. He often left her alone for a month or two at a time.

Her diary ends on November 1, 1963, when she flew to Houston for heart surgery. Whereas she died within two years, Raymond lived until 1998, dying at the age of 89.

In this press & PR photo, director **Victor Fleming** (seated in foreground on the left) guides **Harlow** and **Gable** through an intimate Pre-Code scene in *Red Dust*.

***

"Mary Astor looked like a cold dish until you got her bloomers off…and then she became a wildcat." So claimed Clark, who had a fling with her during the making of *Red Dust* when Jean Harlow wasn't keeping him otherwise occupied.

[Perhaps Gary Cooper heard that remark and uttered a similar declaration when he co-starred with Grace Kelly in High Noon *(1952). The difference in their comments is that Coop said "panties" instead of "bloomers."]*

A daughter of Illinois with German and Portuguese ancestry, Astor had a movie career that spanned decades. She is best remembered today for starring in that classic, *The Maltese Falcon* (1941) with Humphrey Bogart.

Astor was only 17 when she appeared opposite John Barrymore, then in his 40s, in the silent film, *Beau Brummel* (1924). During the making of that movie, he not only took her virginity, but returned for repeats. *[Barrymore was also one of the early seducers of Carole Lombard, Clark's third wife.]*

Barrymore referred to women as "twittering vaginas," His escapades could populate a 12-part TV series, although much of it would not be suitable for general audiences. Take the saga when he spent a month in a whorehouse in Calcutta. His most famous marriage (his third) was to Dolores Costello, his co-star in *The Sea Beast* (1926), a silent film adaptation of Herman Melville's *Moby Dick*.

Astor would go on to have numerous affairs after her fling with Clark. During the crafting of that early movie with Bogie, John Huston seduced her.

Her most notorious affair, later exposed, was with playwright George S. Kaufman.

Her love life went public when her second husband, Dr. Franklin Thorpe *[married 1931-1935]* sued for divorce. A custody battle ensued over their four-year-old daughter, Marilyn.

Astor kept a diary which became notorious during the divorce proceedings. Comments from it were read at the hearings. In one passage about Kaufman, she wrote, "It was wonderful to fuck the sweet afternoon away. I don't know where George gets his staying power. He must have cum three times in just one hour."

Astor's doctor husband claimed that the diary revealed that she would not be a proper mother for their daughter. At the end of the trial, her diary was seized and impounded. Its contents were never revealed to the public, although some passages (some of which were fake) were leaked to the press.

In 1952, a court ordered that her diary be removed from a New York bank vault, where it had been sequestered for sixteen years, and burned.

In her diary, Astor rated her lovers on a star system. She gave Clark zero stars.

Mary Astor played the unhappy, sedate (i.e., boring), and "socially correct" foil to **Clark Gable's** "in the trenches" foreman on a rubber plantation.

To movie audiences' delight, Harlow—the hip, low-class, and loudly boisterous blonde—emerges, romantically as the winner.

***

Reviews of *Red Dust* were mixed. *Ozus World Movie Reviews* reported, "Great performances from the stars make you forget that Gable plays a sexist, and the melodrama borders on camp."

Critic Ken Hanke labeled it "gleefully trashy."

According to MGM's records, *Red Dust* made a profit of $400,000. Today, it's viewed as a Hollywood classic.

More than twenty years after its release, *Red Dust* would be reconfigured, re-released, and retitled, this time as *Mogambo* (1953). Although he'd aged, Clark was once again assigned the male lead. This time, its director was John Ford, and Clark's two leading ladies were Ava Gardner and Grace Kelly.

***

Before Madonna and before Marilyn Monroe, the original "blonde bombshell" was Jean Harlow.

Although she lived only till the age of 26, she made her everlasting mark on Hollywood in a decade-long career in which she starred in three dozen motion pictures. Today, she's ranked no. 22 on the American Film Institute's list of Greatest American Film Legends in the female category.

In 1953, an overhaul of **Red Dust** seemed like a good idea to executives at MGM. It involved relocating it from a rubber plantation in Indochina to the Serengeti plains of Africa and a re-casting of the uninhibited blonde (as portrayed by **Jean Harlow**) with an uninhibited brunette (**Ava Garder**). It also involved recasting the sedate, emotionally anguished brunette (**Mary Astor**) with a blonde (**Grace Kelly**) who gave every impression of just having graduated from an upscale finishing school. **Clark Gable**—older and much more jaded—gamely reprised his original role.

Except for the re-casting of the future **Serene Royal Highness of Monaco (Kelly)** with **The Tarheel Tart (Gardner)**, and some interesting safari shots, it morphed into a boring and occasionally embarrassing reprise of the much more charming Pre-Code original from 1932.

Irving Shulman, a biographer, wrote, "In all the wild, high-stepping history of Hollywood, no star has ever lived as fast and furious, or left such a baffling trail of legend and rumor behind her."

"Clark treated her like a kid sister," said Gene Raymond, one of *Red Dust's* co-stars.

"Like hell he did," responded director Victor Fleming. "He screwed her royally. Actually, that fag, Raymond, wanted Gable for himself."

"Every man I meet who gets close to me gets an obvious erection," Harlow told Gable.

"The thing I like about having sex with Jean is that you can do it without complications," Gable said to Fleming. "Many of the bitches I seduce think I'm going to marry them. After two disastrous marriages, I'm swearing off wives for life."

In one of the most famous scenes from *Red Dust*, a nude Harlow takes a bath in a rain barrel. What the camera didn't show was that when she emerged naked from her bath, Gable was waiting with a big towel to wrap around her and carry her off to his dressing room.

Fleming said, "During the shoot, Jean and Clark could not keep their hands off each other. She felt his cock and balls, and he enjoyed her tits. At one point, I had to tell him, 'Save some of your semen for the screen!'"

Episode 47

The Mysterious Death of
PAUL BERN
the Eccentric Husband of Jean Harlow

Paul Bern was born on December 3, 1889 in what is now Hamburg, Germany. His Jewish parents relocated in New York at the turn of the 20th Century. Julius Levy, Bern's father, died in 1908. His mother later committed suicide by drowning herself.

A young Bern set out at first to become a stage actor, finally fearing he did not have the talent. He decided to try his luck in Hollywood, and moved there early in the 1920s. First, he found work as a film editor and later, as a director for United Artists and Paramount.

His big break came when he moved to MGM and became a production assistant to Irving Thalberg. He climbed the ladder rung by rung, eventually becoming a producer at MGM in his own right.

Little is known about Bern's past, except he had lived with Dorothy Millette, his common-law wife, in New York City. The two had met in Toronto in 1911, and began living together.

He financially supported her but had to send her to a sanatorium in Connecticut because she suffered from mental and emotional problems, and would become violent at times. Even though he left her behind in the East, he continued to make payments to support her.

Bern suffered from an undeveloped penis, which did not make him popular with the actresses at MGM. At best, he developed crushes on female stars. For actual sex, he put young aspirant actors on the casting couch where he fellated them. He always kept his trousers on, not exposing himself.

On Broadway, Bern had seen Clark Gable perform in the play *Machinal* at the Plymouth theatre with his co-star, Zita Johann. He had gone backstage to meet the young actor and had invited him to dinner.

Over a late light supper, he told Clark that if he came to Hollywood, he would aid him in launching a film career.

He held out the prospect of Clark becoming a motion picture star in rugged He-Man roles. It is not known exactly what happened that night between Clark and Bern, but the star maker and the star hopeful began a series of "dates."

Two views of **Jean Harlow** with the ill-fated and unlucky husband, **Paul Bern**.

Upper photo: from immediately before their marriage and *lower photo*: from shortly after.

Reportedly, Clark often ended up on Bern's casting couch, where all he had to do was lie back, dreaming of whomever, while Bern voraciously fellated him. Clark was still in his "gay-for-pay" period, which back then pigeonholed him as a male whore. For surrendering himself to Bern, he was awarded with a $50 bill, when many hustlers at the time were getting no more than ten dollars.

In time, Bern would intervene with his boss, Irving Thalberg, and was said to have helped Clark launch a film career at MGM. That led to him having roles in nine films in the record-breaking year of 1931.

Bern continued to develop crushes on female stars, notably Barbara La Marr. She made it clear she did not want any romance with him but offered to be friends.

Born in Yakima, Washington, in 1896, La Marr was hailed in Hollywood as "The Girl Who Is Too Beautiful." She starred in twenty-seven silent movies between 1920 and 1926.

Douglas Fairbanks Sr. is credited with discovering her, putting her on his casting couch. When he tired of her, he turned her over to his son, Douglas Fairbanks Jr.

John Gilbert, then the pre-eminent rising male star at MGM, was seen seducing La Marr too. One of her breakthrough roles came when she was cast as Milady de Winter in the 1921 silent film, *The Three Musketeers*. She went on to make other movies, two of them with the gay actor, Ramon Novarro.

La Marr was strong competition for the so-called vamps of the 1920s. Theda Bara was the first vamp, but in time, Gloria Swanson competed with Pola Negri for the title.

Two views of the self-destructive silent screen diva **Barbara La Marr**. In the *photo right*, she's with **Ramon Novarro** in *Trifling Women* (1922).

MGM's "fixer" (Howard Strickling) asserted that Paul Bern commissioned and produced a pornographic film starring La Marr and Clark Gable, assuring them it was only intended for himself and his closest circle of friends.

La Marr was a party girl who drank heavily. She told the press that she slept only two hours a night: "I don't want to miss one damn thing by sleeping my life away."

Howard Strickling, "The Fixer" at MGM, later revealed a shocking story: He claimed that Bern hired a yacht to take La Marr and Clark on a long weekend visit to Catalina Island. He invited a cameraman with them and paid the female star and the wannabee male star handsomely for a private shooting of what, back then, was called a "blue movie." He promised them faithfully that the porn film would be only for his personal gratification.

Although it was a reckless thing to do, both Clark and La Marr agreed to do it. According to the script that emerged from Bern's fantasy, Clark breaks into her boudoir late at night and finds that she sleeps in the nude. He strips down and rapes her after demanding that she perform fellatio on him.

The rape seemed to satisfy both Clark and La Marr. Back in Hollywood, he arranged a few private dates with her before her untimely death on January 30, 1926.

During her short life, La Marr was officially married four times. As a wife, she was rarely home. Her marriages were each disastrous. Her first husband, for example, Lawrence Converse, was arrested for bigamy, as he was already married with children. When sent to prison, he committed suicide by constantly banging his head against the bars of his cell.

On January 30, 1926, at the age of 29, La Marr died of complications associated with tuberculosis and nephritis.

In the mid-1930s, Louis B. Mayer, long an admirer of Barbara La Marr, named his newest "discovery," Hedy Lamarr—a recent import from Austria—after the since-deceased film goddess of the 1920s.

***

Paul Bern was introduced to Jean Harlow at the premiere of *Hell's Angels* (1930). After seeing it, he was convinced of her potential star power. Irving Thalberg, his boss, was not impressed. It seems that Bern was the first producer to recognize Harlow's potential.

Around the MGM lot, he had a reputation as the "Father Confessor." Stars such as Joan Crawford could come to him, sharing their fears or even airing complaints, and he would listen. In contrast, Louis B. Mayer often showed the discontents the door.

It can only be wondered why Harlow was attracted to Bern, who was a puny, unattractive man. His sympathetic ear seems to have been his major asset. "Paul was the first person who took me seriously as an actress," she once said.

Scoop artist Ben Maddox asked Harlow what she saw in Bern. "We spend lovely evenings together," she said. "We listen to classical music. We read film scripts together in our search for a suitable breakout role for me. He's the only man I've met in Hollywood who recognized I have a brain--not just a body. He doesn't talk fuck, fuck, fuck all the time."

Since her arrival in Hollywood, Maddox had been following the sexual life of Harlow and would continue to do so as the 1930s rolled on, and as she became a superstar.

Some leading figures on her list included Howard Hawks, Howard Hughes, boxer Max Baer, Clark Gable, Chester Morris (her *Red-Headed Woman,* 1932, co-star); William Powell, gangster Bugsy Siegel, James Stewart, and dozens of members of any film crew, especially the studly ones. Delivery boys, even taxi drivers, were not ruled out.

When Bern proposed marriage to Harlow and she accepted, seemingly everyone at MGM was shocked. "She was nothing but a wise-cracking little harlot, going around with a bottle of hair dye, to use on her head and on her vagina," claimed Joan Crawford, who was a friend of Bern. "I warned him not to marry the bitch, or else he'd spend the rest of his life regretting it. On their honeymoon night, she would probably spend it in bed with William Powell."

Douglas Fairbanks Jr. attended a dinner party at which Bern was to announce his engagement to Harlow. Fairbanks later alleged, "As he made the announcement, Jean's hands were under the table, fondling my basket."

When the news broke to a wider audience the next morning, many Hollywood insiders were stunned "at the palace eunuch planning to marry that platinum slut," in the words of Howard Strickling.

Their marriage took place on July 2, 1932.

Clark Gable's view was that Harlow was "going through with the wedding" for career advancement. He had tapped into that same reasoning when he'd allowed Bern to fellate him.

Gangster Johnny Rosselli, who had a few flings with Harlow, weighed in, too. "Bern was a pansy who for some strange reason liked the company of pretty girls. He could admire their beauty—nothing else."

On September 5, two months into their marriage, Harlow told Bern she was going over to her mother's house to spend the night. She was later awakened with a pre-dawn call from Howard Strickling, who told her that her husband had been found dead from a gunshot wound to his head at their home on Easton Drive in Beverly Hills.

Somehow, his bosses at MGM (they included Strickling, Irving Thalberg, and Louis B. Mayer) had been alerted seven hours before the police were summoned.

There is much debate about exactly what took place that night.

Strickling was ordered by Mayer to come up with a convincing story for the press, something that would not destroy Harlow's rising star. "Do something that will create sympathy for her."

On his desk, he found Bern's diary. There was an entry made, apparently during the course of their honeymoon night, when he had tried to seduce her. It read:

Unfortuately (sic) this is the only way to make up for the frightful wrong I have done you and to wipe out my abject humiliation. I love you.
Paul
You understand that last night was only a comedy.

Strickling and Mayer agreed that Bern perhaps had contemplated suicide on the night he failed her as a husband. Even so, they decided to use it as a recent suicide note, suggesting that he had waited two months before trying to consummate the marriage."

Without alerting his bosses, Strickling searched for the "blue movie" mentioned above. Bern had previously confessed to him that he had ordered a film of Clark having sex with Barbara La Marr.

After a search, he discovered the movie, but didn't alert Thalberg. Strickling had long had a crush on Clark, so he took the movie home with him.

It has never resurfaced. Perhaps it was destroyed after viewings by Strickland. If it still exists, and its new owner wants to make some money, he can put it up for sale. We suggest an auction where the opening bid begins at one million dollars.

The coroner ruled that Bern's death was a suicide. It was noted in his report that the producer had "grossly underdeveloped genitals."

It was later believed that Bern was murdered by his former common law wife, Dorothy Millette. It was reported that she had arrived in the Los Angeles area in September of 1932. She visited Bern. After what was assumed to be a violent argument, she fatally shot him.

Later that morning, she committed suicide by jumping from the *Delta King* steamboat headed for Sacramento.

According to Hollywood legend, Bern's death takes its place with other mysterious deaths, notably that of William Desmond Taylor and Thelma Todd.

Writer Ben Hecht, in a 1960 edition of *Playboy*, wrote this:

Paul Bern, remembered for having committed suicide as the impotent bridegroom of Jean Harlow the great cinema sexpot, did no such thing. His suicide note, hinting that he was sexually incompetent, and had therefore 'ended the comedy' was a forgery. Studio officials, sitting in a conference around the dead body, decided it was better to have Paul a suicide than the murder victim of another woman."

***

Dorothy Millette, "phantom wife" of Paul Bern, followed the film producer in death by leaping in the Sacramento river after she learned he shot himself.

ENDING OF A MYSTERY LIFE

Funeral Service Held for Dorothy Millette.

SACRAMENTO. (INS). "Death is swallowed in victory—". Standing before a white casket, decked simply with two sprays of gladiolas, Rev. J. J. Evans, pastor of the First Christian church at Sacramento, slowly intoned this scriptural passage. It was the funeral eulogy and final rite for Dorothy Millette, socalled "secret bride" of Paul Bern, who followed him in suicide. Before a small group of mourners, none of whom were friends or relatives of the woman, brief funeral services were conducted in the palm chapel of James Garlick, Sacramento county corner. The little cortege of hearse and two automobiles, carrying only the coroner and his staff and the minister, then proceeded slowly to East Lawn cemetery. Thus ended the mystery life of Dorothy Millette as the "phantom bride" of the self-slain husband of Jean Harlow, screen star.

News clipping *(left)* is from the **Nebraska State Journal**, September 18, 1932.

News clipping *right* is from the **Oakland Tribune**, September 15, 1932

Jean Harlow, with family members, at Paul Bern's funeral.

Episode 48

Strange Interlude (1932)

In 1928, during his search for talented new actors with good speaking voices, and for new stage productions with good odds of potential success as screen adaptations, Irving Thalberg, with his wife, Norma Shearer, came to New York. One of the first Broadway plays they saw was Eugene O'Neill's *Strange Interlude*.

It ran for five hours in a format that included starting in the late afternoon and with a dinner break at half-time. Thalberg noticed that many theatergoers did not return for the second half. He, however, was intrigued with the drama and thought that a film adaptation might be successful, but with the clear understanding that O'Neill's drama would require radical editing and shortening.

The play's Broadway original had starred the fabled husband-and-wife team of Lynn Fontanne and Alfred Lunt. In a featured role was Earle Larimore, a long-ago lover of Clark from the 1920s.

Backstage at the theater, Thalberg tentatively proposed a film adaptation in which Fontanne and Lunt would reprise the play on film, as co-stars. Both of them rejected the idea, but in the aftermath of their disinterest, Thalberg arranged for purchase of the play's film rights from O'Neill. He would go through several screenwriters before he trimmed the play drastically down to a "regular" sized running length.

Shearer, it was clearly understood, would be assigned the female lead, and Thalberg acquiesced to his wife's plea that Clark Gable be cast as her leading man. *[She had been very pleased with his performance with her in* A Free Soul *in 1931. The physically ailing Thalberg was fully aware that Clark had seduced Shearer during the course of their work together, but he relented to her wish anyway.]*

When Clark first read the script, he feared that as an actor, he

The American-born son of dysfunctional Irish-American parents (one addicted to alcohol, another to morphine), playwright **Eugene O'Neill** (1888-1953; *depicted above with his older son*) won a Nobel Prize for Literature and four Pulitzer prizes for drama. Once the darling of the theatrical *intelligentsia*, his stage tragedies are dark, filled with anguish, and relentlessly pessimistic.

Whereas both of his sons committed suicide, his estranged daughter, **Oona**, famously married **Charlie Chaplin** for whom (according to **Joan Collins**) she retained "an almost geisha-like deference."

Whereas MGM had amply proven its ability to produce mass-market blockbusters, *Strange Interlude* was more *avant-garde* and self-consciously "artsy" than many of the studio's previous releases.

It was adapted (and brutally condensed) from a complicated five-hour Broadway play by Eugene O'Neill.

Loaded with existential anguish, it's the story of Nina Leeds (**Norma Shearer**). After learning that insanity runs in her husband's family, she produces a love child with a handsome doctor (**Clark Gable**) and tells her husband (**Alexander Kirkland**) that the child is his.

might not be able to meet the standard previously established onstage by Lunt. The director, Robert Z. Leonard, convinced him, however, that he could, reminding him that he had worked effectively with the great Greta Garbo in their film, *Susan Lenox: Her Fall and Rise* (1931).

In *Strange Interlude,* Shearer played Nina Leeds, a complicated, neurotic woman who develops a series of romantic relationships with a number of men. Clark played Dr. Ned Darrell, the love of her life, with whom she has a son, although they never wed, since she was married to another man at the time.

Other roles were cast with Alexander Kirkland as San Evans; Ralph Morgan as Charles Masden; Robert Young as Gordon Evans; May Robson as Mrs. Evans; and Maureen O'Sullivan as Madeline Arnold.

Alexander Kirkland in *Strange Interlude* during a (rare) happy scene with the then-Queen of MGM, **Norma Shearer.**

Kirkland was born in Mexico City in 1901, but grew up in the U.S. After getting an education, he became a stage actor but soon after migrated to Hollywood, where he became a leading man in early talkies. When he appeared opposite Tallulah Bankhead in *Tarnished Lady* (1931), the notorious star lived up to her reputation and seduced him.

In 1942, in the first full year of America's involvement in World War II, Kirkland married Gypsy Rose Lee, the most celebrated stripper in America, the sister of screen actress June Havoc.

Their union lasted only three months. Lee learned that her husband preferred sex with other young (male) actors.

Before their divorce, she gave birth to a son, whose father was director Otto Preminger.

[Forman Brown, the then avant-garde gay novelist, claimed that his novel, Better Angel, *first published in 1933, was inspired by his sexual experiences with Kirkland. Critic Christopher Carey defined it as "the first homosexual novel with a truly happy ending."]*

A New Yorker born in 1883, Ralph Morgan was a stage and film character actor, whose career spanned 1908 to 1953. His brother, Frank Morgan, immortalized himself in his role in *The Wizard of Oz* (1939), starring Judy Garland.

At Columbia University, Ralph earned a law degree, but soon tired of the practice and headed west to Hollywood. His education and early expenses had been financed by his father's profits from the sale of Angostura Bitters.

Clark Gable, emoting here with the film's A-list superstar, **Norma Shearer**, grew a mustache for the filming of *Strange Interlude.* Audiences approved: So he kept it.

He made his debut in silent films in 1915. In the year he worked with Clark, he also starred in *Rasputin and the Empress.*

Off camera, he became one of the founding members of the Screen Actors Guild (SAG).

Clark already knew Robert Young from their experience filming *Hell Divers* (1932). Born on February 22, 1907, in Chicago, he would go on to have a film career that lasted from 1927 to 1988.

He was also a star on radio and television. Two of his TV series made him a household name: *Father Knows Best* (1949-1954) and *Marcus Welby, M.D.* (1969-1976).

Young would also star in 100 motion pictures with such ladies as Katharine Hepburn, Margaret Sullavan, Norma Shearer, Joan Crawford, Helen Hayes, Luise Rainer, Hedy Lamarr, Helen Twelvetrees, Greer Garson, and Loretta Young (not related.)

Long before his appearance in the 1950s TV sitcom *Father Knows Best*, **Robert Young** looked like this.

A native daughter of Australia, born in 1858, May Robson would have an acting career that spanned 58 years, starting in 1883 when she was 25 years old. She is mostly known for all those movies she made in the 1930s when she was in her 70s.

She became the earliest-born person and the first Australian to be nominated for an Oscar. *[Her qualifying film was* Lady for a Day *(1933).]* She lost to Katharine Hepburn.

Thomas Edison, as a luminary in the early film industry, helped launch Robson's career, and rumors spread that they had had an affair.

One of her early lovers was Jack Pickford, brother of Mary.

Upon Robson's death at the age of 84 in Beverly Hills, she was hailed as "the dowager queen of the American stage and screen."

Here, in one of the film's murkier dramatic moments, **Norma Shearer** learns a dark, shame-soaked secret ("*Insanity runs in our family*') from her mother-in-law, as played by **May Robson.**

Irish born in 1911, Maureen O'Sullivan became famous for playing Jane in all those Tarzan movies opposite Johnny Weissmuller: *["Me Tarzan, you Jane."]*

She wasn't confined to just co-starring with "that hunk of beefcake" (her words). Throughout her career, she also appeared opposite Greta Garbo, Laurence Olivier, Fredric March, William Powell, Marie Dressler, Lionel Barrymore, Wallace Beery, the Marx Brothers, and Woody Allen.

O'Sullivan was married twice, once to director John Farrow, with whom she had seven children. One of them, Mia Farrow, married (from 1966 to 1968) Frank Sinatra. "Ol' Blue Eyes should have married me instead of my very young daughter," O'Sullivan said.

As an oddity, in *Strange Interlude,* the actors share oral dialogue, but a voice over reveals what they are really thinking.

Strange Interlude marked Clark's first appearance with a mustache. It became the most famous mustache in the world.

The plot of the movie pours itself quickly across several decades. MGM's makeup department worked wonders in aging the actors for the final scenes of the film.

In a rare visit to one of his film sets, Louis B. Mayer arrived during one of the final days of filming to wish everyone well. He turned to Clark and quipped, "In *A Free Soul,* you knocked Norma around. In this picture, you knock her up."

The Pride of Ireland ("Me Tarzan, You Jane"): Actress **Maureen O'Sullivan**, six-time star, with Johnny Weissmuller, of various Tarzan films.

Like Eugene O'Neill, she, too, produced a very famous daughter. In O'Sullivan's case, it was **Mia Farrow.**

Because Eugene O'Neill's convoluted script had been radically shortened, the movie's plot moved quickly (some said, "confusingly") through many complicated subtleties. O'Neill told the press, "Shearer and Clark Gable are in over their heads in my play." When Clark read the final script, he defined it as "subversive perversity."

Halfway through filming, Clark protested to director Leonard: "Can't I occasionally smile, or be affable, or even romantic—at least once in a while? All I do is look worried and get mad."

As the film opens, Nina Leeds (Shearer) is under the control of her domineering father, Professor Leeds (Henry B. Walthall), but he soon dies.

He opposes her marrying a young soldier named Gordon, who later dies in World War I.

She eventually marries Sam Evans (Kirkland), who doesn't seem able to father a child. She falls in love with Dr. Ned Darrell (Clark) who becomes a mentor to the boy he had previously sired with her, although that secret remains shared only by them.

Depicted as a boy, Gordon Evans was portrayed by the child actor, Ted Alexander. He is instantly hostile to Dr. Darrell (Clark), not knowing that he is his biological father.

Near the end of the film, depicted as a grown man, the film reveals that Gordon remains hostile to Dr. Darrell, never knowing that he is his biological father. At one point, he slaps Darrell's face, hard.

Sam Evans, Nina's husband, suffers a stroke and dies after watching Gordon win a boat race.

Dr. Darrell is now free to marry an aging Nina, but he decides to wish her a loving goodbye and disappears.

Throughout her life, a trusted family friend, Charles Marsden (Ralph Morgan) has always been "waiting for Nina in the wings." Minutes before the film ends, these two aging characters cuddle up in each other's arms to face the final curtain.

Nina, by now, realizes that everyone who mattered has faded from her life except "Dear Ol' Charlie."

***

Photoplay wrote, "Clark Gable and Norma Shearer age beautifully within the short span of an hour and a half. Like vintage wine, they improve with each year."

The *London Film Weekly* found that "Clark Gable's powerful personality shines steadfastly through the misty atmosphere of mixed psychology."

According to MGM records, *Strange Interlude* earned a million dollars in the U.S. and Canada, plus $280,000 abroad. The net profit came to only $90,000.

Here's **Clark Gable** in an MGM press photo being "aged" by a makeup pro for his appearance in the final scenes of *Strange Interlude*.

Four views of **Norma Shearer** and **Clark Gable** at various stages of their aging process during the decades-long span of *Strange Interlude*.

Episode 49

No Man of Her Own (1932)

The casting of Paramount's Pre-Code romantic comedy-drama, *No Man of Her Own,* was mired in confusion during pre-production. Marion Davies was said to be responsible for the lead going to Clark.

As the mistress of William Randolph Hearst, who had strong ties to MGM at the time, she had wanted Bing Crosby for her next picture, *Going Hollywood* (1930).

She got Hearst to make a deal with Louis B. Mayer at MGM to temporarily "swap" Crosby for Clark. [*MGM would lend Clark to Paramount, with Crosby, then under contract to Paramount, temporarily "lent" to MGM.*]

Paramount was very generous to Clark, and even presented him with five choices of scripts.

George Raft, the former New York gangster who had originally been assigned the role, was booted.

Clark was told that his leading lady would be Miriam Hopkins, but she refused the role when she learned that Clark would get star billing over her. Paramount then cast Carole Lombard with Clark, her future husband. It would be the only picture they made together.

On the set, Clark had a reunion with the director, Wesley Ruggles, who had first met him in 1925 when Clark was an extra on the silent film series, *The Pacemakers*.

Clark was assigned the role of "Babe" Stewart, a card sharp and gambling cheat. Lombard would play a small-town librarian, Connie Randall, who falls in love with him. Unaware of his notorious past, she thinks he's a businessman.

Sexually suggestive, even for Pre-Code pottymouths like Lombard.

The role of "the other woman," Kay Everly, went to Dorothy Mackaill.

In fourth billing, Grant Mitchell was cast as Charlie Vane, one of Babe's cronies.

No Man of Her Own was originally based on the 1931 novel by Val Newton, but later drew additional inspiration from a story by Edmund Goulding and Benjamin Glazer.

[*The Gable/Lombard version of* No Man of Her Own *is not related in any way to the 1950 movie of the same name that co-stared Barbara Stanwyck and John Lund.*]

Ruggles, a son of Los Angeles born in 1889, had won acclaim for helming *Cimarron* (1931), based on the Edna Ferber novel. After directing Clark and Lombard, he would go on to helm Cary Grant and Mae West in *I'm No Angel* (1933).

Dorothy Mackaill, born in Yorkshire, England, in 1903, was most active in silent films and in the early Pre-Code movies of the 1930s.

From her birthplace, she gravitated to London at the age of 16 when she was hired as a dancer at the London Hippodrome.

After working for a while in silent movies shot in Paris, she sailed to the Port of New York. At the age of 17, she was dancing on Broadway in the *Ziegfeld Follies*.

Moving to Hollywood she made several silent films with such stars as Rod LaRocque, Anna Mae Wong, John Barrymore, Bebe Daniels, Colleen Moore, Richard Barthelmess, Anna Q. Nilsson, and George O'Brien.

At Columbia Pictures, Mackaill starred in *Love Affair* (1932) with the little-known actor, Humphrey Bogart. She also made several films for MGM, Paramount, and Columbia before retiring to take care of her ailing mother.

In 1955, she moved to Honolulu, living at the luxurious Royal Hawaiian Hotel on the beach. Death came to her there on August 12, 1990 at the age of 97.

A native of Columbus, Ohio, born in 1874, Grant Mitchell was called "Mr. Ordinary." He was comfortable in roles that called for him to be the father of the heroine, a staid businessman, a bank clerk, or school principal.

Photo left: Love in a Library: **Lombard** and **Gable** play-pretend at "meeting cute."

Photo above: **Dorothy McKaill** and **Carole Lombard** play-pretend at the importance of maintaining decorum "within the stacks."

He was the only son of Civil War General John G. Mitchell. His paternal grandmother was the sister of President Rutherford B. Hayes. There were many roles that called for an ordinary American male. This led to his being cast in plays on Broadway that ran from 1902 to 1939, and in films that were released between 1930 and 1948.

He also appeared in minor roles that became classics. They included *Dinner at Eight* (1933), *Mr. Smith Goes to Washington* (1939), *The Grapes of Wrath* (1940), and *Arsenic and Old Lace* (1944).

Mitchell starred with such leading men as Henry Fonda, James Stewart, and Cary Grant.

This archetype for "the ordinary man" remained a bachelor all his life, leading to rumors (unconfirmed) that he was a homosexual.

Prevalent themes of *No Man of Her Own* focused on crime, gambling, dishonesty, love, commitment, and redemption. Babe (Clark) cheats an unsuspecting newcomer, Mr. Morton (Walter Walker) at poker, taking him for thousands of dollars. Police officer "Dickie" Collins (J. Farrell MacDonald) warns Babe that he has told Morton of how he was swindled. Babe decides to get out of town before Morton seeks revenge. Character actor MacDonald had been one of the stars of Clark's first picture, *The Painted Desert* (1931).

Babe escapes to the small town of Glendale, where he meets and eventually falls in love with Connie Randall (Carole Lombard), the town's librarian. Critics later noted that she was the sexiest librarian ever depicted on the screen.

Beefcake, suggestively clad in silk pajamas: **Clark Gable**

He woos her and ultimately marries her. She thinks he is a conventional businessman, not a crooked gambler. Eventually, she learns the truth. While he is serving time in jail, he pretends to be doing business in South America. Fear not....It has a happy ending.

As co-stars, Lombard and Clark were not impressed with each other. At the time, she was in the closing months of her ill-fated marriage to William Powell, Clark's future co-star.

He was put off by her vulgar mouth and her blunt assessments of her husband. He overheard her tell Ruggles, "Bill is a fine, elegant gentleman, but not so good under the sheets."

Clark said, "I once worked with wildcatters in the oilfields of Oklahoma. On Saturday night, when they got stinking drunk, you never heard such curse words—that is, until I met Lombard. She stops them all. Every third word that comes out of that filthy mouth of hers is 'shit.'"

Clark may not have liked Carole's pottymouth, but she was also not impressed with the morality of this married actor. "He has the morals of a wild coyote, chasing anything in a dress. During the making of our film, I spotted three different whores visiting his dressing room."

However, she was pleased that Paramount was paying her almost as much as Clark. He got $4,000 a week, compared to her $3,000.

On his last day on the set, Clark was introduced to Lombard's mother. A devotee of the Bahá'í sect, she kept two astrologers on retainer.

At the end of filming, Lombard and Clark exchanged gifts. He gave her an oversized pair of ballet slippers, suggesting she was a conceited *prima donna*. She gave him a large smoked ham with his picture on it, suggesting what she thought of his ego and his acting.

The film did a mild business, although critics in New York and Boston bashed it for the most part. Father Daniel Lord, the Jesuit priest and writer who helped compile the Hollywood Code of Screen Ethics, claimed "the movie is filthy and violates every tenet of the Code. The bedroom scenes are far too graphic. Lombard not only appears in her underwear, but undresses and showers. Paramount must own stock in lingerie companies."

Lombard with Gable, suggestively splayed in ways that barely made it past the censors.

London Film Weekly wrote: "Gable's impudent love-making exactly fits the character he is playing. Carole Lombard—cool sincere, and intelligent—makes the perfect heroine."

The critic for *Variety,* rather awkwardly, wrote: "Gable is close to the whole picture himself as a swank card-gyp who hits the trail heavy for the women."

Motion Picture Herald found that the film presents "Gable at his best in this sophisticated comedy where he is teamed with luscious Carole Lombard."

***

In Hollywood, Carole Lombard became known as "The Profane Angel" because of her beauty, her ribald humor, and her mischief on and off the camera.

She was born Jane Alice Peters in 1908 in Fort Wayne, Indiana, and was a distant cousin of the famed director, Howard Hawks. Her parents divorced in 1916, and she and her mother and two brothers moved to Hollywood.

She grew up as a tomboy, wrestling with her brothers, before reaching her final height of 5'2".

One day, director Allan Dwan spotted her on a football field and signed her to a contract with Fox. She would appear as a rough-and-tumble tomboy in *A Perfect Crime* (1921).

It was back to school for the next four years. Instead of reading and writing, she preferred track and field. She dropped out of school at the age of 15 and joined a theater troupe.

In 1925, she was given a screen test and signed a contract for her first picture, a silent, *Hearts and Spurs*. In it, she played the female lead.

Tragedy struck in 1926. At the age of 18, she was seriously injured in an automobile accident. Fox canceled her contract. The left side of her face was badly scarred, but she became adept at concealing it behind makeup.

Back at work, she was hired by Mack Sennett to perform in thirteen shorts in just 18 months. This was followed by roles at Paramount.

She encountered Howard Hughes, the aviator and producer, who began a brief affair with her. He promised her the female lead in his upcoming film, *Hell's Angels* (1930).

But by the time shooting began, he'd assigned the role instead to Jean Harlow, who was destined to become one of Clark Gable's leading ladies.

Years later, Lombard learned that her future husband, Clark Gable, had been one of Hughes' (early) sexual conquests.

Right from the beginning, Lombard was not intimated by her bosses, including Harry Cohn of Columbia, who was known for *schtupping* almost every actress he hired. She told him, "I'll make your shitty picture, but fucking you is not part of the deal."

Before appearing on a set, she'd call out to her wardrobe mistress, "Bring me my god damn tits to put on."

One of her close friends, actor William Haines, became her confidant. He told her that in the 1920s, he'd seduced Clark Gable on several occasions.

Lombard began hanging out with him and his homosexual friends, later suffering the label of "fag hag."

Haines said, "Carole photographed like a virginal princess, but she lived like a tiger and fluttered like a butterfly."

In 1931, she made two movies back to back with William Powell: *Man of the World* and *Ladies Man.*

They were a study in opposites. At 22, she was "devil may care." He was 38, a sophisticated intellectual.

Lombard and Powell lived together for several months before deciding to marry in 1931. She claimed, "He was the perfect gentleman, even when he took his shorts off. Always debonair as he was on the screen, especially in all those *Thin Man* movies he made with that dyke, Myrna Loy."

Carole Lombard with then-husband **William Powell.**

In *I Take This Woman* (1931), Lombard starred with Gary Cooper, "The Montana Mule." She had a torrid affair with him before he moved on to his next conquest.

After she appeared with Clark in *No Man of her Own,* she told Garson Kanin, "Clark and I did all sorts of love scenes together. I never got any kind of tremble out of him at all. What a dullard."

After co-starring with him, she appeared with John Barrymore in *Twentieth Century* (1934), which made her a big star. Divorced from Powell at the time, she launched an affair with "The Great Profile."

She "made the biggest mistake of my life" when she turned down co-starring with Clark again in *It Happened One Night* (1934). At the last minute, Claudette Colbert reluctantly accepted the role. To everyone's amazement, *It Happened One Night* was the first film to win the "Big Five" Academy Awards that year—Best Picture, Best Director, Best Actor (Clark Gable), Best Actress (Claudette Colbert) and Best Writing.

In lieu of that, Carole co-starred with George Raft in the musical drama, *Bolero* (1934).

"She is one of the sexiest women I have ever known, and I've known plenty," he said. "She has a sensational figure."

She is credited with nicknaming his penis "Black Snake." He used that "snake" to invade Mae West, Lucille Ball, Betty Grable, Marlene Dietrich, Ann Sheridan, Norma Shearer, and Lana Turner, among hundreds of other showgirls and prostitutes. Early in his career, he used to sodomize his roommate, a very young Valentino, when both of them were "gigolo dancers" for hire in New York.

Raft had been born the same year as Clark. She later admitted, "I am both repelled and attracted to him."

Raft became notorious for the roles he rejected in the 1940s. Humprey Bogart was grateful that he'd turned down *High Sierra* (1941), *The Maltese Falcon* (also 1941), and ultimately, *Casablanca* (1942). Raft also rejected Billy Wilder who wanted him to co-star with Barbara Stanwyck in *Double Indemnity* (1944). Its male lead went to Fred MacMurray.

At the peak of her career in the 1930s, Lombard was hailed as "The Queen of Screwball Comedy," as she flitted from man to man. They included David Niven, Buddy Rogers (husband of Mary Pickford), and David O. Selznick—although she never forgave him for not casting her as Scarlett O'Hara in *Gone With the Wind* (1939).

Her most serious romance ended in a freak discharge of a rifle that caused her lover's death. He was Ross Columbo, a baritone, songwriter, violinist, and actor. Many of the romantic ballads he composed became standards, including "Too Beautiful for Words."

Before his untimely death, he was making forceful inroads as an actor, starring in such films as the romantic "part-talkie" western, *Wolf Song* (1929) with Lupe Velez and Gary Cooper. Cooper and Columbo took turns trying to satisfy the sexual demands of "The Mexican Spitfire."

On Septemb er 2, 1934, Columbo visited the home of his longtime friend, Lansing Brown, who had a large collection of antique guns. As he was examining one of the rifles, it misfired, shooting a bullet into his brain. He was dead at the age of 26. He'd arranged a dinner date with Lombard for later that evening. She was seen weeping at his funeral.

Long after Columbo's death, his songs lived on, emerging from the throats of Perry Como, Frank Sinatra, Lena Horne, Jo Stafford, Bing Crosby, Tiny Tim, and Tab Hunter

After Columbo, two years would go by before Lombard encountered "the love of my life." His name was Clark Gable.

Episode 50

The White Sister (1933)

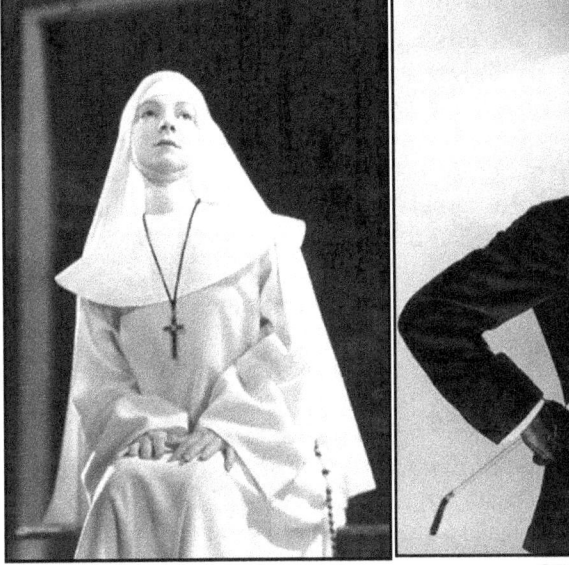

In a candid moment, Helen Hayes, hailed as "the First Lady of the American Theatre," made a confession to gossip maven Louella Parsons. "I'm deeply in love with my husband Charles MacArthur, whom I married in 1928. I'd drop him in a moment if Gary Cooper or Clark Gable asked me to do so."

She had recently co-starred in Ernest Hemingway's *A Farewell to Arms* (1932) with Cooper and was set to appear opposite Clark in *The White Sister*.

When the press announced the Hayes/Gable casting in *The White Sister*, she made references to her title of First Lady of the American Theatre. It was noted by some reporters that the stage actress, Katharine Cornell, held that same title. In a comparison of those two rigorously respectable actresses, one critic commented, "Cornell plays every queen as if she were a woman, and Hayes plays every woman as if she were a queen."

The White Sister, a Pre-Code romantic drama on the verge of production at MGM, had originated in 1901 as a novel by Francis Marion Crawford.

Four years later, producer Walter Hacket adapted it into a play for Broadway, where it ran for two years. In 1915, it reached the screen as an

Audiences couldn't decide if this tale of forbidden love, piety, and death, direct from the trenches of World War I, was a "three-" or a "four-hanky weeper."

Helen Hayes, appropriately clad in white in her capacity as a "bride of Christ" appears on the left; **Clark,** as a horny but gallant red-blooded army officer, on the right.

adaptation that starred Richard Travers and Viola Allen. In 1923, it was remade again as a silent film, this time starring Lillian Gish and Ronald Colman, which launched him as a matinee idol.

Until now, Clark he had never worked with an actress with such credentials as Helen Hayes. She had recently won an Oscar for her star performance in *The Sin of Madeleine Claudet* (1931).

Born at the dawn of the 20th Century in Washington, D.C., Helen Hayes would, in time, become the second person and the first woman to win an Emmy, a Grammy, an Oscar, and a Tony Award.

From the beginning, Clark feared he was miscast as an officer in the Italian Army. As an actor, he was intimidated to be co-starring with such a formidable actress as Hayes.

He was reassured by his favorite director, Victor Fleming: "With your height, you'll tower over the little midget."

Other than casting *The White Sister*'s male and female leads, it was Fleming's job to hire actors for the secondary roles, too. In the third lead, Lewis Stone was assigned the role of Prince Guido Chiaromonte. Other parts featured Louise Closser as Mina Bernardo; May Robson as Mother Superior; Edward Arnold as Father Saracinesca; and Alan Edwards as Ernesto Traversi.

All these roles were re-created from the original scripts by Donald Ogden Stewart, who was born in Columbus, Ohio, in 1894. When he landed in Hollywood, he became known for his sophisticated Golden Age comedies and melodramas, most notably *The Philadelphia Story* (1940), starring Katharine Hepburn, James Stewart, and Cary Grant. The play it was based on had been written by Philip Barry.

Over the course of his career, Stewart worked with George Cukor (his frequent collaborator), Michael Curtiz, and Ernest Lubitsch.

In New York, he was a member of the Algonquin Round Table, with the likes of Dorothy Parker and Robert Benchley.

During the "Red Scare" of 1950, Stewart was blacklisted. In its aftermath, he emigrated to England.

Veteran actor Lewis Stone, born in Massachusetts in 1879, had only one thing in common with Clark. Both of them had co-starred with Greta Garbo—Clark only once, but Stone seven times, in both silent films and talkies. Before *White Sister*, he had co-starred with her in *Queen Christina* (1933).

It would be years before he became even more famous as Mickey Rooney's father in all those Andy Hardy pictures.

Before his death in 1953 at the age of 73, he had appeared in more than 100 films.

On the set, Clark had a reunion with Mae Robson, with whom he had last appeared in *Strange Interlude* (1932).

He was introduced to the burly and formidable Edward Arnold, who had been born in New York in 1890. Overweight, he had a deep voice and an intimidating stare.

As a gruff and likable character actor, Arnold was in heavy demand, particularly in the mid-1930s. He'd go on to be featured in such classics as *Mr Smith Goes to Washington* (1939) with James Stewart and *Meet John Doe* (1941) with Gary Cooper.

Before appearing with Hayes, Eric Portman had warned Clark, "Working with Hayes is like walking barefoot in a room filled with mice."

He found her supportive in every way. She compared him favorably to Gary Cooper. "Unlike you, he has no stage training, and many scenes with him were difficult to pull off. But you were always on the mark, delivering your lines with sincerity. You even convinced me you were really in love with me."

***

In *The White Sister's* much-revised plot, Lewis Stone as Prince Guido Chiaromonte is the stern father of the flighty Angela (Hayes). Fearing she needs to be brought under control, he arranges a marriage for his daughter to Ernesto Traversi (Alan Edwards). Whereas Ernesto, the son of a banker, is stuffy and preoccupied with business, Angela (Hayes) is impulsive, spontaneous, and romantic.

Joining revelers celebrating a saint's feast day, she encounters a handsome, dashing, army lieutenant, Giovanni Severi (Clark). Rather quickly, she falls in love with him, and that love is returned in full measure.

She runs away with Giovanni. When her father pursues her, he dies in a freak car accident. Giovanni is inducted into the military at the start of World War I, and they share a tearful goodbye.

Although he's been captured and is being held in a prison camp, she's told that officially, he has been declared dead.

Filled with sorrow and despair, she enters a convent, where she is trained as a nurse.

Two years go by, and Giovanni, who has been tracking her whereabouts, is shocked to discover that she's now a sister in white, having taken religious vows. She is now a bride of Christ.

In November of 1951, eighteen years after her appearance with Gable in *The White Sister*, LIFE magazine featured **Helen Hayes** with **Lynn Fontanne** and **Katharine Cornell** as the "impossibly famous" leading trio of theatrical *grandes dames* of the American stage.

During the shoot, although standards of etiquette were high, rivalries were ferocious.

Later, she is sent to a villa to help a patient who turns out to be her former lover. Despite being sorely tempted, she refuses to drop out of the convent.

Weeks later, fully recovered, he is hit with a bomb from an Austrian airplane during his exit from the hospital. Angela (Hayes) is called to the bedside of the again-injured soldier, whom she still loves. He dies in her arms.

***

The White Sister, made for $625,000, earned $750,000 in the U.S. and Canada, and $950,000 abroad, showing a profit of $460,000.

Variety wrote, "Clark Gable is a gallant soldier and leaves nothing to be desired."

Hollywood Reporter claimed, "*The White Sister* is a great picture. Hayes and Gable are already stars of the first magnitude, their performances now equal anything of their brilliant past."

Motion Picture Herald found that "Gable is forceful in a story that isn't. Neither he nor Miss Hayes, even with their moving performances, can make the picture the noble effort it pretends to be. There is an anticipation that is never fulfilled."

***

The White Sister was one of the rare films from the 1930s where the male character's hat was consistently better (i.e., more flamboyant) than the female's. Here are two views of Gable with Hayes emoting—before the fall.

The White Sister was Gable's only film in which he was instructed to "impose upon" a nun. Did she retain her wimple and her virtue? According to the filmscript YES!. Audiences, and the Catholic League of Decency, would probably not have accepted it any other way.

Here's director **Victor Fleming** with **Helen Hayes** and **Clark Gable** celebrating a birthday event on the set of *The White Sister*

GABLE VS COOPER

In retrospect, the romantic pairing of **Clark Gable** with **Helen Hayes**, a prim and very grand diva of the American stage, was considered a bit "forced" even at the time.

How? one wonders, did fans who had seen **Hayes** with **Gary Cooper** in the OTHER tearjerker inspired by World War I, *A Farewell to Arms* (1932; *photo right*) compare the two pairings?

No doubt about it. Gable's chief rival for the title of King of Hollywood, **Gary Cooper,** came off better with his pairing with Hayes than Gable did. Many critics thought that Gable was miscast. As Chrystopher J. Spicer wrote: *"Clark looks like he's trying not to crush Hayes rather than being passionate with her. The Gable 'blowtorch' fails to thaw the ice out of The White Sister."*

Episode 51

Hold Your Man (1933)

Clark was rarely pleased with most of the roles he'd been assigned. Privately he accused Louis B. Mayer of "batting me around like I'm a damn tennis ball. Some of the parts I'm forced to play are completely wrong for me."

Hope dawned for Clark when the mogul assigned the very talented screenwriter Anita Loos to write a script for Clark and Harlow as a screen team.

Loos set to work on *Black Orange Blossoms*, a rowdy tale about two con artists trying to survive during the height of a nationwide Depression.

At the time, she was best known for her 1925 comic novel, *Gentlemen Prefer Blondes*. As a writer, Loos was hailed as "The Soubrette of Satire."

Over the course of her career, Loos would write five more films for Harlow, including her final appearance on the screen in *Saratoga* in which she co-starred with Clark for the last time.

In 1919, embarking on her second marriage, Loos had wed John Emerson, a director with whom she worked on several movies starring Douglas Fairbanks Sr. Their films helped make him the biggest star in the world, along with Mary Pickford.

From the beginning, Emerson told her that he had never been faithful to just one woman, and that he had no intention of changing that.

A deal was struck: The couple would be together six days a week, every day except Tuesday. On that day, each of them was free to do whatever either of them desired. When Clark learned about that arrangement, he visited Loos every Tuesday night. Gossip writer Ben Maddox spread the news they were having an affair.

Two views of the sophisticated script writer **Anita Loos**, who sustained an affair with Clark Gable, soothed egos at MGM, and churned out memorable scripts that changed the values of Classic Hollywood.

In the lower photo, **Loos** *(right)* poses for an MGM publicity photo with **Jean Harlow**, star of the script Loos crafted for *Red Headed Woman* (1932). Although Harlow was, at the time she filmed it, the most famous blonde in Hollywood, she gamely posed with Loos as a publicity stunt for her brief association with red-headedness.

From the beginning, they emoted beautifully, with humor and with heat. **Clark Gable** with **Jean Harlow** in *Hold Your Man.*

When Mayer got the script, he had immediate worries that the Hays Office would not allow their heroine to indulge in premarital sex. Before that, the screen antics of both Mae West and Harlow had infuriated censors, who tightened their standards.

In the end, whereas the brass at MGM tolerated the "loose living" of romantic leads, it was determined that before the end of the final reel, they would have "to pay for their misdeeds." With that in mind, the script was revised to include suitable "punishments" for their earlier misdeeds. Harlow spends time in a reformatory, and Gable's character slips in and marries her before he, too, is arrested and forced to spend time in jail. Chastened and somewhat penitent, Harlow's character and his child are waiting for him when he gets out.

To soften her character, Harlow was asked to sing. "My singing was the kind that could get me committed to a long-term prison sentence," she quipped. A real singer, Harriet Lee, was hired as a voice double.

Hold Your Man marked the third film in which Gable and Harlow co-starred. Three more movies lay in their future.

In the Loos plot, a small-town con man, Eddie Nugent, (Clark), trying to hide while pursued by the police, enters the unlocked apartment of Ruby Adams (Harlow). a cynical blonde with a number of boyfriends. At first, they are combative, as in most plots of that era, but in time, she succumbs to his manly charms. Midway through the film, he impregnates her, as we learn later.

As part of a blackmail plot, one of his cronies, Slim (Garry Owen) schemes to catch one of Ruby's admirers in a compromising position with her. At the last minute, to prevent that, Eddie enters the unlocked apartment door and accidentally kills the intended victim.

Eddie escapes but Ruby is arrested by the police and sent to a reformatory. Later, Eddie learns that Ruby is pregnant. His informant is the other woman, Gypsy (Burgess).

Eddie slips into her cell and secretly marries her, but is spotted by an attendant and arrested.

It all ends up happily with Ruby released earlier than Eddie. At last, he can begin life anew as a husband and a father.

Jane Russell *(left)* and **Marilyn Monroe** star in a scene from *Gentlemen Prefer Blondes* (1953), the script for which had also been (brilliantly) crafted by Anita Loos.

Taking advantage of their subjects' respective youth and beauty, studio photographers snapped their shutters often—some said "relentlessly." Here's one of the press and PR photos of Hollywood's then-hottest screen team:— **Gable with Harlow**—that they so effectively captured.

***

Sam Wood was both director and producer of *Hold Your Man*, a dual role he did not relish. He gravitated to the script which he found "sentimental, cheeky, wise-cracking, and swiftly paced."

Mayer allowed Wood to select the supporting players.

Harlow was top billed as Ruby Adams, with Clark cast as Eddie Stuart. Erwin played his buddy, Al Simpson. Dorothy Burgess as Gypsy Angecon was "the other woman," with Garry Owen playing Slim. Louise Beavers was the powder room attendant at a night club.

Other than Victor Fleming, Wood, a son of Philadelphia born in 1883, became one of Clark's favorites. Little did they know at the time, but on the set of *Gone With the Wind*, he would be called upon to direct the film's conclusion. Fleming had to accept another assignment… helming Judy Garland in *The Wizard of Oz* (1939).

In Hollywood in 1919, Wood had been assigned to direct heartthrob Wallace Reid in *Double Speed*. This was the first of five films he helmed with Reid, all of which were released before 1920.

Wood was then assigned to direct Gloria Swanson in her first starring vehicle, *The Great Moment* (1921).

"We started grinding out pictures together," she said, "each one worse than the last. The only thing that changed was the number and the length of the dresses I wore and the face of my leading man."

Actress Barbara Barondess, seventh billed as Sadie Cline, claimed, "Gable was the most gracious gentleman I have ever met." Yet she contradicted herself by adding, "One afternoon when he encountered me on the lot, he called out, 'Hey, Barbara, are you blonde all over?' I managed to suppress an urge to tell him off. I shot back, 'That depends, but you'll never find out.'"

Gradually, Clark got around to meeting other members of the cast and crew. Barondess had been born in Brooklyn in 1907, but her family returned to Russia in 1908. At the time of the Russian Revolution in 1917, the family fled, returning to America.

She grew up to become a star of stage and screen, and a close personal friend of the Off-Broadway producer, Lucille Lortel, owner of the Theatre de Lys on Christopher Street in Manhattan. She received a certain renown when she co-starred in Garbo's best film, *Queen Christina* (1933), the same year she worked with Clark.

As she later told author Darwin Porter, "I was terrified that Garbo was going to try to seduce me."

On the set of *Hold Your Man*, Clark had a reunion with Paul Hurst, cast in it as Aubrey C. Mitchell. They would meet again when he played the lecherous Union soldier shot by Scarlett O'Hara on the staircase of Tara in *Gone With the Wind* (1939).

The stage and movie star, Dorothy Burgess, was a native of Los Angeles born in 1907. George Cukor was one of her early sponsors. He told her indiscreet stories about Clark's private life in the 1920s.

Fox cast her in *In Old Arizona* (1928), one of the first of the outdoor talkies.

One day, Clark's former director, Clarence Brown, who had helmed him in *Possessed* (1931) opposite Joan Crawford, came on the set. Clark was surprised to find that he had unexpectedly proposed marriage to Dorothy Burgess but they soon fell out of love.

Clark even had a couple of beers wth character actor Garry Owen, born in Mississippi in 1902. He is best known today for pLaying the taxi driver in *Arsenic and Old Lace* (1944) with Cary Grant. Amazingly, he would appear in more than 185 films between 1933 and 1951. He was dead at the age of 49.

Clark also bonded with Stuart Erwin, an actor of stage, screen, and later, television. Born in California's Squaw Valley in 1903, he made his first film in 1928. Two years later, he played Joe Palooka in the film *Palooka*. In 1936, he was Oscar-nominated as Best Supporting Actor for *Pigskin Parade*. He worked steadily in character roles until his death at the age of 64 in 1967.

Clark met Louise Beavers, who would also appear later in his career. Born at the dawn of the 20th Century in Cincinnati, Ohio, she was an African American actress who appeared in dozens of films, often as a maid, and later on two hit TV shows.

She won a role in the film *Uncle Tom's Cabin* (1928) and went on to play stereotypical black roles such as those of slaves or domestic servants.

Her most important role was playing a domestic opposite

Two views of **Max Baer** ("Mapcap Maxie"), the son of an Alsatian-Jewish father and a Scottish mother. A "sometimes" actor who held the title of World Heavyweight Boxing Champion (1934-35), he became known for a romance with the recently widowed **Jean Harlow** (pictured with him in the right-hand photo, above.

Baer often credited his physical strength to his teenage years working in a slaughterhouse, carrying heavy carcasses of meat and developing a knack for stunning cattle with a single blow,

Actress **Louise Beavers** got her first taste of Hollywood "ways and means" while working as a maid for silent film diva Leatrice Joy.

After an uncredited role (as a slave at a wedding) in the 1927 silent version of *Uncle Tom's Cabin,* she became a "central casting staple" in dozens of films and TV shows. She often competed with Hattie McDaniel and Ethel Waters for the limited (both in numbers and in scope) roles that were available to her at the time as a woman of color.

Her most famous quote? " *Actors and actresses are all Dr. Jekyll and Mr. Hyde. We play a role...and then we forget it."*

Claudette Colbert in *Imitation of Life* (1934).

Hattie McDaniel was her chief rival for parts. In 1938, when *Gone With the Wind* was first being cast, Beavers met up with Clark, pleading with him to use his influence to get her cast as Mammy. She was disappointed when the part went to McDaniel.

When *Hold Your Man* was released, Frank Nugent of *The New York Times* wrote "The sudden transition from hard-boiled, wisecracking romance to sentimental penitence provides a jolt."

Variety claimed, "Earlier sequences have plenty of ginger, but the torrid details are handled with utmost discretion while conveying a maximum of affect."

London Film Weekly stated, "As a pair of charming toughs, hard as nails, and superbly independent, we have come to know Harlow and Gable on the screen."

The movie made $1.1 million in the U.S. and Canada, and $420,000 abroad, showing a profit of $450,000.

***

During the shoot, Clark offered a distraught Harlow much comfort. She sometimes wanted to talk about the suicide (or murder?) of her late husband, Paul Bern. She revealed that he had left nothing in the bank but a lot of bills (unopened) in the entrance hall of their home. She also complained that her mother and stepfather were spending her money faster than she made it, and that her stepfather was making sexual advances toward her.

Even though she had troubles of her own, she listened patiently as Clark poured out his discontent with Ria Langham and the constant parties she threw.

Sam Wood, the director, claimed, "Jean didn't waste much time satisfying her libido, something that Paul Bern never could do. My hunch was that she was getting royally screwed by Clark during his frequent visits to her dressing room in the afternoon. I soon learned that the boxer, Max Baer, was waiting outside the gate every night to whisk her away, too.

Baer, born in Omaha, Nebraska, in 1909, reigned as the heavyweight boxing champion from 1933 to 1935. In the ring, he was nicknamed "Madcap Maxie."

Harlow indulged in girl talk with Dorothy Burgess. She did not mention Clark, but claimed, "When Max goes to bed with a gal, he satisfies every part of a woman, not only her ears, neck, and mouth, but works his way down to her thighs and big toes. Of course, he hits the target in the rosebud and my honeypot. The only thing I don't like about him is that his Jewish father had his penis clipped over the objections of his Scottish mother. I generally prefer a man who has not been mutilated."

Eddie Mannix, "The Fixer" at MGM, heard that some newspapers were about to reveal the details associated with Harlow's quick recovery from the death of Paul Bern and her torrid affair with Max Baer. It was also going to be reported that her love scenes with Clark weren't confined just to the sceen.

As part of a campaign to "fix" the moral implications of that, Mannix quickly arranged a marriage between Harlow and cinematographer Harold Rosson in 1933. Rosson and Harlow had been friends—not lovers. Although he agreed to go along with this sham marriage, he divorced her eight months later.

A "shotgun marriage," arranged hastily by the studio to offset the exposure that **Jean Harlow** (*left figure in photo above*) was getting for her affairs with (among others) Clark Gable and Max Baer.

The winner who emerged as her next husband was (*right figure, above*) **Harold Rosson**. A cinematographer and (mostly platonic) friend of Harlow, he gamely agreed to the arrangement. He divorced her a few months later.

Today, in addition to his marriage to Hollywood's then-most-famous-blonde, he's best remembered for his work on *The Wizard of Oz (1939)* and *Singin' in the Rain* (1952).

***

Episode 52

Night Flight (1933)

Night Flight was a tribute to the early days of commercial aviation and the brave pilots (as personified by **Clark Gable**, *center photo*) who made it possible.

A Pre-Code aviation drama, *Night Flight* was the first film released by David O. Selznick's new production unit at MGM. It was based on *Vol de Nuit*, a 1931 novel by the French pioneering aviator and anti-Nazi resistance fighter Antoine de Saint-Exupéry. It was inspired by his own experiences of flying across dangerous South American air routes. The film focused on a Trans-Andean airline charged with the emergency transport, during bad weather, of serum that would stem the outbreak of a polio epidemic in Rio de Janeiro.

Selznick told Clark that he wanted *Night Flight* to put *Wings* and *Hell's Angels* to shame. He brought in Clarence Brown, one of the best directors in Hollywood. Brown had previously helmed Clark and Joan Crawford in *Possessed*.

Whereas Brown was assigned the task of casting the film's minor roles, Selznick demanded an all-star cast of dazzling names, including both John Barrymore and his more benign but less handsome brother, Lionel. Each of them was revered as both a stage and film actor. John Barrymore got top billing, followed by Helen Hayes, Clark, Lionel Barrymore, Robert Montgomery, Myrna Loy, and William Gargan.

The film brought Clark together again with Hayes. They had recently co-starred in *The White Sister*. However, in *Night Flight*, there is only one scene of them together. The rest of the movie involved his fatal flight and the face of her anguish waiting to learn if her husband is dead or alive. Actually, these scenes of him were filmed inside the cockpit of an airplane resting securely on tarmac.

As shooting progressed, Selznick interfered annoyingly (and daily) with Brown's direction. He ordered scene after scene reshot, which ran up the budget, increasing the ire of Louis B. Mayer.

On the set, Clark renewed his longtime relationship with Lionel Barrymore, and, once again, at the aging actor's request, they shared the same dressing room. Lionel still liked to give Clark a nude massage at the end of the day's shooting.

John Barrymore, born in Philadephia in 1882, came from one of America's greatest theatrical families. When he played *Hamlet* on Broadway in 1922, he was hailed as "the greatest living American tragedian."

Perhaps John hardly remembered meeting Clark when the revered actor had starred alongside his brother, Lionel, on Broadway in *The Jest*, way back in 1919. At the time, Clark had not been hired as an actor, but as a "callboy." His job involved knocking on the door of the actors in the production and (politely) calling out, "Mr. Barrymore, you're due on the stage in five minutes."

Before working with Clark, John Barrymore had made the film classic, *Grand Hotel* (1932), starring opposite Greta Garbo. After *Night Flight*, he was cast in *Twentieth Century* (1934) opposite Carole Lombard, Clark's future wife.

Clark thought he'd learn something from watching "The Great Profile" (aka John Barrymore) emote on screen. What he learned was that he always seemed to be intoxicated and had to read his lines from cue cards.

John Barrymore was cast as the ruthless A. Rivière, the managing director of the airport, who doesn't seem to mind sending his pilots on life-threatening flights above the Andes at night.

Clark was cast as Jules Fabian, married to Hayes. Lionel was inspector Robneau and Robert Montgomery was the pilot, Augusts Pellerin.

Myrna Loy played the wife of William Gargan, a Brazilian pilot.

Pellerin's girlfriend was played by Dorothy Burgess, who had recently been cast as "the other woman" in the Harlow/Gable movie, *Hold Your Man*. Frank Conway was cast as a radio operator, having appeared before in *Possessed*, a Joan Crawford/Gable vehicle.

Robert Montgomery would be a future co-star with Crawford and Clark in *Forsakng All Others* (1934). Born in 1904 in Beacon, New York, he grew up to become an actor, first on the stage, later drifting to Hollywood. Around the time of his departure, his father jumped off the Brooklyn Bridge to his death after he lost his fortune.

Montgomery co-starred opposite Norma Shearer in *Private Lives* (1931) and with Tallulah Bankhead in *Faithless* (1932).

Scott Eyman claimed, "He is one of the chilliest, most pompous actors to find his way to Hollywood."

Even so, he was elected president of the Screen Actors Guild in 1935.

Born a son of Brooklyn, William Gargan was cast as the husband of Myrna Loy. He'd made his first film when he was seven years old, hired by Vitagraph Pictures at a salary of four dollars a day. Before working with Clark, he had just finished a role in *Rain* (1932), starring Joan Crawford as a prostitute.

Night Flight was the first movie in which Clark would star with Myrna Loy, who would make a series of films with him in their immediate future.

Their relationship got off to a bad start. "At the studio, he was always on the make, after everyone, snapping garters left and right," Loy said.

William Grady, in a supporting role, claimed, "That Clark was one hell of a guy, completely reckless. He'd take on any gal. She didn't have to be pretty or even young. She didn't even have to practice good hygiene."

***

Every month, the Mayfair Club staged a dance. Clark's wife, Ria Langham, was a member, and she asked Clark to go with her to the dance. His agent, Minna Wallis, did not have an escort that evening. Neither did Myrna Loy. So Clark was "enrolled" as the escort of all three of them.

WHEN DIVAS CLASH

According to Robert Osborne, **Helen Hayes** felt intimidated by **John Barrymore**, Barrymore was often notoriously drunk during filming, and relied, sometimes unsuccessfully, on cue cards to remember his lines.)

When they filmed their emotionally fraught scene together, Barrymore refrained from relying on cue cards, "because he didn't want to use a crutch in the presence of a real actress."

Later, Hayes remarked that Barrymore's explanation was the greatest review that she ever received

When the orchestra played "Dancing in the Dark," he asked Loy to dance with him.

"He was no Fred Astaire," Loy recalled, "but sorta okay— except he held me too tight."

At the end of the evening, all four of them got into a chauffeur-driven limousine. Wallis was dropped off first, before the drive to Loy's residence.

"Clark sat in the middle, between Ria and me," Loy said. "He was drunk, right in front of Ria. He edged over to me and tried to feel my breast. I could not believe what was happening right in front of his wife."

"At my house, he walked me to the door, where he insisted on a good night kiss," Loy recalled. "He was very aggressive, giving me a 'monkey bite' on my neck. I shoved him back, and he fell into the bushes off my front porch. It was three days before that monkey bite disappeared."

During the filming of *Night Flight,* they had no scenes together. "I did encounter him one time. He walked right past me without speaking."

At the end of the shoot Clark told Lionel Barrymore, "This damn picture has been a waste of our talent, a complete waste of time and money. I'll never work with any production of Selznick ever again."

[Anyone who has seen Gone With the Wind *knows that wasn't true.]*

The critic for *The New York Herald Tribune* wrote, "Even though with the handsome Clark Gable there is little in *Night Flight* to hold feminine interest, its greatest appeal will be among aviation enthusiasts."

London Film Weekly found "There's too many stars in little parts. Gable, for instance, sits in the plane cockpit throughout his performance. John Barrymore is never seen out of his office."

Variety weighed in: "As to cast, the names are obviously a marquee hypo. Most of 'em are wasted. The sub-people are about on a par with the others as regards histrionic contribution. Gable is almost wholly superfluous as a flyer. John Barrymore is more forceful of the *frères*. Being importantly cast as the brutal managing director of the air service, Lionel is altogether a vague characterization."

Mayer was disappointed at the box office receipts, which generated a profit of only $180,000.

Saint-Exupéry, the author on whose novella the film had been based, sat through a screening of *Night Flight* in Paris and then left the theater in a state of fury. In 1942, the film was withdrawn from circulation as a result of his feud with MGM.

That was when the studio's copyright expired. The public would have to wait until after the legal obstacles had cleared *(i.e., in 2011)* to see it.

Myrna Loy with her love interest in the film, **William Gargan.** In reference to Loy, Gargan said, "She's not a movie queen. Instead of that, she's a real person."

According to Loy, "*Night Flight* was a minor picture for me. Bigger things were on my horizon. But for a girl from Montana with a freckled face, slanted eyes, and red hair, I didn't do too badly."

Aviator, writer, and resistance fighter
Antoine de Saint-Exupéry
(1900-1944)

In terms of book sales, at least, whereas *Vol De Nuit (Night Flight)* was relatively sleepy, **Saint-Exupery's** all-time best seller was *The Little Prince (Le Petit Prince).* A novella, it relays the parable of a young prince who visits various planets, including Earth, and addresses themes of friendship, love, loneliness, and loss.

It became the author's most successful work, selling an estimated 140 million copies worldwide, which makes it one of the best-selling in history. It has been translated into more than 500 languages and/or dialects worldwide, being the second most translated work ever published, trailing only the Bible.

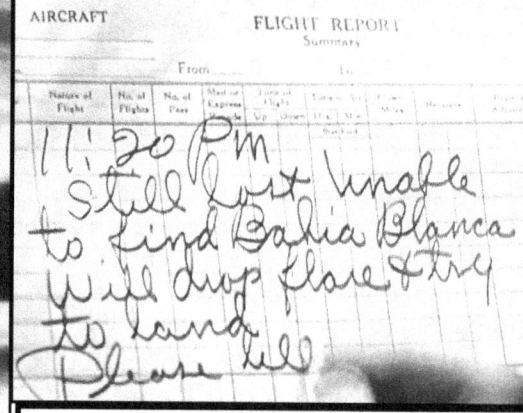

Getting mystical and transcendental with Fabian (i.e., **Clark Gable**), in the moments before his crash in *Night Flight*.

As widely discussed within literary and show-biz circles of the 1930s, the author (**Antoine de St-Exupéry**) of the novel *(Vol de Nuit)* on which *Night Flight* was based was traumatized by MGM's film adaptation.

Recognizing the nuanced complexity of its prose, its producers had opted for less, rather than more, dialogue. Consequently, Clark Gable's character (Fabian) was assigned very few lines. Soldierly and heroically, he endures his fate in silence. Whether that artistic decision succeeded in the transmission of the novel's moments of transcendence became a widely disputed point.

Prior to the release of the film adaptation, St-Exupéry had been largely unknown to the American public. *Night Flight* literally made him famous. Nonetheless, when his agreement with MGM expired in 1942, he refused to renew it. As a reaction, MGM stopped distributing it for 69 years (until 2011), when the legal issues with St-Exupéry's estate were resolved.

At least some of the French author's prose was about transcendental clarity: Inserted below is an English-language translation of the text that describes the pilot's anguish and later, the luminosity he experiences immediately prior to his death:

"And now a wonder seized him. Dazzled by that brightness, he had to keep his eyes closed for some seconds. He had never dreamt the night-clouds could dazzle thus. But the full moon and all the constellations were changing them to light.

"In a flash, the very instant he had risen clear, the pilot found a peace that passed his understanding. Not a ripple tilted the plane, but like a ship that has crossed the bar, it moved within a tranquil anchorage. In an unknown secret corner of the sky it floated, as in a harbour of the Happy Isles. Below him still the storm was fashioning another world, thridded with squalls and cloudbursts and lightnings, but turning to the stars a face of crystal snow.

"Now all grew luminous, his hands, his clothes, the wings, and Fabian thought that he was in a limbo of strange magic; for the light did not come down from the stars but welled up from below, from all that snowy whiteness."

PARLEZ-VOUS FRANÇAIS?

Whereas **Saint-Exupéry's** command of French (his native language) was magnificent, his English was always haltingly inadequate. As relayed in her memoirs by his English-language tutor, Adèle Breaux:

"Saint-Exupéry's prodigious writings and studies of literature sometimes gripped him, and on occasion he continued his readings of literary works until moments before take-off on solitary military reconnaissance flights, as he was adept at both reading and writing while flying. Taking off with an open book balanced on his leg, his ground crew would fear his mission would quickly end after contacting something 'very hard'. On one flight, to the chagrin of colleagues awaiting his arrival, he circled the Tunis airport for an hour so that he could finish reading a novel. Saint-Exupéry frequently flew with a lined carnet (notebook) during his long, solo flights, and some of his philosophical writings were created during such periods when he could reflect on the world below him, becoming 'enmeshed in a search for ideals which he translated into fable and parable'."

Episode 53

Clark Faces Upheavals
At MGM and in His Personal Life as
His Father Returns

Every year, at Christmastime, Louis B. Mayer threw a lavish party for his executives, his stars, and his workers, from electricians to set designers.

After delivering a speech, he left the building. "With him gone and everybody drunk on bootleg liquor, these parties didn't break up until dawn—and turned into orgies," claimed writer Anita Loos. "In the screening rooms, stag films were shown, making everyone horny, often leading to sex without gender preference."

Clark was urged by Eddie Mannix not to attend. "I'm afraid our horny female employees and our multiple homosexuals will tear your clothes off and rape you."

He went anyway, dressed as a preacher with a dog collar around his neck. Accompanying him was Marion Davies wearing her trapeze outfit from their recent movie, *Polly of the Circus* (1932).

Shortly before dawn, Clark was seen heading to his dressing room with two young starlets.

Irving Thalberg's wife, Norma Shearer, wanted to exit from the party at one o'clock, but her husband refused. Whereas she stormed out in a huff, he stayed at the party until 5AM. Normally, because of his heart condition, he drank only a small glass of wine at dinner. But at the party, he became heavily intoxicated, drinking until he passed out.

Two security guards carried him to his chauffeur-driven limousine. They delivered him to his home, where a furious Shearer let them into the house, instructing them to carry him to his bedroom.

Thalberg woke up around one o'clock the following afternoon. Shearer had made repeated

In 1931, a year before the fateful "real life" Christmas party described in this episode, **Clark Gable** had been one of about a dozen MGM stars featured within Louis B. Mayer's "feel-good" Yuletide short film.

Some of the adult actors it included defined it as a 9-minute career-boost for **Jackie Cooper** (shown within the *inset photo, left*). At the time Cooper was MGM's "answer" to the (by today's standards, very annoying) **Shirley Temple** (*inset photo, right*) a proven money-maker for Fox.

The following year, MGM's Christmas party wasn't anything meant for filming and/or public consumption. An all-adult, all-night affair, it broke standards for debauched excess, the after-effects of which profoundly influenced Irving Thalberg, Norma Shearer, Clark Gable, and the future of MGM..

visits to his room before she found him awake. Because he had a high fever, she called the doctor, who visited him every day. Finally, on the third day, Thalberg had a heart attack and was rushed to the hospital.

MGM's "Christmas Party Orgy" was followed that year by a more sedate party on New Year's Eve. Clark attended, accompanied his wife, Ria Langham and the recently widowed Jean Harlow.

Before arriving at the party, he drove them over to visit Thalberg, who had returned from the hospital. Shearer met them at the door, turning them away, asserting that her husband was too ill to receive visitors.

Thalberg needed a long rest to recover, so he and Shearer sailed to Europe, where they stayed at the spa at Bad Nauheim in Germany. It would be a long recovery.

Mayer announced that until Thalberg recovered, he'd be in charge of Thalberg's job overseeing MGM's producers, directors and stars. Instead of one boss telling him what to do, Clark—along with virtually every other star at MGM—met and dealt with an array of different men.

Among them were David O. Selznick, Mayer's son-in-law. He had previously been working at the now nearly bankrupt RKO.

As a result of Thalberg's extended convalescence, Harry Rapf became a major producer for MGM, and the brothers, Lewis and Joseph Schenck, began overseeing (and controlling) the actors' salaries. Around the same time, Hunt Stromberg, a film producer, established a reputation as the producer of some of MGM's most enduring hits, including *The Thin Man* film series (1934-1947).

Long before David O. Selznick cast Clark as Rhett Butler in *Gone With the Wind* (1939), he showed a keen interest in inviting him to join the all-star cast of *Dinner at Eight* (1933). A son of Pittsburgh, Selznick was only a year older than Clark. One of his biggest successes at MGM would be that Pre-Code comedic drama that starred Marie Dressler, John Barrymore, Lionel Barrymore, Wallace Beery, Billie Burke, and others. The only role suitable for Clark was deemed too small, so it went instead to Edmund Lowe.

Many decisions about how to cast Clark in future pictures were decided by Hunt Stromberg. A native son of Louisville, Kentucky, he was born in 1894. His 30-year career in Hollywood began in 1921. He'd begun his career as a newspaper reporter, but in time, headed for Hollywood, where he teamed with film industry pioneer, Thomas H. Ince.

[Ince was believed to have been shot by William Randolph Hearst aboard a yacht. It was rumored that in the dark, he was mistaken for Charlie Chaplin, whom the press baron believed was having an affair with his mistress, Marion Davies.]

Stromberg later joined MGM and became one of the studio's "Big Four" (Mayer, Thalberg, Stromberg, and Harry Rapf.) He produced all of Jean Harlow's films, often teaming her with Clark. He also produced many of Joan Crawford's breakthrough movies. Stromberg's greatest achievement was teaming William Powell with Myrna Loy in all those "Thin Man" sequels, some of the highest-grossing films of the 1930s. Clark had been considered (but later rejected) for the original lead of the private detective and sleuth.

The Treasury Department listed Stromberg as one of the highest-paid executives in the United States. After eighteen years, Stromberg and Mayer had a fight, and he walked away from a contract worth millions.

Photos, clockwise from *upper left*: **Irving Thalberg** with his wife, **Norma Shearer**, onboard a cruise ship hauling them home from Germany after Thalberg's recuperation at Bad Nauheim.

Upper right: **Shearer,** cover girl on a 1936 edition of *Photoplay*, the year of Thalberg's death.

Lower photo: The then very posh spa (*Der Sprudelhof*) at Bad Nauheim, site of Thalberg's prolonged convalescence after the heart attack he suffered in the aftermath of MGM's 1932 Christmas Party.

During Thalberg's enforced convalescence, the *wunderkind* who partially replaced him was **Hunt Stromberg**. He appears above in a 1924 promotion of his cinematic savvy.

A fan and ally of Clark Gable, and before he quit MGM in a rage, he did a lot to promote him during his early casting calls.

Mayer let him go in February of 1942 as American entered World War II. In the aftermath of his (forced) departure, Stromberg launched his own production company, retiring as a rich man in 1951.

In August of 1968, at the age of 74, he died in Santa Monica.

Behind the scenes, Stromberg was instrumental in getting Clark cast in *Manhattan Melodrama* (1934), co-starring with Myrna Loy and William Powell.

Before that, he was instrumental in reteaming Clark with Joan Crawford in *Dancing Lady* (1933). Stromberg also reteamed Clark with Jean Harlow in *China Seas* (1935) and reunited Norma Shearer with Clark in *Idiot's Delight* (1939).

Although Harry Rapf, born in New York City in 1880, became a big-time producer at MGM, he never quite understood the star attraction of Clark Gable. Early in her career, he put Joan Crawford on the casting couch and made her a star. In his first meeting with Clark, he said, "I got the bitch long before you plugged her."

During his 20-year career, Rapf was one of the founding members of the Academy of Motion Picture Arts and Sciences.

***

A disheveled Will Gable, Clark's father, showed up one day in 1933 at the studio gates of MGM. Facing security guards, he claimed he was the father of Clark Gable and demanded to be admitted. Instead, he was refused entry.

Somehow, he got the private address of Ria Langham and Clark Gable and headed there. Tired of tour buses and fans massing outside, Clark and Ria had moved from Beverly Hills to a more secluded colonial-style home in Brentwood, further west. Also living there were Ria's children (Clark's stepchildren), Jana and Alfred.

Surprisingly, a society matron like Ria took Clark's father in and set about transforming him. He had a foul smell to him, but she immediately gave him a room. He had to share a bathroom with her son.

That very day, she ordered carpenters to start building a separate bathroom for her father-in-law. She also found a suitable wardrobe of clothing Clark had grown tired of, and summoned a barber to the house before Clark came home.

Will looked undernourished and in bad health. The following day, she drove him to both her dentist and her doctor in Beverly Hills for checkups and treatments.

Clark's reunion with his father, whom he had not seen in eleven years, did not go well. His last job had been working at a gas station in North Dakota. Clark's last sight of Will was before he fled from the oilfields of Oklahoma heading for Oregon.

With the understanding that Ria had already fed Will shortly after he arrived earlier that day, since he said he hadn't had anything to eat in two days, she also directed her cook to prepare him a big steak dinner.

As the evening progressed, Clark learned that Will still believed that all actors were sissies and fairies. "But I have to hand it to them; some of them know how to make money. You've done well for yourself, son. I made great sacrifices for you as a boy, and I think the time has come for you to pay me back, letting me live the good life after all my struggles to bring you up."

Clark soon learned that his father had seen only one of his fims, *Red Dust* (1932), in which he'd been teamed with Jean Harlow. "That blonde Jean Harlot (mispronouncing her name) looks like one hot piece of ass." So far as it is known, that was the only review Will gave of his son's film

Two views of **the Gables, Clark** and his father, **Will**. In both of them, Clark, at least, seems distinctly uncomfortable.

Clark Gable with his wealthy (and image-conscious) second wife, **Ria Langham**. Having adopted the *persona* of a dutiful wife to her megastar husband, she made concessions for the care and feeding of **Will Gable** (i.e. Clark's errant father) that Clark himself would probably not have made.

Even though Clark had become the King of Hollywood and was hailed as the most masculine man on the screen, his dad asserted again and again that all actors are sissies or fairies.

career in the early 1930s.

Years later, he did offer his comments about *Gone With the Wind:* "I walked out of the movie house halfway through it. It's too damn long. Clark came off looking like some overdressed dandy. I didn't like that English cunt, Vivien Leigh. She wasn't sexy at all. Also, another criticism: Too many niggers."

The Gable family's home life in Brentwood went along largely without Clark, who lived in a different part of the house with its own private entrance. In contrast, Will blended in with the household, eating and living close to Ria and her two children, Jana and Alfred, who called him "Grandpa."

Will discovered a local tavern where he developed some cronies. Clark gave him a $50 bill whenever he was short of cash. He told his newly cultivated friends: "Clark is married to this older broad. He married her for her money since she's far older. I hate to say it, but my son is a gigolo."

One night when he was intoxicated, Will told his cronies, "I'm going home to fuck my daughter-in-law. My son certainly isn't doing it."

Clark was drinking heavily at the time, consuming his daily bottle of gin. He had become disappointed with his agent, Minna Wallis, and was dissatisfied with his recent film scripts. He fired her and hired a much more powerful agent, Bert Allenberg, whose clients included Wallace Beery and John Huston. Other clients included Jack Conway, who had directed Clark in *The Easiest Way* (1931) and Wesley Ruggles, who had helmed him in *No Man of Her Own* (1932). Another client of Allenberg's was the director Sam Wood, who had helmed Jean Harlow and Clark in *Hold Your Man* (1933).

The living arrangements described above came to an end in the spring of 1934. In a lavish wedding financed by Clark, Will married Edna Gable, the widow of Clark's brother, Frank.

For the couple, he purchased a bungalow in North Hollywood for $3,500. He also gave them a monthly living allowance of $500, which he took out of his $3,000 weekly salary.

MOVIE MEDIA: *LET'S GO HOME WITH CLARK*

More than almost any other celebrity of his heyday, **Clark Gable** was lavishly credited by the media for his allegiance with the "home-and-hearth" ideals of the "between-the-wars" middle class.

Here's how his home life with **Ria Langham** was (reverently but mythically) described in the text of the article (**Screenplay Magazine,** July 1934) that accompanied this illustration:

"*Clark—dashing figure of a million romantic dreams—is pretty much like your-man-John around the house. He's a home man. You'd probably find him in old duck pants and a red sweater—how that man loves red!—with a pipe in his mouth and cleaning his gun. Or working in the garden, as I did... Many a morning he's out there at six-thirty digging. And on a day off from the studio if he doesn't trek off to the mountains, he wraps an antique, very faded bandana around his neck, pulls on some blue jeans and starts in hoeing.*

"*But don't picture the Gables as living in the backwoods. They don't! They live on a quiet street in Brentwood about five miles from the Metro studio where he works—as you may have heard. The same street that Joan Crawford and Helen Twelvetrees and several other stars live on. It's like a breath of the country out there, however, and I think that's what sold it to Clark.*"

Episode 54

Dancing Lady (1933)

After Louis B. Mayer ordered Joan Crawford and Clark Gable to end their adulterous affair, he'd been bombarded with "a ton of fan mail" demanding that he recast them together in a new movie. Money won out over morality.

At the time, Crawford was divorcing her first husband, Douglas Fairbanks Jr. Clark, however, was still "up to his neck" in his sham marriage to Ria Langham. Ironically, Crawford sometimes lunched with her, pretending to be her friend.

During the eighteen months Crawford was separated from Clark, she was "heavy dating" the actor, Franchot Tone, who was still a bachelor-at-large.

She had spread the word about his endowment. "Franchot has a ten-inch cock, and he demands that all of his conquests, male and female, pay homage to it." It was rumored that she had nicknamed him "Jawbreaker."

Mayer ordered his son-in-law, David O. Selznick, to come up with a suitable script for a Crawford/Gable "revival." With that in mind, he signed Robert Z. Leonard as director during pre-production. He had recently helmed Clark in *Strange Interlude* (1932) with Norma Shearer.

The Pre-Code musical, *Dancing Lady,* was based on a 1932 novel by James Warner Bellah. It took four scriptwriters, including Robert Benchley, to devise a suitable script.

After it was received by Crawford, she met with Mayer, claiming she didn't like it. He demanded that she do it anyway. She finally gave in to his demand, but insisted that he cast Tone in the third lead

Stars emoting between numbers: . Was it love? **Gable** with **Crawford** in *Dancing Lady.*

[Crawford's last picture had been Today We Live, *an MGM release in 1933. It was her one and only picture with Gary Cooper, and it was directed by Howard Hawks and written by William Faulkner. Franchot Tone had a supporting role.]*

Leonard had no choice in the actors who would be assigned the trio of leading roles, but he was allowed to cast the minor characters. For the fourth lead of Dolly Todhunter, he hired May Robson. She had previously appeared with Clark in *Strange Interlude* (1932) and *The White Sister* (1933).

In other roles, Robert Benchley played Ward King; Eve Arden, Clark's future co-star, was cast in the uncredited role of Marcia, a Southern actress

Making their film debuts were Fred Astaire and the singer, Nelson Eddy. Appearing in a cameo were Ted Healy and the Three Stooges, Curly and Moe Howard and Larry Fine.

After their enforced separation, the renewal of Clark's relationship with Crawford did not go well. She accused him of having an affair with Jean Harlow, "a so-called actress I detest. I kept my bargain with you and I'm divorcing Douglas. Did you forget our bargain? You were to get off your ass and begin divorce proceedings against Langham."

"I can't do it now. I've hired a good-looking young stud to manage our household affairs. I want to catch them in bed together. Otherwise, in the divorce court, she'll bleed me dry in alimony for years to come."

"I don't have years to waste," Crawford said.

"I've heard about Franchot Tone," he said. "Selznick told me that we'll be working with that god damn fairy in this picture."

"Franchot is only a part-time fairy, as you call him. He's also very successful with the ladies."

[Douglas Fairbanks Jr. was fully aware that his wife was having an affair with Clark. In his memoir, Salad Days, *he wrote: "For almost two years, Billie (Crawford) had been having an intense and fully requited love affair with Clark Gable, one of our friends and a frequent dinner guest. Her extra early morning departures for the studio, even when not filming, and her late return home were often the only times they could meet undetected by me or Clark's wife, Ria."*

"I was surprised to learn that one of their favorite trysting places at the studio was the charmingly decorated, very comfortable dressing room that I had given her as a wedding present—and had only recently finished paying for it."

Of course, Fairbanks wasn't wasting any time waiting for Crawford to return from one of her trysts. He might be found in the bed of Tallulah Bankhead, Marlene Dietrich, Elissa Landi, Lupe Velez, Loretta Young, or the ballerina, Vera Zorina.

When Fairbanks Jr. was cited as a party in a divorce action, Jack Warner said, "That guy Fairbanks has so many faggot friends, I was beginning to wonder about him. This scandal will prove that he's not a fairy."

Clark didn't like the script of *Dancing Lady* but agreed to do the picture anyway. He had one demand for Mayer: He wanted to be billed over Crawford. He did not get his wish.

In the script, Janie Barlow (Crawford) is reduced to being a stripper in a burlesque show, which leads to her arrest for indecent exposure.

She is bailed out by Ted Newton (Tone), a millionaire playboy. He gets her a gig in a Broadway musical being directed by "Patch Gallagher," who is rather ruthless with Janie until he falls in love with her, much to the heartbreak of Tone's character.

Robert Benchley, born in Worcester, Massachusetts in 1889, was a writer and humorist best known for his movie shorts and his newspaper column. He was a founding member of the fabled Algonquin Round Table in Manhattan.

Nelson Eddy, born in Rhode Island in 1901, was an actor and baritone singer in nineteen musical films in the 1930s and '40s. Today, he is remembered for the eight musicals he made with soprano Jeanette MacDonald, who became his longtime mistress. In his heyday, he was the highest-paid male singer in the world.

During pre-production, Crawford met Adrian, the fashion designer, who gave her that "broad-shoulder look" that would become her trademark. He would design her wardrobe for the next fourteen years.

Dancing Lady marked the film debut of Fred Astaire, if you discount a brief appearance in a 1916 silent movie when he was only sixteen.

Born in 1899 in Omaha, Nebraska, he became, over the course of his career, the greatest "popular music" dancer of all time, especially in all those RKO musicals of the 1930s where he danced with Ginger Rogers. At the time of his death at the age of 88, the American Film Institute designated him as the fifth greatest star of all time.

He hardly looked like a future movie star. In *Dancing Lady*, he appeared in Bavarian *lederhosen* showing off his bony legs.

Eve Arden emerged from Mill Valley, California, in 1908. Later, as a stage, screen, and television actress, she had a career that began in 1929 and lasted until 1987.

Her first film appearance was in *Stage Door* (1937) with Katharine Hepburn. Her greatest role was in *Mildred Pierce* (1945) opposite Joan Crawford, for which she was nominated for a Best Supporting Actress Oscar.

Her highest profile came on television (1952-1957), when cast as a school teacher, *Our Miss Brooks*, appearing in living rooms across America. *[Prior to that (1948-1957), she'd played the same character in a radio series with the same name. In 1956, she reprised her role in a film, also with the same name.]*

During the filming of *Dancing Lady*, its featured star, **Joan Crawford**, endured torrents of negative publicity from her by-then-estranged first husband **Douglas Fairbanks, Jr**. One detail he wasn't shy about discussing was her prolonged adulterous affair with Clark Gable.

Above, the "then darlings of America" are depicted in a publicity still from the only film they ever made together, ***Our Modern Maidens*** (1929), a silent, Jazz Age morality tale.

Selznick was ordered by Mayer to shoot *Dancing Lady* in just one month, but despite everyone's efforts, it took four months because of the bad health of Clark.

After the first week of filming, he felt great pain in his mouth, especially from his remaining rotten teeth. He drank from a bottle of gin to help relieve the ache.

One night, he woke up in such agony that he was sent to the hospital in an ambulance.

A case of pyorrhea had developed with his forever-troublesome gums and teeth. *[Pyorrhea (aka periodontitis) is a bacterial gum disease. Symptoms include swollen or tender gums that bleed easily, bad breath, and pus between the teeth and gums. It can lead to receding gums, destruction of the tooth's support bone, and tooth loss.]* The infection was spreading rapidly throughout his body.

George Hollenbach Jr., the best dental surgeon in Beverly Hills, was brought in to rescue him. Hollenbach removed all of his teeth, but Clark had to wait for two weeks before he could be fitted with a new set of dentures.

When news of this leaked out, Eddie Mannix, "The Fixer" at MGM, didn't want the public to know that their romantic hero would appear in his next picture with dentures. The story that Mannix released was that Clark had had surgery for appendicitis.

Shortly after Clark returned to work, he was stricken again. During another stay in the hospital, it was discovered that the *pyorrhea* which had devastated his mouth had also invaded his gall bladder, which was removed.

During this delay, with production costs rising, Selznick and Mayer considered replacing Clark with Robert Montgomery.

Finally back at work, Clark was told that because of the delays he had caused, his salary had been cut by $25,000, a huge sum back in those Depression years.

After an early sneak preview, a lot of fans wrote that Clark looked haggard in *Dancing Lady's* final scenes. Selznick called him back to work to reshoot his close-ups with Crawford. By then, his looks, for the most part, had been restored.

At the end of the shoot, Clark was informed that Crawford and Tone had headed to New York on the *Santa Fe Chief--20th Century Limited*, sharing a bedroom suite.

Dancing Lady did well at the box office, generating a profit of $750,000. Mordant Hall in *The New York Times* wrote, "It is for the most part quite a lively affair The dancing of Fred Astaire and Miss Crawford is most graceful and charming. The photographic effects of their scenes are an impressive achievement. Miss Crawford takes her role with no little seriousness."

Variety claimed, "Saying it is a backstage show is hardly enough. There have been plenty of those. But *Dancing Lady* is so basically different that it belongs in a different category. Everything is built upon a fundamental story."

Time magazine wrote: "The versatile Mr. Gable is cast surprisingly as a stage director instead of a gangster. He might make hoofing the rage. Perhaps the film should have been called *Dancing Man* to introduce the new Clark Gable. Although it would be a premature observation, to say that Fred Astaire might have some future competition from Gable, it would not be invalid."

Dancing Lady marked the onscreen debut of **Fred Astaire** *(right)*, appearing here in full-drag Bavarian *schtick* with a dirndl-clad (and blonde) **Joan Crawford**.

Here's **Adrian** (aka Adrian Adolph Greenburg) probably the most influential fashion designer of MGM's very glamourous golden age.

A favorite of Norma Shearer, Katharine Hepburn, and Jean Harlow, he designed the "square-shouldered' look that dominated **Joan Crawford's** fashion identity in 28 of her films.

***

During the making of *Dancing Lady*, Clark became aware of several events taking place that directly or indirectly affected him. First, he got to know Franchot Tone, his future co-star in *Mutiny on the Bounty*

(1935). Any jealousy he might have felt about his affair with Crawford, he concealed.

Unlike Crawford and Clark, who had had bleak childhoods, Tone was born in 1905 in Niagara Falls, New York, into a privileged family. During the time he worked with Clark, he had never married.

His father was Dr. Frank Jerome Tone, president of the Carborundum Company. His socially prominent wife (Franchot's mother) was Gertrude Van Vrancken Tone. With her husband's consent, Gertrude sustained an affair with Dorothy Thompson, hailed at the time as "The First Lady of American Journalism." *Time* magazine claimed that Thompson's influence equaled that of Eleanor Roosevelt. In 1934, because of her writings against Hitler, she was the first journalist expelled from Nazi Germany. News of her expulsion from Germany was publicized around the world. From 1928 to 1942, Thompson was married to Sinclair Lewis, the winner of the Nobel Prize for Literature.

As young Franchot grew up, Thompson appeared frequently at his home. From an early age, he moved within a world of sophisticated people where bisexuality was accepted.

From an early age, movie star **Franchot Tone** (*the upper figure in the photo, right,* where he's embracing his then-wife, **Joan Crawford**, in *Dancing Lady*) was adept at handling forceful and very intelligent women.

His wealthy, socially liberal, and very prominent mother, **Gertrude Van Vrancken Tone**t (*she's depicted in the photo on the upper left*), was a tireless advocate of women's suffrage. She had been a mentor to (and sustained a widely-whispered-about romantic and sexual affair with) the syndicated columnist **Dorothy Thompson** (*lower left photo*).

Thompson, sometimes cited as the most influential woman in America after Eleanor Roosevelt, and "the queen of America's overseas press corps" had been evicted from Nazi Germany because of her printed condemnations of Adolf Hitler during his rise to prominence. In one of her editorials from 1931, she described him as "inconsequent and voluble ... the very prototype of the little man."

Before meeting Crawford, he had a number of affairs with both men and women.

In Hollywood, he fell in love with an actor born in Brooklyn in 1907, Ross Alexander. Alexander had begun his career on Broadway, appearing in plays which included *Let Us Be Gay* (1928). He was signed to a movie contract by Paramount in 1932.

Later, Alexander became a contract player at Warners, where he co-starred with Errol Flynn in *Captain Blood* (1935). Both the bisexual Flynn and Alexander had a torrid affair.

Alexander often appeared on the set of *Dancing Lady* after the day's shoot and headed into the night with Tone. Crawford didn't seem to mind. Months earlier, Clark had learned that Crawford was bisexual herself. That was the real reason he didn't think a marriage to her would work out.

When Tone was sleeping with Alexander, she was bedding Barbara Stanwyck.

Considering his background, Clark could hardly condemn those who had same-sex relationships, although he continued to utter homophobic remarks, hoping it would remove suspicion from his life in the 1920s.

Alexander was heading for doom. To conceal his homosexuality, he married actress Aleta Freel in 1934. In December of 1935, she shot herself in the head with a .22 rifle.

In September of 1936, he married another actress, Anne Nagel, with whom he had co-starred in *China Clipper* and *Here Comes Carter* (both released in 1936).

With his new wife, he had moved to Encino. His personal and professional lives were in disarray, and he was heavily in debt. He used a pistol to commit suicide on January 2, 1937. He was only 29 years old.

***

William Haines, with whom Clark had had an affair in the 1920s, had made the transition from silent film star to a wise-cracking, arrogant leading man at MGM in early 1930s talkies. The 1930 *Quigley Poll* of film exhibitors listed Haines as the top box office attraction in the country.

On a visit to Manhattan in 1926, he met and fell in love with Jimmy Shields and brought him back to Hollywood. They were seen everywhere with each other. The pace of rumors about his life as a homosexual quickened.

To squelch the rumors, Louis B. Mayer ordered Eddie Mannix, "The Fixer", to link Pola Negri, the Polish screen vamp of the 1920s, to a mock engagement with Haines. Negri agreed to go along with the fake news, providing she was justly compensated,

By 1931, she had ended her second marriage to the self-styled Prince George Mdvani, one of the notorious "marrying Mdvanis" who wed prominent women for their money.

Before that, in 1925, she had made a spectacle of herself at the Manhattan funeral of screen idol Rudolph Valentino. She falsely claimed that he had been the love of her life. At the funeral, for the benefit of photographers, she fainted four times.

Tallulah Bankhead claimed, "Negri is a lying lesbo. A Polish publicity hound. She has a mustache and can't act her way out of a paper bag."

Haines, for a while, went along with this *faux* engagement until one afternoon, at the Los Angeles YMCA, he was arrested while fellating a young sailor.

Mannix tried to suppress news of his arrest. Mayer summoned Haines to his office and ordered, "Give up Shields or give up your career."

Haines chose to give up his film career. In the aftermath of that decision, he became the leading interior decorator of Hollywood, re-doing the home of his best friend, Joan Crawford The list of his clients was long, ranging from Jack Warner to Gloria Swanson, from Marion Davies to Ronald Reagan and Nancy Davis.

Haines lived until the age of 73, dying in Santa Monica the day after Christmas in 1973. Jimmie Shields soon followed him into the afterlife by committing suicide.

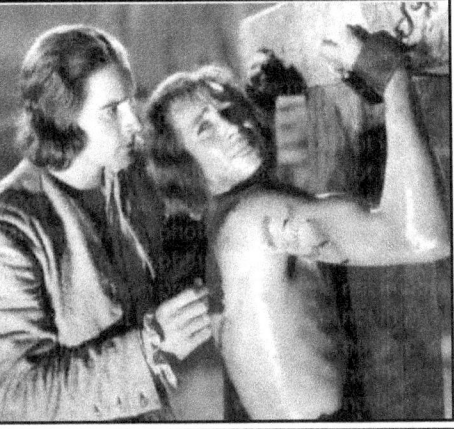

In *Captain Blood* (1935) a film with hints of sadism and undercurrents of homo-eroticism, **Ross Alexander** *(right)* played Jeremy Pitt, a ship navigator and loyal friend to Captain Blood (aka **Errol Flynn**). According to film critic David Bret, Flynn and Ross became lovers during the making of that film.

And as maintained by Lou Lumenick in the *New York Post* "Errol Flynn and Franchot Tone were among the few mourners at Ross Alexander's funeral and were reputed to have spent the night together in memory of the love they (had each) shared."

Loud, proud, and "out," here's **William Haines** as he appeared with **Marion Davies** in *Show People* (1928), during the dizzying peak of his career.

***

THAT'S SHOW BIZ! Some viewers interpret *Dancing Lady* as entertaining but not engrossing, with a charming roster of dance routines evocative of the lavish numbers crafted by Busby Berkely. In the foreground of the upper photo is **Clark Gable** *(HE DANCES!)* bonding with the by-now-seasoned hoofer and top-billed star of the show, **Joan Crawford** amid a rousing cast of intensely competitive chorines.

The lower photo derives from *Dancing Lady's* spectacular, Art Deco-inspired finale.

Episode 55

It Happened One Night (1934)

It seemed that almost every leading actress in Hollywood had no interest in taking the role of the spoiled runaway heiress in *Night Bus*. Its title was later changed to *It Happened One Night,* a Pre-Code screwball comedy.

Louis B. Mayer had originally been offered the screen rights, but he rejected them. He had recently released *Fugitive Lovers* (1934), a "bus drama" starring Robert Montgomery. It had devolved into a major flop at the box office.

Thus, for only $5,000, Harry Cohn of Columbia had acquired the rights to *Night Bus.* The story had first appeared in *Cosmopolitan* magazine, the work of Samuel Hopkins Adams.

Cohn wanted Bette Davis for the role, but Jack Warner refused to lend her. He then sent the script to Miriam Hopkins, who immediately rejected it. He asked Myrna Loy and Robert Montgomery to co-star in the comedy, but each of them turned him down. Margaret Sullavan found it "dull and stupid."

Constance Bennett, then one of the highest-paid stars in Hollywood, would agree to do it only if Cohn would also let her produce it. Of course, Cohn refused such a request. Carole Lombard, Clark's future wife, expressed an interest, but she still had not completed *Bolero* for Columbia, and was (therefore) busy.

Then, after Loretta Young rejected it, Cohn sent the script to the overworked Claudette Colbert, who was planning a much-needed one-month vacation When Cohn doubled her usual fee of $25,000

This scene from *It Happened One Night* establishes the context of **Ellie's** (aka **Colbert's**) dilemma. And who doesn't relate to a story about a girl who flees from her own dysfunctional wedding?

Columbia's set designers brilliantly established it as a ceremony that only a gilded-age fortune—during the depths of the Great Depression—could buy.

Who emerges as her hero after the errant bride flees from her then-very-stylish personal hell?

It was **CLARK GABLE**, on loan to Columbia from MGM for a script that virtually everybody else disliked.

One of the most widely-heralded films of Hollywood's Pre-Code "Golden Age," *It Happened One Night* almost didn't happen.

These publicity stills show the sexual progression of a plot whose protagonists (as played by **Clark Gable** and **Claudette Colbert**) began as quarrelsome antagonists.

per picture, she agreed to star in it.

She was told that Frank Capra would be its director. She had vowed never to work with him again after their first movie, *For the Love of Mike* (1927) had flopped.

It was said that Mayer agreed to give Clark as a "loan" to the low-rent Columbia as a means of punishing him for his arrogance and increased salary demands.

He was getting $2,000 a week. Cohn agreed to give him $2,500, with Mayer getting $500 of that.

Born in 1903 in a suburb of Paris, Colbert learned English as a second language. She spoke it with a Mid-Atlantic accent and she graced the screen with witty dialogues, aristocratic demeanor, and flair, reflected in either light comedies or emotional dramas. She was one of the most popular stars of the 1930s and '40s.

Before Clark, Cecil B. De Mille is credited with turning Colbert into a sex symbol when he starred her in *The Sign of the Cross* (1932). In it, she played the wife of Nero opposite an unappetizing Charles Laughton. Fredric March was much more appealing to her.

He later said, "Claudette was a vixen, a hot hottie after my own heart, or at least another part of my anatomy."

"MGM got really pissed off at me for being a married man and fucking so many of Mayer's leading ladies," Clark said. "So he decided to punish me by lending me out to Columbia for this quickie B film. To add extra punishment, my leading lady would be Claudette Colbert, one of the most famous 'underground lesbians' in Tinseltown. I've heard that she's French and a dwarf." *[Records show her height as 5'5".]*

Actually, the actress was a bisexual who would marry twice, first (1928-1935) to Norman Foster, who later wed Sally Blane, Loretta Young's sister. Colbert later married (from 1935 until his death in 1968) Dr. Joel Pressman. In each case, she lived at addresses separate from those of her husbands. It was believed that she married as a means of deflecting lesbian rumors, especially those associated with her ongoing affair with Marlene Dietrich. Colbert did have a few sexual encounters with males, notably with Gary Cooper, her co-star in *His Woman* (1931). The year before, she'd had a fling with Maurice Chevalier during their filming of *The Big Pond*.

She would later seduce Leslie Howard, the English actor, and also Fred MacMurray when they made *The Gilded Lily* (1935). That was followed in 1942 with a tryst with Preston Sturges in *The Palm Beach Story* (1942).

Director Michael Leisen said, "Colbert always handled herself very well, every inch a lady with a remarkable sense and always graceful under any circumstances."

According to Clark, "Our love affair existed only on the screen. Instead of inviting her to my dressing room, I used the space to seduce many starlets who followed me around with their tongues hanging out and their vaginas dripping."

Apparently, Clark was being discreet, not wanting his wife, Ria Langham, to find out. Months later, Colbert told her friend, Leonard Gershe, "Darling, I did go all the way with Gable. Does that answer your question?"

Perhaps as a "hook" to intrigue viewers, a lot of ink was devoted to the dress **Colbert** wore at the wedding she fled from at the beginning of the film.

Spectacularly expensive, even by the standards of its day, it was described as a bias-cut *charmeuse* crafted from silk *duchesse* with flutter sleeves, a train long enough to reach Cincinnati, and flowers along the neckline. Robert Kalloch, its designer, was imported into the project by Joan Perry (later the wife of Harry Cohn, the director of Columbia Studios), who had for a while been associated with his couture.

In the lower photo, **Colbert** (or a double) flees from the ceremony, thereby establishing a context for the romantic comedy that then develops "on the road" with Clark.

She also had high praise for Clark's "male anatomy."

The American Film Institute lists Colbert as the 12th greatest star of all time. In a career that lasted from 1924 to 1987, she made sixty movies. *Since You Went Away* (1944) was one of the greatest of all the homefront dramas shot during World War II.

If Irving Thalberg had not had a heart attack, Capra might have directed Clark in a different film. He and Capra were in pre-production of a stark drama, *Soviet*. It would reunite Clark with Joan Crawford, Wallace Beery, and Marie Dressler, former co-stars who would also join the cast. That projected film was abandoned, as no one wanted to take over after Thalberg went into recovery in Germany.

Although born in Sicily in 1897, Capra and his family had relocated in Los Angeles when he was only five years old. As he grew up, he became one of the most award-winning directors in Hollywood, churning out such classics as *Mr. Deeds Goes to Town* (1936); *You Can't Take It With You* (1938); *Mr. Smith Goes to Washington* (1939); and *It's a Wonderful Life* (1946).

He frequently worked with Robert Riskin, who was hired to write the screenplay. A New Yorker born in 1897, he was the son of Jewish parents who had escaped from Tsarist Russia. He began his career as a playwright, and later had some small success producing Broadway plays.

At the beginning of Talkies, he moved to Hollywood, where his first collaboration with Capra was *The Miracle Woman* (1931), starring Barbara Stanwyck.

In 1942, Riskin married Fay Wray of *King Kong* fame. She had co-starred with Clark in *The Finger Points* (1931) for First National.

In a nutshell, the plot of *It Happened One Night* focuses on a spoiled, somewhat bratty runaway heiress, Ellie Andrews (Colbert). She is escaping from her tycoon father, millionaire Alexander Andrews (Walter Connolly). She had eloped with pilot and fortune hunter "King" Westley (Jonathan Thomas) but wasn't happy about that either.

In Florida, she boards a Greyhound bus to New York. One of the passengers is Peter Warne (Clark), a recently fired newspaper reporter. When her money is stolen, she is broke, and he comes to her rescue, although his pocket is almost empty, too. Before the film ends, they fall in love.

One scene in *It Happened One Night* became iconic in classic cinema. It was called "The Walls of Jericho." Strapped for cash, the characters portrayed by Colbert and Clark have to share a motel room. He puts up a blanket to protect her privacy. After some interactions, The Walls of Jericho come tumbling down. In that same scene, Gable is seen taking off his shirt, revealing that he's wearing no undershirt. In the aftermath of the film's release, across the nation, sales of men's undershirts plummeted.

Hip, savvy, and Sicilian, and sometimes identified as "The American Dream personified," director **Frank Capra** morphed into one of the greatest directors of Hollywood's Golden Age.

During World War II, his propaganda films were credited with enormous influence on the morale of Americans both on and off the battlefield.

In the aftermath of its success, *It Happened One Night* established **Clark Gable** as a fashion plate and "sales accessory" for a clothing industry that had been battered by the Great Depression. Here are two views of Clark Gable in photos, circa 1934, that were cited for the tastefulness and tailoring of his wardrobe.

Other than the leads, Capra himself cast the supporting players. Walter Connolly was assigned the role of Alexander Andrews, Ellie's millionaire father. Jameson Thomas played "King" Westley, Ellie's *fiancé*, a fortune hunter. Rosco Karns, as Oscar Shapeley, was cast as an annoying bus passenger who tries to hit on Ellie. Alan Hale Sr. is Danker, the singing car driver who wants to steal Ellie's suitcase. Ward Bond appeared in an uncredited role as bus driver #1.

Walter Connolly, born in Cincinnati in 1887, appeared in forty films from 1914 to 1939. Other than

It Happened One Night, his most memorable performance was in *Twentieth Century* (1934) with John Barrymore and Carole Lombard. Connolly also made movies with William Powell, Myrna Loy, Paul Muni, and Mickey Rooney.

Rosco Karns, a native of San Bernardino, California, appeared in 150 movies between 1915 and 1964. He was often cast as a tipsy, wisecracking, cynical character with a rapid-fire delivery. *Twentieth Century* featured one of his best performances.

A Londoner born in 1888, Jameson Thomas, after success in his native land, moved to Hollywood, where he found minor roles—never a big star—until his death in 1939.

Alan Hale Sr., born in Washington, D.C. in 1892, worked as an actor from 1899 to 1950. He is best known for character roles, often as a sidekick to Errol Flynn. "Not only Errol," he said, "but I co-starred with the biggies—James Cagney, Cary Grant, Humphrey Bogart, Ronald Reagan, Wallace Beery, Bette Davis, Lon Chaney, Katharine Hepburn, Barbara Stanwyck, Edward G. Robinson, and Charles Boyer, among others." In all, he was in 235 films. He was also an inventor, his greatest achievement being the greaseless potato chip.

Although Ward Bond, a son of Nebraska born in 1903, starred in 200 films, he is best known for the NBC-TV series *Wagon Train* (1957-1960). Today, he appears every year on TV screens across the nation in the classic *It's a Wonderful Life* (1946), starring James Stewart.

Bond had a reunion with Clark in 1939 when he was assigned a supporting role in *Gone With the Wind.*

Eddy Chandler, a son of Iowa born in 1894, appeared, sometimes uncredited, in more than 350 films between 1916 and 1947. He ofen played police officers and detectives. Many of his early films are lost. On the set of *Gone With the Wind,* in which he had a small role, he, too, had a reunion with Clark.

When, at last, after Frank Capra showed Colbert the final cut of *It Happened One Night,* she stood up in a rage and said, "This is the worst movie ever made!" before storming out of the screening room.

Shot for a budget of $325,000, *It Happened One Night* grossed $2.5 million at the box office. In the beginning, it became a big hit in small towns across America, not playing that well in big cities.

The New York Times wrote, "Clark Gable is at his best, winning new honors for himself. Yet he steals nothing from Colbert."

London Film Weekly found Clark "brilliantly impudent without being the least bit unlikable."

The New Yorker panned it, calling it "pretty much nonsense and quite dreary."

Film Daily gave it a rave, calling it "the finest picture of the year. Gable and Colbert reach new heights, working together as if they had known each other for life."

The big surprise was yet to come. At the Academy Awards, Clark and Claudette Colbert were voted the top actor and actress of the year Not only that, *It Happened One Night* became the first picture to win five Oscars, including Best Picture, Best Director (Capra), and Best Adaptation (Robert Riskin).

Today, it is hailed as one of the greatest films ever made.

For the Best Actor Oscar, Clark beat out Frank Morgan for *The Affairs of Cellini* and William Powell for *The Thin Man.* Colbert won over Grace Moore for *One Night of Love* and Norma Shearer for *The Barretts of Wimpole Street.*

On December 15, 1996, Gable's Oscar statuette was put up for auction. Steven Spielberg placed the highest bid of $607,500. He later donated it to the Motion Picture Academy.

In June of 1997, Claudette Colbert's Oscar for *It Happened One Night* was offered for sale at auction by Christie's, but the sale attracted no bidders.

Foreplay Happened One Night: And then there were all those beefcake shots where a "fit as a fiddle" **Clark** flexes and (partially) strips in a "safe but sexy'" scene devoted to showing **Colbert** "how a man undresses."

Here are views of them engrossed in the mating game.

Episode 56

Men in White (1934)

Back at MGM, Clark was ordered to shave off his mustache so that he could play the role of George Ferguson, a dedicated young doctor who places the welfare of his patients above everything else in his life.

That dedication irritates Laura Hudson (Myrna Loy), his Social Register *fiancée*. She wants him to give up his hospital work and set up an office on Park Avenue catering to her rich society ladies.

George is the *protégé* of Dr. "Hochy" Hochberg (Jean Hersholt), who wants him to study in Vienna at the end of his internship.

He finds solace in the arms of Barbara Dennin (Elizabeth Allan), a student nurse who worships him. Soon they become lovers, and she finds herself pregnant. As the film moves on, Barbara ends up in the operating room for emergency surgery, presumably in the aftermath of a botched abortion. As a surgeon, George tries to save her life, but she develops a blot clot that will be fatal.

This movie was shot just months before the dreaded Hays Code brought a harsh censorship to Hollywood. Because it suggested an illicit romance and the abortion it catalyzed, some scenes were cut before the film was shown in certain towns. Then, the Legion of Decency declared it unfit for showing,

Men in White was based on the play of the same name by dramatist Sidney Kingsley, who won the Pulitzer Prize for his work. It had been a box office smash on Broadway, and the theme on which it was based (an illicit abortion) had caused a scandal.

Kingsley followed his success with the 1935 play *Dead End*, about slum housing and its link to crime. The play spawned the film *Dead End Kids* (1937), another box office smash.

Before its adaptation into a movie starring Clark Gable, and long before the glut of TV medical dramas tthat glutted the airwaves a half-century later, human-interest hospital dramas were fresh, novel, and new.

On the left is a poster advertising **Men in White** as a play that won the 1934 Pulitzer Prize for drama. On the right is artwork issued by MGM promoting the cinematic adaptation it copied in its wake.

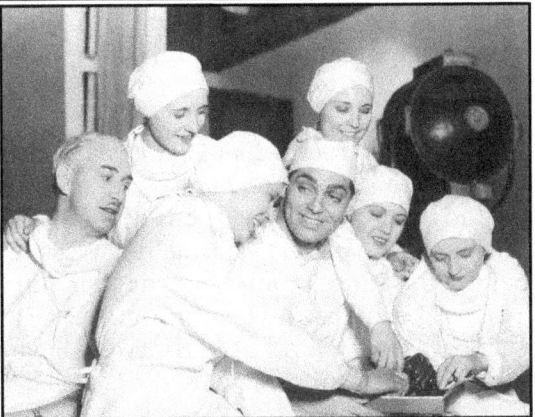

Even dressed in hospital white and within a crowd, **Clark Gable**, imitating a doctor with his medical crew, emerges as a charismatic star.

The playwright married Madge Evans, the actress, in 1939. Their union lasted until her death in 1981.

While shooting *Men in White,* Kingsley visited the set and lunched with Clark and Loy. He was later described as "a powerfully built man with broad shoulders, a big head, and rough-hewn features that made him look like a bust by Sir Jacob Epstein."

Director Richard Boleslawski was born in the Russian Empire in 1889 to a Polish family. As a young man, he was trained as an actor in Moscow by Konstantin Stanislavski. Later, during World War II, he was a cavalry lieutenant fighting on the Tsarist side until the fall of the Empire. He fled Russia in 1917, heading for Poland, where he made his first film.

He arrived in 1922 at the Port of New York, where, in time, he founded the American Laboratory Theatre. Among his students were Stella Adler, Harold Clurman, and Lee Strasberg. All of them became members of the Group Theatre (1931-1940).

He was to die in 1947 but made a few classics such as *Rasputin and the Empress* (1932), starring the three Barrymores: Ethel, Lionel, and John.

The Danish actor, Hersholt, had co-starred with Greta Garbo and Clark in *Susan Lenox: Her Fall and Rise* (1931). Wallace Ford, cast as "shorty," had played a factory worker in pursuit of Joan Crawford in *Possessed* (1931), which also starred Clark.

For the role of the doomed nurse, Barbara Denham, Boleslawski hired Elizabeth Allan, born in England in 1910. She got her start at the age of 17 at London's Old Vic.

A German, Otto Kruger, born in Ohio in 1885, was cast as Dr. Levine. Near the end of the filming of *Men in White,* he told Clark that he had signed to appear as the third lead in his upcoming movie, *Chained (1934),* in which both of them would be vying for the love of Joan Crawford.

Made for a modest budget of $215,000, *Men in White* made $1.5 million at the box office It did that in spite of protests from moral reformers and right-wing religious groups.

Motion Picture Herald found that "Clark Gable does a remarkable acting job. And he has your sympathy all through the episodes with the nurse, who dies as a result of an operation."

Film Daily found that "Gable as a struggling doctor is very real and warm and unlike anything we've seen him doing before. It is unusual, yet very natural, not to see him batting the ladies around in a rough manner. This is, perhaps, the beginning of a Clark Gable as a new kind of hero. We believe it will be a pleasant change."

***

Myrna Loy

From the dust clouds of Montana, like Gary Cooper, Myrna Loy entered the world on a scalding hot day in August of 1905. From such an unlikely beginning, this daughter of Welsh and Scottish ancestry would, in 1937 and 1938, become the busiest and highest-paid actress in Hollywood.

A real estate developer, her father, David Frank Williams, named his daughter Myrna Adela Williams. He became the youngest man ever elected to the Montana State Legislature.

Competing for the love and attention of the handsome doctor (i.e., **Clark Gable**) are the English-born **Elizabeth Allan** *(left)* and his self-involved social-climbing fiancée, **Myrna Loy** *(right)*. The audience, of course, roots for the demure, self-sacrificing nurse...until socialite Myrna realizes that she's on the wrong track.

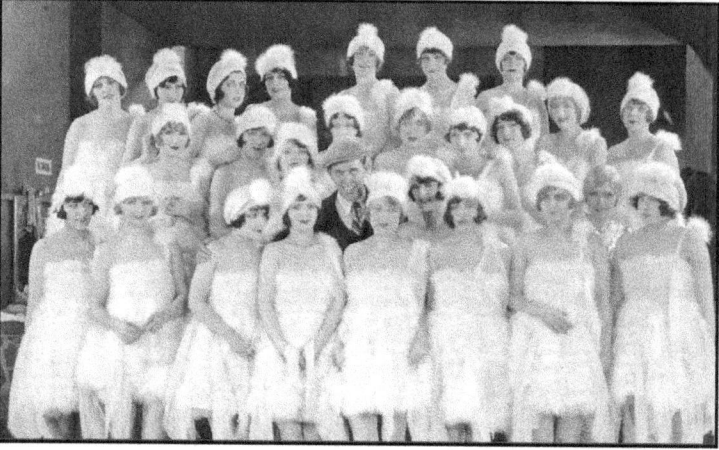

Myrna Loy began her Hollywood career the hard way: As a member of the chorus in the 1925 silent film *Pretty Ladies*. In the upper right photo, she's seen emoting with the Irish-American matinee idol, **Tom Moore**, then a household name.

In the *lower photo* that features the pretty women of the cast, **Loy** (and also **Joan Crawford**) are "faces in the crowd" Where, exactly, we don't precisely know.

On a visit to Los Angeles, Myrna's mother urged her husband to buy real estate. And so he did, later making a load of money when he sold the land to Charlie Chaplin to build his own studio.

As Myrna grew up, she dreamed of becoming a movie sar and deserted her schooling at the age of 18 to try to break into films. She later claimed that when she went to see Eleonora Duse in the play, *Thy Will Be Done*, she was so impressed with her acting technique that she agreed to follow her example for the rest of her career.

At first, Hollywood didn't know what to do with this freckled, slanted-eyed, red-haired beauty. Early in her career, she played Asian or other exotic characters in scenes which are sometimes interpreted as high camp by 21st Century viewers.

Natacha Rambova, the lesbian wife of Rudolf Valentino, put Myrna on the casting couch when she came to audition for the Sheik's next movie, *Cobra*. *[It would be the first independent film that she and her gay husband produced.]* Loy tested for the role, but Valentino rejected her, preferring Gertrude Olmstead.

Soonafter, Loy was hired as an extra for *Pretty Ladies* (1925), an MGM movie. Lucille LeSueur (later Joan Crawford) appeared with her, along with a bevy of other chorus girls dangling from an elaborate chandelier. The two aspirant actresses began a lesbian affair that developed into a friendship that lasted for decades.

Rambova re-entered her life and used her influence to get her cast in a small role opposite Nita Naldi in *What Price Beauty?* (1925). Myrna's exotic makeup and costumes got her into movie magazines and brought her to the attention of Warner Brothers, which signed her to a contract, changing her last name from "Williams" to "Loy."

In silent films, she was most often a vamp or a *femme fatale*, an Asian or Eurasian in such movies as *The Desert Song* (1929). She had not escaped from these exotic roles, even as late as 1932.

She was a villainous Eurasian half-breed in *Thirteen Women* (1932). She also played a sadistic Chinese princess in *The Mask of Fu Manchu* (also 1932) opposite Boris Karloff.

Her career began to change when she was cast in *Night Flight* (1933), which also starred Clark Gable. They did not have any scenes together.

Her career would take a major turn in the 1934 film, *Men in White,* in which she played love scenes with Clark.

After more than 80 films, her career was about to change drastically.

She co-starred with Clark again and William Powell in *Manhattan Melodrama* (1934).

It was with Powell in *The Thin Man* (1934) that launched her into her greatest success. It became one of the biggest hits of the year The Powell-Loy pairing as martini-drinking amateur detectives led to their starring in fourteen films together

All this acclaim led to her facing rumors of being a lesbian. *[It might be more accurate to call her a bisexual.]* She was seduced by Louis B. Mayer and, years

Silent Hollywood's most infamous famous marriage: **Natacha Rambova** (Loy's early mentor and briefly, her lover) with her husband, megastar **Rudolf Valentino**.

An *emigrée* to Hollywood from the big skies of Montana, **Myrna Loy** needed a few roles and a few years to develop *(right photo)* the all-American image that endeared her to Depression-era fans.

At first, producers and directors simply didn't know what to do with her. Steered by the advice and underpinnings of the flamboyantly *avant-garde* **Natacha Rambova**, she began her career as "an exotic" *(photos left and center)* before morphing into the All-American beauty *(right photo)* that she used so effectively in casting calls for the "Americana" venue in which she eventually thrived.

later, by Adlai Stevenson, the two-time presidential candidate running and losing twice to Dwight Eisenhower

Along the way, she managed to seduce two other bisexual actors: Tyrone Power and Montgomery Clift. Rumors of an affair with the gay actor Ramon Novarro were false, she later claimed, but during her filming of *The Barbarian* (1933) with him, Eddie Mannix spread fake news about an affair with him to combat rumors that the 1920s heartthrob was gay.

She did, however, have an affair with the closeted bisexual Spencer Tracy during the filming of *Whipsaw* (1936). Earlier, she had a brief fling with Leslie Howard when they co-starred in *The Animal Kingdom* (1932).

Loy's greatest film was Samuel Goldwyn's *The Best Years of Our Lives* (1946), in which she co-starred with Fredric March, portrayed as her husband.

Loy married four times, most notably to Gene Markey (1946-1950). Famous for marrying A-list movie divas, he also became known as "Mr. Hedy Lamarr" and "Mr. Joan Bennett."

Myrna died in December of 1993 at the age of 88. Before that, she bid *adieu* to the screen after co-starring with Henry Fonda in his last film, a TV drama, *Summer Solstice*.

It was Valentino himself, early in Loy's career, who defined her identity within the Hollywood galaxy: "She was the most voluptuous and least accessible beauty of the cinema world."

MGM ran this ad before the 1941 release of the fourth (***The Shadow of the Thin Man***) of the six films in a mystery series that starred **Myrna Loy** with **William Powell**. The theme of that installment? "Nick and Nora Charles are looking forward to a relaxing day at a racetrack until a jockey accused of throwing a race is found shot to death."

Child star **Dickie Hall** plays their son.

Elizabeth Allan

At MGM, Clark Gable became known for seducing his leading ladies. However, he didn't always get the leading lady—including Myrna Loy during their gig together in *Men in White.* Instead of Loy, he became involved with the fourth lead, Elizabeth Allan, cast as nurse Barbara Denham.

Once, Clark (rudely) walked right past Loy without speaking as he carried coffee and donuts to the English beauty, born in 1910.

At the age of 17, Allan made her stage debut at London's Old Vic. She gained major recognition when she co-starred with Leslie Howard in the British film *Service for Ladies (released as **Reserved for Ladies** in the U.S.)* in 1932. In the final tally, she would appear in fifty films between 1927 and 1967.

In 1932, she married agent William J. O'Bryen, a union that would last until 1977, when he died. O'Bryen, however, was out of town during the filming of *Men in White,* and Allan didn't resist the masculine charms of Clark.

Writer Anita Loos, who visited the set to see Clark, later said, "I adore the man, but he has this Babbit mentality about sex. The old early American idea about what makes a man. A real man, according to that dictate, has to seduce every woman who comes into his path."

One writer claimed that Allan represented "pure English beauty at its best." Other compliments followed: "She had "a pure white complexion, sea-green eyes, the noble nose of royalty, and light hair that evoked Vivien Leigh. She also had a perfect figure like Jean Harlow and a seductive voice that evoked Claudette Cobert."

According to *Men in White's* director Richard Boleslawski, "When Elizabeth wasn't needed on the set and Clark was free, she went immediately to his dressing room. The whole cast knew about it. We just hoped her husband wouldn't find out."

Meanwhile, Allan moved on with her career. She distinguished herself in two memorable film adaptations of a novel by Charles Dickens, playing a young mother in George Cukor's *David Copperfield* (1935). A large number of other stars were featured in it, too. They included W.C. Fields, Freddie Bartholomew, and Lionel Barrymore. Allan played Clara Copperfield.

Jack Conway, Clark's former director, also cast Allan as Lucie Manette in Dickens' *A Tale of Two*

Cities (1935).

As the years went by, she was seen in an occasional film such as *No Highway in the Sky* (1951), starring James Stewart and Marlene Dietrich.

***

Louis B. Mayer never got over his distaste for Clark Gable, but as long as he was generating lines at the box office, he could remain a prize horse in the MGM stable.

Not only that, but Mayer decided to promote him as the studio's biggest attraction, sending him on a cross-country publicity tour beginning in New York. Then, Howard Strickling and Eddie Mannix, MGM's "Fixers," were ordered to launch yet another publicity blitz—this time in Hollywood—before his departure.

Simultaneously, through its "home studio," *It Happened One Night* was also being promoted nationwide by Columbia. It would eventually win for Clark the Best Actor Oscar for 1934.

Mannix was fully aware that the gossip columnist Ben Maddox had long had a crush on Clark and that they had had a fling. He brought them together again for a long weekend together at an exclusive villa in Palm Springs.

It was later rumored that during their brief (shared) vacation, Clark rarely had a chance to put his pants on. Here's an excerpt from one of Maddox's columns:

Early in her career, **Elizabeth Allan** courted a British image as aggressively as Myrna Loy later pursued an All-American one.

In MGM's elaborate period drama ***David Copperfield*** (1935), she was praised (and marketed) as "English Beauty at its best."

In the scene above, she befriends Charles Dickens' juvenile hero, as portrayed by **Freddie Bartholomew.**

Very shortly after that, **Bartholomew** went on to greater glory as the juvenile co-star of Greta Garbo in ***Anna Karenina*** (also 1935) and ***Little Lord Faunteroy*** (1936), and (co-starring with Spencer Tracy) ***Captains Courageous*** (1937).

> *Meet Clark Gable! In the mid-1930s, he occupies the lofty position in the Hollywood galaxy that Valentino did in the 1920s. He is a 'He-Man' with dimples, the screen gangster who went heroic to meet the demands of his screaming female fans. Gable, the most desired of screen lovers, makes Robert Montgomery look like your high school principal."*
>
> *MGM has raised his weekly salary to $3,000. If I were Louis B. Mayer, I would make it $10,000 a week. Other stars are being promoted as a leading man—take Phillip Holmes, for example. He recently starred in* An American Tragedy *(1931). Compared to Gable, Holmes looks like the guy who didn't make the football team. To his ever-growing fans, Gable brings a new brand of love to the screen. He appeals not just to women, but to men as well, who view him as a masculine image they would like to emulate.*

When Mayer read that, he told his secretary, "I think this Maddox queen is in love with Gable."

Mayer liked the publicity so much, he ordered Mannix to arrange a trip with Clark to Manhattan, booking them into adjoining suites at the Waldorf Astoria.

To preserve his *faux* image as a happily married man, Clark was ordered to take his wife, Ria Langham, along on the publicity tour.

He was also ordered to let her occupy the same suite with him. For his escape from her, he had only to knock on the adjoining suite assigned to Maddox.

Beginning with his arrival in New York, Clark was mobbed with dozens and dozens of screaming fans, who seemed to want a piece of him. Some even tried to snatch some of his apparel, including making off with his hat and tie.

He could not walk down the street without attracting a small mob. A few aggressive women even tried to escape with a lock of his hair.

It Happened One Night was the feature film presentation at the 6,200-seat Radio City Music Hall. Less than two blocks away, *Men in White* opened at the Capitol Theatre on Broadway, which had 5,500 seats.

The main competition for the two films was *The Mystery of Mr. X*, starring Robert Montgomery as a jewel thief. Ironically, his leading lady was none other than Elizabeth Allan, who had played the doomed impregnated nurse in *Men in White.* Her husband was with her, keeping things tidy, and with the same intention, Ria was stashed in Clark's suite at the Waldorf Astoria.

Anita Loos was also in town. At this point in their long relationship, she and Clark had become confidants. When she learned that he wanted to slip away on occasion and be with Allan, she arranged for him to use the apartment of her close friend, the rich dowager, Gertrude Patten, who was living at the time at her estate outside Southampton.

The Capitol wanted Clark to appear in a vaudeville show after every screening of *Men in White.* He decided to do a skit from *Dancing Lady,* the movie in which he had co-starred with Joan Crawford. Instead of Crawford, actress Ruth Matteson would be his leading lady.

She had made her first appearance on Broadway that year in *Geraniums in My Window.*

Over the course of her career, she never achieved the stardom she dreamed about. Clark would meet her again when she was assigned a small role in that flop he made called *Parnell* (1937).

The Radio City Music Hall featured a chorus line called The Rockettes. At the Capitol, Clark appeared with the lesser-known "Chester Hale Girls." After his skit, he came back onto the stage as the emcee to introduce each of the acts that followed. They included a male-and-female dancing team, three comics (one of them imitating W.C. Fields), and a man in drag impersonating Mae West. Seats ranged in price from 25¢ to a dollar.

It was an exhausting schedule, with Clark performing from noon to midnight. He never received any bonus—just his regular salary from MGM. The way he calculated, he was getting only $50 per show.

After the end of the publicity tour, he desperately needed a two-week vacation. But to his dismay, he soon learned that almost immediately, he'd be cast as a gangster again. He consoled himself with the fact that at least he'd be billed over William Powell and Myrna Loy.

***

Another of **Clark Gable**'s adoring fans (and lovers) was the renowned Hollywood columnist **Adela Rogers St-Johns**. (*Maria Jane Haggart, the mother of Darwin Porter's mentor, Stanley Mills Haggart, was a close friend and next-door neighbor of hers for many years.*)

The text of the article associated with the photoscans inserted above were—to any hipster who read them—immediately evocative of the slobberingly effusive crush St Johns continued to manifest for him long after their flings had ended. The article specifically described the reaction of his fans to his appearance at the Capitol Theatre associated with the release of **Men In White**.

Here's what Adela Rogers St-Johns, said in print about Clark Gable: "When I first saw him on the screen it was one of the most thrilling moments of mine. So you can see we started off on a remarkable basis...You become a little hesitant about using the word charm. It has been misused so much. But actually, Clark Gable possesses charm—and something more. There is a vital magnetism about Gable—and I think it is because he so definitely and completely enjoys life, enjoys living. You feel it when you are in a room with him, it fills the room and people turn to him where they are conscious of it or not. Good or bad, up or down, hot or cold—he has the real joy of living which is born in only a few people out of each generation, and which is irresistible

"His stay in New York was slightly hectic. Not since the days of Valentino was anyone so besieged by adoring crowds of young ladies. They clustered about the stage door, they waited in the hotel lobby, they followed him wherever he went. He was gracious—he had a lot of fun out of it...

"'But I wish,' Clark said (to me) the other night, 'you'd write me another story. And give me a good lusty heavy to play. You know, I like to play heavies—nice, likable, violent heavies. That's my ideal.'"

Episode 57

How the Saucy Innuendos of
Clark Gable, Jean Harlow, and Mae West
Provoked the Rage of Movie Censors

Here's a replica of the heavy-censored **Seal of Approval** required by the **Hayes Commission** (aka **the Motion Picture Production Code**) before a movie could be screened in any American theater.

The curse of Hollywood, the Motion Picture Production Code, viewed it as their "divine mission" to censor films. It ruled the film industry's endeavors beginning in 1934 and, technically, at least, remained a potent factor in filmmaking until 1968. *[In the sex-crazed 1960s, it was often not adhered to.]*

Sometimes, it was nicknamed the "Hays Code" after its enforcer, Will H. Hays, the buck-toothed, ugliest man in America. He had huge ears, far bigger than Clark's. One critic said, "His left ear begins in Nebraska and stretches to the Mississippi River."

He was a dreaded, disgusting little fiend, trying to regulate the morals of both movie producers and their audiences, dictating what they could—or could not—see on movie screens.

A putrid little creature, who didn't believe in bathing very often, he had been the chairman of the Republican National Committee from 1918 to 1921. He managed the successful presidential campaign of Warren G. Harding (one of the three or four most corrupt Presidents in U.S. history), who later appointed him Postmaster General, en-

Here's **Will Hays**, the mean-spirited bureaucrat who priggishly defined movie censorship in the 1930s. Hays himself blamed the very existence of the Code on **Mae West** (photo far left), **Jean Harlow** (middle photo) and **Clark Gable** (with **Claudette Colbert** in *photo below*.

199

suring that "no filth" could be mailed.

In 1922, Hays resigned that cabinet position to become the first chairman of the Motion Picture Producers and Distributors of America. It wasn't until when he was chairman that the censorship code became more rigorously enforced. By 1934, thanks in part from widespread threats of Catholic boycotts of "immoral" movies, as well as reduced funding from Catholic financiers such as A.P. Giannini of the Bank of America, movie studios granted Hays' organization full authority to enforce the production code on all studios, creating a regime of (rigorously supervised) self-censorship.

Hays later said, "Clark Gable, Jean Harlow, and Mae West really brought on the code."

One critic later described it as "a Jewish-owned business selling Catholic theology to largely Protestant America."

A list of forbidden subjects was included: No nudity, even suggestive; no mention of illegal trafficking in drugs; no reference to "perversions," especially homosexuality; no depictions of white slavery or even miscegenation; no scenes of childbirth; no ridicule of the clergy; no offense to any nation, race, or creed.

Hays hired Joseph Breen, a Catholic and anti-Semite, to censor films, even those protesting Nazism and fascism. Hitler had risen to power in Germany, but producers did not want to offend him and his party because Germany at the time was a lucrative market for Hollywood entertainment.

Weissmuller and **O'Sullivan** get physical in the suggestively titled *Tarzan and His Mate*. The Hays Commission went crazy.

All criminal acts depicted in films deserved punishment, according to the Code. Neither the crime nor the criminal could elicit sympathy from the audience, although Clark elicited a LOT of sympathy for the character he portrayed (a casino owner who pays off the police) in *Manhattan Melodrama* (1934). Defiantly inserting his moral beliefs even further into the creative aspects of filmmaking, Hays distributed a list of about a hundred hard-partying performers whose personal lives "made them unfit to appear in films."

Producers and directors were outraged, some of them asserting that even the Boston Tea Party could not be depicted onscreen.

The first major film to be aggressively censored was the 1934 *Tarzan and His Mate*. Its editors had inserted a brief scene of a body double of Maureen O'Sullivan cast as Jane. Many Pre-Code films, too

Once-notorious for their breakage of some aspects of THE CODE, these films are now considered benign and/or part of the canon of important American films.

risqué to pass the new guidelines, were never screened again. Fortunately, some of them, believed to have been lost, keep turning up in the 21st Century. Others, including the early Pre-Code film, *The Maltese Falcon* was remade in 1941 with Humphrey Bogart.

Warner Brothers was forbidden to make a film about Nazi concentration camps. But in 1938, producer Anatole Litvak, at that studio, defied the ban against offending Nazis and made *Confessions of a Nazi Spy*. That was the year before World War II was declared.

Some critics considered *Casablanca* (1942) as the greatest film ever made, but it ran into trouble. Censors did not want any reference to Rick and Ilsa having slept together in Paris during the "heat" of their romance.

Films made on Poverty Row often ignored the Code. There were not enough censors employed within the Code's enforcement office to even see all the movies being made. *Child Bride,* released in 1938, featured a 12-year-old (Shirley Mills) swimming briefly, nude.

Howard Hughes said "to hell with the god damn code" and shot *The Outlaw* (1941), which was denied a certificate of approval, for the most part because of its emphasis on Jane Russell's breasts. It didn't go into general release until 1946, five years later.

Duel in the Sun, a David O. Selznick Western, that co-starred Jennifer Jones before she married him, was released in 1946 without the approval of the Hays Office.

The power of The Code began to ebb after World War II with the release of *Johnny Belinda* (1946). It depicted a rape and its consequences. The diminished power of the Code was also widely publicized with the release of *Pinky* (1949), whose theme revolved around a black woman passing for white, in love with a white man.

At MGM, after Louis B. Mayer was booted, Dore Schary took over. He demanded films with social realism, and as such, he often defied the Hays Office.

To compete against television, the Code more and more was being ignored Many producers began to loudly evoke their First Amendment rights

Adding fuel to the fire, many films with sexually provocative themes were arriving from Europe, playing to mostly adult audiences in art houses. One of them, the British film *Victim* (1960), starring Dirk Bogarde, dealt with homosexuality.

The Legion of Decency

The performances (and presentations) of both **Jane Russell** (upper photo as she appeared in in *The Outlaw;* 1943) and **Jennifer Jones** lin *Duel in the Sun;* 1946) were considered offensive to the Hays Commission. What do they have in common?

Each of them is positioned in a hayloft, and imply that their character is ready, now and immediately, for a roll in the hay.

In this scene from *Johnny Belinda* (1946), the deaf-mute portrayed by **Jane Wyman** shows both vulnerability and terror at the prospect of being raped. Censors from the Hays Commission worked hard to kill what was later defined as a key episode that later won Miss Wyman an Oscar.

Playing the rapist of Wyman is actor **Stephen McNally.** During the shoot, Wyman, married to Ronald Reagan at the time, had an affair with her leading man, Lew Ayres.

urged Americans to boycott it, but few paid attention anymore.

In 1952, the Supreme Court held that movies and other forms of artistic expression were entitled to First Amendment protection. In the aftermath of that decision, the Production Code's powers were greatly reduced.

Joseph I. Green, a prominent Catholic layman and anti-Semite, was appointed head of the Producers' Guild of America, an organization associated with censorship of public taste and pop culture. Green's rigid leadership lasted until his retirement in 1954.

As time moved on, especially in the 1960s, more and more producers and directors began defying the Code.

Finally, in 1966, a sophisticated liberal, Jack Valenti, took over as the new head of the PGA. Defying the old-fashioned (much loathed) repression of the Production Code, he inaugurated a new rating system. The first film to feature his designation of "For Mature Audiences," was Edward Albee's *Who's Afraid of Virginia Woolf?* (1966), starring a frumpy, bawdy, and sexually explicit Elizabeth Taylor with Richard Burton. Even a much-discussed line within the screenplay, "hump the hostess," became allowed.

In 1969, the sexually provocative Swedish film, *I Am Curious (Yellow),* was banned until the Supreme Court overruled the restriction. Soon, Aristotle Onassis and Jacqueline Onassis were seen leaving a theater together after watching it.

By 1971, with the release of Linda Lovelace's *Deep Throat,* all barriers came tumbling down. Suddenly, theaters were showing hard-core porn. In New York City, Times Square morphed into North America's centerpiece for porn, both straight and gay.

Will Hays, who was born in 1879, died in 1954, "before the revolution." He missed the launch of explicit films that would probably have horrified him: *Charlie Big Dick; Susan the Sword Swallower; Salò— 120 Days of Sodom; Rimmates; Boy Rape; Teenaged Bride;* and *The Cop Who Preferred Sodomy.*

***

CENSORS BE DAMNED

In February of 1961, *Time* Magazine predicted that Edward Albee's two-act Broadway play was too provocative to be filmed. But despite that prediction, audiences flocked to see **Elizabeth Taylor** and **Richard Burton** after they defied the Code and made its provocative celluloid adaptation, *Who's Afraid of Virginia Woolf?*

"Eugene O'Neill once said that you have to have false illusions," its author, **Edward Albee** said. "*Who's Afraid of Virginia Woolf?* says get rid of them. My play is about the battle and the love between George and Martha; the lies, deceits, and false hopes that have held them together."

Darwin Porter, co-author of this biography of Clark Gable, has always been fascinated by the Hays Commission and the changing standards of what's legally obscene.

In 2013, based on interviews with Linda Lovelace while she was still alive, **Blood Moon Productions** published his seminal, award-winning treatise on the film (and the actress) who changed forever how Americans opt to entertain themselves in bed. In addition to showcasing the tragic rise and fall of America's fellatio queen, it went on to win wide endorsements from across the entertainment industry.

Episode 58

Manhattan Melodrama (1934)

The last of his Pre-Code crime films, *Manhattan Melodrama*, was the last crime drama of Clark Gable. He was billed over William Powell and Myrna Loy.

This movie, the first of their fourteen screen pairings, also marked one of the earliest movie roles of Mickey Rooney.

Clark and Powell were polite with each other, but there was some jealousy there. Powell had recently divorced Carole Lombard (Clark's future wife) and was now dating Jean Harlow, with whom Clark had had a fling.

Loy had just co-starred with Clark in *Men in White* (1934), and he was not eager to work with her again. He was still angry about the night, months before, when she had resisted his love-making. From then on, he determined that all his romance with her would be confined to the screen.

In a memoir, Loy wrote, "Clark suffered so much from the macho thing that love scenes were difficult. He was afraid to be sensitive for fear it would contradict his masculine image. I always played it a little bit rough with him."

On his first day on the set, Clark lunched with the director, W.S. Van Dyke, known in the industry as "One Take Woody." Amazingly, he would shoot all of Clark's scenes in twelve days.

A native son of San Diego born in 1889, Van Dyke had just completed *Tarzan and the Ape Man* (1932). The year of 1934 marked one of the hallmarks of his career as a director, as he would helm Powell and Loy in the first of their series, *The Thin Man*, for which he would receive a Best Director Oscar. He respected Clark as an actor, and in the coming months, he would cast him in *San Francisco*, one of Clark's most memorable films, with Jeanette MacDonald and Spencer Tracy,.

Its male lead, Blackie, was the kind of kind-hearted tough guy role at which **Clark Gable** excelled

Because of the rushed schedule, George Cukor was hired to helm some secondary scenes. He and Clark had a tense relationship. Clark knew that the director was fully aware of his gay-for-pay past. Gossipy William Haines was one of Cukor's best friends. At this point, Clark wanted to distance himself from whatever he'd done on the road to stardom, "way back" in the '20s.

During the first week of the shoot, Clark lunched with David O Selznick, the producer of the picture. *[He was years away from producing* Gone With the Wind *(1939).]*

He also met Joseph Mankiewicz, who had just signed a long-term contract with MGM. He had been working in the film industry since 1929, and was moving up the ladder fast. Descended from German Jewish immigrants, he was destined to have a four-decade career in Hollywood.

He would win an Oscar for Best Director and another for Best Adapted Screenplay for *A Letter to Three Wives* (1949) and *All About Eve* (1950), the latter of which was nominated for fourteen Academy Awards, winning six.

Over lunch with Clark, Mankiewicz talked about working on a screen adaptation of *Forsaking All Others*, based on the Broadway play that had been cast with Tallulah Bankhead. He planned to meet with Louis B. Mayer and suggested Clark be re-teamed with Joan Crawford in this romantic melodrama.

The plot of *Manhattan Melodrama*? A trio of East Side kids grow up together in the wake of their parents' drowning in a massive ship disaster. At first, they're depicted as best buddies who, in time, will become Blackie Gallagher (Clark), a crooked gambler and casino operator; Jim Wade (Powell), a district attorney; and Leo Carrillo, a priest ("Father Joe").

As adults, Blackie takes Eleanor Packer (Loy) as his mistress. She pleads in vain with him to marry her and give up his dangerous life. When he doesn't, she finds herself falling for Jim Wade (Powell), the district attorney with ambitions of becoming Governor of New York State.

Blackie later kills Manny Arnold (Noel Madison) for failure to pay his gambling debts. Wade suspects Blackie as the prime suspect, but there is no strong evidence.

When Wade later runs for governor, Thomas Jackson (Richard Snow), a fired and disgraced former Assistant District Attorney, threatens to tell reporters that his former boss covered up a murder committed by his then-friend Blackie.

Eleanor tells Blackie what Jackson is going to do. Blackie shoots him, and Wade becomes Governor of New York State.

This time, Blackie is caught, and Wade becomes the prosecutor who convicts him and sends him to the electric chair. At the last minute, as governor, he offers to pardon his boyhood friend, but Blackie rejects the offer, not wanting to spend the rest of his life in a jail cell.

Wade later appears before New York State Legislators and informs them of the behind-the-scenes murder case. He then shocks the audience by resigning as Governor of New York.

As he is leaving the building, he reunites with Eleanor to chart a new life together. Blackie has died on the electric chair.

***

Van Dyke set about casting the supporting roles. Leo Carrillo was cast as the priest, Father Joe. The Carrillo family had included some of the early settlers of California, and Leo's father later became the first mayor of San Diego.

Cast as Spud, Nat Pendleton, born in Iowa in 1895, had been an American Olympic wrestler and stage performer. He was a descendant of the American Revolutionary General Nathaniel Green. By the mid-1920s, he began appearing in supporting roles, usually as befuddled

In *Manhattan Melodrama*, **Myrna Loy** plays a savvy, well-connected survivor of other mating games. Here, she emotes with the third leg of her love triangle, the State Governor, as portrayed by **William Powell**.

Their onscreen pairing was so successful that MGM eventually co-starred them in 13 movies together.

Here's a latter-day appraisal of **Clark Gable's** style. He appears in these publicity shots for *Manhattan Melodrama* as Blackie, a street-smart casino kingpin with a criminal past and a reputation as a kind-hearted thug. The object of his desire is uptown gal **Myrna Loy**

Upper photo: **Clark and Myrna** "Meet cute." He talks to her like a hipster, not camouflaging his working class diction with upper-class airs. With humor and charm, he conveys to the audience that she's less delicate than her *haute couture* implies, and

Lower photo: Enormously confident, he's not afraid of taking charge. He grabs her early and holds her hard. After that, he systematically amplifies the nuances of the script.

good guys or slow-witted thugs or gangsters. Before working with Clark, he had completed *Horse Feathers* (1932) with the Marx Brothers.

A native daughter of Wyoming, Isabell Jewell, born in 1907, rose to prominence in the 1930s and early '40s. She was years away from playing "that white trash" Emmy Slattery in *Gone With the Wind* (1939).

At the time she met Clark, she was "between husbands." They went out on a few dates in obscure places in San Fernando Valley, often ending up back at her apartment.

Two views of **Isabell Jewell**. *Right photo:* As *nouveau riche* "white trash" Emmy Slattery, is seen here with **Victor Jory**, in *Gone With the Wind* (1939)

Her sexual target on the set of **Manhattan Melodrama** was Clark Gable. Five years later, on the set of *Gone With the Wind*, it was Vivien Leigh.

After Clark moved on from her, she was seen on a few occasions dating the bisexual William Hopper, son of gossip columnist Hedda Hopper.

She would have two husbands after "giving up men."

On April 5, 1972, she committed suicide with an overdose of barbiturates.

Frank Conway, cast as Blackie's lawyer, had co-starred with Clark and Joan Crawford in *Possessed* (1931).

The most controversial bit of casting involved Mickey Rooney in the role of Blackie as a devilish young boy. It was later called "the worst casting of the year." No moviegoer could believe that Clark Gable would grow out of the body of that "pint-sized little brat."

Selznick was so pleased with his discovery (*i.e., Rooney*) that he wanted to cast him in a picture. Because there was no role for him in early versions of *Manhattan Melody's* script, he had his writers insert a scene where Rooney would play Blackie as a kid, along with his best friend, who later morphed into (fully adult) William Powell.

Onscreen, they portrayed boyhood pals whose allegiances got compromised by Blackie's (Clark's) life of crime.

In real-life, **Clark Gable** and **William Powell** retained touches of resentment based on their competition for, among others, Jean Harlow and Carole Lombard.

Rooney had performed on the vaudeville stage from the age of six. At sixteen, he began playing Andy Hardy in sixteen films released between 1937 and 1946 with a final installment released in 1958, which bombed. These films were immensely popular in their heyday, especially when Judy Garland played the object of his adolescent affection. The "midget actor" would have a career marked with successes, declines, disappointments, and comebacks.

He suffered from what is now known as bipolar disorder. He attempted suicide three times.

Rooney was married eight times. He married his first wife, Ava Gardner, in 1942. Their union was a disaster almost from the beginning. He started cheating on her the second night of their marriage.

Gardner, a beauty from North Carolina, would fare better later, after becoming the lover of Clark.

As unlikely as it seemed, Rooney was destined for major stardom. Born in Brooklyn in 1920 as Joseph ("Sonny") Yule Jr., he briefly used the pseudonym Mickey Maguire.

The adult version of Blackie (i.e., **Clark Gable**) with his talented and VERY precocious juvenile counterpart (Baby Blackie), **Mickey Rooney**.

Clark later recalled, "The little squirt told me that he'd lost his virginity when he was ten years old to an 11-year-old female seducer of boys."

In a career spanning nine decades, he would appear in 300 films. He would be among the last survivors of the silent era when he died at the age of 93 in Los Angeles in 2014.

London Film Weekly claimed, "William Powell steals the picture from Gable. By clever acting, Powell also saves the film from lapsing into sentimentality."

Film Daily found that "Gable manages his exciting role with power and appeal."

Hollywood Reporter claimed, "Gable's back in the type of role he does best—a do-good gangster."

Manhattan Melodrama was beginning to sag at the box office, but was rescued by the death of John Dillinger, one of America's leading gangsters during the Great Depression. In his notorious career, he robbed two dozen banks and—get this—four police stations. He courted publicity, and in some quarters was nicknamed "The American Robin Hood."

His favorite actor was Clark Gable because of the gangster roles he played. When he heard that he was again cast as a gangster, he made plans to attend the movie house where *Manhattan Melodrama* was playing. Little did he know that he would be fatally betrayed on that night of July 22, 1934, when he was only 34 years old.

J. Edgar Hoover, director of the F.B.I., had sent a special task force to Chicago to either arrest Dillinger or shoot him if he resisted.

In a hideaway in the city, Dillinger had been living with a prostitute, Polly Hamilton, who worked in the bordello of Ana Akalieva.

Polly informed the madam that she would be attending the Biograph to see the new Gable film. A plot was hatched. Polly was to wear a red dress so that she would stand out and draw attention to Dillinger as he emerged from the theater.

After seeing Clark on the screen, he walked out and looked up and down the street. From a hidden perch, an F.B.I. agent called out to him to surrender.

Dillinger pulled out his gun and ran into an alley which had been blocked off to traffic.

Three agents pursued him into the alley and fired. A bullet hit Dillinger from behind, and he fell, face down. He was shot again, a fatal bullet entering the back of his neck, severing his spinal cord before passing into his brain. He died without saying a word.

He left a pool of blood. Movie-goers coming out heard the word that Dillinger had been shot. As his body was hauled away, the pool of blood remained. Many in the crowd took their handkerchiefs and mopped up the blood to save as keepsakes.

His assassination occurred just two months after the brutal slaying of two other gangsters known as Bonnie and Clyde.

As news of Dillinger's death, and his choice of the last film he saw, reached the front pages of newspapers all over America, the box office for *Manhattan Melodrama* picked up. It grossed $750,000 in the U.S. and Canada, and $500,000 abroad.

Upper left: The FBI WANTED poster for **John Dillinger**,

Upper right: His accomplice (and betrayer), **Polly Hamilton**,

Lower photo: **Spectators on Lincoln Street,** in Chicago, on the sweltering night of July 22, 1934, after witnessing the killing of John Dillinger. Many had just exited from a screening of **Clark Gable** in *Manhattan Melodrama.*

Episode 59

Chained (1934)

Hunt Stromberg as an MGM mogul was at the peak of his career, launching not only *The Thin Man* series with William Powell and Myrna Loy, but also those Nelson Eddy/Jeanette MacDonald operettas.

For the romantic drama, *Chained*, he got the permission of Louis B. Mayer to reteam Joan Crawford and Clark as its principal players. Although Clark's position within MGM had already risen to great heights, he still got second billing to Crawford.

Stromberg hired Clarence Brown as its director. His last picture with Clark had been *Night Flight* (1933) with Helen Hayes and John Barrymore. *Chained* marked the fifth pairing of Crawford with Clark.

"I had divorced Doug Fairbanks and was dating Franchot Tone," Crawford said. "Mayer had his spies out to determine if Clark and I had resumed our fucking. I was free, but he was still married to Ria Langham, at least in name only."

One afternoon in her dressing room, as filming began, Clark confessed he would, in time, divorce Ria. "I'll never marry again. I want to be free, and I don't want to have a collar around my neck. My first two wives were more mothers than lovers."

Clark was not telling Crawford the truth. Secretly, he was trying to set up a rendezvous with the super-rich Mary Pickford, who was divorcing Douglas Fairbanks Sr. as Crawford had divorced Fairbanks Jr.

Clark was worried that a divorce from Ria Langham would leave him broke, and he seemed to be searching for the third older woman who would pay his bills and allow him to live in style.

He'd visited Pickfair on many occasions, and he thought it would make a lavish residence for himself.

Pickford held him at bay and didn't return his phone calls. "I must have been out of my mind," she later said. "I viewed not becoming the third Mrs. Clark Gable as the biggest mistake of my life. We would have made the perfect couple."

Clark was talking to Crawford between takes one afternoon when her brother, Hal LeSueur, had been granted permission to come onto the set. With him was an elderly man who was clean-shaven and modestly dressed in a well-worn suit. He was Thomas LeSueur, her long-lost father, who had abandoned her years ago.

He came up to her and reached for her hand, which he held tenderly, looking into her eyes. His own eyes were tearing up.

He told her how proud he was of her. "Who could have thought it? My little gal is now the most famous star in Hollywood…Bringing in all this money."

She chatted only briefly with him before excusing herself, telling her brother to escort him off the lot. "I have no time to get together. I'm booked up for weeks."

When she returned to where Clark was sitting, she told him, "For my so-called father, it is too late now to show up. He was not there when I needed him, He didn't support me as a little girl growing up. And I have no intention of supporting him now like you're doing with your father."

Chained might have been more appropriately entitled *Love Triangle*. Cast as Diane Lovering, Crawford played the devoted secretary to Richard Field (Otto Kruger), a shipping magnate. She is eager to marry him, but his wife, Louise Field, will not give him a divorce. She has to settle

Chained was **Gable-with-Crawford's** fifth film together. They each had accepted their screen counterpart's murky marital status and proven their skills as photogenic foils. AND they each gave every impression that they genuinely liked one another. The breezy, good-humored result reinforced moviegoers' perception that South America, with its racetracks and fabulous music, was a sophisticated getaway destination for hip, horny millionaires who could afford it.

for being his mistress. He asks her to consider the choice by taking a cruise to Argentina aboard one of his ships. "That way, you'll have time to think over your future."

On board, she meets Mike Bradley (Clark), a handsome American who owns a big ranch outside Buenos Aires. Before they reach port, she has fallen in love with him. The feeling is mutual.

When she returns to the U.S., she learns that Field's wife has agreed to give him a divorce, and he is at last free to marry her. With reluctance, she sends Mike a "Dear John." Then, with even greater reluctance, she marries Field.

A year later, she encounters Mike in a New York gun shop. In spite of his bitterness, he still loves her, and it's obvious that she feels the same about him.

When Field realizes that, he gives Diane her freedom, and he nobly offers to give her a divorce, At long last, she is "unchained," free to move to Argentina to begin a new life on a ranch owned by her new husband.

Otto Kruger as the spurned Richard Field had worked with Clark before on the set of *Men in White* (1934). He told director Brown that he was nervous about starring with Crawford and Clark. "I feel they'll eat up the screen, and no one will even notice me." However, after working with them, he found "both of them very professional. They went out of their way to be kind to me, and didn't try to hog the screen."

Except for the three leads, Brown cast the supporting players. Stuart Erwin as Mike's sidekick provides a bit of comedic relief.

Una O'Conner was Diane's maid. Marjorie Gateson took the role of Field's wife, holding out on granting him a divorce. Akim Tamiroff was Pabin, the chef at the ranch in Argentina.

In uncredited roles, Ward Bond was the ship's steward, and Mickey Rooney is seen in the shipboard swimming pool.

Clark had a reunion with Erwin, who had played the third lead in *Hold Your Man* (1933), with Clark and Jean Harlow.

Clark enjoyed a few drinks of Irish whiskey with Una O'Connor, who was born in Belfast, Ireland, in 1889. This character actress often played a comical wife, servant, or maid.

One of her first films was Alfred Hitchcock's *Murder* (1930). Before working with Clark, she had success in Noël Coward's *Cavalcade* (1933). In James Whale's *The Invisible Man* (1933), she played the publican's wife. In *Bride of Frankenstein* (1935), she was the baron's wife.

Eric Johns described O'Connor as "a frail little woman with enormous eyes that reminded me of a hunted animal."

Born in Brooklyn in 1891, Marjorie Gatson seemed perfect for the role of the shipping magnate's wife. She was profiled in Axel Nissen's book, *Mothers, Mammies, and Old Maids: Twenty-Five Character Actresses of Golden Age Hollywood*. She'd made her film debut in 1931 and would go on to be cast as haughty, aloof women of breeding. Her best-known role was the society matron who attempts to thwart a character played by Mae West in her plans for social climbing in *Goin' to Town* (1935).

An Armenian-American, Akim Tamiroff, born in 1899, was a character actor with a thick accent whose career stretched from 1919 to 1972. Orson Welles, his frequent collaborator, called him "the greatest of all actors."

Crawford was charmed by the work of cinematographer George J. Foley. He discovered the best and most flattering way to light her, spotlighting her large eyes and cheekbones. She was so thrilled at the way he made her appear on the screen that she demanded the same type of lighting in all of her future films.

Chained earned $1.3 million in the U.S and Canada, and $700,000 abroad, showing a profit of $750,000.

Photoplay wrote, "In *Chained*, we are shown a new dimension of Clark Gable's acting skills."

London Film Weekly claimed, "Crawford and Gable hold the screen most of the time, but Otto Kruger gets a fair chance to put in some sound work as the oh-so-sympathetic shipping magnate."

The critic for *The New York Times* said, "So long as Miss Crawford and Mr. Gable are in the picture, it is inevitable as the coming night that the characters they impersonate will not be disappointing in the end. Crawford gives a facile performance, and Gable is as ingratiating as ever. However, *Chained* ends up as just another suspenseless triangle."

The *New York Herald Tribune* said, "The film is little more than a sappy serial in one of the dressier magazines."

Before *Chained* was released, Crawford and Clark were told they would be reteamed again for their next picture.

Episode 60

Forsaking All Others (1934)

In 1933, Edward Berry Roberts and Frank Morgan Cavett wrote a play, *Forsaking All Others*, and took it to Tallulah Bankhead. She'd arrived back in New York after those lackluster films she'd made in early Hollywood. She had last appeared on Broadway eleven years earlier.

The writers took turns reading the play to her, and she agreed to star in it. Finding a producer in the midst of the Great Depression proved too difficult. Bankhead then invested $40,000 of her own money in the production.

Regettably, the play opened on the night that President Franklin D. Roosevelt declared a bank holiday. She kept the show running for fourteen weeks before drawing the final curtain.

Fortunately, she recouped part of her investment when she sold MGM the film rights. Louis B. Mayer wanted it as a vehicle for the reteaming of Clark Gable and Joan Crawford.

W.S. Van Dyke was signed as its director, since he had been successful in helming Clark, along with William Powell and Myrna Loy, in *Manhattan Melodrama* (1934).

Joseph Mankiewicz was assigned the task of adapting the play for the screen. After he finished it, and before he showed it to Van Dyke, he invited Clark and Crawford for a long weekend at his estate in Brentwood. Away from the prying eyes of gossipmongers, he assigned them the same bedroom. When they were not making love, they came downstairs and listened to Mankiewicz read the screenplay, of which both of them approved.

During the course of that weekend, he told them that MGM had originally assigned the script's leading roles to Joel McCrea, George Brent, and Loretta Young. He went on to say that Mayer had later changed his mind, believing it was "safe" to associate Clark with Crawford again, since she was now divorced and therefore less likely to get involved in a scandal

After working with Crawford on *Forsaking All Others,* she would become the favorite star of Mankiewicz and work with him on future movies. Their current project would be the sixth of eight cinematic collaborations between Clark and Crawford.

Over time, Mankiewicz and Crawford would bceome the best of friends—more than that, really. On occasion, they had a number of sexual trysts. He told the press, "Joan Crawford wakes up a movie star. Even when she goes to the john, she is still a movie star."

Crawford was dating the bisexual Franchot Tone on occasion. He had wanted to star in *Forsaking All Others*, but MGM signed the role to Robert Montgomery.

Robert Montgomery, Joan Crawford, and **Clark Gable** feign camaraderie in these onscreen attempts to rearrange their love triangle.

In real life, the dynamic was uncomfortable, despite **Montgomery** and **Gable's** loud, hard-partying efforts onscreen to "male bond."

The last time Crawford had gone out with Tone, he was morbidly depressed. His lover, actor Ross Alexander, had broken from him. He had met Errol Flynn on the set of *Captain Blood* (1935), and had fallen in love with the dashing swashbuckler.

When a copy of the script was sent to the censors at the Production Code, they raised several objections, all of them ridiculous. They objected to the words "sex appeal" and "tramp," and they also objected to a scene in which Crawford takes a shower, even though only her head is shown. They even objected to the main characters in the movie staying in the same hotel, although on different floors.

Unexpectedly, they let a line uttered by Montgomery remain in the script: "I could build a fire by rubbing two Boy Scouts together."

MGM was able to get a seal of approval, even though they had defied all the suggestions to cut certain lines and scenes.

According to the script, Jeff Williams (Clark) has been in love with Mary Clay (Crawford) since they were teenagers. After returning from a trip from Spain, Jeff plans to ask Mary to become his wife. Then he learns that she is planning to marry Dill Todd (Robert Montgomery).

As it turns out, Dill does not show up for the lavish wedding. Mary learns he has run off and married his mistress, Connie Barnes (Frances Drake).

A series of unlikely complications are about to begin: Dill, Mary, Jeff, and Connie spin through various circles before Jeff finally gets his girl. Mary realizes she has been in love with him all along.

The film is enlivened by the jittery Aunt Paula (Billie Burke) who wants to avoid a scandal, particularly when Jeff spends a night with the married Mary at her country house.

W.S. Van Dyke, who had recently helmed Clark in *Manhattan Melodrama*, set about rounding up the supporting cast.

What appears above was one of many ploys by MGM's publicity department to increase consumer involvement in the outcome of *Foresaking All Others*.

It was issued as a "suggestion" (or template) to America's newspaper editors about how a readers' survey might be formatted. The mission involved raising the public's hopes that, indeed, **Clark** would win **Joan** as part of the plot's marital sweepstakes.

Who won in the court of popular opinion? Not surprisingly, it was **CLARK.**

Clark Gable and **Joan Crawford** as they appeared, perhaps at the peak of their respective beauty, in *Foresaking All Others*.

Charles Butterworth, born in 1896 in Indiana, had a key role as Shep, the butler. He specialized in comedic roles. In *Forsaking All Others*, Clark quotes from Benjamin Franklin: "Early to bed, early to rise, makes a man healthy, wealthy, and wise."

Butterworth shoots back, "Ever take a good look at a milkman?"

Sadly, Butterworth was killed in an automobile accident on June 13, 1946, when he lost control of his car on Sunset Boulevard in Los Angeles.

The forever-amusing Billie Burke, often cast as dim-witted and spoiled society types, played Aunt Paula. Born in 1884 in Washington, D.C., and famous in both silent and sound movies, she had an unmistakably high-pitched, quivering, aristocratic voice.

After rejecting a marriage proposal from the operatic tenor, Enrico Caruso, Burke wed Broadway producer Florenz Ziegfeld in 1914, their union lasting until his death in 1932. Today, she is best remembered for playing Glinda, the Good Witch of the North, in *The Wizard of Oz* (1939).

Frances Drake, a New Yorker born in 1912, had the unattractive role of playing Connie Barnes, who marries Bill (Montgomery). *Foresaking All Others* was a departure for her, as she often played "damsels in distress" opposite such stars as Boris Karloff, Bela Lugosi, and Peter Lorre. She is best remembered as the terrified heroine, Eponine, in *Les Misérables* (1935).

Rosalind Russell sometimes lunched with Clark, as they had become friends. He liked her style and sense of humor. "My best chance of becoming a star is getting Myrna Loy's castoffs. Perhaps I don't have what it takes to be a star. Billie Burke, now THAT'S a star. When she arrives at the studio, you see a lot of dogs on leashes. Great trumpets sound as she is followed by a butler and three maids. When Crawford arrives, she, too, has an entourage. As for me, when I arrive, the grips call out to me, 'Hey, gal, how about a game of poker later on?'"

In minor roles were Arthur Treacher, an English actor born in 1894. A veteran of World War I, he became known for playing butlers and manservants. He co-starred with Shirley Temple twice—in *Curly Top* (1935) and in *Heidi* (1937).

He became better known to television audiences when appearing with talk show host Merv Griffin from 1965 to 1970. "And now, here's the dear boy himself, ***Merrrr-vyn!***"

Born in Germany in 1883, Greta Meyer was a dumpy-looking character actress. In Hollywood beginning in 1931, she played a succession of amiable Teutonic or Scandinavian mothers, landladies, domestics, and housewives.

Caustic, astringent, and irrepressibly witty: **Rosalind Russell.**

She appears here dressed "to the nines" in a style that synchs with her celebrity image as a well-connected society gal.

Meyer belonged to a German family that was comparable to the Barrymore family in America. At the age of three, she'd made her stage debut in her father's stock company. Later, she sang for Austria's Emperor, Franz Josef.

In Hollywood, she appeared in many films between 1933 and 1942. She retired because during World War II, anti-German feelings were strong. *[Marlene Dietrich, who prospered despite the ferocious antipathy for German-born entertainers then, was a notable exception.]*

A Londoner, Tom Ricketts, born way back in 1853, was a pioneer in the film industry. In 1908, he was cast as Ebenezer Scrooge in the first American film adaptation of Charles Dickens' *A Christmas Carol*. He also directed one of the first motion pictures ever made in Hollywood, and he also helmed the first movie ever released by Universal. In a career that spanned the years between 1882 and 1939, he was regarded as the oldest working actor in Hollywood. He was assigned movie roles until the year of his death.

He was married to Josephine Ditt, hailed as "the best-dressed woman on the screen."

Character actress Lillian Harmer, born in Philadelphia in 1883, had a brief film career in the 1930s. In *The Bowery* (1933), she played the historic and ferocious teetotaler, Carrie Nation. Other notable movies she played in included *Huckleberry Finn* (1931), starring Jackie Coogan. She also made two films with Fredric March—*A Star Is Born* (1937) and Cecil B. De Mille's historical drama, *The Buccaneer* (1938).

Finally, Ted Healy, born in Texas in 1896, was a performer in vaudeville, a comedian, and character actor. He is chiefly remembered for creating *The Three Stooges* and their form of slapstick comedy. In the 1920s, he was the highest-paid performer in vaudeville, mak-

After Gable and Crawford "re-invented" *Foresaking All Others* through their 1934 celluloid adaptation, **Tallulah Bankhead's** stage version was virtually forgotten. Here's "bad girl" **Tallulah** on the May, 1933 cover of *The Stage* magazine, promoting her Broadway performance as its emotionally flexible protagonist.

ing $4,000 a week. He had first appeared with Clark and Joan Crawford in *Dancing Lady* (1933).

London Film Weekly wrote: "Clark Gable forgoes all that He-Man stuff and clowns and wisecracks his way through this picture with an unbridled sense of humor."

Variety proclaimed, "In the performance of Robert Montgomery, Clark Gable, and Joan Crawford, there is scarcely a shade of preference. All three are superb."

Hollywood Reporter noted, "Surrounding the adventures of the trio (Gable, Joan Crawford, and Robert Montgomery) are comedy situations in which they involved themselves in this triangle."

On an investment of $400,000, *Forsaking All Others* netted a profit of $2.2 million.

True Love, buttressed with friendship, prevail in this publicity photo of **Gable** with **Crawford** in *Foresaking All Others*. Enormously successful, it was the sixth of eight cinematic collaborations between the photogenic pair.

Episode 61

After Office Hours
(1935)

Times in Hollywood had drastically changed since Clark Gable had last appeared in a picture that starred the blonde goddess and superstar, Constance Bennett. She'd hardly noticed him when he had ninth billing in *The Easiest Way* (1931). At that time, she was the highest paid actress in Hollywood, making $30,000 a week.

In *After Office Hours*, Clark shared equal billing with her.

Director Robert Z. Leonard was brought in to helm the screenplay by Herman J. Mankiewicz. He was the older brother of Joseph Mankiewicz. Herman would later write the screenplay for *Citizen Kane* (1941). Leonard had last directed Clark and Joan Crawford in *Dancing Lady* (1933).

In this American drama, Jim Branch (Clark) is a tough-talking managing editor of a newspaper. *[In England in 1932, an unrelated play by John Van Druten was released with the same name;* After Office Hours.*]*

As a lark, Sharon Norwood (Bennett), a rich socialite, takes a job as a reporter on Clark's paper. After a disagreement, he fires her.

That very night, he encounters her in the lobby of a Broadway theater. Her escort is the wealthy man-about-town, Tommy Bannister (Harvey Stephens).

He is about to be named in divorce proceedings by Harry Patterson (Hale Hamilton) against his wife, Julia Patterson (Katharine Aleander). Bannister had been carrying on an affair with her

Jim (Clark) is investigating a murder case, and he thinks Bannister is the killer. It seems that Sharon is friendly with the suspect. He rehires Sharon, and—as would be expected in a movie of that era—they fall in love along the way.

As the plot unfolds, the viewer learns that Jim is right: Bannister is, indeed, the murderer.

Because Clark had, by now, evolved into a super star, Constance no longer treated him

Clark Gable and the very upscale **Constance Bennett** demonstrate **How to Swing** in the Pre-Code months following the repeal of Prohibition. The "permissive" context of the setting—if it had been filmed a few years later—would probably have been censored.

When they filmed *After Office Hours* together (and sustained an affair), Bennett was still married to one of the most prestigious titles in *ancien régime* France: **Henri James Le Bailly de La Falaise, Écuyer**. His title (*Le Marquis de la Coudraye*) prompted Bennett's (many) detractors to sarcastically refer to her as "Madame La Marquise."

like a lowly extra. Originally, when she first met him, she may—one hot afternoon—have summoned him to her dressing room, ordering him to satisfy her. At least, that is what rumors said. Now, she treated him as an equal, like the major-league movie star he was. In the words of their film's director, Robert Leonard, "Constance treated Gable like fresh meat."

Bennett was the daughter of the widely respected stage and silent film star, Richard Bennett. She was also the older sister of actress Joan Bennett.

When Irene Mayer Selznick learned that Constance had seduced her husband, David O. Selznick, she said, "Bennett is crazy about money and sex in that order."

When Clark starred with Constance, she was married to Henry de la Falaise, the French-born Marquis de La Coudraye, the former "Mr. Gloria Swanson."

As Clark was on the dawn of his greatest pictures, Constance's career had begun to decline. In 1941, she co-starred with Greta Garbo in her last film, *Two-Faced Woman*, which was such a flop that after it was released, Garbo disappeared from the screen forever.

Bette Davis cattily remarked, "The face of Constance Bennett was her talent. When it dropped, so did her career." Actually, Davis was wrong. Constance worked in films until 1965, the year of her death. After completing her last film, *Madame X* (1966), in a role secondary to Lana Turner, she collapsed and died of a cerebral hemorrhage at the age of 60.

"I was no female Casanova," she told a reporter after word of her brief fling with Clark leaked out.

One reporter asserted, "Clark and Constance are rehearsing their love scenes in her dressing room."

Later, she admitted to an affair with another leading man, Joel McCrea, who had co-starred with her in *Born to Love* (1931).

In her dressing room one afternoon, waiting for the stagehands to re-arrange the set, Constance confided to Clark, "I made the mistake of my career when I turned down the offer to co-star with you in *It Happened One Night*. You were forced to fall in love on screen with that lez, Claudette Colbert."

Clark happily welcomed Billie Burke, cast as Mrs. Norwood, to the set. He always found her a delight. He had just finished starring in *Forsaking All Others* with her and Crawford.

Stuart Erwin, cast as Hank Parr, had bonded with Clark when they had co-starred with Crawford in *Chained*.

The role of the killer, Tommy Bannister, went to Harvey Stephens, who had made his film debut in *The Cheat* (1931) opposite Tallulah Bankhead. He confessed to Clark, "The horny bitch seduced me."

On a visit to New York, Clark had seen Stephens in the 1930 Broadway production of *Dishonored Lady* starring Katharine Cornell. In Stephens' future, he would be cast with Gary Cooper in *Sergeant York* (1941).

Katharine Alexander, as Julia Patterson, was born in Arkansas in 1898, and was to star in forty-four movies between 1930 and 1951. During the shoot of *After Office Hours*, her husband, William Brady Jr., died. He was the son of the fabled Broadway producer, William Brady Sr. and actress Gladys George.

Hale Hamilton, essaying the role of Henry King Patterson, had appeared with Clark and Crawford in *Dance, Fools, Dance*.

In a very minor role, William Demarest, born in Minnesota in 1892, played a police detective. He usually was cast as crusty but good-hearted characters.

His career lasted from 1906 to 1978, taking in 140 films. But he became best-known on television in the sitcom *My Three Sons* (1965-1972).

Shot for a budget of $375,000, *After Office Hours* took in $1.2 million at the box office.

London Film Weekly wrote: "If Gable had been allowed to do more straight acting, it would have been a better picture. As it is, he is compelled almost to burlesque his art of the tough New York newspaper editor."

Film Daily found that "the clash between Gable and Bennett gives the story a great kick. This is one of the best balanced pix of the season. It has practically everything."

The *Hollywood Reporter* made the claim that "the most forceful asset of the film is Clark Gable."

***

Episode 62

Call of the Wild (1935)

One of Clark Gable's greatest motion pictures, a role that solidified his reign as King of Hollywood, was an adventure film adapted from the 1903 bestseller by Jack London. Producer Darryl F. Zanuck acquired the screen rights and requested that Clark be released by Louis B. Mayer at MGM.

A deal was struck, and a new adaptation of the novel began. Gene Fowler and Leonard Praskins went to work on a screenplay. They were instructed to add a female love interest to the drama, which takes place in the far North.

As a young man, Clark had gone to see a 1923 silent screen version of *Call of the Wild*. Produced by Hal Roach, it had Fred Jackman as the director. In the role of Jack Thornton that Clark would play in 1935, actor Jack Mulhall won the part.

Call of the Wild was first published in 1903 by Macmillan and was a serial in *The Saturday Evenng Post*. It was an immediate bestseller and sent London into orbit as one of the most celebrated authors of the 20th Century. Today, it remains one of the most popular books ever written by an American, and has been translated into eighty languages.

Born in San Francisco in 1876, London was the illegitimate son of William H. Chaney, who soon abandoned mother and child. The future author took his surname from John London, his stepfather.

As a young man, the future novelist spent a year (1897-1898) in the Klondike in search of gold.

MGM's 1935 screen adaptation of Jack London's bestselling novel, *Call of the Wild* was marketed with the force and frenzy of everything the studio could muster. Its drama was matched (some said "surpassed") by the complications that transpired on location during filimg.

He failed as a gold miner and developed a severe case of scurvy. [*Scurvy is a life-threatening form of malnutrition based on deprivation of Vitamin C, in most cases from a dietary lack of fresh fruits and vegetables.*] He turned his harsh experiences there into gold by writing *Call of the Wild.*

In the beginning, he had little faith in his own novel, calling it "another dog story." He sold the book rights to Macmillan for only $2,000.

[*Over the years, there have been seven movie adaptations of* Call of the Wild, *the most notable of which was the Clark Gable version.*]

A handsome youth, London was both restless and courageous, eager for adventures in the frozen North or sailing across rough seas to exotic, uncharted lands. He became a romantic legend in his short lifetime. Somehow, he managed to write fifty books, both fiction and nonfiction, as well as a few hundred short stories.

He used his own experiences as a seaman to write *The Sea Wolf* in 1904. Some critics define it as his best work. Most of his stories were about men and animals fighting harsh weather conditions in brutal terrains.

Ernest J. Hopkins in the *San Francisco Bulletin* wrote: "No writer, unless it were Mark Twain, ever had a more romantic life than Jack London. His untimely death in 1918 profoundly shocked a world that expected him to live for many more years."

***

The year of 1935 was a milestone in both the life and career of Clark Gable. He'd won the Best Actor Oscar for *It Happened One Night.* For *Call of the Wild,* he would be nominated for another Best Actor Academy Award, too.

On location for the movie, he would sustain an affair with his co-star, Loretta Young. It would lead to the birth of a daughter.

Heading north from Los Angeles, Clark boarded a train to Portland, Oregon, where in the 1920s, he'd worked as a newspaper reporter and a struggling actor.

Reporters were on hand to greet him at the railway station there, along with a horde of female fans. Still sleepy and tired from the ride, he was friendly and even welcomed questions: "Who is your favorite actress?" one newsman asked.

"Joan Crawford," he said. "I've never worked with Loretta Young before, so we'll see how that works out. From seeing her in the movies, I think she has a radiant beauty. Incidentally, neither Miss Young or myself will be the star of the movie. It'll be the dog."

He was referring to a 225-pound St. Bernard named Buck. When Buck and Clark eventually came together, it would be love at first sight. Buck was often seen nestled at Clark's feet. If he got up, the dog rose, too, to follow him. If people approached Clark, Buck growled to warn he was ready to attack if anybody wanted trouble

Clark had traveled to the remote, high-altitude location, north of the town of Bellingham, Washington, near the Canadian border. Some members of the company were

"The function of a man is to live, not to exist."
                                    --**Jack London** (photo above)

A reviewer of his work once remarked, "The greatest story **Jack London** ever wrote was the story he lived." His 1903 overview of survival in the frozen north, ***Call of the Wild*** sold a million copies and made him the most popular American writer of his generation.

Late in his life, he confessed to being barely able to think about the abuse he experienced as a runaway teenager in prison. "What I found there was unprintable, and almost unthinkable," he said. Radicalized, he joined the Socialist Party, read hundreds of books, and quit after one semester at the University of California at Berkeley. In 1897, he joined the Klondike Gold Rush.

After a brutalizing winter, he returned with only a few dollars worth of gold and a priceless lode of stories. The novel that evolved tells the story of Buck, a kidnapped St. Bernard sold to Gold Rush prospectors, who brutally "train" him.

Here's an excerpt from *Call of the Wild* describing Buck's abuse:

"A dozen times he charged, and as often, the club broke the charge and smashed him down. After a particularly fierce blow, he crawled to his feet, too dazed to rush. He staggered limply about, the blood flowing from nose and mouth and ears, his beautiful coat sprayed and flecked with bloody slaver."

housed in Mount Baker Lodge in Heather Meadows, at the foot of towering Mount Shukshan.

The cast and crew consisted of 175 people, mostly men. Not everybody could be housed at the lodge. Many of the townspeople slept in their kitchens so that they could rent bedrooms to the crew as a means of making extra money during the Depression years.

Clark met at breakfast one morning with Loretta Young, his co-star. She was obviously in an emotionally disturbed state. She did not speak of what was causing her such emotional pain, but he knew the reason, since it was being widely gossiped about in Hollywood.

For Columbia Pictures during the shooting of *A Man's Castle* (1933), she had fallen in love with her co-star, Spencer Tracy. Both of them were devout Catholics, and he already had a wife.

At the end of the shoot, she had to break off the affair, although she still loved him. She'd arrived heartbroken in the North. Privately, Clark planned to help her get over her romantic pain by bringing a new man into her life, although he, as she well knew, was also married.

Filming *Call of the Wild* took much longer, because of blizzards, than the schedule and budget had called for. At one point, cast and crew were cut off from the world. Emergency food suppies had to be flowin in from Seattle in a helicopter and dropped onto the film location by parachute.

Clark often spent the cold, long, and dark winter nights with Young "all bundled up." He was determined to make her get over Tracy, who would soon be his co-star in another film.

When she wanted to be alone, he gave her time to be by herself. She told him she could not afford to fall in love with another married man.

When that happened, he and Jack Oakie somehow managed to travel south to check out one of the three "cathouses" in the little town of Bellingham.

They checked into the classiest of the whorehouses, one run by Sadie Hawkins, a former burlesque queen. She had aged badly, looking like a cross between Marjorie Main and Marie Dressler.

Months later, a savvy reporter visited the same bordello and requested the prostitute that Clark had hired. She gave her fake name of "Mabel Mondo."

He asked her about her night with Clark. "That's all bullshit!," she said. "I've seen five of Gable's films, and that unshaven bastard who visited me might have vaguely resembled Gable, but he was not Clark Gable. I'm not dumb. This brute looked like some guy who shovels coal for a train. I know what I'm talking about. After all, he lay on top of me nose to nose. Gable is the idol of millions and a known womanizer. The stinking roughneck who screwed me was no movie star. He didn't smell like one either."

After their adventure in Bellingham, even though Clark and Oakie had left early to return to the set, they were hampered by bad weather. Although Clark had been scheduled for filming early that morning, they didn't arrive at the set till 3PM.

That afternoon marked the outbreak of what morphed into a feud between Clark and his director, William A. Wellman. During the first week of filming, there had been an uneasy hostility between them. Clark didn't know why but found out later.

Before *Call of the Wild*, Wellman had worked on three previous films with Young, during which time they'd had a sexual fling. He was hoping to repeat their affair during those long, cold nights in the North—until he discovered that Clark had already moved in and around her.

Back on the set, Wellman, in front of the cast and crew, denounced Clark. "Why don't you tend to

"**Buck**," a 225-pound St. Bernard, was the real star of *Call of the Wild*.

"I wasn't jealous of him upstaging me," **Clark Gable** said. "The dog was madly in love with me, following me around the wilderness with his tongue hanging out."

Loretta Young and **Clark Gable** are in love on and off the screen in *Call of the Wild*.

"I wanted to help her mend a broken heart caused by my friend Spencer Tracy. I later learned that our director, William A. Wellman, had planned—until I thwarted him—to spend long winter nights in her arms."

business instead of monkey business? How dare you hold up the shoot on a good day when we could get some film in the can?"

"Why don't you go fuck a tiger?" Clark answered. "I'm going to what you call a dressing room and get into costume."

"Forget it, you jerk. It's too dark now."

Clark turned menacingly on him, as if ready to slug him.

"If the asshole had struck me, I was going to strike back," Wellman later told Reginald Owen. "I weigh only 150 pounds, but I can take the bastard on. After I get through with his face, he can only take character roles in the future." He was smart enough to know that if he'd bashed in the face of Clark Gable, he might never get another job as a director.

Clark knew little about Wellman until he later read an article about him. He'd been born in Massachusetts in 1896. He'd grown up to be an adventurous youth, joining the French Foreign Legion during World War I. Later, he flew with the Lafayette Escadrille.

Back in the States, he became a stunt flyer and barnstormer.

Douglas Fairbanks Sr. was instrumental in launching Wellman's film career. After he directed *Wings* (1927) with Clara Bow and Buddy Rogers, he was on his way, especially when that film won the first Best Picture Oscar.

Later, Wellman helped kick off the 1930s era of gangster pictures when he cast James Cagney in *The Public Enemy* (1931).

One of his biggest achievements was crafting the original story of *A Star Is Born* (1937), starring Janet Gaynor and Fredric March.

For the rest of the shoot, Clark feigned politeness to Wellman. Both were eager to finish the film so that they could return to civilization.

One of Clark's best acting moments came when he shared, onscreen and during a scene with Young, his philosophy of life: "Wishing never got anybody anyplace. It's owning something that counts, and taking it is when you can't get it any other way. That's all right, too. It's the law up here. The law of the Klondike. If there is something you want, get it! Take it away from the other guy. It's a good law. It works."

***

Other than "Clark and Loretta," the real star, in the eyes of some movie goers, was Buck, a St. Bernard who finds that his once-loving master, Mr. Smith, is drunkenly threatening to kill him. He is rescued by Jack Thornton (Clark).

Together, they head out into the Klondike on a search for gold. For Jack's sidekick, he teams up with "Shorty" Hollahan (Jack Oakie), who is fresh out of prison for stealing other people's mail. He has a map indicating the location of a gold mine.

Of course, a woman has to be introduced as a love interest. Jack meets and falls in love with Claire Blake (Young), who is searching for her husband who has headed for their gold mine claim and has not returned. She hires Jack and Shorty to search for him and to locate the mine site he had discovered.

The adventure through the winter of blizzards is just beginning, with the dog stealing every scene in which he appears.

Jack Oakie, born in Missouri in 1903, was tabbed "The Oakie from Missouri" when he and his family moved to Oklahoma when he was five years old.

As Eve Golden wrote, "He was hardly a matinee idol, as he was a little short, a bit pudgy, with a grinning moon face and tiny, sparkling eyes. But he was one of the most likable players of the 1930s and '40s. Indeed, he was rarely out of work. He made a total of 87 films, from big budget comedies to B Westerns and football flickers, Oakie was always a bracing breath of fresh air."

He made his debut on Broadway as a chorus boy in 1923. There, he met and seduced fellow chorister Lucille LeSueur, who became Joan Crawford.

In Hollywood, he became known as "The World's Oldest Freshman" because of his numerous appearances as a collegiate in such films as *The Wild Party* (1931). He was an inveterate socializer and became good friends with Clara Bow, Lucille Ball, Bing Crosby, and Robert Benchley. He also became a best buddy to the ill-fated Joseph Kennedy Jr. He nicknamed his pal "Jackie-O" long before Jacqueline Kennedy became more famously associated with it.

Oakie is best remembered for his role of Il Duce of "Bacteria," in *The Great Dictator* (1940), a spoof of the Italian fascist Benito Mussolini. In it also appeared Charlie Chaplin with a devasting impression of Hitler. Oakie later claimed, "By the time our movie opened in theaters, Hitler was no laughing matter."

Later, Oakie summed up his career: "I was always second banana to—most notably—my good friend Clark Gable in *Call of the Wild*."

In 1927, Oakie had made it to Hollywood, just as silent pictures were on life support. Wesley Ruggles, Clark's former director, cast Oakie in *Finders Keepers* (1927) opposite Laura LaPlante. He was on his way. Over the course of his career, he would be a scene stealer in 86 motion pictures.

His first time with Clark was in *Manhattan Melodrama* in which he was cast as a defense attorney.

Other notable roles included appearances in *The Gorgeous Hussy* (1936) with Joan Crawford; *Lady of Burlesque* (1943) with Barbara Stanwyck; *The Ox-Bow Invident* (1943) with Henry Fonda; and *The Snakepit* (1948) with Olivia de Havilland.

Reginald Owen, in the role of the evil Mr. Smith, was born in London's West End in 1887. He made his stage debut in 1905 and worked steadily in plays in England for twenty years. Finally, he arrived at the Port of New York, where he later found work on Broadway. Hollywood beckoned, and for the next forty years he became stereotyped as an Englishman, essaying roles that ranged from aristocrats to seedy villains.

Every Christmas, he appears on TV as Charles Dickens' Ebenezer Scrooge, a role into which he was cast at the last minute, replacing the ailing Lionel Barrymore. The year was 1938.

One of his most notable roles was as the bombastic Admiral Boom, the bizarre, cannon-crazed neighbor of *Mary Poppins* (1964) as portrayed by Julie Andrews.

Frank Conroy, born in England in 1890, was cast as John Black. After he emigrated to the United States, he was both an actor and director of many Off-Broadway productions, later establishing the Greenwich Village Theatre.

Katharine De Mille, cast as Marie, was Canadian, born in 1911. The adopted daughter of Cecil B. De Mille, she made twenty-five credited film appearances from the mid-1930s to the late 1940s. A dark beauty, the actress was cashing in on her famous father's name.

Notable roles came when she was cast as Molly Bryant, the nemesis of Mae West's character in *Belle of the Nineties* (1934). She also had the second female role in *All the King's Horses* (1935) at Paramount. The role of Princess Alice of France in *The Crusade* (1935) was a Christmas gift from her father.

In 1937, she famously wed actor Anthony Quinn, with whom she would produce five children. Their first child was found drowned in the lily pond of W.C. Field's home. He was only two years old.

Her marriage was rocky, in part because Quinn once claimed, "I want to impregnate every woman in the world."

Instead of being home in bed with Katharine, Quinn migrated between the boudoirs of such stars as Mae West, Susan Ball, Ingrid Bergman, Claire Bloom, Rita Hayworth, mobster moll Virginia Hill, Margaret Leighton, Pia Lindstrom (daughter of Ingrid Bergman), Carole Lombard (before Clark got her), Maureen O'Hara, Inger Stevens, Ruth Warrick, Shelley Winters, and even director George Cukor.

"There was simply too much of Tony," claimed Evelyn Keyes. "Yes, down there, too."

Sidney Toler, cast as Joe Groggins, was born in Missouri in 1874. In 1929, *The Unfaithful Husband* launched his film career.

Although he was 65 years old in 1938, he accepted the role of the Chinese Hawaiian detective, Charlie Chan, a part he would play in numerous pictures for the next nine years. He became the second non-Asian to essay the role of the famed detective. He was of Scottish ancestry, but makeup added a slant to his eyes. His films rivaled those of another master detective, Sherlock Holmes.

A New Yorker born in 1886, James Burke was cast as "Ole" in *Call of the Wild*. He continued to work in films until four years before his death in 1968. In the final count, he was cast in 205 motion pictures, maybe more. (He may have forgotten some appearances.) With the face of an Irishman and a broguish voice, he often played "a big-city flatfoot."

His most notable role was in *Nighmare Alley* (1947), in which he had a fine scene as the flinthearted sheriff moved to tears by the persuasive patter of carnival barker, Tyrone Power.

Charles Stevens emerged from the womb in Arizona in 1893. He was cast as François, the henchman of Mr. Smith. He was half-Apache, half-Mexican, and the grandson of the Apache warrior, Geronimo. When he moved to Hollywood, he was cast, uncredited, in *Birth of a Nation* (1915), that notorious film of D.W. Griffith.

Stevens became friends with Douglas Fairbanks Sr. and appeared in some of his swashbuckling movies. It took him a lifetime, but he had roles in 140 motion pictures, hardly a record, but impressive. He was best known for playing menacing tribal chiefs or bandits in serials and in cheap B-list flickers.

If a director needed a "seedy, drunken redskin," Stevens was chosen. Sometimes, he got a part in an A-list production such as John Ford's *My Darling Clementine* (1946).

Lalo Encinas, born in Arizona in 1886, was cast as another of the henchmen of Mr. Smith. He bridged the gap between silents and talkies. One of his first sound movies was as General Grant's secretary in *Only the Brave* (1930).

Herman Bing, born in Germany in 1889, arrived in Hollywood at the birth of the talkies. In 1931, he had a role in *Anna Christie*, starring Greta Garbo in her first talkie. He also had a minor part in *Dinner at Eight* (1933) with its all-star cast. Regrettably, his interactions with Clark Gable in *Manhattan Melodrama* (1934) were cut, but he popped up in *Twentieth Century* (also 1934), co-starring John Barrymore and Carole Lombard.

His last film appearance was in *Night and Day* (1946), starring Cary Grant as the tormented composer, Cole Porter. Because of the Production Code at the time, it was necessary to conceal Porter's homosexuality.

In all, Bing would pop up in 120 motion pictures before committing suicide in Los Angeles in January of 1947.

***

The world premier of *Call of the Wild* was held at the Cathay Circle Theatre in Los Angeles. However, according to survey cards distributed at the end of the screening, movie goers objected strongly to the death of the character played by Jack Oakie. The film was recalled and a new ending was filmed, thereby keeping Oakie alive.

Author Darragh O'Donoghue wrote: "There are some brilliant things in *Call of the Wild,* such as the vivid portrait of frontier life at the turn of the century. This is, though, largely a disappointing version of Jack London's novel. Much of his anti-capitalism is here, but reduced to the emotional progress of Clark Gable. The theme of tame/wild is invoked—dog, woman, nature—but the crucial Buck plot is sidelined and made cute. The acting irritates in its refusal of depth, although Loretta Young's entrance could be straight out of Cocteau. The landscape is beautiful to look at, but there is little sense of nature as devouring or malevolent."

Gable with Young: Happy together...at least until he got her pregnant.

Another critic wrote, "I doubt that Jack London would have approved of the comic role Jack Oakie played, but I found it a relief from the perfectly coiffed, glamorously lit, and dramatically deficient Loretta Young, who alternated clenched-jaw determination while looking adoringly at Clark Gable (who was doing his usual raffish lovable rogue thing)."

The film was a big hit. *Time* magazine wrote, "Gable is no stranger to the rugged life that Jack London wrote about."

Photoplay claimed that "the picture with Clark Gable, Loretta Young, Jack Oakie, and Reginald Owen gives you top-notch entertainment."

Film Daily suggested that the co-stars, Owen and Oakie, "are vivid and stimulating and hold their own against Gable and Young."

London Film Weekly found that Clark's character "as a bearded, gold-prospecting master, is a figure compounded of virility, stern silence, and innate nobility."

The Klondike at the turn of the (20th) Century: Cold, Rough, and Tumble.

***

Episode 63

Clark Impregnates Loretta Young During the Filming of *Call of the Wild*

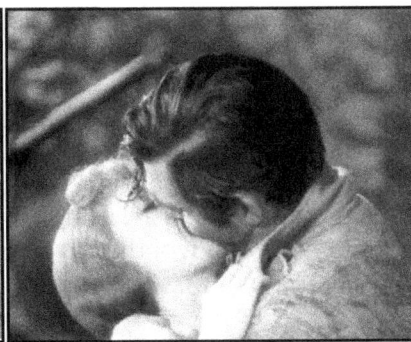

Does art really imitate life? Here are two views of **Loretta Young** with **Clark Gable** as they appeared onscreen in *Call of the Wild*. Privately, their onscreen passion was replicated offscreen. Their lovemaking led to Loretta's unplanned pregnancy and a convoluted saga that has, since then, been widely reported in the mainstream press.

We take no prurient glee in any of it. We present it here, however, with the perspective that had the situation evolved in modern times, it would have transpired in very different ways, with less shame and subterfuge.

Therefore, with the clear understanding that all parties involved are no longer living, post-mortem and with deep respect, we extend our empathy and this rundown on what really happened.

"If you want a place in the sun, you have to expect a few blisters."
—Loretta Young

Loretta Young, a native daughter of Salt Lake City born in 1913, would go on to reign as one of the leading ladies of the Golden Age of Hollywood. She later became a star on television.

Billed originally as Gretchen Young, she and her three sisters were dragged to the studios of that day to appear in bit parts. Major stardom would come only to Loretta.

She made her screen debut in *Sirens of the Sea* (1917). After that, she co-starred with Lon Chaney in *Laugh, Clown, Laugh* (1928).

In 1930, when she was only 17, she eloped with actor Grant Withers. Their union was annulled the following year after they co-starred in the aptly titled *Too Young to Marry*.

In time, she became a much-awarded actress, but not in the beginning. If you looked quickly enough, you might have seen her face in Rudolph Valentino's *The Sheik* (1921).

After spending a few months with Young as his wife, Withers labeled her as "The Steel Butterfly." In the press, she was sometimes referred to as "Hollywood's Beautiful Hack." Bosley Crowther, in *The New York Times*, noted, "Whatever it is that this screen actress never had, she still hasn't got it."

In 1934, she co-starred with Cary Grant in the Pre-Code drama, *Born to Be Bad* for Fox. The Hays Office tried to prevent its release, but did not succeed. The next year, she found herself co-starring with Clark Gable in *The Call of the Wild*. It would change her life forever. During its filming in the far North, she was notified that Cecil B. De Mille wanted her to play the Princess of Navarre in his latest epic, *The Crusades* (1935).

Young was 23 when she first encountered Clark. He was very attracted to her beauty, and was often seen staring into her eyes, which held such promise for him. Seduction was obviously on his mind, as the cast and crew saw the begin-

Here's an early view of **Loretta Young** with the daughter, **Judy Lewis**, she produced with Clark Gable during the filming of *Call of the Wild*.

Gable was (unhappily) married to Ria Langham at the time of Lewis's conception. With the approval (and pressure) from their studios, Lewis was placed in an orphanage a few weeks after her birth. After 19 months in orphanages Lewis was reunited with her mother and defined, to the world at large, as Loretta's adopted daughter.

Four years later, Young married radio producer Tom Lewis, and Judy took his last name. Young and Lewis went on to have two sons of their own, Christopher and Peter Lewis.

ning of a love affair emerging before them. Between takes, and clad in furs, they often sat huddled together. After a few days, they were sharing a cabin together.

Soon, word reached Ria Langham that her errant husband was having an affair with his co-star. By now, she was used to hearing of his adulterous romances, and she continued her lifestyle as the socialite that she was, embracing the title of Mrs. Clark Gable.

Back in Hollywood, Young realized that she was pregnant. As a devout Catholic, she opposed abortion, and she didn't tell Clark that he had impregnated her one snowy night.

Then she announced to the press that she was about to embark on an extended vacation, as she had been making one film after another.

Judy Lewis came into the world on November 6, 1935 in Venice, California in a seaside cottage that Young owned. Shortly after the child's birth, Young placed her in an orphanage. Later, still unmarried, she re-appeared in Hollywood with two young girls, having adopted both of them.

She had not seen Judy in nineteen months. Later, she got rid of the unrelated (and unwanted) daughter, sending her back to the orphanage. Her biological daughter's name was registered as Judith Young.

When Judy was four years old, Loretta married radio producer Tom Lewis and changed her daughter's name to Judy Lewis.

Judy didn't know, at the time, who her biological father was, although she had inherited big ears. At the age of seven, she underwent painful surgery to pin her ears back.

Before Loretta's marriage to Lewis, she had had a string of affairs with famous men. Biographer Edward Epstein claimed that Young was never as saintly as she pretended to be. "She was ruthless and determined to have things her way, no matter if it meant pushing others aside, even her own family. In fact, she was deserving of the title of Attila the Hun."

To "name drop" a bit, her lovers had included George Brent, Louis Calhern, Ricardo Cortez, Douglas Fairbanks Jr., Joseph P. Mankiewicz, handsome hunk Wayne Morris, beautiful boy Tyrone Power, horny Gilbert Roland, heavy-hung David Niven, Josh Whitney (fresh from the bed of Tallulah Bankhead), Darryl F. Zanuck, and Spencer Tracy, with whom she fell in love.

Loretta would make one more film with Clark named *Key to the City* (1950) in which they were cast as mayors attending a convention.

During its filming, Loretta invited Clark home to meet his daughter, without telling her that he was her father. As the girl remembered it, "We talked pleasantly for a few minutes, then he got up, kissed me on the forehead, and disappeared from my life forever."

By the time Judy married Joe Tinney in 1958, Judy had finally figured out who had fathered her. She confronted her mother one afternoon about it. Loretta confessed Clark's involvement, admitting,

Actress and therapist **Judy Lewis** in a 1977 press and PR photo.

On November 6, 1935, Loretta sent Clark an anonymous telegram informing him of the birth of a blonde, blue-eyed daughter. He was said to have flushed the note down the toilet. On her birth certificate, Loretta listed the father as **William Clark**, leaving off the "Gable." The only thing his daughter inherited from Clark was his dimpled grin and big ears.

In 1950, years after **Loretta's** pregnancy with the child **Gable** had fathered, MGM opted to re-team the still-amicable pair in a sexually suggestive political comedy entitled *Key to the City*.

Although by then involved with other partners, each of them rose to the challenge of re-igniting at least a semblance of their former passion. Studio publicists rushed to link it with taglines that almost everyone interpreted as Freudian. One of them was **"They click like a key in a lock!"**

Here's a replica of a *First National Studios Christmas Card* from the early 1930s, a "Seasons Greetings" that featuring an ingenue —and very photogenic—**Loretta Young** as Santa's helper.

"Yes, you are my sin."

A bright and attractive woman, Judy went on to become an actress, writer, producer, and later, a therapist. Her longest-running TV serial role *(1964, with interruptions, till 1972)* was as Susan Ames on *The Secret Storm,* then one of the most popular of CBS's daytime soap operas.

As for Loretta, she continued to work in films or on television until 1994. She died in Los Angeles in 2000 at the age of 87.

In general release on television today, viewers can see her in her most famous performance as *The Farmer's Daughter* (1947), for which she won that year's Best Actress Oscar. She was also nominated for another Best Actress Oscar for her role in *Come to the Stable* (1949), but lost to Olivia de Havilland for *The Heiress.*

In spite of all that film work, she became best known on the then-new medium of television by (glamourously) hosting a dramatic anthology series, *The Loretta Young Show.* It ran from 1953 to 1961.

Loretta Young was not the first (or last) Hollywood megastar whose career was jolted by an unplanned pregnancy, How she coped was not unusual for the era. Our "non-judgmental point is that after the brouhaha had quieted, Miss Young moved on to other adventures in show-biz.

Below, and on the page that follows, we present a photo-montage of post-pregnancy Loretta, the "fashion-plate envy" of Classic Hollywood and the Age of Sputnik that followed.

Suez (1935), a romanticized rundown of how the Suez Canal got financed and built, starred **Loretta Young** as the French Empress, **Eugenie de Montijo**, the Spanish-born wife of **Napoleon III**. Loretta, as Eugenie, co-starred with **Tyrone Power** as Lessups, the canal's architect. Although its plot of *Suez* is confusing and tiresome, fans of costume dramas interpret it as one of the greatest "frock flicks" of all time.

Here's an overview of how **Loretta Young** zestfully contributed to the aesthetic success of an otherwise rather ponderous and silly film.

Eugénie de Montijo (1826-1920) became Empress of the French through her marriage, in 1853, to Napoleon III. Born to Spanish nobility, she was educated in France, Spain, and England. As Empress, she used her influence to champion "authoritarian and clerical policies." With Napoleon III, she produced only one child, Louis-Napolean, Prince Imperial (1856–1879). After the fall of France's Second Empire, the three lived in exile in England; Eugénie outlived both her husband and son and spent the remainder of her life setting fashion styles and working to commemorate the glories of France's Second Empire. In the ***left photo above***, she appears in courtly splendor, as depicted by Franz Xaver Winterhalter in 1857.

Center photo: In 1935, Hollywood studios selected **Loretta Young** as the clotheshorse who tried to replicate, with overkill and lots of *oooh-la-la* schmaltz, the dress code of the French Empress. In the center photo, Miss Young reacts, as a spectator at a tennis match, to her first view of **Tyrone Power,** cast as de Lessups *(right photo)*, the traumatized architect of the Suez Canal. After the film's release in France, citing the fictionalization of the script, de Lesseps' descendants sued (unsuccessfully) for libel.

And then, there was an even better venue for Loretta Young's talent as a FASHION ICON. It was

THE LORETTA YOUNG SHOW

After she retired from filmmaking in 1953, during the peak years of the Cold War, Loretta hosted a sentimental drama anthology television series that was famously broadcast, at weekly intervals, into living rooms across America. Hosted on NBC television, and running for almost eight consecutive years, it was *The Loretta Young Show*. Though she acted in many of its weekly episodes, it's remembered primarily for her swirling entrances, during which she showcased—in a style better than that of most runway models, all sides of her glamorous very *haute,* couture. Simultaneously, she pattered along with relentlessly charming conversational segues.

Presented below are views of some of them. They were said at the time to have contributed to more self-loathing of the "average" American woman than any other TV show of its era. Ironically, Miss Young's acting skills were soon overshadowed by her image as "the perfect American woman" and/or "the perfect corporate (or "country club") wife."

In 1993, **Loretta Young** entered her third and final marriage to the famous French designer **Jean Louis**, originator of many of the fashions worn by MGM stars during their Classic Hollywood heydays. At the time, the groom and bride were 86 and 80 years old, respectively. Fashion columnists described her wedding dress as a "bamboo silk suit " and the groom's wardrobe as "impeccable, as always." A Catholic priest (*photo right*) presided over the ceremony.

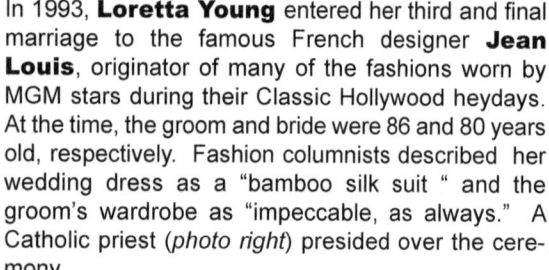

And then there was **Miss Young's** niche as a *film noir* diva. In *Accused,* (1949) Wilma Tuttle (Loretta Young) is a college professor who unintentionally arouses the sexual interest of her student, as portrayed by Douglas Dick. When he tries to rape her, she accidentally beats him to death with an auto part. It afforded Young the chance to play a genuine film noir dame. She got the role after Barbara Stanwyck dropped out, claiming that the script was "too stupid" to ever get filmed.

Episode 64

Joan Crawford Marries

No, Not Clark Gable…

He's Franchot Tone

Franchot Tone (left) with his soon to be wife, **Joan Crawford** *(right)*, as she appeared in the first of seven movies they filmed together, *Sadie McKee* (1934).

In the 1930s, Clark Gable and Franchot Tone were the most frequent partners of Joan Crawford both on and off the screen. She would actually marry Tone after her divorce from Douglas Fairbanks Jr.

"I was far cozier with Clark than those two grandmas he married," she later claimed. "Until Carole Lombard came along, I was his main squeeze. Unlike all of his other affairs, my liaison with him lasted on and off for three decades. If he had ever gotten around to proposing to me, I would have accepted. I would have said, 'Put that damn ring on my finger.' But he never did, only talking about it instead. Frankly, he told me he didn't want to marry a movie star, fearing too much competition in the family. He obviously changed his mind when he married Lombard. In the beginning, I was a much bigger star than Clark, and got top billing. Maybe he was right. Our marriage might have doomed our ongoing love affair, ending in the divorce courts."

Tone had been captivated by Crawford when he had third billing in Faulkner's *Today We Live* (1933). "She was spending a lot of time in the dressing room of the star of that picture, Gary Cooper," Tone claimed.

On the set, Tone kept staring at her, day after day. Finally, he decided to approach her, finding her head buried in a script. She had been demanding that their director, Howard Hawks, sharpen her dialogue.

"Gosh," he said to her. "You're one hell of a dame."

She looked up at him. "Don't call me a dame. I hate that word. I'm a lady."

"Indeed you are, and I respect that. You're also a great beauty. Those eyes…"

"Excuse me," she said "I've got to learn some new lines in the script." Then she walked away.

Her opinion of him changed when they co-starred with Clark in *Dancing Lady* (1933), in which he played a rich playboy enamored of her.

"We began to date," Tone said, "going out to nightclubs. During the day, she and Clark could bang-bang, but he couldn't take her out to nightclubs, and be photographed with her because he was still married to that Ria Langham dame. I became Joan's escort. A lot more than escort."

"I'd take her out on at least three occasions and got no more than a good night kiss," Tone recalled. "I decided to change things. Before she emerged from the car, I took her hand and placed it on my crotch. That accomplished my aim. She invited me to spend the night. After all, Bette Davis gave me the name of 'Jawbreaker,' and word spread fast through the Hollywood colony."

By the time they made *Sadie McKee* (1934, the third of seven films they'd make together), Crawford and Tone had begun to see each other on alternate nights. "Joan played a maid in this one, and I was the master of the house. Its male star was Gene Raymond."

"Gene had lusted after Clark Gable when they shot *Red Dust* (1932)," Crawford later claimed. "Now he went for Franchot big time."

Tone was engaged in another torrid affair with Bette Davis, which marked the beginning of the famous Crawford/Davis feud. Tone and Davis were co-starring in the film *Dangerous* (1935), which would bring Davis a Best Actress Oscar, putting the saucer-eyed star on the road to being the long-reigning Queen of Warner Brothers.

Davis told Tone, "You're the first man who has satisfied me sexually. My first husband, Ham Nelson, was a chronic masturbator and given to premature ejaculation."

Davis would soon drop Tone, giving him back to Crawford, as she pursued other game, notably George Brent, Howard Hughes, Henry Fonda, and director William Wyler, who would helm her in *Jezebel* (1938).

In 1935, Tone co-starred with Crawford again in MGM's *No More Ladies* with his screen rival, Robert Montgomery. "Louis B. Mayer told me that I was the stand-in to take over a Montgomery role in the future if he gave the studio any trouble," Tone said. "I hated the stuck-up bastard. Once, when I heard him talking to the crew and calling me a fairy, I wanted to punch him."

"When Tone proposed marriage, I didn't agree at first," Crawford claimed. "Maybe Clark was right. Two movie stars in the same family was a recipe for disaster. Maybe we'd be too competitive. However, he convinced me that his friends, Alfred Lunt and Lynn Fontanne, were doing very well, indeed."

On October 11, 1935, Tone and Crawford were married in Fort Lee, New Jersey, by that city's mayor, Herbert J. Jenkins.

Their honeymoon transpired within a suite at Manhattan's Waldorf Astoria. Their first night together was interrupted when a blackmail note was delivered to her. A man was demanding $50,000, claiming he had a copy of a "blue movie" in which she had starred. She immediately called Eddie Mannix, "The Fixer at MGM" to get her out of the jam.

Back in Hollywood after her honeymoon, Crawford said, "I need sex for a clear complexion, but I'd rather do it for love."

"Instead of sexy screen sirens, some new actresses coming along are being promoted as the girl next door," she said. She had an answer for that. "If you want to see the girl next door, go next door."

Clark was among the first to greet her after her return. He promised her, as she later admitted, "I won't let your marriage to Tone interrupt what we have going. We'll get together on the nights he's out with some male lovers."

Crawford and Tone were not pleased with her new picture, a costume drama, *The Gorgeous Hussy* (1936), in which her leading man was Robert Taylor, hailed as the handsomest actor in Hollywood.

In it, Crawford was cast (and, some said, frumpily costumed) as Peggy O'Neal, an innkeeper's daughter, in the 1830s.

At one point, Tone propositioned Robert Taylor and was cruelly rejected. Taylor, however, would sexually submit to far bigger players—notably Howard Hughes, Errol Flynn, and Tyrone Power.

Taylor was cast in *Small Town Girl* (1936) where Thelma (Pat) Ryan, then a minor actress, developed a powerful crush on him and pursued him. As she later admitted, "To put it delicately, I had my eye trained on him. I failed to get him and settled for Richard M. Nixon."

When gossip columnist Ben Maddox asked Clark if he were jealous of Tone, he answered, "I'll probably have to fuck him one night just to show him who's boss."

Crawford said, "Sometimes, Franchot and I were very domestic. I would, in our living room, be hooking a rug . He'd read to me from the works of Shaw, The Bard, or Ibsen. Some smartass claimed I was his Eliza Doolittle to his Professor Higgins."

A lot of Tone's friends from New York began to arrive in Hollywood, seeking work in motion pictures. Adhering to Tone's wishes, Crawford entertained them at dinners or parties she hosted.

She preferred her own friends, however. Frequent guests were William Haines and his lover, Jimmy Shields. Frank Fey and his wife Barbara Stanwyck were also visitors. Crawford often had sexual trysts with Stanwyck.

Helen Hayes and her playwright husband Charles MacArthur sometimes showed up, as did the Gary Coopers. Perhaps Irving Thalberg or Fred Astaire would be guests, too.

Always the honored guest at any of Crawford's suppers would be Clark himself. When he began to show up in the months to come with Carole Lombard, Crawford did her best to conceal her jealousy.

During their early days in Hollywood, both Lombard and Crawford were sometimes called "fag hags."

As the 1930s moved on, some of the film industry's most bankable stars included Clark, Crawford, Robert Taylor, Garbo, Joe E. Brown, Dick Powell, and Shirley Temple. Mickey Rooney was on his way up the ladder, too.

Tone often suffered long bouts of depression. He was disappointed at the direction of his career, especially whenever Crawford got angry with him and reminded him that he was drawing a paycheck of only $1,000 a week, as compared to her $250,000 per picture.

On a few occasions when he was in a dunken stupor, he physically assaulted her. He had grown bored with being called "Mr. Joan Crawford."

Director Clarence Brown once reported seeing Crawford arriving at the studio with bruises from one of Tone's recent attacks.

When Clark heard about it, he said, "I'll give Tone a few bruises of his own. I hear from many sources he's a mean drunk. Joan likes to swig down more than a few drinks herself. But somehow, while doing so, she always manages to be a lady at the same time."

***

Episode 65

China Seas (1935)

Clark's next picture, a sea adventure saga, cast him as a brave captain, sailing a tramp steamer in the Orient with a shipment of gold that he needs to protect from pirates.

It would become the reason for a re-teaming of him with Wallace Beery and Jean Harlow.

At MGM, Irving Thalberg was in charge of production, although he didn't usually oversee adventure pictures. He had high hopes for this story, and frequently showed up on the set to interfere with production. It was based on a novel published in 1931 by Crosbie Garstin. MGM had acquired the film rights for it a few months after its publication.

Thalberg was disappointed at the draft submitted "by a pack of hack writers." He assigned the task of rewriting it to Jules Furthman, who had had great success with *Shanghai Express* (1932), starring Marlene Dietrich.

The new scriptwriter was horrified that entire pages had been plagiarized from the works of W. Somerset Maugham, and lines directly from Mark Twain.

On his first day at work, Clark was introduced to his new director, Tay Garnett, a son of Los Angeles born in 1894. Both a screenwriter and a director, he would have a career that spanned from 1920 to 1975.

He got his start by working with such producers as Mack Sennett, Samuel Godwyn, and Hal Roach, often in comedies with Laurel and Hardy.

Garnett made the leap from comedies to dramas and wrote for Cecil B. De Mille Motion Pictures.

After a long absence from MGM, Garnett would return to helm Claudette Colbert in *Since You Went Away* (1944) and also to direct *The Postman Always Rings Twice* (1946) with Lana Turner and John Garfield.

As the sea captain, Alan Gaskell (Clark) is the abrasive, gambling-addicted captain

Competitive teams of writers labored over the script of *China Seas*. The atmosphere that resulted, as implied by this "on location" harborside photo of stars **Clark Gable, Jean Harlow,** and **Wallace Beery**, reeked of the fetid, sweaty, opium-soaked stench of venues that were wildly exotic to American movie audiences at the time.

of the steamer, the *Kin Lung*, as it chugs between Singapore and Hong Kong with a shipment of gold. He is shocked to find Dolly Portland (aka "China Doll") as portrayed by Jean Harlow. She is his former girlfriend and is still in love with him. Her competition is the aristocratic Sybil Barclay (Rosalind Russell), who plans to marry Clark when the steamer docks.

James McArdle (Wallace Beery) is the corrupt passenger in league with a gang of pirates planning to steal the shipment of gold. Dolly discovers the plot and attempts to warn the captain against McArdle, but he deflects her conspiracy theory.

Before the final reel, the captain has to face a violent typhoon and a raid by Malay pirates who capture and torture him. It will all work out in the end, and China Doll gets the rugged sea captain.

Garnett selected the supporting cast, many of whom had starred with Clark in films before. Lewis Stone played Tom Davids; C. Aubrey Smith was Sir Guy Wilmerding; Robert Benchley was Charlie McCaleb; and Akim Tamiroff was Paul Romanoff.

As was his custom, Clark liked to greet familiar faces in the cast or crew. This was his fourth picture with Jean Harlow. Their sexual fling in the film was a scene drawn from their collective past.

Since encountering her again, she had fallen for William Powell, and they were secretly living together. Instead of sexually pursuing her, Clark now treated her like a protective older brother.

"We're getting a paycheck" she said, "but I fear *China Seas* will not be another *Red Dust*."

"Was your movie, *Bombshell*, based on your life or on that of Clara Bow?" he asked.

"A little bit of both," she answered. "Lee Tracy and Franchot Tone were two horny bastards."

At this point in her short career, Harlow seemed to be riding high at MGM, one of the studio's biggest box office draws. Louella Parsons hailed her as "the next Greta Garbo."

"Our Louella must have spiked her tea when she wrote that," Clark said. "You are a red-hot siren and Garbo is the ice goddess."

When Wallace Beery encountered Clark again, the veteran actor tried to conceal his rage. He complained to director Garnett about getting third billing after Gable and Harlow. "In *Hell Divers* he was billed after me. I don't know why I'm being demoted. *Dinner at Eight* (1933) with Harlow and a roster of big-name stars went over like gangbusters. *Tugboat Annie* (also 1933) with Marie Dressler was massive. When I played Long John Silver in *Treasure Island* (1934), it was MGM's third biggest hit of the season. So what in hell is going on here?"

"You're talking to the wrong man," the director answered. "Mayer and Thalberg cast the lead roles. I just work here."

Clark met with Lewis Stone, who seemed depressed. "My day as a leading man has come to an end. I had a good run, crowned by my appearing in seven films with Garbo, including the most recent, *Queen Christina* (1933). Now I'll be lucky to play father roles."

Indeed, he was lucky. In his imminent future, MGM would cast him as Judge Hardy, the father of

Jean Harlow, at the time the most notorious blonde in the world, was at the peak of her fame during the filming of *China Seas*,

In the lower photo, as an earthy but empathetic girl who knows how to get along, she comforts the brooding, melancholy captain of her ship, as portrayed by **Clark Gable.**

the character played by Mickey Rooney in a series of box office smashes. Stone took over the role from Lionel Barrymore, who was in poor health.

Months later, when he encountered Clark he said, "Look at me and you'll get a preview of yourself when you're no longer a leading man. You'll be the father of the latest romantic matinee idol."

"I don't know. When that dreaded Hays Code is junked forever, movies can get wild. Perhaps I'll play the horny coach of a high school football team lusting after the young cheerleaders."

Rosalind Russell, who had recently starred with Clark and Joan Crawford in *Forsaking All Others* (1934), lunched with him. She was still years away from becoming his leading lady herself.

"I liked the dame," Clark recalled, "but not in *that* way. I heard she was lez oriented. She was amusing and a great pal to hang out with, but I certainly didn't have the kind of equipment that would turn her on."

When interviewed years later, Russell said, "No director ever could direct Clark Gable. I don't mean that he would not take direction. When he went before the camera, he became what he always was: Clark Gable in the flesh, oozing masculine charm. Nobody wanted him to be anybody else. He and John Wayne were screen personalities—not Laurence Olivier. A personality is an asset. You don't try to destroy it. You live with it."

The Londoner, C. Aubrey Smith, who had co-starred with Clark and Marion Davies in *Polly of the Circus* (1932), invited Clark for a game of cricket. [*Clark turned down the offer.*]

"I hear your Hollywood Cricket Club is going great," Clark said, "attracting everyone from Olivier to Boris Karloff. I also hear you're up for the sound version of *The Prisoner of Zenda*."

"Would you believe my first major stage role was in 1896?" Smith said to him. "You guessed it: The Prisoner of Zenda."

Clark also had a reunion with Robert Benchley, who had last appeared with him in *Dancing Lady* (1933) with Joan Crawford.

"Are you still the brilliant wit at the Algonquin Round Table in Manhattan?" Clark asked. "At least you have the most humor, or so I hear. I also understand that Tallulah Bankhead is the most vulgar."

"For a while, she rented a suite in the hotel and used to invite guests to one of her private parties," Benchley answered. "The first time I attended, she opened the door totally nude. Instead of shaking my paw, she grabbed it and pessed it into her snatch."

Clark had last seen the Armenian-American actor, Akim Tamiroff, on the set of *Chained* (1934), a movie in which he had appeared with Crawford. He would later see Tamiroff again in *The Lives of a Bengal Lancer* (1935). "How was it working with that bastard Gary Cooper, my major competition?"

"It was a bit wild. One afternoon, that crazy *Mexicana*, Lupe Velez, came onto the set. She and Coop were shacking up at the time. In front of the crew, he exposed one of her breasts. Then, with her tube of lipstick, he drew a face around the tit, letting her nipple be the nose."

"Lupe told us that Coop could blast off four times in just six hours."

"That's Coop!" was all Clark had to say, barely concealing the jealous look on his face.

A Scot, Donald Meek was that "forever worried" little man. As a pas-

Two views of **Clark** with that trenchant, witty brunette, **Rosalind Russell**, in *China Seas*

Robert Benchley, famously skilled at arbitering the literary land mines of the Round Table at the Algonquin Hotel in NYC.

senger aboard Clark's steamer, his role was so small, he was uncredited. His film career stretched from 1886 to 1946, the year of his death at 68. His most notable screen appearances were in Frank Capra's *You Can't Take It With You* (1938) and in John Ford's *Stagecoach* (1939) with John Wayne.

Also cast in *China Seas*, Hattie McDaniel was four years away from playing Mammy in *Gone With the Wind* (1939). In this current movie, she played Isabelle McCarthy, the outspoken maid to Harlow's "China Doll."

As biographer Jill Watts wrote in a biography, "No respectable white woman would employ such a servant. Isabelle languishes seductively in an elaborate dressing gown. When the Harlow character asks her, 'Would you say I look like a lady?' Hattie answers, "No's Miss Dolly. I've been with you too long to insult you that way."

China Seas was a big hit at the box office, earning $1.7 million in the U.S. and Canada. Abroad, it took in another $1.2 million, generating an overall profit of $675,000.

A critic for *The New York Times* wrote: "Clark Gable is the two-fisted skipper of a tramp steamer, a role that demands vigor, an infectious devil-may-care attitude, and the passion of distempered blood. It is one of Gable's most convincing portrayals."

Hollywood Reporter said, "Clark Gable plays the captain of the ship with ease and assurance that will win him many new admirers. The role of the captain is a natural for Gable."

The critic for *Photoplay* gave a more serious appraisal: "Action and thrills, striking photography, and the glitter of the well-known team of Gable and Harlow only partly obscure the sordidness of the tale of a white man's deterioration in the fetid moral atmosphere of the Orient. It is not sufficiently adroit in its handling to make its coarseness and brutality even slightly palatable."

Puttin' on airs on the China Seas: **Hattie McDaniel** (*left;* later known for her portrayal of Mammie in *Gone With the Wind*) as **Jean Harlow**'s uppity maid in *China Seas*.

Jean Harlow

As the 1930s moved on, and as the popularity of MGM's top female stars—Joan Crawford, Greta Garbo, and Norma Shearer—began to wane a bit, Harlow's movies continued to make huge profits at the box office, even during the middle of the Depression. Films made with Clark were especially successful.

After her third marriage to cameraman Harold Rosson collapsed in 1934, she met William Powell, another MGM star doing well, in part because of those *Thin Man* movies. They fell in love, and began living together. For two years, they were engaged. Their disagreements derived, in part, from Powell's past marriages. He was reluctant to enter into another marriage.

In spite of their vast differences, they seemed to move in harmony, as was evident when they costarred in *Reckless,* released the same year as *China Seas* (1935). It was her first movie musical, her voice dubbed with that of the skilled vocalist, Virginia Verill.

Clark Gable in a love scene with **Jean Harlow** from *China Seas*.

"After reading the script, I knew I'd be playing a thinly disguised whore," she said. "The movie turned out to be my first big hit since *Bombshell*, and *Time* magazine put me on the cover, claiming I was the foremost U.S. embodiment of sex appeal. I wore a wig in the picutre. A rumor had spread that I had lost most of my real hair from too much bleaching. Instead of a China Doll, I felt I looked like a deranged kewpie."

Powell came into Harlow's life when she could no longer handle the pressure cooker existence she'd endured with "Mama Jean" and her stepfather, Marino Bello, who was making frequent sexual advances toward her.

Biographer Edward Epstein wrote "Powell's older, refined, and knowledgeable manner, his suave, cultured, sexy male baritone, and his distinguished position as a film star of long standing appealed to Jean. He had real class. And, of course, he could not help being attracted to the sexy, famous young bombshell who respected him and sought his advice about the direction of her career."

Between 1927 and 1937, Harlow would make 36 movies, playing only minor roles in her first outings. Never a great actress, she was known as "The Blonde Bombshell," a woman whose beauty and energy ate up the scenery.

As in the case of Valentino, James Dean, and Marilyn Monroe, the public never got to know what she could do if she had lived.

Clark opted not to quiz her, but he'd heard that she'd aborted a child. Powell had been the father.

She told Clark she always wore a lucky ankle bracelet on her left leg and had a lucky mirror in her dressing room. She always looked in that mirror before departing to face a camera.

Everyone who worked with her had an opinion: "She didn't want to be famous. She wanted to be happy." Or so claimed Clark.

Spencer Tracy asserted that Harlow was, "a square shooter if there ever was one."

James Stewart said, "When it came to kissing, Harlow was the best."

Groucho Marx weighed in with: "I'd have liked to have gone to bed with Harlow. She was one beautiful broad. The fellow who married her was impotent, and he killed himself. I would have done the same thing."

Harlow told Clark, "My career is going well, but I've made a few mistakes."

"Haven't we all?" he answered.

"I turned down the lead in *King Kong* (1933). Fay Wray got it."

"She always came up with amusing stories about her life to relay to me," Clark said. "She claimed that when the superstar canine, Rin Tin Tin, died at the age of 16 (112 in doggie years), she lived across the street from his master, Lee Duncan. I came over and cradled the dog's head in my lap before he drifted off to that doggie Heaven in the sky."

One day over lunch, she said, "Men like me because I don't wear a *brassière*. Women like me because I don't look like a gal who would steal their husband—at least not for long."

In many ways, *China Seas* marked the apex in Harlow's far too brief career. *Time* magazine put her on the cover of its August 19, 1935 edition. She wore a white *négligée* with ostrich-trimmed sleeves. The caption read: "FINE FEATHERS ARE FINE FANS."

With Harlow no longer available, Gable "indulged himself with starlets, extras, and high-priced call girls," wrote Nigel Cawthorne. "To protect his male stars, Mayer had MGM run an establishment called The Cat House. It was staffed with former starlets who were regularly checked for venereal disease. That way, Mayer could protect his stars' reputation and health."

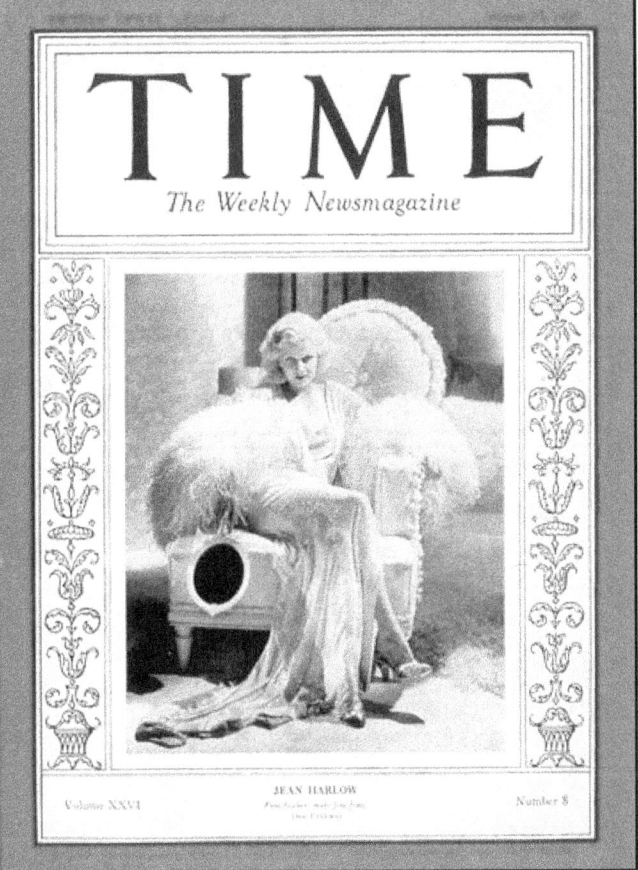

At least back then, blondes did, indeed, have more fun. Here's **Harlow** on the cover of the August 19, 1935 edition of *Time* magazine.

"Clark was like a kid in a candy store," Cawthorne continued. "At a party, he would size up every woman in the room. Within minutes, he knew which one was leaving with him, even though he had not met her yet."

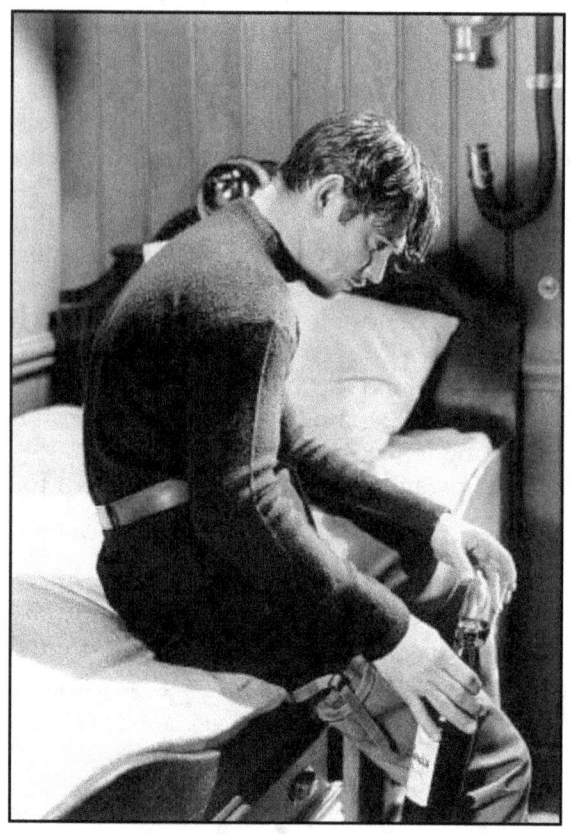 

Indeed, *China Seas* presented **Clark Gable** as an action-adventure hero who battled pirates and typhoons with aplomb, and navigated his way with rough-and-tumble success through the fleshpots of the exotic East. It also presented him as an alienated, All-American hero with a brooding and tormented sense of anguish, much in the style of a character by Hemingway—then at the peak of his popularity, too.

On the left, **Gable**, as an expatriate captain of a grungy China steamer, broods in alcohol-sodden anguish.

On the right, with courage, resignation, and aplomb, he faces torture from a Malay goon squad.

Episode 66

Mutiny on the Bounty
(1935)

A sea adventure released by MGM, *Mutiny on the Bounty*, directed by Frank Lloyd, became the highest-grossing film of 1935. Clark Gable originally didn't want to star in it, and he especially disliked working with scene-stealer Charles Laughton. He agreed with Tallulah Bankhead's assessment that Laughton "was a repulsive, fat mess of glop!"

He was also warned that Laughton, a notorious homosexual, would be lusting after him, the way he did with Gary Cooper in *Devil and the Deep* (1932).

Clark at first refused to be cast in the role of Fletcher Christian, based on the best-selling novel by Christian Nordhoff, published in 1932. It's a saga about a mutiny in the British navy in the early 1800s.

In a tense meeting with his boss, Irving Thalberg, Clark complained, "I'll look like a fag in knee breeches, with my hair in pigtails. Also, I'll have to shave off my mustache."

Gable, as Fletcher Christian, with **Charles Laughton** as the villainous Captain Bligh.

After a tense talk that went on for an hour, Thalberg made a final plea: "Come on, Clark. Give me a break. I've been good to you. My doctors told me I don't have long to live. One last favor. I'm pleading with you."

"Well, Irving, if you put it that way, I'm your star, pigtails and all."

Thalberg had hired three scriptwriters to create this sea adventure: Jules Furthman, Carey Wilson, and Talbot Jennings.

Furthman had been the chief writer of Clark's recent picture, *China Seas*, and he'd also written the screenplay for *Shanghai Express* (1932) in which Marlene Dietrich played a prostitute.

Frank Lloyd was chosen as director, since he had acquired the original rights to the novel. Born in Scotland in 1886, he was not only a director, but an actor, scriptwriter, and producer. He'd been President (from 1934 to 1935) of the Academy of Motion Picture Arts and Sciences, and he'd won Oscars for his direction of *The Divine Lady* (1929), and Noël Coward's *Cavalcade* (1933).

In upcoming years, he would helm such stars as Claudette Colbert, Joel McCrea, Ronald Colman, Douglas Fairbanks Jr., Cary Grant, James Cagney, Lon Chaney, and Leslie Howard. Before working with Clark, he had directed Clara Bow in *Hoop-La* (1933), her last motion picture.

Top billing of *Mutiny* would go to the English actor, Charles Laughton, who had been born in Yorkshire, in England, in 1899. He had already starred in *The Private Life of Henry VIII* (1933). Although he was a homosexual, he had married veteran actress Elsa Lanchester in 1929. She was very understanding about his outside seductions of young men,

Near the end of the film, Laughton, as Captain Bligh, performs one of the greatest feats of navigation after having been set adrift in a small boat, with some of his loyal officers after the mutiny aboard his ship, *The Bounty*.

Actually, in real life, Laughton was afraid of the water, and he was seasick throughout most of the shoot.

Right from the beginning, he and Clark did not get along. Calling him (in private) "a disgusting old fag," Clark said, "I hear he eats shit sandwiches as one of his sexual fetishes. Surely that could not be true. How repulsive can you get?"

On the set, Laughton never concealed his sexual preference for men. With him was a blonde and handsome young man in his early 20s. Laughton introduced him as "my masseur."

Director Lloyd expected "fireworks" between Tone and Clark. The well-bred (younger) actor had just married Joan Crawford, and Clark wasn't certain whether or not she planned to continue their affair. *[Tone had recently ended his affair with Bette Davis during their co-starring performances in* Dangerous *(1935).]*

In Hollywood circles, both Crawford and Tone were widely known as bisexuals. Clark told Lloyd, "The two of them seem evenly matched. While she's getting off with a woman, like Barbara Stanwyck, Tone can be screwing, say, Robert Taylor."

Actually, no feud developed between the two stars. From what Lloyd noted, "They became the best of buddies, hanging out together. On Catalina Island, they asked to room together."

A variation of *Mutiny* had been first filmed in Australia. Entitled *In the Wake of the Bounty* (1933), it had starred an unknown actor born in Tasmania, Errol Flynn.

In 1962, *Mutiny on the Bounty* would be remade with Marlon Brando cast in the role of Fletcher Christian, with Trevor Howard playing the sadistic captain. Again in 1984, Mel Gibson would star as Fletcher, with Anthony Hopkins as the monstrous captain.

To prepare for one scene, Tone and Clark were to be fitted with loincloths for a scene on the island of Tahiti. "Seeing Tone jaybird naked," Clark recalled, "I saw why he was nicknamed 'Jawbreaker.' I feared Crawford would not ever return to my bed again after she had Tone available every night."

Instead of the South Pacific, Lloyd chose Catalina Island, 22 miles west of the California mainland, as the filming's location. There, art director Cedric Gibbons re-created the waterfront of an 18th Century English colonial port.

Upper photo: Two officers from the Royal Navy (Gable, left, and Tone) controlling their sunburns on a tropical beach and dreaming of freedom.

Lower photo: Lobby card showcasing how naval blokes should abandon their starchy uniforms and stop thinking of England. *left to right,* **Mamo, Franchot Tone,** and **Clark Gable.**

The plot opens in Portsmouth, England, in 1787, as a gang raids a local beer tavern and presses several of the stoutest men into enforced naval service.

The *HMS Bounty* is set to sail to the South Pacific. Its mission involves the transport of breadfruit trees from Polynesia to the British West Indies, as a food source for slaves forcibly transported there from Africa for forced labor in sugarcane fields.

Captain William Bligh (Laughton) is a brutal tyrant who administers harsh punishment to the men under his command, even for the slightest infractions.

Fletcher Christian (Clark) is the ship's second-in-command, and Roger Byam (Tone) is an idealistic midshipman.

During the arduous voyage, the enmity between Christian and Bligh rapidly escalates. It finally leads to the mutiny promised in the title.

After Captain Bligh and a few of his officers are forcibly ejected and set adrift in a small boat, the deposed captain vows revenge.

In the meantime, Fletcher orders the *Bounty* to return to Tahiti, where they begin life anew.

Fletcher marries a native girl, Maimiti (Mamo Clark) and has a child with her. In a native ceremony, Byam weds Tehanni, as portrayed by the Mexican-Amerian actress, Movita Casteneda), another native beauty.

There is yet more heavy drama to come. Byam voluntarily returns to England, where he faces a court martial and is found guilty of mutiny. He is later pardoned by King George III.

Meanwhile, Fletcher discovered the uninhabited yet sustainable island of Pitcairn. He takes his new family and the rest of the mutineers to this remote place to begin life anew. He orders that *The Bounty* be burned, based on fears that it will be sighted by passing European expeditions, and with hopes that it will help to erase the nightmarish memories of Captain Bligh.

Here's **Donald Crisp** with **Charles Laughton**, presenting alarming views of authoritarian cruelty within His Majesty's Navy.

***

Mutiny became celebrated for its supporting cast, which contained not a lot of famous actors, but character players suitable for the portrayal of rugged, 18th-century seamen.

Although Tone marries Tehanni (Movita Casteneda) in the movie, off-screen it is Clark himself who has a brief fling with the exotic beauty. Of Mexican descent, she was born in Arizona in 1916. She had been cast with Fred Astaire and Ginger Rogers in *Flying Down to Rio* (1933).

In the late 1950s, following Marlon Brando's breakup with Anna Kashfi, Motiva and Marlon, the future Fletcher Christian in the remake of *Mutiny on the Bounty,* got married. The union was annulled in 1968, when it was discovered that she had never divorced her previous husband, Jack Boyle.

Mamo Clark, cast as Maimiti, was born in Honolulu in 1914. Her mother was a descendant of the famous 15th Century Hawaiian chief, Liloa. In *Mutiny*, Fletcher marries her and they produce a child.

One ship, thousands of stories, and oceans of anguish: **Eddie Quillan** on the verge of a mutinous breakdown getting himself under control, thanks to Fletcher Christian (**Clark**).

After *Mutiny*, she was cast as a Polynesian princess in *Robinson Crusoe of Clipper Island*. She retired after appearing in a minor role in *Seven Sinners* (1940) with John Wayne and Marlene Dietrich.

An English character actor, Herbert Mundin, cast as "Smith," was born in 1898. In the 1930s, he was frequently typecast in films like *The Adventures of Robin Hood* (1938).

He was a cheeky eccentric, a type with jowled features and a cheerful disposition.

Eddie Quillan, a son of Philadelphia, born in 1907, was a film actor and singer. As a child, he performed in vaudeville and silent movies. His 1928 comedy-drama, *Show Folks*, was a modest success, starring Carole Lombard. His breakout role came in the 1929 silent film, Cecil B. De Mille's *The Godless Girl*.

Quillan was gay, and he often bonded with other bisexual or gay actors or members of the crew for parties on Catalina Island. Clark and Tone were honored guests. Herbert Mundin (see above) was also gay, as was Donald Crisp, cast as Burkitt.

Crisp was a Londoner born in 1882. He had a career that began in the early silents and went on into the 1960s. In 1942, he won a Best Supporting Actor Oscar for his performance in *How Green Was My Valley*. Early

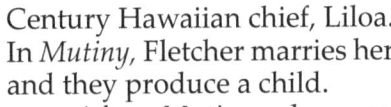

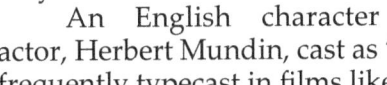

In Hollywood's sexual history, the actress **Movita Casteneda** has a unique position. She seduced both actors who played the role of Fletcher Christian: Clark Gable (in 1935) and Marlon Brando (in 1962)..

Known for her portrayal of exotic women, she became the second wife of Brando. Their union, however, was annulled in 1968 after it was discovered that she was still married to the Irish boxer Jack Doyle, whom she'd wed in 1939.

Movita and Brando were the parents of two children.

235

in his career, he traveled west with director D.W. Griffith, who later cast hm as General Grant in *Birth of a Nation* (1915).

In time, Crisp became a director himself. He was accused of making frequent use of the casting couch, seducing handsome young men who wanted roles in his films.

Over the years, he directed seventy motion pictures, including *Don Q, Son of Zorro* (1925), starring Douglas Fairbanks Sr. In the years to come, Crisp developed crushes on many of his leading men, including Henry Fonda, Gregory Peck, and Laurence Olivier. He got lucky only once, and that was with Errol Flynn during the shoot of *The Private Lives of Elizabeth and Essex* (1939).

(*Left photo*) **Bette Davis** with **Errol Flynn** in that ode to the eccentricities to the Virgin Queen, and (*right photo*) its director, **Donald Crisp**.

Cast as Joseph Banks, Henry Stephenson was born in 1871 to British parents in Grenada, then a British colony within the West Indies. He portrayed many friendly and wise gents in motion pictures of the 1930s and '40s. Memorable roles included his performance in *Oliver Twist* (1948).

Stephenson made his Broadway debut in 1901, later starring in more than thirty plays. Beginning in 1917, he worked in silent movies, but made his mark mostly as an elderly man in sound pictures. In all, his career endured for more than half a century.

Cast as Captain Nelson, Francis Lister was a Londoner born in 1899. He got his start in silents beginning with *Branded* in 1920. He was sometimes cast as a duke, lord, or prince in films that continued until 1951. From 1924 to 1932, he was married to the famous English actress, Nora Swinburne. Her career also began in 1920, lasting until her farewell to the screen in 1974.

Spring Byington, cast as Mrs. Byam, emerged in 1886 in Colorado Springs and would have a long career stretching from 1904 to 1968. Her biggest success was her seven-year radio and television gigs on the sitcom, *December Bride*, a featured serial broadcast by CBS Radio (1952-1953) and later, by CBS TV (1954-1959). Zsa Zsa Gabor was occasionally hauled in for a guest appearance.

All-American **Spring Byington,** cast with Clark in *Mutiny on the Bounty* as a virtuous, proudly patriotic example "Hail Britannia's" home & hearth.

In 1938, Byington won a Best Supporting Actress Oscar for *You Can't Take It With You.* She co-starred in it with James Stewart and Jean Arthur.

Although she was once married, Byington was later outed as a lesbian. As her best friend, Marjorie Main, claimed, "Spring just didn't have much use for men."

An Irishman born in 1884, Byron Russell, cast as Quintal, was a character actor who moved to the United States in 1911. He worked on Broadway and in silent films as part of a career that stretched from 1913 to 1960. *Mutiny on the Bounty* became his best-known work. He eventually turned to television as his film career in Hollywood faded.

David Torrence, as Lord Hood, born in Edinburgh in 1864, appeared in more than a hundred motion pictures between 1913 and 1939. His first role was as the Duke of Strelsau in the first version of *The Prisoner of Zenda* (1913). He was the brother of the far more famous actor, Ernest Torrence, who played cold-eyed, imposing villains.

Notable films from his repertoire include *Mantrap* (1936) with Clara Bow, and *Fighting Caravans* (1931) with Gary Cooper and Lili Damita.

Born in 1909 in Toronto, Douglas Walton, as Stewart, was a gay actor who worked in films from 1931 to 1950—in all, a total of sixty appearances. Tall, blonde, and elegant, he was often cast in aristocratic roles or that of a man of sophistication.

One of his most noted performances was opposite Katharine Hepburn in *Mary of Scotland* (1936). He played the effeminate and cowardly "Lord Darnley."

Ian Wolfe, as Maggs, born in Illinois in 1896, was a character actor who appeared in an astonishing 400 films and TV series between 1934 and 1990.

In Hollywood, he made his first screen appearance in *The Barretts of Wimpole Street* (1934). He often worked in *Sherlock Holmes* dramas. Today, he is still seen on the screen in the James Dean movie, *Rebel Without a Cause* (1955).

A son of Missouri, born in 1871, DeWitt Jennings was both a Broadway and film actor, appearing in seventeen plays and more than 150 movies between 1915 and 1937. His best-known role was as Sailing Master Flyer in *Mutiny on the Bounty*. Most of his silent films, including his performance in *Fighting Fitzgerald* (1921), are lost.

A son of Glasgow born in 1875, Ivan F. Simpson, cast as Morgan, emigrated to America, where he worked on and off on Broadway from 1906 until his death in 1951. In between, he had a film career, often appearing with George Arliss, his co-star in *Disraeli* (1929). In all, he would star with Arliss in nine films. He often played servants or priests. He also made four films with Errol Flynn, including *Captain Blood* (1935).

In *Mutiny on the Bounty*, Vernon Downing appeared as Hayward. A British actor born in 1913, he had minor roles in motion pictures from 1934 to 1954. In many of his roles, he was uncredited. In 1938 and 1939, he appered in three film classics: *Marie Antoinette, Wuthering Heights,* and *Pride and Prejudice*.

Bill Bambridge, as "Hitihiti," was born in 1892 in Papeete, Tahiti. His parents had nine children. He later moved to America, where, in addition to *Mutiny*, he starred in *Tabu: A Story of the South Seas* (1931).

Marion Clayton, as Mary Ellison, was born in British Columbia, Canada, in 1907. As an actress, her most notable movies were *Mutiny*, along with *The Barretts of Wimpole Street* (1934), and *Ladies Love Danger* (1935).

Stanley Fields, cast as Muspratt, came from Pennsylvania, where he was born in 1883. First focusing on roles on Broadway (from 1908 to 1911), later performing with Frank Fay (the first husband of Barbara Stanwyck) and a vaudeville troupe.

He made his screen debut in *New York Nights* (1929). He was perfectly cast in *Ladies Love Brutes*, a talkie, in 1930. His nose was broken during a stint as a boxer, and he used his ugly mug to his advantage during his subsequent career in films.

A Londoner born in 1881, Crawford Kent, cast as Lt. Edwards in *Mutiny*, was a stage actor in England before emigrating to the United States. Between 1915 and 1952 (the year before his death), he showed up in 208 Hollywood films, many without screen credit. He could be seen in such pictures as Oscar Wilde's *The Picture of Dorian Gray* (1945); *The Dolly Sisters* (1945) with Betty Grable and June Haver; and *Pat and Mike* (1952) with Spencer Tracy and Katharine Hepburn.

Alec Craig, cast as McCoy in *Mutiny*, fitted the bill when a producer needed a stereotypically tight-fisted Scotsman. He'd emerged in Fife, Scotland, in 1884. One of his best-known performances, widely screened today on home television, was in *National Velvet* (1944), starring Elizabeth Taylor.

A native of Washington, D.C., born in 1897, Pat Flaherty played Churchill in *Mutiny*. As a young man, he was both a professional baseball and football player.

After that, he relocated to Hollywood, where he worked with Joseph P. Kennedy during the mogul's involvement in an affair with Gloria Swanson.

At one point in his 200-film career, he specialized in baseball-themed pictures based on the lives of, among others, Babe Ruth and Lou Gehrig.

Harry Allen went uncredited in *Mutiny* in the role of Wherryman. He'd emigrated to America from Australia, where he was born in 1877. In Hollywood, his first film performance was in *The Last Moment* (1923). Even though he had only small roles, he appeared in many classics such as *Of Human Bondage (1934)*, starring Bette Davis and Leslie Howard; *Mrs. Miniver* (1942) with Greer Garson; and *Jane Eyre* (1944) with Orson Welles and Joan Fontaine. His career lasted until 1949. In total, he appeared in more than a hundred motion pictures.

Dick Winslow, cast as Tinkler, born in Louisiana in 1915, got an early start in the film industry when he was five years old. By 1934, he had appeared in 75 films. He was also a master musician skilled at the pipe organ, the marimba, bagpipes, the accordion, and drums.

Another Irishman, born in 1887, Charles Irwin, was cast in *Mutiny* as Thompson. Quite by chance, he appeared in a number of award-winning films that included *Mrs. Miniver, The Adventures of Robin Hood, The Wizard of Oz, The Great Dictator, The Letter, Kitty Foyle, Yankee Doodle Dandy, Pride of the Yankees,* and *The King and I*.

As a footnote to casting, James Cagney, on a hiatus from Warner Brothers, appears uncredited at the beginning of *Mutiny*. Also uncredited were David Niven and the singer, Dick Haymes. Haymes later married Rita Hayworth.

Photoplay wrote, "*Mutiny on the Bounty* is a brutal, sweat-and-blood tale of man's inhumanity to man and its tragic consequences. It is not a pretty film, but it is grand and real and so are its characters, especially Laughton, Gable, and Tone."

Film Daily had high praise: "*Mutiny on the Bounty* is one of the most important productions since the inception of talking pictures. It is grim, gripping, and pictorially perfect."

London Film Daily published a review that instantly became Clark's favorite: "Gable's Fletcher Christian is a brilliant characterization. It is the most worthy of praise because he could so easily have been merely a violent crusader against the captain's sadism. But Gable presents first and foremost a naval man, who, until the final outrage, strives hard to maintain discipline and tradition in spite of his feelings and who, even when he has taken the fateful step, still regrets that he has been forced to break the ideals of the service. A fine, natural performance, full of those small touches that make a character live."

Hollywood Reporter raved that "*Mutiny* is one of the greatest films of all time, with the epic sweep of the sea itself."

Life magazine noted, "Tahitian sweethearts seem snatched right out of the Vassar daisy chain."

At the Academy Award ceremony, *Mutiny on the Bounty* won Best Picture.

Unique in Hollywood history, three stars in the same picture—Laughton, Gable, and Tone—were nominated for Best Actor, all of them losing to Victor McLaglen for his performance in *The Informer*. In part because of that, the Academy later created the category of Best Supporting Actor in which Tone would almost certainly have been nominated for his contribution to *Mutiny*.

Mutiny on the Bounty cost $2 million to make, and generated some $5 million worldwide at the box office.

***

Episode 67

How Merle Oberon Seduced Clark Gable

Again… and Again…and Again

During the first three months of 1936, Clark Gable characterized himself as "a married-but-separated bachelor-at-large."

The first screen goddess to take advantage of his new reputation was Merle Oberon. This was the year that would see the release of one of Clark's most memorable motion pictures, *San Francisco*. Oberon's most memorable film was four years away, when she would co-star with Laurence Olivier in *Wuthering Heights* based on Emily Brontë's classic novel.

One moonlit night in Hollywood, when Clark danced with Oberon at a chic party, he became entranced with her. Before midnight, they were seen leaving the party together. At that time, she was also having affairs with producer Joseph Schenck as well as actors David Niven and Leslie Howard.

After he poured himself a drink in her living room, he was summoned to her boudoir, where he found her in lingerie from Paris. Draped around her beautiful body was a silk robe with ostrich trim. It would be a night of soft Rudy Vallee music, champagne, and a midnight snack of caviar. Her hazel eyes welcomed him, as he mounted her by candlelight.

There were two smells in the room: Incense and Chanel No. 5 from her luscious body. The silk sheets were the color of beige.

Cecil Beaton, the photographer and designer, claimed, "Merle is almost a nymphomaniac. She makes love because she likes it. She's as promiscuous as a man, enjoying a quickie behind the door."

Two views of **Merle Oberon**, a spectacularly promiscuous grand diva with well-rehearsed theatrics and a "winning formula" of social pretentions from the dying days of the British Empire. *PSSST!!* In Hollywood, THEY WORKED!

A jealous Marlene Dietrich was very outspoken: "This so-called princess, an Indian half-caste, puts on airs like a great lady. In reality, she's a common piece, seducing nearly all her leading men and some important producers."

When Oberon heard that, she told Louella Parsons, "Ms. Dietrich is no one to criticize me. Her whorish list of lovers—men and women—would fill a phone book."

Years later, Oberon said, "Dietrich, as it is well known, seduced both Joseph Kennedy and his son, John Kennedy. I never seduced one of the Kennedy boys. However, I did get a call from Ted Kennedy one night asking me out for a date. I turned him down. That was only

Clark Gable ("The King') with **Merle Oberon** (*aka* "Queenie") at the 1936 Academy Awards.

The divine, the irreplaceable: **Marlene Dietrich**, who privately referred to Miss Oberon as a "strumpet" and a "tramp."

days before he had that dreadful accident over a rickety old bridge on Chappaquidick. His girlfriend drowned. It was such a big scandal, but it didn't wreck his political career."

Biographer Charles Higham went rhapsodic in describing Oberon: "She was one of the magic princesses of the 20th Century. That rich black hair, that high, noble forehead, the smoky, opalescent hazel eyes, the sensual lips, the exquisite neck and shoulders, and the full, generous, voluptuous body—all remain fascinating and desirable."

"Clark and Merle" were seen at premieres and on the night club circuit. Their romance captured the most attention when they appeared together on the red carpet at the 1936 Academy Award presentations. Clark had won the Best Actor Oscar two years before for *It Happened One Night*.

That night, Paul Muni won for his portrayal of the title character in *The Story of Louis Pasteur*, beating out Gary Cooper, Spencer Tracy, and William Powell.

Oberon watched in envy as Luise Rainer took home the Best Actress Oscar for *The Great Ziegfeld*. Masking their disappointment were Norma Shearer, Irene Dunne, and Carole Lombard, Clark's future wife.

Oberon had arrived in England when she was 17 in 1928. She lied about her birth, claiming she was born in 1912 in Tasmania. Actually, she was born in Bombay in British India and given the nickname of "Queenie" after Queen Mary. She was "half caste," a prejudiced reference to children born to a white father and a mother who was native to India. Her father was a Welsh mechanical engineer, and her mother came from Ceylon (now Sri Lanka).

She lived in Australia, France, and Italy before being discovered by producer and director Alexander Korda, who changed her name to Merle Oberon and cast her as Anne Boleyn in *The Private Life of Henry VIII* (1933) opposite Charles Laughton as the monarch.

She moved on from there, starring in *The Battle* (1934) opposite Charles Boyer. Korda, in 1939, would become the first of her four husbands. Their union lasted until the end of World War II in 1945.

Oberon provided little information about her long-running affair with Clark, which began in 1936. In the late 1930s, when he was not spending his nights with Carole Lombard, he was often with Oberon. He once slipped away for a week's vacation with her at her lavish villa at Acapulco, in Mexico.

***

Early in her career in London, Oberon began an affair with the producer and director, Alexander Korda. She was never faithful to him

The Private Life of Henry VIII (1933) was followed by *The Private Life of Don Juan* (1934), starring Douglas Fairbanks Sr. They had an affair. Years later, she would also seduce his son, Douglas Fairbanks Jr.

That was followed by *The Scarlet Pimpernel* (1934) in which she had a crush on her leading man, Leslie Howard. That led to seduction.

One afternoon, as Howard was seducing Oberon in his dressing room, his wife, Ruth Evelyn Martin, paid an unannounced visit. As she opened the door, she caught her husband on top of Oberon.

He rose up in embarrassment with a full erection. "We were just rehearsing," was his reply.

Later, Oberon agreed with Blondell. "Leslie was adorable, but the

Louis Rainer emotes with **William Powell** in *The Great Ziegfeld* (1936). Her win of the Oscar for Best Actress enraged every other (female) player in Hollywood.

THE TALK OF LONDON: Anglo-Hungarian film producer **Sir Alexander Korda** with his *protégée* (and later wife) **Merle Oberon**

A portly and debauched **Charles Laughton** plays a portly and debauched English autocrat with **Merle Oberon** as Anne Boleyn ("enjoying her neck while she can") in *The Private Life of Henry VIII (1933)*.

little devil could not keep his hands off any woman around."

Like Clark himself, the future Ashley Wilkes in *Gone With the Wind* (1939) seduced his leading ladies, notably Mary Pickford in *Secrets* (1933). Before that he'd had flings with Ann Harding in *Devotion* (1931) and later that same year, with Marion Davies in *Five and Ten*.

In the months to come, he seduced Myrna Loy in *The Animal Kingdom* and Ingrid Bergman in *Intermezzo* (1939). He even managed to lure Claudette Colbert to his bed, although she was more lesbian-oriented.

In Hollywood, Oberon was cast opposite the French actor, Maurice Chevalier in *Folies Bergère* (1935). He lured her to his dressing room on the second day of the shoot.

Chevalier later bragged, "I had the most beautiful women in Hollywood." He didn't name them, but a few of them included Claudette Colbert, Lili Damita (wife of Errol Flynn), Marlene Dietrich, Kay Francis, Jeanette MacDonald, Marilyn Miller, and Miriam Hopkins, plus "half of the women in Montmartre in Paris" (his words).

Maurice Chevalier with **Merle Oberon** in the English comedy, *Folies Bergere de Paris* (1935).

As she moved along with her Hollywood career, Oberon's list of lovers read like a *Who's Who* of Hollywood, including producer Darryl F. Zanuck at Fox.

At any of her lavish dinner parties, you might encounter Laurence Olivier, Frank Sinatra, Norma Shearer, Greer Garson, Cole Porter, and, later on, Ronald Reagan and Nancy, the former MGM starlet Nancy Davis. Clark Gable was always an honored guest.

To her opulent mansion in Acapulco, she invited Prince Philip, who planned only a three-day visit, stretching it out to a week. Her staff later reported that the consort of Elizabeth II shared the boudoir of their mistress.

Two views of **Merle Oberon** in *Wuthering Heights*, the romantic "frock flick" with which she was indelibly associated for the rest of her life. *Left photo:* with the relatively benign character played by **David Niven**, and *right*, with **Laurence Olivier** as the melancholy, brooding, probably insane Heathcliff.

Tongues wagged on both sides of the Atlantic when the tragic and "magnificently bipolar" **Vivien Leigh** *(aka* Scarlett O'Hara—*right figure in photo below)* visited her then-husband, **Laurence Olivier** *(center figure)* and **Merle** on the set during its filming.

Oberon also had an on-again, off-again affair with John Wayne that lasted from 1938 to 1947. When he was asked who was his alltime best lover, he named Marlene Dietrich. "I never spoke to the bastard after that," Oberon said.

"I couldn't be a philanderer," Wayne claimed. "I tried it, but it made me feel cheap and dirty."

Wayne got down, "cheap," and "dirty," however, with Clara Bow, Joan Crawford, "Get him out of the saddle—you got nothing," Marlene Dietrich (*Pittsburgh; 1942);* and Paulette Goddard *(Reap the Wild Wind)* (also 1942).

In 1939, as Clark Gable starred in *Gone With the Wind*, Wayne appeared in *Stagecoach,* the Western that

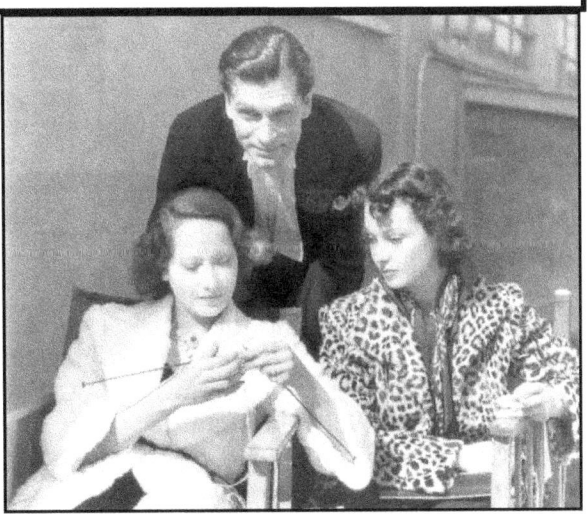

made him a star. He managed to seduce Claire Trevor, who got top billing over him.

Born in England in 1902, Brian Aherne made it to Hollywood to appear as a leading man in the 1930s and 1940s. Later, he would be famously married to Joan Fontaine.

Oberon later admitted to an affair with him. He also managed to seduce Wendy Barrie, Ruth Chatterton, and Marlene Dietrich while co-starring in *Song of Songs* (1933). He was even lured into the bedchamber of tobacco heiress Doris Duke.

Author John Van Druten found him terribly *naïve*: "He didn't believe that homosexuals could have sex. 'How could they?' he asked. 'They both have a penis.'"

"The first time I met Merle, I fainted at her awesome beauty," Aherne said. "I found the great women stars of the 1930s to be monsters. All the women I seduced were too demanding, even Merle."

Left photo: **Brian Aherne** with **Merle Oberon** in *First Comes Courage* (1943). In addition to many other actresses, Aherne went on to seduce one of the world's then-richest (and most notorious) women, tobacco, electric, and aluminum heiress **Doris Duke**. The *photo right* presents her as she appeared in 1951.

***

Oberon later admitted that as a teenager growing up in poverty in Calcutta, she stole enough money to buy a ticket at a ramshackle movie house playing *Dark Angel* (1925), starring Ronald Colman.

"I developed a big crush on him and was looking forward to meeting him in California."

In the spring of 1935, Samuel Godwyn met with Oberon and told her he wanted her to play the female lead opposite Colman in a remake of *Dark Angel*.

She was delighted to work with her childhood crush, especially in the upcoming kissing scenes. She and Colman met and had a brief fling. As she recalled, "He was the smoothest lover who ever seduced me…and that seductive voice of his…"

Shooting of *Dark Angel's* remake, however, was delayed, and Colman was cast in another picture. Her new co-star was Fredric March. "The first time we met, he put his hand up my dress," Oberon claimed. "After that, the bastard never got lucky."

Merle Oberon and Fredric March created a stir at Mocambo when they waltzed in with a party. Merle (now Lady Korda since King of England knighted hubby Alex) constantly requested "Marie."

***

"Once I met Gary Cooper, nicknamed 'The Montana Mule.' He couldn't get enough of me," Oberon claimed. She had been introduced to him by David Niven at a party at the Santa Monica beach house of Marion Davies, Clark's friend and former co-star.

Among the guests were Norma Shearer, Gloria Swanson, Joan Bennett, Charles Boyer, and Douglas Fairbanks Jr.

Inset photo: Handsome **Ronald Colman**, British star of the silent (1925) version of the tragic romantic drama he filmed with Vilma Banky, *Dark Angel.*

Ten years later, **Merle Oberon** was cast as Colman's co-star in a remake of the same script. To her chagrin, because of a last-minute scheduling conflice, Colman was replaced with another male lead, the gauche and sexually aggressive **Fredric March,** whom she disiked.

Despite their onscreen tensions, **Oberon** nonetheless appeared with **March** in a "society page puff piece," posted above. Its caption described the venue like this: *"Merle Oberon and Fredric March created a stir at Mocambo when they waltzed in with a party. Merle (now Lady Korda since the King of England knighted her hubby, Alex) constantly requested (that the dance band play the Big Band Fox Trot)* "Marie."

Cooper arrived at the party without his wife, Veronica ("Rocky") Balfe.

After only one dance, Cooper was seen leaving the party early with Oberon. As she later confessed, "We spent the weekend together. I don't think he ever let me get out of the bed except to go into the bathroom to freshen up before another assault."

"In Hollywood, Cooper found he was good at two things: Riding a horse and fucking," said gossip columnist Sheilah Graham, who also was one of Coop's conquests.

From the 1930s to the 1950s, Cooper compiled one of the biggest name-dropping lists of conquests in Hollywood. Tallulah Bankhead claimed she only came to Hollywood "to seduce that divine Gary Cooper."

His star-studded list also included photographer Cecil Beaton, Ingrid Bergman, Clara Bow, Lupe Velez, Claudette Colbert, Marlene Dietrich, Howard Hughes, director Edmund Goulding (who had to have him twice a day), William Haines, Cary Grant, Randolph Scott, Rod La Rocque, producer David Lewis, Barbara Stanwyck, Carole Lombard, Mae West, and Anna Sten.

Coop's more enduring affairs were with Patricia Neal, his co-star in *The Fountainhead* (1949)., as well as the tobacco heir, Anderson Lawler, who lived with him during his early days. He also had a much-publicized affair with the Countess di Frasso, who said, "I'm certain that Gary had had a man on occasion. They wouldn't let him alone."

Oberon's opinion? "Gary was divine. Later on, even Grace Kelly fell for him when they co-starred in *High Noon* (1952)."

***

David Niven became her lover, too. He had been an extra on Clark's *Mutiny on the Bounty* (1935) and had become a star in his own right soon thereafter. He was a housemate of Errol Flynn, and he lured Oberon onto Flynn's notorious yacht, *Sirocco*, on a sail to Catalina Island.

When Oberon came face to face with the dashing swashbuckler, Flynn, it was obvious what was on his mind. "He lived up to his legend. During our yachting trip, I don't think those boys allowed me to come up on deck one time. I was bed-ridden, if you get my drift."

Niven later bragged that, unlike Clark Gable, he did not have to visit bordellos, especially "The Cat House" that had been built and paid for by Louis B. Mayer.

Instead of prostitutes, Niven preferred movie stars: Alice Faye, Ava Gardner, Paulette Goddard, Rita Hayworth, Grace Kelly, Deborah Kerr, Evelyn Keyes, Hedy Lamarr, Ann Todd, Loretta Young, Ann Sheridan, Ida Lupino, Norma Shearer, Ginger Rogers, and even Mae West. He even managed to seduce America's two richest women: tobacco heiress Doris Duke and Woolworth heiress Barbara Hutton.

Around this time, George Brent also entered Oberon's life when they co-starred in *'Till We Meet Again* (1940). He had satisfied his co-star Bette Davis, in the 1930s, but he didn't please his fourth wife, Ann Sheridan, who disliked his equipment: "Brent bent."

Other stars did not seem to have complained too much about Brent: Ruth Chatterton (his second wife), Diana Barrymore, Kay Francis, Olivia de Havilland, Ilona Massey, Loretta Young, and even Greta Garbo, with whom he co-starred in *The Painted Veil* (1934).

Also in 1940, Oberon co-starred with Rex Harrison in *Over the Moon*. As she later confessed, "Rex and I had a brief fling, but he was not my greatest. He was efficient, on cue, and always the gentleman."

Harrison had begun his sex life in Liverpool when he was a "young gent." He became a frequent paying guest at a local bordello, where he

"Yup!" "Nope!" and *"Aw, shucks, ma'am!"*

Here's "The Montana Mule" **(Gary Cooper)** hauling **Merle Oberon** off to his home on the range in *The Cowboy and the Lady* (1938)

The swashbuckler film, *Captain Blood*, made **Errol Flynn** an overnight sensation. He was hailed as "the greatest shot in the arm that Hollywood has had in years—move over Gable!"

He also seduced Merle, but infuriated her by revealing to the public that, "She too, is from Tasmania and her real name is **Queenie O'Brien**."

had become enamored of a black prostitute, always demanding her.

Harrison would have five wives, three of them actresses: Lilli Palmer, Kay Kendall, and Rachel Roberts. Outside affairs featured Vivien Leigh, Carole Lombard, Romy Schneider, and even Tammy Grimes.

Oberon's sexual tryst with James Cagney did not work out. She'd met him on a War Bond tour during World War II. They checked into the same hotel. He slipped next door and invaded her room, where she welcomed him in a nightgown. During intercourse, she said, "I can't believe I'm getting fucked by that great movie gangster, James Cagney himself."

As he later reported, "Somehow, hearing that, I lost my erection."

Turhan Bey, hailed as "The Turkish Delight" by his fans, seduced Oberon when they co-starred in *A Night in Paradise* (1945). According to Oberon, "Turhan told me that during the making of *Arabian Nights* (1942) with Maria Montez, he 'plugged her'" (his words). "I figured if he could satisfy that bitch, he could take me on."

Oberon reportedly fell madly in love with the rugged Robert Ryan during their filming of *Berlin Express* (1948). A former U.S. Marine during World War II, Ryan was appraised by her as "A little prettier and he might have been one of the golden boys of Hollywood. But there was something menacing about his face (sometimes open and sweet, too), which bunched as tight as a fist. He stood 6 feet, 4 inches, at times looming like a threat."

Even the titles of her films contributed to her image as a sex goddess:

Here's **Turhan Bey** with **Merle Oberon** in *A Night in Paradise (1945)*.

***

Born in 1911, Oberon would live until 1979, dying at the age of 68. As she aged, she spent a lot of time looking into the mirror

Whenan actress reached 40, and most definitely 50, it meant retirement age for most of them, with the exception of Joan Crawford, Bette Davis, and Barbara Stanwyck.

One summer, she decided to head for Switzerland for a controversial treatment from a German-speaking doctor, Paul Niehans (1882-1971). He was said to be capable of removing years off the faces of his clients, who had included Christian Dior, the Aga Khan, and Pope Pius XII.

Adjacent to the doctor's office was a small slaughterhouse where animals, mostly cows, were housed. The sound of their screeching could be heard as the doctor cut into their wombs, removing embryos, which, after processing, he would inject into his patients, including Oberon—a painful process.

Back in Hollywood, she threw a chic party for her friends for the purpose of introducing "the new Merle Oberon," who was looking more youthful.

[Niehan's "fresh cell therapy" incorporated the use of fresh (or sometimes dried) animal cells which were injected directly into the muscles of humans. He promoted it as an "alternative medicine" and as a cure for cancer, homosexuality and/or sexual dysfunction, anemia, diabetes, impotence, heart disease, and in some cases, a form of breast enhancement. During his heyday, he operated clinics in Vevey, Montreux, and Aigle, in Switzerland.

Thereis no evidence it is useful for any health problem. The American Cancer Society found "no evidence that treatment with the Fresh Cell Therapy or "CT" results in any objective benefit in the treatment" There have been several instances of severe adverse effects including death, and The World Health Organization does not recognize its usefulness as a form of medical treatment.]

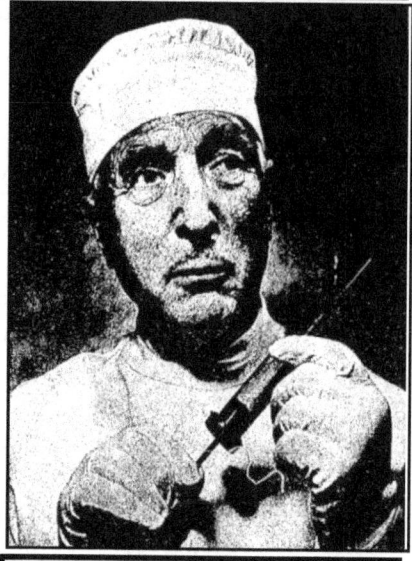

How did Merle Oberon retain her legendary beauty? In part, it might have been the work of **Dr. Paul Niehans.** Later derided as a quack, his cosmetic procedures involved injecting cells from the placentas and embryos of calves directly into the sagging flesh of his patients (or victims, depending on your point of view). His very costly clinics—until they were forcibly closed, operated out of three scenic sites in the French-speaking Swiss Alps. **Miss Oberon** was a frequent recipient.

For sex, Oberon turned to younger actors, since her previous lovers, including Clark Gable, had not aged as gracefully as she had.

At the party, she met a handsome young actor, Rod Taylor, who was from Australia, where she had once lived. She said, "There is just something about men from Down Under. They seem more macho and have more seductive appeal than most men from other countries. They also have a direct approach to a woman. No fancy pampering. They just come right up to a woman, put a strong arm around her waist, and announce, 'Babe, you're coming away with me.'"

That night marked the beginning of a six-week affair that she pronounced "torrid and most gratifying. I wondered where he'd been all my life. Well, the answer to that was he was not yet born. He didn't come into the world until 1930. He was a most thrilling lover, beginning at your neck, and working his way to your toes."

Their romance (for her) ended far too soon. Around the corner appeared Anita Ekberg, the sexpot from Sweden who lured him out of Oberon's love nest.

However, she had such fond memories of Taylor that she made the down payment on a new home for him.

Taylor and Oberon remained friends, and on that rare occasion, would have lunch together in Beverly Hills. He once told her that he had been asked to play James Bond in an early film. "The role I found stupid, outrageous, beneath me. Today, whenever I go see Sean Connery as Bond, I want to tear my hair out for being such an idiot and turning it down."

As a young boy, actor Richard Harris—born in Limerick, Ireland, in 1930—kept a sexy picture of Merle Oberon in his bedroom. Every night while looking at it, he "jerked off" (his words).

As an actor, Harris rose in prominence during the British New Wave. By 2020, he was listed as No. 3 on the list of Ireland's greatest film actors, as compiled by *The Irish Times*. He received two Oscar nods for his performances in *This Sporting Life* (1963) and *The Field* (1990).

The press learned he could always be counted on for a good provocative quote. "I was always a horny bastard," he claimed. "When I'm in trouble, which is most of the time, I'm an Irishman. When I turn in a good performance, I'm an Englishman."

Richard Burton, a Welshman, had a comment to make: "Richard Harris makes me look sober."

"Richard was a real bad boy," Oberon recalled. After our first night together, he told me, "You have fulfilled my boyhood fantasies. He was proud of his tool, which seemed to stay perpetually hard. He liked to display it to anyone interested."

"Good-looking, sexy, and hung," was Merle Oberon's assessment of the Aussie actor **Rod Taylor**. He is mostly remembered today for his starring role in Alfred Hitchcock's *The Birds* (1963), in which he tried to protect girlfriend Tippi Hedren from feathery onslaughts. He later recalled his fling with Oberon: "She wanted it four times before the sun rose in the sky."

Wanna know more about **Merle Oberon's** links to **Peter O'Toole**?

In 2015, Blood Moon published Darwin Porter's definitive, award-winning overview of his life, times, and love affairs with an astonishing range of show-biz and social-register bigwigs, including Merle Oberon.

As fans and detractors said about him at the time: "He was the biggest, most lecherous, and most original British-Empire bad boy since Lord Byron,"

Bad bay Irish actor **Richard Harris** as he appeared in 1965. He was another of Oberon's love interests.

"I was always a horny bastard," he confessed. "My ideal woman is a beautiful, mute nymphomaniac who runs the local boozer."

One night, Oberon confessed to Lady Sylvia Ashley, wife of Clark Gable, "I shouldn't admit this, but one night, Richard lured me into a *ménage à trois* with another roustabout Irishman, Peter O'Toole. Unspeakable acts were committed that night, which I can't reveal."

When Oberon first met Eddie Fisher backstage at a concert, he was still married to Debbie Reynolds. That was before he dumped her and married Elizabeth Taylor.

"He was a very naughty little boy," Oberon said. "He flitted from bed to bed, ending up in my boudoir one rainy night after he drove me home from a party. He was doped up a bit on cocaine. He told me he'd been 'screwing around with chicks' since the age of fourteen. He was a competent lover, nothing special. I didn't want a repeat."

This little boy had many other holes to fill.

She could have cited everyone from Marlene Dietrich to Judy Garland. The list of Fisher's sexual/romantic involvments included Hope Lange, Ann-Margret, Juliet Prowse, Mia Farrow, Edie Adams, Pier Angeli, Mamie Van Doren, Maria Schell, and Stephanie Powers. He later married Connie Stevens.

Oberon's last stand was with George Hamilton. She became friends with the perpetually suntanned actor when he was dating Lynda Bird Johnson, the daughter of President Lyndon B. Johnson, who objected to their relationship. "All male movie stars are pansies," he said in private.

Oberon was seen together with them at Truman Capote's gala masked ball at the Plaza Hotel in Manhattan in 1964.

Oberon invited Hamilton and Linda Bird to her villa in Acapulco, and they accepted. Occupying Oberon's bed during their visit was a young Spanish actor whose name was never revealed.

While there, Oberon and her guests went sailing on John Wayne's yacht.

Ultimately, Lynda Bird and Hamilton would break up, and she'd go on to marry Charles Robb.

Somewhere along the way, Hamilton and Oberon linked up in bed. Their rumored affair was so brief it is hardly worth defining.

He moved on. Stars who included Elizabeth Taylor lay in his future.

So did Imelda Marco of the Philippines, singer Mary Wilson of the Supremes, Vanessa Redgrave, Julie Newmar, Britt Ekland, and Catherine, the daughter of the Duchess of Bedford.

Near the end of her career, when Oberon had a reunion with Nancy Reagan, her longtime friend, both of them lamented that Clark was "The Man Who Got Away." Each of them admitted she would have married him if he had proposed.

***

Merle Oberon (1911-1979), the Anglo-Indian actress/adventuress who made it big in show biz, as she appeared in 1943.

Rest in Peace

"Mine was, in fact, no better than a hundred other faces, but it did possess a fortunately photogenic quality."
—**Merle Oberon**, as relayed to a journalist at *Film Weekly* in 1939

Episode 68

HAL LeSUEUR
Joan Crawford's "Brother from Hell"

Two views of **Hal LeSueur**. *Left*, in a carefully posed studio shot where both siblings (especially **Joan Crawford**) "made nice" for the camera.

On the set of *Mutiny on the Bounty* (1935), Clark Gable was approached one afternoon by Hal LeSueur, who had an uncredited role in the film.

"Hello, Mr. Gable," he said. "You don't know me, but I'm Lucille's brother."

"And what Lucille might that be?" Clark asked.

"You know…Lucille LeSueur, or should I say, Joan Crawford."

"Oh, yes. She has told me many stories about you, especially about when you were growing up together."

"She told me tales about you, too," Hal said. "Could we get together tonight? You know, have a little fun? William Haines has told me about your dalliances, and I'm available— one hundred percent government-inspected beef."

"Why, you little shit," Clark said, pushing him aside. "Get out of my sight."

So far as it is known, this may have been the only encounter Clark ever had with the notorious Hal LeSueur.

Myrna Loy, a close friend of Crawford's, once said, "If she had lived, she could have written a book called *Brother Dearest* that would make that dreaded Christina Crawford's *Mommie Dearest* look like *Rebecca of Sunnybrook Farm* with Shirley Temple."

Crawford's childhood memories would haunt her for the rest of her life. Hal was born in 1901 in San Antonio, Texas, the first child of Thomas F. LeSueur and Anna Bell Johnson. He would soon abandon his family.

Crawford, then known as Lucille Fay LeSueur, was born on March 23, 1904. A severe mother, Anna preferred her son over her daughter, whom she beat frequently.

Anna later divorced Thomas and married businessman, Henry J. Cassin (1868-1922). The family lived in Lawton, Oklahoma, later migrating to Kansas City, Missouri. Henry didn't like the name of Lucille, so during his marriage to her mother, he dubbed her "Billie Cassin."

"Marilyn Monroe had a difficult childhood," Crawford said during her later years. "It was nothing compared to what I endured…a litany of horrors."

Clark Gable was the only person in Hollywood with whom Crawford dared to discuss her tawdry existence as a young girl. At the age of eleven, she began having frequent sex with her stepfather.

One afternoon, Anna came home early and found her husband in bed, seducing her daughter. She exploded in violence, ultimately divorcing him.

Crawford's incestuous relationships weren't over yet. As a teenager, Hal began to seduce his sister frequently. When he needed extra money, he would bring members of his gang for sustained rapes while he held her down. He threatened her with violence if she ever told their mother. He charged his gang members $2 each for forcibly penetrating his sister.

He was married twice, first to Jessie Burress (1923-1929), and later to Kasha Haroldi (1931-1935). He was never faithful to either of them. Both wives reported that he was often drunk and abusive, sustaining numerous affairs on the side, not only with women, but with men, whom he charged for his services.

Clark had met Crawford before she changed her name. He remained the only person she could share her past and present difficulties with Anna and Hal.

Once news reached her brother and mother that Crawford was on the way to stardom, they took the train to Los Angeles, where, without permission, they moved into her bungalow.

One of the first things he did, living with his sister, was to take her roadster—without her permission—and crash it into a lamppost one drunken night.

He told her, "If you can become a film star, with those big eyeballs, your funny face, and all those freckles, I can become an even bigger one. After all, I'm god damn good-looking, and—as you know all too well—very well endowed. Rumor has it that you're using the casting couch to advance yourself. Well, so can I."

She introduced him to Paul Bern, the MGM executive who later married Jean Harlow. That afternoon, Crawford spotted Hal leaving the studio to spend the weekend with Bern.

Hal began to get occasional work in Hollywood as an extra. When money was tight, he found he could hustle gay men. One of his conquests was director George Cukor, who invited him to his Sunday afternoon parties, where he was passed along from one homosexual to another Many wanted him not just for his looks, but because he was the brother of Joan Crawford.

One afternoon, Hal appeared uninvited on the set of *Across to Singapore* (1928), a picture in which Joan's co-star was Ramon Novarro. Four hours later, as the set shut down for the day, Crawford noticed her brother leaving the studio with Novarro for the weekend.

She found living with her brother and mother intolerable. "Hal would bring his tricks home at night, and I'd find some stranger, one of his johns, sitting at my breakfast table. In the meantime, my mother was running up bills all over Hollywood."

She finally moved out, asking for a private address and giving them her bungalow.

After appearances as an uncredited extra in one film after another, Hal eventually found stardom out of his reach.

Tired of this, Hal was later hired by the makeup department at MGM, where he met and hustled many upcoming stars, some of whom had arrived from Broadway at the advent of the Talkies.

In 1954, when tracked down by a reporter, he said, "for personal reasons, I must refrain from saying why I never see my sister. I don't feel it is the proper time to talk."

Their mother, Anna, died in August of 1958 in Los Angeles at the age of 74.

"My mother never loved me," Crawford confessed to Clark. "She only wanted what I could do for her."

Later in life, Hal was discovered working as a desk clerk in a motel, and living in a small room in the rear. He died of a ruptured appendix on May 3, 1963, at the Los Angeles General Hospital.

In Manhattan at the time, Crawford did not attend the funeral. When queried about it by a reporter, all she said was, "My brother and I parted a long time ago."

In reference to her mother, **Anna Bell Johnson** (1884-1958), **Joan Crawford** said to one of her biographers, Roy Newquist:

"I don't think she really loved me, but when you consider the life she led, what the hell. She married too young and too often. She was a little Swedish girl who wasn't too bright. All the way along, the wrong men appealed to her, and she worked her ass off, more often supporting them than they supported her. She was old and tired by the time she was 49, and when she came out here [to Hollywood] at least a few of the fires had been put out, and she could be Hal's [Joan's brother] servant and my friend.

"She was a good woman, even though she ignored me when I was a kid, and she found life a lot easier during her last years... We weren't really close—we never had been...I let her live her own lifestyle, and that style included Hal, and I simply wouldn't have him around, so her loyalties had to have been divided."

When Johnson died in 1958, Joan flew from Bermuda, where she was vacationing with her then-husband **Alfred Steele** (president and later chairman of the board of Pepsi-Cola Company from 1950 until his death in 1959) to attend her funeral.

Anna Bell Johnson is buried in Los Angeles at Forest Lawn Cemetery. She appears in the inset photo with her wise and sensitive but ferociously tough-minded daughter, **Joan**.

Episode 69

Lupe Velez
The Mexican Spitfire

Funny, irrepressible, street smart, and hip, **Lupe Velez** appears as the center of attention with **Jimmy Durante** (in white dinner jacket) and **The Mills Brothers** in *Strictly Dynamite* (1934). Audiences loved her. A lot of A-list actors did, too.

Maria Guadalupe Villalobos Vélez was born on July 18, 1908 in a little town in Mexico called San Luis de Potosi. It was not a good day to be born. Four hours later, a fierce hurricane swept through the town, destroying buildings and damaging others. The roof was torn off the adobe house in which the future Lupe Vélez came into the world.

Her father, Jacobo Villalobos Reyes, was a colonel in the armed forces of dictator Porfirio Díaz. His wife, Josephine Vélez, was a singer. It was a time of great political upheaval in Mexico, and Díaz, who had ruled the country for three decades, was overthrown. Lupe was only two years old when Pancho Villa, a cattle rustler, took over.

At the age of 13, Lupe was sent to a convent school in San Antonio, across the border in Texas. There, she learned to dance. She had to return to her home at the age of 15 when her father was shot in a battle on the outskirts of Mexico City.

Forced to drop out of school to help support her family, which included two sisters, she made $4 (in U.S. currency) a week as a salesgirl. She still pursued dancing lessons which cost 37¢ per session.

At the age of 17, Lupe was dancing in extremely revealing costumes in rowdy burlesque houses. At this time in her life, her widowed mother, still attractive, was a streetwalker.

When a john wanted someone much younger, her mother forced her daughter to go away for a night of sex. On many occasions, her seducer took her back to a room where two or three other men were waiting.

Her first big break, or at least what appeared to be, came when the aging matinée idol, Richard Bennett, summoned her to Hollywood to play a Mexican cantina dancer in his upcoming play, *The Dove*. He was the father of two future movie stars, Constance and Joan Bennett.

By the time Lupe arrived in Hollywood, he'd assigned the role to another actress.

She was later discovered by an impresario who cast her in Hollywood's Music Box Theatre. There, she met

Two views of the remarkable seductive charms of **Lupe Velez**. Part of her charm derived from her ability to self-satirize. As one of the rare Latina actresses to thrive in Hollywood of her era, she elevated Mexican schtick to a high (and non-pejorative) art form.

Fanny Brice (*left*), the eccentric Funny Girl who recognized the brilliant comic timing of another eccentric Funny Girl (i.e., **Lupe Velez**), *right*.

the legendary Fanny Brice, who spotted her talent.

Brice was ending her terrible marriage to Nicky Arnstein. She summoned Lupe to her dressing room, where she was feeding her caged pet, a large rat, ham and eggs.

The show lasted for nine weeks, after which Brice said she would recommend her to Florenz Ziegfeld for his upcoming Broadway show. As she was preparing to leave Los Angeles for New York, a call came in from producer Hal Roach, who offered her a screen test.

At Pathé, she met other aspirant stars Jean Harlow and Carole Lombard. After the test. Lupe made her screen debut in 1927 in a comedy short, *What Women Did for Me.* That was followed by a two-reeler, *Sailors Beware!* starring the comedy team of Laurel and Hardy.

Lupe was eager for stardom, and she soon got her wish. A talent scout introduced her to Douglas Fairbanks Sr., the reigning male star of Hollywood, who cast her in his upcoming film, *The Gaucho,* in 1927. He did more than that. He had a sexual fling with her.

Perhaps news of it reached his wife, Mary Pickford, the reigning female star of Hollywood. "America's Sweetheart," as she was known, came on the set and was introduced to Lupe. She walked past her without speaking.

Months later, Fairbanks introduced her to his son, Douglas Fairbanks Jr., with instructions for her to take his son's virginity.

Fairbanks Sr. also introduced Lupe to Charlie Chaplin, marking the beginning of her affair with "The Little Tramp." He told her that "there is no more beautiful thing in life than a very, very young girl who was first starting to bloom." He called his penis "the eighth wonder of the world."

After a fling with Lupe, he dropped her to marry 16-year-old Mildred Harris, who claimed to be pregnant with his child.

Chaplin's favorite form of amusement involved visits to the hideaway brothels that illegally hired pre-teen orphaned girls or runaways from home. "There is nothing better that a man can do than take a young girl's virginity and introduce her to the thrills that a man can provide."

In no time at all, Lupe developed a reputation as "the leading nymphomaniac of Hollywood."

A three-way comic schtick: **Lupe Velez** (left) as "The Baroness Behr," flummoxing **Laurel and Hardy** in *Sailors Beware!*

Randy and raunchy **Douglas Fairbanks Sr.**, as an Argentinian rancher with ingenue **Lupe Velez** in The Gaucho (1927).

Married at the time to "America's Sweetheart," (Silent Screen diva Mary Pickford), he nonetheless sustained an affair with "The Mexican Spitfire."

Mega-star and silent screen icon **Charlie Chaplin**, the sexually insatiable child molestor, as he appeared in the film he wrote and directed in 1915, The Tramp.

As confided by Lupe to character actor Leon Ames, "I never met a man I didn't like unless he was a *mariposa*. I began to seduce at random. I find it hard to turn a man down when he wants the sexual thrill that I can provide. One night at a club, I met Clark Gable at the right time. He'd taken a chorus girl to the club, but they had a fight. He was free for the night, and I made myself available. That night, on and off, would stretch on for years. Sometimes, months would pass before we hooked up again."

Another of Clark's conquests, Adela Rogers St. Johns, wrote: "In the studios of Hollywood, there has never been a girl like Lupe Vélez except for Clara

Marion Morrissey (aka **John Wayne**) before he got jowly and gruff.

Cowboy in white: **Tom Mix,** the most acclaimed Western star of the Silents.

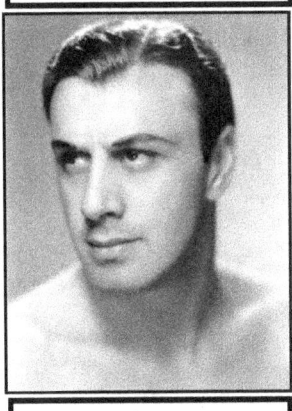

Big Band Singer **Russ Columbo.** Noted for charismatic talent and an affair with Lupe Velez, he died young and tragically in a gun accident, much to the consternation of his many fans.

Bow. I dub her 'The Mexican Spitfire." So stormy, so merry, so warmhearted."

When Lupe read that, she said, "My heart may be warm, but another part of my anatomy is red hot, especially for Gable."

"Clark and I had something in common," Lupe said. "He wanted to fuck all of his leading ladies, even the lesbians like Greta Garbo and Claudette Colbert, and I wanted to seduce my leading men. Even the ugly ones. That included in my near future, Edward G. Robinson. He appeared with me in *East Is West* (1930)."

"Rumor has it that I fuck all my leading men," she continued. "That's a damn lie. I didn't fuck Rin Tin Tin, 'The Wonder Dog' when I starred with him in my first talkie, *Tiger Rose* (1929)."

One of Lupe's early conquests in Hollywood was Tom Mix, the then-leading Western star in motion pictures. "He shared something in common with his horse, if you get my drift," she claimed.

Once a knife thrower in a circus, and later a soldier of fortune, Mix ended up in Hollywood, where he was soon making $17,500 a week when the average annual salary in America, in 1925, was $2,100 a year.

He always wore a white cowboy outfit with a large leather belt with a diamond-studded buckle. When they went out together, he insisted she wear white, too.

Once, when she visited his dressing room late one afternoon, a young man was shining his black boots. As he rested in an armchair, he still had them on. He introduced her to Marion Morrison. Later, she watched as they each donned a pair of trunks and staged a boxing match in the studio's boxing ring.

She was very attracted to Morrison. Later, he and Lupe would have a brief affair after he'd changed his name to John Wayne.

Mix's business partner at the time was Joseph P. Kennedy, a leading bootlegger from back East, in Hollywood at the time to make it as a producer. Recognizing the beginning of the decline of Mix's popularity, Kennedy signed him to a salary of $15,000 per week—still a very generous salary at the time.

Kennedy was involved at the time in an affair with Gloria Swanson. Even so, the future head of the Kennedy political clan in Massachusetts slipped away for a short fling with Lupe.

One night during one of her dates with

Lupe Velez with **Clark Gable**.

Although she was married at the time to Johnny Weissmuller, rumors spread that they were having an affair, She vehemently denied it at the time.

Later, however, she told her co-star Leon Errol, "Anybody who believes *(that we didn't have one)* also believes that the moon is pure gold, and that its mountains are covered in diamonds."

Lupe Velez with then-famous matinee idol **Monte Blue** in her breakthrough film, *Tiger Rose* in 1929.

This publicity photo captures the charm and comedic zest that some of her fans describe as "endearing."

Clark, Lupe attended a performance of Bing Crosby at the Cocoanut Grove. When Russ Columbo came out to sing a duet with him, Lupe later admitted, "Even though I was with Clark, I had the hots for this handsome young crooner, especially when he sang 'Too Beautiful for Words.'"

She secretly tipped an usher to leave a note with her phone number in his dressing room.

For a while at least, she forgot all about Clark as she and Columbo began a torrid affair. "I got him years before Carole Lombard put her mangy paws on him."

Ironically, Victor Fleming, by coincidence, cast both Columbo and Lupe in *Wolf Song* (1929), starring Gary Cooper.

Within two days of meeting Fleming, she was in his bed in a hotel room. "He was a real man's man during the day, but at night he could be a woman's delight."

After four nights of sex, he introduced her to the star of *Wolf Song*, a young Gary Cooper, who became "the love of my life." After sampling his endowment, although it's in some dispute, Lupe is credited with nicknaming him, "The Montana Mule."

She could talk openly with him about her affair with Clark, as he freely discussed his own conquests. "I don't know how I have any energy left to perform on the screen," she said. "Servicing Columbo, Coop, and Victor is more than a full-time job."

Clark later met Fleming and was so impressed with him that a decade later, he would want George Cukor fired as director of *Gone With the Wind* and Fleming hired in his place.

A fellow director, Henry Hathaway claimed, "Every dame Vic directed fell on her ass for him. His lists of conquests sometimes equaled that of a matinée idol, every actress from Clara Bow to Norma Shearer."

"Clark did not disappear from my life, and we ran into each other in the years to come," Lupe said. "Every now and then, we had a quickie, nothing serious. The bastard kept promising me he'd get Irving Thalberg to cast me as his leading lady in a picture, but he never did. If the part I could play, a hussy, perhaps, came along, he lobbied for Jean Harlow of the hair dye."

A widely respected director and behind the scenes authority figure: **Victor Fleming.**

This publicity photo of **Gary Cooper** with **Lupe Velez** from *Wolf Song* (1929) captures the intensity of their offscreen, sometimes psychotic, love affair. In at least two separate incidences, Lupe tried to kill him, once with a knife, another time, in public, with a gun.

***

No doubt about it Gary Cooper—not Clark Gable—became the love of Lupe's life. She found him her most passionate and satisfying lover. However, he was not always available. A number of actors and actresses also wanted a piece of "The Montana Mule."

"I'm nuts about her," he said. "A man cannot help falling for Lupe. I'm as much in love as one can get with one so quicksilver. She flashes, storms, and sparkles like diamonds."

When Louella Parsons asked Cooper who was the most exciting woman he'd ever dated, he responded at once, "Lupe Velez! Yes, Lupe Velez! But she's like a wildcat...hard to control."

He was not always available for Lupe. She constantly heard rumors of his other affairs. When he was shooting *Morocco* (1930) with the luscious goddess from Germany, Marlene Dietrich, Lupe showed up one afternoon on the set. She headed for Dietrich's dressing room for a violent confrontation and had to be restrained.

Coop and Lupe became an item in the tabloids, with

A competitor who consistently sent Lupe into paroxysms of rage and jealousy was **Marlene Dietrich**, who appears here in *Morocco* (1930), at the peak of their respective beauty, with **Gary Cooper.**

Hedda Hopper predicting marriage. But, as detailed in many biographies, she had an unexpected competitor: Not Clara Bow. Not Dietrich. He was the tobacco heir, Anderson Lawler, who eventually moved in with Cooper and who bestowed wonderful gifts on him, including a custom-made automobile.

They went on hunting and fishing trips together, and even on double dates with Lupe before she began to suspect the true nature of their friendship. Lawler sometimes found himself in the position of refereeing some of her frequent fights with Cooper.

The night Lupe realized that Cooper and Lawler were lovers, Cooper had come over for dinner. He was in her kitchen, reaching up into her cupboard for a bottle of bourbon. Suddenly, she lunged at him with a butcher knife, missing his heart but stabbing him in his arm. Bleeding profusely, he was rushed to the nearest hospital in an ambulance with dome lights flashing.

She later claimed, "I sure left my mark on *Garee*."

"A lot of people, even Clark, admired Cooper's "cool," she said. "But like me, he, too, had a violent streak in him. Just ask Clara Bow. Ask Carole Lombard. He can knock a woman across the room. He has beaten me furiously."

When Cooper decided to leave Vélez, he was in ill health and had lost a lot of weight, which he could not afford to do. He needed a six-month break from turning out one picture after another

Another implacable foe for Lupe was "the *Mexicana* with the perfect skin," **Dolores del Rio**. Whereas Lupe excelled at wild, impulsive, amusingly crazy *latinas*, Del Rio played it cooler and more "aristocratic." Here's a view of her from the late 1920s.

Somehow, she learned that he was to board the *Twentieth Century* on its cross-country route to Chicago. He did not say goodbye. He was leaving with Lawler.

Lupe showed up at the railway station in Los Angeles just as he was boarding the train. She carried a revolver and fired it at him, narrowly missing his head. Had she hit her target, the history of Golden Age Hollywood would have had to be rewritten.

Fearing arrest, she dropped her weapon and fled. After the violence had receded, Cooper and Lupe did get together on and off through the 1930s for sexual trysts—"for old times' sake."

In 1931 and 1932, Cooper was in Rome dating the socialite, the Countess di Frasso, whom he had met through producer Walter Wanger.

Cooper married Veronica ("Rocky") Balfe on November 5, 1933. It would be Cooper's one and only marriage. He left her temporarily for Patricia Neal, his co-star in *The Fountainhead* (1949). After that, he continued to have affairs but remained married nonetheless.

***

Lupe had not always been known just as "The Mexican Spitfire." By the time she'd turned 20, she was hailed as the hottest sex symbol in Hollywood, dubbed by her lovers as "Hot Tamale" (Clark's favorite name for her.) Otherwise, she was "The Wildcat from Mexico."

One night at a club, Clark was on a date with another fabled Latin beauty, Dolores del Rio. Lupe's date that night was Bruce Cabot,

Lupe was always very jealous of Del Rio, viewing her as her major competition in the movie business. Lovely, elegant, and ladylike, Del Rio could play a beautiful woman of refinement, whereas Lupe was assigned more whorish roles.

Lupe had another reason to be jealous: Del Rio had seduced Cabot, her date, and was now out with Clark.

Not only that, but both had been involved with the German novelist Erich Maria Remarque. "Every part of Dolores was beautiful—even her feet," he claimed.

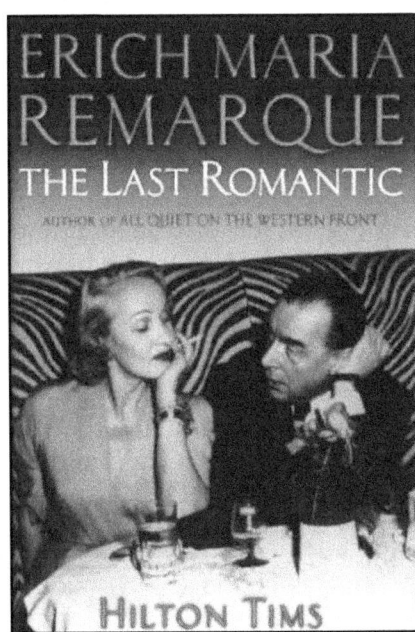

No other writer of his era managed to "occupy" niches of high glam and literary acclaim as fully as **Erich Maria Remarque**, author of *All Quiet on the Western Front*. Here, he appears with German-born **Marlene Dietrich**, who opposed Hitler's Nazi regime and fled to America.

Orson Welles told the press, "She is the most beautiful woman I've ever seen."

So what did Lupe do, face to face with her competitor? She picked up a glass of Scotch and soda from a nearby table and tossed it into Del Rio's face.

Clark spent the night with Del Rio, apologizing for Lupe.

After a night of *amour*, they had a late breakfast and retired to her garden and pool for a nude swim.

He was surprised when lunch was served at three o'clock. It was a plate of beautiful gardenias. When he saw her pick them up, petal by petal, and eat them, he, too joined for the first lunch of his life where the main course was gardenias.

The following night, Del Rio replaced Clark in her bed with Greta Garbo.

***

During her tumultuous life, Lupe would marry only once: to the screen Tarzan, Johnny Weissmuller.

Born in 1904 in the Kingdom of Hungary (in a town that's now part of Romania), he later won fame as an Olympic swimming champion, setting one of the most outstanding Olympic records of the 20th Century.

After he retired from swimming, he moved to Hollywood, where he played Edgar Rice Burrough's *Tarzan* in a dozen motion pictures between 1932 and 1948.

Fan magazines wrote that at long last, **Lupe Velez** could be "tamed," thanks to her marriage to **Johnny Weissmuller** (Tarzan).

Less than four months after their wedding, they announced the first of their separations. But they soon made up. "All he had to do was strip naked in front of me, and I'd forgive him for anything."

He had won the role of Tarzan by beating out Clark Gable, who later said, "I'm delighted I lost the role of Tarzan. Imagine how my career would have gone if I'd been chosen."

Weissmuller claimed, "All I have to do is utter that famous yell, swing on a vine, be fitted with a jockstrap to conceal my huge manhood behind a loincloth, say, 'Me Tarzan, you Jane,' and then go home with a million."

Before Lupe, other stars sampled the Jungleman's "package."

Early in the 1930s, Tallulah Bankhead worked in Hollywood, making one failing picture after another. She told him, "*Dah-ling*, you're the kind of man a woman like me must Shanghai and keep under lock and key until both of us are entirely spent. Prepare to be locked up for ten days."

Joan Crawford was next: "Unlike Clark Gable, Johnny likes to have his foreskin sucked."

From the beginning, the Weissmuller/Vélez marriage was rocky. They fought in private, and they fought in public.

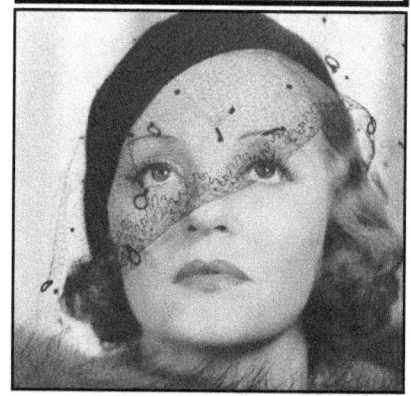

It was rumored that Lupe in bed, inflicted more wounds on Weissmuller than the jungle animals he tangled with in his movies. She was rumored to be a "wildcat" herself.

Biographer David Fury wrote, "In bed, Lupe was so ferocious that Johnny looked like a wildcat had attacked him. He arrived on the Tarzan set, his magnificent body covered with strawberry-sized hickeys, scratches, and annular bites on his pecs. The studio had to use extensive makeup before he was ready to shoot."

When word reached Lupe Velez that the formidable **Tallulah Bankhead** was seducing Johnny Weissmuller, Lupe issued a threat: "If I ever come across that Alabama whore, I'll use my claws to tear out each of her eyeballs and toss them across the room."

He also wrote, "Johnny and Lupe had a classic 'love-slash-hate' marriage. When they loved, they were happy. But when they hated, they fought long and loud in battles that echoed throughout Hollywood."

After four months, they separated and planned to divorce. But they reconciled.

Their marriage endured throughout most of the 1930s, although they were never faithful to each other. When temporarily separated from him, she slipped around to seduce Cooper and, on occasion,

Clark.

In August of 1938, Lupe filed for a divorce from Weissmuller for the third time, charging him with cruelty. The divorce was finalized a year later, in 1939.

By then, she was involved in a torrid affair with "Big Boy" Williams. After dumping him, she took up with the German novelist, Erich Maria Remarque. He told Oscar-winner Luise Rainer, "I find her volatility wonderful. When she gets mad at me, she takes off my shoe and hits me on the head with it."

***

For another episode with Clark, let's wander back to the time he had finished *Mutiny on the Bounty* (1935). Irving Thalberg asked him to spearhead a publicity tour of South America with journalist Ben Maddox, his on-again, off-again lover who continued to write gushing praise of Clark's films. At the time, his most formidable challenger at the box office was Shirley Temple, "Little Miss Lollipop" herself.

Not since the death of Valentino had a male star attracted so many women as fans from coast to coast, plus thousands upon thousands of devoted homosexual worshippers, too.

"Clark Gable is the man that every woman dreams about", claimed Claire Ellen, president of the Gable Fan Club's New Jersey chapter.

Beginning in Mexico City, Clark and Maddox winged their way to such cities as Bogotá, Lima, Santiago, Buenos Aires, and Rio de Janeiro. As his films were very popular south of the border, wherever Clark went, he was mobbed by adoring fans.

Maddox—who announced as Clark's press agent—and Clark shared a suite wherever they stopped. One night, Clark received a secret (and coded) message from Howard Strickling at MGM. Loretta Young had given birth to a baby daughter. He'd become the unacknowledged father.

Maddox and Clark planned to sail back to the Port of New York from Rio. Surprise of surprise, in the suite next to them aboard the *SS Pan America* was Lupe Vélez.

They sailed north. A steward spread rumors that they were engaged in a *ménage à trois*, since Maddox also serviced women.

One night on deck, Lupe admitted that she had resumed her affair with "*Garee*," as she called Cooper.

To complicate matters when they arrived at New York harbor, Johnny Weissmuller was waiting for her. Hearing that, Clark and Maddox waited in their suite for 90 minutes before disembarking.

Clark arrived in New York in time for the premiere of *Mutiny on the Bounty*, which morphed into a smashing success.

When he finally made it back to Los Angeles with Maddox, he returned to his suite at the Beverly Wilshire Hotel.

He characterized himself as "a married man with the privileges of a bachelor-at-large."

***

Near the end of her career, Lupe was offered a series of Mexican Spitfire movies, eight comedies for RKO between 1940 and 1943. The series began with *The Girl from Mexico* in 1939. It introduced the character of Carmelita Fuentes, a sympathetic but temperamental Mexican singer.

Her leading men were Donald Woods, Buddy Rogers, and Walter Reed. She hated the role and felt trapped in the series, but she needed the money. The last of the Spitfire movies was *Mexican Spitfire's Blessed Event* (1943).

In popular culture, these films have been compared and contrasted to the *I Love Lucy* TV series in the 1950s., Both feature a Latino-Anglo couple, one of whom is a sweet troublemaker wife.

***

Lupe's life ended in tragedy whose details were announced in Second Coming headlines across the nation. During the last week of her life, she told a member of her staff, "I learned today from my doctor that I'm pregnant. The father is Gary Cooper. Maybe Clark Gable."

On December 14, 1944, she retired to her bedroom for the final time. There, she swallowed 75 Seconal pills washed down with a large glass of brandy. It is believed that she died within fifteen minutes.

The Mexican Spitfire left the world at the age of 36.

Her fame died with the deaths of her once-devoted fans of long ago.

THE SPITFIRE SERIES: AN HOMAGE TO LUPE VELEZ

Lesser actresses, with weaker egos, might have drowned in their own stereotypes. But **Lupe Velez** managed to transcend, with humor, the limitations of her roles. Here's how some of her films were marketed to mostly white, mostly Anglo, and mostly conventional mainstream audiences.

Her timing was brilliant, and almost everyone laughed—especially Lupe.

Lupe Velez, as a scatterbrained *Latina* named Carmelita, in collaboration with the very talented vaudevillian *schtickster,* **Leon Erroll.**

REST IN PEACE, LUPE

Episode 70

The Death of Irving Thalberg

Upper photo: **Pallbearers** at Thalberg's funeral in Los Angeles, Lower photo: **Obits,** nationwide.

In September of 1936, "starmaker" Irving Thalberg, who once said "I created Clark Gable," attended an outdoor concert in Hollywood. There, he developed a cold, which later led to Lobar pneumonia. *[Lobar pneumonia is an acute bacterial infection involving a large portion of one lobe or an entire lobe of a human lung.]*

At home, his wife, Norma Shearer, confined him to bed for a week, and summoned his doctor every day. He was pronounced dead on September 14.

He had forced Clark to star in *Mutiny on the Bounty* (1935). Clark later said, "I was wrong for resisting. Irving was right, although I still didn't like wearing that damn pigtail."

Louis B. Mayer announced a day of mourning at MGM, shutting down the studio on September 16, the date of the funeral of "The Boy Wonder."

Clark was asked to be an usher at the funeral. He was reluctant to do so, since he had not spoken to Thalberg all year. The producer and his star had had a feud when Clark refused to be cast opposite Shearer in Shakespeare's *Romeo and Juliet*.

"I don't look like Romeo. I'm too old. While we're on the subject, your wife, Ms, Shearer, is far too old to play Juliet. She might play Juliet's mother." Then he stormed out of Thalberg's office.

Eventually, Thalberg hired the English actor, Leslie Howard, to take on the role of Romeo, although he, too, was far too old for the part.

Most of the big stars at MGM showed up for the funeral, although Garbo bowed out. Figures from other studios attended, including Carole Lombard, Mary Pickford, Gary Cooper, Fredric March, and even the Marx Brothers. Director Erich von Stroheim was there, even though Thalberg had fired him.

In the congregation sat Joan Crawford, still harboring resentment of Thalberg for assigning several choice roles she wanted to his wife, Norma Shearer.

Cecil B. De Mille said "the passion of Irving Thalberg is the greatest conceivable loss to the motion picture industry, and I say that absolutely without qualification. There are hundreds of executives, but only six men with the genuine genius for making motion pictures. Mr. Thalbeg was the greatest of those. I have long considered him the most competent and inspired producer in the business."

At least three thousand fans gathered outside, not necessarily to mourn Thalberg, but to watch the parade of stars filing into the temple. Mayer showed up and was given an honored front-row seat. The funeral had the grandeur of a film premiere. Howard Strickling was in charge of assigning seats, sending "the nobodies" to the rear.

At the funeral, Clark and Douglas Fairbanks Jr. acknowledged each other. He still harbored resentment toward Clark for frequently seducing Crawford during their ill-fated marriage.

Shortly after Thalberg's death, F. Scott Fitzgerald, the novelist, began writing *The Last Tycoon*, a fictionalized overview of Thalberg's life. (He died before he completed it.)

Two weeks after the death of her husband, Shearer summoned Clark to her residence. Even though her producer husband was dead, the actress still had great power at MGM since she had inherited huge holdings in MGM's parent company, Loews, Inc.

Clark felt he had better heed her command, and he arrived late Saturday morning and didn't leave until noon on Monday. "I need you to comfort me," she told Clark.

Most of that "comforting" took place in her boudoir.

"For the last few months of his life," she told him, "Irving was not capable of performing. I'm looking forward to co-starring with you in my future films."

***

Happier Times for the "Ultimate Insiders": **Thalberg** with **Norma Shearer** and MGM's studio chief, **Louis B. Mayer**.

Thalberg's funeral was enormously important, both professionally and emotionally, to everyone associated with MGM.

Here's **Franchot Tone** with his wife, **Joan Crawford**, expressing their grief (and emphasizing their claim) to their coveted status within the firmament of MGM bigwigs.

Whereas Clark had reluctantly (but wisely) accepted Thalberg's plea for him to star in **Mutiny on the Bounty** (1935), a year later, he refused to play **Romeo** opposite Norma Shearer's **Juliet**. "Too fussy, too highbrow...and definitely not my style," Clark said.

Clark remained resistant, despite Thalberg's ongoing pressure, with the full understanding that it would cool the friendship he'd developed with Thalberg and his ambitious (and too old to convincingly play Juliet) wife, **Norma Shearer**.

MGM eventually cast "that sissy Englishman," **Leslie Howard** as Romeo to Shearer's Juliet in a film that eventually bombed. In the upper photo, he appears in full Shakespearan drag with **Norma Shearer** in a self-satirization of their respective roles, having switched chairs. Regrettably for everyone involved, Thalberg died on the night of its Los Angeles premier, plunging everyone involved into deep uncertainties.

The lower photo, snapped in 1932, shows (*left to right*) **Norma Shearer** with her all-powerful husband, **Irving Thalberg**; and a dowdy-looking **Ria Langham** with her philandering husband, **Clark Gable** during the peak years of their respective collusions and collaboraltions.

Episode 71

Wife vs. Secretary (1936)

Clark was enjoying the distance he'd cultivated not only from Ria Langham and her kids, but from his father. He had settled comfortably into his suite at the Beverly Wilshire, which cost only $150 a month.

Late one afternoon, Joan Crawford put through a call to him, inviting him to spend the weekend at her home with her husband, Franchot Tone. Clark had recently co-starred with him in *Mutiny on the Bounty.*

Somehow, Louis B. Mayer was tipped off about this arrangement. He asked Eddie Mannix, "Do you think those three whores, each a bisexual, are going to have a three-way? I wouldn't put it past them."

More news was on the way. On November 14, 1935, Ria Langham Gable confirmed to the press that she and Clark were separated. "We will seek a divorce sometime in the future. Difficulties in our domestic life arose because Mr. Gable has to work so long, and so hard, in his movie roles."

The plot of his next picture, a wife being jealous of her husband's secretary, had been filmed many times before. After reading Faith Baldwin's short story in *Cosmopolitan*, director Clarence Brown thought it had a twist that might appeal to Clark's large fan base of women. Harlow and Loy's involvement would add more dollars at the box office.

A romantic comedy, it marked the fifth of six motion pictures Clark would make with Harlow, and the fourth of seven films in which he would co-star with Loy. Harlow and Loy would soon appear with each other in *Libeled Lady* (1936), in which Harlow would be billed over Spencer Tracy and her current lover, William Powell.

The plot of *Wife vs. Secretary* centers on Jake (Clark), a publisher. Loy, his wife, suspects that he's having an affair with "Whitey" (Harlow). He isn't.

When the wife confronts the secretary, Harlow warns her, "If you leave him now, you'll never see him again, and you're not going to get him back. If he turns to me, I won't turn away."

Eventually, Loy realizes her suspicions are not founded, and she reconciles with Clark. Meanwhile, Harlow returns to her beau, as played by James Stewart.

***

Harlow's brief marriage to cameraman Harold Rosson had ended in divorce. She was now being courted by the debonair William Powell, who had become a frequent visitor to the set, often arriving to take

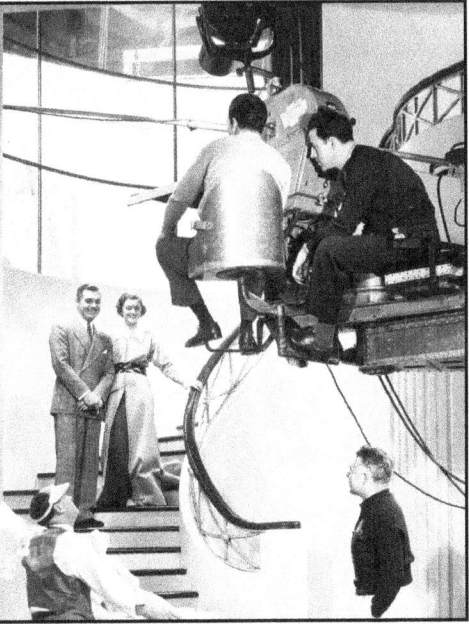

The technical savvy of the movie industry had increased exponentially since the early careers of all three of the stars of *Wife Vs. Secretary.*

This, Clark's fifth movie with Jean Harlow, and the fourth of the seven he'd make with Myrna Loy, marked a period of facile grace and ease among all three of them. In the *photo above*, the object of the cameraman's "affection" are **Clark Gable** with his "wife," **Myrna Loy**.

This photo, released to the press as a backlot curiosity showcasing director **Clarence Brown's** skill with cameras and cranes, gave movie audiences an insight into how movie-making involved more than beauty, brawn, romance, and drama.

his new lover to lunch.

Meanwhile, producer Hunt Stromberg had hired a trio of screenwriters to adapt Baldwin's short story for the screen. Making the largest contribution was Norman Krasna, aided by John Lee Mahin and Alice Duer Miller.

The relationship between Clark and Loy had gotten off to a bad start when she had rejected his sexual advances. On the set of *Wife vs. Secretary*, their newest movie, a friendship developed between them. "He's gotten over my rejection, or else forgotten about it. We had our morning chats when he brought me freshly brewed coffee."

In many articles and biographies, Loy is outed as a lesbian. Yet she was known to have had a number of affairs with men, most notably with Louis B. Mayer himself. She had also had an affair with William Powell, her *Thin Man* co-star.

She managed to seduce two otherwise homosexual actors, Ramon Novarro and later, Montgomery Clift. In her future on the set of *The Rains Came* (1939), she seduced the bisexual matinee idol, Tyrone Power.

Early in her career, she'd had a fling with Leslie Howard, her co-star in *The Animal Kingdom* (1932).

Her most unusual affair was with Adlai Stevenson, the Democratic candidate for president, who ran against Dwight Eisenhower twice in the 1950s.

In *Wife vs. Secretary*, she played Linda, the wife of high-end magazine publisher, Van ("Jake") Stanhope. "This was one of my sexiest roles," she claimed. "A lot of smooching going on. The woman I played had one foot in the bed all the time. Even though we were a married couple, the Breen office wanted some scenes reshot or cut altogether."

In one scene, Clark appears in bed without his shirt. Presumably, he is nude. The Breen office wanted it reshot with him wearing an undershirt. He'd been bare-chested in *It Happened One Night*.

Harlow's beau in *Wife vs. Secretary*, James Stewart, was appearing in one of his early roles. A son of Indiana, born in 1908, he had a certain drawl that Clark felt would hinder him. "How wrong I was," he later said.

From 1935 to 1991, Stewart would make 80 motion pictures. The American Film Institute ranked him as No. 3 among the screen's greatest actors.

Stewart was captivated by the beauty of Harlow, describing her skin as "pink ivory...I didn't know what glamour was until I encountered her."

"Our director got pissed off at me," Stewart said. "He didn't like my on-screen smooching with Harlow. He made us repeat the kissing scene countless times. I botched it on purpose. That dame was one hell of a kisser. She aroused 'Old Henry' in my pants. He was rock hard. Our kissing led to other things."

When they weren't needed on the set, Stewart was often seen going into her dressing room. Of course, he timed such trysts for days when Powell was tied up in filming his latest picture,

"At first, I thought Jimmy was too shy and awkward to attract many women," Clark said. "Before

In *Wife Vs. Secretary*, **THE WIFE** (**Myrna Loy**, *left*)—at least in public—is relentlessly restrained, upper-class, and *bourgoise*. Meanwhile, **THE SECRETARY** (**Jean Harlow**, *right*) portrays a spontaneous, street-smart, lower-middle-class confection of platinum coiffe and satin.

In some ways, the division between the rivals for **Clark Gable**'s affection morphs into a backstory overview of class distinctions during the Great Depression.

SPOILER ALERT: It's the rich brunette (the one he's already married to) who wins **Gable** in the end.

Here's **Jean Harlow** with then-newcomer **James Stewart**, suggestively alone together in a car. Cars were something that moralists and movie censors of that era sometimes denounced as "motel rooms on wheels."

The sexually suggestive setting wasn't lost on movie audiences of that era. Neither was the "come hither" look in Stewart's eyes.

he married Gloria, his one and only, he later estimated he had deflowered some 250 stars and starlets."

"My bachelor years—those were the days," he said. "It was wonderful."

To name-drop a bit, he seduced Marlene Dietrich, leading her to have an abortion, along with Olivia de Havilland, Loretta Young, Lana Turner, Margaret Sullavan, Diana Barrymore, June Allyson, Grace Kelly, Ginger Rogers, Norma Shearer, Rosalind Russell, and Jeanette MacDonald.

***

In the supporting cast of *Wife vs. Secretary*, May Robson played Mimi Stanhope. She and Clark had worked together on *Strange Interlude* (1932).

George Barbier, in the role of J.D. Underwood, was born in Philadelphia in 1864. Both a stage and a screen actor, he would appear in 88 motion pictures. He shot his first film in the first year of the 20th Century. He worked until 1945, dying only weeks before World War II came to an end. He was usually cast as weighty, white-haired, often pompous patriarchs.

Hobart Cavanaugh, in the role of Joe, was born in Nevada in 1886. He'd made his film debut in 1928 and had worked steadily until 1950, the year of his death.

In many of his films, the roles were so small, he went uncredited. He appeared with Errol Flynn in *Captain Blood* (1935), but was usually cast as a downtrodden, henpecked husband.

John Qualen, born in Vancouver in British Columbia in the closing days of the 19th century, was of Norwegian heritage. That made him ideal when a director wanted a Scandinavian. Over the course of his career, he appeared in more than 100 films and enjoyed a long association with director John Ford.

Tom Dugan, as Finney, was born in Dublin in 1889. He was seen in 270 motion pictures between 1927 and 1955, the year of his death. He was most often cast as an Irish cop, a gangster, or a taxi driver. He is mainly seen today as the Polish actor who disguised himself as Hitler in Ernst Lubitsch's *To Be or Not To Be* (1942), Carole Lombard's last film.

Gilbert Emery, as Simpson, was born in central New York State in 1875 and worked in films from 1921 until his death in 1945. He was also a playwright and wrote seven Broadway plays, including *Far-Away Horses* in 1933.

Marjorie Gateson, as Eve Merritt, had previously worked with Clark and Crawford in *Chained* (1934).

Gloria Holden was a Londoner born in 1903. She often played chic-but- chilly society women. Her best-known role was as *Dracula's Daughter* in 1936. She is also known for playing Mme. Zola in *The Life of Émile Zola* in 1937.

Exponentially Frumpy: Here's **Myrna Loy** with her onscreen mother, **May Robson**, a character actress who was invariably wonderful in every movie she graced.

Together, they're dressed in the sartorial splendor of their era. It's a hair-trigger alliance soaked in Depression-era privileges.

Perhaps just to prove that the implied threat of a marital rift wasn't an issue offscreen, the studio released this press photo of the film's love triangle.

Basking in the innocent bliss of an ice-skating session (*Why ice skating, one wonders?*) **Jean Harlow, Clark Gable, and Myrna Loy** each seem intent on conveying that their romantic competitons weren'r real, and that everything that had happened onscreen had been wholesome, healthy, and fun.

[*Harold A. Winston, Gloria Holden's third husband, was a studio scout who is credited with discovering a then-unknown actor known at the time as Bill Beadle. Winston, according to legend, was still smitten with his then-estranged wife, Gloria Holden. It was he who invented the name "William Holden" (aka "Golden Boy") and helped "assign" it to the man (Bill Beadle, aka William Holden) who later emerged as a major A-list movie star.*]

On December 11, 1936, Harlow collapsed while shooting a scene. She took a long weekend off, but returned to work that morning. Her collapse was just a harbinger of what was to come

"I sat through the first screening of *Wife vs. Secretary*," Loy said. "I came to believe that *double entendre* and ambiguity are more effective than being too explicit."

Made on a budget of $526,000, the film grossed $2 million at the box office.

Photoplay wrote, "Clark Gable is effective and affectionate enough for his most romantic admirer.".

Variety praised both Clark and Loy, but claimed, "It is Harlow who profits the most. She clicks in every scene without getting spectacular."

London Weekly weighed in too: "Here is one of the best films seen for a long time in which next to nothing seems to happen. Gable works hard but is more convincing as a high-spirited husband than as a hustling man of Big Deals."

In Irving Schulman's appraisal, he wrote, "This time, Jean Harlow played a sympathetic Miss Typewriter, who did not raise her voice above a conversational tone even in scenes of stress. So that for once, her voice was rated excellent by important reviewers. She handled her dialogue naturally, with such bright humor that she excited some consideration at the studio for roles other than that of a scatter-brained, good-hearted chippy."

Gloria Swanson and **William Holden** immortalized themselves when they co-starred in the memorable ***Sunset Blvd.*** (1950). In her greatest role, she played the faded silent screen star Norma Desmond.

Holden later said, "I actually played a male whore. I had practice as a whore. When I was a young actor starting out in Hollywood, I 'serviced' many actresses much older than me."

Stars of ***Wife Vs. Secretary***, with **Clarence Brown**, their director—proof that everyone at MGM was a lighthearted place where everyone got along.

But Myrna, the setting was a hot and sunny day in southern California...So WHY did you wear that fur coat?

Episode 72

San Francisco (1936)

One of Clark Gable's alltime greatest box-office hits was *San Francisco,* a musical drama disaster film depicting the horrifying San Francisco earthquake of April 18, 1906.

It starred Clark with singing star Jeanette MacDonald. Spencer Tracy had third billing. The earthquake sequences and the inclusion of MacDonald helped make the film a blockbuster.

Once again, Clark played a rough-and-tough character named Blackie, the same name he'd been assigned for his portrayal of the gangster in *Manhattan Melodrama* (1934).

As Blackie Norton, he owns a wild Barbary Coast club where he hires Mary Blake (MacDonald), who would probably have been better suited to an opera stage. Father Tim Mullin (Tracy) is a Catholic priest who warns Mary that Blackie "is as unscrupulous with women as he is with men."

He also warns her about San Francisco: "It's the wickedest, most corrupt, and most godless city in America." Originally, Tracy didn't want the role, telling director W.S. Van Dyke "I'm too virile to play a priest for God's sake."

Despite her priest's warning, she falls in love with the charismatic saloon owner. There will be much melodrama and their inevitable separation before the earthquake unites them again. As a preface to the ending, he frantically searches for her as the buildings of San Francisco tumble down around him.

Although Tracy had at first disliked the project, many critics felt that his performance as a rugged but understanding priest stole the picture from Clark and MacDonald

The earthquake itself, one of the most dramatic ever simulated until then on film, was the highlight of the picture.

It was ominous, frightening, and spectacular. The earth seemed to open up and swallow its victims. Deadly showers of masonry, timbers, and plaster rained down as water mains burst. Live wires exposed fleeing residents to electrocution. Columns collapsed and gargoyles tumbled from roofs. Dozens of extras were injured.

[*As a footnote, two famous directors, D.W. Griffith and Erich von Stroheim, both of them uncredited, collaborated with Van Dyke. Griffith directed*

San Francisco, till then the most realistic disaster film ever made, was released a mere 30 years after the 1906 earthquake that had devastated the City on the Bay. To many viewers, its memory was still vivid, fresh, and traumatic.

It reprised **Clark Gable**'s rough-tough saloonkeeper, a character with a name ("Blackie") that he'd originated two years years earlier in **Manhattan Melody.**

A rousing musical, *San Francisco* teamed him with **Jeanette MacDonald** *(center)*, an operatic *grand diva* who, for decades after, was an object of ridicule for her unapologetic belting, at "reaching to the rafters volumes" of what became San Francisco's theme song as the city crashed down around her.

Emotionally tormented, and in real life a hard-core alcoholic and bisexual **Spencer Tracy** convincinglty played a parish priest battling human frailties in the city that the script defined as the then-most-corrupted city in America, *San Francisco.*

some of the mob scenes, and Von Stroheim contributed to the screenplay.]

In the end, Blackie and Mary join the survivors as they march through the shattered city singing "The Battle Hymn of the Republic." The screen then switches to the rebuilt San Francisco as it looked in 1935.

The film's title song, "San Francisco," became a standard. It was composed by Walter Jurmann and Bronislaw Kaper, with lyrics by Gus Kahn. As part of the finale, as the city crumbles around her, MacDonald repeats the lyrics, with gusto, about a half-dozen times, morphing it into an anthem for the survivors.

Today, it remains a theme song for the City on the Bay. *[The city's "other" most familiar song is* "I Left My Heart in San Francisco," *especially the version sung by Tony Bennett.]*

The script was mainly written by Anita Loos, with whom Clark had had an affair. She would later generate a million dollars from the filmscript she crafted for *Gentlemen Prefer Blondes* (1953).

As a director, Van Dyke had recently helmed Joan Crawford and Clark in *Forsaking All Others* (1934).

***

Spencer Tracy didn't like taking third billing. *San Francisco* was the first of three films in which he would co-star with Clark. In spite of their carefully concealed mutual jealousy, Tracy and Clark bonded during the filming.

Sometimes, they would sneak away and have a few drinks in one of their dressing rooms, although during the day, that was forbidden by Van Dyke. Their friendship didn't extend after quitting time. In private, they went their separate ways.

Tracy was born at the dawn of the 20th Century in Milwaukee and reared as a devout Catholic.

In his early years, he developed a career in stock companies and on Broadway before migrating to Hollywood. His breakthrough came in the play *The Last Mile* (1930), in which he played "Killer Mears," a hotheaded convict.

As author Barry Monush wrote: "For 37 years, Spencer Tracy was one of Hollywood's greatest stars, but he never seemed to behave like one. Although he could be cantankerous, demanding, and difficult on the set, what the world saw was the finished product, a stocky, average-looking guy who projected strength, decency, and intelligence. For an industry steeped in phoniness, he seemed to rise above all the nonsense and sell a straight and honest bill of goods."

He'd married Louise Treadwell in 1923, although in time, they lived apart. He never divorced her because of his strict Catholic upbringing.

For years, Hollywood was fed the fake story of a passionate romance between Katharine Hepburn and Tracy. George Cukor, in private, shot that down, claim-

Jeanette MacDonald, shaking, rattling, and rolling in a (some said) bizarre blend of high opera with showbiz schmaltz. Drag queens, decades later, built entire onstage repertoires around her, and latter-day comedians made her a butt of endless jokes.

Spencer Tracy, as a strong and sustaining priest, counseling a member of his flock, a saloon singer **(MacDonald)** in a city devoted to sin—until the Judgment Day of a devastating quake.

San Francisco in 1906, after the quake. The film sequences were so realistic that some survivors became ill and had to be escorted out of the theater.

ing that their relationship was platonic, and that each of them was the other's best friend.

Today, in numerous books and film documentaries, they are "outed" as bisexuals. Scotty Bowers, Hollywood's leading pimp, revealed that over the course of many years, he supplied 150 girls to Hepburn—"no blemishes, please." He even pimped himself to Tracy.

When all those *exposés* of Tracy were broadcast from television sets or streamed from mobile devices in the 21st Century, many of his old fans had a hard time accepting Tracy's homosexual life. Their image of what a gay man was like did not conform to Tracy's screen image.

It wasn't until film documentaries came out in 2020 that television fans learned that Tracy was "passionate" about pretty boy John Derek. A ladies' man, Derek worshipped Tracy as an actor and rewarded him by letting him fellate him on occasion while he closed his eyes and thought perhaps of the many women he seduced and/or those he eventually married—notably Pati Behrs (married 1948-1956); Ursula Andress (1957-1966); Linda Evans (1968-1974); and Bo Derek (1976–1998).

The illusion that **Spencer Tracy** and **Katharine Hepburn** were a conventional heterosexual couple was useful during the peak of their respective celebrities.

Once, a reporter asked Hepburn what her big attraction for Tracy was. She said, "He makes the best cup of coffee in Hollywood."

In addition to his secret life as a homosexual, Tracy was actually bisexual. But instead of "banging" Hepburn, he seduced such female stars as Joan Bennett, Ingrid Bergman, Joan Crawford, Paulette Goddard, Myrna Loy, Grace Kelly, and Loretta Young, who fell in love with him.

He did all this when he wasn't drunk. Sometimes he would sneak away and check into a remote hotel with a suitcase filled with liquor.

After one of his epic binges, he'd sober up and began filming again, turning out such hits as *Captains Courageous* (1937) or *Boys Town* (1938), in which he taught pint-sized Mickey Rooney who the boss was.

Director George Cukor once said, "Movie fans during the Golden Age were so innocent. Americans are far more sophisticated these days. Back then, they believed all that publicity puff put out about the stars. If a matinée idol liked to get fucked, they turned him into a ladies' man like they did with poor Tab Hunter. If a woman was a lez, they linked her with male idols. At night, she might be going down on Marlene Dietrich or Greta Garbo. I know all about them. They had no secrets from me. I knew every time a rat crossed Hollywood Boulevard."

***

The female lead of *San Francisco* was Jeanette MacDonald. Born in Philadelphia in 1903, she would, in time, become one of the most influential sopranos of the 20th Century. She introduced opera to film-going audiences of the 1930s and inspired a generation of singers.

She is best remembered for all those movies she made with her co-stars, Maurice Chevalier and Nelson Eddy. In all, she starred in 29 motion pictures, four of which won Oscar nominations for Best Picture, including *San Francisco*.

After seducing her, Chevalier said, "She didn't have one ounce of humor."

MacDonald asserted, "Maurice was the fastest *derrière* pincher in Hollywood."

In contrast, her frequent co-star, Nelson Eddy, became the love of her life, although they never married. According to MacDonald, "All my other co-stars were either old enough to be my

And then again, at her best, **Jeanette MacDonald** was lovely, indeed.

She detested her love scenes with Clark Gable. He disliked her so much he made a point of eating raw garlic before kissing her.

father or queer."

"Jeanette was the easiest lay in Hollywood," claimed director Rouben Mamoulian.

MacDonald had gone to great trouble and expense to secure Clark as her co-star in *San Francisco*, even going without pay for several weeks while he finished another picture.

After one week of working with him, she regretted her decision: "I should have gone with either Robert Young or William Powell."

"Never in my career have I been so disappointed in a co-star as I was with Gable. He's terribly jealous of me and doesn't bother to conceal it. He seems to think that Van Dyke is favoring me in our scenes together. He is so sulky."

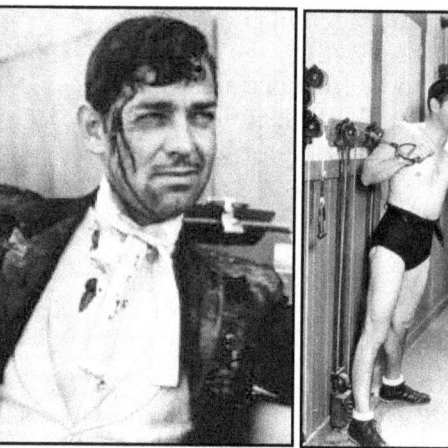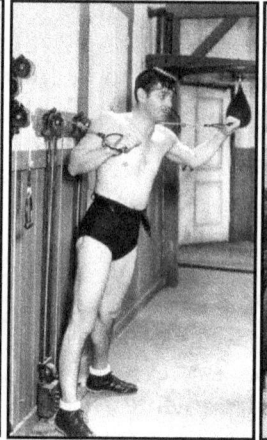

Left and right photos: **Gable**, as Blackie, the gentleman thug admired and/or hated by everyone in San Francisco, soiled and bloodied by the forces of nature.

Center photo: Gable, working out at a Hollywood gym, mid 1930s.

Years later, another (much younger) singing star at MGM, Judy Garland, was not impressed with MacDonald. "That silly horse is *yakk*ing, *yakk*ing about her wooden-peg, Nelson Eddy, with all that glycerine running down her Max Factor makeup."

MacDonald might have looked like a perpetual virgin, but she'd lived a notorious past. She'd worked as an "escort" along Hollywood Boulevard in the 1920s.

She'd also had affairs with both Henry Fonda and James Stewart, who lived together in the same house a block away from her.

Her list of other lovers was ever so varied, ranging from Louis B. Mayer to Duke Ellington. Ernst Lubitsch seduced her when he helmed her in *The Love Parade* (1929).

Clark was not impressed with MacDonald, either: "I disliked her on sight. I usually screw my leading ladies, but not this one. As for the plot, I'm no singer. I didn't want to stand around showing the back of my neck to the camera while she sang to me. She goes around with her nose so high in the air that she can't smell an oncoming pile of shit she's about to step into."

Rehearsing the Art of Love

The stance and pose **Clark Gable** adopted here with **Jeanette MacDonald** in 1936 seems like a precursor for his 1939 embrace of Vivien Leigh in *Gone With the Wind* three years later.

Perhaps it's not accurate, but Clark is sometimes given the dubious honor of having assigned, to MacDonald, the nickname "The Iron Butterfly." She often delayed production, blaming it on her menstruation. During the shoot, he was also suffering from a bad case of hemorrhoids.

MacDonald married actor Gene Raymond in 1937. The gay actor had fallen in love with Clark when they'd co-starred in *Red Dust* (1932) with Jean Harlow and Mary Astor. Raymond's mother refused to attend the wedding, claiming that her son's new wife, aged 34 at the time, was a "cradle snatcher." Raymond was 29 at the time.

Nelson Eddy's love affair with MacDonald stretched from 1935 to 1965, the year of her death.

In his heyday, Eddy was the highest-paid singer in the world, starring in nineteen movie musicals in the 1930s and '40s. His career spanned the era from 1922 to 1967, the year of his death. In 1941, Franklin D. Roosevelt invited him to sing at his third inauguration.

MacDonald reportedly spent her honeymoon night alone, fretting over the fact that it was Gene Raymond—not Nelson Eddy—whom she had married. As for her new husband, he spent his honeymoon night in bed with Buddy Rogers, the husband of Mary Pickford.

MacDonald reached the pinnacle of her career in 1939 when was named "Queen of the Movies." *[As the title's counterpart, matinée idol Tyrone Power was named "The King."]*

She invited him to spend the evening with her, but he turned her down. He was seen later getting into a car piloted by Errol Flynn. MacDonald watched as those two stars drove away into the night.

"That's Hollywood for you," she reportedly said.

***

Jack Holt as Jack Burley topped the list of *San Francisco's* supporting players. Born in the Bronx in 1888, and known for his dapper mustache, prominent jaw, and quick-with-his fists manner, he became a familiar face on the screen. He personified rugged masculinity, often appearing in open-air scenes in Westerns. He was one of the actors Margaret Mitchell recommended for the casting of Rhett Butler in *Gone With the Wind* (1939).

Jessica Ralph, cast as Mrs. Burley, was born in Massachusetts in 1864. She'd made her stage debut in stock theater in 1880. She didn't arrive in Hollywood until 1933, when she could play only matronly roles. She was Garbo's maid in *Camille* (1936), and W.C. Field's battle axe of a mother-in-law in *The Bank Dick* (1940). In *San Francisco,* she was cast as a society matron.

The actress Shirley Ross had recently appeared with Clark in *Manhattan Melodrama* (1934) in which he'd co-starred with Myrna Loy and William Powell. Most often, Ross appeared with Bob Hope and Bing Crosby.

Cast as "Babe," Harold Huber was born in 1909 to Jewish immigrants from Imperial Russia. He'd last appeared with Clark and Joan Crawford in *Forsaking All Others* (1934).

Cast as the sheriff, Edgar Kennedy was born in Monterey County, California, in 1890. During his career, he set something of a record by appearing in some 500 motion pictures (both silent and sound) from 1911 to 1948. One of the original Keystone Cops, he worked with such stars as Charlie Chaplin, Fatty Arbuckle, Laurel and Hardy, the Marx Brothers, and W.C. Fields.

On a minor note, Clark was rumored to have had a brief fling with actress Margaret Irving, cast as Delia Bailey. A daughter of Pittsburgh, born in 1898, she was a seductive blonde. She had appeared uncredited in his latest picture, *Wife vs. Secretary* (1936).

She'd been working steadily since 1922. She is best remembered as Mrs. Whitehead in *Animal Crackers* (1930) with the Marx Brothers.

She later recalled, "I once encountered Clark at a party after the war, and I came up and introduced myself to him. It was obvious he had no memory of me. I was disappointed, but he'd gone through the war and I'm sure many more important memories clogged his brain. As for me, I viewed it as a peak in my love life, having been bedded by 'The King' himself."

Margaret Irving
"I seduced Clark Gable. He didn't seduce me."

Irving lived with her memories until the age of 90, when she died in San Francisco.

Ted Healy, the vaudeville performer who created The Three Stooges, had appeared with Clark and Joan Crawford in *Dancing Lady* (1933). In *San Francisco,* he had a character role as "Matt."

On December 21, 1937, when he was 41, and about a year after the release of *San Francisco*, he went to the Trocadero Club on Sunset Strip. Later that night, he was murdered outside its back entrance, as patrons were celebrating the upcoming Christmas. Reportedly, he was also celebrating the recent birth of his son.

According to Moe Howard, one of the Stooges, "Ted was nuts about kids. He used to visit our homes and envied the fact that all of us were married and had children. He often gave Christmas parties for underprivileged youngsters and spent hundreds of dollars on toys."

Left to right: **Gable,** seated, as he appeared in *San Francisco* with the vaudevillian, **Ted Healy,** and **Jeanette MacDonald** belting out yet another rousing song

The circumstances of his death that night remain controversial even to this day. Eddie Mannix at MGM announced that he died of a heart attack.

However, he was badly beaten with a serious injury to his left eye and a deep cut on his forehead, as if he'd been struck with a blunt instrument.

After a night of heavy drinking, he'd stepped outside. According to an unverified report, he was followed by actor Wallace Beery, producer Albert Broccoli (who later produced James Bond films), and agent/producer Pat DiCicco. It is said that Healy was clubbed to death. His murder was hushed up, but the scandalous rumors associated with his death have never died.

***

Prior to *Gone With the Wind* (1939), *San Francisco* was MGM's biggest box office draw. Shot on a budget of $1.3 million, it grossed $5.5 million.

The New York Times found that "Clark Gable reflects an arrogant godlessness as the picture's Blackie Norton."

The *New York Sun* pronounced the picture "another He-Man role for Clark Gable."

The *New York Herald Tribune* claimed, "Mr. Gable as Blackie is the most successful member of the cast. Spencer Tracy is not so fortunate in his role of the Holy Father."

Newsweek cited a love triangle, cabaret dancing, opera, comedy, religion, morality, and politics as the overriding themes. "Without the rest of the picture, the earthquake sequences would be worth the admission price."

W.S. Van Dyke was Oscar nominated as Best Director, losing to Frank Capra for *Mr. Deeds Goes to Town*. Spencer Tracy was nominated for Best Actor, losing to Paul Muni for *The Story of Louis Pasteur*.

***

W.S. Van Dyke *(center figure, standing)* directs **Jeanette MacDonald** *(in the froufrou frock)* during the filming of ***San Francisco*** (1936). He was known as "One Take Woody," never wanting to do a second take even though both Gable and MacDonald wanted certain of their scenes reshot.

Episode 73

Cain and Mabel (1936)

Conceived as an acting vehicle for Marion Davies, whose career was financially supported by her very wealthy lover, press baron William Randolph Hearst, *Cain and Mabel* (1936) was a reincarnation of an earlier, silent film, *The Great White Way* (1924). Produced by Hearst's production company, Cosmopolitan, it had co-starred Anita Stewart and Oscar Shaw.

In its recycled 1936 version, Davies opens the film—as produced by Warner Brothers—as a waitress and ends up, before the final reel, as Mabel O'Dare, a Broadway star.

Production was delayed over confusion associated with who would be her leading man. Eventually, Davies demanded—and, thanks to her influence over Hearst, received—Clark Gable as her co-star.

[A few years earlier, during the making of Polly of the Circus *(1932), she and her then co-star, Clark, had enjoyed a short but torrid affair, conducted for the most part at her lavish beachfront house in Santa Monica.]*

Achieving her goal required lots of backlot intrigue, all of it "facilitated" by Hearst himself, who agreed to pay for the enlargement of one of Warner's sound stages. (*For more on that, see below*). It also involved Hearst having to persuade MGM to release Clark from his long-term contract for this production at Warners.

Based on a screenplay by Laird Doyle, producers Hal B. Wallis and Jack L. Warner hired Lloyd Bacon to helm it

Clark was cast as Larry Cain, a garage mechanic turned prize fighter. His fans were delighted to see him stripped down to black boxing trunks.

Aloysius K. Reilly (Rosco Karns, as a publicist) invents a phony romance between the boxer and the Broadway star as a means of beefing up their sagging careers. A big problem immediately looms: Each of them intensely dislikes the other.

At this point in filmmaking history, that plot device had evolved into *cliché*. Many other films had started, and would start, with the protagonists disliking each other before falling madly in love.

Although Dick Powell was the original choice for the male lead,

When **Marion Davies** starred with **Clark Gable**, her fabled film career was coming to an end. When she made this movie, she was struggling with alcoholism, and would soon leave the screen to devote her life to tending to her mentor, William Randolph Hearst, the ailing press baron who was to die in 1951.

She waited only 11 weeks before marrying sea captain Horace Brown, a union that lasted until her death a decade later.

269

Hearst learned that Davies (his *protégée* and mistress) had developed a powerful attraction for him. As such, Powell was booted from the picture.

Inspired by Busby Berkeley, the film's dance director, Bobby Connolly, staged lavish musical production numbers. One was so extravagant and oversized that it would not fit under the 45-foot high ceiling of the sound stage that had been designated to house it. Consequently, Hearst spent $100,000 to have its roof and ceiling raised to more than twice its original height.

For the wedding scene, a 90-foot organ with 165 pipes was moved into the studio, and Davies was extravagantly outfitted in the world's most expensive wedding gown. Weighing more than sixty pounds, it was said to have exhausted her during the scalding heat of a Los Angeles summer.

 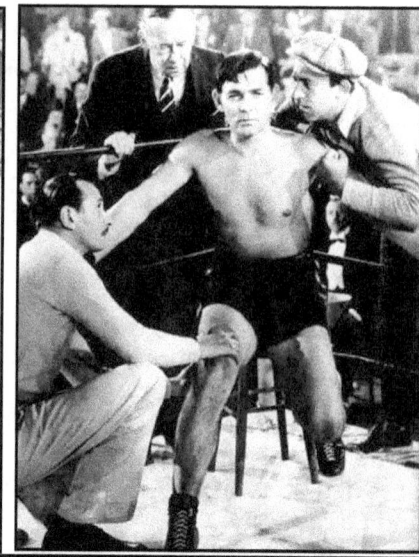

No pain, no gain, no rehearsals, no final scenes. **Here's Clark** *(left photo)* in training, off the set, and *(right photo)* filming the finished result, post-training, on celluloid.

Clark and Davies opted not to repeat the fling they'd started during their filming of *Polly of the Circus* four years before. Since then, Clark had become good friends not only with Davies, but also with Hearst himself. This time around, perhaps for reasons associated with his career, Clark dropped the idea of a secret affair, opting instead to remain good friends with each of them.

Lloyd Bacon, the film's director, had been born in San Jose, California, in 1889. He was active in the film colony from 1914 to 1955, the year of his death at the age of 65.

He'd also been an actor in vaudeville, on the Broadway stage, and in films. Throughout the picture, both Davies and Clark trusted his direction.

Bacon had made his reputation at Warners and was known for his gritty, torn-from-the-headlines dramas. His most famous work was the musical, *42nd Street,* which remains a classic even today. As an actor, he had appeared in two Chaplin movies, *The Champion* (1915) and *The Tramp* (also 1915). He also helmed Ronald Reagan in *Knute Rockne—All American* (1940).

In a supporting role, Hobart Cavanaugh, cast as Milo, the stage manager, had recently worked with Clark in *Wife vs. Secretary* (1936).

Allen Jenkins, as "Dodo," had been born on Staten Island, New York, in 1900. He'd started out as a stage actor in 1922. In Hollywood, he most often appeared as a gloom-faced wisecracker in comedies, dramas, and musicals.

He was also a member of the "Irish Mafia" in Hollywood, a drinking fraternity whose members included Spencer Tracy, James Cagney, and Pat O'Brien.

Walter Catlett, as Jake Sherman, was born in San Francisco in 1899. He started out in vaudeville but made his stage debut in 1906. He appeared in a few silents, but his career didn't really take off until

Three sequences showing **Gable** and **Davies'** shared sense of comedy and fun: The scene is a library and the goal involves remaining incognito.

the advent of talkies, where he often played excitable, meddlesome, temperamental, and officious blowhards.

Roscoe Karns, cast as Aloysius K. Reilly, was born in San Bernardino, California, in 1891. He had the fourth lead in *Cain and Mabel*. Between 1915 and 1964, he would appear in 150 motion pictures, often as cynical, wisecracking, and often tipsy, characters with rapid-fire deliveries. He appeared in the silent film classic, *Wings* (1927) with Clara Bow. He was also cast in *It Happened One Night* (1934) as the annoying bus passenger trying to pick up Claudette Colbert.

Cast as Aunt Mimi, Ruth Donnelly was born in Philadelphia in 1896. She made her first film in 1914, but it wasn't until 1931 that she found steady work in Hollywood. Often, she was just comic relief, but she managed to appear in a classic every so often, notably *Mr. Smith Goes to Washington* (1939) and *The Bells of St.Mary's* (1945) with Bing Crosby and Ingrid Bergman.

Robert Paige in the role of Ronny Cauldwell was born in Indianapolis in 1911. Between 1934 and 1963, he made 65 films. He was noted for his handsome features and his assured speaking voice. He had a brassy charm and was very versatile, at home in films as diverse as *Son of Dracula* (1943) or *Bye Bye Birdie* (1963).

William Colliber Sr., a New Yorker born in 1964, ran away from home at the age of eleven and joined a touring company run by Eddie Foy. As a teenager, he was often molested by gay actors. Eventually, he escaped to Hollywood, where producer Mack Sennett put him under contract. He also became a writer and director. In *Cain and Mabel*, he played "Pops" Walters. In all, he had roles in 89 motion pictures.

Pert Kelton as Toddy Williams was a Montana belle born in 1907. She started out in vaudeville later working on the stage in films, and on radio and television. She was the original Alice Kramden on the TV series *The Honeymooners* starring Jackie Gleason. Sadly, she was blacklisted during the communist witch hunt of the early 1950s and was fired, the role going to Audrey Meadows.

Kelton became part owner of the Warner-Kelton Hotel in Los Angeles, where she lived with her parents during the late 1920s. Its clientele consisted mainly of actors, writers, and musicians. Guests included costume designer Orry-Kelly and his young lover, Cary Grant, as well as Rodgers and Hart. In the garden was a small wishing well that inspired the standard "There's a Small Hotel."

Robert Middlemass, a son of Connecticut, born in 1883, was cast as Mr. George, the owner of a café.

Cain and Mabel tried to be all things to all audiences: A fight film, a frothy romance, and a big screen extravaganza in a style inspired by Busby Berkeley.

Here are two views of an 18th century costume ball, *left photo*, as depicted in the final cut and *right photo*, as camera techies worked to make it happen backstage.

Blood, muscle, bridal veils, and lace, all of it transpiring in the ring to a rough-tough crowd of fight enthusiasts. Perhaps the implication is that love and marriage—as embraced by *Cain and Mabel*—is just another spinoff of a fight scene.

He was both a playwright and an actor, playing minor roles in about a hundred motion pictures, often cast as a detective or policeman. In 1940, he appeared in a play, *The Man Who Wouldn't Talk*. The drama even today remains a favorite with amateur or local theater groups.

Joseph Crehan appeared as the manager of Fighter Tom Reed (cast with Allen Pomeroy). Born in Baltimore in 1883, Crehan appeared in more than 300 films between 1916 and 1965.

He is best remembered for playing General Ulysses S. Grant in nine movies between 1939 and 1958—most notably, in *They Died with Their Boots On* (1941).

***

Cain and Mabel flopped at the box office.

Time wrote, "This is the end of some very fine feelings for Miss Davies and Mr. Gable, and musical comedy, too. You see it at your own risk."

Newsweek wrote that the film set "a new low. Gable and Davies fit into this picture like a fat hand squeezed into a small glove. Too much talent for such a skimpy, thinly woven plot that unravels in a trite series of moments rather than a well-constructed tale."

Film Daily had a different view: "Like the fistic champ that Clark Gable portrays in it, this Cosmopolitan feature matched very top-flight current films. Not only does Miss Davies give a vibrant and exquisite performance—but the surrounding cast is flawless, production values lavish. The swiftly paced screenplay copiously packs romance, tuneful melody, pathos, and humor, providing audiences with 90 minutes of flittering entertainment."

After this film with Clark, Davies appeared in only one more picture, *Ever Since Eve* (1937), before retiring from the screen. She settled into retirement, dying on September 21, 1961, at the age of 64. Hearst had died in 1951.

Mabel (*aka* **Marion Davies**), checking for (and showing) telltale signs of age.

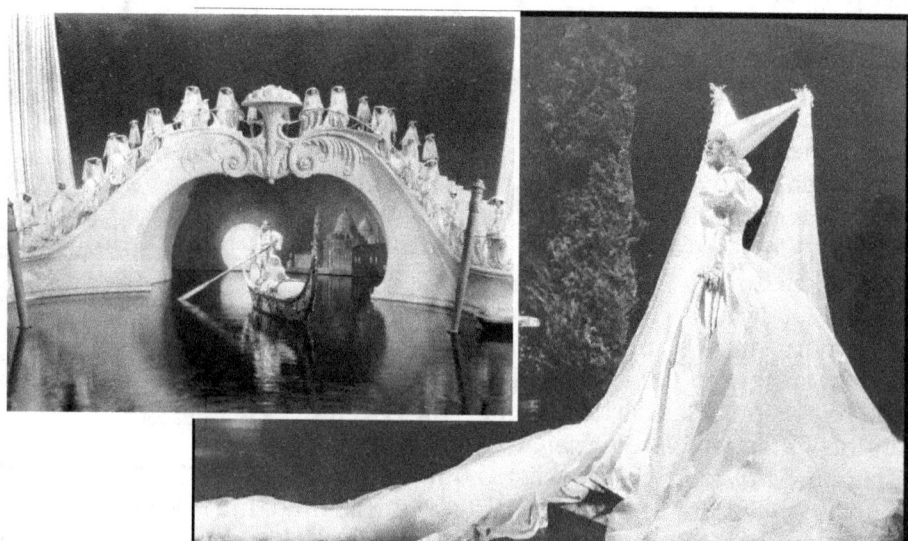

Cain and Mabel: An ambitious, oddly disjointed *potpourri* of themes and styles.
Clark's job involved keeping it macho.
RIP Marion Davies (1897-1961)

Episode 74

Marlene Dietrich & Clark Gable

How and Where She Added Him to Her Long List of Lovers

As her first American film, Marlene Dietrich made *Morocco* (1930) for Paramount. In it, she starred, opposite Gary Cooper, as Amy Jolly, a cabaret entertainer. Cooper played Legionnaire Tom Brown, the "ladykiller" of his military outpost.

She shocked audiences of her day when she came out onto a cabaret stage wearing a man's tuxedo and plants a kiss on the mouth of a woman in the audience.

Dietrich's fame would be greatly enhanced in 1931 when *Der Blaue Engel (The Blue Angel)* was released. Both it and *Morocco* were directed by her mentor, Josef von Sternberg. He's credited with "discovering" Dietrich during his search for "the eternal woman." Up to that point, she had been confined mostly to pictures in German.

Films to Review wrote: "The theme of the soldier and the lady (who eventually becomes a camp follower), following her man into battle or wherever he goes is a familiar one, but Von Sternberg did it first and best. *Morocco* is a love story written, directed, and aimed for intelligent audiences.

The humor of *Morocco* is wry, subtle, and perverse. In part because of it, Dietrich was launched into a Hollywood career that would make her, like Clark himself, one of the legends of its Golden Age.

Although frequently compared to Greta Garbo, Dietrich was very different in her style and looks. They had each been associated, in very minor roles (in Dietrich's case, uncredited), in the same German film, *The Joyless Street* (aka *Die freudlose Gasse; 1925*). During the course of its filming, they had a lesbian affair.

During the filming of *Morocco*, Cooper and Dietrich had a sexual fling. To his surprise, he found that her favorite form of sex was fellatio. "That way, I can be in control of the situation," she later claimed.

"She had sex without gender preference," claimed Kenneth Tynan.

Of all the Hollywood female stars, her list of lovers

> In September of 1936, **Marlene Dietrich** and **Clark Gable** performed together in a radio rendition of her then-celebrated hit film, *Morocco*, which in 1930, had indelibly associated her—on-screen, at least—with Gary Cooper.
>
> Before the program began, there was a last-minute shuffling of seating charts, stage angles and credits: Whereas Dietrich preferred to face her radio audience directly, Gable would have preferred himself positioned in profile. There was also a tussle about whose name would appear first in the credits. Clark won.
>
> Eventually, perhaps both of them won. Within a few hours of the program's ending, they'd morphed their onstage romance into a private party within the private villa that Dietrich had rented from the Countess di Frasso, Gary Cooper's former lover.

As an expatriate European with a wildly successful career in Hollywood, foreign audiences were endlessly fascinated by every daring, iconoclastic thing **Dietrich** ever did. Here is some German-language *(left)* and Spanish-language *(right)* publicity for her till-then most celebrated film, *Morocco*, with **Gary Cooper**, was arguably the most impressive. It might have begun with Coop, but it hardly ended there. To name-drop a bit: Joseph (senior) and John F. Kennedy, Yul Brynner, Maurice Chevalier, baseball player Joe DiMaggio, singer Eddie Fisher, Edith Piaf, novelist Erich Maria Remarque, Barbara Stanwyck, Adlai Stevenson, John Wayne, James Stewart (who made her pregnant), Orson Welles, George Raft, Edward G. Robinson, Burt Lancaster, Ronald Colman, French novelist Colette, George Bernard Shaw, John Gilbert, Kirk Douglas, and director Otto Preminger, to name only a few.

Dietrich proclaimed, "No man falls in love with me that I don't want to have fall in love with me."

It seemed inevitable that Clark Gable would be added to her list of lovers.

She and Clark were selected to star in the June 1, 1936 radio presentation of *The Legionnaire and the Lady*, a voice-only adaptation of *Morocco*.

Cooper was offered the male role, but he turned it down. However, Clark eagerly accepted because he had been enchanted with the films by Dietrich he'd seen. This would mark the only time they ever worked together. Cecil B. De Mille was the presenter of the show.

[Around the time of the broadcast, Dietrich had returned from Arizona, where she had starred in a desert drama, The Garden of Allah *(1936) with Charles Boyer.]*

In a strong, masculine voice, Clark sounded like the powerful soldier he was portraying. And whereas Dietrich did not replicate Amy Jolly's "drag king act," she maintained the controlled cadence of her silver screen character.

The radio presentation was a huge success, reaching a vast audience. Comments began pouring into the studio: One of them stated, "Loved listening to Dietrich and Gable. Her wonderful voice must have enchanted listeners sitting by the radio imagining the tale—minus Cooper, plus Gable. Her beauty isn't underrated, but I think her talent and ability often is."

Another listener wrote in, "It's unfortunate that Dietrich and Gable never teamed up on the screen, because on radio, their chemistry is superb. Clark works well with all sorts of leading ladies, and it seems Marlene drew that out as well as anyone. And both are better at their craft than people give them credit for."

Another view: "As for Clark Gable and Dietrich's chances of working together again, Gable's nearly exclusive professional relationship with MGM limited such a possibility. Dietrich worked for MGM only once, in *Kismet* (1944), which failed to garner the box office success that would have convinced MGM to sign her for another film."

No one could rise to the challenge of exaggerated hyperbole better than Marlene Dietrich. Inserted below is an enlargement of the text that appeared in this, an original print ad for Marlene Dietrich's *The Garden of Allah*.

QUESTION: What did the middle-aged Marlene Dietrich say to Darwin Porter when she first introduced herself to him—an obvious, slobberingly adoring fan—at a party in Hollywood in the 1970s?

ANSWER: "*Helloooooooo*. My name is Marlene Dietrich. I am a cabaret entertainer."

None knew the overflowing, bursting gladness, the singing joy these two, who had never loved before, found deep in the heart of the desert. The lavish brush of Technicolor reveals the golden beauty of Marlene Dietrich, the burning emotions of Charles Boyer with an intensity never before seen on the screen.

Another review *[this one posted by "Chas" in 2001]* asserted: "This show has atmosphere. It will take you right back to the days when you regularly visited your favorite movie theater and became so involved with the story which was unfolding on the silver screen. It makes you realize that changes have taken place throughout the world in the last fifty or sixty years with regards to heroes and their ladies. Incidentally, make sure you settle down to listen with a coke or something cool. It's thirsty work in the desert."

Although he had rejected any involvement in the radio spot, Gary Cooper was in the studio audience that night. Backstage, he greeted Clark and Dietrich. The trio were seen leaving the studio in separate cars but heading for her rented residence. Rumors spread that they would collectively orchestrate a short-term *ménage à trois* that weekend.

Actually, Coop stayed for only an hour, leaving early for a torrid weekend with Lupe Velez, "The Mexican Spitfire." Clark, however, remained until Monday morning.

[Cooper was familiar with the mansion which Marlene had rented. It was owned by the Countess Dorothy di Frasso, with whom he'd sustained an extended affair. Within this same house, Di Frasso had also sustained an affair with the notorious gangster, Bugsy Siegel.

During his weekend there with Dietrich, Clark became intimately familiar with its master bedroom.

The countess died aboard the Union Pacific Rail Line en route to Los Angeles on January 4, 1954. Her gay friend, actor Clifton Webb, discovered her body. It was clad in an evening gown, a mink coat, and $250,000 worth of jewelry.

Fellow socialite and hostess, Elsa Maxwell, remembered di Frasso to her readers: "She was a fabulous countess, a great broncobuster of the banal, pathos, and hypocrisy—that makes up for what we call modern society today."]

Dietrich and Clark never worked together again. Director George Marshall thought Clark would be ideal in a co-starring role in a Western film entitled *Destry Rides Again* (1939). Whereas it was already clear that Dietrich would tackle the role of Frenchy, a saloon singer, Marshall and the film's producer, Joe Pasternak, were hot in pursuit of a suitable actor for the film's male lead, Tom Destry, Jr., the new deputy in a Western outpost.

When Clark was reached through his agent about "claiming" the role, it was too late. He had already signed as the male lead of an upcoming blockbuster, *Gone With the Wind* (1939).

James Stewart became Dietrich's co-star in *Destry*. During the course of filming, he impregnated her, leading to an abortion.

Countess Dorothy di Frasso (1888-1954; *née* Dorothy Cadwell Taylor), former patron, lover, and muse to Gary Cooper.

The American-born and occasionally Fascist heiress is seen here in 1952 at El Morocco in NYC with an unknown companion, long after her affair with Cooper had ungracefully ended. Others of her lovers had included Rudolph Valentino and Bugsy Siegel.

In 1938, **Marlene Dietrich,** along with Katharine Hepburn and Joan Crawford, was labeled "Box Office Poison."

Joe Pasternak to the rescue. He met with her on the French Riviera and proposed a radical idea: He wanted her to star in a remake of a Tom Mix Western released seven years previously, ***Destry Rides Again***, opposite James Stewart.

It took a lot of convincing, but she finally agreed to play a saloon entertainer named "Frenchy" at the Last Chance Saloon in the town of Bottleneck, where Stewart is the sheriff.

Ironically, the plot of the 1939 remake had almost nothing to do with the novel on which the 1932 version had been based. But her fading career was rescued.

In honor of one of the
Greatest International Movie Stars of all Time,
and in memory of a style that inspired artists, lovers,
anti-Fascists, and movie fans from around the world:

MARLENE DIETRICH

(1901-1992)   REST IN PEACE, MARLENE

"Though we all might enjoy seeing Helen of Troy as a gay cabaret entertainer, I doubt that she could be one quarter as good as our legendary, lovely Marlene."

So said **Noël Coward** as he introduced her at the Café de Paris in London in the summer of 1954.

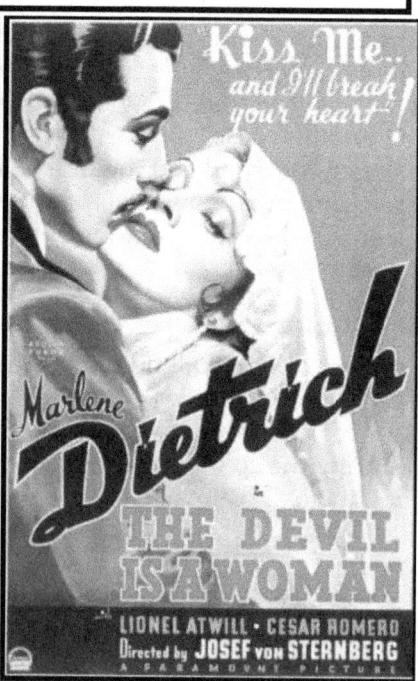

Episode 75

Love on the Run (1936)

The press was predicting fireworks when producer Joseph L. Mankiewicz and director W.S. Van Dyke cast Joan Crawford (still getting top billing), Clark Gable, and Franchot Tone as the leads in *Love on the Run*.

It was well known in Hollywood circles that Crawford and Clark had been engaged in a clandestine affair that had stretched over a period of years. But since 1935, she'd been married to Tone.

"The question was, would Franchot and Clark go at each other's throats?" Ben Maddox asked, in private. "If they do, my money's on Clark making mincemeat out of Tone."

To the surprise of the other members of cast and crew, Tone, Crawford, and Clark hung out like a friendly trio when not needed on camera. They lunched together, and chatted between takes. The threesome also spent a lot of time together in Crawford's dressing room with the door locked.

When they got a four-day break in the shooting schedule, the trio went on a sailing cruise to Catalina Island.

All this bonding gave rise to a rumor that spread along the Hollywood grapevine: All three of them were said to be engaged in sexual bonding, since each of them had a bisexual background.

The screenplay for this daffy chase comedy was by John Mahlin, a writer otherwise known for his racy dramas. It was based on a story that had first run in *Cosmopolitan* magazine. Mahlin had recently written the script for *Wife vs. Secretary* (1936) in which Clark had co-starred with Jean Harlow and Myrna Loy.

Clark, in the role of Mike Anthony, and Tone as Barney Pells, are rival newspaper reporters, but friendly enough. The movie opens as they are waking up in bed together.

Both have been assigned to cover the upcoming marriage of Sally Parker (Crawford) to Prince Igor (Ivan Lebedeff), who is a fortune hunter. At the wedding ceremony, and at the last minute, she realizes she doesn't love him and flees from the church.

The fun in this wacky comedy has just begun as she hooks up with Mike, unaware that he is a reporter. The plot will take the viewer on a roller coaster ride that's "accessorized" with a stolen airplane, a spy ring, and a break-in of the Château de Fontainebleau outside Paris for a night's frolic.

The Crawford and Gable characters eventually fall in love, of course…It's a movie, after all.

Nearly all critics interpreted *Love on the Run*—a story about a runaway heiress and a newspaper reporter—as a "rip-off of the Oscar-winning *It Happened One Night* (1934), which had starred Clark with Claudette Colbert.

Almost everyone's favorite scene was set in Fontainebleau, where the caretaker, as portrayed by Donald Meek, views them (Gable and Crawford) as the reincarnations of Louis XIV and Madame de Maintenon.

The Scottish actor in the caretaker role had first worked with Clark as an uncredited extra in *China Seas* (1935). Clark had first met him in 1929 when he appeared on Broadway opposite Bette Davis in

In its way, the casting of **Love on the Run** represented some of the most sophisticated (or indulgent) sexual couplings of an onscreen trio in the history of Hollywood. In reference to who was (or wasn't) sleeping with whom, no one outside the triangular pairing of the co-stars was entirely sure.

Middle photo: **Clark Gable** with his on-again, off-again *inamorata*, **Joan Crawford.**

Lower photo: **Clark Gable** dressed in formal splendor with *(right)* **Franchot Tone**—at the time, Joan Crawford's amicably estranged husband.

Broken Dishes.

An airplane was essential to the film's convoluted plot. In part because aviatrix Amelia Earhart was one of the then-most-famous women in the world, Mankiewicz hired aerial coordinator Paul Mantz to replicate her airplane for the film's ground sequences. Mock-ups of studio cockpits were added to other scenes. Eerily, moviegoers later recognized the prop as identical to the plane she flew a year later (in 1937) when she disappeared during the course of her final expedition. Earhart's death still remains one of the great unsolved mysteries of the years leading up to World War II.

In the fourth-billed role of Baron Otto Spandermann, Reginald Owen had last co-starred with Clark in *Call of the Wild* (1935).

Cast as the greedy and ambitious Prince Igor, Ivan Lebedeff had been born in 1894 in the Russian Empire in what is now Lithuania. His on-screen wife, Baroness Hilda, was portrayed by Mona Barrie, a Londoner born in 1905. After emigrating to the United States, she played secondary roles for the most part in more than fifty movies. During the filming of *Love on the Run,* she made several passes at Clark, but they were not intercepted,

William Demarest, who had recently appeared with Clark in *Wife vs. Secretary*, was assigned the role of the crusty newspaper editor, Lees Berger. He was such a familiar figure on the Paramount lot that in the 1950 movie, *Sunset Blvd.,* his name is mentioned as the potential star of the unsold baseball screenplay that the fast-failing Joe Gillis (William Holden) is peddling.

Love on the Run marked the seventh of eight motion pictures in which Crawford and Clark would be paired. Made for a budget of $580,000, it earned almost $2 million at the box office.

The New York Times suggested that *Love on the Run* is "a slightly daffy cinematic item of absolutely no importance, with Crawford, Gable, and Tone in roles that are a bit stale. The film ought to bow, in turn, to several distinguished antecedents, for it has borrowed liberally here and there from tried-and-true screen devices and situations."

Howard Barnes in *The New York Herald Tribune* found "it is a lot of gay nonsense strung together to make a delightful addition to the season. It's continuously amusing and frequently hilarious."

Variety found it "crowded with ludicrous situations and suffering from a meandering story development, some slipshod dialogue, and several vapid moments."

The New Yorker claimed, "Everybody works very hard, especially Crawford and Gable, reteamed once again."

Also in *The New Yorker,* John Mosher wrote, "The film only succeeds in seeming pretty pitiful."

***

Crawford hated to admit it, but by now, Clark's star at MGM had risen higher than hers, even though she got top billing over both her lover and her husband, and even though *Photoplay* had recently hailed her as "The Queen of the Movies."

***

Tone's final film with his wife was when he played her leading man in *The Bride Wore Red* (1937) with Robert Young in the third spot. In it, Crawford played a beautiful, talented, embittered cabaret performer in Trieste.

Producer Joseph L. Mankiewicz hired the lesbian director Dorothy Arzner—one of the rare female directors in Hollywood—to helm it.

During the course of its filming, Crawford and her director had an affair.

According to Tone, "Joan didn't have to lie on the casting couch anymore. This time, she went willingly."

Here's **Dorothy Arzner,** widely acknowledged as the most influential female director of her era,

About a year after *Love on the Run* was finished, Arzner directed a film that for the last time paired **Crawford** with her "anything but true-blue" husband, **Franchot Tone**. That didn't mean that Crawford and Tone had redefined their swinging marriage. During its filming, Crawford sustained an affair with Arzner, too.

Arzner is interpreted today as a perfectionist with a gift for slanting films to the "women's angle." According to Arzner, "My philosophy is that to be a director you cannot be subject to anyone, even the head of the studio. I threatened to quit each time I didn't get my way, but no one ever let me walk out."

Episode 76

Parnell (1937)

Clark's latest motion picture, *Parnell*, was based on the life of Charles Stewart Parnell (1846-1891), a land reform agitator and a member (1875-1891) of the British Parliament. Hailed by thousands of (usually Irish) fans as the uncrowned "King of Ireland," he's remembered today as one of the most effective Parliamentarians and political organizers of his age. Dead of pneumonia at the age of 45, four years after a stint in jail for his political activism, his funeral was attended by 200,000 mourners, and the day of his death is still commemorated as Ivy Day.

Parnell is celebrated today as one of the most formidable, admired, and loathed figures in Parliamentary history. Both Parnell Street and Parnell Square in Dublin are named after him

Yet despite the fame and nostalgia associated with his name, Clark Gable's film adaptation of his life, *Parnell* (1937), is listed in the book of *The Fifty Worst Films of All Time*. It has also been blasted as the most horrendous film that Clark and Myrna Loy ever made together. Upon its release, thousands of letters poured into MGM with complaints.

In response, Loy protested, "We're actors, for God's sake. What are we to do? Play Blackie Norton and Nora Charles for the rest of our lives?"

Clark had wanted Joan Crawford as his leading lady, but she had rejected the script. MGM had recently released *The Gorgeous Hussy* (1936), in which she had co-starred with Robert Taylor, Franchot Tone, and (in a portrayal of Andrew Jackson), Lionel Barrymore. Crawford played an innkeeper's daughter of the 1830s in a role noted for its frumpy costumes. It had flopped and she got bad reviews. In its aftermath, she vowed never to make another costume drama. "I'm too modern for that type of thing."

Originally, Loy had been cast as the female lead in *The Last of Mrs. Cheyney*, an MGM drama/romance about a jewelry heist set for a 1937 release with co-stars William Powell and Robert Montgomery. But Crawford made a deal with MGM to do a switch, "annexing" for

Perhaps it was its frumpish prudery that doomed **Parnell** to failure. Or perhaps by now, **Myrna Loy** and **Clark Gable** were too hip and liberated to convincingly play lovers trapped in the belief patterns of the *haute* Victorian age.

Regardless, despite the public's overwhelming yawn, as a scrren team, they'd already been defined as the Queen and King of the Movies, as the print ad (lower photo) screamed prior to the release of the film.

The cheesy-looking object in the center of the *lower photo* replicates the "crown" that each of them would wear at an upcoming press event.

herself Loy's role in *Mrs. Cheyney* and persuading MGM to assign Loy to another picture with Clark. That "other picture with Clark" eventually morphed into *Parnell*.

Like Crawford, Clark was not thrilled at appearing in another costume drama. Charles Parnell, the Parliamentarian, was known for his beard, but Clark refused to either grow one or be outfitted with one. Instead, attired in dour Victorian frock coats, he settled for "mutton-chopped sideburns."

As his co-star (again), Loy was uncomfortably costumed with "bonnets, bows, bustles, and floor-length taffeta gowns."

Around this time, Clark and Loy were voted "King and Queen of the Movies."

Although the film addresses the sexual scandal that destroyed Charles Stewart Parnell's career, its treatment of his indiscretions was oblique, sanitized, and consistent with the dictates of the Hays' Commission's dreaded Production Code.

Parnell (Clark) falls in love with Katie O'Shea (Loy). At what he hopes will be his moment of political glory, advocating Irish Home Rule, a scandal breaks. Katie's husband, Captain William O'Shea (Alan Marshal) cites him in a divorce court, publicly exposing him as a fornicator and the lover of his wife.

Parnell's career is ruined. Suffering from a heart attack and a sense of frustration and shame, he dies in the arms of his Katie, declaring his love for her.

Loy later recalled, "During our time together, I learned about another side of Gable. He was a man who loved poetry and fine literature, He read it and knew it. He would read poetry to me during our breaks, but he didn't want anyone to know it."

Parnell was based on a play by Elsie T. Schauffer, a Kansas City-based writer who died before she could see its movie adaptation. It was produced by John M. Stahl, who had been born to a Jewish family in Baku, Azerbaijan. He'd directed his first silent film in 1913 and was part of the Louis B. Mayer team which had founded Metro-Goldwyn-Mayer.

Left: **Charles Stewart Parnell,** Irish parliamentarian and advocate of home rule who was "brought down" by a marital scandal that could only have survived during the Victorian age.

Right: **Clark Gable,** slogging through an uninspired replication of Parnell's complicated struggles as a Parliamentarian walking a fine line between patriotism and treason.

Parnell included great (albeit frumpy) costumes and supremely talented secondary players. What it lacked was a "connection" between its megastars (Gable and Loy) and the murky diplomatic maneuverings of a murky historical era.

Above, left, **Clark** begins what might have morphed into an engaging subplot (but didn't).

Right, he woos "darlin' Katie," (an inconveniently married and WAY overdressed and overstarched **Myrna Loy**)

One of Stahl's biggest hits had involved directing Claudette Colbert in *Imitation of Life* (1934).

MGM hired two top writers (John Van Druten and S.N. Behrman) to adapt Schauffer's play to the screen. Van Druten, born in London in 1901, was one of England's most successful playwrights. Hollywood adapted several of his plays into movies, notably *Old Acquaintance* (1943), with Bette Davis and *The Voice of the Turtle* (1947) with Ronald Reagan.

***

Parnell had a strong supporting cast, with Edna May Oliver as Aunt Ben Wood taking the third lead. Born in Massachusetts in 1883, she became famous in films of the 1930s, often cast as tart-tongued spinsters. She had worked on Broadway before moving to Hollywood. There she starred in such films as *Little Women* (1933). David O. Selznick cast her in film adaptations of two novels by Charles Dickens—*A Tale of Two Cities* (1935), with Ronald Colman, and *David Copperfield* (also 1935). Oliver also co-starred with Norma Shearer, Leslie Howard, and John Barrymore in *Romeo and Juliet* (1936), and she later won an Oscar for Best Supporting Actress in *Drums Along the Mohawk* (1939).

Edmund Gwenn took the fourth lead as Campbell. Born in London in 1877, he is remembered today for his role as Kris Kringle in the Christmas classic, *Miracle on 34th Street* (1947), for which he won a Best Supporting Actor Oscar. Gwenn launched his stage career in 1895 and was still working in 1959, the year of his death. In all, he would appear in more than eighty movies, including four directed by Alfred Hitchcock.

In *Parnell,* as the cuckholded husband, Captain William O'Shea, Alan Marshal took fifth billing. Born in 1909 in New South Wales, Australia, he came from a theatrical family. His parents left their native land, emigrating to other parts of the world, when he was five years old. At the age of 15, Marshal made his Broadway debut.

As so many stage actors do, he

The Triumph of Frump: Two character-actress superstars, **Edna May Oliver** *(left)* with **Billie Burke**, showcase what months of historical research and hours of padding, primping, and cosseting can produce.

Here, as congenial, gossip-soaked Victorian monsters with Irish accents, they have a LOT to say about the scandals associated with Katie O'Shea.

Alan Marshal *(left)* as the cuckolded husband, Captain William O'Shea, and *(right)* **Myrna Loy** and **Clark Gable** as the radical transgressors.

ended up in Hollywood, where he made a notable appearance in *Garden of Allah* (1936), starring Marlene Dietrich and Charles Boyer. He also appeared with William Powell and Myrna Loy in *After the Thin Man* (1934). Marshal also starred with Greta Garbo in *Conquest* (1937).

Luise Rainer had won two back-to-back Best Actress Oscars, but when Marshal co-starred with her in *Dramatic School* (1938), it was a big flop.

Marshal would continue to work with such stars as Cary Grant, Ginger Rogers, Anna Neagle, Merle Oberon, Basil Rathbone, Ida Lupino, and Loretta Young. One of his biggest hits was *White Cliffs of Dover* (1944) with Irene Dunne. After a nervous breakdown and a departure from acting for several years, Marshal re-emerged as a television actor during the 1950s.

Billie Burke, cast as Clara Wood, had previously appeared with Clark in *Forsaking All Others* (1934) and *After Office Hours* (1935). Donald Crisp as Davitt had been cast as a member of the mutinous crew in *Mutiny on the Bounty* (1935).

Donald Meek, as Murphy, had worked with Clark during the filming of *Love on the Run* (1936).

Montagu Love, cast as the British Liberal Parliamentarian, William Gladstone, was born in England in 1877. He'd gotten his start in vaudeville, later morphing into a stage actor on Broadway. When Hollywood beckoned, he found himself cast with Valentino in *The Son of the Sheik* (1926). Love also starred with John Barrymore in *Don Juan* (1926) and with Lillian Gish in *The Wind* (1928).

His career survived the entertainment industry's transition into talkies, as he played Henry VIII's son *[Edward VI, who died at the age of 16 in 1553]* in the first talking version of *The Prince and the Pauper* (1937), starring Errol Flynn.

Barton Churchill, as O'Gorman Mahon, had last appeared with Clark in *Love on the Run* (1936).

In the uncredited role of Pat, Lee Strasberg would later become famous as the director of the Actors Studio in Manhattan.

***

Parnell flopped at the box office, often receiving scathing reviews. MGM suffered a loss of $640,000.

After *Parnell*, Clark vowed never to appear again in a costume drama. Vows, however, are sometimes not meant to be kept. Waiting around the bend was *Gone With the Wind*.

John Mosher, in *The New Yorker*, wrote, "I must say that the two leading players, Clark Gable and Myrna Loy—expert though they may be in their way—give not the slightest indication of trying to understand anything."

F. S. Nugent of *The New York Times* wrote: "For all the dignity of its production, the imposing cast at its command, *Parnell* struck me as being singularly pallid, tedious, and an unconvincing drama. The sets are rich and solid, the costuming is splendid. But it lacks vitality, completely missing the emotional surge that swept the play out across the footlights into the hearts of its audience when it was put on last season."

Bob Wagner in *Script* claimed, "*Parnell*? No! Clark Gable appears in his worst miscasting. Nor is Myrna Loy any help to him, for she is equally stodgy and unbending Too bad, because the story is good, the direction fine, and the production all we have learned to expect from MGM. It is the secondary characters who give the picture what little life it has. The whole show is splendid, except for the unfortunate casting of the principals."

Parnell hardly diminished the careers of either Loy or Gable. The next two pictures in which they co-starred, *Test Pilot* and *Too Hot to Handle* (both released in 1938), each made money.

It was during this period that Loy became one of the busiest and highest-paid actresses in Hollywood. Both in 1937 and 1938, she was listed in the annual Quigley Poll of the "Top Ten Money-Making Stars."

While working for MGM, Loy told the press, "Why does every black person have to play a servant? How about a black person walking up the steps to a courthouse carrying a briefcase?"

A movement to memorialize **Charles Parnell** was organized by his political successor John Redmond in 1898. It was funded largely by Irish and American subscribers.

Sculpted by **Augustus Saint-Gaudens**, and set at the north end of O'Connell Street in Dublin, it bears an inscription lifted from one of Parnell's fiery advocacies for Irish self-rule: *"No man has a right to fix the boundary to the march of a nation. No man has a right to say to his country thus far shalt thou go and no further. We have never attempted to fix the ...progress of Ireland's nationhood and we never shall."*

Cited as one of the most brilliant Parliamentarians in Anglo-Irish history, Parnell's rise to prominence ended abruptly after revelations about his links to Katharine O'Shea, a married woman.

Saint-Gaudens, at his studio in New Hampshire, USA, began work on it in 1903, hoping "that it will endure for generations, when idiosyncrasies will have been forgotten and the monument will count as a whole regardless of any personal peculiarities," the sculptor assured.

Unveiled in 1911, it was cast in bronze six weeks before Saint-Gaudens' death.

Episode 77

The Origin of Clark Gable's Passionate Romance with

CAROLE LOMBARD

"When Clark Gable and I hooked up, both of us were getting used goods," claimed **Carole Lombard**. "Okay, so he wasn't the great lover his devoted fans dreamed about. But'he had a glorious time trying."

Quite by chance, Clark Gable encountered Eadie Adams one afternoon in January of 1936 as he strolled across the studio lot at MGM.

As she came toward him, his roving eye focused on her blonde hair and shapely figure. She came up to him and asked him for his autograph, claiming, "I'm your biggest fan."

He invited her for a hamburger and a coke in the commissary, where he learned that she was a singer and actress who had signed a two-year contract with the studio.

Born in Chicago in 1907, she later became a singer with Kay Kyser's Orchestra. While performing one night, she caught the attention of an MGM talent scout.

Their meeting led to Hollywood and a contract that got her cast in a number of motion pictures between 1935 and 1937. They included an appearance in *After the Thin Man*, starring William Powell and Myrna Loy. The chief reason MGM needed her was to dub the on-screen voices of actresses such as Jean Harlow, who could not sing.

After Clark finished work for the day, he invited Adams to go out with him that night. He drove her home, where he waited in his car for her to change her dress into a gown. Then he drove her over to his hotel suite, where he got dressed.

After a night at the Trocadero, he took her back to his suite, where she accepted his invitation to spend the night.

[Incidentally, some writers have confused Eadie Adams with the similarly named Edie Adams, whose first name is spelled differently. Edie Adams, born in Pennsylvania in 1927, would by 1950 be voted "Miss U.S. Television" in a beauty contest. Edie Adams became famous on TV during her appearances with Ernie Kovacs, whom she later married.]

With Eadie Adams on his arm, Clark arrived on the night of January 21, 1936 at Victor Hugos in Beverly Hills. Hosted by Carole Lombard, the Mayfair Club was staging a lavish gala there. Accompanying Clark and his date were press baron William Randolph Hearst and his mistress, Marion Davies, with whom Clark had had an affair.

He was unpleasantly surprised at the sight of his estranged wife, Ria Langham, sitting at a table with her society friends. At another table, Loretta Young was the center of a party. She had given birth to his daughter, whom Young was pretending was a bio-

Eadie Adams (not to be confused with Edie Adams), the cabaret & nightclub singer Clark was dating the night he deepened his friendship with Lombard.

logically unrelated infant whom she had adopted.

Clark deliberately avoided both the Langham and the Young tables.

Everything, including all the decorations, was white. Lombard had requested that men show up in white tuxedos and that women wear flowing white gowns. She was furious when Norma Shearer defied her and showed up in a stunningly low-cut (scarlet) gown.

As the orchestra struck up dance music, Clark fulfilled his obligation by asking Eadie to dance, followed by escorting Davies onto the dance floor. Then he excused himself and walked over to the hostess table and invited Lombard onto the floor. He had not seen her since they had made love on camera in *No Man of Her Own* (1932).

On the floor, he warned her, "I'm not much of a dancer."

"You'll have no argument from me about that," Lombard shot back.

After the dance, she invited him to a pre-dawn rendezvous at her residence, giving him her address. He later dropped off Eadie for the night and hurried over to Lombard's home.

There, he was disappointed when he found her getting ready for one of those "parties that last till dawn breaks over California."

She had invited about 35 guests from the Mayfair Club, and they began to arrive. Perhaps as a deliberate act of provocation, Lombard had made Loretta Young the guest of honor.

Not wanting to call attention to their former affair, Young and Clark stayed on opposite sides of Lombard's large living room.

Clark had an early call at the studio, so he left the party a few hours before dawn. Two days later, he placed a call asking Lombard for a date.

"Sorry, I'm too busy," she said. "Can't talk now." Then she put down the receiver.

They would not see each other again until February, when they were each invited to the "Nervous Breakdown Ball" at the mansion of John Hay Whitney, nicknamed "Jock."

The party began at noon, but the host asked all the guests to arrive in formal wear. As the party got underway, the guests heard an emergency siren from an ambulance arriving, with its dome light flashing, at the front door. A body covered with a sheet was wheeled into the main hallway as the curious crowd gathered around it. Then Whitney ripped off the sheet to reveal Lombard jumping up, fully gowned. "Surprise!" she shouted at the guests.

Clark later told his host, "I thought that Lombard gal was the one for me. But I don't think we'll be compatible. I hate such childish stunts."

Nevertheless, she later sought him out for a chat, suggesting they should team up for another picture together. He soon learned that she was known for her sharp wit and acid tongue. As her friends, such as William Haines, knew, "Every other sentence contained the words 'shit' or 'fuck.'"

But as the days went forth, it was Carole who began to show a romantic interest in Clark. "For fun, I like to be a fag hag, but for sex, I turn to he-men like Gable."

"He needs work," she confided to Myrna Loy, "and I think I'm the gal to do it."

To show her interest in him, she decided to send him a gift for Valentine's Day. For $15, she bought a broken-down Model T Ford and had it painted all white before hiring an artist to paint hearts all over the vehicle.

On the morning of February 14, he found the Model T parked next to his Duesenberg. Her Valentine's note was "vintage Lombard."

"Wanna fuck, Buster?" it read. "Give me a call."

He found her message both amusing and provocative. It was an invitation he could not ignore. He phoned her later that afternoon and asked her out for dining and dancing at the Trocadero,

To pick her up, he showed up in that Model T for transit to the Trocadero, where stars and moguls arrived in the most expensive vehicles in America, many of them custom-made.

The posh and impossibly well-connected **John Hay (Jock) Whitney** as he appeared, limbering up for a polo match, on the cover of the March 27, 1933 cover of *Time*.

She spent the night with him, and it was the beginning of his greatest love affair. As she later confessed to William Powell, her former husband, "I'd had better fucks than Clark, but I think I'm falling in love with the big lug."

She continued to surprise him. He showed up at her studio to take her out that night and arrived at the door to her dressing room. She invited him in and told him he could come into her bathroom.

There, he found to his surprise that she was completely nude, applying a solution of peroxide to her pubic hair. "Relax, Clark," she said. "I'm just making my collar and cuffs match."

At the time she began her affair with Clark, she was still involved sexually with Robert Riskin, a screenwriter eleven years her senior. "Bob was an intellectual who taught me to read books. Have you ever heard of this Southern boy, William Faulkner?"

Clark began to spend nights at her home, moving some of his stuff over from his hotel suite.

Their busy schedules often kept them apart. He was filming *San Francisco* (1936) with Jeanette MacDonald, and she was shooting *My Man Godfrey* (also 1936) with her former husband, William Powell.

One night, Louella Parsons, the era's leading gossip columnist, approached Lombard at a party and asked her if she were serious about Clark. Her (unprintable) answer shocked Parsons: "He's okay, I guess, except he's not circumsized. I guess that's okay with me. Perhaps I'll urge him to get it clipped."

Carole Lombard *(left)* was said to have had a knack for marrying famous men. Here she is with her first husband, actor **William Powell**. She co-starred with him in the screwball comedy, *My Man Godfrey* (1936).

Clark was also asked how he felt about Lombard: "I dig the way she wiggles her ass in a white satin gown. She doesn't have much in the tit department, so she never wears a bra. She also doesn't wear panties, which makes it easier for me when I reach up her dress."

Even though he was falling in love with Lombard, he had not lost his interest in other women. Nor would he give up other conquests, even though he admitted, "Carole is the love of my life." In the meantime, when she was busy, he was also engaged in a torrid affair with Merle Oberon.

Noel Busch, in *Life* magazine, wrote a description of Lombard at the beginning of her torrid romance with Clark.

She gets up too early, plays tennis too hard, wastes time and feelings on trifles, and drinks Coca-Cola the way Samuel Johnson used to drink tea. She is a scribbler on telephone pads, inhibited and a nail-nibbler, toe-puller, pillow-grabber, head-and-elbow scratcher, and chain cigarette smoker.

When she talks, her conversation, often brilliant, is punctuated by screeches, laughs, growls, gesticulations, and the expletives of a sailor's parrot."

As author Lyn Tornabene put it, "Clark must have felt he had a bobcat by the tail, or that a bobcat had him by the tail. All evidence indicates that he started out as the pursuer but ended up as the pursued."

By April, when Hollywood was in full bloom, so was the romance between Lombard and Clark. He had not divorced Ria Langham because her financial demands were too excessive for his limited bank account.

Lombard began to adjust her schedule to his priorities. She'd never gone hunting before, but she set out on her first hunting trip with him, sleeping with him in a tent at night.

Although she didn't say anything, she was privately horrified at his shooting down of birds.

Before that, she thought one of the miracles of life involved seeing birds in flight. "It was an amazing feat of nature that brought joy to me. I didn't want to see these lovely creatures shot down in their glorious flight."

During one of their first dates, they were seen dancing cheek to cheek to the music of Cab Calloway. At one point, she grabbed his genitals. "You bastard, you've got a hard-on."

"Guess who gave it to me?" he shot back.

The table next to them was amused.

On another night, she tried to teach him the rhumba to a tune orchestrated by composer Irving Berlin. He'd written a new song for the upcoming musical, *Follow the Fleet* (1936), co-starring Fred Astaire and Ginger Rogers.

One night at a party in Beverly Hills hosted by Jack L. Warner, Lombard became furious when she saw "pretty boy" Robert Taylor monopolizing Clark.

"He was hovering over him, even getting his drinks. He seemed very possessive. I decided to break it up."

"Later, I told Clark, "Can't you see what's happening? The swish is in love with you."

On the following night at the Trocadero, the orchestra began to play the song, "You Were Meant for Me."

Clark an Lombard were on the floor dancing cheek to cheek. "From now on, that is going to be our theme song," they mutually agreed.

Sexy, foul-mouthed, enigmatic, controversial, and funny, **Carole Lombard** would morph into Clark Gable's "true love." Much more about her will be relayed in Volumes Two and Three of this three-volume overview of the life of Clark Gable.

Episode 78

Saratoga (1937)

Saratoga, a romantic comedy, starred Clark Gable and Jean Harlow in her last motion picture. She died before filming was completed, and it was finished using a stand-in with dyed blonde hair. Amazingly, it became MGM's highest-grossing film of the year and the most financially successful movie Harlow ever made.

A patch-up job was done on the film's final scene. In it, as a means of concluding the plot, a Harlow clone moved quickly through a long-distance clip that skillfully managed to conceal the stand-in's face.

This racetrack drama was directed by Jack Conway and produced by Bernard Hyman.

Clark and Conway were old buddies, ever since he'd directed him in *The Easiest Way* (1931), starring Constance Bennett. The men would get to know each other a lot better in years to come, since Conway would also be assigned to helm him in some of his alltime best films: *Too Hot to Handle* (1938) with Myrna Loy; *Boom Town* (1940) with Claudette Colbert, Hedy Lamarr, and Spencer Tracy; and *Honky Tonk* (1941) with Lana Turner.

MGM may have lost one of its biggest money-makers with the death of Harlow, but another box office champ was on the way: Walter Pidgeon, born in 1897 in New Brunswick, Canada, would become a leading man in the Golden Age of Hollywood, at his best when teamed with Greer Garson.

He became known for his portrayals of men who prove to be both sturdy and wise. Twice, he would be nominated for Best Actor Oscar for performances in *Mrs Miniver* (1942) and *Madame Curie* (1943).

Pigeon's career would span eras that stretched from 1925 to 1977. At the age of 87, he would die in 1984.

Clark had the lead as a bookie, Duke Bradley, with Harlow cast as Carol Clayton.

In the third lead was Lionel Barrymore as Grandpa Clayton. Frank Morgan was Jesse Kiffmeyer, with Walter Pidgeon as Hartley Madison.

In minor roles were Una Merkel as Fritzi; Cliff Edwards as Tip, George Zucco as Dr. Harmsworth Bierd. Jonathan Hale played Frank Clayton.

On the set, Clark renewed his friendship with Hattie McDaniel. In their near future, both of them would immortalize themselves in *Gone With the Wind* (1939). In an uncredited role in *Saratoga* as "Maizie," Margaret Hamilton was also headed for glory as the Wicked Witch of the West in *The Wiz-*

Jean Harlow never completed the film *Saratoga* with co-star Clark Gable. On the screens of the 1930s, she evoked youth and life. her death set off a whirlpool of fake rumors unmatched in Hollywood history. One had her begging for medical help while her Christian Scientist mother refused, praying for her instead. Another claimed she had a botched abortion, having been impregnated by Gable. Brain poisoning from hair dye was another charge, as was that she came down with syphilis by fellating a man with veneral disease. Others claimed "she drank herself to death."

Kidney disease, the cause of her death, was not well understood in 1937.

ard of Oz (1939).

During his reunion with McDaniel, Clark hugged the fat black woman and gave her a light kiss on the lips. She later told director Conway, "I'd hook up with that white dude any time of the day or night. I would even marry him if he was the right color."

Born in New York in 1890, Frank Morgan is still known today for his performance as *The Wizard of Oz*, the object of the quest "at the end of the rainbow" for Dorothy (Judy Garland). He had that well-rehearsed *schtick* that would see him through many a drama or comedy. He would soon be working with Clark again in *Boom Town* (1940).

Clark's friendship with Lionel Barrymore dated back to the 1920s. Their bonding had held up over the years. When they weren't needed on the set, they shared many memories.

Una Merkel was born in 1903 in Kentucky. Because of her resemblance to Lillian Gish, she had been cast as Gish's youngest sister in the never completed, never released silent film *World Shadows*, whose production was abandoned when the producers ran out of money.

At one point, she headed back to New York, where her biggest triumph was a role in *Coquette* (1927), a Broadway play which starred her idol, Helen Hayes.

Back in Hollywood, Merkel was often cast as the wise-cracking best friend of such stars as Harlow, Carole Lombard, Loretta Young, or Eleanor Powell.

Merkel became known for her kepie-doll look, Southern accent, and witty line deliveries. Her most famous performance occurred in 1939, when she staged a "cat fight" with Marlene Dietrich in *Destry Rides Again*.

Cliff Edwards and Clark dated back to when they had worked together on the set of *Dance, Fools, Dance* (1931), starring Joan Crawford.

George Zucco, born in England in 1886, was a character actor who appeared in almost a hundred films from the 1920s to 1951. He often played suave villains, members of the nobility, or mad doctors.

Jonathan Hale, born in Ontario, Canada, in 1891, was both a TV and a film actor, known for such series as *Blondie, The Saint,* and *The Cisco Kid*. He also worked in two episodes of *The Adventures of Superman*.

On February 28, 1966, at the age of 74, he committed suicide in his room at the Motion Picture & Television Country House and Hospital in Woodland Hills, Los Angeles. A .38 caliber pistol was found beside his dead body.

Two great character actors who each went on to greater glory in 1939's *The Wizard of Oz*. On the *left* is **Frank Morgan** (who played the mendacious but kind-hearted Wizard) and **Margaret Hamilton**, famous forever after for her rendition of the Wicked Witch of the West.

Lionel Barrymore reflexively portraying one of crusty, kind-hearted characters for whom he'd become famous.

***

The plot of *Saratoga* is intricate and complicated, better seen on film than reiterated in print. Suffice it to say that Duke Bradley (Clark) is a bookmaker always betting on the horses. Harlow is the snooty granddaughter of Frank Clayton (Jonathan Hale).

In the beginning, she is engaged to Wall Street mogul Hartley Madison (Pidgeon). The viewer knows that before the final reel, Duke will "get the gal."

As the film opens, a bank is foreclosing on the stud farm of Grandpa Clayton (Barrymore). Duke comes to the rescue.

Louis B. Mayer originally wanted the film to be another Gable/Crawford vehicle, but Crawford, at the time, was committed to another film.

Then, after a strong demand from Clark, MGM tried to get Paramount to release Carole Lombard for the female lead. But despite Lombard's newest lover's best efforts, because of contractual difficulties, that casting never happened.

[At the time Carole Lombard was co-starring with Fredric March in her first Technicolor film, Nothing Sacred (1937), for David O. Selznick. Lombard had already read Gone With the Wind, the novel by Margaret Mitchell, and shortly after finishing it, she was one of the first actresses in the entertainment industry to seek the screen role of the novel's heroine, Scarlett O'Hara.]

Consequently, Jean Harlow was eventually assigned the female lead in *Saratoga*, and Pidgeon was "borrowed" from Universal for the filming.

During the shoot, a tragedy occurred for Lionel Barrymore when he tripped over a cable on the set, breaking his hip for the second time in two years. He also broke his kneecap. By 1951, because of these injuries, he would need a wheelchair for the rest of his life.

MGM rushed to release *Saratoga* in an attempt to capitalize off Harlow's death on June 7, 1937, of renal failure at the early age of 26. Consequently, the final cut reached movie theaters only seven weeks after her death made "Second Coming" headlines around the nation.

Produced on a budget of $1.1 million, *Saratoga* grossed $3.3 million in worldwide box office sales.

Writing in *Night and Day*, Graham Greene said, "*Saratoga* is of more interest than just curiosity value over Harlow's death. She totes breasts like a man totes a gun. Her acting represents a star point in her short career. The film has been skillfully showed in such a way that the missing scenes with its female star lend an air of originality, which the original project might not have had. The story proceeds fast and less obviously. The heroine is less unduly plugged."

Marguerite Tazelaar, in the *New York Herald Tribune*, wrote: "The movie made me feel sad at the death of Jean Harlow. In a way, it is an obituary of a lovely person and a talented actress. The picture is entirely Miss Harlow's. She is surrounded by a fine and loyal cast, notably Clark Gable, with whom she has appeared in five motion pictures before."

Motion Picture Herald said, "Jean Harlow takes her final curtain call as the least boisterous and the most attractive heroine in her career. This comedy of the racetrack is well staged and directed by an excellent cast headlined by Clark Gable."

***

Just before Lombard got serious about Gable, film merchandisers had made feverish attempts to merge **Fredric March** and **Carole Lombard** into a charming, spontaneous, and romantic screen team.

It wasn't overwhelmingly successful.

Lombard's greatest disappointment was her failure to get cast as Scarlett O'Hara opposite Clark Gable in *Gone With the Wind*.

Saratoga was **Walter Pidgeon's** *(left)* first major screen role. He appears here with **Jean Harlow**, a few weeks before her death, and **Clark Gable**.

She was the first (and in her heyday, most famous) of Hollywood's megastar blondes. *Saratoga* was her last film.

Rest in Peace
JEAN HARLOW
(1911-1927)

Episode 79

The Death (1937) and Burial of JEAN HARLOW

On the first day of the filming of *Saratoga*, Clark had paid an early morning call on Jean Harlow, with whom he'd had an affair. Since then, he'd morphed into a kind of big brother.

Before *Saratoga*, he had made five movies with her. "The Blonde Bombshell" had been his favorite leading lady, beating Norma Shearer, Myrna Loy, Greta Garbo, and even Joan Crawford for that honor.

His affair with Harlow had reached its peak intensity during the filming of *Red Dust* (1932). Now, co-starring with him again, she was romantically involved with William Powell, the former husband of Carole Lombard.

In her dressing room, he immediately noticed that something was seriously wrong. Her skin, once hailed as "pink ivory," actually looked chalky. She complained of a headache and confessed that she was feeling tired all the time.

Jack Conway, their director, privately discussed it with Clark as shooting progressed: "There's something wrong with Jean. Around two o'clock every afternoon, her body just seems to shut down. She really should be examined by the studio doctor."

"I've told her that several times," Clark said. "Mama Jean, her mother, runs her life and is an ardent Christian Scientist. I hear they don't believe in doctors."

"Well, something has to be done," Conway said, "or else our gal is in big trouble."

On May 8, 1937, Harlow posed in a pink silk *négligée* designed by Dolly Tree. It was to have been used in a romantic scene with Clark. She didn't know it at the time, but it was the outfit that would drape her corpse at her funeral.

As filming progressed, there were more and more signs of failing health, including the fact that some of her hair had fallen out. She was putting on weight and looked bloated, which caused problems for both her director and the film's cameramen.

Jean Harlow's funeral was mobbed with both grief-stricken fans and the "idly curious." Many—already intrigued by the tabloid scandals of the deceased 27-year-old's convoluted private life, wanted to see the emotional reactions of the many film-industry bigwigs who made it a point to attend the ceremony.

In the lowest photo, **Clark Gable**, accompanied by **Carole Lombard**, seems to react to the ironies of celebrity, fame, and show-biz.

Clark visited her every day. One afternoon, he was appalled to discover that she had the shakes. Against her wishes, he summoned the studio doctor, who gave her a superficial examination, suggesting that she might be having trouble with her gall bladder. He recommended that she enter a hospital at the end of the shoot for a complete and total examination.

It was then that Clark told him that Mama Jean, an ardent practitioner of "faith healing," did not believe in doctors.

During the opening scenes of *Saratoga*, it's clearly established that Walter Pidgeon was her character's beau.

"I will always remember the date," Pidgeon later said. "It

was May 29. Jean fainted in my arms while we were trying to film a love scene. Two members of the crew carried her to her dressing room. Little did I know at the time, but that afternoon would be the last time I would ever see Jean Harlow."

Clark was not on the set at the time, but he learned later that Harlow had been sent home. Conway told him that she had complained of needing a long weekend of total rest. She promised, "I'll be fit as a fiddle come Monday morning."

But when Harlow did not show up on either Monday or the following Tuesday, Clark sensed that something was wrong. He knew that "Mama Jean" was a staunch Christian Scientist, and he feared that she might have put Harlow to bed without getting her the proper medical attention.

He had her private phone number, and he frantically called her, but she did not pick up the receiver.

Telling Conway what he was up to, he drove to the Harlow residence. Mama Jean opened the door but refused to admit him.

He shouldered his way past her and bolted up the stairs to her bedroom. What he found shocked him: The actress had ballooned to almost twice her weight. When he bent over to gently kiss her lips, her breath smelled of urine.

As he learned later, she could not urinate. The waste in her body was escaping through her sweat glands and through her mouth, overflowing with saliva.

Walter Pidgeon with **Jean Harlow** in *Saratoga*. Their pose is equivalent to the kissing scene they were filming just before Harlow collapsed, was rushed to the hospital, and shortly thereafter, died.

He later told Conway, "It was like kissing a rotten corpse."

Back at MGM, he reported on Harlow's condition to Howard Strickling. "The Fixer" immediately phoned Louis B. Mayer, who called the police to escort an ambulance to the Harlow home to have her rushed to a hospital.

With sirens blaring and dome lights flashing, the ambulance, flanked by police cars, arrived. Three attendants barged past Mama Jean and headed upstairs to carry Harlow out on a stretcher.

She was rushed to the Good Samaritan Hospital in Los Angeles. It was too late. Harlow died on June 7, 1937, her death generating screaming headlines across the nation. Three hours later, doctors released a statement that the actress died of uremic poisoning. She was only 26 years old.

Two views of **William Powell**, widely reported as the most "emotionally destroyed" mourner at **Jean Harlow's funeral.**

Upper photo: as they appeared together in *Reckless* (1937), and

Lower photo: with his mother, entering the chapel.

Harlow's mother, mourning and ostentatiously clad in fur during the peak of a Los Angeles summer, at her daughter's funeral.

Her death sent Clark into a deep depression. What began as a sexual liaison had morphed into a very sincere and loving friendship.

William Powell, who had had plans to marry her, was devastated.

He went into a deep mourning. At her funeral, he could barely conceal his pain and distress.

He wrote her a card and put it inside her casket. It read, "Good night, my dearest darling."

In honor of Harlow's death, Mayer shut down MGM for the day. Across the nation many theaters dimmed their lights for two minutes.

Even those critics who had labeled Harlow "A tart with a heart" felt empathy for her dying so young.

***

When Mayer was alerted to Harlow's death, he was making a deal with Darryl F. Zanuck at Fox. Mayer had wanted to borrow Tyrone Power for an upcoming project, *Madame X*. In return, he'd lend Fox Harlow for an upcoming film entitled *In Old Chicago*.

[The filming of In Old Chicago, *one of the most expensive movies ever made till then, was delayed until 1938, when it was released as a fictionalized account of 1871's Great Chicago Fire. It starred Alice Brady as the owner of both the cow and the burning lantern which started the fire, along with Tyrone Power, Alice Faye, Don Ameche, and Andy Devine.]*

Mayer had no great love for Harlow, but before her death, he had decided that she was MGM's best bet for super sales. His two most famous leading ladies at the time, Greta Garbo and Joan Crawford, had each been labeled "box office poison" by theater exhibitors across the country.

Still smarting from the recent death of Irving Thalberg, an uncharacteristically subdued **Norma Shearer**, accompanied by **Louis B. Mayer**, attend Harlow's funeral.

In addition to losing one of his proven money-makers, Mayer faced the daunting challenge of having to complete *Saratoga* without its female lead. It was a film in which MGM was already over-invested.

Mayer had an array of scripts waiting to be filmed, each of which he wanted to star Harlow. As of yet, he had no leading man for *The Best Dressed Woman in Paris* and *The Shopworn Angel*. Maybe Clark Gable would be cast.

These two films would be followed by *Spring Tide* with Robert Taylor; *Tell It to the Marines* with Spencer Tracy; and *The World's Our Oyster* with William Powell.

Mayer learned that after Harlow's death, a copy of a novel she was reading was found on her nightstand. It was Margaret Mitchell's *Gone With the Wind*.

Clark was asked to be a pallbearer at her funeral at Forest Lawn's Wee Kirk of the Heather Chapel. Carole Lombard appeared with Clark at the funeral. After the casket was put in place, he sat beside Lombard.

They were surrounded by the elite of MGM, all except Garbo, as well as a host of movie stars from other studios.

Jeanette MacDonald sang "Indian Love Call," a Harlow favorite. Her frequent co-star, Nelson Eddy sang "Oh, Sweet Mystery of Life."

Genevieve Smith, a Christian Science leader, read from Mary Baker Eddy's *Science & Health with a Key to the Scriptures*.

William Powell paid $25,000 for a vault for Harlow in the Sanctuary of Benediction Mausoleum, where her body was placed "for eternal rest."

***

At MGM, Mayer faced a dilemma. Some $850,000 had already been invested in *Saratoga*, and its female star had died before its completion. For at least a day, he considered abandoning it com-

Here's a press and PR photo of **Jean Harlow** as she appeared in *Saratoga*, wearing the diaphonous, semi-transparent *négligée* in which (tastefully or not) she was eventually buried.

Here's **Harold Rosson**, appearing at her funeral with an unidentified companion. He had been Harlow's third and final husband, though she had divorced him in 1935.

In light of the multiple romantic dramas swirling around the megastar at the time of her death, his presence seemed almost embarrassing.

pletely and storing its unfinished footage in a vault. However, MGM was swamped with mail from Harlow fans demanding that he release whatever footage he had. He screened it for himself.

He considered reshooting it completely with a number of actresses, notably Virginia Grey, Rita Johnson, and Gladys George. Virginia Bruce was also a contender. He feared that none of these choices had any box office power. He then decided that Jean Arthur would be the best choice—that is, if she were available. She wasn't.

In his final decision, he decided to hire Mary Dees—who looked a bit like Harlow—for filming of interim scenes that would bind the rest of the footage into a more-or-less continuous plot. It was clearly understood that Dees' hair would be dyed blonde, and she would only be shown with her back to the camera.

Filming the final scenes of *Saratoga* wrapped on June 29, 1937. On July 28, the film opened in big city theaters across the country. Ironically, Clark's *Parnell* had just opened in some houses. Managers yanked *Parnell*, which was playing to sparse audiences, and subbed *Saratoga* instead.

Harlow was dead but her legend was just being born. Hollywood insiders and her fans had different theories. Even Cary Grant got in on the act, telling the press that he was convinced that Harlow died from peroxide poisoning, a result of the chemical seeping into her brain.

Harlow with Gable, her favorite (and most compatible leading man), as they appeared around the time of **Red Dust** (1932), critically perceived today as their greatest collaboration

Jean Harlow: The eminently likable blonde perceived during her heyday as the prototypically hip, street-smart, fun, sexually accessible, and eminently desirable American woman.

Episode 80

Test Pilot (1938)

As Margaret Mitchell's best-seller, *Gone With the Wind*, swept the nation, polls showed that Clark Gable was the No. 1 favorite of fans to star as Rhett Butler in the film version. Runners-up were Ronald Colman, Gary Cooper, and Errol Flynn.

Producer David O. Selznick had acquired the film rights, and Carole Lombard was working for him at the time. Clark feared that Selznick would enroll her in his campaign to persuade him to play Rhett Butler.

"No damn way," he said. "It's a woman's picture."

Whenever the "in love and showing it" couple could find some time off, they went swimming and horseback riding at the Arrowhead Springs Hotel in San Bernardino.

Back in Los Angeles, they were seen dancing and dining together at the High Hat Club, where they celebrated her 29th birthday. She kept urging him to divorce Ria Langham, and he kept putting it off. "The bitch is demanding all the gold stored at Fort Knox."

After a long vacation, MGM summoned Clark back to work to star with Spencer Tracy and Myrna Loy in *Test Pilot*, an aviation drama to be directed by Victor Fleming. With a budget of $2 million, *Test Pilot* would be the most expensive aviation picture made since billionaire Howard Hughes had produced and directed *Hell's Angels* (1930).

Clark and Tracy had recently co-starred in *San Francisco* (1936), and Loy had been Clark's co-star in his first big flop, Parnell. [Parnell *was a flop in spite of the fact that its stars had recently been widely publicized as the King and Queen of Hollywood.*]

As a celebration of the era's progress in engineering, especially aviation, MGM opted to position its moneymaking pros into positions where they could dramatize (and romanticize) its glories and dangers.

So whereas **Clark Gable, Spencer Tracy,** and **Myrna Loy** were enlisted as the "face" of the new frontiers, the real star of *Test Pilot* was **Boeing's Y1B-17**, then the "*ne plus ultra*" of the Air Force. One of them, soaring over Manhattan in the late 1930s, is depicted above.

Victor Fleming, during the months ahead, would be directing Clark as Rhett Butler in *Gone With the Wind* (1939). He had last helmed Clark in *The White Sister* (1933) opposite Helen Hayes.

Four writers, John Lee Mahin, Howard Hawks, Waldemar Young, and Vincent Lawrence based the script of *Test Pilot* on an original story by Frank Wead, a former Naval aviator.

Clark, as the reckless and dashing test pilot, Jim Lane, took top billing. His aircraft, called *The Drake Bullet*, is forced to land on farmland in Kansas. There, he meets "the farmer's daughter," Ann ("Thursday") Barton (Myrna Loy). They spend the day together, falling in love. In no time at all, he'll marry her.

His best friend, Gunner Morris (Tracy), arrives at the homestead with spare parts. He's a mechanic sent to repair the plane.

Later, Jim is fired by his boss, Drake (Lionel Barrymore).

Tracy and Gable maintained some sort of friendship, even though they were rivals. Tracy envied Clark's looks and masculine appeal, and Clark envied him as a scene-stealing acting pro. Before filming began, Tracy warned Fleming, "I'm gonna steal every god damn scene from that stuck-up stud."

He lived up to his threat, especially in the last scene, where he dies in Clark's arms.

One critic noted that Tracy's film character followed Clark around "like a love-sick puppy." When viewed today, their relationship might be called a bromance. The gay scriptwriter, Waldemar Young, had inserted several other emotionally explicit scenes between Tracy and Clark, but Clark objected, ordering that they be rewritten. "I'm not going to say all that faggy dialogue."

Because Clark was widely acknowledged as the King of Hollywood, Tracy bowed every time he encountered Clark, referring to him as "Your Majesty." To retaliate, Clark called him "The Wisconsin Ham." Loy was referred to as "Queenie."

Paul Mantz, a noted air-racing and movie stunt pilot, was brought in as a consultant/technical advisor. Before working on *Test Pilot,* he had acted as a navigator for the doomed aviatrix, Amelia Earhart

On March 17, 1937, Earhart set out on the first leg of her around-the-world flight, during the course of which, she disappeared.

"I was set to fly with Earhart on her final voyage," Mantz said. "Thank God I didn't. My buddy, Frederick Noonan, went with her. As the world knows, those two were never heard from again."

For some of the aerial scenes in *Test Pilot,* Mantz had 18 cameramen at work.

During the shoot, Clark spent time with Lionel Barrymore, his longtime friend. As far as it is known, there was no mention made of his long-ago seduction of the young actor.

"Yesterday, as they say, is dead and gone," he told Clark. "If only I could live it all over again. One's youth rushes by all too fast."

After he is fired by Drake, Clark lands a very dangerous job flying experimental aircraft. His new wife (Loy) is forced to live with the anxiety that every time she kisses him goodbye before he boards an airplane, that he might not return.

As a celebration of American patriotism and prowess, *Test Pilot* morphed into a BIG movie with BIG sets, BIG budgets, and BIG egos.

Here's a view of *(left to right)*, **Loy, Tracy**, and **Gable** between takes at Lindbergh Field, San Diego, surrounded by then-high-tech accessories and dozens of technicians and technical consultants.

Clark Gable emerged from *Test Pilot* with a reinforcement of the perception that he represented "The Best of America." At this point in his career, he excelled at portrayals of smart, technically savvy, and brave American men with a talent for overcoming adversity.

Ticket sales soared as the United States strengthened its self-image as a military fortress.

She defines her rival for Clark's love not as another woman, but as "his love for a lady with wings," a reference to the experimental airplanes he flies on test missions.

Test Pilot used authentic U.S. Army Air Corps airfield settings and was able to obtain access to Boeing's new Y1B-17 airplanes. Principal photography took place at Van Nuys, California; at Lindbergh Field (San Diego), and at March Field (also in California). Some scenes were shot at the Cleveland National Air Races.

The conclusion of the film is when Clark and his co-pilot (Tracy) take off in an aircraft, trying to ascend to a death-defying 30,000 feet. *[Audiences are told that the plane has been loaded with sandbags substituted for the weight of bombs, and that at altitudes that high, pilots need to wear oxygen masks.]*

Disaster is around the corner. During the airplane's descent, the straps holding the sandbags break and start sliding toward the cockpit. Both pilots are in mortal danger of being crushed against their instrument panels.

In a desperate move, Clark fights to keep the aircraft under control He also throws sandbags out the window.

The plane is forced to crash land. Clark is seen dragging his co-pilot away from the crash site before the plane explodes in flames.

Tracy is seen dying in Clark's arms. The scene had to be reshot because Tracy kept dragging it out. Finally, Clark said, "Die, goddamn it, Spence. I wish to Christ you would!" Then he dropped Tracy's head with a thud.

"Okay, guys, let's do it all over again," Fleming shouted at them. "Remember, Spence, you're not Greta Garbo dying in *Camille*."

In the hands of lesser actors, the scene where Spencer Tracy dies in the arms of his bromance buddy, Clark Gable, might have sunk into the maudlin.

Even so, it became the subject of suppressed ridicule—at least for a while.

Here's **Greta Garbo**, portraying a *demi-mondaine* and courtesan in mid-19th-Century Paris, dying in the arms of **Robert Taylor** in *Camille*. It had been released only two years previous to *Test Pilot*, in 1936.

***

Test Pilot was Clark's first picture with character actress Marjorie Main. She was cast in the rather lackluster role of "The Landlady." She would also have a supporting role in his next picture, *Too Hot to Handle* (1938).

Born in Indiana in 1890, Main got her start in vaudeville. She began to appear in stage plays, such as *Cheating Cheaters* (1916), starring John Barrymore. She also played Mae West's mother in *The Wicked Age* (1927). The following year, she appeared on stage with Barbara Stanwyck in the long-running play, *Burlesque*.

Samuel Goldwyn hired her to reprise her stage role in the film version of *Dead End* (1937). Humphrey Bogart was cast as her son. In the all-star female cast, *The Women* (1930), Main operated a dude ranch/resort hotel for out-of-state residents seeking a divorce in Reno.

In the 1940s, MGM tried to repeat the success of Wallace Beery and Marie Dressler in the 1930s. Main played opposite Beery in six films, including *Barnacle Bill* (1941).

It would be the *Ma and Pa Kettle* comedies with Percy Kilbride that would garner for Main her greatest box office hits These movies grossed at least $3 million each, saving Universal from bankruptcy.

Main was married to Staney Fevre from 1921 until his death in 1935. But they hardly lived together. Her longest-term relationship was with the lesbian actress Spring Byington,

Louis Jean Heydt, in the role of Greg Benson, was born in New Jersey in 1903. For a time, he was a reporter on the *New York World*. It was during his performance as a reporter that he made his Broadway debut in the 1930s. He later traveled to Hollywood, where he got cast in *Gone With the Wind* as one of the hungry soldiers at Tara. Actress Gloria Holden was cast as his wife, Mrs. Benson. When Heydt first met Clark, he was reading a copy of Margaret Mitchell's *Gone With the Wind*.

Arthur Aylesworth, cast as Frank Barton, was born in Rhode Island in 1883. He made his Broadway debut in 1911, and for years, he appeared on the stage. He arrived at Warner Brothers in Hollywood in the 1930s, where he signed on as a character actor. Often uncredited, he popped up in 130 motion pictures.

Two views of **Marjorie Main**, the golden-age character actress who defined hillbilly chic.

In *Test Pilot*, Fay Hoden was uncredited as a lingerie saleslady. She was born in England in 1893, but left in 1929, heading for Canada. Eventually, she moved to Hollywood, where between 1935 and 1953, she appeared in 46 films.

Fame came when she was cast as the mother of Mickey Rooney in all those Andy Hardy movies.

For a change of pace, she played the mother of Samson (Victor Mature) in Cecil B. De Mille's *Samson and Delilah* (1949) starring Hedy Lamarr.

***

Since Carole Lombard was busy making pictures and often coming home late, Clark had time for a sexual fling with a minor actress, Virginia Grey. She was a beautiful woman born in 1917 in Edendale, California. She never made it as a top-flight star, but continued to work until 1977, appearing in 100 films and a number of radio and TV shows. She became the best friend of Lana Turner.

At the age of 10, she made her silent film debut as Little Eva in *Uncle Tom's Cabin* (1927). For many years, she was a contract player at MGM, where she was seduced by a number of its male stars, ranging from William Powell to Mickey Rooney.

Later, she freelanced, appearing in such popular films as *All That Heaven Allows* (1955) with Rock Hudson and Jane Wyman; *Back Street* (1961) with Susan Hayward and John Gavin; and *Madame X* (1966) with Lana Turner.

She never married, but often seduced her co-stars, including Johnny Weissmuller (Tarzan) and both Gene Autry and Roy Rogers. Buster Crabbe was her favorite.

These were mere passing flings. Her alltime love affair was with Clark. It is not known for certain, but she may have first met him on the set of *Test Pilot* (1938), in which she had a minor role as Sarah.

He seduced her, which marked the beginning of an affair that lasted on and off for years. She was next seen as one of his chorus girls in *Idiot's Delight*, released in 1939, the year he starred as Rhett Butler in *Gone With the Wind*.

Gay and counterculture hipsters of the late 1930s instantly recognized the subtle love triangle that lurked, subliminally, in *Test Pilot*.

Here, the very heterosexual characters portrayed by **Gable** and **Loy** make nice, while the (possibly gay) "third wheel" (as portrayed by **Spencer Tracy**) looks on with suppressed envy.

***

Test Pilot was a hit, *The New York Times* defining it as "one of those irresistible MGM productions of the 1930s that coast along on sheer star power. *Variety* noted that "the story bespeaks authority in detail, obviously explained by the fact that Captain Frank Wead, who authored the original, had a practical aviation background."

"Victor Fleming got exact performances that verged on reality," *Time* magazine wrote. "First there was actress Myrna Loy, and a loud, slam-bang Clark Gable. And then there's amenable, sandy Spencer Tracy, currently cinema's No. 1 actors' actor."

Cue magazine wrote: "As the trio, Clark Gable, Spencer Tracy, and Myrna Loy turn in probably the best performances of their career."

Made for a budget of $1.7 million, *Test Pilot* earned $4 million at the box office.

By this point in his career, Tracy had become big box office, which was noticed at the Academy Awards.

In 1936, he was nominated for playing the priest in *San Francisco* opposite Clark Gable. That was the year that Paul Muni won for *The Story of Louis Pasteur*. The Tracy/Gable movie, *San Francisco*, was nominated for Best Picture that year, losing to *The Great Ziegfeld*, starring William Powell.

In 1937, Tracy won the Best Actor Oscar for *Captains Courageous*. This time, he beat out Paul Muni for *The Story of Emile Zola*.

In the 1938 race, *Test Pilot* was nominated for Best Picture of the Year, losing to *You Can't Take It With You*, starring James Stewart, Jean Arthur, and Lionel Barrymore.

Tracy won the 1938 Oscar for Best Actor, a movie in which he'd co-starred with Mickey Rooney. He beat out James Cagney, Charles Boyer, Robert Donat, and Leslie Howard.

After meeting him on the set of *Test Pilot*, actress **Virginia Grey** fell in love with Clark Gable, and never stopped loving him. Over the years, he continued to visit her on occasion for romantic trysts.

After Gable's wife, Carole Lombard, died in a plane crash in 1942, he turned to Grey for love and comfort. She expected a proposal of marriage at that time, but he shocked her by wedding Lady Sylvia Ashley.

When she died at the age of 87, she'd never married. "Clark was the only man I ever loved."

Episode 81

Too Hot to Handle
(aka *Let 'Em All Talk;* **1938**)

Hollywood insiders had long known of the Gable/Lombard affair. However, in May of 1938, *Photoplay* magazine introduced their romance to the general moviegoing public. Reporter Eddie Doherty wrote an article entitled "Can the Gable-Lombard Story Have a Happy Ending?":

> *A beautiful blonde girl, witty and winsome and wise, in love with a debonair actor who has been married a number of years and whose wife is unwilling to divorce him. What will happen? How will the characters react? How will the story end? Will the wife step gracefully aside, someday, and allow her husband to marry the younger woman? Will she wait in patience, knowing that time oft withers infatuation, or will the girl, tired of waiting, give the man up? Will there be tragedy? Or will the last reel of the drama be played to the chime of wedding bells?"*

Louis B. Mayer was horrified by this kind of publicity, having his top male star, a married man, involved in an affair with a famous actress. In the 1930s, this was considered scandalous.

Even so, MGM wanted to make money. Since Clark Gable and Myrna Loy had been crowned King and Queen of Hollywood, Mayer wanted to co-star them in another movie, since *Test Pilot,* their latest vehicle, had been a big hit.

He called Jack Conway, who had recently helmed Clark and the doomed Jean Harlow in *Saratoga* (1937), to his office.

"I want to team Gable and Loy again," he said, handing over the script of *Too Hot to Handle* to the director. It was the work of Lawrence Stallings and John Mahin. Mayer had already cast the three leads. Clark played what one writer called "a waggish and thoroughly sneaky newsreel reporter," Christ Hunter. Walter Pidgeon, cast as Bill Dennis, was his main competitor. Loy, as female aviatrix Alma Harding, was influenced by Amelia Earhart, who had disappeared during an around the-world flight fourteen months before shooting began.

Loy had played an aviatrix before in *Wings in the Dark* (1935) in which she was personally instructed by Earhart herself. Cary Grant had been her co-star.

Conway was directly affected by Harlow's death: "It was a sad day for me. Mayer met with me and had me in mind to direct more films with Harlow. We'd gotten along

smoothly when I directed her in *Libeled Lady* (1936).

The script *Too Hot to Handle* called for Loy to enlist the help of both the Gable and Pidgeon characters to finance a search in South America for her missing brother. Her brother was played by Johnny Hines.

The action moves to voodoo country where the natives need a white woman for one of their rituals. With a brother held captive and now Alma (Loy) also a prisoner, it is Chris Hunter (Clark) to the rescue.

"My role wasn't much of a part," wrote Myrna Loy. "It was rather routine. It was Clark Gable's picture. He's wonderful, very comical, as the newsreel reporter who fakes stories. The whole thing was fun, though and a bit hazardous. Clark supposedly saved my life on that picture. The script called for him to rescue me from a burning plane wreck after causing it. They turned on a controlled fire from a valve behind the cameras, and Clark ran over to pull me out. He yells, 'Come on, those gas tanks will blow at any minute.'"

"I counter, 'What did you expect them to do, you clumsy jackass?' Supposedly, the controlled fire went wrong at this point. Clark kept coming and yanked me out as the plane burst into flames. Ten seconds later, I might have been burned to death."

For inspiration, scriptwriters Laurence Stallings and John Mahin drew upon the exploits of Earhart, the Pearl White series and the comedies of Buster Keaton, who wrote some of the comic scenes himself, although he was not credited.

In the silent film era, Keaton had been a big star, performing amazing stunts with his deadpan expression that earned him the title of "The Great Stone Face." During the Roaring '20s, he was called "the greatest actor-director in the history of the movies."

A son of Kansas, born in 1895, Keaton got his start as a child in vaudeville. The silent film *The General* (1926) is viewed as his masterpiece.

His career declined in 1928 as he descended into alcoholism.

The third lead of Bill Dennis went to the then fast-rising star, Walter Pidgeon. He had recently starred with Clark and Harlow in *Saratoga* (1937). When he wasn't needed on camera, he and Clark discussed her untimely death.

One afternoon, quite by accident, Clark spotted Pidgeon fellating a studly member of the crew behind a wall of scenery.

Here's **Clark** rescuing his onscreen lady love (**Myrna**) from burning wreckage. During its filming, the immediate danger of her burning alive was greater than anyone off the set knew at the time.

PR teams within the studio seemed at odds during the crafting of *Too Hot to Handle*. Some of them wanted to stoke the (somewhat tired) onscreen chemistry between **Myrna Loy** and **Clark Gable**. Others thought a media emphasis on the newer and earthier gig blossoming between Clark and Carole Lombard might be more profitable.

With that (confusing) dynamic in full flower, Gable and Loy gamely made another stab at witty sexual tension under stress. For **Loy**, at least, that style had worked beautifully with **William Powell** in their long-running *The Thin Man* detective series a half-decade earlier. [Lower photo shows them together in that series a half-decade earlier.]

Here's Loy with Gable, immersed in the then-newfangled world of scoop-chasing for newsreels. For movie audiences, the onscreen tensions were heightened as Europe and Asia each moved closer to war.

Loy & **Powell**, *The Thin Man*

Later, he mentioned it to the film's director, Jack Conway, who responded, "To each his own."

***

On the set of *Too Hot to Handle,* Walter Connolly, cast as Gabby MacArthur, had a reunion with Clark. He had starred as the tycoon father of Claudette Cobert in *It Happened One Night* (1934). He had just appeared in *Libeled Lady* 1936) with William Powell, Myrna Loy, Jean Harlow, and Spencer Tracy.

He had also played the worthless uncle of the Paul Muni character in *The Good Earth* (1937).

He confessed to Clark, "I don't know how much longer I can keep working. My clock is ticking."

"Chin up," Clark said. "You're just getting started."

In May of 1940, Connolly died at the age of 53, following a stroke.

Leo Carillo, cast as José Estanza, had a beer with Clark one afternoon. They talked over their last picture together, *Manhattan Melodrama* (1934), in which they'd worked with Myrna Loy and William Powell.

Joining them for a beer was Al Shean, who had a very minor role as "Gumpy" Gumpert. He had played the piano player, known as "the Professor," in Clark's *San Francisco* (1936) with Spencer Tracy and Jeanette MacDonald.

Also joining them for a round of beer was Marjorie Main, who had the role of Miss Kitty Wayne. She and Clark had just completed *Test Pilot* (1938).

Johnny Hines, as Mr. Parsons, was a son of Colorado, born in 1895, He'd starred in silent films, but was reduced to minor parts in the Talkies. In all, he would appear in 50 motion pictures between 1914 and 1938, when he left the screen. He was granted only six roles in the 1930s.

He confessed to Clark, "I just don't have what it takes for talkies. Directors tell me to find another profession."

After *Too Hot to Handle,* he would have a bit part in one more movie, *Magnificent Doll* (1946), starring Ginger Rogers and David Niven.

Virginia Weidler, born in Los Angeles in 1927, was a child actress who rose to a quirky kind of fame beginning in the 1930s. In *Too Hot to Handle,* she played Hulda Harding. Her family had emigrated from Germany in 1923, her father an architect, her mother an opera singer.

She became known as "the little girl who could hold her breath until she got her way." Clark would later see her in *Souls at Sea* (1938) starring Gary Cooper and George Raft.

Here's the "amicably crabby" **Walter Connolly** getting "handled," as **Clark**'s character adroitly maneuvers around him.

Connolly was one of several GREAT character actors from the golden age of filmmaking in the late 1930s.

The charming but unlucky **Virginia Weidler** in *Bad Little Angel* (1939), a year after filming *Too Hot to Handle.*

She became a member of the all-female cast in the 1939 film, *The Women,* as Norma Shearer's daughter.

Her greatest fame derived from her performance as the outspoken (i.e. "bratty") younger sister of Katharine Hepburn in *The Philadelphia Story* (1940).

Her major competitors were the then-adolescent actresses Shirley Temple and Jane Withers. As Weidler grew out of her teen years, she sank into retirement, granting no more interviews. She had suffered from a bad heart for many years. In July of 1968, she had a heart attack and died at the age of 41.

Gregory Gaye was cast as "Popoff." Born in St. Petersburg, Russia, in 1900, he had a remarkable career that ranged from 1928 to 1979. After the Russian Revolution, in 1923, he escaped to Hollywood, where he would appear in small roles in more than a hundred movies.

His first role was in the silent film *Tempest* (1928) starring John Barrymore. He appeared in three movies with Will Rogers before John Ford gave him a bit part in *The Black Watch* (1929). He worked with other bit players, notably John Wayne and Randolph Scott.

In 1930, he was cast as a suave violinist chasing Gloria Swanson in the romantic comedy *What a Widow!*. He would go on to work with Bela Lugosi, Boris Karloff, Claudette Colbert, and Peter Lorre.

He popped up in many classic movies such as *Ninotchka* (1939) starring Greta Garbo. During World War II, he often played Nazis, including an official of Hitler's Reichsbank in *Casablanca* (1942).

Henry Kolker, cast as Pearly Todd, born in 1874 in Quincy, Illinois, was a director and a stage and film actor. He launched his career in stock theater in 1895 and began making films in 1915, including the Pre-Code hit, *Baby Face* (1933), starring Barbara Stanwyck.

His best-known work as a director was *Disraeli* (1921), starring George Arliss. Only one reel of it has surfaced, the rest of it lost to film history.

Betsy Ross Clark *(aka Betsy Ross Clarke)* cast as Mrs. Ruth Harding, escaped the cold winds of North Dakota, where she was born in 1892. Her maternal grandfather had been a Union brigadier general during the Civil War.

She set out to become a ballet dancer, but life had other plans for her. Instead, she morphed into a stage and film actress, finding work from 1920 to 1940.

After living in England and in Australia, she returned to the United States in 1929 at the dawn of the Talkies.

Many of her films are lost to history. One that survived was her (silent) 1921 appearance with Fatty Arbuckle in *The Traveling Salesman*.

Cosmopolitan and spectacularly international: **Gregory Gaye.**

THE IRONIES OF FAME

Betsy Ross Clark as she appeared as a Cover Girl in 1922.

***

Too Hot to Handle was the sixth and final Gable/Loy picture. It earned $1,630,000 in the United States and another $775,000 in Canada. Even so, it recorded a loss of $35,000.

Critic Frank Nugent, in *The New York Times*, wrote: "*Too Hot to Handle*" is one of a dozen fairly entertaining melodramas you might have seen in the last five years. Gable plays Chris Hunter with his customary blend of bluster and blubber. Loy's lady-like flier turns into a completely insincere performance."

Variety noted, "Adventures of newsreel cameramen are the basis for this Gable/Loy co-starrer. It's a blazing action thriller aimed as a follow-up to the same pair's click in *Test Pilot*. It has driving excitement, crackling dialogue, glittering performances, and inescapable romantic pull."

The 1930s were coming to an end, as was the on-screen pairing of **Clark Gable** with **Myrna Loy.**

In *Too Hot to Handle*, she struck a blow for women's equality in her role as an aviatrix. She'd played another pilot in **Wings in the Dark** (1935), for which she had been coached by Amelia Earhart herself.

Episode 82

Idiot's Delight
(1939)

This comedy-drama by Robert E. Sherwood had been a big hit on Broadway in 1936 when it co-starred the husband-and-wife acting team of Alfred Lunt and Lynn Fontanne. They later took it on a nation-wide tour, playing to packed houses.

In London's West End, it was also a success, co-starring Raymond Massey with Tamara Geva.

Born in New Rochelle, New York, in 1896, Sherwood was one of America's most distinguished playwrights and screenwriters. In addition to *Idiot's Delight*, he also wrote such classics as *Waterloo Bridge* (1931 and 1940), *Abe Lincoln in Illinois* (1940), *The Best Years of Our Lives* (1946), and *The Bishop's Wife* (1947).

He received Pulitzer Prizes for Drama in 1936, 1939, and 1941, as well as an Academy Award for Best Screenplay of 1947. Sherwood was one of the members of the famed Algonquin Round Table, towering over the other members at 6 feet, 8 inches.

Groucho Marx once asked him, "What do you say to people who ask you how's the weather up there?"

He replied, "I spit in their eye and tell them it's raining."

During World War II, Sherwood became a speechwriter for Franklin D. Roosevelt. He originated the phrase "Arsenal of Democracy" that the President often used in his wartime speeches.

It was Louis B. Mayer who demanded that Norma Shearer and Clark Gable be cast as the female and male leads, with Shearer taking top billing. *[Although Clark viewed himself as a star now big enough to take top billing, she owned a huge block of MGM stock, willed to her by her late husband, Irving Thalberg.]*

It started as a hit Broadway play with a message permeated with the murky existential anguish being discussed by the leading intellectuals of its heyday. Then It fast-evolved into a big-budget celluloid extravaganze promoted by the full might and power of MGM.

It had something for everyone: Continental intrigue, dancing showgirls, and über-glam mega-stars in love—specifically **Clark Gable** and **Norma Shearer**. What came out of it all? A show with pacifist undertones and a romantically stylish, *"Here's lookin' at ya, kid"* ending that nobody really liked: **IDIOT'S DELIGHT**.

Clarence Brown signed on as director. He had once helmed Clark alongside a star much "bigger" than Norma Shearer: That had occurred in 1931, when he cast Clark with Greta Garbo in *Susan Lenox: Her Fall and Rise*.

Even before regular rehearsals began, Clark had to spend six weeks with dance instructor George King. It was in preparation for his appearance in front of six chorus girls called "Les Blondes." Their big number was "Puttin' on the Ritz."

Author Jean Stokes wrote: "All his life, Clark Gable made it a point to keep his feet planted firmly on solid ground. He always had been self-conscious about his feet. He wore 11-Cs, a heritage of his barefoot farm days in Ohio. Awkward as a kid, he shied away from dances. During his early days on the stage, when eating regularly was of primary importance, he had neither the time nor the inclination to dance. He could waltz in a pinch, but until recently, that was the full extent of his terpsichorean activity."

Clark warned his director, Brown, "I'm no Fred Astaire. I was pissed off when I got Sherwood's latest revised script. At least fifteen pages are devoted to my dance routine. A couple of jokers were added too, one called *The Buck-Schottische*, another with me in tails and top hat like Astaire himself."

The script called for him, at the end of his finale, to toss his straw hat into the air before being carried off by the six chorus girls.

Some nights, when he returned home for dinner, Carole Lombard, his mistress, insisted he spend another two hours rehearsing his dance steps with her.

Whenever she could, a jealous Lombard visited the set, fearing that Clark might be tempted to seduce one of the gorgeous young women of the chorus.

Late one afternoon, she spotted one of the dancers flirting with Clark. She turned to Brown and said, "Get that god damn whore out of here before I tear her hair out."

The transgressing dancer was fired and quickly replaced. Lombard, however, never picked up on the actress (i.e., Virginia Grey) with whom Clark was having an affair.

Grey had had a sexual fling with Clark when she was cast in a minor role in his film *Test Pilot* (1938) with Spencer Tracy and Myrna Loy. *[Also, Clark had been instrumental in getting Brown to cast Grey as one of the chorus girls in* Idiot's Delight.*]*

Against her better judgment, Grey had fallen in love with Clark. "He was the man for me, even though I knew he was married, he didn't love his wife, but he seemed mad about Lombard. Even so, that didn't stop him from making love to me every chance we got to slip away. I wanted Clark any way I could get him."

The most enduring stage of their long-running affair, however, did not begin until Clark returned from the battlefields of World War II. However, it was another actress also named Virginia, that got mentioned in the press.

At the time, gossip columnist Louella Parsons wrote, "I expect Clark Gable will soon be announcing his wedding date to Virginia Field any day now. The couple is seen at night clubs and chic restaurants. They make a lovely pair. The starlet, Miss Field, seems to be the woman to make Clark get over the

"Defiant hooferism" on the eve of World War II: **Gable** with a straw hat, a cane, and **"Les Blondes."**

Here, **Gable**, as the overseer of a troupe of vaudevillian dance hall hostesses fresh from a gig in Romania, unleashes their feminine charm on the scary and humorless **Commandante**. It doesn't work.

In advance of the film's release, **MGM** did somersaults trying to make the film's pacifist message palatable to the Fascist governments rattling sabers in Europe at the time. The specific alpine nation whose freedom was in peril remained unnamed and hazy, and the language spoken by "the enemy" was scrupulously limited to Esperanto.

All of MGM's efforts were in vain—the then-Fascist governments of Germany, Italy, and Austria banned the movie anyway.

DID YOU KNOW? That **Lana Turner** was cast as one of "Les Blondes" and dyed her hair for the role. A bout of appendicitis forced her to withdraw from the film, but she left her hair blonde and it became her signature look.

tragic death of Carole Lombard."

***

As *Idiot's Delight* opens, Harry Van (Clark) is a World War I veteran performing a mentalist act in a vaudeville act in Omaha. There, he meets Irene (Shearer), a trapeze artist They share a romantic fling.

Twenty years go by before they meet again, when he is performing onstage with six dancing girls. They are detained at the Swiss border *en route* to the swanky hotel where they'll be performing. There's talk that war is imminent.

Irene arrives with Achille Weber, a munitions king. Harry suspects this is the same woman he knew back in Omaha. Now she's an *über-glam* platinum blonde with an exaggerated Russian accent.

As the plot unfolds, Irene admits that she's that woman from long ago, back in Omaha. Her munitions king deserts her, and she reunites with Clark.

She vows her love for him as the bombs begin to fall.

In the original ending, the curtain goes down on Harry and Irene as they sing "Onward Christian Soldiers," Bombs explode outside, leaving their survival an open question.

However, at a premiere showing in January of 1939, the preview audience hated it, and MGM was bombarded with protest mail.

Consequently, Louis B. Mayer ordered Clarence Brown to do retakes

Two different endings were reshot. The one most often shown depicts the couple singing "Abide By Me," with their backs turned to the furious aerial bombings going on outside their picture window.

"I've loved you all the time," he says.

"Thanks for telling me, darling," she replies.

The explosions suddenly stop. "Look, Harry, they've gone away!" She is in tears as they embrace.

THE END.

***

The script initially ran into trouble with the film censor, Joseph Breen—not because of any flagrant sex scenes, but for political reasons. Its theme—laced with anti-war references—

Left photo: **Clark** confronts his trapeze artist, "that lying redhead," after a one-night stand long ago and far away, back in Omaha. It's **Norma Shearer,** who, twenty years later, has morphed herself into:

Right photo: **THE COUNTESS**, supposedly a Romanoff refugee, fetchingly (albeit improbably) outfitted in Karakul lamb and *haute* everything by MGM's best costume designer, **Adrian**.

Idiot's Delight was the third film in which **Clark** had co-starred with beautiful and ever-so-chic **Norma Shearer.**

Although their chemistry in their previous films had always been magical, her new position as owner of much of her late husband's stock in MGM now made her more politically delicate (and more politically dangerous) than ever.

contained diatribes against militarism, fascism, and munitions. America hadn't yet entered World War II, and Breen feared that *Idiot's Delight* might cause reprisals against distributors.

Mussolini was the first to ban the film in Italy, followed by Hitler refusing to allow it to be shown in Germany and Austria.

***

Edward Arnold, cast as Achille Weber, born in New York in 1890, was both a stage and screen actor active from 1907 until his death in 1956 at the age of 66.

At the age of 12, he appeared onstage as Lorenzo in *The Merchant of Venice.* In 1927, he had the second lead to George Jessel in *The Jazz Singer.*

He made his debut in talkies with *Okay America!* (1932).

In 1935, he appeared as *Diamond Jim,* which sent him on the road to stardom. He reprised the role of Diamond Jim Brady in the 1940 biopic, *Lillian Russell.*

He survived being labeled "box office poison" in 1938 and went on to make 150 movies. "I long ago gave up losing weight," he recalled. "The bigger I got, the better character roles were offered." He was so sought after that on occasion, he worked on two pictures at the same time.

Another character actor, Charles Coburn, was cast as Dr. Waldersee. Born in Georgia (USA) in 1877, he made his Broadway debut in 1901. After that, he would work steadily for the rest of his life, dying in 1961 at the age of 84.

He was nominated for Best Supporting Actor Oscars three times for performances in *The Devil and Miss Jones* (1941), *The More the Merrier* (1943), and *The Green Years* (1946).

He and Clark did not get along: "The old devil was the most blatant racist I ever encountered."

Joseph Schildkraut, as Captain Kirvline, was born in Vienna in 1896 into a Jewish family. He received stage training with Max Reinhardt in Berlin and made several appearances there before moving, in 1920, to the United States, where he became a Broadway star.

In Hollywood, he found work in silent films, such as the role of Chevalier de Vaudrey in D.W. Griffith's *Orphans of the Storm* with Lillian Gish (1922). Cecil B. De Mille, in his 1927 epic, *The King of Kings,* cast the actor as Judas Iscariot.

At the time he worked with Clark and Shearer, he had completed the role of Alfred Dreyfus in *The Life of Emile Zola* (1937). He had also appeared with Shearer in *Marie Antoinette* (1938).

He is perhaps best remembered today for playing Otto Frank in both the stage and the 1959 film version of *The Diary of Anne Frank.*

Laura Hope Crews, cast as Madame Zuleika, shocked Clark by her appearance. She was no longer the stage actress he'd seduced back in the 1920s when he was her guest in her New York apartment. In fact, she was getting ready to play the obese and eccentric Aunt Pittypat in *Gone With the Wind* (1939).

Burgess Meredith, born in Cleveland, Ohio, in 1907, was the first to admit that "God knows, I was not a dashing swain, but a kind of mongrel for the way I chased the foxes." He got many of them, too, seducing Norma Shearer during the shooting of *Idiot's Delight.*

He not only accomplished that, but also bedded Tallulah Bankhead, Ingrid Bergman, Olivia de Havilland, Marlene Dietrich, Hedy Lamarr, and Ginger Rogers.

He also indulged in a *ménage à trois* with a rich German lady and her lesbian lover,. Among his four

The Wages of Sin: Here's **Edward Arnold** as a tuxedo-clad armaments king, on the verge of dumping his mendacious mistress, as portrayed by **Norma Shearer**.

What alternative does she have, on the verge of mass destruction, but to re-approximate herself with her Omaha he-man of long ago, **Clark Gable**?

Here are the four male leads of *Idiot's Delight*. left to right: **Skeets Gallagher, Clark Gable, Burgess Meredith, and Charles Coburn**.

This talented quartet was given one script that was later withdrawn to tone down the antifascist sentiments. Many European countries, including Italy, threatened to ban it.

wives was a marriage (from 1944-1949) to the sultry Paulette Goddard.

Meredith found work as an actor from 1929 to 1997, the year of his death at 89. He has been hailed as "one of the most accomplished actors of the 20th Century, and he was heavily awarded with, among others, two separate nominations for Best Supporting Actor Oscars. A younger generation got to know him when he portrayed "The Penguin" in the 1960s TV series, *Batman*.

***

During the filming of *Idiot's Delight*, Clark had a reunion with "Skeets" Gallagher, with whom he had appeared before in *Possessed* (1931) alongside Joan Crawford. In the studio gym, he and Clark had a few rounds in the ring, boxing. "He had the best southpaw I ever saw," Clark said. "One time in the ring with him was enough. After all, he was once crowned the 'unofficial amateur flyweight champion of the world.'"

Although Pat Paterson, born in England in 1910, made more than fifty films, she was best known as the wife of Charles Boyer, whom she'd married in 1934.

She arrived in Hollywood in 1929 at the dawn of the Talkies and was signed by Fox.

In 1939, the Boyers spent much of their time supporting the war efforts of France and Britain.

She gave birth to their only child, Michael Charles Boyer, who committed suicide when he was 21 years old. His girlfriend had just told him, "We're through."

Pat Patterson died in Phoenix in 1978. Two days later, Boyer committed suicide by overdosing on drugs.

At this point in his sexually promiscuous career, Clark Gable had known **Laura Hope Crews** for a long long time.

Here she is as she appeared as Madame Zuleika in *Idiot's Delight*. Later, looking even frowsier and more eccentric, she'd immortalize herself as one of the best-remembered character actresses in ***Gone With the Wind***, Aunt Pittypat.

Peter Willes, cast as Mr. Cherry, was a British actor/producer born in 1913. Although he morphed into a talented actor in his own right, until his dying day he was most famous for having forged a relationship with Frank Vosper, an actor and playwright best known for playing urbane villains on the London stage. He appeared with such stars as Alec Guinness, Dame Edith Evans, Margaret Rutherford, and Jack Hawkins.

Vosper achieved a certain fame on London's West End for his stage appearance in the 1933 production of *The Green Bay Tree*. In it, he played a homosexual aristocrat (described by one critic as "a rich, hothouse sybarite) who adopts a working-class boy and remodels him in his own image.

On March 6, 1937, "Frank (Vosper) & Peter (Willes)" returned to England from New York aboard the *SS Paris*. On board, they were seen, over drinks, chatting with Ernest Hemingway.

Later that night, Vosper disappeared. Several weeks later, the remains of his body were found 200 miles away, near East Dean, on the coast of Sussex, in England.

Was it suicide, murder, or an accident?

Vosper's death gave rise to a cruel saying, "Never get on a ship with Peter Willes." That quip was still in circulation (and widely understood) as late as the 1960s.

William Edmunds as Dumpsty was born in Italy

Tragedy-soaked British expats thriving (or not) in Hollywood in the late 1930s.

Left photo: **Pat Patterson,** wife of Charles Boyer, appears with **Peter Willes** in *Idiot's Delight*.

Willes was briefly suspected of foul play associated with the disappearance at sea of his partner *(right photo)*, the distinguished English actor **Frank Vosper**, famous for his portrayals of rich (gay) sybarites onstage.

The inquest into Vosper's death aboard the *SS Paris* in 1937 generated newspaper headlines on two continents and dragged on for months.

in 1886. He beame a character actor playing roles that required a heavy Italian, Spanish, or French accent. He is best known for his performance as Giuseppe Martini in *It's a Wonderful Life* (1946). His first credited role was in Bob Hope's *Going Spanish* (1934). He worked steadily from 1910 to 1959.

His brief appearance in *Casablanca* (1942) is still seen on the screen today. *[In Rick's Bar, he gives instructions to a man seeking illegal passage out of the city.]*

Fritz Feld, as Pittatek, was born in Berlin in 1900, and eventually came to Hollywood, where he appeared in 140 motion pictures over the course of 72 years, both silents and talkies. His trademark involved slapping his mouth with the palm of his hand to create a "pop" sound. He could play every role from a *maître d'hotel* to an eccentric aristocrat. In 1938, at the time he worked with Clark, he also starred in the screwball comedy, *Bringing Up Baby* with Cary Grant and Katharine Hepburn.

Paula Stone, cast as Beulah, was born in New York in 1912 as the daughter of Fred Stone, the owner of the Fred Stone theatrical stock company. Though her parents, she became an actress, making her stage debut at the age of 13. She toured the country in plays, including *Idiot's Delight*, before getting cast in its screen adaptation.

Bernadene Hayes, born in St. Louis, Missouri, in 1912, became known as a singer on radio, her career stretching from 1934 to 1956. In September of 1930, she was named "the most beautiful radio performer in America."

Her great success was on radio and television. Although she tried out for a film career, she only managed to get hired as an extra for $10 a day.

During the filming of *Idiot's Delight*, she revealed that "Clark made a pass at me, and I expressed interest, but then he didn't follow through with an actual invitation."

***

Idiot's Delight cost $1.5 million to make. MGM was very disappointed at the final gross it generated: $1.7 million worldwide.

Gavin Lambert expressed it like this:

Costumed with wonderful tongue-in-cheek furs and frippery by Adrian, Norma Shearer creates a larger-than-life portrait of a femme fatale, a seductive fake with snaky gestures, smoky laugh, accented drawl, and a pretentious cigarette holder."

On February 3, 1939, The New York Times critic raved in a long review: "It is with boundless enthusiasm, with uncritical hornpipes in the street, and wild huzzas of approval that finally, at long last, we hail the arrival of an adult picture on the local screen. As a profoundly bitter preview—profound because its bitterness wears the mask of comedy—of the trivial circumstances which will undoubtedly attend the beginning of the next World War, Idiot's Delight is as timely as tomorrow's front page.

By the very nature of its theme, (it) exposes the essential idiocy and pointlessness of militarism. The suicidal greed, the monstrous complacency toward death and destruction which are not racial, but universal; not individual, but mass phenomena, as ugly and as international as hate. As for the chief characters, they have retained their considerable, if somewhat pat, theatrical charm, and they are still Mr. Sherwood's. We are ready to suppose that the present American ending, on what can only be described as a note of defiant hooferism, with Gable pounding on the piano and Miss Shearer ecstatically "trucking" as the walls collapse, was the best that was cinematically available.

TCM.com observes: "This was the only film in which Clark Gable performed a dance number. He spent six weeks rehearsing the steps with the dance director George King and practicing at home with Carole Lombard. Because of his fear of messing it up during a take, the set was closed during the filming of this sequence. When Gable had to sing 'Puttin' on the Ritz,' he actually had to be carried off by *Les Blondes* so they saved that *[scene]* for last, in case he was injured. On the day of shooting, Lombard came to watch and was amazed that it only took one take."

The Nation was harsh: "Miss Shearer is even more pretentious than her pretentious past."

Newsweek declared, "Clark Gable, a hard-boiled hoofer, is a fine dramatization."

The Hollywood Reporter found that "Clark Gable and Norma Shearer give their brightest performances to date."

Episode 83

Clark Divorces
RIA LANGHAM

& Marries
CAROLE LOMBARD

Two views of **Clark Gable** with then-wife **Ria Langham**. *Left*, looking irritated and bored at the Santa Anita racetrack and *right*, puttin' on the Ritz in a socially pretentious setting he probably hated.

In March of 1939, the usually astute Adela Rogers St. Johns wrote a column about the breakup of the marriage of Clark Gable and Ria Langham, his second marriage.

It was subjected to ridicule among Hollywood insiders. It made Carole Lombard furious and sent Langham to bed in tears.

It gave Clark a "belly laugh." He told friends, "Adela knows better than to write such gush."

According to Adela:

The parting of the Gables makes my heart ache a little. Why did it have to happen? Why did two such swell people, both of them real, both of them deserving of happiness, have to come to the end of what seemed to all of us who knew them well, who'd been close friends, an ideal marriage? I've been sitting here looking out at trees that are bare, but that will be green again in the Spring, at lilac bushes that today are brown twigs, but that in April will be fragrance and colour once more, and trying to figure it out. You see, it was like this with the Gables. You felt a wholeness of self when they were together. They weren't sentimental or gushing. They were too modern for that. But your heart felt a little warmer because they were joined in their own way, and the world is often a lonely place and men and women were meant to be one, so that loneliness would roll back like a wave and stand trembling at the command of love. So the world, and fame, and all its petty trials and tribulations caught up with them. The very virility that had won Rhea [sic] in the beginning tortured her. The very elegance and charm that had won Clark began to smother him. And beauty drifted away and left hunger on both sides, a hunger that had sent them out to begin all over again.

Adela Rogers St-Johns with **Clark Gable**. He had been "the object of her affection" for years. Gossips said that she'd been infatuated, even obsessed, with him ever since their affair before he became a movie star.

Kirtley Baskette, a muckraking reporter for *Photoplay* magazine, had been investigating the private lives of major stars who were living together without benefit of a marriage license. Carole Lombard and Clark Gable were at the top of his list.

In the January, 1939 issue of *Photoplay*, he wrote an *exposé* entitled "Hollywood's Unmarried Husbands and Wives."

In it, he also "outed" Barbara Stanwyck and Robert Taylor, Constance Bennett and Gilbert Roland, and Charlie Chaplin and the much younger Paulette Goddard.

Baskette summed up his opinion of the Gable/Lombard liaison:

Carole Lombard is not Clark Gable's wife, either. Still, she has remodeled her whole Hollywood life for him.

> *"Nowhere has domesticity, outside the marital state, reached such a full flower as in Hollywood. Nowhere are there so many unmarried husbands and wives."*
>
> --Kirtley Baskette
> *Photoplay*

She calls him "Pappy," goes hunting with him, makes his interests dominate hers. Whoever heard of a woman in love with a man giving him a gun for Christmas? Or a man, crazy about one of the most glamourous, sophisticated and clever women in the land hanging a gasoline scooter on her Christmas tree? For Clark, Carole stopped almost overnight being a Hollywood playgirl. People are expected to change when they get married. All Clark and Carole did was strike up a Hollywood twosome. Nobody said, 'I do!' Clark Gable doesn't like nightspots or parties, social chitchat or the frothy pretensions of society. He has endured plenty of it, but it makes him fidget. Carole, quite frankly, used to eat it up. She hosted the most charming and clever parties in town. These things were the caviar and cocktails of Carole Lombard's life—before she started going with Gable. But look what happened! Clark didn't like it! Carole has practically abandoned all her Hollywood social contacts. She doesn't keep up with the girls in gossip as she used to. She doesn't throw parties that hit the headlines and the picture magazines. She and Clark are all wrapped up in each other's interests. Yes, Carole Lombard is a changed woman since she tied up with Clark Gable, but her name is still Carole Lombard.

So-called "morality groups" throughout the nation responded to the Baskette's *exposé* with outrage. They included The General Federation of Women's Clubs; the National Catholic Legion of Decency; The American Legion, the Knights of Columbus; and the Daughters of the American Revolution.

The response of Louis B. Mayer, delivered directly to Gable, was harsh: "Get a divorce, get remarried—or else I won't renew your contract."

David O. Selznick had already signed Clark for the male lead (Rhett Butler) in *Gone With the Wind*, and he began to receive mail from outraged women threatening to boycott the picture. He, too, joined the chorus of Hollywood bigwigs who wanted Clark to get a divorce and remarry.

In the aftermath of Baskette's article, Selznick's current frontrunner for Scarlett, Paulette Goddard, was dropped. His notice of dismissal was brief: "Because of the scandal, I cannot grant you the role of Scarlett O'Hara. I'm so sorry for giving you such hope. Please forgive me."

Two weeks after publication of the *Photoplay* editorial/*exposé*, Clark announced he was divorcing Langham. She was outraged, demanding that she should be the one to divorce him.

Her financial demands were tough: She wanted $300,000, the equivalent of $5 million in 2024 currency.

Mayer would lend him the money, deducting a certain percentage of it from his weekly paychecks, which had by now risen to $7,500.

Langham flew to Las Vegas, where, on March 8, 1939, she was granted a divorce by Judge William E. Orr. The court hearing lasted only four minutes.

She told the press, "Clark always knew he could divorce me at any time. But he never seemed to want to. He is a miser when it comes to money, and he knew the divorce would cost him plenty. I believe

The catalyst that finally broke **Clark Gable's** stagnant marriage to **Ria Langham** was a "call to arms" editorial in *Photoplay's* edition of March, 1939. *[Its cover, showcasing Hedy Lamarr, appears as the inset photo on the lower right.]* Citing the movie community's *blasé* indifference about marital infidelities, it enraged fans nationwide. Their protests galvanized **Louis B. Mayer** to demand that Clark divorce Ria and make Carole Lombard "an honest woman." The exposé's sensationalist and muckraking author was **Sheilah Graham**, writing under the *nom de plume* of Kirtley Baskette.

a marriage between a society woman and a male movie star has a better chance of surviving than a marriage between two top-ranking motion picture stars. I doubt very seriously his marriage to Lombard, if it comes off, will last two years…maybe not even that!"

After the divorce, Langham stuck around Hollywood for two or so years, but found that being the former Mrs. Clark Gable did not have the prestige she'd had during her marriage. Invitations dwindled down to a precious few.

For a while, she dated the ex-gangster (now movie star) George Raft—that is, when he wasn't involved with Betty Grable, Lucille Ball, or Marlene Dietrich.

Langham finally decided to return to Houston, Texas, her former residence. There, she faded from public view, but she kept up with news about Clark through newspaper clippings of his exploits. She shared them with her children and her grandchildren, often talking about "the glory days of Old Hollywood."

A forgotten figure, she died on September 24, 1966 and was buried the Glenwood Cemetery in Houston. Clark had died six years earlier.

Left photo: **Poor, prim, pretentious Ria**: Her dress code evoked a Hollywood that had already gone out of favor and out of style. Think Mary Pickford and Douglas Fairbanks in all their frumpy finery during the glory days of Pickfair.

More hip, more avant-garde, and with a better sense of humor was the girl cited as having "the foulest potty-mouth in Hollywood" *(right photo)* **Carole Lombard.**

***

When the time came for Clark to marry Lombard, neither of them wanted it to become a press event. They decided to slip out of town and drive to Kingman, Arizona, population 2,000.

They drove there with Otto Winkler, who worked for Howard Strickling at MGM. He would also be Clark's best man.

When they applied at the town hall for a license, the young woman who greeted them almost fainted at seeing Clark Gable. He was her favorite movie star.

On the marriage license, Clark gave his age as 38, whereas Lombard listed hers as 29, shaving one year off her actual age. Winkler had already made arrangement for the modest ceremony to be performed at the small First Methodist Episcopal Church. Since Lombard had been married before, she felt "virginal white" was not for her, so she appeared in a grey flannel suit.

After the brief ceremony, Clark phoned to announce the marriage to Lombard's mother. "This is your new son-in-law talking, Mom."

The newlyweds had to get back to Hollywood, 800 miles away. Winkler, in his blue DeSoto coupe, was the driver.

One of the movie industry's premier but oft-ridiculed columnists, **Louella Parsons** (1881-1972) was hired by newspaper mogul **William Randolph Hearst**, in part because she helped him cover up the killing of Thomas Ince, and partly because she lavishly (and constantly, in print) praised Hearst's mistress, **Marion Davies**. During her folksy but flamboyant heyday, her columns were read by 20 million people in 400 newspapers worldwide. She remained Queen of Hollywood until the arrival of Hedda Hopper, with whom she feuded viciously for years.

Here's **Louella** interviewing **Lana Turner** about her skills at boosting the morale of American soldiers en route to the battlefields of Europe and the Pacific.

Winkler called Strickling at MGM to announce the news to the press. Louella Parsons never forgave them for not letting her have the scoop.

On the road back to California they stopped at a roadside Harvey House Restaurant for their wedding dinner. They ordered juicy steaks and sat at the counter, preferring it to being seated at a table.

Patrons instantly recognized them and kept interrupting their meal to ask for autographs. For the first time in her life, she wrote "Carole Gable."

At three o'clock in the morning, they arrived at her residence in Bel Air. They had to get some sleep, since a press conference had been set up for that very morning.

The press showed up *en masse,* all except for Louella Parsons. She later said "I don't attend press conferences. I'm a scoop artist."

The house on Gable and Lombard's ranch near Encino, displayed here as a commemorative postcard for his fans. Publicists soon began referring to it as "**The House of the Two Gables.**"

Secretly, Lombard told Winkler, "I am in love with Clark. It's not just for the sex. I can't say he's a helluva good lay. I've had better."

The newlyweds had already made plans to move out of Bel Air and into a ranch at Encino in the San Fernando Valley. Lombard had bought it from the director Raoul Walsh, paying him $50,000 of her own money, since Clark's bank account had been flattened by his divorce.

The white brick farmhouse had been built in 1926 and stood on twenty acres of undeveloped land with a wide variety of trees, predominantly orange but also fig, apricot, peach, plum, avocado, and eucalyptus.

On their first night by the fireplace of their new home, he said, "I plan to spend the happiest years of my life here with you. I'm about to play Rhett Butler. I know the role will make or break me. If I'm laughed off the screen, I'll still be happy to return here with you and fade into oblivion."

"Pa," as she'd nicknamed him. "You and I would be perfectly cast as has-beens growing old together."

"What will you do when I can no longer cut the mustard?"

"Don't worry about it. You've got forty good years ahead of you…at least."

***

Clark Gable and **Carole Lombard** sit outside, covered with blankets against the cold winds blowing over their ranchland. Both stars had found the love of their lives.

Regrettably, some of the great love affairs in history—or in Hollywood—are destined to end tragically.

Darwin Porter

As a precocious nine-year-old, **Darwin Porter** began meeting entertainers through his mother, Hazel, a charismatic Southern girl whose husband had died in World War II. Migrating from the Depression-ravaged valleys of western North Carolina to Miami Beach during its most ebullient heyday, Hazel became a personal assistant to the vaudeville comedienne **Sophie Tucker**, the kind-hearted "Last of the Red Hot Mamas."

Loosely supervised by his mother, Darwin was regularly dazzled by the likes of **Judy Garland, Dinah Shore, Frank Sinatra, Ronald Reagan** (at the time near the end of his Hollywood gig), and **Marilyn Monroe**. Each of them made it a point, whenever they were in Miami (either on or off the record), to visit and pay their respects to "Miss Sophie."

At the University of Miami, Darwin edited the school newspaper, raising its revenues, through advertising and public events, to unheard-of new levels. He met and interviewed **Eleanor Roosevelt** and later invited her, as part of a sponsored event he crafted, to spend a day ("Eleanor Roosevelt Day") at the university, and to his delight, she accepted. Years later, in Manhattan, during her work as a human rights activist, he escorted her, at her request, to many public functions.

On another occasion, he invited **Lucille Ball and Desi Arnaz**, then at the pinnacle of their fame and popularity, to the University. On campus, after the photographers and fans departed, Lucille launched a bitter attack on her husband, accusing him of having had sex the previous night with two showgirls. Because of that and other upsets that unfolded that day, Darwin learned early in his life that Lucille Ball and Desi Arnaz were definitely not Ricky and Lucy Ricardo.

After his graduation, Darwin, in a graceful transition from his work as editor of the University's newspaper and his sponsorship by **Wilson Hicks** (Photo Editor and then Executive Editor of Life magazine) became a Bureau Chief of The Miami Herald (the youngest in that publication's history) assigned to its branch in Key West. At the time the island outpost was an avant-garde literary mecca and—thanks to the Cuban missile crisis—a flash point of the Cold War.

Key West had been the site of Harry S Truman's "Winter White House" and Truman returned a few months before his death for a final visit. He invited young Darwin for "early morning walks" where he used the young emissary of The Miami Herald to "set the record straight."

Through Truman, Darwin was introduced and later joined the staff of **Senator George Smathers** of Florida. Smathers' best friend was a young senator, **John F. Kennedy.** Through "Gorgeous George," as Smathers was known in the Senate, Darwin got to meet Jack and Jacqueline in Palm Beach. He later wrote two books about them—The Kennedys, All the Gossip Unfit to Print, and one of his all-time bestsellers, Jacqueline Kennedy Onassis—A Life Beyond Her Wildest Dreams. (A commemorative new edition was released in 2022 as JKO: Her Tumultuous Life & Her Love Affairs).

Buttressed by his status as The Miami Herald's Key West Bureau Chief, Darwin met, interviewed, and often befriended **Tennessee Williams. Ernest Hemingway, Tallulah Bankhead, Gore Vidal, Truman Capote, Carson McCullers,** and a gaggle of other internationally famous writers and entertainers: **Cary Grant, Rock Hudson, Marlon Brando, Montgomery Clift, Susan Hayward, Warren Beatty, Christopher Isherwood, Anne Bancroft, Angela Lansbury,** and **William Inge.**

Eventually transferred to Manhattan, Darwin worked for a decade in television advertising with the producer and arts-industry socialite **Stanley**

Yesterday, When He Was Young

DARWIN PORTER
A social historian fascinated by biographies and the ironies of the American Experience.

Mills Haggart. In addition to some speculative ventures associated with Marilyn Monroe, they also jointly produced TV commercials that included testimonials from **Joan Crawford** (then feverishly promoting Pepsi-Cola); **Ronald Reagan** (General Electric); and **Debbie Reynolds** (Singer sewing machines). Other personalities they promoted, each delivering televised sales pitches, included **Louis Armstrong, Lena Horne, Rosalind Russell, William Holden,** and **Arlene Dahl,** each of them hawking a commercial product.

Beginning in the early 1960s, Darwin joined forces with the then-fledgling **Arthur Frommer** organization, playing a key role in researching and writing more than 50 titles and defining the style and values that later emerged as the world's leading travel guidebooks, **The Frommer Guides.** Darwin's particular journalistic expertise on Europe, New England, California, and the Caribbean eventually propelled him into authorship of (depending on the era and whatever crises were brewing at the time), between 70 and 80% of their titles. Even during the research of his travel guides, he continued to interview show-biz celebrities, discussing their triumphs, feuds, and frustrations. At this point in their lives, many were retired and reclusive. Darwin either pursued them (sometimes though local tourist offices) or encountered them randomly as part of his extensive travels. **Ava Gardner, Lana Turner, Hedy Lamarr, Ingrid Bergman, Ethel Merman, Andy Warhol, Elizabeth Taylor, Marlene Dietrich, Bette Davis**, **Judy Garland,** and **Paul Newman** were particularly insightful.

Porter's biographies—at this writing, they number sixty-three— have won thirty first prize or "runner-up to first prize" awards at literary festivals in cities or regions which include New England, New York, Los Angeles, Hollywood, San Francisco, Florida, California, and Paris.

Darwin, also a magazine columnist, can be heard at regular intervals as a radio and podcast commentator, reviewing the ironies of celebrities, tabloid culture, politics, and scandal.

A resident of New York City, where he spent years within the social orbit of the Queen of Off-Broadway (the eccentric and very temperamental philanthropist, **Lucille Lortel),** Darwin is currently at work on a series of books with eyebrow-raising revelations about the dazzling personalities who kept the lights sparkling both On and Off Broadway in the 70s and 80s.

Danforth Prince

Danforth as a Young Turk

For years, Danforth Prince was one of the "Young Turks" of the post-millennium publishing industry. He's president and founder of Blood Moon Productions, a firm devoted to researching, salvaging, compiling, and marketing the oral histories of America's entertainment industry.

One of Prince's famous predecessors, the late Lyle Stuart, founder of Barricade Press, was self-described as "the last publisher in America with guts." Stuart once defined Prince as "one of his natural successors." In 1956, that then-novice maverick launched himself with $8,000 he'd won in a libel ludgment against gossip columnist Walter Winchell. It was Stuart who published Linda Lovelace's two memoirs—*Ordeal* and *Out of Bondage.*

"I like to see someone following in my footsteps in the 21st Century," Stuart told Prince. "You publish scandalous biographies. I did, too. My books on J. Edgar Hoover, Jacqueline Kennedy Onassis, and Barbara Hutton stirred up beehives. You do, too."

Prince launched his career in journalism in the 1970s at the Paris Bureau of *The New York Times*. In the early '80s, he resigned to join Darwin Porter in the research, development, and publishing of various titles (including *Frommer's France* and *Frommer's Paris*) within *The Frommer Guides.* As a collaborative team, they reviewed the travel scenes of more than 50 nations for Simon & Schuster. Authoritative and comprehensive, the guides they spearheaded were perceived as indispensable "travel bibles" for millions of readers with recommendations (hotels, restaurants, shopping, nightlife, and "what to see and do" for the nations of Western Europe, the Caribbean,

Bermuda, New England, The Bahamas, Georgia, the Carolinas, and California.

Prince, with Porter, is also the co-author of many celebrity biographies, each configured as a title within Blood Moon's Babylon series. These have included *Hollywood Babylon—It's Back; Hollywood Babylon Strikes Again; The Kennedys: All the Gossip Unfit to Print; Frank Sinatra, the Boudoir Singer,* and *Elizabeth Taylor, There is Nothing Like a Dame.*

Prince, in tandem with Porter, has also co-authored four books on film criticism, along with provocative "postmodern" biographies of, among many others, Lana Turner and Peter O'Toole. With Porter, he also co-authored *Pink Triangle: The Feuds and Private Lives of Tennessee Williams, Gore Vidal, Truman Capote, and Famous Members of their Entourages.*

Prince, a graduate of Hamilton College and a native of Easton and Bethlehem, Pennsylvania, is the president and founder (in 1996) of the Georgia Literary Association, and of the Porter and Prince Corporation. Founded in 1983, the Porter and Prince Corp. produced dozens of travel titles for both Prentice Hall and John Wiley & Sons. In 2011, he was named "Publisher of the Year" by a consortium of literary critics and marketers spearheaded by the J.M. Northern Media Group.

According to Prince, "Blood Moon provides the luxurious illusion that a reader is a perpetual guest at some gossipy dinner party populated with brilliant but occasionally self-delusional figures from bygone eras of the American Experience. Our success at salvaging, documenting, and articulating the (till now) orally transmitted histories of the Entertainment Industry—in ways that have never been seen before—is one of the most distinctive aspects of our backlist."

During the years he published in collaboration with the National Book Network, he electronically documented some of the controversies associated with his stewardship of Blood Moon. From that collaboration emerged more than fifty videotaped documentaries, book trailers, public speeches, and TV or radio interviews. Any of these can be watched, without charge, by performing a search for Ðanforth Prince" on YouTube.com; checking him out on Facebook *[either "Danforth Prince" or "Blood Moon Productions]*, on Twitter (now X) (#BloodyandLunar); or by clicking on BloodMoonProductions.com.

During the rare moments when he isn't writing, editing, neurosing about, or promoting Blood Moon, he works out at a New York City gym, rescues stray animals, talks to strangers, and maintains the physical plant and gardens of his historic home in St. George, Staten Island.

Since 2004, under Danforth's stewardship, Blood Moon titles have been awarded dozens of nationally recognized literary prizes. They've included both silver and bronze medals from the IPPY (Independent Publishers Assn.) Awards, four nominations and two Honorable Mentions for BOOK OF THE YEAR from Forward Reviews; nominations from the Ben Franklin Awards; and Awards and Honorable Mentions from the New England, the Los Angeles, the Paris, the New York, the San Francisco, and the Hollywood Book Festivals. Two of its titles have been Grand Prize Winners for Best Summer Reading, as defined by the Beach Book Awards.

Feisty, Scrappy, Prolific and Independent, We're Blood Moon Productions.

Blood Moon Productions originated in 1997 as *The Georgia Literary Association*, a vehicle for the promotion of obscure writers from America's Deep South. Today, Blood Moon is based in New York City, and staffed with writers who previously devoted their energies to **THE FROMMER GUIDES**, a trusted name in travel publishing.

Blood Moon has demonstrated a remarkable knack for publicity. Its titles have been widely reviewed by the U.S. and U.K's broadsheet newspapers and/or tabloids, and four of its biographies were extensively serialized by the largest-readership publications of the U.K., *The Mail on Sunday* and *The Sunday Times*. Other serializations of Blood Moon's titles have appeared in Australia's *Women's Weekly* and *The Australian*.

Our corporate mission involves researching and salvaging the oral histories of America's entertainment industry--those "off the record" events which at the time might have been defined as either indecent or libelous, but which are now pertinent to America's understanding of its origins and cultural roots.

The pages that follow document a few of the other guides and show-biz biograpies we've written and produced. Thanks for your interest, and Happy Reading.

Blood Moon Productions:
Challenging the Status Quo's Beliefs about Celebrity and Fame

Are you tired of GenZ Actors, and worried that you can't get enough of Clark? FEAR NOT! Two additional volumes documenting his status as King of H-wood are breathlessly waiting in the wings, scheduled for production SOON:

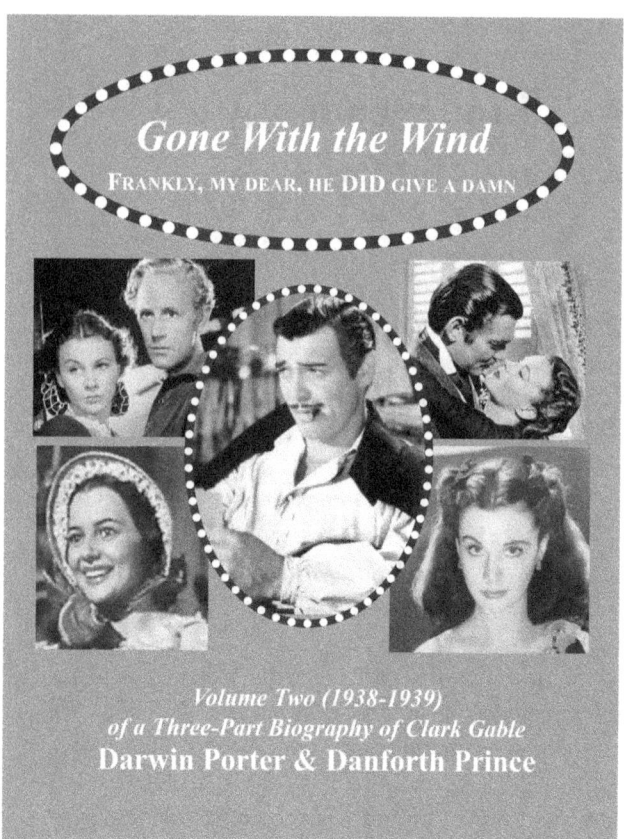

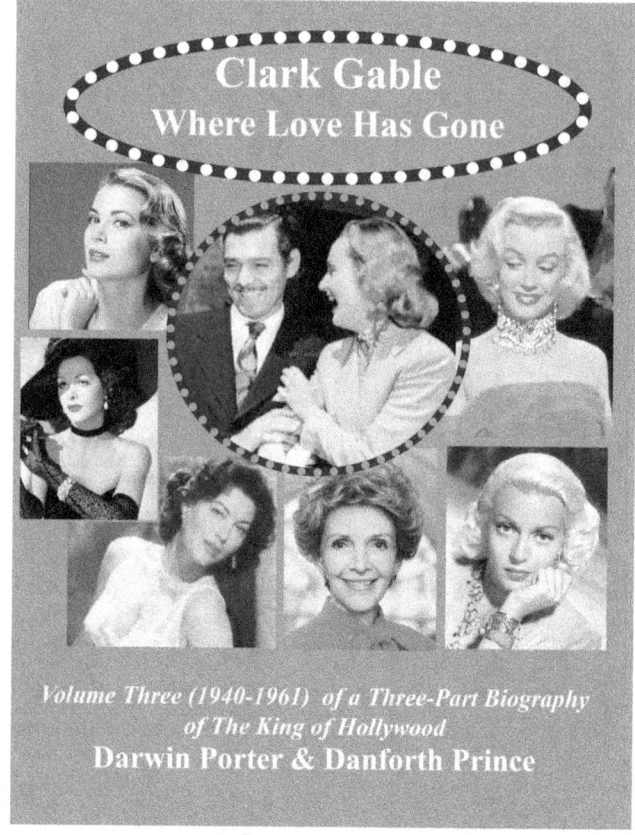

COMING SOON
Volume Two (1938-1939):

Everything you never dared to ask about the story behind the stories of the most profitable movie of the 20th Century

GONE WITH THE WIND, FRANKLY MY DEAR, HE DID GIVE A DAMN

COMING SOON
Volume Three (1940-1961):

After the death of Lombard, the King carries on with a daunting set of show-biz adversaries, embraced by a mind-bending menage of feminine charms. The 20th Century was never, after that, the same.

CLARK GABLE, WHERE LOVE HAS GONE

GABLE! He's here, alive and thriving, the beneficiary of years of research from the creative team at Blood Moon. So complicated is his story that no single tome can contain all that's needed to say in this ULTIMATE OVERVIEW of CLARK, GLORIOUSLY GABLED, the focal point of a major trilogy spearheaded by film historian Darwin Porter.

WHAT DO WE RECOMMEND AS A "PREQUEL," before you dive into our coverage of Clark as Rhett Butler in GONE WITH THE WIND? It would be our biography of VIVIEN LEIGH, the tragic Englishwoman forever after identified as:

SCARLETT O'HARA,

DESPERATELY IN LOVE WITH HEATHCLIFF,

TOGETHER ON THE ROAD TO HELL

Here, for the first time, is a biography that raises the curtain on the secret lives of **Lord Laurence Olivier**, often cited as the finest actor in the history of England, and **Vivien Leigh**, who immortalized herself with her Oscar-winning portrayals of Scarlett O'Hara in *Gone With the Wind*, and as Blanche DuBois in Tennessee Williams' *A Streetcar Named Desire*.

Dashing and "impossibly handsome," Laurence Olivier was pursued by the most dazzling luminaries, male and female, of the movie and theater worlds.

Lord Olivier's beautiful and brilliant but emotionally disturbed wife (Viv to her lovers) led a tumultuous off-the-record life whose paramours ranged from the A-list celebrities to men she selected randomly off the street. But none of the brilliant roles depicted by Lord and Lady Olivier, on stage or on screen, ever matched the power and drama of personal dramas which wavered between Wagnerian opera and Greek tragedy. Damn You, Scarlett O'Hara is the definitive and most revelatory portrait ever published of the most talented and tormented actor and actress of the 20th century. Darwin Porter is the principal author of this seminal work.

"The folks over at TMZ would have had a field day tracking Laurence Olivier and Vivien Leigh with flip cameras in hand. Damn You, Scarlett O'Hara can be a dazzling read, the prose unmannered and instantly digestible. The authors' ability to pile scandal atop scandal, seduction after seduction, can be impossible to resist."

—THE WASHINGTON TIMES

DAMN YOU, SCARLETT O'HARA

THE PRIVATE LIFES OF LAURENCE OLIVIER AND VIVIEN LEIGH

Darwin Porter and Roy Moseley

Winner of four distinguished literary awards, this is the best biography of Vivien Leigh and Laurence Olivier ever published, with hundreds of insights into the London Theatre, the role of the Oliviers in the politics of World War II, and the passion, fury, and frustration of their lives together as actors in the West End, on Broadway, and in Hollywood.

ISBN 978-1-936003-15-0   Hardcover, 708 pages, with about a hundred photos.

AS THEY RELATE TO BLOOD MOON'S PUBLISHING AGENDAS

Let's talk about

Twosomes, Twins, Triplets, and (GASP) Quintets that we, as content creators, have birthed.

Blood Moon has been cited as "dauntingly prolific," with a knack for multiple children. Here are some of our titles bound together into "matched sets," Each is described under the "OUR BOOKS" tab of www.BloodMoonProductions.com

LUCY X2
(I.E., THE RICARDOS, INCLUDING DESI)

A JUICY TRIPTYCH OF BABYLONS

TRIPLE-PLAY GUIDES TO GLBTQ FILMS

OUR DOUBLE DOSE OF DONALD MEANS DOUBLE THE FUN!

THE FONDAS: TRIPLE EXPOSURE IN TWO VOLUMES

BOGIE X2: WE'VE COVERED HIS YOUTHFUL INDISCRETIONS AND HIS VERY ADULT INDISCRETIONS, TOO.

GOMORRAH ON THE POTOMAC
(A ROLLICKING PRESIDENTIAL QUINTET)

LUCILLE BALL & DESI ARNAZ
BECAME THE MOST CELEBRATED DUO IN THE HISTORY OF TELEVISION

Half of America gathered every Monday night around the little black box in their living rooms to watch the antics of Lucy and Ricky Ricardo, a Cuban bandleader with his wacky, high-spirited wife.

The early struggles of Lucy and Desi were epic. As a girl, she at times was literally chained in her backyard in Jamestown, New York. As a teenager, she broke away and earned a reputation as "The Jamestown hussy," riding around with Johnny DeVita, a local hoodlum.

Born to wealth and privilege in Cuba, Desi, at the age of twelve, was escorted to the local bordello by his father to lose his virginity.

His family lost everything in the Cuban Revolution and fled to America. In Miami, Desi got a job cleaning out canary cages. He was eventually hired by bandleader Xavier Cugat because, "I beat hell out of those Afro-Cuban drums."

Meanwhile, in Manhattan, Lucy was struggling to break into show business, hustling "sugar daddies" and stage-door Johnnies who gave her money and gifts. Once, when desperate, she became a nude model. "A gal's gotta eat."

In the 1930s, she made it to Hollywood and worked making films for RKO. The executives used her as a gussied-up hooker to "entertain" out-of-town film exhibitors.

[Ultimately, she got her revenge. In one of the most ironic "fiscal revolutions" in show-biz history, she bought the studio.]

Drifting to Hollywood, Desi spotted Lucy on a sound stage "dressed like a two-dollar whore who had been badly beaten by her pimp." Their tempestuous marriage, characterized by long separations, staggered along for two decades.

By the early 1950s, the careers of both Desi and Lucy had headed south. There was a lot of resistance among TV executives who objected to his Cuban accent. But *I Love Lucy* was launched nevertheless and shot up in the ratings like a rocket, morphing into the most successful sitcom in TV history.

"With gold arriving in wheelbarrows" (Desi's words), they bought the four-block RKO Studios. Desilu Productions was launched, becoming the largest motion picture and television studio in the world.

In 1960, after their divorce, Lucy appraised her husband: "He is a Jekyll and Hyde type. He drinks, gambles, and chases the broads from thirteen to thirty, even Carrie Fisher. He's awash in broads, lots of booze, and that gay actor, Cesar Romero, is his devoted slave. Desi is destructive, but always building something. If it's big, he has to break it down."

"Love?" she asked. "I was always falling in love with the wrong man. Even Desi."

Desi, too, summed up his many years of marriage: "We were anything but Lucy and Ricky Ricardo on the tube. Those guys had nothing to do with us. Lucy and I dreamed of success, fame, and fortune. Guess what? ***It all led to hell.***"

LUCILLE BALL & DESI ARNAZ

THEY WEREN'T LUCY AND RICKY RICARDO

VOLUME ONE (1911-1960)
OF A TWO-PART BIOGRAPHY

Darwin Porter and Danforth Prince
ISBN 978-1-936003-71-6
Softcover, 530 pages, with photos,
available everywhere now

THE SAD & TRAGIC ENDING OF LUCILLE BALL

VOLUME TWO (1961-1989)
OF A TWO-PART BIOGRAPHY

Darwin Porter and Danforth Prince
ISBN 978-1-936003-80-8
Softcover, 550 pages, with photos, available
everywhere now

Judy Garland & Liza Minnelli

Too Many Damn Rainbows

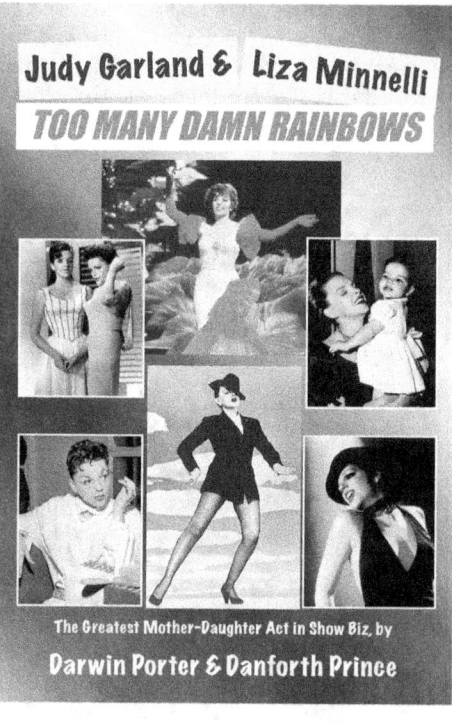

Judy and Liza were the greatest, most colorful, and most tragic mother-daughter saga in show biz history. They live, laugh, and weep again in the tear-soaked pages of this remarkable biography. Darwin Porter and Danforth Prince have compiled a compelling "post-modern" spin.

According to Liza, "My mother—hailed as the world's greatest entertainer—lived eighty lives during her short time with us."

Their memorable stories unfold through eyewitness accounts of the typhoons that engulfed them. They swing across glittery landscapes of euphoria and glory, detailing the betrayals and treachery which the duo encountered almost daily. There were depressions "as deep as the Mariana Trench," suicide attempts, and obsessive identifications on deep psychological levels with roles that include Judy's Vicky Lester in *A Star is Born* (1954) and Liza's Sally Bowles in *Cabaret* (1972).

Lesser known are the jealous actress-to-actress rivalries. Fueled by klieg lights and rivers of negative publicity, they sprouted like malevolent mushrooms on steroids.

As Judy faded into the 1960s, Liza roaringly emerged as a star in her own right. "I did it my way," Liza said. She survived the whirlwinds of her mother's drug addiction with a yen for choosing all the wrong men in patterns that weirdly evoked those of Judy herself.

For millions of fans, Judy will forever remain the cheerful adolescent (Dorothy) skipping along a yellow brick road toward the other side of the rainbow. Liza followed her down that hallucinogenic path, searching for the childhood, the security, and the love that eluded her.

Judy Garland, an icon whose memory is permanently etched into the American psyche, continues to thrive as a cult goddess. Revered by thousands of die-hard fans, she's the most poignant example of both the manic and depressive (some say "schizophrenic") sides of the Hollywood myth.

Deep in her 70s, Liza is still with us, too, nursing memories of her former acclaim and her first visit as a little girl to her parents at MGM, the "Dream Factory," during the Golden Age of Hollywood.

Judy Garland & Liza Minnelli: Too Many Damn Rainbows
Darwin Porter & Danforth Prince
Softcover, 6" x 9", with hundreds of photos.   ISBN 9781936003693
Available Everywhere Now

The Seductive Sapphic Exploits of
Mercedes de Acosta
Hollywood's Greatest Lover

IF YOU ASSUMED THAT THE GREATEST LOVERS ARE MEN, some of the most famous "cult goddesses" of the early- and mid-20th-Century might emphatically disagree.

At Magnolia House, in the final years of her life, the celebrated, notorious, and once-fabled Spanish beauty, **MERCEDES DE ACOSTA** (1892-1968) was a frequent visitor. To Darwin Porter, she confessed and recited fabulously indiscreet stories about her romantic same-sex exploits among the theatrical and cinematic elite of New York, London, Paris, and Hollywood.

*It reveals "Sapphic Standards" from the heyday of Silent Film and the early Talkies that no other book—even her own (*Here Lies the Heart, *published in 1960)— ever dared to make public.*

Mercedes de Acosta's love affairs were with women, each a figurehead in art, the theater, and the filmmaking and literary scenes. They included Greta Garbo, Marlene Dietrich, Nazimova, Gertrude Stein, Alice B. Toklas, Eva Le Gallienne, Tallulah Bankhead, Jeanne Eagels, Katharine Cornell, Eleanora Duse, Isadora Duncan, and both of Valentino's wives. This is probably the best portrait of *avant-garde* Broadway and early 20th-century filmmaking ever published.

Read all about it in the most recent installment of Blood Moon's MAGNOLIA HOUSE SERIES

The Seductive Sapphic Exploits of
Mercedes de Acosta
Hollywood's Greatest Lover

Darwin Porter and Danforth Prince   ISBN 978-1-936003-75-4.
A pithy, photo-packed softcover with 474 pages and many dozens of photos
available now from Ingram's Lightning Source and Amazon.com

TIRED of HORROR STORIES ABOUT DONALD TRUMP?
Cheer Up, because here's
BOOK AGENDA NEWS about Blood Moon Productions'
NEWEST BOOK RELEASES--Biographies to Die For!!!
CELLULOID NOSTALGIA, HOLLYWOOD GLAMOR, & SEX
THEY'RE BACK!!!

Blood Moon proudly announces the release of radical new biographies of two of the sexiest stars of Hollywood's Dream Machine:

LANA TURNER & ROCK HUDSON

Drawing on firsthand interviews and on information never before published, each is the most complete, comprehensive, and unvarnished portrait of these great American movie stars ever published.

LANA TURNER: Everything that no one ever told you about The Sweater Girl, Hollywood's OTHER most famous blonde, LANA TURNER, Hearts & Diamonds Take All. Available everywhere now. Softcover, 6" x 9";.622 pages with hundreds of photos and dozens of unvarnished insights into LUSCIOUS LANA. ISBN 978-1-936003-53-2, and

ROCK HUDSON: A former naval ensign & truck driver, Roy Fitzgerald charmed every casting director in Hollywood (and movie-goers throughout America) as the mega-star we most wanted to share PILLOW TALK with. ROCK HUDSON EROTIC FIRE--a biography loaded with never-before published information about America's Sexiest and Most Secretive All-American Heartthrob, delectably available for consumption by enquiring minds on 32nd anniversary of his death in November of 2017. Softcover, 6" x 9", 650 pages with hundreds of photos. ISBN 978-1-936003-55-6.

For more information, click on
BloodMoonProductions.com

or contact
DanforthPrince@gmail.com

THIS BOOK ILLUSTRATES WHY *GENTLEMEN PREFER BLONDES*, AND WHY MARILYN MONROE WAS TOO DANGEROUS TO BE ALLOWED TO GO ON LIVING.

Less than an hour after the discovery of Marilyn Monroe's corpse in Brentwood, a flood of theories, tainted evidence, and conflicting testimonies began pouring out into the public landscape.

Filled with rage, hysteria, and depression, "and fed up with Jack's lies, Bobby's lies," Marilyn sought revenge and mass vindication. Her revelations at an imminent press conference could have toppled political dynasties and destroyed criminal empires. Marilyn had to be stopped…

Into this steamy cauldron of deceit, Marilyn herself emerges as a most unreliable witness during the weeks leading up to her murder. Her own deceptions, vanities, and self-delusion poured toxic accelerants on an already raging fire.

"This is the best book about Marilyn Monroe ever published."
—**David Hartnell**, Recipient, in 2011, of New Zealand's Order of Merit (MNZM) for services to the entertainment industry, as defined by Her Majesty, Queen Elizabeth II.

Winner of literary awards from the New York, Hollywood, and San Francisco Book Festivals

"Darwin Porter is fearless, honest and a great read. He minces no words. If the truth makes you wince and honesty offends your sensibility, stay away. It's been said that he deals in muck because he can't libel the dead. Well, it's about time someone started telling the truth about the dead and being honest about just what happened to get us in the mess in which we're in. If libel is lying, then Porter is so completely innocent as to deserve an award. In all of his works he speaks only to the truth, and although he is a hard teacher and task master, he's one we ignore at our peril. To quote Gore Vidal, power is not a toy we give to someone for being good. If we all don't begin to investigate where power and money really are in the here and now, we deserve what we get. Yes, Porter names names. The reader will come away from the book knowing just who killed Monroe. Porter rather brilliantly points to a number of motives, but leaves it to the reader to surmise exactly what happened at the rainbow's end, just why Marilyn was killed. And, of course, why we should be careful of getting exactly what we want. It's a very long tumble from the top."

—ALAN PETRUCELLI, Examiner.com, May 13, 2012

MARILYN: DON'T EVEN DREAM ABOUT TOMORROW
SEX, LIES, MURDER, AND THE GREAT COVER-UP, BY DARWIN PORTER
ISBN 978-1-936003-79-2   A Revised Edition of Darwin Porter's Investigative Classic from 2012
MARILYN AT RAINBOW'S END

CARRIE FISHER & DEBBIE REYNOLDS
PRINCESS LEIA & UNSINKABLE TAMMY IN HELL

It's history's first comprehensive, unauthorized overview of one of the greatest mother-daughter acts in showbiz history, Debbie Reynolds ("hard as nails and with more balls than any five guys I've ever known") and her talented, often traumatized daughter, Carrie Fisher ("one of the smartest, hippest chicks in Hollywood"). Evolving for decades under the unrelenting glare of public scrutiny, each became a world-class symbol of the social and cinematic tastes that prevailed during their heydays as celebrity icons in Hollywood.

It's a scandalous saga of the ferociously loyal relationship of the "boop-boop-a-doop" girl with her intergalactic STAR WARS daughter, and their iron-willed, "true grit" battles to out-race changing tastes in Hollywood.

Loaded with revelations about "who was doing what to whom" during the final gasps of Golden Age Hollywood, it's an All-American story about the price of glamour, career-related pain, family anguish, romantic betrayals, lingering guilt, and the volcanic shifts that affected a scrappy, mother-daughter team—and everyone else who ever loved the movies.

"Feeling misunderstood by the younger (female) members of your gene pool? This is the Hollywood exposé every grandmother should give to her granddaughter, a roadmap like Debbie Reynolds might have offered to Billie Lourd."
—Marnie O'Toole

"Hold onto your hats, the "bad boys" of Blood Moon Productions are back. This time, they have an exhaustively researched and highly readable account of the greatest mother-daughter act in the history of show business: Debbie Reynolds and Carrie (Princess Leia) Fisher. If celebrity gossip and inside dirt is your secret desire, check it out. This is a fabulous book that we heartily recommend. It will not disappoint. We rate it worthy of four stars."
—MAJ Glenn MacDonald, U.S. Army Reserve (Retired), © MilitaryCorruption.com

"How is a 1950s-era movie star, (TAMMY) supposed to cope with her postmodern, substance-abusing daughter (PRINCESS LEIA), the rebellious, high-octane byproduct of Rock 'n Roll, Free Love, and postwar Hollywood's most scandal-soaked marriage? Read about it here, in Blood Moon's unauthorized double exposé about how Hollywood's toughest (and savviest) mother-daughter team maneuvered their way through shifting definitions of fame, reconciliation, and fortune."
—Donna McSorley

Winner of the coveted "Best Biography" Award from the 2018
New York Book Festival

CARRIE FISHER & DEBBIE REYNOLDS,
UNSINKABLE TAMMY & PRINCESS LEIA IN HELL
Darwin Porter & Danforth Prince

630 pages Softcover with photos. Now online and in bookstores everywhere
ISBN 978-1-936003-57-0

LANA TURNER

THE SWEATER GIRL, CELLULOID VENUS, SEX NYMPH TO THE G.I.s WHO WON WORLD WAR II, AND HOLLYWOOD'S OTHER MOST NOTORIOUS BLONDE

BEAUTIFUL AND BAD, HER FULL STORY HAS NEVER BEEN TOLD. UNTIL NOW!

Lana Turner was the most scandalous, most copied, and most gossiped-about actress in Hollywood. When her abusive Mafia lover was murdered in her house, every newspaper in the Free World described the murky dramas with something approaching hysteria.

Blood Moon's salacious but empathetic new biography exposes the public and private dramas of the girl who changed the American definition of what it REALLY means to be a blonde.

Here's how CALIFORNIA BOOKWATCH and THE MIDWEST BOOK REVIEW described the mega-celebrity as revealed in this book:

"Lana Turner: Hearts and Diamonds Take All belongs on the shelves of any collection strong in movie star biographies in general and Hollywood evolution in particular, and represents no lightweight production, appearing on the 20th anniversary of Lana Turner's death to provide a weighty survey packed with new information about her life.

"One would think that just about everything to be known about The Sweater Girl would have already appeared in print, but it should be noted that Lana Turner: Hearts and Diamonds Take All offers many new revelations not just about Turner, but about the movie industry in the aftermath of World War II.

"From Lana's introduction of a new brand of covert sexuality in women's movies to her scandalous romances among the stars, her extreme promiscuity, her search for love, and her notorious flings - even her involvement in murder - are all probed in a revealing account of glamour and movie industry relationships that bring Turner and her times to life.

"Some of the greatest scandals in Hollywood history are intricately detailed on these pages, making this much more than another survey of her life and times, and a 'must have' pick for any collection strong in Hollywood history in general, gossip and scandals and the real stories behind them, and Lana Turner's tumultuous career, in particular."

Lana Turner, Hearts & Diamonds Take All
Winner of the coveted "Best Biography" Award from the San Francisco Book Festival

By Darwin Porter and Danforth Prince
Softcover, 622 pages, with photos. ISBN 978-1-936003-53-2
Available everywhere, online and in bookstores.

DONALD TRUMP
WAS THE MAN WHO WOULD BE KING

This is the most famous book about our incendiary ex-President you've probably never heard of.

Winner of three respected literary awards, and released three months before the Presidential elections of 2016, it's an entertainingly packaged, artfully salacious bombshell, a scathingly historic overview of America during its 2016 election cycle, a portrait unlike anything ever published on CANDIDATE DONALD and the climate in which he thrived and massacred his political rivals.

Its volcanic, much-suppressed release during the heat and venom of the 2016 Presidential campaign has already been heralded by the Midwestern Book Review, California Book Watch, the Seattle Gay News, the staunchly right-wing WILS-AM radio, and also by the editors at the most popular Seniors' magazine in Florida, BOOMER TIMES, which designated it as one of their BOOKS OF THE MONTH.

TRUMPOCALYPSE: *"Donald Trump: The Man Who Would Be King* is recommended reading for all sides, no matter what political stance is being adopted: Republican, Democrat, or other.

"One of its driving forces is its ability to synthesize an unbelievable amount of information into a format and presentation which blends lively irony with outrageous observations, entertaining even as it presents eye-opening information in a format accessible to all.

"Politics dovetail with American obsessions and fascinations with trends, figureheads, drama, and sizzling news stories, but blend well with the observations of sociologists, psychologists, politicians, and others in a wide range of fields who lend their expertise and insights to create a much broader review of the Trump phenomena than a more casual book could provide.

"The result is a 'must read' for any American interested in issues of race, freedom, equality, and justice—and for any non-American who wonders just what is going on behind the scenes in this country's latest election debacle."

Diane Donovan, Senior Editor, California Bookwatch

DONALD TRUMP, THE MAN WHO WOULD BE KING
WINNER OF "BEST BIOGRAPHY" AWARDS FROM BOOK FESTIVALS IN
NEW YORK, CALIFORNIA, AND FLORIDA
by Darwin Porter and Danforth Prince
Softcover, with 822 pages and hundreds of photos. ISBN 978-1-936003-51-8.

Available now from Ingram, Amazon.com and other purveyors, worldwide.

LINDA LOVELACE
INSIDE LINDA LOVELACE'S DEEP THROAT
Degradation, Porno Chic, and the Rise of Feminism

The most comprehensive biography ever written of an adult entertainment star, her tormented relationship with Hollywood's underbelly, and how she changed forever the world's perceptions about censorship, sexual behavior patterns, and pornography.

Darwin Porter, author of more than thirty critically acclaimed celebrity exposés of behind-the-scenes intrigue in the entertainment industry, was deeply involved in the Linda Lovelace saga as it unfolded in the 70s, interviewing many of the players, and raising money for the legal defense of the film's co-star, Harry Reems.

In this book, emphasizing her role as an unlikely celebrity interacting with other celebrities, he brings inside information and a never-before-published revelation to almost every page.

"This book drew me in..How could it not?"
Coco Papy, Bookslut.

THE BEACH BOOK FESTIVAL'S GRAND PRIZE WINNER FOR BEST SUMMER READING OF 2013"

RUNNER-UP TO "BEST BIOGRAPHY OF 2013" THE LOS ANGELES BOOK FESTIVAL

Another hot and insightful commentary about major and sometimes violently controversial conflicts of the American Century, from Blood Moon Productions.

Inside Linda Lovelace's Deep Throat, by Darwin Porter
Softcover, 640 pages, 6"x9" with photos.
ISBN 978-1-936003-33-4

PINK TRIANGLE

The Feuds and Private Lives of
TENNESSEE WILLIAMS, GORE VIDAL, TRUMAN CAPOTE,
& Famous Members of their Entourages

Darwin Porter & Danforth Prince

This book, the only one of its kind, reveals the backlot intrigues associated with the literary and script-writing *enfants terribles* of America's entertainment community during the mid-20th century.

It exposes their bitchfests, their slugfests, and their relationships with the glitterati—Marilyn Monroe, Brando, the Oliviers, the Paleys, U.S. Presidents, a gaggle of other movie stars, millionaires, and international débauchés.

This is for anyone who's interested in the formerly concealed scandals of Hollywood and Broadway, and the values and pretentions of both the literary community and the entertainment industry.

"A banquet... If PINK TRIANGLE had not been written for us, we would have had to research and type it all up for ourselves...Pink Triangle is nearly seven hundred pages of the most entertaining histrionics ever sliced, spiced, heated, and serviced up to the reading public. Everything that Blood Moon has done before pales in comparison.

Given the fact that the subjects of the book themselves were nearly delusional on the subject of themselves (to say nothing of each other) it is hard to find fault. Add to this the intertwined jungle that was the relationship among Williams, Capote, and Vidal, of the times they vied for things they loved most—especially attention—and the times they enthralled each other and the world, [Pink Triangle is] the perfect antidote to the Polar Vortex."

—Vinton McCabe in the NY JOURNAL OF BOOKS

"Full disclosure: I have been a friend and follower of Blood Moon Productions' tomes for years, and always marveled at the amount of information in their books—it's staggering. The index alone to Pink Triangle runs to 21 pages—and the scale of names in it runs like a Who's Who of American social, cultural and political life through much of the 20th century."

—Perry Brass in THE HUFFINGTON POST

"We Brits are not spared the Porter/Prince silken lash either. PINK TRIANGLE's research is, quite frankly, breathtaking. PINK TRIANGLE will fascinate you for many weeks to come. Once you have made the initial titillating dip, the day will seem dull without it."

—Jeffery Tayor in THE SUNDAY EXPRESS (UK)

PINK TRIANGLE—The Feuds and Private Lives of Tennessee Williams, Gore Vidal, Truman Capote, and Famous Members of their Entourages

Darwin Porter & Danforth Prince
Softcover, 700 pages, with photos   ISBN 978-1-936003-37-2   Also Available for E-Readers

THOSE GLAMOROUS GABORS
BOMBSHELLS FROM BUDAPEST

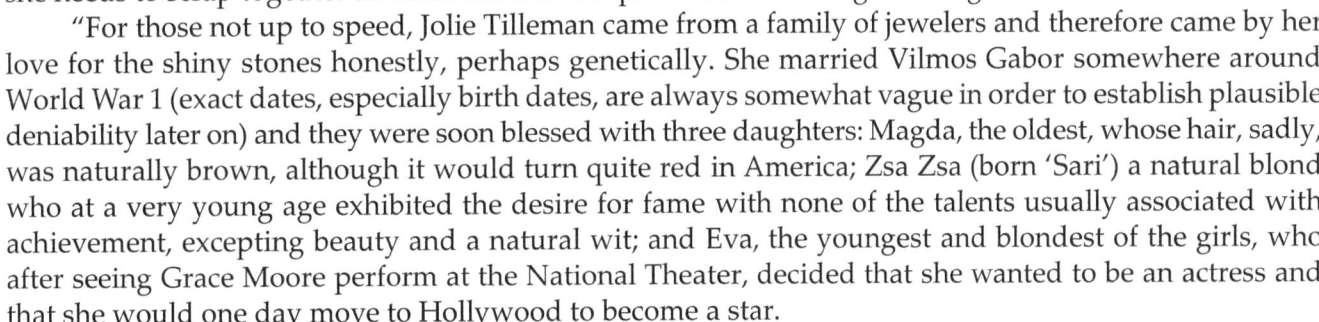

Zsa Zsa, Eva, and Magda Gabor transferred their glittery dreams and gold-digging ambitions from the twilight of the Austro-Hungarian Empire to Hollywood. There, more effectively than any army, these Bombshells from Budapest broke hearts, amassed fortunes, lovers, and A-list husbands, and amused millions of voyeurs through the medium of television, movies, and the social registers. In this astonishing "triple-play" biography, designated "Best Biography of the Year" by the Hollywood Book Festival, Blood Moon lifts the "mink-and-diamond" curtain on this amazing trio of blood-related sisters, whose complicated intrigues have never been fully explored before.

***

"You will never be Ga-bored…this book gives new meaning to the term compelling. Be warned, Those Glamorous Gabors is both an epic and a pip. Not since Gone With the Wind have so many characters on the printed page been forced to run for their lives for one reason or another. And Scarlett making a dress out of the curtains is nothing compared to what a Gabor will do when she needs to scrap together an outfit for a movie premiere or late-night outing.

"For those not up to speed, Jolie Tilleman came from a family of jewelers and therefore came by her love for the shiny stones honestly, perhaps genetically. She married Vilmos Gabor somewhere around World War 1 (exact dates, especially birth dates, are always somewhat vague in order to establish plausible deniability later on) and they were soon blessed with three daughters: Magda, the oldest, whose hair, sadly, was naturally brown, although it would turn quite red in America; Zsa Zsa (born 'Sari') a natural blond who at a very young age exhibited the desire for fame with none of the talents usually associated with achievement, excepting beauty and a natural wit; and Eva, the youngest and blondest of the girls, who after seeing Grace Moore perform at the National Theater, decided that she wanted to be an actress and that she would one day move to Hollywood to become a star.

"Given that the Gabor family at that time lived in Budapest, Hungary, at the period of time between the World Wars, that Hollywood dream seemed a distant one indeed. The story—the riches to rags to riches to rags to riches again myth of survival against all odds as the four women, because of their Jewish heritage, flee Europe with only the minks on their backs and what jewels they could smuggle along with them in their decolletage, only to have to battle afresh for their places in the vicious Hollywood pecking order—gives new meaning to the term 'compelling.' The reader, as if he were witnessing a particularly gore-drenched traffic accident, is incapable of looking away."

—*New York Review of Books*

THOSE GLAMOROUS GABORS
Bombshells from Budapest,
by Darwin Porter & Danforth Prince
Softcover, 730 pages, with hundreds of photos
ISBN 978-1-936003-35-8

ROCK HUDSON

IN THE DYING DAYS OF HOLLYWOOD'S GOLDEN AGE, ROCK HUDSON WAS THE MOST CELEBRATED PHALLIC SYMBOL AND LUST OBJECT IN AMERICA.

THIS BOOK DESCRIBES HIS RISE AND FALL, AND THE INDUSTRY THAT CREATED HIM.

Rock Hudson charmed every casting director in Hollywood (and movie-goers throughout America) as the megastar they most wanted to share PILLOW TALK with. This book describes his rise and fall, and how he handled himself as a closeted but promiscuous bisexual during an age when EVERYBODY tried to throw him onto a casting couch.

Based on dozens of face-to-face interviews with the actor's friends, co-conspirators, and enemies, and researched over a period of a half century, this biography reveals the shame, agonies, and irony of Rock Hudson's complete, never-before-told story.

In 2017, the year of its release, it was designated as winner ("BEST BIOGRAPHY") at two of the Golden State's most prestigious literary competitions, the Northern California and the Southern California Book Festivals.

It was also favorably reviewed by the *Midwestern Book Review, California Book Watch, KNEWS RADIO, the New York Journal of Books,* and the editors at the most popular Seniors' magazine in Florida, *BOOMER TIMES.*

ROCK HUDSON EROTIC FIRE
By Darwin Porter & Danforth Prince
Softcover, 624 pages, with dozens of photos, 6" x 9"
ISBN 978-1-936003-55-6

Available everywhere now

BILL & HILLARY
So This Is That Thing Called Love

Confused about how to interpret their raucous pasts?
This uncensored tale about a love affair that changed the course of politics and the planet is of compelling interest to anyone involved in the slugfests and incendiary wars of THE CLINTONS.

"This is both a biographical coverage of the Clintons and a political exposé; a detailed, weighty exploration that traces the couple's social and political evolution, from how each entered the political arena to their White House years under Bill Clinton's presidency.

"Containing gossip, scandal, and biographical sketches, it delves deeply into the news and politics of its times, presenting enough historical background to fully explore the underlying controversies affecting the Clinton family and their choices.

"Sidebars of information and black and white photos liberally peppered throughout the account offer visual reinforcement to the exploration, lending it the feel and tone of both a gossip column and political piece - something that probes not just Clinton interactions but the D.C. political milieu as a whole.

"The result may appear weighty, sporting over five hundred pages, but is an absorbing, top recommendation for readers of both biographical and political pieces who will thoroughly enjoy this spirited, lively, and thought-provoking analysis."

—THE MIDWEST BOOK REVIEW

***

Shortly after its release in December of 2015, this book received a literary award (Runner-up to Best Biography of the Year) from the New England Book Festival. As stated by a spokesperson for the Awards, "The New England Book Festival is an annual competition honoring excellence in books, with particular focus on projects that deserve closer attention from the academic community. Congratulations to Blood Moon and its authors, especially Darwin Porter, for his highly entertaining analysis of Clinton's double-barreled presidential regime, and the sometimes hysterical overreaction of their enemies."

Bill & Hillary—So This Is That Thing Called Love
Softcover, with photos. ISBN 978-1-936003-47-1

BURT REYNOLDS
PUT THE PEDAL TO THE METAL
How a Nude Centerfold Sex Symbol Seduced Hollywood

In the 1970s and '80s, Burt Reynolds represented a new breed of movie star.

Charming and relentlessly macho, he was a good old Southern boy who made hearts throb and audiences laugh. He was Burt Reynolds, a football hero and a guy you might have shared some jokes with in a redneck bar. After an impressive but tormented career, rivers of negative publicity, a self-admitted history of bad choices, and a spectacular fall from Hollywood grace, he died in Jupiter, Florida, at the age of 82 in September of 2018.

For five years, both in terms of earnings and popularity, he was the number one box office star in the world. *Smokey and the Bandit* (1977) became the biggest-grossing car-chase film of all time. As he put it, perhaps as a means of bolstering his image, "I like nothing better than making love to some of the most beautiful women in the world." Perhaps he was referring to his romantic and sexual involvements with dozens of celebrities from New Hollywood. More unusual dalliances occurred with Marilyn Monroe, whom he once picked up on his way to the Actors Studio in New York City. Love with another VIP came in the form of that "Sweetheart of the G.I.s," Dinah Shore, sparking chatter. "I appreciate older women," he once said in a moment of self-revelation. According to Sally Field, "Burt still lives in my heart." But then she expressed relief that, because of his recent death, he never read what she'd said about him in her memoir.

Men liked him too: He played poker with Frank Sinatra; shared boozy nights with John Wayne; intercepted a "pass" from closeted Spencer Tracy; talked "penis size" with Mark Wahlberg; went "wench-hunting" with Johnny Carson; and threatened to kill Marlon Brando, to whom his appearance was often compared. He also hung out with Bette Davis. ("I always had a thing for her.")

His least happy (some said "most poisonous") marriage—to Loni Anderson—was rife with dramas played out more in the tabloids than in the boudoir. According to Reynolds, "She's vain, she's a rotten mother, she sleeps around, and she spent all my money."

This biography—the first comprehensive overview of the "redneck icon" ever published—reveals the joys and sorrows of a movie star who thrived in, but who was then almost buried by the pressures and insecurities of the New Hollywood. A tribute to "truck stop" America, it's about the accelerated life of a courageous spirit who "Put His Pedal to the Metal" with humor, high jinx, and pizzazz. He predicted his own death: "Soon, I'll be racing a hotrod in Valhalla in my cowboy hat and a pair of aviators." On his tombstone, he wanted it writ: "He was not the best actor in the world, but he was the best Burt Reynolds in the world."

BURT REYNOLDS
PUT THE PEDAL TO THE METAL

Darwin Porter & Danforth Prince; ISBN 978-1-936003-63-1; 450 pages with photos.
Available Everywhere Now

JAMES DEAN
Tomorrow Never Comes

Honoring the 60th Anniversary of His Violent and Early Death

America's most enduring and legendary symbol of young, enraged rebellion, James Dean continues into the 21st Century to capture the imagination of the world.

After one of his many flirtations with Death, which caught up with him when he was a celebrity-soaked 24-year-old, he said, "If a man can live after he dies, then maybe he's a great man." Today, bars from Nigeria to Patagonia are named in honor of this international, spectacularly self-destructive movie star icon.

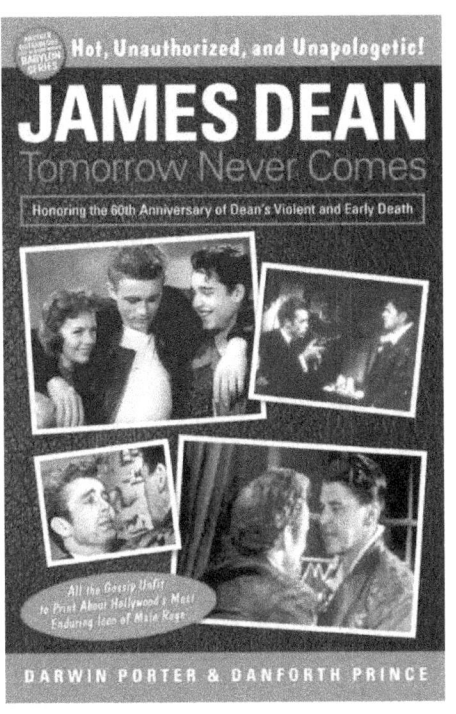

Migrating from the dusty backroads of Indiana to center stage in the most formidable boudoirs of Hollywood, his saga is electrifying.

A strikingly handsome heart-throb, Dean is a study in contrasts: Tough but tender, brutal but remarkably sensitive; he was a reckless hellraiser badass who could revert to a little boy in bed.

A rampant bisexual, he claimed that he didn't want to go through life "with one hand tied behind my back." He demonstrated that during bedroom trysts with Marilyn Monroe, Rock Hudson, Elizabeth Taylor, Paul Newman, Natalie Wood, Shelley Winters, Marlon Brando, Steve McQueen, Ursula Andress, Montgomery Clift, Pier Angeli, Tennessee Williams, Susan Strasberg, Tallulah Bankhead, and FBI director J. Edgar Hoover.

Woolworth heiress Barbara Hutton, one of the richest and most dissipated women of her era, wanted to make him her toy boy.

Tomorrow Never Comes is the most penetrating look at James Dean to have emerged from the wreckage of his Porsche Spyder in 1955.

Before setting out on his last ride, he said, "I feel life too intensely to bear living it." *Tomorrow Never Comes* presents a damaged but beautiful soul.

JAMES DEAN—TOMORROW NEVER COMES
Darwin Porter & Danforth Prince
Softcover, with photos. ISBN 978-1-936003-49-5

Available Now From Blood Moon: The Comprehensive, Unauthorized Exposé that Every Survivor of the Sexual Revolution Will Want to Read

Hugh Hefner, the most iconic Playboy in human history, was a visionary, an empire-builder, and a pajama-clad pipe-smoker with a pre-coital grin.

In 1953, he published his first edition of *Playboy* with money borrowed from his puritanical, Nebraska-born mother. Marilyn Monroe appeared on the cover, with her nude calendar inside.

Rebelling against his strict upbringing, he lost his virginity at the age of 22.

His magazine, punctuated with nudes and studded with articles by major literary figures, reached its zenith at eight million readers. As a "tasteful pornographer," Hef became a cultural warrior, fighting government censorship all the way to the U.S. Supreme Court. As the years and his notoriety progressed, he became an advocate of abortion, LGBT equality, and the legalization of pot. Eventually, he engaged in "pubic wars" with Bob Guccione, the flamboyant founder of Penthouse, which cut into Hef's sales.

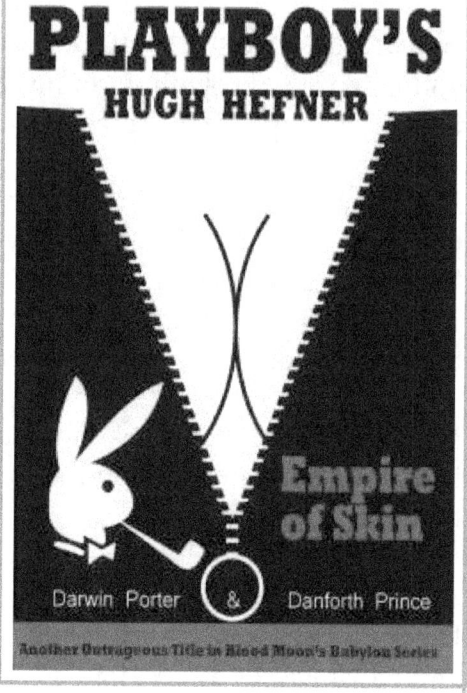

Lauded by millions of avid readers, he was denounced as "the father of sex addiction," "a huckster," "a lecherous low-brow feeder of our vices," "a misogynist," and, near the end of his life, "a symbol of priapic senility."

During his heyday, some of the biggest male stars in Hollywood, including Warren Beatty, Sammy Davis, Jr., Mick Jagger, and Jack Nicholson, came to frolic behind Hef's guarded walls, stripping nude in the hot tub grotto before sampling the rotating beds upstairs. Even a future U.S. president came to call. "Donald Trump had an appreciation of Bunny tail," Hef said.

Hefner's last Viagra-fueled marriage was to a beautiful blonde, Crystal Harris, 60 years his junior. "There's nothing wrong in a man marrying a girl who could be his great-granddaughter," he was famously quoted as saying.

This ground-breaking biography, the latest in Blood Moon's string of outrageously unvarnished myth-busters, was the first published since Hefner's death at the age of 91 in 2017. It's a provocative saga, rich in tantalizing, often shocking detail. Not recommended for the sanctimonious or the faint of heart, and loaded with ironic, little-known details about the trendsetter's epic challenges and the solutions he devised.

PLAYBOY'S HUGH HEFNER
EMPIRE OF SKIN

by Darwin Porter and Danforth Prince
978-1-936003-59-4

Blood Moon Productions proudly announces its compilation of lurid, vintage scandals from the Golden Age of Camelot.

It's in the form of a new edition of Darwin Porter's classic 2014 biography of the most watched, most enigmatic, and most controversial woman of the 20th Century,

JACQUELINE KENNEDY ONASSIS
HER TUMULTOUS LIFE & HER LOVE AFFAIRS

JACKIE INVADES WASHINGTON BABYLON, EUROPE, and BEYOND

This is a new edition of the most compelling compilation of cash-soaked ambition, sexual indiscretion, and social embarrassment about a former first lady ever published,

Available now from **Ingram** and from **Amazon.com** worldwide, in honor of one of

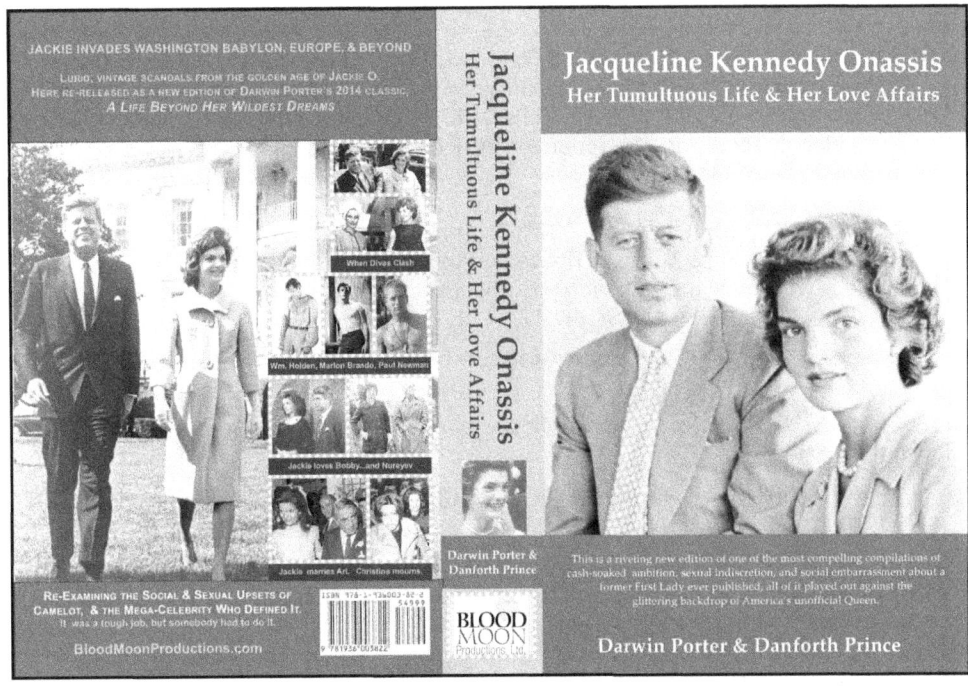

America's favorite Valentines

JAQUELINE KENNEDY ONASSIS
HER TUMULTUOUS LIFE & HER LOVE AFFAIRS
ISBN 978-1-936003-82-2   Originally published in 2014 as
A LIFE BEYOND HER WILDEST DREAMS by Darwin Porter & Danforth Prince
700 fascinating pages with hundreds of photos

Conceived in direct and sometimes defiant contrast to the avalanche of more breathlessly respectful testimonials to the life and legacy of "America's Queen," this book is the latest installment in Blood Moon's endlessly irreverent MAGNOLIA HOUSE series.

RE-EXAMINING THE SOCIAL AND SEXUAL UPSETS OF CAMELOT AND THE MEGA-CELEBRITY WHO DEFINED IT.

IT WAS A TOUGH JOB, BUT SOMEBODY HAD TO DO IT.

INTRODUCING BLOOD MOON'S

MAGNOLIA HOUSE

AND THE SERIES THAT BEARS ITS NAME

TWO TURN-OF-THE-20TH-CENTURY VIEWS OF STATEN ISLAND'S HISTORIC MAGNOLIA HOUSE

HOW DO YOU DESCRIBE A BOOKISH, MAGNOLIA-SCENTED LANDMARK?

As depicted below, **Volumes One and Two** of Blood Moon's **Magnolia House Series** were conceived as affectionate testimonials to a great American monument, **MAGNOLIA HOUSE,** our company's nurturing and very tolerant historic home in Staten Island (NYC) It has a raft of stories to tell—some of them about how it adapted to the publishing industry's radically changing tastes, times, circumstances, and values.

VOLUME ONE (ISBN 978-1-936003-65-5) focuses on its construction by a prominent lawyer during the booming (Northern) economy before the Civil War; its Gilded-Age purchase by the widow of the Surgeon General of the Confederate States of America; and later, its role as a branch office of THE FROMMER GUIDES during the heyday of the American travel industry. It was an era rich with insights into the celebrity secrets their reporters on the job in "London, Paris, and "Hollywood on the Tiber" (privately, until now) unveiled, years later, through Blood Moon Productions.

VOLUME TWO (ISBN 978-1-936003-73-0) is an *haute* celebrity romp through the half-century of Broadway, Hollywood, and publishing scandals swirling around Magnolia House's visitors and their frenemies…a "Reporters' Notebook" with everything that arts industry publicists didn't want fans and critics to know about at the time.

**Each of these books is a celebration of the fast-disappearing
PRE-COVID AMERICAN CENTURY,**
And both are available now through internet purveyors worldwide.

**from BLOOD MOON PRODUCTIONS at MAGNOLIA HOUSE
Award-Winning Entertainment about
America's Legends, Icons, & Celebrities**

DID YOU KNOW? That Blood Moon's **Darwin Porter** "rolled around in the hay" with the legacy of Humphrey Bogart not once, but TWICE.

Both of the **"BOGART BIOPSIES'** he produced generated massive tabloid publicity, in part because their revelations at the time were NEW, SCANDAL-SOAKED, and directly culled from the HOLLYWOOD UNDERGROUND.

Left photo:
Humphrey Bogart, The Early Years (1899-1931),
back when his films were Pre-Code and *risqué*
ISBN 0-9668030-5-1

Right photo:
Humphrey Bogart, the Making of a Legend.

What was the secret of his spectacular popularity? and what REALLY lay benearth his trenchcoat?
ALL of that's here, as aggressively promoted the week of its publication by some of the biggest newspapers and tabloids
in the world.
ISBN 978-1-936003-14-3

HOW THE TABLOIDS HUMPED FOR BLOOD MOON'S PAIRED OVERVIEWS OF BOGIE

In the early stages of its publishing life, Blood Moon's frenemies sometimes rebuked it for "Courting and Romancing" the Tabloids. But our humping paid off. The Daily Mail and its weekend counterpart,The Mail on Sunday, along with the National Enquirer, The Globe, The Examiner, The New York Daily News, and publications across Europe all delivered SCADS of early publicity. We've replicated some of the coverage that the press lavished on our double-volumed release of revelations about "Hunky Humpy" Bogart.

LOVE TRIANGLE
Ronald Reagan, Jane Wyman, & Nancy Davis

HOW MUCH DO YOU REALLY KNOW ABOUT **THE REAGANS?**

THIS BOOK TELLS EVERYTHING ABOUT THE SHOW-BIZ SCANDALS THEY DESPERATELY WANTED TO FORGET.

UNIQUE IN THE HISTORY OF PUBLISHING, THIS SCANDALOUS TRIPLE BIOGRAPHY focuses on the Hollywood indiscretions of former U.S. president Ronald Reagan and his two wives. A proud and Presidential addition to Blood Moon's Babylon series, it digs deep into what these three young and attractive movie stars were doing decades before two of them took over the Free World.

As reviewed by Diane Donovan, Senior Reviewer at the California Bookwatch section of the Midwest Book Review: "Love Triangle: Ronald Reagan, Jane Wyman & Nancy Davis may find its way onto many a Republican Reagan fan's reading shelf; but those who expect another Reagan celebration will be surprised: this is lurid Hollywood exposé writing at its best, and outlines the truths surrounding one of the most provocative industry scandals in the world.

"There are already so many biographies of the Reagans on the market that one might expect similar mile-markers from this: be prepared for shock and awe; because Love Triangle doesn't take your ordinary approach to biography and describes a love triangle that eventually bumped a major Hollywood movie star from the possibility of being First Lady and replaced her with a lesser-known Grade B actress (Nancy Davis).

"From politics and betrayal to romance, infidelity, and sordid affairs, Love Triangle is a steamy, eye-opening story that blows the lid off of the Reagan illusion to raise eyebrows on both sides of the big screen.

"Black and white photos liberally pepper an account of the careers of all three and the lasting shock of their stormy relationships in a delightful pursuit especially recommended for any who relish Hollywood gossip."

In 2015, LOVE TRIANGLE, Blood Moon Productions' overview of the early dramas associated with Ronald Reagan's scandal-soaked career in Hollywood, was designated by the Awards Committee of the HOLLYWOOD BOOK FESTIVAL as Runner-Up to Best Biography of the Year.

LOVE TRIANGLE:
Ronald Reagan, Jane Wyman, & Nancy Davis
Darwin Porter & Danforth Prince
Softcover, 6" x 9", with hundreds of photos.   ISBN 978-1-936003-41-9

BOOK RELEASE NEWS

Blood Moon's
Hollywood Remembered
Glitz, Glamour, Triumph, & Tragedy

*How Blood Moon Productions captured the attention of
The American Tabloids during the decline of
The Entertainment Industry's Golden Age*

Blood Moon Productions (www.BloodMoonProductions.com) proudly announces the release of *Hollywood Remembered*, a 500-page compendium of "short stories" inspired by **Darwin Porter's** long exposure to the backlot intrigues of the entertainment industry's "Hollywood Heyday."

It's envisioned as an oversized coffee table book of enduring interest to anyone who ever loved classic films and the scandalous intrigues associated with its players. It's not for the timid. Pages are splashed with incisive commentary and photographs of a fabulous era swept away by changing times.

Its inspiration derived from twenty years of Darwin Porter's monthly contributions to *Boomer Times*, a glossy magazine and "Sunday supplement" of *The Miami Herald's* subscribers in Dade and Broward Counties, Florida. It was spearheaded by **Anita Finley**, a South Florida gerontologist who doubled as a spokesperson for her state's "politically connected' population of Baby Boomers.

According to Blood Moon's president, Danforth Prince, "The core values of **Anita Finley** and **Darwin Porter**—who define Baby Boomers as "Old-Time Hollywood's Greatest Fans"—always dovetailed neatly. This book is envisioned as a joint celebration of the staggering literary output of both *Boomer Times* and **Blood Moon Productions**. As such, we've dedicated it to **Ms. Finley**. The *Grande Dame* of Florida's Boomers.

"We also envision this as an **autobiography of Blood Moon Productions** and an end-of-life tribute to its creative director, **Darwin Porter**. If not for his archival skills, many once-underground truths about The American Century would have died with their last first-hand witnesses. But thanks in part to Porter's staggering descriptive output, thousands of once-repressed facts have been recorded and digitalized for future historians and fans. In fact, for the Library Trades, we've categorized this one-of-a-kind new book as a resource for MEDIA STUDIES.

"With a release expected on that Greatest of American Holidays, The 4th of July, Blood Moon's *HOLLYWOOD REMEMBERED* will challenge traditional beliefs about celebrities and the sociologies that nurtured them. "

With a special tribute to the celebrities whose luminous images still enthrall us on movie screens today, thanks for taking a look at this portrait of the ferociously unfettered "indie" that briefly reigned as a magnet for tabloid publicists, and as one of the hottest independent publishing ventures in the world.

**Blood Moon's HOLLYWOOD REMEMBERED:
Glitz, Glamour, Triumph, & Tragedy**

By Darwin Porter with Danforth Prince
ISBN 978-1-936003-92-1

In bookstores everywhere and online, worldwide, on the 4th of July 2024

Here's the back cover of HOLLYWOOD REMEMBERED, the award-winning title we described on the previous page.

This is the story behind the story of the small, scrappy independent press,
Blood Moon Productions,
whose celebrity *exposés* (more than 50 of them) generated *tsunamis* of tabloid flash during the decline of the entertainment industry's golden age.

It's a story about Media, the Hollywood Dream Factory, and the clumsy, treacherous juggernaut known as FAME. It's about the fantasies that the entertainment industry crafted, and the secrets it conspired to conceal.

It offers an "on the down low" view of entertainers who delighted us, who captured our imaginations, and who paid heavy prices for the pedestals on which we placed them.

It's also a memorial to belief systems and values that in many cases have
Gone With the Wind.

From "Deep in December" of our lives *(or, if we're lucky, from Deep in September)*,
we offer it as a tribute to the way we were.

Here it is…*Hollywood Remembered*…an idiosyncratic, scrappy anthology
like nothing that's ever been seen before. It says a lot about the American version
of Fame and/or Infamy that you might not have expected.

Happy reading…and may your memories burn bright.

www.BloodMoonProductions.com

CHALLENGING THE STATUS QUO'S
BELIEFS ABOUT CELEBRITY
AND THE IRONIES OF FAME

IT'S A TOUGH JOB,
BUT SOMEBODY'S GOT TO DO IT.

www.ingramcontent.com/pod-product-compliance
Lightning Source LLC
Chambersburg PA
CBHW081438070526
44586CB00019B/2167